Gary.
Romain

SECOND EDITION

Quantitative Concepts for Management

Decision Making Without Algorithms

G.D. Eppen

University of Chicago

F.J. Gould

PRENTICE-HALL, INC., Englewood Cliffs, New Jersey 07632

Library of Congress Cataloging in Publication Data

EPPEN, GARY D., (date)
    Quantitative concepts for management.

    Includes bibliographical references and index.
    1. Management—Mathematical models. I. Gould,
F. J. (Floyd Jerome), (date). II. Title.
HD30.25.E66 1985   658.4′033   84-17940
ISBN 0-13-746637-4

Editorial/production supervision by Rick Laveglia and Susan Fisher
Interior design : Anne T. Bonnano and Rick Laveglia
Cover design : Anne T. Bonnano
Manufacturing buyer : Ed O'Dougherty

Printed in the United States of America

10 9 8 7 6 5 4 3 2 1

ISBN 0-13-746637-4 01

Prentice-Hall International, Inc., *London*
Prentice-Hall of Australia Pty. Limited, *Sydney*
Editora Prentice-Hall do Brasil, Ltda., *Rio de Janeiro*
Prentice-Hall Canada Inc., *Toronto*
Prentice-Hall Hispanoamericana, S.A., *Mexico*
Prentice-Hall of India Private Limited, *New Delhi*
Prentice-Hall of Japan, Inc., *Tokyo*
Prentice-Hall of Southeast Asia Pte. Ltd., *Singapore*
Whitehall Books Limited, *Wellington, New Zealand*

To Ann and Katharine

CONTENTS

v

CHAPTER 3
Constrained Optimization Models 30

CHAPTER 4
Formulation of Constrained Optimization Models 48

CHAPTER 5
Geometric Representation
of the Linear Programming Model *104*

CHAPTER 6
Linear Programs: Computer Analysis
and Interpreting Sensitivity Output *146*

CHAPTER 7
Special LP Topics:
Duality, V(b) and V(c)   198

CHAPTER 8
Management Science in Action:
Optimizing Production, Marketing, and
Distribution at PROTRAC   252

CHAPTER 11
Integer Programming and Network Models 321

CHAPTER 12
Project Management: PERT and CPM 379

CHAPTER 13
Calculus-Based Optimization and an Introduction to Nonlinear Programming 422

CHAPTER 14
Decision Theory and Decision Trees 448

CHAPTER 15
Inventory Control
with Known Demand 501

CHAPTER 16
Inventory Models
with Probabilistic Demand 536

CHAPTER 17
Forecasting 556

CHAPTER 18
Simulation Models 593

CHAPTER 19
Queuing Models *632*

CHAPTER 20
Dynamic Programming *656*

APPENDIX A
The Simplex Algorithm *678*

INDEX *691*

VIGNETTES AND APPLICATIONS

PREFACE

This book is the 2nd edition of *Quantitative Concepts for Management—Decision Making Without Algorithms* (Prentice-Hall, 1979). The nonalgorithmic approach of the first edition is retained with dedication—to the extent that in this revision even the sacred cow, the simplex method, has been put to pasture in the appendix. Now, almost ten years after beginning to think more than casually about texts and needs in this field, we continue to believe there is much rationale for this nonalgorithmic approach. Our thinking about this topic is stated in the preface to the first edition. The bottom line would seem to be, "Is it useful to teach algorithms, and does management science have anything else to offer?" Our answer to both parts of this question is "Yes." There are zealots who would say that algorithms are pen and pencil exercises which in reality exist only in textbooks. But some education begins with pen and pencil exercises and indeed we would quickly agree that there exist groups of students for whom an algorithmic emphasis, or at least exposure, is useful. It is precisely for that reason that our alternative text, *Introductory Management Science* (Prentice-Hall, 1984) has been written. This second edition of *Quantitative Concepts* (QC) has much in common with *Introductory Management Science* (IMS). The main differences are (i) IMS includes all of the usual textbook algorithms and QC contains only an illustration of the simplex method in the appendix; and (ii) in QC the coverage of topics such as LP is extended to a higher level in terms of concepts and depth.

The first edition of QC represented a new approach to the traditional teaching of management science. One response we initially encountered was, in blunt form, "If you don't teach algorithms, what else is there to do in a management science class?" This is essentially the second half of the previously posed question. Indeed our initial entry into the textbook arena was prompted by our belief that there is much else to offer, in the way of appropriate nonalgorithmic material, for large sectors of students. Candidly, our first effort at designing a nonalgorithmic exposition, at a uniform level of depth, was marked with nontrivial imperfections. And yet the first edition of QC has established a respectable niche in the market. Our goals for this revision have been:

(I) To make the level and depth of treatment more uniform throughout.

(II) To enhance the number of "teaching tools" in the text.

A more detailed discussion of these two items will suggest the nature of this revision.

I. *Level of Treatment.* Perhaps the most common criticism of the first edition was that our goals in the first half of the book, which was very strong in mathematical (especially linear) programming, were more successfully achieved than in the second half. In this revision, most of the LP material has been retained intact, with some minor reorganization such as introducing some geometric discussion before the computer output interpretation. We've found that for probably a majority of students some preliminary geometric intuition, imparted at the outset, facilitates the comprehension of the sensitivity portion of the printout. In order to upgrade the second half of the book, there has been extensive revision. Some of the key features are:

(1) A new chapter (Chapter 10) on goal programming has been added.

(2) The material on IP and networks (Chapter 11) has been expanded and rewritten at a less abstract level with more specific examples in the context of real world vignettes.

(3) Coverage on PERT and inventory control has been expanded to three chapters (Chapters 12, 15, and 16) which emphasize the relation between the model and the real problem.

(4) The calculus-based chapter on NLP (Chapter 13) has been rewritten with many more numerical examples and a more practical orientation.

(5) The decision theory material (Chapter 14) has been rewritten as a single chapter more orthodox in presentation.

(6) The forecasting chapter (Chapter 17) has been entirely rewritten with many more numerical examples and problems. The discussion is practically oriented, comparing various techniques.

(7) The material on simulation (Chapter 18) has been completely rewritten with more concrete illustrations and applications to specific problems in inventory, marketing, and queuing.

(8) New chapters on Queuing Models and Dynamic Programming have been added (Chapters 19 and 20, respectively).

Throughout the material we have endeavored to retain the uniform view that in the real world the solution of a model is always performed on computers. For this reason we stress, wherever possible, the interpretation of computer solutions. Nearly 40 computer printouts are scattered throughout the text. In the first edition these printouts were almost exclusively in the LP chapters. Now they are more evenly distributed throughout the exposition of such topics as IP, inventory, PERT, goal programming, and simulation. The theme, wherever possible, is to stress the various levels of interplay among a numerical example of a real problem, the symbolic model of the specific problem, the computer solution, and the geometric interpretation which provides intuition for a deeper level of problem understanding and output interpretation. As stated earlier, missing by design is a technical exposition of the algorithms which underlie the computer solutions.

II. *New Teaching Tools.* In part the unusual length of time between the first edition and this second edition is due to the preparation and extensive class testing of new teaching materials. These are:

1. Each chapter contains a "Major Concepts Quiz" with answers located at the end of each chapter. These true-false/multiple choice questions serve two purposes. First, they are pedagogical tools designed to sharpen and reinforce the student's understanding of the main concepts introduced in the chapter. Second, they provide a way for the student to evaluate his or her progress. Numerous quarters of class testing have made us painfully aware of the difficulty of writing clear, useful, and unambiguous questions of this sort. However, the payoff has been well worth the effort. Indeed, materials extrapolated from these major concepts quizzes provide major portions of our exams. An extensive exam bank is included in the new *Instructor's Resource Manual.*

2. Appropriate chapters have a "Notes on Implementation" section in which the real-world application of the techniques is discussed.

3. Five carefully pruned cases are included in the text to move students closer to working on real problems. In our view, these cases are important and deserve some comment. Experience leads us to believe that a good case will serve at least two roles. The first is the usual analytic training, separating the relevant from the irrelevant, etc. Equally difficult to design is a second and less traditional role: namely, to convey institutional knowledge which the student feels is germane to professional interests. For example, in the *Municipal Bond Underwriting* case (Chapter 11) the enthusiasm generated by learning, via the case, some details of this bond market makes integer programming itself take on new value. For the instructor who covers IP, we suggest that the use of this case will produce surprising rewards.

Experience also indicates that there is scarcely the time in a one-quarter or even one-semester introduction to management science to dwell on long cases. Consequently our materials tend to be rather short, almost in the realm of minicases. Not only are they short, but they are focused. Too often cases leave students too frustrated (for our taste) and floundering in a sea of generalities. In this text, cases are followed by questions requiring specific analytic responses.

4. Eight "Diagnostic Assignments" are also included in the text. These vignettes typically present a dialogue within a scenario in which one major point has been misunderstood or incorrectly treated. Students are asked to comment on the presentation. The purpose is to stress the evaluative role of the manager. These as well as the cases are useful as take-home assignments and provide good opportunities for student presentations and classroom discussion.

Discussion and answers for these Diagnostic Assignments appear in the *Instructor's Resource Manual*.

5. Eleven "Applications Capsules" briefly summarize successful applications of management science models. Such discussions help build the bridge from classroom to practice.

6. Finally, the problem set has been revised and expanded. Again, all answers appear in the *Instructor's Resource Manual*.

Organization for Various Courses. The text has been designed to permit a maximum degree of flexibility so as to be useful in a wide variety of course configurations. Chapters 4 through 9 are sequential, although 5 and 6 can be interchanged. The heart of the LP presentation—formulation, geometry, and dealing with printout analysis and sensitivity interpretations—is included in Chapters 4 through 6. Chapters 7, 8, and 9 provide additional LP depth, mainly in applications of sensitivity analysis. Some users who plan to cover a variety of other models will choose to omit these three chapters. The inventory chapters (15 and 16) are in sequence, but for all of the remaining chapters the sequence is relatively unimportant, as each of these remaining chapters is self-contained. However, study of the simulation chapter (18) will be most meaningful if it follows a study of Chapter 16 which deals with probabilistic inventory models. The fact that most chapters are self-contained and include a good supply of problems makes it possible to accommodate many types of introductory courses. A packed one-quarter course devoted to mathematical programming can be created by selecting Chapters 3 through 11 and then Chapters 13 and 20. For a strong emphasis on operations management topics, the instructor would select Chapters 12, 15, 16, 17 and 18. An emphasis on stochastic models comes from Chapters 12, 14, 16, 17, 18 and 19.

A Note on the Computer Printouts. The LP printouts appearing in the text have all been produced by the interactive LINDO code created by Linus Schrage. The code has been widely distributed and is easily adapted to use on different machines. For futher information on LINDO, contact Professor L. Schrage, Graduate School of Business, The University of Chicago, 1101 East 58th Street, Chicago, IL 60637. Because the text contains numerous printouts, it is not essential to have a computer on-site. However, if at all possible we strongly urge, for the student's benefit, the enrichment of some hands-on computer contact at least during the LP portion of the course. The form of LP output is more or less standard, and the variation in format in the LP software on different computers is trivial. A student who follows the discussion in the text will be able to read, with minimal reorientation, any LP output encountered.

Acknowledgments. This book is a product of many combined years of teaching, research and consulting, and most importantly, what we've learned from the use and response to the first edition. We are indebted to many for their ideas and assistance. The following professors contributed reviews and/or comments on materials which in some form appear in this text: Robert Abrams, Donald L. Adolphson, John J. Bernardo, J. J. Brennan, Thomas A. Carrerale, Robert L. Childress, William Cooper, Roger G. Dean, Richard Disconza, John P. Evans, Marshall Fisher, Robert Jeroslow, Edward Kao, Marvin Jay Karson, Anne B. Koehler, Charles Kriebel, Irwin Kruger, Victor McGee, Louis W. Miller, Gary R. Reeves, John ReVelle, David Rubin, Mitchell L. Stolnick, Ralph Steuer, Harish L. Verma, and Harvey M. Wagner.

Colleagues at Chicago provide a continuous source of ideas, comments and criticism. We are especially indebted to Linus Schrage, as well as Robert Graves, Kipp Martin, Sam Savage and Willard Zangwill.

These acknowledgments would be incomplete without an expression of our gratitude for the opportunity to work with an exceptional staff at Prentice-Hall. The support and guidance of our editor, Dennis Hogan, has been deeply appreciated, as well as the efforts of Rick Laveglia and Susan Fisher in creating the final product. Finally, our heartfelt thanks to Patricia Combs for the typing and retyping of the seemingly endless flow of paper that launched this revision.

CHAPTER 1

An Introduction to Models

1.1

MODELS, COMPUTERS, AND PLANNING

Facing today's economic upheavals and the uncertainties of the future, companies are scrambling for new and better planning techinques. They are relying more and more on the use of computers and quantitative models. At the same time, they are becoming more knowledgeable about what models can do. One thing is certain: computer print-outs are becoming as common as pencils and paper, and the combination of modeling and computer analysis is here to stay.

Whether a modeler's recommendations are accepted or rejected, they must be questioned and understood. If they are accepted, it had better be on grounds other than blind faith. If they are rejected, forceful and equally quantitative arguments may be required to contradict the modeler's analysis. No matter what surprises the future holds in store, the planner who utilizes computers and formulas must be reckoned with. Whether his or her recommendations are implemented or shelved, they must be clearly interpreted in the proper perspective and context.

Although computers and models are separate entities conceptually, in terms of use they usually go hand in hand. Managers are seldom interested either in models or computers, per se. In today's managerial setting, no one uses a model without a computer, and anyone who uses a computer is familiar with at least some kind of model.

This book is about the model part of the picture. We shall refer to computer analyses, and we shall examine and discuss computer printouts. Since models tend to be sterile without the use of machines for computation, computer-related considerations are obviously important. But for our purposes, the computer is treated as a given tool that can be used without much requisite knowledge or skill in the same way that you can use the telephone without understanding the complexities of the Bell System.

The emphasis in future chapters is on the role of models in the decision-making context. But in order to work in detail with models, you must understand some of the basic concepts and tools of mathematics. The level of mathematics required to work effectively with the material varies somewhat with the various chapters in the text. Throughout it is assumed that you approach this text with a solid background in elementary algebra. By *elementary*, we mean algebra at the level commonly taught in high school. Although this is sufficient for most chapters, the mathematical maturity that comes with a course in calculus will stand most students in good stead. It is especially useful to have been exposed to calculus as preparation for Chapters 10 and 19.

1.2

DIFFERENT TYPES OF MODELS AND THREE EXAMPLES

In our world, many kinds of models are associated with many kinds of activities. Engineers build model airplanes, urban planners build model cities, designers make model dresses, and stage managers make model sets. Physicists construct models of the universe, and economists build models of the economy. Business managers and corporate planners work with models of their own particular environments. Such an environment may be a complex multinational corporation or it may simply be a one-room shop where three products are assembled on four machines.

Despite the diversity of these models, they have one aspect in common. They are all idealized and simplified representations of reality. Another way of saying the same thing is that

---

A model is a selective abstraction of reality.

An artist looks at reality, filters it, and creates a selective representation. A modeler does the same thing.

Three Examples: Gravity, Supply and Demand, Break-Even Analysis

Based on observation, Sir Isaac Newton hypothesized the notion of gravitational force. Based on experimentation, Galileo quantified this model, stating that a falling body, no matter what its mass, falls a distance of

$$D = gt^2/2$$

feet in t seconds, where g is called the constant of acceleration. This quantitative statement is a *selective representation of reality* that explicitly describes the quantitative relation between distance D and time t. This equation, $D = gt^2/2$, is an excellent example of a model. It states an idealized numerical relationship. It is *idealized and simplified* because it ignores (or, putting it differently, "assumes away") everything else that is happening in the world and focuses only on a particular relationship between the two distinguished entities, D and t. Although the relationship set forth in the model is not *exactly* satisfied in any real situation (because of, for example, air friction, wind storms, and other variable factors), the model is certainly useful, important, and simple. Its very simplicity represents a level of achievement often sought but seldom realized, for it is frequently the case that the best models are the simplest ones—those that are easiest to use and understand.

In economics, a well-known model describes the equilibrium price of a given commodity. This model is based on two functions: the supply function and the demand function. Figure 1.1 shows the supply function. It specifies the per unit price that must be offered to persuade suppliers to bring a quantity of the commodity to market. Note that

Suppliers will ask a per unit price p to entice the production (per unit time) of the quantity q. As q increases, p will increase in accordance with the relationship $p = S(q)$.

Figure 1.1

Supply Function

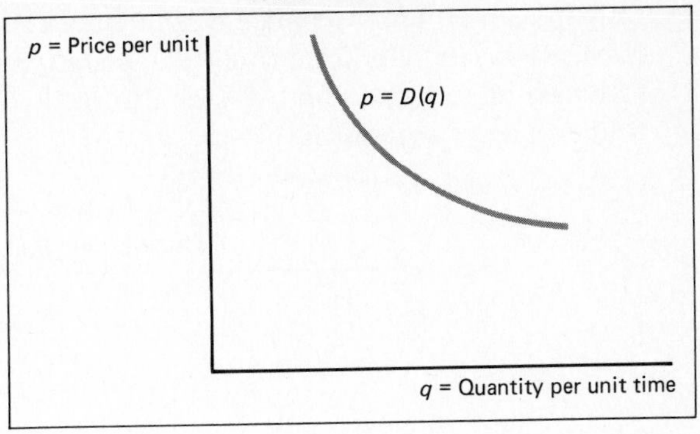

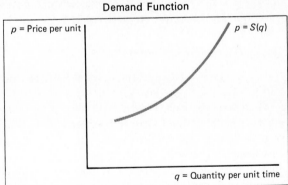

p = Price per unit

$p = D(q)$

q = Quantity per unit time

The demand function is shown in Figure 1.2. It shows the price per unit that must hold in order for a total quantity q to be sold (per unit time). Note that

A per unit price p must hold for a total quantity q to be purchased (i.e., demanded by buyers). If a larger total quantity is to be purchased, the unit price must fall. As q increases, p will decrease in accordance with the relationship $p = D(q)$.

Figure 1.2

Demand Function

p = Price per unit

$p = S(q)$

q = Quantity per unit time

A graphic view of the interaction between the supply function and the demand function is provided in Figure 1.3. We see that the equilibrium price, according to this model, is that price at which the supply and demand curves intersect (i.e., the price where quantity supplied equals quantity demanded). In other words, at the equilibrium price, denoted p^*,

quantity supplied by producers $= q^* =$ quantity demanded by consumers

or, more concisely,

supply = demand

This simple quantitative model is certainly a selective representation of reality. It ignores most of the world and describes only three entities of interest: price, quantity supplied, and quantity purchased. Price is related to supply. Price is related to demand. In equilibrium, says the model, price will find a level at which supply equals demand. It is a beautifully simple model, but it is also an idealization, for the world we live in is never truly in equilibrium. The price of an item varies from store to store, from day to day, from city to city, and from country to country. Nevertheless, the model has been found to be useful as a first approximation to reality and it is considered to be fundamental to the study of economics.

Figure 1.3
Market Equilibrium Model

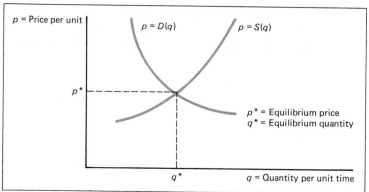

The model *supply = demand* has several features in common with the model $D = gt^2/2$. Both are extremely simple. Both are quantitative. That is, both models describe a *quantitative relationship* between entities of interest.

A third example of a simplified quantitative model is provided by *break-even analysis* (sometives called cost–volume–profit analysis) for a firm. This model determines the *volume of sales* at which

$$\text{total revenue} = \text{fixed cost} + \text{variable cost}$$

This volume of sales is called the *break-even point* (BEP). Since at the break-even point, total revenue = total cost, it must be true that (1) at this point profit (i.e., revenue − cost) is zero; (2) for volumes less than BEP, the firm will incur a loss; and (3) for volumes that exceed BEP, the firm will accrue profits. These relationships are shown by the model represented in Figure 1.4. This simplified model shows quantitative relationships between various entities of interest. For example, because of previous commitments management may wish to focus on a sales volume of q units. You can conveniently read from Figure 1.4. that at this volume

$$\text{total cost} = T$$

$$\text{variable cost} = T - F$$

$$\text{total revenue} = R$$

$$\text{profit} = R - T$$

In the business environment, many of the useful models are quantitative in nature.

Figure 1.4
Break-Even Analysis Model

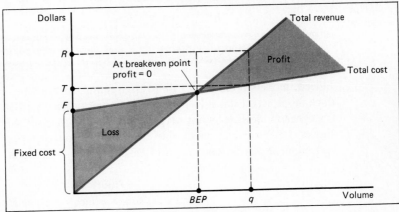

Our exclusive interest in this text is in quantitative models. Unfortunately, most quantitative models in practice are much more complicated than the three examples given above. Although models used in business may become simpler in the future, it is notable that computation costs have been historically decreasing and that the current trend in model building is toward greater complexity.

1.3
QUANTITATIVE DECISION MODELS

Models and
Numbers

Quantitative models start with, operate on, and produce numbers. That is, numbers play many roles in the creation, solution, and use of quantitative models. Consider, for example, the fact that most models of interest to management are what we call *decision models*. Every decision model contains *decision variables*. The solution of the model yields numerical values for these decision variables. These values imply specific decisions. *It follows that selecting a decision amounts to determining numerical values for decision variables, and vice versa.* In other words,

In the context of quantitative decision models, decisions are numbers.

In such models, it is also the case that

Decisions are based on an evaluation of numerical data.

Consider the following commonplace examples. A model to evaluate the alternatives of buying a house versus renting an apartment, considers the down payments required, mortgage rates, cash flow, appreciation—in brief, numerical data. A model to help you decide whether or not to work for an MBA degree would consider length of time required, the tuition and other expenses, salary potential—numerical data. In short, numerical data are the guts of quantitative models.

We have seen that quantitative models are based on numerical data and that decision models produce numbers that are decisions. Models also serve as generators of numbers that are not, in their own right, decisions. For example, a model may reveal the maximum possible profit a certain enterprise can yield. In other words, what we have been saying is:

Models evaluate numerical data and they provide additional numerical data.

Indeed, models often do no more than refine, or evaluate, crude data in order to produce more useful data. In fact, the outputs of some models may be used as the inputs for other models. It is not atypical for models to be linked together, as illustrated in Figure 1.5. Notice, for example, that the marketing model has as its output a forecast of next year's demand, and this forecast is an input to the production model.

Figure 1.5
Analysts Use Models as Inputs to Other Models

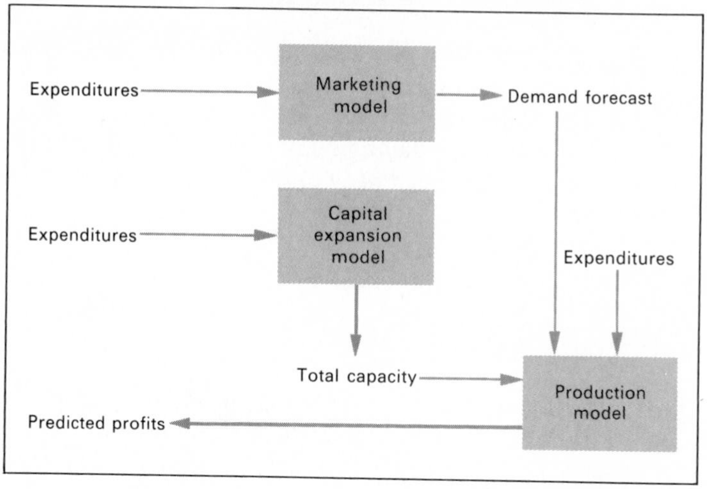

Objectives   In order to evaluate data, most decision models contain, as well as decision variables, what we call an *objective*. The model symbolically specifies the ways in which various decisions will affect the objective. As simple illustrations of objectives, consider the following examples:

1. *Salesforce allocation model:* The decisions (i.e., decision variables) might be how many salespeople to assign to each territory. Alternative objectives might be to minimize costs, to make sure that the best salespeople get the best accounts, and so on.
2. *Job-shop scheduling model:* The decisions (decision variables) might be how many hours to schedule given parts on given machines, and in what sequence. Alternative objectives might be to minimize costs, to minimize the total completion time for all parts, to minimize tardiness on deliveries, and so on.
3. *Cash-management model:* The decision variables might be the amount of funds to be held in each of several categories (cash, Treasury bills, bonds, stocks) each month. Alternative objectives might be to minimize the opportunity cost of holding more liquid assets, to minimize the probability of short-term debt given other constraints, and so on.

It is not difficult to think of many other types of decision models with different objectives. For example, consider policy-planning models. Often the objective is to forecast GNP, unemployment, or inflation under assumptions about various government policies. Or consider a corporate-planning model where the problem is whether to invest in oil from the North Sea or in synthetic fuels.

A Framework and Classification

All these examples of decision models fit into a general framework that we are beginning to establish. Namely:

1. Decision models selectively describe the environment.
2. Decision models designate decision variables.
3. Decision models designate objectives.

We shall discuss these three points in more detail in the following pages and in other chapters. For now, it suffices to state that the models we shall be concerned with in this text are called *quantitative decision models*. Many models satisfy this description. In Figure 1.6, 12 different kinds of models are listed, all of which are used in real-world quantitative decision problems. The list is not exhaustive; it will simply

Figure 1.6
Decision Models by Uncertainty Class and Corporate Use (D, Deterministic; P, Probabilistic; H, High; L, Low)

MODEL TYPE	UNCERTAINTY CLASSIFICATION	FREQUENCY OF CORPORATE USE
Linear programming	D	H
Network (induding PERT/CPM)	D, P	H
Inventory, production, and scheduling	D, P	H
Econometric, forecasting, and simulation	D, P	H
Integer programming	D	L
Dynamic programming	D, P	L
Stochastic programming	P	L
Nonlinear programming	D	L
Game theory	P	L
Optimal control	D, P	L
Queuing	P	L
Difference equations	D	L

give you an idea of the breadth of the field of quantitative modeling. Figure 1.6 also shows two other important features. The first is a classification scheme in terms of degree of uncertainty. Some of the models in management science are called *deterministic models*. This means that all the relevant data (i.e., data that the model will use or evaluate) is assumed to be known. Other types of models are *probabilistic* (also called *stochastic*) models. In such models, some of the relevant data (such as future demand, for example) is considered uncertain. In the latter type of model, probabilities may have to be specified for the uncertain data. Examples of both these types of models, deterministic and probabilistic, are treated in the text. Also, as you can see in Figure 1.6, some models, such as inventory and production, can be either of a deterministic or a probabilistic nature.

The second type of information provided by Figure 1.6 concerns *frequency of use* of these models in corporate settings. Based on three studies of this topic,[1] we have indicated, for each type of model, whether it tends to be used with high (H) or low (L) frequency by corporate managers. Such information was obtained by sampling large companies. You can see that of the many different types of models, there are only four which seem to be frequently employed in applications. Most of the chapters in this text will deal with these four categories.

1.4
MODEL BUILDING

Whether a model is simple or complex, it is a representation that idealizes, simplifies, and selectively abstracts reality, and this representation is something that is built, or constructed, by individuals. Unfortunately, there are no easy rules or automatic methods for model building. Model building involves art and imagination as well as technical know-how.

In a business environment, quantitative modeling involves the specifications of interactions between many variables. In order to accomplish this "quantification," the problem must be stated in the language of mathematics. We shall see many examples of model building in the chapters to follow. Do not be misled by the specific examples in the text, for *in the complexity of real-world problems there is usually no single "correct way" to build a model. Different models may address the same situation in much the same way that paintings by Picasso and Van Gogh would make the same view look different.*

As an overall guide, we can break down the process of building a quantitative decision model into three steps:

1. The environment is studied.
2. A selective representation of the problem is formulated.
3. A symbolic (i.e., mathematical) expression of the formulation is constructed.

Let us analyze the foregoing breakdown in more detail. Then we will talk about the *use* of models.

Study the Environment   The first of the three model-building steps, a study of the environment, is often under-valued by those new to modeling. The stated problem is often not the real problem. A variety of factors, including organizational conflicts, a difference between personal and organizational goals, and simply the overall complexity of the situation, may stand between the modeler and a clear understanding of the problem. Experience is probably the most essential ingredient for success—experience both in building models as well as a working experience in the environment to be studied.

[1]W. Ledbetter and J. F. Cox, "Are O.R. Techniques Being Used?" *Journal of Industrial Engineering*, Vol. 9, February 1977, pp. 19–21; Efraim Turban, "A Sample Survey of Operations Research Activities at the Corporate Level," *Operations Research*, Vol. 20, May–June 1972; F. C. Weston, "O.R. Techniques Relevant to Corporate Planning Function Practices: An Investigative Look," *Operations Research Bulletin*, Vol. 19, Suppl. 2, Spring 1971.

Formulation The second step, formulation, involves basic conceptual analysis, in which *assumptions and simplifications usually have to be made*. It is sometimes stated that until a model can be formulated the very problem under consideration is unclear. During the model formulation, pertinent relationships are conceptualized in much the same way that Galileo thought about the interactions among distance, time, and the rate of acceleration due to gravity in the falling-object problem. The process of formulation also requires the model builder to *select* or *isolate* from the total environment those aspects of reality relevant to the problem scenario. Since the problems we are concerned with involve decisions and objectives, these must be explicitly identified and defined. In some of the problems to be considered in future chapters it will become apparent that there are many applications in which the definition of the decision variables and the objective is a major task in itself. There may be various ways to define the decision variables, and the most appropriate definition may not be apparent initially. For example, it may be unclear whether a certain model should include amounts produced of every product or of only some subset of products. To keep the model suitably small for computational purposes, it may even be desirable to combine all products into one aggregate class. Moreover, the objectives may be unclear. Even the most capable managers may not know precisely what results they want to achieve. Equally problematic, there may be too many objectives to be satisfied, and it may be necessary to choose one out of many. (It will become evident that it is often impossible to optimize two different objectives at the same time, and thus, generally speaking, it is nonsensical to seek to obtain "the most return for the least investment.")

Formulation requires selecting and isolating the decision variables and the objective.

Construction of the Symbolic Model Once a logical formulation is accomplished (and this may be a verbal process), a symbolic form of the model must be constructed. In a sense, formulation and construction are integrated processes, with formulation the conceptual logical aspect and construction the actual symbolic representation of the logical relationships. All models are constructed of some medium. A dress designer constructs models out of fabric. The model city is made of clay. The conceptual formulation (a compact radial city with inner and outer hubs, underground parking, moving sidewalks, etc.) takes on a physical representation in the clay model. The conceptual and verbal relationships among distance, time, and acceleration due to gravity are represented via the medium of mathematical symbols in the statement $D = gt^2/2$.

In a decision-making environment, models are usually constructed in the symbolic language of mathematics. Also, construction may involve a good deal of data collection and computer programming. The construction of the model may, however, be less critical than the formulation. The reason is this: Formulation requires analysis, selectivity, and decisions about relevance and objectives, whereas construction is usually a more technical process, involving a translation into mathematics and the adaptation and use of known tools.

Construction translates the formulation into mathematics.

The interactions between formulation and construction are usually critical. For example, a formualtion of a corporate-planning model may involve a decision on whether to look 3, 5, or 10 years into the future. It may involve judgments on which divisions and subsidiaries to include. It may then turn out that the model as formulated is far too complex to be constructed in a way that can be useful. Perhaps the required data simply do not exist. Or perhaps the data can be found, but it turns out that with existing techniques it would take three days to run the model on the computer. This embarrassment can make the cost of using the model outweigh any potential gain. Unemployed management scientists can testify to the fact that, all too often, models are formulated that simply cannot be built.

Does this process of model building sound like too much for one person to accomplish? Often, it is. When operations research (for all practical purposes, today, the terms "operations research" and "management science" are synonymous) began, during World War II, logistic models were built by teams of mathematicians, statisticians, economists, physicists, engineers, and generalists. Today, the picture is not much different, except that econometricians, computer scientists, and management scientists have been added. Usually, management scientists train in the *theory* and *development* of models. They are also concerned with the development of *algorithms*, which are techniques for solving models. Thus, models are frequently built by heterogeneous and interdisciplinary teams of experts from various fields. A management scientist working alone has a very limited repertoire and limited capabilities.

1.5

ON THE USE AND IMPLEMENTATION OF MODELING

Models are used in as many ways as there are people who build them. They can be used to sell an idea or a design, to order optimal quantities of nylon hosiery, to better organize our knowledge of the universe, or to better organize an economy or a firm.

Models and Executive Judgment

In the firm, models are increasingly synonymous with executive planning. Planning models are used to forecast the future, to explore alternatives, to develop multiple-contingency plans, to increase flexibility and reaction time—in short, to provide planners with all sorts of data. However, although models are used for planning, it must be stated that *no model can ever be guaranteed to give a high-level planner the "best decision."* In fact, as will be discussed in Chapter 3, the very notion of "best decision" is, strictly speaking, a mathematical rather than a real-world idea. You must remember that *a model is not reality. It is only a symbolic approximation, a selective approximation, of reality.* A model can produce a "best decision," but only within the limited context of the model. No model can completely capture the real world. Some considerations will always be left out. And because of the fact that no model can be guaranteed to produce a "best real-world decision," *the model is not a substitute for executive judgment and intuition.* But models do provide interesting data for executives to evaluate. They are, in the final analysis, used only as tools to aid in the decision-making process. Figure 1.7 shows one way of portraying the interaction between the model and the manager. You can see from this picture that *one aspect of the manager's role is to evaluate the model itself.* It is not unusual for the modern manager to be faced with a significant decision, after all is said and done, as to how much weight should be assigned to the recommendations of a particular model. The need for managerial decisions often arises out of conflict or adversary confrontations, and quantitative models are often used as tools

Figure 1.7
Feedback Interaction between Model and Manager

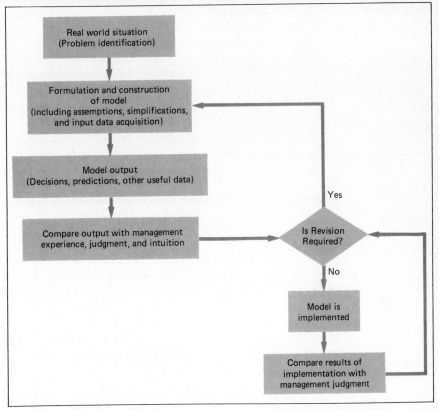

in this process. The manager's decision may well influence his or her career. This fact in itself provides a not insignificant incentive for the study of models and their proper employment in the managerial setting.

Concerning "the use of models," it can also be said that models often play different roles at different levels of the firm. At the top levels, models more typically provide data and information, not decisions. They are useful as strategic planning tools. At lower levels, models are actually used to provide decisions. In many plants, for example, assembly-line operations are completely computerized. Decisions are produced by a model of the operation.

Models have different uses at different levels of the firm for a number of reasons. At progressively lower levels of an organization, alternatives and objectives are apt to become clearer. Interactions are easier to specify quantitatively. Data are often more available and the future environment more certain. For example, at the bottom of the hierarchy a decision may concern the scheduling of a particular machine. We know the products that will be run on it and the costs of changing the machine from the production of one product to any other product. The goal of the model may be to find a schedule that produces the necessary amounts by the due dates and minimizes changeover and storage costs.

Contrast the clarity and explicitness of that problem with a multibillion dollar, top-management decision between "invest and grow" and "produce and generate current earnings." Models can certainly be applied to such broad and fuzzy problems, but the models themselves are loaded with assumptions and uncertainties. In such sases, the validity of the model may be as difficult to determine as the desired decision.

In spite of these different uses of models at different levels of the firm, a few generalities apply to all quantitative decision models. All such models provide a framework for logical and consistent analysis. More specifically,

1. Models force managers to be explicit about objectives and assumptions.
2. Models force managers to identify and record the types of decisions (decision variables) that influence objectives.
3. Models force managers to identify and record pertinent interactions between decision variables.
4. Models force managers to record constraints on the values that the variables may assume.

It follows from these features that a model, in a sense, provides a way of establishing a verifiable record, and it also provides a *consistent tool* for evaluating different policies. That is, each policy or set of decisions is evaluated by the same objective according to the same formulas for describing interactions and constraints. Moreover, models can be explicitly adjusted and improved with historical experience.

A final point: Models provide the opportunity for a systematic use of powerful mathematical methods. They can handle a large number of variables and interactions. The mind is capable of storing only so much information. Models allow us to use the power of mathematics hand in hand with the storage and speed of computers.

1.6
MAJOR CONCEPTS QUIZ

True–False

1. **T F** The more complicated the model, the more useful it generally is.
2. **T F** Models usually ignore most of the world.
3. **T F** Decision models produce numerical values for decision variables and hence, in this sense, decisions are numbers.
4. **T F** A decision model often captures interactions and trade-offs between certain variables or quantities of interest.
5. **T F** A model can be thought of as a particular simplification of reality, and thus there is usually no single correct way to build a model of a realistic problem.
6. **T F** One advantage of the modeling approach is that it often eliminates the need to be very familiar with the environment being studied.
7. **T F** In practice, models are often built by teams of individuals drawn from different disciplines.
8. **T F** The purpose of models is to help provide a good decision for the real problem.
9. **T F** A model is a good substitute for executive judgment and experience.
10. **T F** An important role of management can be the evaluation of a model (determination of whether or not a model should be used and its results implemented).
11. **T F** In stochastic models, all components of the model are known with certainty.
12. **T F** Break-even analysis determines the profit-maximizing volume.

13. **T F** "Operations research" and "management science" are synonymous.

14. **T F** For most real-world problems, there will be a correct model that produces a best decision.

Multiple Choice

15. A model is
    a. a selective representation of reality
    b. an abstraction
    c. an idealization
    d. all of the above

16. Models
    a. are rarely used in the strategic planning process
    b. play different roles at different levels of the firm
    c. are a costly way of making routine daily decisions
    d. are used only to produce decisions

17. Decisions are often based on
    a. an evaluation of numerical data
    b. numbers produced by models
    c. executive judgment and intuition
    d. all of the above

18. A model
    a. is a tool for the decision maker
    b. forces a manager to be explicit about objectives
    c. forces a manager to identify interactions and trade-offs between various quantities (such as production and resource consumption)
    d. all of the above

19. In the modeling process, assumptions
    a. are rarely required
    b. are made in the formulation stage
    c. are difficult to justify
    d. all of the above

20. Break-even analysis
    a. is synonymous with cost–volume–profit analysis
    b. is a simplified quantitative model
    c. determines the volume at which revenue = cost
    d. all of the above

Answers

1. F	8. T	15. d
2. T	9. F	16. b
3. T	10. T	17. d
4. T	11. F	18. d
5. T	12. F	19. b
6. F	13. T	20. d
7. T	14. F	

1.7
PROBLEMS

A major goal of this text is to give you an appreciation for what models do and how they are made. The following questions are intended to provoke discussion and to help pull together the ideas we have introduced in Chapter 1. Most of these questions do not have clear-cut answers, but with a certain amount of thought and imagination, they can be interesting for you to pursue, especially in group discussions. As the course develops, your perspective will expand, and you will find it worthwhile to reapproach some of these problems.

1-1. Suppose that you want to become a managerial decision maker but your special abilities and interests are far from the quantitative field. What is the point to your studying an introductory quantitative-modeling text?

1-2. List several specific ways in which the use of models might be superior to a more conventional kind of reasoning.

1-3. List decision problems that involve a choice between only two or three discrete alternatives rather than a choice among a continuous spectrum of alternatives.

1-4. List several kinds of corporate-planning decisions. Compare these with specific operational decisions.

1-5. What reasons can you think of to explain the fact that many models are built and never implemented? Does the absence of implementation mean that the entire model-development activity was a waste?

1-6. What is your interpretation of the phrase "a successful application of a model"?

1-7. "Different models are often applied to the same situation." Give several interpretations to this assertion. What makes one model different from another?

1-8. What do you think it means to "solve" a model?

1-9. Suppose that a model has been constructed to represent a specified segment of the firm's activity. Discuss how the type of activity might be related to the number of times the model is used. That is, think about kinds of models that might be used on a regular schedule, such as hourly, daily, weekly, or monthly, versus kinds of models that might be used on a very sporadic basis.

1-10. Try to imagine some ways in which existing models might have to be updated, as opposed to not tampered with.

1-11. Do you have any specific ideas why interdisciplinary teams might be an asset in building models? Can you think of specific instances that might draw on different disciplines?

1-12. What is your understanding about the ways in which models might be used at different levels in the firm?

1-13. To many people the terms *management science*, *operations research*, and *systems analysis* all mean the same thing. Are you aware of any different connotations that, at least to some extent, distinguish these professions?

1-14. In the text we interpret decisions, in the context of quantitative models, as being numbers. But consider a model designed to help determine whether a new facility should be located in Philadelphia or Pittsburgh. How might such a decision be represented in the model as a decision variable and as a number?

CHAPTER 2

Data and Models

INTRODUCTION

In most enterprises, decisions are based to a large extent on the evaluation and interpretation of data. Models provide a way to evaluate and interpret data consistently. Models can also be used to generate data, and a certain amount of data is usually required to bulid a model. In fact, it is not exceptional for the success or failure of a modeling effort to be data-related. Because of these intimate and varied linkages, a great deal of attention centers on the subject of data in the practical use of models. In this chapter, we introduce some of the considerations pertinent to the use of data in model building. In particular, we discuss forms and sources of data, along with the related topics of aggregation, refinement, and data display. We apply the use of data tables, plots, and graphs—each a vehicle for data display—to problems involving marginal, average, and total cost functions.

Data tables, plots, or graphs are the simplest types of models managers work with. Consequently, we devote a substantial portion of this chapter to illustrating the use of tables, plots, and graphs in a business environment. The scenario for this discussion, and others in this book, is a hypothetical firm called *PROTRAC*.

2.2
PROTRAC: HISTORICAL SKETCH

PROTRAC started in the late nineteenth century as a partnership between a blacksmith and a financier. The site was a two-story, 80- by 100-foot factory in Chicago. The firm employed about 100 men in the manufacture of a narrow line of harvesting equipment. The business developed on principles of product quality, aggressive marketing, and efficient distribution. For example, PROTRAC was one of the first firms to issue money-back guarantees, the first to advertise standard as opposed to bartered prices, and it assured quick deliveries at harvest time by locating storage agencies at key distribution points throughout the country.

15

By 1916, PROTRAC's net income (total earnings minus all expenses, depreciation, interest) was $4,932,024.72 from a product line that had expanded to include manure spreaders, lime and fertilizer sowers, hay loaders, corn shellers, grain elevators, hillside plows, hay stackers, corn binders, cotton and corn planters (two-row and single-row), beet lifters, four-row beet and bean planters, walking cultivators, light tractor disc plows, walking gang plows, and self-dumping hay rakes.

These products were manufactured in 14 factories, located as follows: 6 in Moline, Illinois; 1 in Horicon, Wisconsin; 1 in Syracuse, New York; 1 in Ottumwa, Iowa; 1 in Welland, Ontario; 1 in Fort Smith, Arkansas; 1 in St. Louis, Missouri; 1 in Waterloo, Iowa; and 1 in Malvern, Arkansas. In addition to these assets, the company owned hardwood timber lands in Arkansas and Louisiana.

PROTRAC's major sales activities were conducted through offices in 24 U.S. cities and 5 Canadian cities. Its export business was handled through a special office in Moline, with a forwarding office in New York; the amount of export outside Canada was negligible.

The Product Line

Since 1916, growth has been substantial. In the past year, PROTRAC had record net sales of $1.03 billion; net income was $62.3 million. The product line has diversified, now including over 200 items distributed among farm machinery, industrial and construction machinery, chemical products, and lawn and garden equipment. The main source of revenue is the sale of machine tools for agriculture, construction, forestry, landscaping, earth moving, and materials handling.

For the most part, these products are made in the same 14 factories. There are now only 14 sales offices in U.S. cities, still 5 in Canada. However, foreign business has grown considerably. There are now 45,434 employees throughout the world, 32,414 in the United States and Canada.

In analyzing the success of PROTRAC, two factors deserve considerable weight. One is enlightened management. The other is the gradual but significant increase in demand for its products caused by the growth in population.

Considering the future, it is estimated that world population will double by the year 2000. This growth will create additional demand for food, clothing, and housing. In addition, increasing affluence will cause more people to want better food, clothes, and housing.

2.3
DATA AS A MODEL: AN EXAMPLE

As is the case in most firms, decisions in PROTRAC are based to a large extent on available information, that is, on the evaluation and interpretation of data. In Chapter 1, we stated that from the modeling point of view, a decision is defined to be a number. Keep this very precise definition in mind. We also want you to be very clear on what we mean by *data*. For our purposes, the word *data* also means "numbers."

To see how numbers and models become intimately connected, consider a PROTRAC management decision on how much money to allocate to European marketing. Before making such a decision, management may want to have some idea of the effect of this allocation on total European sales. Therefore, an executive requests data on European marketing expenditures and total European sales for a 12-year period. These data are presented in Figure 2.1.

Figure 2.1

PROTRAC European Marketing Expenditures
and Sales, 1963–1974 (thousands of dollars)

YEAR	MARKETING EXPENDITURES	SALES
1963	0	0
1964	50	400
1965	100	750
1966	200	1200
1967	150	1000
1968	250	1390
1969	400	1800
1970	300	1565
1971	350	1715
1972	450	2025
1973	500	2140
1974	550	2200

This table is simply one means of conveying the requested data. The format of the table is purely a matter of convenience; it is not intended to connote any special relationship between the various numbers. However, suppose that after studying the data in Figure 2.1, the executive hypothesizes some relationship between marketing expenditures and sales. He may feel, for example, that the total sales in a given year depend directly on the marketing expenditure in that year. (The words "depend directly "imply that a higher expenditure on marketing leads to higher sales.) Thus, the executive may feel that sales of $1.8 million in 1969 were significantly related to the marketing expenditures of $400,000 in 1969. Alternatively, he may feel that the 1969 sales are more truly related to the marketing expenditure in 1967. Or, he may hypothesize that 1969 sales depend equally on the 1967, 1968, and 1969 marketing expenditures.

Formulating a Model

Numerous possible relationships could be hypothesized. The appropriate relationships would obviously depend on many factors associated with the actual PROTRAC environment. Also, we have phrased the hypothesized relationships, or interactions, in vague, semiquantitative language. That is, we hypothesized that 1969 sales "depended directly" on 1969 marketing expenditures, but we did not hypothesize a specific quantitative relationship. We could make a specific quantitative statement: actual sales in 1969 are 4.5 times the marketing expenditure in the same year. This means that in 1969, there were, *on the average*, 4.5 dollars of sales for each dollar of marketing. However, this fact *by itself* certainly does not permit us to conclude that a $600,000 marketing expenditure in 1969 *would have* led to a $2.7 million level of sales. Furthermore, does the 1969 factor of proportionality have any bearing on the current decision? In 1974, for example, the factor of proportionality was 4.0, not 4.5. How do the 1974 data relate to the 1969 data? Are current PROTRAC marketing techniques more like they were in 1974 than in 1969? Or has the operation basically remained unchanged between 1969 and 1974?

And what about other relevant factors, such as general economic conditions? If we hypothesize some causal relationship between marketing and sales in each year t, then the data reveal that *on the average* each dollar expended on marketing in 1969 was more effective than in 1974. What real-world factors might lie behind these different degrees of effectiveness in the different years? That is, what real-world interactions are reflected by the data? There could be differences in advertising techniques, differences in market softness and demand that, in turn, could be due to different economic conditions, weather, government policies, and so on.

The manager must consider these kinds of questions as soon as he begins to "interpret" the data in the table. But the point of the present discussion is this: **as soon as the manager begins to hypothesize even a semiquantitative relationship between the numbers in Figure 2.1, he is beginning to formulate a model.** He is beginning to interpret the data as a reflection of important interactions. Figure 2.1 takes on a special significance to the manager: **it becomes a selective representation of reality.** As such, the table of data fits one of our earlier definitions of a model. It is important to emphasize that the numbers by themselves do not represent the model. In fact, the numbers by themselves do not mean anything aside from records of fact (e.g., in 1969, total European sales were $1.8 million). It is only when some relationship or interaction is ascribed to the numbers that a model, at least in embryonic form, exists.

2.4

DATA-RELATED CONSIDERATIONS

Forms of Data

These numbers, which we call data, may be encoded on a magnetic tape or stored in coded form in a computer. They may be recorded on punched cards or in tables like the phone book or the almanac. The numbers may be in pounds or tons, francs or dollars. Questions of units are often important in working with data. For example, in what currency should PROTRAC management measure European sales? If the answer is dollars, what exchange rates should be used to convert foreign currencies into dollars? These rates vary from time to time, and the effect of these variances could be insignificant wrinkles in our calculations, or they could cause the world to look significantly different.

Sources of Data

Data may come from records of the past. Data may be generated by making direct observations or estimates in the present. In particular, the data may be produced by a model that requires certain decisions as inputs. Or, finally, data can be produced by making forecasts of the future.

Planning and Data

It is difficult to say which comes first, quantitative planning or the gathering of data. Certainly, data are required for effective planning. Efforts toward better planning often lead to the acquisition and storage of new types of data. The existence of data increases the potential for the use of models. One of the characteristics of advanced civilization, at least in terms of technology, seems to be the acquisition and use of data.

Aggregation of Data

One of the key considerations in using data is the degree of aggregation desired. For example, does a model require data on total yearly sales over the past five years, or on total yearly sales per country over the past five years, or on total yearly sales per plant over the past five years, or on total yearly sales per plant per product over the past five years? This list of requirements describes data in increasingly *disaggregated* form. Disaggregated data are more detailed and are generally more difficult to obtain. However, they are also more valuable because they contain more information. Furthermore, it is possible to aggregate disaggregated data, but it is not possible to go the other way. Thus, if total yearly sales per plant per product are known, it is possible to obtain total sales per product per country, or total sales per country, or total sales per product, or total sales per plant. However, it is clearly not possible to go from the aggregated down to the disaggregated numbers.

Although disaggregated data are desirable because they contain much information, it is also true that data may be too disaggregated for an individual decision maker's use. In terms of a decision on whether or not to build new plants in Europe, PROTRAC executives may want to compare a small select collection of aggregated data. That is, their decision may be based on a "mental model" in which they selectively represent reality with a few chosen numbers.

It should be obvious that more information can only lead to better decisions. (If this is not obvious, at least it should be clear that more information cannot lead to worse decisions.) However, it is also true that the degree of disaggregation an individual decision maker can digest is limited. Models and computers can work with much more detail than an individual; this is a major reason for their use. As activities become more complex and sophisticated, *details* become increasingly important. However, the sword is double-edged. Though models typically like to have disaggregated data, sometimes the disaggregation itself creates insurmountable problems. Disaggregation may create too many decision variables, thus making the model too large and impossible to use. In this respect, the balance is between the ideal of using the most information available (highly detailed, disaggregated data) and the practical matter of implementation.

Refinement of Data

The term *refinement* is often used synonymously with disaggregation. Thus *highly refined data* (often called *highly structured*) refers to highly disaggregated data. However, refinement has another meaning. A considerable amount of data may be available. The data may be relevant to the problem under study but they may not be in the correct form. We may have yearly data on total sales volume and yearly data on total number of plants operating, but for our model we may require average sales per plant in each year. It is possible to obtain the figures we need by preforming some simple algebraic manipulations on the existing data. This process of manipulating or "massaging" data is also termed *refining* the data. Such refinements can be quite extensive, depending on what is available and what is needed. The refining of data is usually a job relegated to computers and, in fact, computers can be reasonably described as powerful "data refineries."

All data, once accumulated, must be stored. In order to examine data, they must be displayed. Most data are stored on paper, on mangetic tapes, in magnetic discs, or in computers. For our purposes, the storage is less important than the display.

The same numbers can be displayed in various alternative ways. Numbers can be displayed in tables, by plots, or by graphs. The choice may be dictated by convenience or the reasons may be more basic. For example, a table is a display of a finite amount of data. A graph is a display of an infinite amount of data. In the remainder of this chapter, we discuss various displays and their uses in the decision process.

2.5
PLOTS AND GRAPHS

Tables, plots, and graphs provide alternative ways of displaying data. You have already seen a tabular representation in Figure 2.1. Let us return to these data to demonstrate the use of plots and graphs. Recall that these data represent a historical record of marketing expenditures and sales over time. The name for data that represent observations over time is a **time series.**

Suppose PROTRAC's manager believes that neither marketing techniques nor product demand has changed in any significant way during the period over which the data were recorded. As a result, the manager considers the time element to be of minor importance in terms of capturing the interaction between marketing and sales. He hypothesizes that there is some direct relationship between marketing expenditures in year t and total sales in year t. He does not know exactly what the relationship is, but he feels that it is reflected by the numbers in Figure 2.1. However, he also feels that the appropriate relationship does not depend on the year. For example, he may have a rough idea that sales volume should be "*about* four times" marketing expenditures, regardless of the year. This factor of proportionality, 4, is hypothesized to be *independent* of time. We use the phrase "about four times" because the manager knows that the factor may be somewhat less than 4 in some years and somewhat greater than 4 in others, because of random events. In this linguistic sense, of course, the factor does *Dependent vs* depend on time. However, from the viewpoint of mathematics, the words **dependent** *Independent* and **independent** have special and important meanings. In the mathematical sense, the hypothesis that the factor of proportionality is "independent of time" means that time has no consistently recognizable or identifiable influence.

Suppose, however, that the manager feels that marketing efficiency has been improving year by year, because of such factors as new knowledge, shifting tastes leading to increased product demand, greater sales potential because of government policies, and so on. Many of these influences are difficult to measure and quantify directly, and the manager may therefore lump them together into a single factor or influence he thinks of as "time." Thus, time becomes a surrogate for other quantities not explicitly in the model. In that case, the factor of proportionality between marketing and sales would depend explicitly on the year. In other words, the relationship between marketing and sales would be *dependent* on time.

Let us return to our original scenario. The manager has hypothesized that the factor of proportionality is "about four." In order to pin the value down more closely, or, as we sometimes say, in order to get a better feeling for the data, it is often convenient to **plot** the numbers, as in Figure 2.2. Explicit reference to time is deliberately omitted because we are operating under the manager's assumption that the essential quantitative relationship is independent of time.

Figure 2.2
PROTRAC European Sales versus Marketing
Expenditures

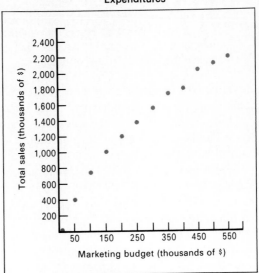

The information presented in data tables, or the plots associated with them, is **discrete** rather than **continuous**. In other words, in Figure 2.2 the value of total sales is given for only a selected number of values of the marketing budget.

In some cases, the discreteness of the data is a conceptual necessity dictated by the type of phenomenon being considered. After all, the phone company has few alternatives to listing its subscribers and their phone numbers. Similarly, data on crawler tractor production must occur in discrete units, since fractions of tractors are not produced.

In many other cases, however, there is no conceptual problem with having a very large number of possible values for the quantities considered, and indeed with having an infinite number or a continuum of values. For example, there is no conceptual reason why a refinery manager cannot think of processing 156.984215 barrels of crude oil per day.

Although there is no conceptual problem with a relationship between two continuous quantities or variables, there are substantial practical problems in determining such relationships. Many textbooks on quantitative methods are devoted to deriving "optimal" decisions assuming that we are given various quantitative relationships, but the truth is that

In many applied situations the most difficult problem is knowing the precise quantitative form of the relationships of interest.

The problem of deriving relationships from data cannot be "assumed away." Moreover, in real problems relevant data often do not exist, or, when data are available, they may not reveal anything meaningful or causal about the particular relationship of interest to management.

The present scenario provides a case in point. Let's review the logic:

1. The data in Figure 2.1 provide a historical record. That much is clear and indisputable.

2. It seems reasonable to feel that there are interactions of a causative nature between marketing expenditures and total sales. These interactions may or may not be deduced from the data in the table.

3. Now the manager makes several big assumptions. He does not actually "believe" these assumptions, but he considers them to be at least reasonable "first approximations." First, he assumes that the interactions *can* be deduced from the numbers in Figure 2.1. Second, he assumes that sales in year *t* depend only on marketing efforts in year *t*, and not on past marketing expenditures. (In technical language, he assumes that *lags* are unimportant.) Third, he assumes that the relevant interaction between sales and marketing is independent of time.

Given this logic, an important question for our purposes is: How is it possible to compute the total sales anticipated with a marketing budget of $324,579.36? Before you read on, try to answer this question. Consider how you would go about getting a specific number from Figure 2.2. You cannot read this number directly from the figure. You will have to do a certain amount of reasoning and "fudging."

Specifying a Graph

There are two reasonable approaches to this problem. The first approach is very intuitive and simple. Take a ruler and draw a straight line "close" to all the points. This straight line, called a **graph,** provides a means for representing continuous data. The equation of the line can be computed, and from then on it is fairly easy to obtain the total sales associated with the marketing expenditure of $324,579.36. Figure 2.3 shows this approach. The straight line in this figure is a model for the relationship between marketing expenditure and sales.

The equation of the line in Figure 2.3 is

$$\text{sales} = 4 \times \text{marketing} + 200$$

Therefore, the total sales associated with a marketing value of $324,579.36 is $1,498,317.44.

Obviously, we could draw other straight lines or graphs that would be close to the points in Figure 2.2. The study of which line is "best" is a separate topic that lies in the domain of statistics and is called **linear regression analysis**. In the empirical analysis of data, regression is a very important topic which is typically covered in some detail in statistics courses.

The data could also be approximated by a curve rather than a straight line. This topic of curve fitting is called **nonlinear regression.** The equation of a curve is often difficult to compute, and the statistical theory becomes much more complicated. This does not mean that curved graphs are not used in practice. Quite to the contrary, they are often essential in representing nonlinear phenomena.

But for our present purposes, it is sufficient to draw any straight line that looks close to the points on the plot. After all, we have already acknowledged the existence of random disturbances from year to year, and we are seeking only a reasonable first approximation to the interaction between marketing and sales.

The second intuitive approach we can use for continuous estimation in this situation is simply to connect each data point with a straight line. The result, which is linear in segments, is shown in Figure 2.4. This type of graph is called a **piecewise linear approximation.**

Using this method, we can compute the total sales associated with the marketing value of $324,579.36 from the particular linear segment that connects the marketing expenditures of 300 and 350 to the appropriate sales, 1565 and 1715. The

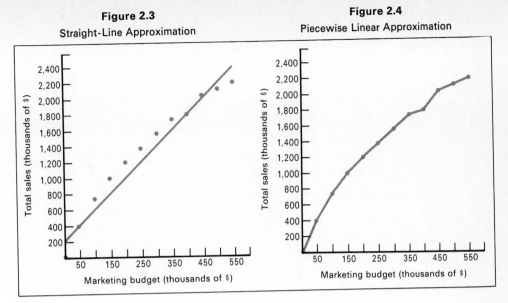

Figure 2.3
Straight-Line Approximation

Figure 2.4
Piecewise Linear Approximation

equation of this segment is

$$\text{sales} = 3 \times \text{marketing} + 665$$

Consequently, the total sales associated with a marketing value of $324,579.36 is $1,638,738.08. The piecewise linear approximation differs from the straight-line approximation value by $140,420.64, which is certainly not an insignificant amount. It is important for the manager to be aware of the possibility of *alternately plausible estimates*.

The fact is that in this example the two approaches may not be equally plausible, and the second estimate may be preferable to the first. Look at Figure 2.4 again. Notice that between the marketing expenditures of 0 and 400 the linear segments decrease in steepness. At the marketing level 400 the steepness sharply increases, but then the decreasing pattern continues.

Decreasing steepness in a piecewise linear graph is sometimes called **decreasing (or diminishing) marginal returns** (also called diminishing returns to scale). It reflects real-world phenomena of concern to management. For example, in the present scenario, decreasing marginal returns could be explained by market saturation, meaning that most of the market has already been captured. An additional dollar spent on advertising must convince ever more reluctant customers and consequently yields a smaller amount of revenue than the last dollar spent. Also, market saturation may mean that financial incentives such as lower payments and carrying charges may have to be offered to attract more customers.

The Manager's Interpretation

Since the number 324,579.36 is in an area of decreasing marginal returns, it may mean that some of the foregoing phenomena are at work at that level of marketing. In other words, if the manager "believes" the decreasing marginal returns pattern, then Figure 2.4 should be used to represent the interactions of interest.

The key consideration is the manager's interpretation of the shapes of the graphs. If he believes that the quantitative relationship is basically linear and that the deviations from the straight line (in Figure 2.3) are due to random factors such as bad weather, then Figure 2.3 should be accepted. If he believes that Figure 2.4 reflects a real-world operational phenomenon in the form of decreasing marginal returns in the budget region of interest, then Figure 2.4 should be accepted. His interpretation and judgment are crucial in his use of these graphs as tools.

2.6

AN EXAMPLE: PROTRAC ANNUAL PRODUCTION DECISIONS

PROTRAC utilizes a matrix type of organization. For example, the large crawler tractor (LCT) manager in the Moline plant reports both to the LCT manager in corporate headquarters and to the Moline plant manager. The LCT manager in corporate headquarters is responsible for recommending an overall annual level of LCT production to the corporate vice-president.

Let us consider the corporate LCT manager's problem. Although there are really three different LCT types, the P-7, P-8, and P-9, for purposes of determining the general level of activity they are treated as a common "unit of production." Also, in short-term planning (planning for next year) the capacity is considered to be more or less fixed within a given range. In other words, expanding capacity by capital investment (new plant and equipment) requires more than a year. Moreover, LCT production is sufficiently specialized so that it is impossible to sublet any significant part of the process. As a result of these considerations, there are relatively inflexible upper limits to which next year's capacity can be extended. The allowable variations are controlled by

1. Determining the number of shifts the assembly line will work
2. Allowing workers to work overtime
3. Increasing the speed of the assembly line, which entails hiring additional assemblers and material handlers

In attempting to recommend a desirable annual level of production, the corporate LCT manager has gathered some data on the historical relations between *quantity produced, total revenue, total cost, profit, average revenue, average cost, average profits, marginal revenue,* and *marginal cost.* The definitions of these quantities are:

$$\text{Average revenue} = \frac{\text{total revenue}}{\text{quantity produced}}$$

$$\text{Average cost} = \frac{\text{total cost}}{\text{quantity produced}}$$

$$\text{Profit} = \text{total revenue} - \text{total cost}$$

$$\text{Average profit} = \text{average revenue} - \text{average cost}$$

$$\text{Marginal revenue} = \text{additional revenue from last unit produced}$$

$$\text{Marginal cost} = \text{additional cost from last unit produced}$$

The data on total revenue, total cost, and profit are presented in Figure 2.5. In Figure 2.6, the data for total revenue and total cost are plotted against quantity produced, and then the points are connected by straight lines to obtain piecewise linear graphs of total revenue and total cost.

Note that this method of connecting points creates a number of corners on the graphs. Remember that these graphs are only approximations. A truer picture of

Figure 2.5

Data on PROTRAC Totals

QUANTITY PRODUCED	TOTAL REVENUE (MILLIONS OF $)	TOTAL COST (MILLIONS OF $)	PROFIT (MILLIONS OF $)
0	0	14[a]	−14
500	60	36	24
1000	120	58	62
1500	166	80	86
2000	200	103	97
2500	224	134	90
3000	243	165	78
3500	255	196	59
4000	265	227	38
4500	273	262	11
5000	280	297	−17

[a]Cost of producing 0 units at $14 million represents the fixed costs to the firm of maintaining plants, equipment, and so on.

Figure 2.6

Total and Marginal Graphs
for PROTRAC Revenue and Cost

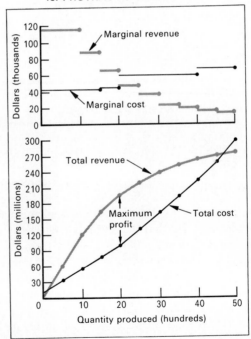

the underlying relationships could conceivably be smooth and without corners.[1] However, for the present problem the question of which method to use to connect the points should be considered in the perspective that a certain amount of uncertainty and imprecision in the underlying real-world relationships is inevitable. From this point of view, it is relatively unimportant whether we use straight lines, as in Figure 2.6, or whether we sketch a smooth graph through or near the points, as with the regression type of

[1]In mathematics, this terminology is redundant, for the word *smooth* means "without corners."

approximation we mentioned in Section 2.5. For the present purpose, we can obtain marginal information very easily from a piecewise linear approximation; therefore, it is convenient to use this method. These marginal data derived from the total cost and total revenue curves are also displayed in Figure 2.6. For example, the marginal revenue obtained from producing unit 2200 is equal to the steepness, or *slope*, of the total revenue graph at the same point. Reading from Figure 2.5, this slope is

$$\frac{224(10^6) - 200(10^6)}{500} = \frac{24}{5}(10^4) = 48,000$$

This calculation shows that the revenue added by unit 2200 is $48,000. All the marginal figures can be obtained from the slope of the total graphs in this way. At the corners, the *slope from the left* is used to define the marginal data; for example, the magrinal revenue at 1500 units is $92,000.

Marginal Cost and Revenue

In analyzing these data, it is important to note that marginal revenue is nonincreasing and marginal cost is nondecreasing. At all production levels less than 2000 units, marginal revenue is greater than marginal cost. This means that the return on each unit is greater than the cost of producing that unit. Consequently, for each of the first 2000 units produced, a profit results. For each unit of production after the first 2000, marginal revenue is less than marginal cost and hence a loss results from each such unit. This implies that the maximum profit occurs at the quantity 2000. You can verify this from either Figure 2.5 or from the graphs in Figure 2.6. We have just observed in these figures that

---

Profit is maximized by selecting the largest production level for which marginal revenue is greater than marginal cost.

As a final comment on marginal data, recall our earlier discussion that the graphs on totals could have been sketched as smooth curves rather than as piecewise linear approximations. Regardless of which choice had been made, the graphs would have looked more or less the same. However, this statement is not true for the graphs on marginal data. Explanations for this phenomenon go beyond our scope and intent. It is enough to say that if the totals had been graphed as smooth curves, then the marginal curves[2] would look very different from those in Figure 2.6. Marginal revenue would be a continuous decreasing graph, and marginal cost would be a continuous increasing graph. However, these two graphs would cross over somewhere near a production level of 2000, and this crossover point, where marginal revenue equals marginal cost, would give the quantity at which maximum profit is indicated by the smoothed total curves.

Data on averages are displayed in Figure 2.7 and plotted in Figure 2.8. Note that according to our analysis, although total profit is maximized at a production level of 2000 units with a corresponding profit of $97 million, the average profit is maximized at a production level of 1000 with the total profit at only $62 million. Although production of 1000 units produces the largest profit per unit, **most firms are interested in obtaining a maximum level of total profit, even though the profit per unit may be smaller.** The corporate LCT manager's view is consistent with overall profit maximization, and he therefore recommends a production level of 2000 units.

---

[2] In the language of calculus, the marginal curve is the first derivative of the total.

Figure 2.7
Data on PROTRAC Averages

QUANTITY PRODUCED	AVERAGE REVENUE	AVERAGE COST	AVERAGE PROFIT
500	$120,000	$72,000	$48,000
1,000	120,000	58,000	62,000
1,500	110,666	53,333	57,333
2,000	100,000	51,500	48,500
2,500	89,600	53,600	36,000
3,000	81,000	55,000	26,000
3,500	72,857	56,000	16,857
4,000	66,250	56,750	9,500
4,500	60,666	58,222	2,444
5,000	56,000	59,400	−3,400

Figure 2.8
PROTRAC Average Revenue, Cost,
and Profit Graphs

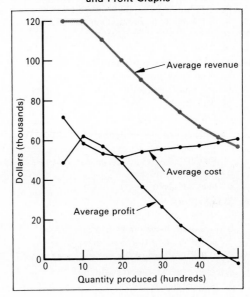

2.7

MAJOR CONCEPTS QUIZ

True–False

1. **T F** Data are used in building models.
2. **T F** A model provides a consistent means to interpret and evaluate data.
3. **T F** Aggregated data contain more information than do disaggregated data.
4. **T F** ''Highly structured data'' means the opposite of ''highly refined data.''
5. **T F** In order to plot data, they must be continuous as opposed to discrete.

6. T F A graph is one means of representing discrete data.

7. T F Discreteness of data may be a conceptual necessity.

Multiple Choice

8. Data can be represented by
   a. tables
   b. plots
   c. graphs
   d. all of the above

9. Discrete data can often
   a. be represented as a plot
   b. be the basis for a piecewise linear representation
   c. arise from a time series
   d. all of the above

10. Continuous relationships
    a. can be represented by a table
    b. can be estimated with a regression fit to discrete data
    c. cannot be plotted or graphed
    d. none of the above

11. For smooth revenue and cost curves, maximum profit occurs when
    a. average revenue equals average cost
    b. marginal revenue equals marginal cost
    c. average profit is maximized
    d. none of the above

12. Most firms wish to maximize
    a. total revenue
    b. average revenue
    c. total profit
    d. profit per unit sold

13. To maximize profit per unit sold, management must maximize
    a. total profit
    b. marginal profit
    c. marginal revenue
    d. average profit

14. Marginal cost
    a. is the intercept of the total cost curve
    b. is the profit-maximizing cost value
    c. is the slope of the total cost curve
    d. is the intercept of the average cost curve

15. A piecewise linear representation
    a. is a linear approximation
    b. is linear in segments
    c. is always an approximation
    d. is a form of regression line

16. For a function of a single continuous variable, diminishing marginal returns
    a. means that the graph of the function has increasing slope
    b. means that the underlying phenomenon experiences saturation
    c. would have little real-world relevance
    d. all of the above

Answers

1. T	7. T	12. c
2. T	8. d	13. d
3. F	9. d	14. c
4. F	10. b	15. b
5. F	11. b	16. b
6. F		

2-1. What is the relationship between data and models?

2-2. Define the terms *decision* and *data*.

2-3. At what point do entries in a data table, such as Figure 2.1, begin to take on the role of a model?

2-4. List some of the forms and sources of data.

2-5. What is the advantage of having disaggregated data? What is the advantage of aggregated data?

2-6. What is the distinction between a time-dependent relationship and one that is time independent?

2-7. Name some types of data that are conceptually discrete as opposed to continuous. Name two quantities that are inherently continuous. Is money continuous or discrete?

2-8. What is meant by "diminishing marginal returns"? What type of data might exhibit such a phenomenon, and how might it be explained?

2-9. What is the relationship between the shape of the marginal graph and a total graph that exhibits the following characteristics?
(a) Diminishing marginal returns
(b) Increasing marginal returns

2-10. Does *profit maximization* generally mean the same thing as *maximize average profit*?

CHAPTER 3

Constrained Optimization Models

3.1
INTRODUCTION

Many of the models to be studied in this text fall under the broad category of constrained optimization models. In this chapter we provide an overview of such models, emphasizing the concept of constrained optimization and some of the language used in dealing with constrained optimization models.

At the outset, it is to be noted that most people make many of their personal and professional decisions in situations where the set of allowable decisions has been restricted in some way. In the language of modeling, a restriction on the set of allowable decisions is called a **constraint.** Constraints may be self-imposed or dictated by others. A person with a strict budget must buy groceries for the week without spending too much money. A production manager must plan production schedules without exceeding the capacity of plant and equipment. A speculator is constrained in his or her trading by the amount of margin on deposit with a broker. A parent of three teenagers can let only one of them take the family car Saturday night. A plant superintendent can assign only unoccupied maintenance crews to unanticipated repairs. A member of Alcoholics Anonymous declines an invitation for cocktails. The list is endless. It is perhaps not surprising, therefore, that **constrained optimization,** which means achieving the best possible result considering the restrictions, has been the most active area of management-science research. Indeed, one of the most commonly employed management-science tools, linear programming, is a special model for carrying out constrained optimization.

The Meaning of Optimality Constrained optimization models, when solved, provide what are called **optimal,** or best, **decisions,** but this statement calls for the strongest possible caveat.

Optimization models produce the optimal answer to a mathematical problem posed by a model.

This may or may not be a good (to say nothing of optimal) answer in the real context. Whenever we use words like "real" or "true" we are referring to the real-world problem that underlies the mathematical model. The term *optimality* is a theoretical (i.e., mathematical), as opposed to a real-world concept. The truth is that rarely is it meaningful to talk about optimal decisions for the complicated problems of business, and *one of the worst mistakes a manager can make is blindly to allow a model to make his or her decisions.* In fact, in management problems, two plus two do not always equal four. Rather than seeking the quantitatively superior solution, the mature manager will often be more concerned with the optimal political solution. This, however, does not by any means imply that quantitative models do not play an important role in the overall decision-making process. In order to appreciate this role, it is necessary to appreciate some of the relationships between the real problem, the problem analyst, the decision maker, and the model.

Complicating a Model

And so, let us begin to explain the assertion that the complicated problems of business (and even more so, of government) have no optimal solution. There are always considerations that cannot be built into the model, for to include everything would complicate the model enormously and make it impossible to solve. What do we mean by "complicate the model"? This will become clearer as we proceed. For now, it suffices to mention two major complicating factors: (1) form, or mathematical structure, and (2) size. For example, in terms of form it is often important to keep all expressions in the model linear. But it simply may not be possible to capture some of the interactions with linear expressions, and consequently such interactions may not be included. In terms of size, models with too many constraints and too many variables cannot be solved even on high-speed computers. This consideration can also lead to simplifications, and a limited and incomplete representation of the real problem may result. These facts help to amplify our assertion in Chapter 1 that models are selective representations of reality. In any realistic application, the ultimate effect of this selectivity is the following truth:

> **The word "optimal" is strictly a mathematical concept. An "optimal (or best) decision" produced by a model should be interpreted as being hopefully a "good decision" for the real problem.**

Consequently, the decision maker has to blend the output of the model with his own personal interests and his own perceptions about the nature and credibility of the model and its correspondence with the real problem.

In fact, one of the most important applications of models is to provide reinforcement for the intuition of the decision maker. This reinforcement can be positive. It can provide quantitative support for the decision maker's preconceived notions. It can bolster his confidence in his own intuition. It can show him explicitly how to go about implementing his preferred policy (regardless of the motivation for that policy) and what results, in quantitative terms, might be expected. On the other hand, the model's reinforcement can be negative. The results can challenge the intuition. Previously hidden or overlooked relations may become apparent. The decision maker may be forced to choose between his intuition and the model. The better and more credible the model, the more difficult the choice.

Aside from these considerations, there are also technical ways of determining how good a model may be and how relevant its recommendations may be for the real-world problem at hand. These technical aspects are in the realm of what is called **sensitivity analysis** and thus will be emphasized wherever possible in our exposition.

At this point let us explicitly turn to the general form of a constrained optimization model.

3.2
MATHEMATICAL FORMULATION AND INTERPRETATION

The terms **constrained optimization** and **mathematical programming** are often used to describe the same general model. Although the explicit meaning of this model can be described in words, the symbolic or mathematical representation is the most unambiguous way to depict all that it says. In symbolic form, the constrained optimization model is

$$
\begin{aligned}
&\text{maximize (or minimize)} \quad f(x_1, x_2, \ldots, x_n) \\
&\text{subject to the constraints that} \\[1em]
&g_1(x_1, x_2, \ldots, x_n) \;\; {\textstyle\begin{matrix}\leq\\=\\\geq\end{matrix}} \;\; b_1 \\[1em]
&g_2(x_1, x_2, \ldots, x_n) \;\; {\textstyle\begin{matrix}\leq\\=\\\geq\end{matrix}} \;\; b_2 \\
&\qquad\qquad \vdots \qquad\qquad\qquad \vdots \\
&g_m(x_1, x_2, \ldots, x_n) \;\; {\textstyle\begin{matrix}\leq\\=\\\geq\end{matrix}} \;\; b_m
\end{aligned}
$$

When all the functions in this model are linear, we have the important special case of a **linear programming model.** Ultimately, we will pay specific attention to linear programs, but for now the discussion is quite general.

Components of a Constrained Optimization Model

The function f is called the **objective function,** or the **payoff function,** or simply the **return.** The model states that the problem is to make the value of this function as large (or as small) as possible, provided that the **constraints,** or restricting conditions, are also satisfied. The value of the objective function is often measured in quantities like dollars of profit (in a maximization problem) or dollars of cost (in a minimization problem). The variables $x_1, x_2, \ldots, x_n$ are called **decision variables.** Recall our earlier definition that, for our purposes, decisions are numbers. The numerical values of the decision variables represent actions or activities to be undertaken at various levels. The decision maker has the values of these variables under his direct control. Any choice of these values indirectly assigns a numerical value to the objective function. The functions $g_1, \ldots, g_m$ are called **constraint functions.** Any selection of numerical values for the decision variables also indirectly assigns values to the constraint functions. The model requires that each of these constraint function values must satisfy a condition expressed by a mathematical inequality or an equality. The first constraint, for example, is one and only one of the following conditions:

32

$$g_1(x_1, x_2, \ldots, x_n) \leq b_1$$
$$g_1(x_1, x_2, \ldots, x_n) = b_1$$
$$g_1(x_1, x_2, \ldots, x_n) \geq b_1$$

where b_1 is a parameter with a specified numerical value. In other words, in the language of models, *a constraint is a mathematical equality or inequality which must be satisfied.* The numbers b_i, $i = 1, 2, \ldots, m$, taken together are called the **right-hand sides** (abbreviated RHS). The number b_1 is called the right-hand side of the first constraint, and so on. The set of all m of the constraints taken together, that is, the group of relations

$$g_i(x_1, x_2, \ldots, x_n) \overset{\leq}{\underset{\geq}{=}} b_i \qquad i = 1, \ldots, m$$

indirectly restricts the values that can be assigned to the decision variables.

For example, suppose the model contains the requirement that

$$g_1(x_1, x_2, \ldots, x_n) \leq b_1$$

Consider a vector $x = (x_1, \ldots, x_n)$ of decisions that imply that

$$g_1(x_1, x_2, \ldots, x_n) > b_1$$

This choice of decisions will be forbidden by the model since it violates one of the constraints. The model will consider only those decisions that satisfy **all** the constraints.

In summary, we have seen that

Every constrained optimization model has an objective function, constraints, decision variables, and parameters.

3.3
THE HYDE PARK POLICE CAPTAIN

The problems of the captain of the Hyde Park police force will help to illustrate the meaning of the constrained optimization model. The police captain wants to penetrate one of the city's most pernicious dope rings. His tactic is to select a patrolman to impersonate a hurdler on the University of Chicago track team. Since he has neither the time nor the inclination to interview each patrolman individually, he will ask the personnel department to screen the employee files. Recalling from the Olympics that most hurdlers are young and tall, he instructs the personnel department to send to his office the tallest patrolman between the ages of 20 and 28. His selection procedure is described by the following constrained optimization model:

Find an x that maximizes $f(x)$

subject to

$$20 \leq g_1(x) \leq 28$$

where the decision variable x represents a patrolman and

$$f(x) = \text{height of patrolman } x$$
$$g_1(x) = \text{age of patrolman } x$$

Note that the constraint $20 \leq g_1(x) \leq 28$ is equivalent to two constraints in standard form, namely, $g_1(x) \leq 28$ and $g_1(x) \geq 20$. This problem is illustrated by the lineup in Figure 3.1. As this figure shows, although there are points where the objective func-

Figure 3.1

Selecting a Hurdler: The Model with One Decision Variable and One Constraint

tion $f(x)$ takes on larger values, the captain has limited the search to those values of x for which $g_1(x)$, the patrolman's age, is between 20 and 28. Among those constrained values of x he seeks one that maximizes his objective function. The optimal solution to the model is provided by the patrolman with badge number 34. When the personnel department sends the optimal solution to his office, the captain is disappointed to discover that the man weighs 310 pounds and looks more like King Kong than a hurdler. Although the solution is optimal in terms of the model, the captain's intuition tells him it is far from optimal in terms of his real problem. Rather than reject his intuition, he decides to reject his model. He decides that it must be an inaccurate portrayal of his problem. One of his management consultants suggests that they modify the instructions to the personnel department so as to find the tallest man between the ages of 20 and 28 who *also* weighs between 150 and 180 pounds (i.e., the tallest man who satisfies *two* conditions). The new model is

Illustrating
"Optimality"

$$\text{Find an } x \text{ that maximizes} \quad f(x)$$
$$\text{subject to}$$
$$20 \leq g_1(x) \leq 28$$
$$150 \leq g_2(x) \leq 180$$

where x, $f(x)$, and $g_1(x)$ are defined as before and $g_2(x)$ is the weight of patrolman x.

Figure 3.2

Selecting a Hurdler: The Model with One Decision Variable and Two Constraints

This problem is illustrated in a three-dimensional portrayal in Figure 3.2. In this figure, height is represented vertically above the two-dimensional plane representing age and weight. Whereas formerly there were three *allowable decisions* (badge numbers 2, 34, and 18), there are now only two allowable decisions (badge numbers 2 and 18). Number 34 has been rejected because he does not satisfy *both* constraints. The new optimal solution is number 2.

If we now generalize f and g_1 to be functions defined on, say, all nonnegative numbers x, then a generalized version of Figure 3.1 will provide a reasonable geometric representation of a constrained optimization problem with one decision variable x and one constraint. Figure 3.3 illustrates the following generalized problem and the solution, x^*:

$$\text{Maximize} \quad f(x)$$
$$\text{subject to}$$
$$g_1(x) \geq b_1$$
$$x \geq 0$$

In Figure 3.3, you can see the numerical values of x at which the value $g_1(x)$ is not less than b_1. These are the so-called **feasible,** or **allowable values** of x. Considering all these allowable values of x, the value $f(x^*)$ is the largest objective value. This means that x^* is the optimal value of x (the solution) for the given model.

Let us now complicate the model by adding a second constraint, say $g_2(x) \leq b_2$. The model becomes

$$\text{Max} \quad f(x)$$
$$\text{s. t.} \quad g_1(x) \geq b_1$$
$$g_2(x) \leq b_2$$
$$x \geq 0$$

Figure 3.3
Constrained Optimization Problem with One
Variable and One Constraint

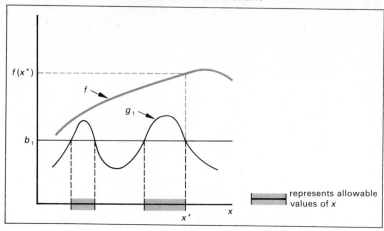

Effect
of Adding
a Constraint

This problem is shown along with the new solution, $\hat{x}$, in Figure 3.4. You can see that the set of x values that simultaneously satisfy both constraints (the hatched and shaded region) is a subset of the x values that satisfy either constraint individually. You can also note that in the problem with two constraints, the solution is not "as good"—that is, $f(\hat{x}) < f(x^*)$—as it was for the problem with a single constraint. In other words, adding a constraint to a problem can "hurt" the objective. But don't forget the Hyde Park police captain. Adding a constraint to his model did, in fact, hurt the model's objective (to maximize height), but it actually improved the decision maker's objective (to find the best impersonator of a hurdler). Thus, adding a constraint served to make the model more credible. We shall return to this point later in this chapter. For now, you have some idea of what a model looks like (symbolically and geometrically) and what it says.

Figure 3.4
Constrained Optimization Problem with One
Variable and Two Constraints

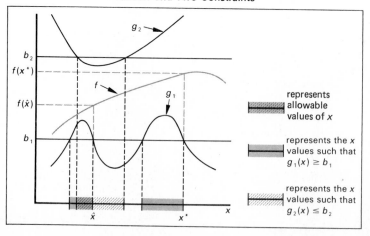

ANOTHER EXAMPLE: ASTRO/COSMO

The Hyde Park Police Captain was conceptual fun. Here is another very simple example of a constrained optimization model, but one that is a better preview of the type of problem we will begin to see much more of in the next chapter. The problem is first stated in words:

A TV company produces two types of TV sets, the Astro and the Cosmo. There are two production lines, one for each set, and there are two departments, both of which are used in the production of each set. The capacity of the Astro production line is 70 sets per day. The capacity of the Cosmo line is 50 sets per day. In department A picture tubes are produced. In this department the Astro set requires 1 labor hour, the Cosmo set requires 2 labor hours. Presently in department A a maximum of 120 labor hours per day can be assigned to production of the two types of sets. In department B the chassis is constructed. In this department the Astro set requires 1 labor hour and the Cosmo also requires 1 labor hour. Presently, in department B a maximum of 90 labor hours per day can be assigned to production of the two types of sets. The profit contributions are 20 and 10 dollars, respectively, for each Astro and Cosmo set. These data are summarized in tabular form as follows:

		LABOR UTILIZATION PER SET (hr)		
	DAILY CAPACITY	Dept. A	Dept. B	PROFIT PER SET
Astro	70	1	1	$20
Cosmo	50	2	1	10
Total labor availability		120	90	

If the company can sell as many Astro and Cosmo sets as it produces, what should be the daily plan (i.e., the daily production) for each set?

To formulate a constrained optimization model for this problem we define two decision variables:

Defining the Decision Variables

$$A = \text{daily production of Astros (sets/day)}$$
$$C = \text{daily production of Cosmos (sets/day)}$$

The objective is to maximize profit, where

$$\text{profit} = 20A + 10C$$

The constraints are

$$A \leq 70 \quad \text{(capacity of the Astro line)}$$
$$C \leq 50 \quad \text{(capacity of the Cosmo line)}$$
$$A + 2C \leq 120 \quad \text{(limitation on labor available in department A)}$$
$$A + C \leq 90 \quad \text{(limitation on labor available in department B)}$$

The complete model is thus

$$\text{Max} \quad 20A + 10C \qquad \text{Objective function}$$

$$\left.\begin{array}{r} \text{s.t.} \quad A \le 70 \\ C \le 50 \\ A + 2C \le 120 \\ A + C \le 90 \end{array}\right\} \quad \text{Constraints}$$

$$A \ge 0, \quad C \ge 0 \qquad \text{Nonnegativity conditions}$$

Several observations are to be made:

1. This is an example of a **linear program**, since all expressions in the model are linear.
2. It has been assumed that A and C are continuous variables, so that fractional numbers of TV sets make sense. Forcing A and C to be integer values turns this into a much different type of model, called an **integer program**. Integer programs are dealt with later in the text. Until then it will often be assumed that fractional values make physical sense or, if not, it is assumed that the solution will be rounded for purposes of implementation.
3. Notice that since negative production does not make sense, so-called nonnegativity conditions have been imposed.

In the same way that Figures 3.3 and 3.4 show graphic solutions to constrained optimization models with one decision variable, the Astro/Cosmo problem, with two decision variables, can also be graphically analyzed. Specifically, Figure 3.5 portrays the set of nonnegative decisions that satisfy all constraints simultaneously and we also see the location of the optimal production plan, $A^* = 70$, $C^* = 20$.

Figure 3.5
Astro/Cosmo Feasible Region

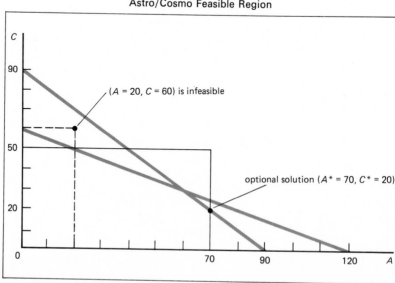

The details of this graphical approach are presented in Chapter 5. For now, our goal is to enrich your understanding of the *meaning* of constrained optimization. In particular, the shaded region represents points (A, C) which satisfy the four inequalities and the nonnegativity conditions. Any pair of decisions (A, C), lying in this shaded region, is termed **allowable** or **feasible.** The shaded set is called the **feasible region,** also called the **constraint set.** Any pair such as $(A = 20, C = 60)$ lying outside the feasible region is termed **infeasible.** Since such a pair will violate at least one constraint, it is not allowed.

The constraint optimization problem is this: Of all the allowable pairs (A, C), find one that maximizes profit. Such a pair is an **optimal solution** to our model. For now we will merely state that the optimal solution occurs at the point $(A^* = 70, C^* = 20)$.

3.5
APPLICATIONS OF CONSTRAINED OPTIMIZATION MODELS

Constrained optimization models were first used in decision making in the 1940s. Among the major applications were logistic problems in World War II. The fields of operations research and management science arose from these early defense applications.

Now, applications of constrained optimization models range across all sorts of planning activities in both the public and private sectors. Applications in government are frequent. They currently include modeling efforts in the areas of defense, health planning, transportation, energy planning, and resource allocation, to name only a few. In the private sector, applications vary from long-term planning to daily, or even hourly, scheduling of activities. Specific applications in long-term planning include capital budgeting, plant location, long-range marketing strategy, and long-range investment strategy. Shorter-term applications include production and work-force scheduling, inventory management, machine scheduling, aircraft routing, chemical blending, product design, media selection, statistical estimation, feed-mix blending, tanker scheduling, waste disposal, site selection, and project scheduling in the construction of nuclear submarines or major shopping centers. The list could go on and on.

In all these applications, there are decisions to be made in order to carry out an activity or collection of activities optimally according to some criterion (such as minimizing cost, time, waste, or delay, or maximizing profit or total amount shipped). Also, in all these applications, there are limitations imposed either by scarce resources that must be allocated or by certain requirements that must be satisfied, or a combination of both. These limitations or requirements place constraints on the decisions that can be made. Other constraints may exist in the form of logical relations or physical laws that must be satisfied by the decision variables. Thus, decisions must be found that optimize the objective subject to all the constraints.

3.6
CONSTRAINED VERSUS UNCONSTRAINED OPTIMIZATION

Most professionals in management science or operations research believe that constrained optimization models capture the essence of management decision making. Others do not. One dissident group adheres to what is sometimes labeled the *economist's*[1] or the *price*

---

[1]In this context, we cheerfully acknowledge the inaccuracy of this label since many economists have a deep interest in constrained optimization. For example, Tjalling Koopmans, a Nobel Prize winner in economics, was one of the early users of linear programming.

theorist's point of view. This point of view was most succinctly put forth by a former colleague at Chicago who emphatically stated, "There is no such thing as a truly constrained optimization problem."

The disputed issue concerns the role of parameters in the decision-making process. In the constrained optimization approach, the right-hand-side (RHS) parameters play a role in defining the constraints in the model, and values for these parameters are viewed as being temporarily fixed. The modeler seeks to find the best decision (for example, the one that maximizes the objective function) within the limits prescribed by these parameters. We shall see that he or she may want to explore the effects of varying these parameters, but in a single execution of the model they are fixed. For example, in a production-planning model it might be specified that the capacity of a certain department or production facility is fixed, and the goal would be to maximize profits within that limit.

In the price theorist's view, constraining parameters simply do not exist. For example, in a box-manufacturing plant, the capacity of the printing department is not considered fixed. It is "always" possible to purchase additional printing capacity. Perhaps we can hire more workers or work another shift or send boxes out to another printer. Symbolically, the difference between these points of view is experssed as follows. Suppose that $g_4(x_1, x_2, \ldots, x_n)$ is the printing time required if we produce x_1 units of product 1, and so on, and let b_4 be an RHS parameter whose value is the capacity of the printing department. Then, instead of employing a constraint $g_4(x_1, x_2, \ldots, x_n) \leq b_4$, the price theorist prefers to use a function

$$C_4[g_4(x_1, x_2, \ldots, x_n)]$$

that yields the cost to the firm of obtaining $g_4(x_1, x_2, \ldots, x_n)$ hours of printing time. This term along with many similar terms makes up a profit function to be used as the objective for the firm. There are no constraining parameters in the model. The value of the objective function is maximized without constraints; this is thus called an **unconstrained optimization model.** The assumption in such a model in that anything can be had at the right price.

In summary, the two approaches can be compared as follows:

The constrained optimizer imposes conditions that irrevocably rule out some decisions and then optimizes.

The unconstrained optimizer allows the potential for any decision to occur at an appropriate cost.

In the abstract, the unconstrained model is rational and it may be conceptually satisfying, for there are probably few things in life that cannot be changed at some price. However, the empirical fact is that many problems in reality are solved either formally or informally as constrained optimization problems.

Why is there this seeming paradox between the unconstrained view of decision making and what many people actually do? We believe that the answer is this:

Although the unconstrained model has theoretical appeal, it frequently cannot be implemented in practice.

More precisely, the unconstrained approach is frequently *uneconomical* to implement in practice. In the following section you will learn why the constrained approach, on the other hand, offers a pragmatic alternative.

3.7
WHY CONSTRAINTS ARE IMPOSED

The analyst confronts a real-world problem. His or her apparent goal is to construct a quantitative optimization model. A more correct description is: *The analyst's goal is to provide some quantitative rationale and support in the decision-making process.* In pursuit of this goal, analysts employ constraints for a variety of subtle reasons. The reasons generally have a great deal to do with *practicality*, and they may differ one from the other only in matters of degree or interpretation. They generally have little to do with any philosophical conviction about the virtues of the constrained versus the unconstrained approach. The following illustrations will help you to establish a perspective for the use and relevance of constrained models in real life.

Immutable Technology and Laws of Nature

In short-term planning situations, technological constraints may be inevitable. Consider an equilibrium-pricing model that attempts to forecast average regional prices of wheat during a given crop year along with total net imports of wheat in that same period for a number of countries. The total global supply of wheat is fixed. In the real world, there is no way it can be changed until the next crop is harvested. Agricultural technology and botanical laws cannot be altered, no matter what price the planner would pay to do so.

Bottlenecks

A steel strike has just occurred. There is no way we can increase our supplies for the next planning period. "Wrong!" you say. "Pay a high enough price and you can import more supplies!" However, it turns out that import quotas exist. "Change the law!" you say. Great idea. Unfortunately, the manager must have a production plan on his boss's desk by tomorrow morning. In such a scenario, the resource (steel) is genuinely scarce. Bottlenecks such as this are a common cause for the appearance of constraints.

The Cost of Search

An important practical factor in problem solving involves the cost of finding the solution. Constraints are often used to reduce this cost. Consider the parent whose child asks for help in using a book of state topography maps to locate the highest point in the United States. The problem could be tackled by an unconstrained search through the entire book. But with no more than an average knowledge of geography, the parent confidently ignores the maps of Ohio, Michigan, Indiana, Wisconsin, Iowa, Nebraska, and a host of others.

As another example, consider the U.S. distributor of a new French perfume. In making the product available to the public, the distributor wants to select an advertising campaign that maximizes the ratio

41

$$\frac{\text{total sales}}{\text{total advertising expenditure}}$$

The advertising options are numerous:

1. Advertising on buses in major cities
2. Advertising on radio in major cities
3. Advertising on network TV
4. Advertising in selected magazines
5. Passing out handbills

The distributor decides on the basis of intuition to eliminate the first, second, and fifth possibilities and then sponsors a study to determine the best way to allocate dollars to specific advertisements within the remaining two categories. The funds for such a study are limited. By imposing constraints, the distributor is able to specialize the study and, hopefully, obtain better results.

This example takes us fairly close to a danger point. What if the decision maker's intuition is wrong? What if radio advertising is the approach with the largest payoff? Maybe the distributor will discard the best alternative after a few minutes of introspection and spend his time and money selecting among inferior options.

Here is an actual case in point. Years ago, most automobile insurance was sold through individual agents, and most studies on how to optimize sales were constrained by the conventional wisdom that this was the best way to do things. Then, Allstate began over-the-counter sales in Sears stores and dramatically captured a substantial portion of the market.

Thus, we do not suggest that a good way to minimize the search cost is to slap constraints blindly into the model. You should always be aware of the fact that you may be pushing yourself out on a limb. The constraints can end up costing more than the saving.

Uncertainty, Nonlinearity, and Parametric Analysis

A firm has constructed a constrained optimization model of its distribution system. The model includes a yet to be constructed warehouse in Tampa. The capacity (in cubic feet) of the warehouse is specified as a parameter C, the value of which remains undetermined at the time the model is formulated. Indeed, part of the problem is to determine an appropriate value for C. Assigning different values to C and successively rerunning the model will provide results that indicate the extent to which the optimal solution is sensitive to capacity. This technique is called "performing a parametric (or sensitivity) analysis on C." Such an analysis will enable us to say, "If the capacity is so and so, then these are the results we can expect." This is one way of incorporating uncertainty into a deterministic model.

Surrogate Objectives and Pushing the Solution

We have seen, in our previous discussion, that in some sense **a model can be thought of as a "surrogate" or a replacement for reality.** Often this is particularly true of the objective function. Let us give an illustration. A study was to be undertaken for a client involved in several projects of interest to the old Department of Health, Education, and Welfare (HEW). The client wanted to determine the "optimal locations" for 16 proposed health care clinics. The clinics were to have a modular design and were architecturally rather innovative. But what does it mean to "optimize locations"? What is the appropriate measure? Some suggestions are:

1. Minimize the distances between locations and dense, low-income population areas.
2. Maximize the geographic coverage without regard to population density or income distribution.
3. Minimize the level of government subsidy required.
4. Maximize the aesthetic exposure (the visibility of the architect).

The alternatives are numerous. The problem in a study like this is not just how to quantify the objective. Actually, it is not even clear what HEW was looking for. Unless an appropriate objective function can be defined, *at least verbally*, it seems hopeless to embark on a quantitative study. When there is a *verbal* consensus as to the proper objective (e.g., maximize profit) let us then say that is the *verbal objective* for the problem at hand.

Assuming that a verbal objective can be determined, a modeler is faced with the task of then quantifying this objective in order to get it into the model (i.e., the modeler must make the transition from words into symbols or, in our previous language, the transition from formulation to construction). In many problems, the verbal objective and the model objective will be the same (e.g., to maximize profit). In other instances, the verbal objective may not be directly quantifiable. In such cases, an **indirect** or **surrogate measure** may be chosen.

In cases where the verbal objective is imprecise or unquantifiable, the decision maker may be able to justify imposing constraints in order to "push" the solution in the right direction. Even though the verbal objective cannot be quantified, the decision maker may feel that he or she understands some of the properties that would hold for an optimal solution. The use of constraints provides assurance that the solution to the model (with the surrogate objective function) will satisfy these properties. This use of constraints can thus be viewed as a kind of insurance, or hedging, against an inability to quantify the verbal objective function.

Nest Feathering

On September 13, 1976, the editorial page of the *Wall Street Journal* featured a story on the new political power of a New York City councilman. The gist of the story was that the councilman used the federal antipoverty programs to build a powerful political machine for his own purposes. Whether funds were illegally used or not is unimportant to us. This item reports on a situation in which a subordinate achieves his own ends in spite of his boss. This situation is called the **underling problem**.

The underling's aspiration is that like everyone else in life, he wants to maximize his own well-being. As a result, he has a personal objective function that differs in at least some respects from that of the organization (i.e., his boss). The underling's solution strategy is to disguise his own self-interest in a constraint and then argue for the constraint. The constraint looks innocuous to the boss—neither good nor bad. The underling's contrived justification seems plausible; so the boss innocently accepts the constraint, unaware of the full implications. The results of the constraint may be costly to the boss but will benefit the underling.

In many cases, constraints of this nature impose a kind of prescreening in order to limit the alternatives that reach the final stage of the decision-making process. A prominent charitable foundation developed a program of fellowships to give management training in the United States to promising young civil servants from a developing African country. Dossiers were assembled for each candidate, and then a committee of representatives from the participating American universities selected the individuals to receive the fellowships. Ten winners were selected annually from a field of over 200 applicants, and everyone thought the program was a great success. A review of the program after several years revealed that unbeknown to the selection committee all fellowship winners (and indeed, all applicants) had been members of the same tribe (and political party). This tribe had traditionally held the important administrative positions in the colonial government and thus controlled the application process. The group was in an ideal position to feather its own nest.

Or, for example, imagine how easy it is for a department head to draw up a job description that calls for a recent university graduate who majored in hieroglyphics, minored in engineering, and has work experience as a canoeing instructor. Would you be surprised to learn that her second cousin's son, with exactly those qualifications, was looking for a job?

The 1976 tax reform bill has been described as having at least 60 special-interest provisions. According to Senator Edward Kennedy (*Time*, August 16, 1976), some of these provisions were so finely drawn that they resembled legislation for a "one-eyed bearded man with a limp." You are invited to speculate on the motivation for the inclusion of so many special provisions.

As a final and less specific example, notice that in large firms, major capital-investment decisions are typically made by the board of directors. They consider a group of alternatives that have reached them after passing a large number of reviews (departmental, divisional, regional, etc.). There are thus numerous opportunities for subordinates to impose various "nest feathering" constraints in order to influence the set of alternatives from which the final decision will be made.

Hierarchical Structure and the Delegation of Authority

Constraints seem to be an inherent part of organizational structure. **The necessity to delegate authority and responsibility for certain activities while maintaining overall responsibility for an entire operation almost always dictates the use of constraints** and, consequently, the constrained optimization approach.

A good example is provided by the purchasing activity in multinational firms. When a firm has plants in several nearby countries, a question arises as to who should do the buying for each plant. In some multinational corporations, a centralized purchasing department buys for all plants. Many firms, however, use a decentralized system with a buying group for each plant. In this case, central management usually constrains the activities by insisting that all purchases be from centrally approved suppliers and that certain standard receiving and testing procedures be followed. The buyer at an individual plant then tries to minimize costs subject to the given constraints on delivery time, the quality of the material, and on the set of possible suppliers.

The process of passing down constraints occurs at all levels in organizational hierarchies. The government constrains the corporation, which constrains its divisions, which constrains their plants, which constrains their departments, and so on. The net result is that most decision makers in organizations find themselves facing problems in constrained optimization. The constraints may change as firms reorganize to meet competition, and the variables may change for an individual as he or she progresses through an organization. But it is difficult to imagine a world in which the delegation of *limited* responsibility and authority is not a critical part of the management process.

Definitional or Balance Equations

Often in a model certain relations between variables will be defined in the constraints. For example, in a model with inventory variables we may have a constraint that says

$$\left(\begin{array}{c}\text{inventory at}\\\text{the end of month } t\end{array}\right) = \left(\begin{array}{c}\text{inventory at}\\\text{beginning of month } t\end{array}\right) + \left(\begin{array}{c}\text{production in}\\\text{month } t\end{array}\right) - \left(\begin{array}{c}\text{sales in}\\\text{month } t\end{array}\right)$$

As another example, a logistics model may have a "material balance" constraint that says

$$\text{amount entering a depot} = \text{amount leaving a depot}$$

Many examples of such constraints will be encountered.

3.8
INTUITIVE VERSUS FORMAL MODELING

In concluding this chapter, let us compare the type of models we have been discussing with what we have referred to as **intuitive models.** We believe that most decisions in life are made in accord with some internal and intuitive optimization model of the problem at hand. Such models, though less formal than the ones we have considered, also try to capture certain trade-offs and interactions. They are also composed of objectives and constraints—the same fabric as formal models—but in mental rather than external symbolic form.

Within their structure, these internal models tend to incorporate diffuse, hard-to-quantify considerations that pertain to individual tastes and dispositions. To a degree, you are observing a person's outlook on life by seeing the reflection of his model in the way he searches for solutions and in the quality of the solutions he actually finds. The constraints in a formal model serve to define the environment within which we will seek to maximize our objective. The same is true of intuitive internal models.

As an illustration of the kinds of unquantifiable conditions or perceptions that are incorporated in intuitive models, consider the following quotations. Each statement suggests a way to constrain the search for wealth and success.

> **No man ever lost money underestimating the intelligence of the American people. H. L. Mencken**
> **There's a sucker born every minute. P. T. Barnum**

These statements reflect a major difficulty with intuitive modeling. Intuitive models generally are not explicit. They are difficult to challenge, or criticize, or subscribe to because what such models say is ambiguous. Are the quotes assertions of fact? If so, how would you go about verifying either one beyond dispute?

By contrast, the formal model at least aspires to "laying it all out" and then, hopefully, "putting it all together." The objective can be disputed or accepted. It may not be the ideal, but it is what it is, and, as we have seen, it may be manipulated and modified. The constraints are a matter of record. They can be challenged, modified, augmented, or eliminated. **Because of their explicit and unambiguous nature, formal models provide individuals and groups with a tool for eliminating inconsistency.** In this way, the use of formal models is an arm of rational behavior in the quest for good decisions.

3.9
MAJOR CONCEPTS QUIZ

True–False

1. **T F** A constraint is a restriction on the problem data.
2. **T F** Constrained optimization embodies the price-theoretic approach to problems.
3. **T F** Parameters and decision variables are either numbers or symbols that represent numbers, either to be input or determined.
4. **T F** Surrogate objectives are useful when the true objective is well defined.
5. **T F** Devious motives can lead to the imposition of constraints.
6. **T F** Unconstrained optimization is typically more useful than the constrained approach in real-world managerial settings.
7. **T F** The term *optimal* is a mathematical as opposed to a real-world concept.
8. **T F** For problems in one or two decision variables, the feasible region can be represented graphically.
9. **T F** A feasible production policy, as in the Astro/Cosmo problem, is any policy that satisfies at least one constraint.
10. **T F** "Constraint set" is synonymous with "constraint function."
11. **T F** "Nest feathering" refers to a situation in which a subordinate achieves his or own ends in the underlying problem.

Multiple Choice

12. Constraints may be imposed
    a. because total sales are less than total advertising expenditures
    b. to deal with uncertainty
    c. to deal with immutable short-term technology
    d. b and c
13. A constrained optimization model
    a. provides a best decision in a mathematical sense
    b. provides a best decision within the limited context of the model
    c. can provide a consistent tool for evaluating different policies
    d. all of the above
14. Constrained optimization means
    a. the model is an overly simplistic representation of reality
    b. achieving the best possible value of the objective function, considering the restrictions
    c. both of the above
    d. neither a nor b
15. A constraint
    a. is a mathematical equality or inequality that must be satisfied
    b. involves a constraint function and a right-hand side
    c. is formulated in terms of decision variables
    d. all of the above

16. "Pushing" the solution refers to
    a. a technique for solving an optimization problem
    b. a "hedging process" of imposing constraints in a scenario when the objective function is not clear
    c. is another term for "surrogate objective function"
    d. none of the above

Answers

1. F	7. T	12. d
2. F	8. T	13. d
3. T	9. F	14. b
4. F	10. F	15. d
5. T	11. T	16. b
6. F		

3.10

PROBLEMS

3-1. What is a constraint? How is it expressed in mathematical terms? Distinguish between a constraint, a right-hand side, and a constraint function.

3-2. Profit maximization is commonly taken as the objective function for the firm. Is this a surrogate objective or a real objective? For example, consider a firm such as ITT. Can you think of other objectives that might be appropriate? Do not worry about whether or not they are quantifiable.

3-3. Write out the general form of a constrained optimization model with n decision variables and m constraints. Write out the same model for the case where all functions are linear.

3-4. What is the difference between a real objective function and a surrogate objective function?

3-5. We have said that there are no optimal decisions for the complex problems of business. And yet optimization models produce "optimal decisions." In what sense, then, are such decisions optimal?

3-6. Consider the following statement: "Our production policy should be to achieve maximum output at minimum cost." Comment on this misunderstanding.

3-7. "An optimization problem has been solved but some of the constraints are violated." Discuss this assertion.

3-8. What is the meaning of a mathematical constraint when the data (parameter values) are not known with precision? What kinds of assumptions would tend to justify the use of models in such situations?

3-9. Consider an optimization model involving something called *units of effectiveness* (E), and suppose that this cannot be realistically translated into dollars. However, greater effectiveness results from expending more dollars (C). It is desired to obtain high effectiveness, but at not too great a cost. Discuss the pitfalls in
    (a) Maximizing $E - C$
    (b) Maximizing E/C
    How might you analyze such a problem?

3-10. What is meant by the assertion that one model is more structured than another?

3-11. Can you think of any resource that cannot be obtained at *some* price?

3-12. Compare constrained and unconstrained optimization models. Try to give some real-life illustrations of each model.

3-13. List as many motives as you can for the appearance of constraints. For each motive, discuss whether the use of a constraint is constructive or deleterious.

CHAPTER 4

Formulation of Constrained Optimization Models

ALLOCATING A SCARCE RESOURCE*

The 1973 world fuel crisis was a double whammy for the American airline industry: (1) the government restricted an airline's monthly fuel supply to a percentage of its 1972 monthly consumption, and (2) fuel prices for domestic trunk airlines jumped by more than 50% in the 5-month interval from December 1973 to May 1974. To add to the problem, fuel vendors were often unable to meet the airlines' demands at specific cities. The overall impact of these forces was canceled flights and exceptionally high prices paid for spot purchases. The airlines found themselves with record increases in operating costs and fuel became the largest percentage of an airline's costs.

National Airlines constructed and implemented a linear programming model to attack this problem. This model took into account:

1. The flight schedule
2. The price and availability of fuel at each station
3. The reserve requirement for each plane
4. The upper bound on weight for each plane
5. The distance for each segment of a flight
6. The fuel remaining when a plane arrives at a station
7. Fuel consumption for each plane as a function of weight, flight altitude, weather, and speed

It is interesting to note that it may not pay for a plane to take on extra fuel

*Wayne D. Darnell and Carolyn Laflin, "National Airlines Fuel Management and Allocation Model," *Interfaces*, Vol. 7, No. 2, February 1977, pp. 1–16.

early in a flight even though the cost per gallon is relatively low. This is because the additional weight of the fuel can increase fuel consumption enough to produce a larger total cost.

National's LP model included 800 constraints and 2400 variables for a flight schedule of 350 flight segments, 50 station/vendor combinations, and multiple aircraft types. In the first month it was used, National's fuel costs dropped from an average of 16.35 cents to 14.43 cents per gallon. This was the largest percentage decrease realized by any of 11 domestic airlines during the same period. Indeed, 6 of the other 10 airlines suffered an increase in the average cost per gallon at that time. It is estimated that total fuel savings to National Airlines over a 2-year period was multimillions of dollars. In addition, sensitivity analyses available with the linear programming solution were most helpful in informing management as to when a change in policy might be required.

4.1

INTRODUCTION

Specific rules that tell you exactly how to formulate an optimization model are doomed to fail, for the technique is largely an art that is developed with practice. However, we can offer loose guidelines. The diagram in Figure 4.1 provides a useful schema for our

Figure 4.1

The Modeling Process

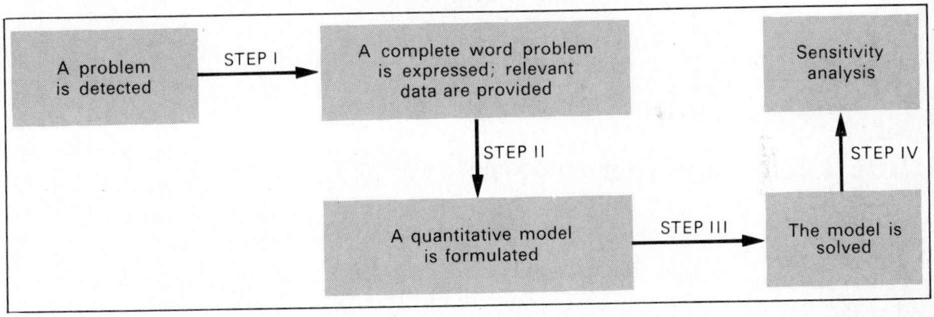

discussion. For the purpose of this discussion, we can think of the real-world transition from problem detection through solution and analysis as a four-stage process. In step I, the first signal of a problem evolves into a carefully worded description of the problem and the appropriate environment. Relevant data are provided. Step II is purely a translation from words into mathematical symbols. A quantitative model is the result. In step III, the model is solved. In step IV, numerous "sensitivity" properties of the solution are analyzed.

A Guideline to Formulation

The initial problem detection may be simple observations like "profits should be larger," "resource use appears to be inefficient," or "our inventories are too high." The first big step in model building is the evolution from this signal into a careful description of the problem and the environment. Clearly, in many realistic situations only select parts of the environment can be included in the description. This process is the first step in creating a selective representation of reality. In step II, further selection may occur in choosing the form of the mathematical approximation. The transition via steps I and II results in a quantitative model that *approximates* reality. This model will hopefully be a useful aid in management's efforts to surmount the problem initially detected. It is worth bearing in mind that in a complex real-world situation, two different individuals starting at the beginning and working independently will almost surely construct different models. The reason is that the specific transitions that occur during steps I and II are, to a large extent, determined by the background, training, perceptions, preferences, and special interests of the modeler. The question of whether one model turns out to be better than the other is answered by purely pragmatic considerations. The better model is the more useful model (i.e., the one that yields the greatest net return to the user). You should keep that goal in mind from the start.

This chapter focuses on step II of the transition. We will present a number of word problems along with the relevant data and then transform them into constrained optimization models.

The Manager's Role

"Why," we hear you cry, "is this worth doing? As a manager, won't I be able to hire a specialist to do this sort of thing?" To some extent this may be true. However, the modern manager may be required to translate vague verbal descriptions of objectives or constraints into meaningful quantitative formulations. The ability to do so helps to create a basis for communication with the specialist. In addition, on a more pedagogical level, every model is an abstraction, and we believe that a good way to begin learning about models is to actually participate in the creation of this abstraction. To do so will force you to think logically about trade-offs and interactions and to give a formal symbolic expression to your thoughts. At the outset this may not be easy, but the experience of working through a number of formulations will help to develop your skill in formulation.

4.2
GUIDELINES AND COMMENTS ON MODEL FORMULATION

In translating a word problem into a formal model, you may find it helpful first to create a verbal model corresponding to the given problem. That is, you might proceed as follows:

1. Express each constraint in words; in doing this, pay careful attention to whether the constraint is *a requirement* of the form $\geq$ (at least as large as), *a limitation* of the form $\leq$ (no larger than), or $=$ (exactly equal to).
2. Then express the objective in words.

Steps 1 and 2 should then allow you to

3. Verbally identify the decision variables.

Often a careful reading of the problem statement will reveal that the decision variables and the objective are given to you in the exact form that you need. It is usually of great importance that your decision variables be correctly defined. Sometimes you may feel that there are several possible choices. For example, should they represent pounds of finished product or pounds of raw material? One guideline that is often useful is to ask yourself the question: "*What decisions must be made in order to optimize the objective function?*" The answer to this question will help lead you to identify the decision variables correctly.

Having accomplished steps 1 through 3, invent symbolic notation for the decision variables; following this:

4. Express each constraint in symbols (i.e., in terms of the decision variables).
5. Express the objective function in symbols (in terms of the decision variables).

At this stage it is advisable to check your work for consistency of units. For example, if the coefficients in the objective function are in dollars per *pound*, the decision variables that appear in the objective function should be in pounds, not tons or ounces. Similarly, check that for each constraint the units on the right-hand side and the units on the left-hand side are the same. For example, if one of the constraints is a limitation of ≤ form on labor hours, the right-hand side will be labor hours. Then if, as above, the decision variables are pounds, the data for this constraint function (i.e., the numerical coefficients for each decision variable on the left-hand side of the constraint) should be in labor hours per pound. To put it quite simply, you do not want to end up with hours on one side and minutes or seconds or pounds or tons on the other.

At this point it would be a good idea to comment on one other aspect of model formulation. We have seen that inequality constraints may be of the form ≥ or ≤. Students often ask whether or not a linear programming problem can have a *strict inequality* constraint, such as < or >. The answer is a resounding *no*. The reason for this is mathematical in nature. It is to assure that a well-formulated problem will have a solution. The mathematical details required to justify this assertion lie outside our scope of interest. This is not a costly prohibition, for in just about any real-world situation you can imagine, involving inequality constraints, it is almost always true that the ≤ or ≥ representation entirely captures the real-world meaning.

Let us now discuss one final aspect of model formulation. This deals with the nature of the cost data to be employed.

4.3
SUNK VERSUS VARIABLE COST

In many real-world problems there are often two types of costs: *fixed costs*, also referred to as *sunk costs*, and *variable costs*. Contrary to the first impressions that students sometimes have, *it is only the variable costs that are relevant in optimization models*. The sunk or fixed costs have already been paid, which means that no future decisions can affect these expenditures. For example, suppose that 800 pounds and 500 pounds of two grades of aluminum (grade 1 and grade 2) have been purchased for future delivery, at specified prices, $5 and $10 per pound, respectively, and that the contract has been signed. Management's problem is, in part, to determine the optimal use of these 1300 pounds of aluminum so as, perhaps, to maximize profit obtained from producing aluminum knuckles and aluminum conduits. Associated with these two products there will be revenues and variable costs incurred in their production (costs of machining, stamping, etc.). In formulating this type of model the fixed, or sunk, costs of $9000 associated with the contracted purchase are irrelevant. This amount has already been spent and hence the *quantities to be purchased* are no longer variables. The variables will be how much product should be produced, and the relevant cost in this determination is only the variable cost. More specifically, the formulation corresponding to the description above might be as follows. Let

$$K = \text{number of knuckles to be produced (decision variable)}$$
$$C = \text{number of conduits to be produced (decision variable)}$$
$$10 = \text{revenue per knuckle}$$
$$30 = \text{revenue per conduit}$$
$$4 = \text{cost of producing a knuckle (variable cost)}$$
$$12 = \text{cost of producing a conduit (variable cost)}$$

For each product we must calculate what accountants call the *unit contribution margin*, that is, the difference between per unit revenue and per unit variable cost. The unit contribution margins are

$$\text{for knuckles: } 10 - 4 = 6$$
$$\text{for conduits: } 30 - 12 = 18$$

Suppose that each knuckle uses 1 unit of grade 1 aluminum and 2 units of grade 2 aluminum. Each conduit uses 3 units of grade 1 and 5 units of grade 2. Then we obtain the following **linear programming model**:

$$\text{Max} \quad 6K + 18C$$
$$\text{s.t.} \quad K + 3C \le 800 \quad \text{(grade 1 limitation)}$$
$$2K + 5C \le 500 \quad \text{(grade 2 limitation)}$$
$$K \ge 0, \quad C \ge 0$$

Another way to see the irrelevance of the sunk cost is to note that the objective function in the formulation is the total contribution margin. The net income, or profit, would be

$$\text{net profit} = \text{contribution margin} - \text{sunk cost}$$
$$= 6K + 18C - 9000$$

However, finding feasible values of K and C that maximize $6K + 18C - 9000$ is the same as finding feasible values that maximize $6K + 18C$. The constant term of 9000 can therefore be ignored. The bottom line here is that maximizing a function plus a constant, or even a positive constant times a function, gives in either case the same result, in terms of optimal values of decision variables, that you would obtain without the constant. However, adding (or subtracting) the same constant to each coefficient in the objective function may change the result. This is all nicely illustrated in the Red Brand Canners case at the end of this chapter. This case is a good illustration of how both sunk and variable costs arise in real-world problems.

Learning to Formulate Models

The remainder of this chapter contains examples of formulations that you can use to cement your ability to make the transition between the real-world problem and the mathematical model. This transition—the way in which the model has been set up, the way the constraints and the objectives have been formulated—is of prime importance.

Try to work the following problems on your own. Set them up as quickly as possible and **do not read more into a problem than precisely what is given.** Do not, for example, introduce additional constraints or logical nuances or flights of imagination of your own which might in your opinion make the model more realistic. Do not, for example, worry about "what happens next week" if the problem never refers to "next week." The problems that we pose are chosen to help you develop a facility for formulation. In order to do this, and so that you may check your work and gauge your progress, it must be true that within the described context the correct formulation should be unambiguous. In other words, there is a "right answer." Later, when you have more experience, the latitude for shades of interpretation will be broader. Because the topic of formulation is so important, and because practice is the only way to master this topic, an especially long list of problems appears at the end of this chapter.

One final word of advice. Do not simply read the problem and then immediately read the solution. That would be the best way to deceive yourself about what you understand. Do not read the solution until either (1) you are certain you have correctly solved the problem on your own or (2) you are absolutely convinced that you have hit an impasse.

4.4

PRODUCT-MIX EXAMPLES

In problems of this type, a collection of products can be sold and the set of resources from which these products are made is limited. Each product contributes to profit and utilizes resources. The objective is to find a mix of products to produce (i.e., the amount of each product to produce) so as to maximize profit subject to the constraints that resource availabilities are not exceeded.

Example 1

PROTRAC produces the largest member of its earth-moving equipment line (the E-9) and the largest member of its forestry equipment line (the F-9) with essentially the same equipment. Demand for these items is very high at this time, and management believes it is possible to sell as many of both as the firm can produce. The profit is $5000 for an E-9 and $4000 for an F-9. In planning production for the next 2 weeks, management knows it is necessary to produce a total of at least five E-9s and F-9s in order to meet previous commitments. Each of these products requires processing in department A and department B. Over the next 2 weeks, these departments have 150 and 160 hours of available time, respectively. Each E-9 requires 10 hours in department A and 20 hours in department B, whereas each F-9 requires 15 hours in department A and 10 hours in department B. In order to honor the labor contract, the total labor hours used in testing finished products cannot fall more than 10% below the agreed goal of 150 hours. (This is independent of the processing requirements in departments A and B.) Each E-9 requires 30 hours of testing and each F-9 requires 10. Finally, in order to maintain the current market position, management feels that it is necessary to build at least one F-9 for every three E-9s produced. How much of each product should PROTRAC produce in the next 2 weeks to maximize profit? Formulate this problem as a constrained optimization model. Remember, you are entitled to make no assumptions other than those explicitly stated in the preceding description. Also you must proceed on the principle that *all* relevant data and assumptions are included in this description.

Solution to Example 1

Diagram

Figure 4.2

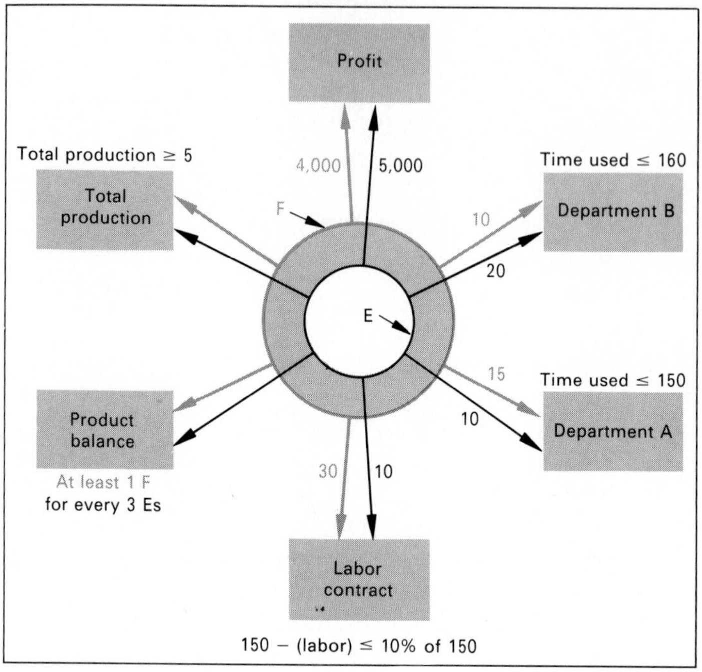

Verbal Model

Maximize   profit

subject to

total production	$\geq$	5	(1)
time used in department A	$\leq$	150	(2)
time used in department B	$\leq$	160	(3)
labor used testing	$\geq 150 - 10\%$ of 150		(4)
at least 1 F-9 for every 3 E-9s			(5)

Although we have created a verbal model, the fifth constraint is not yet in a form easily convertible to an inequality. To see how to convert such a verbal statement into a mathematical inequality, it is often useful to think through some example cases with numbers plugged in. Suppose that we made 3 E-9s. Then we would need *at least* 1 F-9. Now suppose that we made 21 E-9s. We would need at least 1 F-9 for every 3 E-9s, or at least 7 F-9s. In general, you can see that

$$\text{number of F-9s} \geq \frac{\text{number of E-9s}}{3}$$

or

$$3(\text{number of F-9s}) \geq (\text{number of E-9s})$$

Decision Variables

$$E = \text{number of E-9s produced in the next 2 weeks}$$
$$F = \text{number of F-9s produced in the next 2 weeks}$$

The Model

$$\text{Max} \quad 5000E + 4000F$$

s.t.	$E + F \geq 5$	(1)
	$10E + 15F \leq 150$	(2)
	$20E + 10F \leq 160$	(3)
	$30E + 10F \geq 135$	(4)
	$E - 3F \leq 0$	
	$E, F \geq 0$	

Rather arbitrarily, the nonnegativity conditions, $E, F \geq 0$, are usually thought of as being spearate from the constraints. Thus, the constrained optimization model has an objective function, constraints, and, when appropriate, nonnegativity conditions.

At this point, we once again note the fact that unless we put in a specific constraint forcing the decision variables to be integers, we must in general be prepared to accept fractional answers. Your first reaction is apt to be to add constraints forcing E and F to be integers since in all likelihood a solution that sets E equal to 3.41, (i.e., to produce 3.41 E-9s in the next 2 weeks) would not be physically meaningful. When such so-called **integrality conditions** are added, the problem becomes an **integer program.** Unfortunately, integer programming problems are much more difficult to solve. We shall frequently formulate models such as the one above without paying attention to integrality conditions. This assumes that either fractional solutions are meaningful or else (for the purpose of implementation) they will be rounded to integers. In a later chapter we will take a careful look at this assumption and at types of problems where such a simplification is not justified and hence where integrality conditions simply cannot be ignored.

Example 2

A plant can manufacture five different products (A, B, C, D, E) in any combination. Each product requires time on each of three machines as shown in Figure 4.3. Each machine is available 128 hours per week. Products A, B, C, D, and E are purely competitive, and any amounts made may be sold at respective per pound prices of $5, $4, $5, $4, and $4. Variable labor costs are $4 per hour for machines 1 and 2, and $3 per hour for machine 3. Material costs for each pound of products A and C are $2. The material costs are $1 for each pound of products B, D, and E. You wish to maximize profit to the firm. Formulate this problem as a constrained optimization model, using as few variables as possible.

Figure 4.3

Machine Time (minutes per pound of product)

PRODUCT	MACHINE		
	1	2	3
A	12	8	5
B	7	9	10
C	8	4	7
D	10	0	3
E	7	11	2

Solution to Example 2

Diagram

Figure 4.4

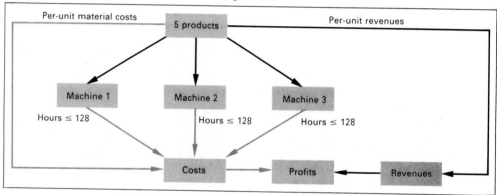

Verbal Model

$$\text{Maximize} \quad \text{profit} = \text{revenue} - \text{cost}$$

subject to

hours used on machine $1 \leq 128$ (1)

hours used on machine $2 \leq 128$ (2)

hours used on machine $3 \leq 128$ (3)

Decision Variables

A = pounds of product A produced per week

B = pounds of product B produced per week

C = pounds of product C produced per week

D = pounds of product D produced per week

E = pounds of product E produced per week

The Model   First, in order to calculate the cost of machine usage, we must determine the time used on each machine.

$$\text{total hours used on machine } 1 = \frac{12A + 7B + 8C + 10D + 7E}{60}$$

$$\text{total hours used on machine } 2 = \frac{8A + 9B + 4C + 11E}{60}$$

$$\text{total hours used on machine } 3 = \frac{5A + 10B + 7C + 3D + 2E}{60}$$

We divide by 60 to convert minutes used on each machine into hours. We do this because the processing times were given in minutes but the cost parameters are in dollars per hour. Hence, the model is

$$\text{Max} \quad 3(A + B + C + D + E) - 4\left(\frac{12A + 7B + 8C + 10D + 7E}{60}\right)$$

$$- 4\left(\frac{8A + 9B + 4C + 11E}{60}\right)$$

$$- 3\left(\frac{5A + 10B + 7C + 3D + 2E}{60}\right)$$

Capacity on Machine 1   s.t. $\quad \dfrac{12A + 7B + 8C + 10D + 7E}{60} \le 128$

Capacity on Machine 2 $\quad \dfrac{8A + 9B + 4C + 11E}{60} \le 128$

Capacity on Machine 3 $\quad \dfrac{5A + 10B + 7C + 3D + 2E}{60} \le 128$

$$A, B, C, D, E \ge \quad 0$$

The objective function in this example could be simplified by collecting terms. However, this translation into a more finished form is purely mechanical algebra. Our object was just to obtain a logically correct formulation and so it suffices to leave the model in this raw form. We should point out, however, that the formulation of this problem is parsimonious in the sense that we employ the fewest possible number of variables. For an equivalent but less parsimonious approach, see Problem 4-19.

Example 3

A firm operates four farms of comparable productivity. Each farm has a certain amount of usable acreage and a supply of labor to plant and tend the crops. The data for the upcoming season are shown in Figure 4.5.

Figure 4.5

Acreage and Labor Data by Farm

FARM	USABLE ACREAGE	LABOR HOURS AVAILABLE PER MONTH
1	500	1700
2	900	3000
3	300	900
4	700	2200

The organization is considering three crops for planting. These crops differ primarily in their expected profit per acre and in the amount of labor they require, as shown in Figure 4.6. Futhrermore, the total acreage that can be devoted to any particular crop is limited by the associated requirements for harvesting equipment.

Figure 4.6

Acreage, Labor, and Profit Data by Crop

CROP	MAXIMUM ACREAGE	MONTHLY LABOR HOURS REQUIRED PER ACRE	EXPECTED PROFIT PER ACRE
A	700	2	$500
B	800	4	200
C	300	3	300

In order to maintain a roughly uniform work load among the farms, management's policy is that the percentage of usable acreage planted must be the same at each farm. However, any combination of the crops may be grown at any of the farms as long as all constraints are satisfied (including the uniform work-load requirement). Management wishes to know how many acres of each crop should be planted at the respective farms in order to maximize expected profit. Formulate this as a constrained optimization model.

Solution to Example 3

Diagram

Figure 4.7

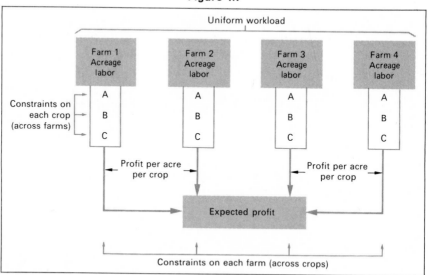

Verbal Model

Maximize   expected profit

subject to

acres of crops planted on farm 1 $\leq$ 500   (1)

acres of crops planted on farm 2 $\leq$ 900   (2)

acres of crops planted on farm 3	≤ 300	(3)
acres of crops planted on farm 4	≤ 700	(4)
labor hours per month required on farm 1	≤ 1700	(5)
labor hours per month required on farm 2	≤ 3000	(6)
labor hours per month required on farm 3	≤ 900	(7)
labor hours per month required on farm 4	≤ 2200	(8)
acres planted with crop A	≤ 700	(9)
acres planted with crop B	≤ 800	(10)
acres planted with crop C	≤ 300	(11)

$$\frac{\text{acres planted on farm 1}}{500} - \frac{\text{acres planted on farm 2}}{900} = 0 \qquad (12)$$

$$\frac{\text{acres planted on farm 1}}{500} - \frac{\text{acres planted on farm 3}}{300} = 0 \qquad (13)$$

$$\frac{\text{acres planted on farm 1}}{500} - \frac{\text{acres planted on farm 4}}{700} = 0 \qquad (14)$$

Decision Variables

$$A_i = \text{acres devoted to crop A at farm } i \qquad i = 1, 2, 3, 4$$
$$B_i = \text{acres devoted to crop B at farm } i \qquad i = 1, 2, 3, 4$$
$$C_i = \text{acres devoted to crop C at farm } i \qquad i = 1, 2, 3, 4$$

The Model

$$\text{Max} \quad 500 \sum_{i=1}^{4} A_i + 200 \sum_{i=1}^{4} B_i + 300 \sum_{i=1}^{4} C_i$$

s.t. $A_1 + B_1 + C_1$	≤ 500	(1)
$A_2 + B_2 + C_2$	≤ 900	(2)
$A_3 + B_3 + C_3$	≤ 300	(3)
$A_4 + B_4 + C_4$	≤ 700	(4)
$2A_1 + 4B_1 + 3C_1$	≤ 1700	(5)
$2A_2 + 4B_2 + 3C_2$	≤ 3000	(6)
$2A_3 + 4B_3 + 3C_3$	≤ 900	(7)
$2A_4 + 4B_4 + 3C_4$	≤ 2200	(8)
$\sum_{i=1}^{4} A_i$	≤ 700	(9)
$\sum_{i=1}^{4} B_i$	≤ 800	(10)
$\sum_{i=1}^{4} C_i$	≤ 300	(11)

$$\frac{A_1 + B_1 + C_1}{500} - \frac{A_2 + B_2 + C_2}{900} = 0 \qquad (12)$$

$$\frac{A_1 + B_1 + C_1}{500} - \frac{A_3 + B_3 + C_3}{300} = 0 \tag{13}$$

$$\frac{A_1 + B_1 + C_1}{500} - \frac{A_4 + B_4 + C_4}{700} = 0 \tag{14}$$

all variables ≥ 0

Note that constraints (1), (12), (13), and (14) taken together imply that constraints (2), (3), and (4) must be satisfied. For this reason, constraints (2), (3), and (4) are termed **redundant,** and they could just as well be omitted from this particular model. Such redundant constraints are not usually easy to identify, and there is no harm in including them in the model.

4.5

A BLENDING EXAMPLE

In this type of problem, it is necessary to mix or blend a collection of raw materials into a finished product, such as cereal grains into dog food, phosphates into fertilizer, or several metals into a high-strength alloy. The objective is to minimize the cost of the finished product subject to minimum requirement constraints (e.g., percent protein in the blend ≥ 15). These problems usually have a constraint stating that the sum of the parts equals the whole. In other words, the proportions of all components must add up to 1. Care must often be exercised in keeping the units consistent throughout the problem. That is, variables may be either percentages or quantities, and the constraints and the objective must be formulated accordingly. Moreover, if the variables are in quantities, the quantity units must be consistent within all the constraints and the objective. For example, if the variable x is in units of pounds in the objective function, it must also be in units of pounds in every constraint in which it appears.

Example 4: The Crawler Tread Problem

The iron ore from four different locations is blended to make crawler tractor treads. Analysis has shown that there are minimum requirements on three basic elements in order to produce a suitable blend. The ore from each location possesses each of these three elements in different amounts and has a different cost for PROTRAC.

Figure 4.8 gives the number of pounds of each basic element per ton of ore from each location, the minimum requirements of each element per ton of final blend, and the cost per ton of ore from each location. Assume that the quantities of the basic elements are additive; that is, if 1 ton of ore from location 1 includes 10 pounds of element A and 1 ton of ore from location 2 includes 3 pounds of element A, then an equal parts blend of these two ores would have 13 pounds of element A for each 2 tons of blend, or 6.5 pounds per ton. PROTRAC wants to know what blend will satisfy the constraints at minimum cost.

Present a constrained optimization model that will answer this question.

Figure 4.8
Data for Ore-Blending Example

BASIC ELEMENT	LOCATION				MINIMUM REQUIREMENTS PER TON
	1	2	3	4	
A	10	3	8	2	5
B	90	150	75	175	100
C	45	25	20	37	30
Cost per ton	$800	$400	$600	$500	

Solution to Example 4

Diagram

Figure 4.9

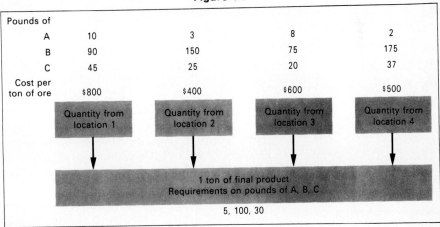

Pounds of				
A	10	3	8	2
B	90	150	75	175
C	45	25	20	37
Cost per ton of ore	$800	$400	$600	$500

Quantity from location 1 · Quantity from location 2 · Quantity from location 3 · Quantity from location 4

1 ton of final product
Requirements on pounds of A, B, C

5, 100, 30

Verbal Model

Minimize   cost per ton of final blend

subject to

pounds of A	$\geq$ 5	(1)
pounds of B	$\geq$ 100	(2)
pounds of C	$\geq$ 30	(3)
total tons of ore from all locations per ton of final blend =	1	(4)

Decision Variables

T_i = fraction of a ton of ore from location i in 1 ton of the final blend

62 *The Model*

CHAPTER 4
Formulation
of Constrained
Optimization
Models

$$\text{Min} \quad 800T_1 + 400T_2 + 600T_3 + 500T_4$$

$$\text{s.t.} \ 10T_1 + \quad 3T_2 + \quad 8T_3 + \quad 2T_4 \geq \quad 5 \tag{1}$$

$$90T_1 + 150T_2 + 75T_3 + 175T_4 \geq 100 \tag{2}$$

$$45T_1 + \quad 25T_2 + 20T_3 + 37T_4 \geq \quad 30 \tag{3}$$

$$T_1 + \quad T_2 + \quad T_3 + \quad T_4 = \quad 1 \tag{4}$$

$$T_i \geq \quad 0 \qquad i = 1, 2, 3, 4$$

4.6
MULTIPERIOD INVENTORY EXAMPLES

This important class of models applies to inventories of materials, cash, and employees carried from one period to the next. Multiperiod models are sometimes referred to as **dynamic** problems. They reflect the fact that the decisions made this period affect not only this period's returns (or costs) but the allowable decisions and returns in future periods as well. For this reason, multiperiod problems cannot be treated as if they were merely a collection of single-period problems. The topic of inventory management is considered in some detail in later chapters.

Example 5

This is a classical, so-called deterministic, single-product inventory problem. It is called *deterministic* because we assume that the demand (i.e., number of orders to be satisfied) in each future period is known at the beginning of period 1. For example, a producer of polyurethane has a stock of orders for the next 6 weeks. Let d_i be a parameter that denotes this known demand (say, in terms of number of gallons that must be delivered to customers during week i), and assume that $d_i > 0$ for all i. Let C_i denote the cost of producing a gallon during week i, and let K_i denote the maximum amount that can be produced (because of capacity limitations) in week i. Finally, let h_i denote the per unit cost of inventory in stock at the end of week i. (Thus, the inventory is measured as the number of gallons carried from week i into week $i + 1$.) Suppose that the initial inventory (at the beginning of period 1 and for which no carrying charge is assessed) is known to be I_0 gallons. Find a production and inventory-holding plan that satisfies the known delivery schedule over the next 6 weeks at minimum total cost.

Before formulating the constrained optimization model, it will be useful to develop an expression for the inventory on hand at the end of each period. Since there is an inventory carrying charge, this quantity will clearly play a role in the objective function.

Let I_i be the inventory on hand at the end of week i. Define the decision variable x_i to be the gallons of polyurethane produced in week i. We note that

$$I_1 = I_0 + x_1 - d_1$$

That is, the inventory on hand at the end of week 1 is equal to the inventory on hand at the end of week 0 (the beginning of week 1) plus the production in week 1 minus the deliveries in week 1. (We are assuming that all demand must be satisfied. Hence, the known demand in week i, d_i, is by definition the amount delivered in week i.)

Similarly,

$$I_2 = I_1 + x_2 - d_2$$

and, in general, the same reasoning yields, for any period t,

$$I_t = I_{t-1} + x_t - d_t$$

This important inventory equation says that

inventory at end of t = inventory at beginning of t + production in t − demand in t

Note that if we substitute the known expression for I_1 into the equation for I_2, we obtain

$$I_2 = \underbrace{I_0 + x_1 - d_1}_{I_1} + x_2 - d_2 = I_0 + \sum_{i=1}^{2} x_i - \sum_{i=1}^{2} d_i$$

We could then substitute the foregoing expression for I_2 into the equation for I_3 to obtain

$$I_3 = I_0 + \sum_{i=1}^{3} x_i - \sum_{i=1}^{3} d_i$$

Repeating this procedure leads to an equivalent inventory equation

$$I_t = I_0 + \sum_{i=1}^{t} (x_i - d_i)$$

for any period t.

Note that this last expression relates the inventory at the end of period t to all previous production (the x values). The equation simply says that the inventory at the end of period t is equal to the initial inventory, plus the total production through period t, minus the total deliveries through period t. The variable I_t is sometimes referred to as a **definitional variable** because it is defined in terms of other decision variables (the x_i values) in the problem. The use of definitional variables sometimes makes it easier to see the proper formulation. Before writing the verbal model for this problem, we must figure out a way of saying that production in each period must be *at least* great enough so that demand (i.e., the delivery schedule) can be satisfied. In period 1 this means that $I_0 + x_1 \geq d_1$, or $I_0 + x_1 - d_1 \geq 0$. Since $I_0 + x_1 - d_1$ is the same as I_1, this is the same as saying that the inventory at the end of period 1 is nonnegative. Satisfying period 2 demand means that inventory at the beginning of period 2 (the end of period 1) plus period 2 production $\geq d_2$. That is,

$$I_1 + x_2 \geq d_2 \qquad \text{or} \qquad I_1 + x_2 - d_2 \geq 0$$

which is the same as saying that the inventory at the end of period 2 is nonnegative. It should now be possible to see the pattern. **The condition that demand in period t must be satisfied is equivalent to the condition that inventory I_t at the end of period t must be nonnegative.**

Solution to Example 5

Diagram

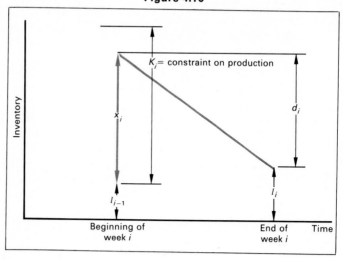

Figure 4.10

Verbal Model

Minimize   production cost + inventory cost

subject to

inventory at the end of week t ≥ 0 $t = 1, 2, \ldots, 6$ (1)

production in week t $\leq K_t$ $t = 1, 2, \ldots, 6$ (2)

Decision Variables

$$x_t = \text{production in week } t$$

The Model

$$\text{Min } \sum_{t=1}^{6} C_t x_t + \sum_{t=1}^{6} h_t I_t$$

$$\text{s.t. } I_t = I_{t-1} + x_t - d_t \qquad t = 1, 2, \ldots, 6$$

$$\left. \begin{array}{l} x_t \leq K_t \\ x_t \geq 0 \\ I_t \geq 0 \end{array} \right\} \qquad t = 1, 2, \ldots, 6$$

In general, the structure of such models is fairly complex. That is, interactions are occurring between large numbers of variables. For example, inventory at the end of a given period t is determined by all production decisions in periods 1 through t. This

64

is seen from the inventory equation

$$I_t = I_0 + \sum_{i=1}^{t} (x_i - d_i)$$

Therefore, the cost in period t is also determined by all production decisions in periods 1 through t. In models such as this, simplified versions can often provide considerable insight into the interactions. This will be illustrated in Problem 4-26. Finally, it is noted that the formulation above can be written in an equivalent form without the I_t variables appearing. Try to do this on your own.

Example 6

In a calculated financial maneuver, PROTRAC has acquired a new blast furnace facility for producing foundry iron. The management science group at PROTRAC has been assigned the task of providing support for the quantitative planning of foundry activities. The first directive is to provide an answer to the following question: How many new slag-pit personnel should be hired and trained over the next 6 months?

The requirements for trained employees in the pits are 8000 labor hours in January, 9000 in February, 7000 in March, 10,000 in April, 9000 in May, and 11,000 in June. Trainees are hired at the beginning of each month. One consideration we wish to take into account is the union rule that it takes one month of classroom instruction before a person can be considered well enough trained to work in the pits. Therefore, it is mandatory that a trainee be hired at least a month before he is actually needed. Each classroom student uses 100 hours of the time of a trained slag-pit employee, so that 100 less hours of his time are available for work in the pit. We are also informed that, by contractual agreement, each trained employee can work up to 150 hours a month (total time, instructing plus in the pit). If maximum total time available from trained employees exceeds a month's requirements, each man works fewer than 150 hours, and none are laid off. From historical data, we have learned that by the end of each month approximately 10% of the trained men at the beginning of the month have quit their jobs. A trained employee costs the company $800 a month (i.e., he is paid for a full 150 hours per month, whether or not he actually works the full amount) and a trainee costs $400 a month in salary and other benefits. There are 60 trained employees available at the beginning of January. Formulate the hiring-and-training problem as a constrained optimization model.

Solution to Example 6

Verbal Model

Minimize   total salaries paid

subject to

hours available from trained employees for work in each month $\geq$ number required in each month   (1)–(6)

66 *Diagram*

CHAPTER 4
Formulation
of Constrained
Optimization
Models

Figure 4.11

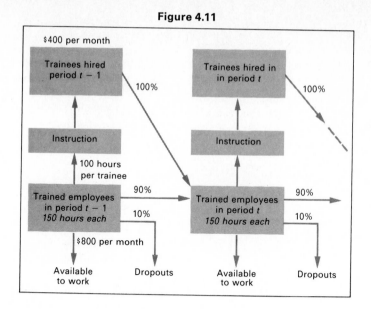

Decision Variables

$$y_t = \text{number of trainees hired in period } t$$

It is also convenient to have a definitional variable,

$$x_t = \text{number of trained employees on hand at the beginning of month } t$$

By definition, *this also equals the number of trained employees on hand at the end of month $t - 1$.*

Relating these definitional variables x_t to the decision variables y_t will require six constraints, which we label (7)–(12).

The Model

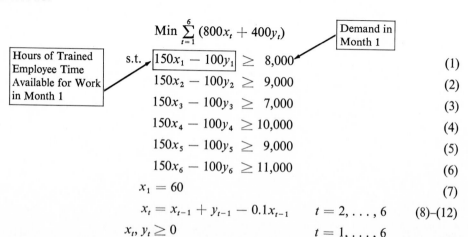

$$\text{Min} \sum_{t=1}^{6} (800x_t + 400y_t)$$

Demand in Month 1

Hours of Trained Employee Time Available for Work in Month 1

$$\text{s.t.} \quad 150x_1 - 100y_1 \geq 8,000 \tag{1}$$
$$150x_2 - 100y_2 \geq 9,000 \tag{2}$$
$$150x_3 - 100y_3 \geq 7,000 \tag{3}$$
$$150x_4 - 100y_4 \geq 10,000 \tag{4}$$
$$150x_5 - 100y_5 \geq 9,000 \tag{5}$$
$$150x_6 - 100y_6 \geq 11,000 \tag{6}$$
$$x_1 = 60 \tag{7}$$
$$x_t = x_{t-1} + y_{t-1} - 0.1x_{t-1} \quad t = 2, \ldots, 6 \tag{8--12}$$
$$x_t, y_t \geq 0 \quad t = 1, \ldots, 6$$

Example 7

Suppose that we add to the preceding problem new contract provisions proposed by the union:

1. In each month, all trained employees should work the same number of hours. This number can differ from month to month but, as before, cannot exceed 150 hours.
2. Each trained employee should be paid only for the hours he works instead of for 150 hours.
3. The hourly rate for trained employees will be r dollars (where r is a fixed number given by the union).
4. As before, the per unit cost per month for each trainee is $400.

Assuming the same dropout rate as before, management wants to know whether to accept this new contract or whether it would be preferable to renew the previous contract. How can such a determination be made? Suppose that management would be willing to accept the proposed new contract if it were possible to negotiate the value of r. How might a *maximum* acceptable value of r be determined?

Solution to Example 7

Reformulate the model of Example 6 so that employees receive pay only for hours worked subject to constraints that the hours actually worked by trained employees do not exceed the maximum available amount in any given month. Thus

$$\text{Hours actually worked by trained employees in period } 1 = 8000 + 100y_1$$

and so on.

$$\text{Maximum hours available in period } 1 = 150x_1$$

and so on. The total cost becomes

$$(8000 + 100y_1)r + (9000 + 100y_2)r + (7000 + 100y_3)r + (10{,}000 + 100y_4)r$$
$$+ (9000 + 100y_5)r + (11{,}000 + 100y_6)r + \sum_{t=1}^{6} 400y_t$$
$$= 54{,}000r + \sum_{t=1}^{6} (400 + 100r)y_t$$

The Model

$$\text{Min} \ \sum_{t=1}^{6} (400 + 100r)y_t + 54{,}000r$$

$$
\begin{align}
\text{s.t.} \quad 150x_1 - 100y_1 &\geq 8{,}000 \tag{1} \\
150x_2 - 100y_2 &\geq 9{,}000 \tag{2} \\
150x_3 - 100y_3 &\geq 7{,}000 \tag{3} \\
150x_4 - 100y_4 &\geq 10{,}000 \tag{4} \\
150x_5 - 100y_5 &\geq 9{,}000 \tag{5}
\end{align}
$$

$$150x_6 - 100y_6 \geq 11,000 \tag{6}$$

$$x_1 = 60 \tag{7}$$

$$x_t = x_{t-1} + y_{t-1} - 0.1x_{t-1} \qquad t = 2, \ldots, 6 \qquad (8)\text{--}(12)$$

$$x_t, y_t \geq 0 \qquad t = 1, \ldots, 6$$

If the optimal objective value for the reformulated problem is less than the original optimal objective value (in Example 6), management should accept the new contract.

A *maximum* acceptable value of r can be determined by modifying the foregoing model, and treating r as a nonnegative *variable* rather than a parameter. The objective becomes Max r and the constraint

$$\sum_{t=1}^{6} (400 + 100r)y_t + 54,000r = V$$

is added, where the number V is the optimal value of the objective function in the model formulated in Example 6.

It is noteworthy that the reformulation above, treating r as a variable, has a nonlinear constraint because of the term ry_t. In other words, *the reformulation produces a nonlinear programming (NLP) model. All the previous examples have been linear programs (or LP problems), which means that all functions in the models (objectives and constraints) have been linear.*

4.7

CAPITAL-BUDGETING PROBLEMS

Deciding how to allocate funds to alternative projects that require capital is a major management decision in most firms. One aspect of this process is assigning funds in order to maximize the total present value of the investment while not exceeding a limit on the total amount of investment. The next four examples provide a mathematical programming approach to increasingly more realistic problems in the area of capital budgeting.

Example 8

This example considers a simple, one-period problem. Suppose that there are N projects $1, 2, 3, \ldots, N$, and that each project may be undertaken in any fractional amount between zero and one. Let R_i be the present value of the return if project i is selected at a 100% level of investment, and assume that the returns on each project are directly proportional to the level of investment. Thus, if project i is undertaken at the 50% level, then the present value of the return will be $0.5R_i$, and so on. Also let C_i be the cost of selecting project i at the 100% level, and let the costs be proportional to the levels, just as for returns. Finally, let C be the limit on the total investment in projects $1, 2, \ldots, N$. Formulate the problem of maximizing total present value as a linear program.

Solution to Example 8

Diagram

Figure 4.12

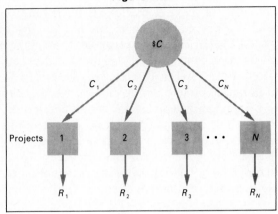

Verbal Model

Maximize   total present value

subject to

total capital investment $\leq C$

Decision Variables

$x_i =$ fraction of project i selected

The Model

$$\text{Max} \quad \sum_{i=1}^{N} R_i x_i$$

$$\text{s.t.} \quad \sum_{i=1}^{N} C_i x_i \leq C$$

$$x_i \leq 1 \qquad i = 1, \ldots, N$$

$$x_i \geq 0$$

This model deserves several comments. First, it is clear that in many cases fractional values of x_i are meaningless. The decision maker may be constrained either to accept project i completely ($x_i = 1$) or to reject it ($x_i = 0$). It may simply be unrealistic or impossible to accept half the project ($x_i = 1/2$). For example, assume that project i is building a bridge. **Introducing constraints that x_i must equal either zero or one (*instead of $x_i \leq 1$, $x_i \geq 0$*) makes this an integer programming problem.**

In particular, the foregoing problem, with the added constraints that each x_i must be either zero or one, is called a **knapsack model,** or a **knapsack problem.**[1] Although the

[1] Management scientists have created an enigmatic, if not amusing, taxonomy of phyla and genera. These so-called canonical problems include the knapsack problem, the traveling salesman problem, the streetwalker's dilemma, the cutting-stock problem, the newsboy problem, the capacitated transportation problem, minimal spanning trees, and a host of others. A few of these will be mentioned at appropriate points in the text.

slight difference in formulation (i.e., requiring x_i to be either zero or one) may appear to be little more than cosmetic, the mathematical implications turn out to be very significant, and it is generally true that integer programming problems are much more difficult to solve than ordinary linear programs.

As a final comment, we note that if the integer constraints are ignored so as to make the problem continuous, there is a simple algorithm to solve the foregoing problem. To find the optimal solution, you first calculate the return per dollar of investment for each project (i.e., compute each ratio R_i/C_i). The projects are ranked according to the decreasing order of these ratios. Then the highest-ranked project is undertaken at the 100% level, if its cost does not exceed the budget constraint; similarly for the next ranked project, and so on. Eventually, a project is encountered for which a 100% undertaking would violate the budget constraint. (Otherwise, all projects can be selected at the 100% level and the problem is uninteresting.) At this point, the last-contemplated project is undertaken at the fractional level that would bring total cost exactly up to the budget limit, and the algorithm terminates. All remaining projects are discarded because the limit on capital expenditures has been reached. This procedure for obtaining the *continuous solution* may not yield an optimal solution when the integer constraints are imposed. Can you create a simple example to illustrate this fact?

Example 9

Consider a multiperiod version (say T periods) of the problem presented in Example 8. In this case, each project yields a return in each period. In addition, each project also requires a capital expenditure in each period, and there is an upper limit on the total allowable capital expenditure in each period. Let r_{it} and c_{it} be the return and the capital investment, respectively, associated with maximal commitment ($x_i = 1$) to project i in period t, and assume that α is the interest rate, independent of time. Assume that the cash flows r_{it} (i.e., the returns) occur at the *end* of period t and that the investments c_{it} occur at the *beginning* of period t. Finally, let C_t be the upper bound on capital investment in period t. For a given project, it is assumed that the fractional commitment in each period is the same (for instance, we cannot make a 50% commitment to project 1 in period 1 and a 25% commitment to project 1 in period 2). Formulate the problem of maximizing the total present value of the returns as a linear program.

Solution to Example 9

Diagram

Figure 4.13

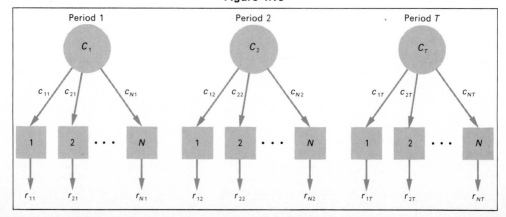

Maximize total present value

subject to

capital expenditure in period $t \leq C_t$ $t = 1, \ldots, T$

Decision Variables

$$x_i = \text{fraction of project } i \text{ selected}$$

The Model   Note that the objective is to maximize total present value. By definition, the present value of project i (if fully undertaken) is

$$\sum_{t=1}^{T} \frac{r_{it}}{(1 + \alpha)^t}$$

For notational convenience, let us introduce the variable R_i defined by

$$R_i = \sum_{t=1}^{T} \frac{r_{it}}{(1 + \alpha)^t}$$

Thus R_i is the present value of project i when fully undertaken. Then the model is

$$\text{Max} \quad \sum_{i=1}^{N} R_i x_i$$

$$\text{s.t.} \quad \sum_{i=1}^{N} c_{it} x_i \leq C_t \qquad t = 1, 2, \ldots, T$$

$$x_i \leq 1 \qquad i = 1, 2, \ldots, N$$

$$x_i \geq 0 \qquad i = 1, 2, \ldots, N$$

We note that the concern about noninteger solutions continues to exist in this problem, and we may need to complicate the model further (depending on the application) by substituting the constraints $x_i = 0$ or $x_i = 1$ for the last $2N$ inequalities. We also note that the simple technique we used to find an optimal solution to the *continuous* version of the single-period problem in Example 8 does not work for this multiperiod problem. With T c_{it} values for each project and T constraints on capital expenditures, there is no straightforward analogue of the ratio-ranking technique suggested in Example 8.

Example 10

Consider the problem presented in Example 9 with the additional complication that there are contingency relationships among some of the projects. Let us assume we are considering models where the integrality conditions $x_i = 0$ or 1 must be imposed. Now, as an example of contingency relationships, let us assume that project 3 cannot be selected unless project 4 is also selected and that project 5 cannot be selected unless projects 6 and 7 are both selected.

Solution to Example 10

The only difference between the new model and the one in Example 9 is that constraints have to be added to ensure that the contingency relationships are enforced. The first contingency requirement states that project 3 cannot be selected unless project 4 is also selected. If project 3 is selected, then $x_3 = 1$. Thus, to force project 4 to be selected whenever 3 is selected, we can use the inequality

$$x_3 \le x_4$$

Similarly, the second contingency requirement can be enforced by adding the constraint

$$2x_5 \le x_6 + x_7$$

Example 11

Here is an excellent example of an LP financial model in which the integrality conditions need not be imposed. Winston-Salem Development Management (WSDM) is trying to complete its investment plans for the next 3 years. Currently, WSDM has $2 million available for investment. At 6-month intervals over the next 3 years, WSDM expects the following income stream from previous investments: $500,000 (6 months from now), $400,000; $380,000; $360,000; $340,000; and $300,000 (at end of third year).

There are three development projects in which WSDM is considering participating. The Foster City Development would, if WSDM participated fully, have the following projected cash-flow stream at 6-month intervals over the next 3 years (negative numbers represent investments, positive numbers represent income): −$3,000,000 (beginning of period 1); −$1,000,000; −$1,800,000; $400,000; $1,800,000; $1,800,000; $5,500,000. The last figure is its estimated value at the end of 3 years.

A second project involves taking over the operation of some old lower-middle-income housing on the condition that certain initial repairs be made and that the housing be demolished at the end of 3 years. The cash-flow stream for this project, if participated in fully, would be: −$2,000,000 (beginning of period 1); −$500,000; $1,500,000; $1,500,000; $1,500,000; $200,000; −$1,000,000.

The third project, the Disney-Universe Hotel, would have the following cash-flow stream at 6-month intervals if WSDM participated fully (again, the last figure is the estimated value at the end of the 3 years): −$2,000,000 (beginning of period 1); −$2,000,000; −$1,800,000; $1,000,000; $1,000,000; $1,000,000; $6,000,000. WSDM can borrow money for half-year intervals at 3.5% interest per half-year. At most, $2 million can be borrowed at one time; that is, the total outstanding principal can never exceed $2 million. WSDM can invest surplus funds at 3% per half-year. If WSDM participates in a project at less than 100%, all the cash flows of that project are reduced appropriately. Formulate as an LP model the problem of maximizing the net worth of these investments to WSDM after six periods.

Solution to Example 11

We have the following LP formulation of the problem of maximizing WSDM's net worth at the end of 3 years.

Decision Variables

$F =$ fractional participation in the Foster City project

$M =$ fractional participation in lower-middle-income housing

$D =$ fractional participation in Disney-Universe Hotel

$B_i =$ amount borrowed in period i, $i = 1, \ldots, 6$

$L_i =$ amount lent in period i, $i = 1, \ldots, 6$

$Z =$ net worth after the six periods

The Model With all numbers measured in units of 1000, the model is

$$\text{Max} \quad Z \tag{1}$$

s.t.

$$-3000F - 2000M - 2000D + B1 - L1 \geq -2000 \tag{2}$$

$$-1000F - 500M - 2000D + B2 - L2 + 1.03L1 - 1.035B1 \geq -500 \tag{3}$$

$$-1800F + 1500M - 1800D + B3 - L3 + 1.03L2 - 1.035B2 \geq -400 \tag{4}$$

$$400F + 1500M + 1000D + B4 - L4 + 1.03L3 - 1.035B3 \geq -380 \tag{5}$$

$$1800F + 1500M + 1000D + B5 - L5 + 1.03L4 - 1.035B4 \geq -360 \tag{6}$$

$$1800F + 200M + 1000D + B6 - L6 + 1.03L5 - 1.035B5 \geq -340 \tag{7}$$

$$5500F - 1000M + 6000D \qquad\qquad + 1.03L6 - 1.035B6 - Z \geq -300 \tag{8}$$

$$B1, B2, B3, B4, B5, B6 \leq 2000 \tag{9--14}$$

$$F, M, D \leq 1 \tag{15--17}$$

$$\text{all decision variables} \geq 0 \tag{18}$$

Note that in this example the objective function has been given the label (1). The constraints (2) through (7) state that the amount of money spent must not exceed the amount on hand at the beginning of periods (1) through (6), respectively. The constraint labeled (8) is used to define Z, the net worth at the end of period 6 (year 3). The remaining constraints are self-explanatory.

4.8

A MEDIA-PLANNING EXAMPLE

Example 12

A radio network wants to establish revenue-maximizing prices for advertising time. This example presents a simplified version of its pricing problem. Assume that there are three classifications of network advertising time: prime-evening, weekday, and Saturday/Sunday afternoon (before 6 P.M.). Let P_1, P_2, and P_3 be the respective prices per minute for each of these time slots.

The network sells large blocks of time to K major advertisers, who have a significant effect on the determination of prices. The network knows that major advertiser k wants to purchase a package consisting of a_{1k}, a_{2k}, and a_{3k} minutes in the three time slots and is willing to pay up to A_k dollars for this package. Each term a_{ik} is assumed to be a function of price, as follows:

$$a_{ik} = \frac{c_{ik}}{P_i + d_{ik}}$$

where c_{ik} and d_{ik} are specified parameters. Finally, H_i is the total number of hours that can be sold in time slot i. Formulate the network's problem as a constrained optimization model.

Diagram

Figure 4.14

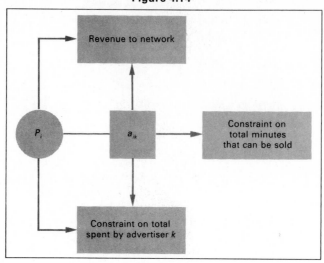

Verbal Problem

Maximize   total revenue

subject to

total spent by advertiser k $\leq A_k$ $k = 1, \ldots, K$

total minutes sold in time slot $i \leq 60H_i$ $i = 1, 2, 3$

Decision Variables

$$P_i = \text{price per minute in time slot } i$$

The Model

$$\text{Max } \quad P_1 \sum_{k=1}^{K} \frac{c_{1k}}{P_1 + d_{1k}} + P_2 \sum_{k=1}^{K} \frac{c_{2k}}{P_2 + d_{2k}} + P_3 \sum_{k=1}^{K} \frac{c_{3k}}{P_3 + d_{3k}}$$

$$\text{s.t. } \quad \sum_{i=1}^{3} P_i \frac{c_{ik}}{P_i + d_{ik}} \leq A_k \qquad k = 1, \ldots, K$$

$$\sum_{k=1}^{K} \frac{c_{ik}}{P_i + d_{ik}} \leq 60H_i \qquad i = 1, 2, 3$$

$$P_i \geq 0 \qquad i = 1, 2, 3$$

Note that this is a nonlinear programming model. The objective function and all constraints are nonlinear.

ADDITIONAL EXAMPLES AND SOLUTIONS

The rationale for the previous examples was to teach you model formulation by enabling you to read the example and then read a detailed discussion of the solution. By now, you should have acquired enough facility to operate more effectively on your own. In this section, then, examples are presented for you to solve, both to check your progress and to further develop your formulation skills. We also provide the solutions to the examples in this section, but with minimal discussion. Again, we strongly recommend that you devote considerable effort to deriving the model on your own before looking at the solution. Agreeing that a model proposed by someone else is correct and creating the model yourself are quite different processes.

Example 13: Diablo/Red Baron

McNaughton Inc. produces two steak sauces, spicy Diablo and mild Red Baron. These sauces are both made by blending two ingredients, A and B. A certain level of flexibility is permitted in the formulas for these products. Indeed, the restrictions are that (1) Red Baron must contain no more than 75% of A and (2) Diablo must contain no less than 25% of A and no less than 50% of B. Up to 40 quarts of A and 30 quarts of B could be purchased. McNaughton can sell as much of these sauces as it produces at a price per quart of $3.35 for Diablo and $2.85 for Red Baron. A and B cost $1.60 and $2.05 per quart, respectively. McNaughton wishes to maximize its net revenue from the sale of these sauces. Formulate their problem as an LP problem.

Solution to Diablo/Red Baron Example

$$D = \text{quarts of Diablo to be produced}$$
$$R = \text{quarts of Red Baron to be produced}$$
$$A_1 = \text{quarts of A used to make Diablo}$$
$$A_2 = \text{quarts of A used to make Red Baron}$$
$$B_1 = \text{quarts of B used to make Diablo}$$
$$B_2 = \text{quarts of B used to make Red Baron}$$

$$\text{Max} \quad 3.35D + 2.85R - 1.60(A_1 + A_2) - 2.05(B_1 + B_2)$$

$$
\begin{aligned}
\text{s.t.} \quad & A_1 + B_1 - D && = 0 \\
& A_2 + B_2 - R && = 0 \\
& A_1 + A_2 && \leq 40 \\
& B_1 + B_2 && \leq 30 \\
& A_1 - 0.25D && \geq 0 \\
& B_1 - 0.50D && \geq 0 \\
& A_2 - 0.75R && \leq 0 \\
& A_1, A_2, B_1, B_2, D, R && \geq 0
\end{aligned}
$$

As an alternative but equivalent formulation, we can use the relationships

$$D = A_1 + B_1$$
$$R = A_2 + B_2$$

to eliminate the variables D and R from the objective function and to reduce the number of constraints. This yields

$$
\begin{aligned}
\text{Max} \quad & 1.75A_1 + 1.30B_1 + 1.25A_2 + 0.80B_2 \\
\text{s.t.} \quad & A_1 + A_2 \leq 40 \\
& B_1 + B_2 \leq 30 \\
& 0.75A_1 - 0.25B_1 \geq 0 \\
& 0.50B_1 - 0.50A_1 \geq 0 \\
& 0.25A_2 - 0.75B_2 \leq 0 \\
& A_1, B_1, A_2, B_2 \geq 0
\end{aligned}
$$

The next scenario gives an example of a so-called transportation model. The particular form of this problem is even more "special" than linear. For example, if your formulation is correct, you will note that all of the nonzero coefficients in the constraints are 1. Other examples of transportation models will appear later in the text. In fact, a transportation model is an example of an entire special class of linear programs called *network problems*. These are discussed in a later chapter.

Example 14: Transportation Model

A company has two plants and three warehouses. The first plant can supply at most 100 units and the second at most 200 units of the same product. The sales potential at the first warehouse is 150, at the second warehouse 200, and at the third 350. The sales revenues per unit at the three warehouses are 12 at the first, 14 at the second, and 15 at the third. The cost of manufacturing one unit at plant i and shipping it to warehouse j is given in Figure 4.15.

Figure 4.15
Manufacturing and Shipping Data

	WAREHOUSE		
PLANT	1	2	3
1	8	10	12
2	7	9	11

The company wishes to determine how many units should be shipped from each plant to each warehouse so as to maximize profit. Formulate an LP model for this problem.

Solution to Transportation Model Example

$$x_{ij} = \text{units sent from plant } i \text{ to warehouse } j$$

$$\text{Max} \quad 4x_{11} + 5x_{21} + 4x_{12} + 5x_{22} + 3x_{13} + 4x_{23}$$

$$\text{s.t.} \quad x_{11} + x_{12} + x_{13} \leq 100$$

$$x_{21} + x_{22} + x_{23} \leq 200$$

$$x_{11} + x_{21} \qquad\quad \leq 150$$

$$x_{12} + x_{22} \qquad\quad \leq 200$$

$$x_{13} + x_{23} \qquad\quad \leq 350$$

$$x_{ij} \geq 0 \qquad \text{all } i, j$$

Example 15: Tape Recorders

A tape recorder company manufactures models A, B, and C, which have profit contributions of 15, 40, and 60, respectively. The weekly minimum production requirements are 25 for model A, 130 for model B, and 55 for model C. Each type of recorder requires a certain amount of time for the manufacturing of component parts, for assembling, and for packaging. Specifically, a *dozen* units of model A require 4 hours for manufacturing, 3 hours for assembling, and 1 hour for packaging. The corresponding figures for a dozen units of model B are 2.5, 4, and 2, and for a dozen units of model C are 6, 9, and 4. During the forthcoming week, the company has available 130 hours of manufacturing, 170 hours of assembling, and 52 hours of packaging time. Formulate as an LP model the problem of scheduling production so as to maximize profit.

Solution to Tape Recorder Example

$$A = \text{units of A produced per week}$$

$$B = \text{units of B produced per week}$$

$$C = \text{units of C produced per week}$$

$$\text{Max} \quad 15A + 40B + 60C$$

$$\text{s.t.} \quad A \qquad\qquad\qquad \geq 25$$

$$B \qquad\quad \geq 130$$

$$C \geq 55$$

$$4\frac{A}{12} + 2.5\frac{B}{12} + 6\frac{C}{12} \leq 130$$

$$3\frac{A}{12} + \quad 4\frac{B}{12} + 9\frac{C}{12} \leq 170$$

$$1\frac{A}{12} + \quad 2\frac{B}{12} + 4\frac{C}{12} \leq 52$$

$$A, B, C \geq 0$$

Example 16: Fertilizer Mix

The University of Chicago is planning to put fertilizer on the grass in the quadrangle area early in the spring. The grass needs nitrogen, phosphorus, and potash in at least the amounts given in Figure 4.16. Three kinds of commercial fertilizer are available; analysis and price are given in Figure 4.17.

Figure 4.16
Total Grass Requirements

MINERAL	MINIMUM WEIGHT (lb)
Nitrogen	10
Phosphorus	7
Potash	5

Figure 4.17
Fertilizer Characteristics (per 1000 lb)

FERTILIZER	NITROGEN CONTENT (lb)	PHOSPHOROUS CONTENT (lb)	POTASH CONTENT (lb)	PRICE
I	25	10	5	$10
II	10	5	10	8
III	5	10	5	7

The university can buy as much of each of these fertilizers as it wishes and mix them together before applying them to the grass. Formulate an LP model to determine how much of each fertilizer to buy to satisfy the requirements at minimum cost.

Solution to Fertilizer Mix Example

F_1 = pounds of fertilizer I to purchase

F_2 = pounds of fertilizer II to purchase

F_3 = pounds of fertilizer III to purchase

$$\text{Min} \quad \frac{10}{1000}F_1 + \frac{8}{1000}F_2 + \frac{7}{1000}F_3$$

$$\text{s.t.} \quad 25\frac{F_1}{1000} + 10\frac{F_2}{1000} + 5\frac{F_3}{1000} \geq 10$$

$$10\frac{F_1}{1000} + 5\frac{F_2}{1000} + 10\frac{F_3}{1000} \geq 7$$

$$5\frac{F_1}{1000} + 10\frac{F_2}{1000} + 5\frac{F_3}{1000} \geq 5$$

$$F_1, F_2, F_3 \geq 0$$

Example 17: Security Force

The security and traffic force at PROTRAC's Moline plant must satisfy the staffing requirements shown in Figure 4.18. Officers work 8-hour shifts starting at each of the 4-hour intervals shown, that is, midnight, 4:00 A.M., 8:00 A.M., and so on. How many officers should report for work at the beginning of each time period in order to minimize the total number of officers required to satisfy the staffing requirements? Formulate this as an LP problem.

Figure 4.18
Security Staff Data

TIME	NUMBER OF OFFICERS REQUIRED
0:01– 4:00	5
4:01– 8:00	7
8:01–12:00	15
12:01–16:00	7
16:01–20:00	12
20:01–24:00	9

Solution to Security Force Example

The secret to solving this example is to choose the decision variables in an appropriate manner. Let

$$x_i = \text{number of officers who start in shift } i$$

Note that officers who start in one shift are also available to satisfy demand in the next shift. The stated goal is to minimize the number of officers required. The problem then becomes

$$\text{Min} \quad x_1 + x_2 + x_3 + x_4 + x_5 + x_6$$
$$\text{s.t.} \quad x_1 + x_2 \geq 7$$
$$x_2 + x_3 \geq 15$$
$$x_3 + x_4 \geq 7$$
$$x_4 + x_5 \geq 12$$
$$x_5 + x_6 \geq 9$$
$$x_6 + x_1 \geq 5$$
$$x_i \geq 0 \quad i = 1, \ldots, 6$$

Example 18: Marketing at PROTRAC

This problem is instructive in a special sense. It shows how LP can be applied to a **piecewise linear**, as opposed to linear, objective function.

Figure 4.19

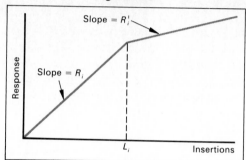

The marketing department at **PROTRAC** is deciding how to allocate an advertising budget among N different media. In particular, management wishes to determine how many times to use each medium. In marketing jargon, each use of a medium is called an *insertion*. For each medium, say i, there is an assumed response R_i for each insertion until a specified number of insertions, say L_i, is reached. After this, the response rate per insertion becomes R_i', where $R_i' < R_i$. The general shape of a typical response curve is shown in Figure 4.19. The objective of the advertising campaign is to maximize total response.

If C_i is the cost per insertion in medium i and the total advertising budget is B, create an LP model that determines the optimal number of insertions per medium (optimal in the sense of response maximizing) without violating the advertising budget.

Solution to Marketing Problem Example

$x_i =$ number of insertions in medium i with a response of R_i

$y_i =$ number of insertions in medium i with a response of R_i'

$$\text{Max} \quad \sum_{i=1}^{N} (R_i x_i + R_i' y_i)$$

$$\text{s.t.} \quad \sum_{i=1}^{N} C_i(x_i + y_i) \leq B$$

$$x_i \leq L_i \qquad i = 1, \ldots, N$$

$$x_i, y_i \geq 0$$

Try to convince yourself that the variable y_i will never be positive until x_i has hit its upper bound of L_i. This is because $R_i > R_i'$. A piecewise linear objective function with the shape shown above (decreasing slopes) is called **concave**. Had the curve been **convex** (i.e., increasing slopes), then the foregoing formulation would not work. The general rule is this:

A piecewise linear objective function with decreasing marginal returns (a concave function) can be treated in a maximization LP context. A piecewise linear objective function with increasing marginal costs (a convex function) can be treated in a minimization LP context.

Example 19: Paint Finishes

In ordering a product from **PROTRAC**, customers may choose among three finishes, hard, luster, and regular. These finishes are blended from four raw paints purchased by PROTRAC. Since each raw paint has different characteristics, there are constraints on the amounts of each that can be used in making a finish. The paint department at PROTRAC receives transfer price revenues for the various finishes it produces. Paint data are given in Figure 4.20, finish data in Figure 4.21.

Figure 4.20
Paint Data

RAW PAINT	BARRELS AVAILABLE	COST PER BARREL
1	6,000	$9
2	8,000	6
3	12,000	8
4	9,000	4

Figure 4.21
Finish Data

FINISH	COMPOSITION CONSTRAINTS	TRANSFER PRICE REVENUE PER BARREL PRODUCED
Hard	Not more than 20% of 1 Not less than 30% of 2 Not less than 15% of 3	$15
Luster	Not more than 50% of 4 Not less than 18% of 2 Not more than 25% of 3	12
Regular	Not more than 40% of 2 Not more than 30% of 1	13

Let the net revenue be the transfer price revenue minus the expense for the raw paints used. Create a linear program that determines the amount and blend of each finish that should be made from the supply of raw paints available in order for the paint department to maximize net revenue.

Solution to Paint Finish Example

Let b_{ij} be the number of barrels of raw paint i used in the total production of finish j. Note that $b_{1H} + b_{2H} + b_{3H} + b_{4H}$ is the total amount of hard finish (H) paint produced, whereas $b_{1H} + b_{1L} + b_{1R}$ is the total amount of raw paint 1 used, and $b_{1H}/(b_{1H} + b_{2H} + b_{3H} + b_{4H})$ is the proportion of raw paint 1 used in finish H.

These observations lead to the following LP model:

$$\text{Max} \quad 15(b_{1H} + b_{2H} + b_{3H} + b_{4H}) + 12(b_{1L} + b_{2L} + b_{3L} + b_{4L}) + 13(b_{1R} + b_{2R}$$
$$+ b_{3R} + b_{4R}) - 9(b_{1H} + b_{1L} + b_{1R}) - 6(b_{2H} + b_{2L} + b_{2R}) - 8(b_{3H}$$
$$+ b_{3L} + b_{3R}) - 4(b_{4H} + b_{4L} + b_{4R})$$

These constraints ensure using no more raw paint than is available

s.t.

$$\begin{cases} b_{1H} + b_{1L} + b_{1R} \le 6{,}000 \\ b_{2H} + b_{2L} + b_{2R} \le 8{,}000 \\ b_{3H} + b_{3L} + b_{3R} \le 12{,}000 \\ b_{4H} + b_{4L} + b_{4R} \le 9{,}000 \end{cases}$$

These constraints ensure that the blend for hard finish satisfies the percentage requirements

$$\begin{cases} \dfrac{b_{1H}}{b_{1H} + b_{2H} + b_{3H} + b_{4H}} \le 0.20 \\[2ex] \dfrac{b_{2H}}{b_{1H} + b_{2H} + b_{3H} + b_{4H}} \ge 0.30 \\[2ex] \dfrac{b_{3H}}{b_{1H} + b_{2H} + b_{3H} + b_{4H}} \ge 0.15 \end{cases}$$

These constraints ensure that the blend for luster finish satisfies the percentage requirements

$$\begin{cases} \dfrac{b_{4L}}{b_{1L} + b_{2L} + b_{3L} + b_{4L}} \le 0.50 \\[2ex] \dfrac{b_{2L}}{b_{1L} + b_{2L} + b_{3L} + b_{4L}} \ge 0.18 \\[2ex] \dfrac{b_{3L}}{b_{1L} + b_{2L} + b_{3L} + b_{4L}} \le 0.25 \end{cases}$$

These constraints ensure that the blend for regular finish satisfies the percentage requirements

$$\begin{cases} \dfrac{b_{2R}}{b_{1R} + b_{2R} + b_{3R} + b_{3R}} \le 0.40 \\[2ex] \dfrac{b_{1R}}{b_{1R} + b_{2R} + b_{3R} + b_{4R}} \le 0.30 \end{cases}$$

$$\text{All } b_{ij} \ge 0$$

The problem is now formulated. Note that the constraints appear to be nonlinear. However, by using simple arithmetic we obtain the following linear format. Note that terms in the objective function have also been collected.

$$\text{Max} \quad 6b_{1H} + 9b_{2H} + 7b_{3H} + 11b_{4H} + 3b_{1L} + 6b_{2L} + 4b_{3L} + 8b_{4L} + 4b_{1R} + 7b_{2R}$$
$$+ 5b_{3R} + 9b_{4R}$$

s.t.

$b_{1H} +$	$b_{1L} +$	b_{1R}	$\le 6{,}000$
$b_{2H} +$	$b_{2L} +$	b_{2R}	$\le 8{,}000$
$b_{3H} +$	$b_{3L} +$	b_{3R}	$\le 12{,}000$
$b_{4H} +$	$b_{4L} +$	b_{4R}	$\le 9{,}000$

$$0.8b_{1H} - 0.2b_{2H} - 0.2b_{3H} - 0.2b_{4H} \le 0$$
$$-0.3b_{1H} + 0.7b_{2H} - 0.3b_{3H} - 0.3b_{4H} \ge 0$$
$$-0.15b_{1H} - 0.15b_{2H} + 0.85b_{3H} - 0.15b_{4H} \ge 0$$
$$-0.5b_{1L} - 0.5b_{2L} - 0.5b_{3L} + 0.5b_{4L} \le 0$$

$$-0.18b_{1L} + 0.82b_{2L} - 0.18b_{3L} - 0.18b_{4L} \geq \quad 0$$
$$-0.25b_{1L} - 0.25b_{2L} + 0.75b_{3L} - 0.25b_{4L} \leq \quad 0$$
$$-0.4b_{1R} + 0.6b_{2R} - 0.4b_{3R} - 0.4b_{4R} \leq \quad 0$$
$$0.7b_{1R} - 0.3b_{2R} - 0.3b_{3R} - 0.3b_{4R} \leq \quad 0$$
$$\text{all } b_{ij} \geq \quad 0$$

Example 20: Crankshafts at PROTRAC

Crankshafts for earth-moving equipment are produced in only three of PROTRAC's factories because of the high capital investment necessary to produce these parts economically. The crankshafts, however, are assembled into the engines in six different plant locations. The assembly schedule for the coming month is given in Figure 4.22.

Figure 4.22
Assembly Schedule

ASSEMBLY PLANT	NUMBER OF CRANKSHAFTS REQUIRED
1	20
2	60
3	90
4	30
5	50
6	70
Total	320

Figure 4.23 gives the characteristics of the crankshaft department of each of the three producing factories. The overhead costs are independent of the quantity produced; however, if no production is scheduled in a particular plant for the month, the overhead cost falls to zero.

Figure 4.23
Production Data

FACTORY	MONTHLY PRODUCTION CAPACITY	FIXED (OVERHEAD) PRODUCTION COSTS PER MONTH	PRODUCTION COST PER UNIT
A	180	$900	$18
B	130	600	20
C	90	400	22

Figure 4.24 gives the per unit transportation costs for crankshafts from each factory to each assembly plant.

The vice-president of production has currently scheduled 160 units of production for factory A, 120 units for factory B, and 40 units for factory C. The manager of factory C calculates his per unit cost to be [400 + $22(40)]/40 = $32. He feels that this is

Figure 4.24
Transportation Costs (dollars)

FROM FACTORY	\multicolumn{6}{c}{TO PLANT}					
	1	2	3	4	5	6
A	1.50	1.75	2.00	2.25	2.50	2.75
B	2.60	2.40	2.10	1.90	2.90	3.20
C	1.45	1.25	1.95	2.15	1.60	1.80

uneconomical. If the vice-president would transfer 20 units from factory B to him, his per unit cost would become $[400 + \$22(60)]/60 = \$28.67$, a decrease of $3.33. The increase in per unit cost at plant B due to this transfer of 20 units would be $1, from $25 to $26. The net saving per unit from the transfer would be $\$3.33 - \$1.00 = \$2.33$. Thus, for the 20 units transferred, a reduction of $46.40 would occur in the costs.

1. Define the appropriate variables and set the allocation problem up as a cost-minimizing LP problem.
2. Comment on the logic of the plant manager's argument.

Solution to the Crankshaft Example

At first glance, it may appear that this is not an LP problem because of the presence of fixed overhead costs. Since these overhead costs in a particular factory depend on the existence of any production in that factory, we must consider the possibility of satisfying the demands most economically by producing in just two or perhaps just one of the factories. We note, however, that monthly demand is 320 units and that no combination of less than three factories is able to satisfy demand. We, therefore, must assume that all three factories will be operating and attempt to find the best allocation of production among them. Let

x_{ij} = number of crankshafts produced in factory i and sent to assembly plant j

$i = A, B, C$

$j = 1, 2, 3, 4, 5, 6$

The problem then is to minimize production and shipment costs while satisfying demand and not exceeding production capacities.

$$
\begin{aligned}
\text{Min} \quad & (18 + 1.50)x_{A1} + (20 + 2.60)x_{B1} + (22 + 1.45)x_{C1} \\
& + (18 + 1.75)x_{A2} + (20 + 2.40)x_{B2} + (22 + 1.25)x_{C2} \\
& + (18 + 2.00)x_{A3} + (20 + 2.10)x_{B3} + (22 + 1.95)x_{C3} \\
& + (18 + 2.25)x_{A4} + (20 + 1.90)x_{B4} + (22 + 2.15)x_{C4} \\
& + (18 + 2.50)x_{A5} + (20 + 2.90)x_{B5} + (22 + 1.60)x_{C5} \\
& + (18 + 2.75)x_{A6} + (20 + 3.20)x_{B6} + (22 + 1.80)x_{C6}
\end{aligned}
$$

These
constraints
ensure that
capacity is
not exceeded

s.t.

$$\begin{cases} x_{A1} + x_{A2} + x_{A3} + x_{A4} + x_{A5} + x_{A6} \leq 180 \\ x_{B1} + x_{B2} + x_{B3} + x_{B4} + x_{B5} + x_{B6} \leq 130 \\ x_{C1} + x_{C2} + x_{C3} + x_{C4} + x_{C5} + x_{C6} \leq 90 \end{cases}$$

These
constraints
ensure that
demand is
satisfied

$$\begin{cases} x_{A1} + x_{B1} + x_{C1} = 20 \\ x_{A2} + x_{B2} + x_{C2} = 60 \\ x_{A3} + x_{B3} + x_{C3} = 90 \\ x_{A4} + x_{B4} + x_{C4} = 30 \\ x_{A5} + x_{B5} + x_{C5} = 50 \\ x_{A6} + x_{B6} + x_{C6} = 70 \end{cases}$$

$$\text{all } x_{ij} \geq 0$$

The plant manager presents an erroneous argument. First, his analysis depends basically on the overhead costs. Since we have seen that any feasible solution must involve operating all three plants, any reasonable solution cannot be centered on these costs.

Furthermore, his solution cosiders only production costs and ignores transportation costs. Clearly, these latter costs should be considered in the solution. Note that the decision variables in this model are more disaggregated than "what to produce in each plant." They are "what to produce in each plant and where to ship it."

4.10

MAJOR CONCEPTS QUIZ

True–False

1. **T F** In the context of modeling, restrictions on the allowable decisions are called constraints.
2. **T F** Not every LP has to have constraints.
3. **T F** Any model with an objective function, constraints, and decision variables is an LP.
4. **T F** A limitation is expressed as a $\geq$ constraint.
5. **T F** The nonnegativity conditions mean that all decision variables must be positive.
6. **T F** Since fractional values for decision variables may not be physically meaningful, in practice (for the purpose of implementation) we often round the optimal LP solution to integer values.
7. **T F** All the constraints in an LP are inequalities.
8. **T F** Properly defining the decision variables is an important step in model formulation.
9. **T F** The objective function of a cost-minimization model need only consider variable, as opposed to sunk, cost.
10. **T F** The way in which a problem has been formulated as a model is of considerable interest to the manager, who may one day have to pass judgment on the validity of the model.
11. **T F** For most real-world problems, a good test of the "correctness of a model" is whether different analysts would come up with the same model.
12. **T F** Adding the same constant to each coefficient in an LP objective function will not change the optimal values of the decision variables.

13. T F Adding a constant to the objective function in an LP gives a new objective function whose optimal value will be the same as the optimal value of the original objective function.

14. T F When integrality conditions appear in a formulation, the problem is no longer an LP.

15. T F In a correctly formulated model, each variable must explicitly appear in each constraint and in the objective function.

16. T F In a dynamic problem, the end of period $t - 1$ is considered the same as the beginning of period t.

Multiple Choice

17. A constraint directly or indirectly limits the values that
   a. the objective function can assume
   b. the decision variables can assume
   c. neither of the above
   d. both a and b

18. Constraints may represent
   a. limitations
   b. requirements
   c. balance conditions
   d. all of the above

19. Linear programming is
   a. a constrained optimization model
   b. a constrained decision-making model
   c. a mathematical programming model
   d. all of the above

20. In an LP max model
   a. the objective function is maximized
   b. the objective function is maximized and then it is determined whether or not this occurs at an allowable decision
   c. the objective function is maximized over the allowable set of decisions
   d. all of the above

21. The *distinguishing* feature of an LP (as opposed to more general mathematical programming models) is
   a. the problem has an objective function and constraints
   b. all functions in the problem are linear
   c. optimal values for the decision variables are produced

22. In translating a word problem into a formal model, it is often helpful to
   a. express each constraint in words
   b. express the objective in words
   c. verbally identify the decision variables
   d. all of the above

23. Model formulation is important because
   a. it enables us to use algebraic techniques
   b. in a business context, most managers prefer to work with formal models
   c. it forces management to address a clearly defined problem
   d. it allows the manager to better communicate with the management scientist and therefore to be more discriminating in her hiring policies

24. The nonnegativity requirement is included in an LP because
   a. it is included in the model the computer solves
   b. in most cases it makes the model correspond more closely to the real-world problem
   c. neither of the above
   d. both a and b

25. In a multiperiod production problem, the requirement that demand must be satisfied in each period can be enforced by
   a. the carrying of inventories
   b. properly defining inventory variables

    c. nonnegativity of inventory variables
    d. b and c

26. Blending problems often
    a. are integer problems
    b. include a balance constraint
    c. minimize cost
    d. b and c

27. LP problems with integrality conditions
    a. are special cases of LP
    b. are often treated by dropping the integrality conditions, solving the LP, and rounding
    c. ignore integrality conditions
    d. none of the above

Questions 28 through 35 refer to the following problem.

    Three Latvian terrorists, Lotta Crapp, Claire Voyante, and Fickle Finger, are en route to Hollywood to seek their fortune. The flight time is 40 hours at a fuel cost of $100 per gallon. In a Hollywood deli they strike up a quick friendship with the notorious Hymen Putter. Hymen's total income per year is $40,000—his alimony payments are $60,000. Knowing almost everyone in town, Hy is able to spin out a stairway to the stars for our three fortune seekers. They are now inspecting capsule medicine products by passing the capsules over a special lighting table where they visually check for cracked, partially filled, or improperly tainted capsules. Currently, any of our three moguls can be assigned to the visual inspection task. These ladies, however, differ in height, accuracy, and speed abilities. Consequently, their employer (Flora Fortune) pays them at slightly different wage rates. The significant differences are summed up as follows:

INSPECTOR	SPEED (units/hr)	ACCURACY (%)	HOURLY WAGE	HEIGHT
Lotta	300	98	$2.95	7 ft 2 in.
Claire	200	99	2.60	4 ft 3 in.
Fickle	350	96	2.75	5 ft 2 in.

Operating on a full 8-hour shift, Flora needs to have at least 2000 capsules inspected with no more than 2% of these capsules having inspection errors. In addition, because of the devastating Latvian autoimmune syndrome, no one lady can be assigned this task for more than 4 hours per day. Let

$$X_1 = \text{number of hours worked by Lotta}$$

$$X_2 = \text{number of hours worked by Claire}$$

$$X_3 = \text{number of hours worked by Fickle}$$

The objective is to minimize the cost of 8 hours of inspection. Assume that the inspection process must be in operation for all 8 hours. In other words, continuous production must occur during the 8-hour period. In addition, Lotta, Claire, and Fickle are the only inspectors, no more than one inspector can work at a time, and the plumber works at most 4 hours per day.

28. A correct accuracy constraint is
    a. $(0.98)(300)X_1 + (0.99)(200)X_2 + (0.96)(350)X_3 \geq 2000$
    b. $(0.02)(300)X_1 + (0.01)(200)X_2 + (0.04)(350)X_3 \leq (0.02)(2000)$
    c. $-2X_2 + 7X_3 \leq 0$
    d. none of the above

29. The production requirement constraint is correctly written as $300X_1 + 200X_2 + 350X_3 = 2000$.
    a. true
    b. false

30. Excluding the nonnegativity conditions, a proper formulation for this problem will contain six constraints.
    a. true
    b. false

31. It is possible that the correct formulation for this problem will have no feasible decisions. (Answer this question for the given data.)
   a. true
   b. false

32. If it were not for the accuracy requirement and the 4-hour limitation, the optimal solution would have only Fickle working.
   a. true
   b. false

33. The optimal solution will require that at least two of the three employees inspect.
   a. true
   b. false

34. A feasible policy is provided by
   a. 4 hours Claire, 4 hours Fickle
   b. 4 hours Lotta, 4 hours Claire
   c. both a and b

35. Let policy A be $x_1 = 4$, $x_2 = 4$, $x_3 = 0$. Let policy B be $x_1 = 3$, $x_2 = 4$, $x_3 = 1$. Note that each policy is feasible. Since A produces 2000 capsules and B produces 2050, A is preferred.
   a. true
   b. false

Answers

1. T	13. F	25. d
2. F	14. T	26. d
3. F	15. F	27. b
4. F	16. T	28. c
5. F	17. d	29. b
6. T	18. d	30. a
7. F	19. d	31. b
8. T	20. c	32. b
9. T	21. b	33. a
10. T	22. d	34. b
11. F	23. c	35. b
12. F	24. d	

4.11

PROBLEMS

Warm-Up Exercises

4-1. The Swelte Glove Company manufactures and sells two products. The company makes a profit of $12 for each unit of product 1 and a profit of $4 for each unit of product 2 sold. The labor-hour requirements for the products in each of the three production departments are summarized in Figure 4.25. The supervisors of these departments have estimated that

Figure 4.25

Swelte Glove Company Production Data

	PRODUCT	
DEPARTMENT	1	2
1	1	2
2	1	3
3	2	3

the following number of labor hours will be available during the next month: 800 hours in department 1, 600 hours in department 2, and 2000 hours in department 3. Assuming that the company is interested in maximizing profits, show the linear programming model of this problem.

4-2. Cori Ander's Spice Company has a limited supply of two herbal ingredients that are used in the production of seasonings. There are 8000 ounces of ingredient HBO 1 and 7000 ounces of ingredient HBO 2 available. Cori uses the two ingredients to produce either turmeric or paprika. Each bottle of turmeric uses 1 ounce of HBO 1 and 2 ounces of HBO 2. In addition, the marketing department reports that although the firm can sell all of the jars of paprika it can produce, it can only sell up to a maximum of 6000 bottles of turmeric. If Cori makes a profit of $0.05 on each bottle of turmeric and $0.02 on each jar of paprika, what mix of these two products will maximize her firm's profits?

4-3. Willie Maykit is president of a one-person investment firm that manages stock portfolios for a number of clients. A new client has just requested the firm to handle a $100,000 portfolio. The client would like to restrict the portfolio to a mix of the three stocks shown in Figure 4.26. How many shares of each stock should Willie purchase to maximize the estimated total annual return?

Figure 4.26
Portfolio Mix

STOCK	PRICE PER SHARE	ESTIMATED ANNUAL RETURN PER SHARE	MAXIMUM POSSIBLE INVESTMENT
Gofer Crude	$60	$7	$60,000
Can Oil	25	3	25,000
Sloth Petroleum	20	3	30,000

4-4. Doug E. Starr, the manager of Heavenly Dog Kennels, Inc., provides lodging for pets. The kennel's dog food is made by mixing two soybean products to obtain a "well-balanced dog diet." The data for the two products are shown in Figure 4.27. If Doug wants to be sure that his dogs receive at least 5 ounces of protein and 2 ounces of fat per day, what is the minimum cost mix of the two dog food products?

Figure 4.27
Well-Balanced Dog Diet

SOYBEAN PRODUCT	COST PER OUNCE	PROTEIN (%)	FAT (%)
1	$0.05	40	15
2	0.02	15	18

4-5. Suppose that forestry equipment produces a net revenue of $802 per unit and requires 700 pounds of iron, 50 hours of labor, 1 transmission, and 30 hours of heat treatment per unit. Earthmoving equipment yields a net revenue of $660 per unit and requires 4200 pounds of iron, 110 hours of labor, 1 transmission, and 12 hours of heat treatment per unit. The company's capacity during this period is 680,000 pounds of iron, 21,000 hours of labor, 290 transmissions, and 6000 hours of heat treatment. Define the decision variables, and formulate this as a revenue-maximizing linear program.

4-6. Two products are manufactured on each of three machines. A pound of each product requires a specified number of hours on each machine, as presented in Figure 4.28. Total hours available on machines 1, 2, and 3 are 10, 16, and 12, respectively. The profit contributions per pound of products 1 and 2 are 4 and 3, respectively. Define the decision variables and formulate this problem as a profit-maximizing linear program.

Figure 4.28

Machine-Time Data (hours)

	PRODUCT	
MACHINE	1	2
1	3	2
2	1	4
3	5	3

4-7. Identify the decision variables and formulate the following model as a cost-minimizing linear program. A corporation has decided to produce two new products. Three branch plants now have excess production capacity. The unit manufacturing costs of each product in each plant are shown in Figure 4.29. Sales forecasts indicate that 100 units of product 1 and 150 units of product 2 can be sold and therefore should be produced each day. Plants 1, 2, and 3 have the respective capacities to produce 100, 200, and 200 units daily, regardless of the product or combination of products (except that plant 1 cannot produce product 2). The corporation wishes to determine how much of each product should be produced at each plant in order to minimize total manufacturing cost.

Figure 4.29

Manufacturing Data

	PRODUCT	
PLANT	1	2
1	$26	a
2	28	$33
3	24	28

[a]Plant 1 cannot produce product 2.

4-8. Pearce Dears, former encounter group trainer, has turned into a feedlot operator. He desires to feed his animals in such a way as to meet their nutritional requirements at minimum cost. Pearce is considering the use of corn, soybeans, oats, and alfalfa. Figure 4.30 shows the relevant dietary information per pound of grain (e.g., 1 pound of corn

Figure 4.30

Nutrients per Pounds of Grain

NUTRIENT	CORN	SOYBEANS	OATS	ALFALFA	RECOMMENDED DAILY ALLOWANCE
Protein (mg)	10	9	11	8	20 mg
Calcium (mg)	50	45	58	50	70 mg
Iron (mg)	9	8	7	10	12 mg
Calories	1000	800	850	9000	4000 cal
Cost per pound	55	94	50	55	

provides 10 milligrams of protein). Formulate an LP model to determine a dietary mix that will satisfy the recommended daily allowances at minimum cost.

4-9. *Portfolio Planning*   An investment company currently has $10 million to invest. The goal is to maximize expected return earned over the next year. Their four investment possibilities are summarized in Figure 4.31. In addition, the company has specified that at least 30% of the funds must be placed in common stock and treasury bonds, and no more than 40% in money market and municipal bonds. All of the $10 million currently on hand will be invested. Formulate an LP model which tells how much money to invest in each instrument.

Figure 4.31
Summary of Investment Possibilities

INVESTMENT POSSIBILITY	EXPECTED EARNED RETURN (%)	MAXIMUM ALLOWABLE INVESTMENT (millions)
Treasury bonds	8	$5
Common stock	6	7
Money market	12	2
Municipal bonds	9	4

4-10. An investment company must choose among four projects which are competing for a fixed investment budget of $1,200,000. The net investment and estimated returns for each project are shown in Figure 4.32. Each of these projects can be funded at any fractional level ≤ 100%. Formulate an LP model which tells what fraction of each project should be undertaken so as to maximize expected returns.

Figure 4.32
Investment Projects

PROJECT	INVESTMENT	ESTIMATED RETURNS
Shopping centers	$400,000	$575,000
Shale oil	500,000	750,000
Office buildings	350,000	425,000
Low-income housing	450,000	510,000

4-11. Bob Frapples packages holiday gift-wrapped exotic fruits. His packages are wrapped in two different locations from which they are sent to five different wholesalers. The cost of packaging his product at locations 1 and 2 is 5.25 and 5.70, respectively. Bob's forecasts for demand indicate that shipments must be as indicated in Figure 4.33. Wrapping capacity at location 1 is 20,000 packages and at location 2 is 12,000 packages. The distribution costs from the two locations to the five wholesalers are given in Figure 4.34. Formulate an LP

Figure 4.33
Wholesaler Demand

WHOLESALER	1	2	3	4	5
SHIPMENT REQUIRED	4000	6000	2000	10,000	8000

model to determine how many packages Bob should send from each location to each wholesaler.

Figure 4.34

Distribution Costs

FROM LOCATION	TO WHOLESALER				
	1	2	3	4	5
1	0.06	0.04	0.12	0.09	0.05
2	0.15	0.09	0.05	0.08	0.08

More Challenging Problems

4-12. A certain restaurant operates seven days a week. Waitresses are hired to work six effective hours per day. The union contract specifies that each waitress must work five consecutive days and then have two consecutive days off. Each waitress receives the same weekly salary. The restaurant requires at a minimum the following number of waitress hours: Monday, 150; Tuesday, 200; Wednesday, 400; Thursday, 300; Friday, 700; Saturday, 800; Sunday, 300. Assume that this cycle of requirements repeats forever and ignore the fact that the number of waitresses hired must be an integer. The manager wishes to find an employment schedule that satisfies these requirements at minimum cost. Formulate this problem as a linear program.

4-13. Consider the restaurant discussed in Problem 4-12. A new union rule will allow management to hire up to one-half the waitresses who have the day off on an overtime basis. Overtime pay is 1.5 times the usual pay, and any waitress who works overtime must be paid for the entire day. How should the LP problem be modified to take this new rule into account?

4-14. An investor has two money-making activities, coded Alpha and Beta, available at the beginning of each of the next four years. Each dollar invested in Alpha at the beginning of a year returns $1.40 two years later (in time for immediate reinvestment). Each dollar invested in Beta at the beginning of a year returns $1.80 three years later. A third investment possibility, construction projects, will become available at the beginning of the second year. Each dollar invested in construction returns $1.20 one year later. (Construction will be available at the beginning of the third and fourth years also.) The investor starts with $10,000 at the beginning of the first year and wants to maximize the total amount of money he has available at the end of the fourth year.
(a) Identify the decision variables and formulate an LP model.
(HINT: Let M_i be the money available at the beginning of year i and maximize M_5 subject to the appropriate constraints.)
(b) Can you determine the solution by direct analysis?

4-15. A manufacturer has four jobs, A, B, C, and D, that must be produced this month. Each job may be handled in any of three shops. The time required for each job in each shop, the cost per hour in each shop, and the number of hours available this month in each shop are given in Figure 4.35. It is also possible to split each job among the shops in any proportion. For example, one-fourth of job A can be done in 8 hours in shop 1, and one-third of job C can be done in 19 hours in shop 3. The manufacturer wishes to determine how many hours of each job should be handled by each shop in order to minimize the total cost of completing all four jobs. Identify the decision variables and formulate an LP model for this problem.

Figure 4.35
Job-Shop Data

SHOP	HOURS REQUIRED PER JOB				COST PER HOUR OF SHOP TIME	SHOP TIME AVAILABLE (hr)
	A	B	C	D		
1	32	151	72	118	$89	160
2	39	147	61	126	81	160
3	46	155	57	121	84	160

4-16. Identify the decision variables and formulate an LP model for the following problem. A vineyard wishes to blend wine of five different years ($i = 1, 2, \ldots, 5$) to make three types of blended wine. The available supply (in gallons) of wine from year i is S_i, $i = 1, 2, \ldots,$ 5. Blend 1 is considered a premium blend and, therefore, no more than 100 gallons are to be made. Restrictions on each of the blends are given in Figure 4.36.

Figure 4.36
Wine-Blend Data

BLEND	RESTRICTION	PROFIT PER GALLON
1	At least 60% must be from years 1 and 2, no more than 10% from years 4 and 5	c_1
2	At least 50% must be from years 1, 2, and 3	c_2
3	No more than 50% from year 5	c_3

4-17. A speculator operates a silo with a capacity of 5000 bushels for storing corn. At the beginning of month 1, the silo contains 2000 bushels. Estimates of the selling and purchase prices of corn during the next four months are given in Figure 4.37.

Figure 4.37
Selling and Purchase Price Data

MONTH	PURCHASE PRICE PER 1000 BUSHELS	SELLING PRICE PER 1000 BUSHELS
1	$40	$35
2	50	50
3	70	60
4	70	70

Corn sold during any given month is removed from the silo at the beginning of that month. Thus 2000 bushels are available for sale in month 1. Corn bought during any given month is put into the silo during the middle of that month, but it cannot be sold until the following month. Given the above sales and purchase prices, and the assumptions on storage costs presented in parts (a) and (b) below, the speculator wishes to know how much corn to buy and sell each month so as to maximize total profits shortly after the beginning of the fourth month (which means after any sale that may occur in that month).

To aid in defining the assumptions on storage cost, let

A_t = bushels in the silo immediately after the quantity sold in period t is removed (t = 1, 2, 3, 4)

B_t = bushels in the silo immediately after the quantity purchased in period t is put into the silo (t = 1, 2, 3)

(a) Assume that the storage cost in period t (t = 1, 2, 3) is

$$\$0.005\left(\frac{A_t + B_t}{2}\right)$$

Define the decision variables and formulate an LP model for this problem.

(b) Assume that no storage cost is incurred for corn removed at the beginning of the month immediately following the month of its acquisition, so that corn sold in month t is taken out of purchases in month $t - 1$, to the greatest extent possible. That is, the storage cost in period t (t = 1, 2, 3) is

$$\$0.005 \quad \max(A_t, A_{t+1})$$

Demonstrate that this mathematical expression represents the verbal description of the storage cost. Then define the decision variables and formulate a *nonlinear* programming model for this problem. Can you convert this to an LP model?

4-18. As one phase of its spare parts operation, PROTRAC produces two parts (1 and 2) that are sold as part of three separate components (A, B, and C) and also as individual units. Figure 4.38 indicates the number of parts required by each component.

Figure 4.38
Part/Component Data

COMPONENT	PART 1	PART 2
A	2	0
B	0	1
C	1	3

Each part and each component is processed in each of three departments and requires time (in minutes) as shown in Figure 4.39. Note that the processing time for a component does *not* include the processing times for the parts that will later be included in the component. The components also require time in the assembly department.

Figure 4.39
Processing-Time Data (min)

PART	COMPONENT	DEPARTMENT 1	DEPARTMENT 2	DEPARTMENT 3	Assembly
1		16	20	24	
2		25	21	18	
	A	27	30	25	15
	B	12	18	21	24
	C	17	22	28	19

In one period there are 8000, 9000, 10,000, and 12,000 minutes available in departments 1, 2, 3, and assembly, respectively. To satisfy current commitments, PROTRAC must produce at least 5 of component A, 7 of component B, and 8 of component C, as well as 20 of part 1 and 60 of part 2. The net profit from selling the components and individual parts is: component A, $30; component B, $38; component C, $45; part 1, $10; part 2, $15.

(a) Assuming that PROTRAC can sell as much of each of these items as it produces, create an LP problem that yields the optimal production plan.

(b) Each unit of part 1 and each unit of part 2 requires a single aluminum bearing purchased from outside PROTRAC. How many bearings in total must be ordered to implement the optimal production plan obtained from part (a)?

4-19. Consider the problem presented in Example 2 of Section 4.4. Define three additional variables $M1$, $M2$, and $M3$ as follows:

$$M1 = \text{total hours used on machine 1}$$
$$M2 = \text{total hours used on machine 2}$$
$$M3 = \text{total hours used on machine 3}$$

(a) Reformulate the model from Example 2 of Section 4.4 with these variables included. The relations between these new variables and the former ones must appear in the reformulation.

(b) A variable whose values are directly determined by the values of other variables is sometimes referred to as a "definitional variable." Show that this is the case for $M1$, $M2$, and $M3$.

● (c) In what sense is the reformulated model equivalent to the formulation in the text?

(d) For what reasons might definitional variables be employed?

(e) Suppose that the revenue parameters in Example 2 of Section 4.4 are modified as follows. "Products A, B, and C are purely competitive and any amounts made may be sold at respective per pound prices of $5, $4, and $5. The first 20 pounds of products D and E produced per week can be sold at $4 each, but all made in excess of 20 can only be sold at $3 each." Reformulate the model as modified, using the variables $M1$, $M2$ and $M3$.

4-20. The Party Nut Company has on hand 550 pounds of peanuts, 150 pounds of cashews, 90 pounds of brazil nuts, and 70 pounds of hazelnuts. It packages and sells four varieties of mixed nuts in standard 8-ounce (half-pound) cans. The mix requirements and net whole-sale prices are shown in Figure 4.40. The firm can sell all that it can produce at these prices. How many pounds of each type of nut should be used in each mix? Formulate this problem as a profit-maximizing LP model.

Figure 4.40
Nut Mix Data

MIX	CONTENTS	PRICE PER CAN
1 (peanuts)	Peanuts only	$0.26
2 (party mix)	No more than 50% peanuts; at least 15% cashews; at least 10% brazil nuts	0.40
3 (cashews)	Cashews only	0.51
4 (luxury mix)	At least 30% cashews; at least 20% brazil nuts; at least 30% hazelnuts	0.52

4-21. A small firm has two processes for blending each of two products, charcoal starter fluid and lighter fluid for cigarette lighters. The firm is attempting to decide how many hours to run each process. For 1 hour of process 1, an input of 3 units of kerosene and 9 units of benzene produces an output of 15 units of starter fluid and 6 units of lighter fluid. For an hour of process 2, an input of 12 units of kerosene and 6 units of benzene produces an output of 9 units of starter fluid and 24 units of lighter fluid. Let x_1 and x_2 be the number of hours the company decides to use of process 1 and process 2, respectively. Because of a federal allocation program, the maximum amount of kerosene and benzene available is 300 units and 450 units, respectively. Sales commitments require that at least 600 units of starter fluid and 225 units of lighter fluid be produced. The per hour profits that accrue from process 1 and process 2 are p_1 and p_2, respectively. Formulate this as a profit-maximizing constrained optimization model.

4-22. In the human diet, 16 essential nutrients have been identified. Suppose that there are 116 foods. A pound of food j contains a_{ij} pounds of nutrient i. Suppose that a human must have N_i pounds of each nutrient i in the daily diet and that a pound of food j costs c_j cents. What is the least-cost daily diet satisfying all nutritional requirements? Use summation notation in the formulation of this problem. Aside from the question of palatability, can you think of an important constraint that this problem omits?

4-23. The Pittsburgh Steel (PS) Company has contracted to produce a new type of steel that has the tight quality requirements shown in Figure 4.41.

Figure 4.41
Steel Content Requirements

MINERAL CONTENT	AT LEAST (%)	NOT MORE THAN (%)
Carbon	3.0	3.5
Chrome	0.3	0.45
Manganese	1.35	1.65
Silicon	2.7	3.0

PS has materials available for mixing a batch as shown in Figure 4.42.

Figure 4.42
Data on Available Materials for Steel Blend

AVAILABLE MATERIAL	COST PER POUND	CARBON (%)	CHROME (%)	MANGANESE (%)	SILICON (%)	AVAILABLE AMOUNT (lb)
Pig iron 1	$0.03	4.0	0	0.9	2.25	Unlimited
Pig iron 2	0.0645	0	10.0	4.5	15.0	Unlimited
Ferrosilicon 1	0.065	0	0	0	45.0	Unlimited
Ferrosilicon 2	0.061	0	0	0	42.0	Unlimited
Alloy 1	0.10	0	0	60.0	18.0	Unlimited
Alloy 2	0.13	0	20.0	9.0	30.0	Unlimited
Alloy 3	0.119	0	8.00	33.0	25.0	Unlimited
Carbide (silicon)	0.08	15.0	0	0	30.0	20
Steel 1	0.021	0.4	0	0.9	0	200
Steel 2	0.02	0.1	0	0.3	0	200
Steel 3	0.0195	0.1	0	0.3	0	200

How much of each of the 11 materials should be blended in a 1-ton batch so as to satisfy all the foregoing requirements at minimum cost? Formulate this as a constrained optimization model.

4-24. An airline must decide on the amounts of jet fuel to purchase from three oil companies. The airline refuels its aircraft regularly at the four airports it serves. The oil companies have said that they can furnish up to the following amounts of fuel during the coming month: oil company 1, 250,000 gallons; oil company 2, 500,000 gallons; oil company 3, 600,000 gallons. The minimal required amounts of jet fuel are: 100,000 gallons at airport 1; 200,000 gallons at airport 2; 300,000 gallons at airport 3; 400,000 gallons at airport 4.

　　When transportation costs are added to the price per gallon supplied, the combined cost per gallon is as shown in Figure 4.43.

Figure 4.43
Oil Cost-per-Gallon Data (dollars)

OIL COMPANY	AIRPORT			
	1	2	3	4
1	12	11	11	11
2	9	10	8	13
3	15	12	12	14

(a) Formulate this problem as a cost-minimizing constrained optimization model.
(b) Note that the total supply from all companies will not be used. Is it possible to tell by inspecting the data which companies will sell all their fuel?
(c) Suppose that company 3 wishes to become more competitive. One way would be to reduce transport costs. Instead, management decides to offer a bulk discount of the following form: if the airline purchases at least 400,000 gallons then the company will reduce its price per gallon by $2. How can the airline determine whether or not to accept the discount?

4-25. A firm wants a production plan that will minimize costs for the next three periods. Let

d_i = quantity demanded in period i
c_i = cost of producing a unit in period i
h_i = cost per unit of inventory on hand at the end of each period i

There is a 10% spoilage. That is, 10% of the inventory available at the end of period i must be discarded. It is not available to satisfy demand in period $i + 1$. Let

P_i = production in period i
I_i = inventory on hand at the end of period i

(a) Assume that I_0 is known and formulate an LP problem that yields the optimal production plan.
(b) Management feels that the model derived in part (a) is inadequate because it does not incorporate the cost of adjusting labor and production facilities from one rate of production to another. An operations analyst thus proposes introducing this adjustment cost into the model by utilizing a factor K_i, where K_i is the cost per unit change in the production from period $i - 1$ to period i. For example, if production in period 1 is 300 units and in period 2 it is 100 units, a cost of $200K_2$ is incurred. Similarly, if production in period 1 is 100 units and production in period 2 is 200 units a cost of $100K_2$ is incurred. Assume that I_0, P_0, and P_4 are known. The analyst suggests that

the solution to the new problem can be found by replacing the objective function of the problem in part (a) by the expression

$$\text{Min} \quad c_1 P_1 + c_2 P_2 + c_3 P_3 + h_1 I_1 + h_2 I_2 + h_3 I_3 + K_1(P_0 - P_1)$$
$$+ K_2(P_1 - P_2) + K_3(P_2 - P_3) + K_4(P_3 - P_4)$$

Will the solution to this LP problem provide the correct answer to the question posed by management? If not, state why.

4-26. Consider Example 5 of Section 4.6. Let $I_0 = 0$, $K_t = \infty$, and $h_t = 0$ for all t. That is, assume no initial inventory, no holding costs, and infinite capacities. Also assume demand in each period is positive.

(a) Suppose that per unit production costs are the same in each period. That is, $C_t = C$ for all t. Can you, by inspection, discover an optimal production schedule? What is the total cost of this schedule? Is this schedule unique? (That is, can you discover more than one optimal schedule?)

(b) Suppose that the per unit production costs are increasing $(0 < C_1 < C_2, \ldots, < C_6)$. Can you discover an optimal policy in this case? Can you discover more than one?

● (c) Suppose that in part (b) the holding cost h_1 is increased from zero by a very slight amount. Would you think that the optimal policy will change? Suppose that h_1 is now continuously increased further. Try to discuss the trade-offs that will occur. What happens as the capacity in period 1 is continuously reduced from ∞?

(d) Suppose that the per unit production costs are decreasing $(C_1 > C_2, \ldots, > C_6 > 0)$. Answer the questions in part (b).

● (e) For the case $C_1 > C_2, \ldots, > C_n > 0$, answer the questions in part (c).

● (f) Suppose that the initial inventory is 12 and the remaining parameters for the problem are as specified in Figure 4.44. Can you discover an optimal production plan?

Figure 4.44

Parameter Data

t	1	2	3	4	5	6
d_t	100	100	100	100	100	100
C_t	15	13	14	9	10	8
h_t	0	0	0	0	0	0
K_t	500	500	500	500	500	500

4-27. Consider Example 6 of Section 4.6. Show how to eliminate the x_t variables from the model given in this example (for $t = 2, \ldots, 6$).

4-28. Consider Example 7 of Section 4.6. The objective function in the model developed in the first part of Example 7 can be replaced with

$$\sum_{t=1}^{6} (400 + 100r)y_t$$

In other words, the term $54,000r$ can be ignored. Why is this so? (How do the optimal decision variables compare in each formulation? What about the optimal objective values?)

● **4-29.** Each year, the parts department of PROTRAC takes a physical count of its parts inventory in each of its main warehouses. This work is done during the second shift (4 P.M. to midnight) by trained members of the clerical staff, called counters. However, it is possible to train additional members of the staff to be counters. Training is done in classes of size 20 by one of the already trained staff who serves as an instructor. The staff is unionized, and the following work rules are strictly enforced:

1. Only trained personnel can count.
2. A job as a counter is taken for a 1-week interval.
3. A person who serves as a counter in a given week can serve as neither an instructor nor a counter in the following week.
4. Any trained person can serve as an instructor.
5. An instructor always handles a class of exactly 20 persons.
6. A training class lasts one week.
7. Once a person has served as an instructor, he cannot serve as either an instructor or a counter again that year.

It is estimated that 900 person-weeks of counting must be done during the next 4 weeks. There are 400 trained personnel on hand who can act as counters or instructors during the first week. Counters are paid $320 per week. Instructors are paid $600 per week. All trained persons are paid $40 per week if they are not used as either counters or instructors. Express as a linear program the problem of minimizing the total cost of supplying the 900 person-weeks.

4-30. *A Scheduling Problem*   While it is operating out of Stockholm, the aircraft carrier *Mighty* is on maneuvers from Monday through Friday and in port over the weekend. Next week the Captain would like to give shore leave for Monday through Friday to as many sailors as possible. However, he must carry out the maneuvers for the week and satisfy Navy regulations.

The regulations are:

1. Sailors work either the A.M. shift (midnight to noon) or the P.M. shift (noon to midnight) any day they work, and during a week they must remain on the same shift every day they work.
2. Each sailor must be on duty exactly four days, even if there is not enough "real work" on some days.
3. A sailor *cannot* work more than three consecutive days.

Figure 4.45
Sailors per Shift Day

	M	T	W	T	F
A.M.	900	300	700	750	500
P.M.	400	800	650	850	1000

The number of sailors required each shift of each day is shown in Figure 4.45. Formulate this problem as a linear programming problem. Define your variables in such a way that it is obvious how to implement the solution if one were to solve the LP you suggest (i.e., so that one would know how many sailors work on each day).

4-31. Consider three plants, and let b_i be a decision variable denoting the budget allocated to plant i ($i = 1, 2, 3$). Let $f_i(b_i)$ be a function denoting the revenue obtained by plant i, given budget b_i. Consider the following two models:

100

CHAPTER 4
Formulation
of Constrained
Optimization
Models

$$\text{Profit Maximization Model} \quad \begin{cases} \text{Max} & \sum_{i=1}^{3} (f_i(b_i) - b_i) \\ \text{s.t.} & \sum_{i=1}^{3} b_i = 5.5 \\ & b_i \geq 0 \quad i = 1, 2, 3 \end{cases}$$

$$\text{Revenue Maximization Model} \quad \begin{cases} \text{Max} & \sum_{i=1}^{3} f_i(b_i) \\ \text{s.t.} & \sum_{i=1}^{3} b_i = 5.5 \\ & b_i \geq 0 \quad i = 1, 2, 3 \end{cases}$$

(a) Are these two models the same or different? That is, will they produce the same or different decisions?

(b) What is wrong with the following procedure? In the profit maximization model, since the constraint says

$$\sum_{i=1}^{3} b_i = 5.5$$

substitute this into the objective function and then solve

$$\text{Max} \quad \sum_{i=1}^{3} f_i(b_i) - 5.5$$
$$\text{s.t.} \quad b_i \geq 0 \quad i = 1, 2, 3$$

(c) Suppose that the equality constraints in each of the models are changed to $\leq$. What effect, if any, could such a change have?

CASE

RED BRAND CANNERS*

Here is a simple but interesting case that captures several points that are important in real-world problem formulation. In any real problem it is important for the manager to distinguish between those facts and data which are relevant and those which are not. This may be especially difficult because on occasion confused or incorrect concepts will be strongly held by members of the management team. This case is designed to reproduce such a setting. The present task will simply involve model formulation. You will deal with this case again, however, after Chapter 6, where you will be asked to produce solutions, analysis, critiques, and interpretations.

On Monday, September 13, 1965, Mr. Mitchell Gordon, vice president of operations, asked the controller, the sales manager, and the production manager to meet with him to discuss the amount of tomato products to pack that season. The tomato crop, which had been purchased at planting, was beginning to arrive at the cannery, and packing operations would have to be started by the following Monday. Red Brand Canners was a medium-sized company which canned and distributed a variety of fruit and vegetable products under private brands in the western states.

*Reprinted from *Stanford Business Cases 1977* with the permission of the publishers, Stanford University Graduate School of Business. Copyright © 1977 by the Board of Trustees of the Leland Stanford Junior University.

Mr. William Cooper, the controller, and Mr. Charles Myers, the sales manager, were the first to arrive in Mr. Gordon's office. Dan Tucker, the production manager, came in a few minutes later and said that he had picked up Produce Inspection's latest estimate of the quality of the incoming tomatoes. According to their report, about 20 percent of the crop was grade "A" quality and the remaining portion of the 3,000,000-pound crop was grade "B."

Gordon asked Myers about the demand for tomato products for the coming year. Myers replied that for all practical purposes they could sell all the whole canned tomatoes they could produce. The expected demand for tomato juice and tomato paste, on the other hand, was limited. The sales manager then passed around the latest demand forecast, which is shown in Exhibit 1. He reminded the group that the selling prices had been set in light of the long-term marketing strategy of the company, and potential sales had been forecasted at these prices.

Exhibit 1
Demand Forecasts

PRODUCT	SELLING PRICE PER CASE	DEMAND FORECAST (cases)
24–2½ Whole tomatoes	$4.00	800,000
24–2½ Choice peach halves	5.40	10,000
24–2½ Peach nectar	4.60	5,000
24–2½ Tomato juice	4.50	50,000
24–2½ Cooking apples	4.90	15,000
24–2½ Tomato paste	3.80	80,000

Bill Cooper, after looking at Myers's estimates of demand, said that it looked like the company "should use the entire crop for whole tomatoes and should do quite well (on the tomato crop) this year." With the new accounting system that had been set up, he had been able to compute the contribution for each product, and according to his analysis the incremental profit on the whole tomatoes was greater than for any other tomato product. In May, after Red Brand had signed contracts agreeing to purchase the grower's production at an average delivered price of 6 cents per pound, Cooper had computed the tomato products' contributions (see Exhibit 2).

Dan Tucker brought to Cooper's attention that, although there was ample production capacity, it was impossible to produce all whole tomatoes as too small a portion of the tomato crop was "A" quality. Red Brand used a numerical scale to record the quality of both raw produce and prepared products. This scale ran from zero to ten, the higher number representing better quality. Rating tomatoes according to this scale, "A" tomatoes averaged nine points per pound and "B" tomatoes averaged five points per pound. Tucker noted that the minimum average input quality for canned whole tomatoes was eight, and for juice it was six points per pound. Paste could be made entirely from "B" grade tomatoes. This meant that whole tomato production was limited to 800,000 pounds.

Gordon stated that this was not a real limitation. He had been recently solicited to purchase any amount up to 80,000 pounds of grade "A" tomatoes at 8½ cents per pound and at that time had turned down the offer. He felt, however, that the tomatoes were still available.

Exhibit 2
Product Item Profitability

COSTS	PRODUCT					
	24–$2\frac{1}{2}$ Whole Tomatoes	24–$2\frac{1}{2}$ Choice Peach Halves	24–$2\frac{1}{2}$ Peach Nectar	24–$2\frac{1}{2}$ Tomato Juice	24–$2\frac{1}{2}$ Cooking Apples	24–$2\frac{1}{2}$ Tomato Paste
Selling price (per case)	$4.00	$5.40	$4.60	$4.50	$4.90	$3.80
Variable costs						
Direct labor	1.18	1.40	1.27	1.32	0.70	0.54
Variable overhead	0.24	0.32	0.23	0.36	0.22	0.26
Variable selling	0.40	0.30	0.40	0.85	0.28	0.38
Packaging material	0.70	0.56	0.60	0.65	0.70	0.77
Fruit[a] (cost per case)	1.08	1.80	1.70	1.20	0.90	1.50
Total variable costs	3.60	4.38	4.20	4.38	2.80	3.45
Net profit (per case)	0.40	1.02	0.40	0.12	2.10	0.35

[a]Product usage is as given below.

PRODUCT	POUNDS PER CASE
Whole tomatoes	18
Peach halves	18
Peach nectar	17
Tomato juice	20
Cooking apples	27
Tomato paste	25

Exhibit 3
Marginal Analysis of Tomato Products

Z = cost per pound of "A" tomatoes in cents

Y = cost per pound of "B" tomatoes in cents

(1) $(600,000 \text{ lb} \times Z) + (2,400,000 \text{ lb} \times Y) = (3,000,000 \text{ lb} \times 6)$

(2) $\dfrac{Z}{9} = \dfrac{Y}{5}$

Z = 9.32 cents per pound

Y = 5.18 cents per pound

PRODUCT	CANNED WHOLE TOMATOES	TOMATO JUICE	TOMATO PASTE
Selling price	$4.00	$4.50	$3.80
Variable cost (excluding tomato costs)	2.52	3.18	1.95
	$1.48	$1.32	$1.85
Tomato cost	1.49	1.24	1.30
Marginal profit	($0.01)	$0.08	$0.55

Myers, who had been doing some calculations, said that although he agreed that the company "should do quite well this year," it would not be by canning whole tomatoes. It seemed to him that the tomato cost should be allocated on the basis of quality and quantity rather than by quantity only, as Cooper had done. Therefore, he had recomputed the marginal profit on this basis (see Exhibit 3), and from his results, Red Brand should use 2 million pounds of the "B" tomatoes for paste, and the remaining 400,000 pounds of "B" tomatoes and all of the "A" tomatoes for juice. If the demand expectations were realized, a contribution of $48,000 would be made on this year's tomato crop.

Questions

1. Why does Tucker state that the whole tomato production is limited to 800,000 pounds (i.e., where does the number 800,000 come from)?
2. What is wrong with Cooper's suggestion to use the entire crop for whole tomatoes?
3. How does Myers compute his tomato costs in Exhibit 3? How does he reach his conclusion to use 2,000,000 pounds of B tomatoes for paste, the remaining 400,000 pounds of B tomatoes, and all of the A in juice? What is wrong with Myers's reasoning?
4. Without including the possibility of the additional purchases suggested by Gordon, formulate as an LP the problem of determining the optimal canning policy for this season's crop. Define your decision variables in terms of pounds of tomatoes. Express the objective function in cents per pound.
5. How should your model be modified to include the possibility of the additional purchases suggested by Gordon?

CHAPTER 5

Geometric Representation of the Linear Programming Model

INTRODUCTION

Geometry can be used as a "picture" to illustrate many of the concepts of constrained optimization. This chapter develops the geometric tools that will enable us to illustrate some important aspects of the LP model. We restrict this geometric presentation to only two decision variables. As you already know, real-world problems are always in higher dimensions, but the general concepts we want you to understand can be clearly represented in two-dimensional space. Our purpose here is not to solve LP problems with geometry—indeed, real-world problems are solved algebraically by computers. The purpose of this approach is to provide you with an understanding of the interrelationships of the model, an understanding that will enable you to use a computer-generated solution more intelligently and to answer conceptual questions about the problem that the computer does not answer.

The Two-Dimensional Case Although two-dimensional geometry is obviously a very special case, many general concepts can be nicely represented with two-dimensional pictures. For example, pictures will show what happens when the data in the model are changed. And a picture will intuitively answer the question: Why is the number of positive variables in an LP solution equal at most to the number of constraints? As another side of the same coin, a picture will show why a linear profit-maximization problem with n products (n variables) and $m > n$ inputs (m resource constraints) will normally have at least $m - n$ resources in excess. In more general models (not necessarily linear), geometric tools can be used to show what can happen if a constraint is added to a problem or if a constraint is tightened or relaxed by changing the right-hand side or if a constraint is unintentionally left out of the model, or included, but in the wrong way.

When you have acquired facility in transforming these and related conceptual questions to a pictorial representation, you will have a good tool for problem analysis. The geometric approach developed and used in this chapter will help you to rely with greater confidence on your own reasoning to answer questions the computer will not answer for you.

At the outset we briefly recall the technique for plotting inequalities and contours. This material can be quickly skimmed by many readers.

5.2
PLOTTING INEQUALITIES AND CONTOURS

Let us begin by plotting the set of points (x_1, x_2) that satisfies the **inequality**

$$2x_2 - x_1 \leq -2 \tag{5.1}$$

Plotting Inequalities To accomplish this we will use the following general procedure for plotting inequalities.

■ *Step 1: Plot equality.*   Convert the inequality to an equality and plot the straight line that represents this equation. In our example the equality is $2x_2 - x_1 = -2$. The plot of this equation is shown in Figure 5.1.

Figure 5.1
Plotting $2x_2 - x_1 \leq -2$

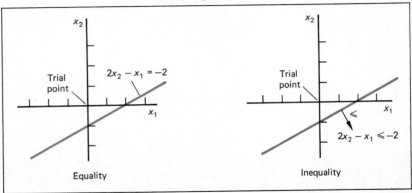

■ *Step 2: Choose trial point.*   Choose any trial point that is not on the line. If the point $x_1 = 0$, $x_2 = 0$ is not on the straight line, then it is a convenient point. In our example, we select $x_1 = 0$, $x_2 = 0$ as the trial point (see Figure 5.1).
■ *Step 3: Evaluate left-hand-side expression.*   Substitute the trial point into the expression on the left-hand side of the inequality. In the example, the expression is $2x_2 - x_1$. Substituting the values $x_1 = 0$, $x_2 = 0$ yields a numerical value of 0.
■ *Step 4: Determine if the trial point satisfies the inequality.*
    a. If the trial point **satisfies** the original inequality, then the straight line plotted in step 1, and all points on the **same** side of the line as the trial point, satisfy the inequality.
    b. If the trial point **does not satisfy** the original inequality, then the straight line, and all points **not** on the same side as the trial point, satisfy the inequality.

In our example, since 0 *is not* ≤ -2, the trial point does *not* satisfy the inequality. Condition b above holds and the straight line and all points on the opposite side of the line from $(0, 0)$ satisfy the inequality. This set is shown in Figure 5.1. Note the convention of denoting the relevant side of the equality line with an arrow and $\leq$ or $\geq$, as appropriate.

106

CHAPTER 5
Geometric
Representation
of the Linear
Programming
Model

Although the idea of "less than" is algebraic and not geometric, students will often confuse the algebraic and the geometric concept with an incorrect impression that the $<$ side of an inequality plot is always "below" the equality line. Hence, to plot the points satisfying a $\leq$ relation, they change the $\leq$ to $=$, graph the equality, and then hastily include all points that lie below the equality line. Figure 5.2 shows a case where the $<$ side is "above" the line. A comparison of Figures 5.1 and 5.2 should convince you that there is no general relationship between the sense of the inequality (i.e., $\leq$ or $\geq$) and the *above* or *below* side of the equality plot. The appropriate side can always be found using a trial point, as we have demonstrated.

Figure 5.2
Plotting $2x_1 - x_2 \leq 2$

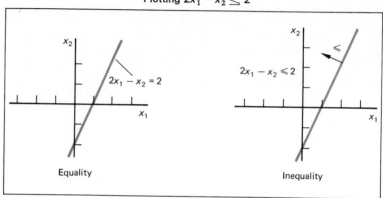

Equality   Inequality

Plotting   The technique described above provides the basic tool for plotting the constraints in
Contours   an LP, for recall that such constraints are always mathematical equalities or inequalities. In order to be well prepared for geometric analysis, it will be useful also to recall the notion of a **contour** (also called an **isoquant**) of a function. A **contour** of a function f of two variables is the set of all pairs (x_1, x_2) for which $f(x_1, x_2)$ takes on some specified **constant value**. When f is a profit function, the contours are often referred to as **isoprofit** lines, and when f is a cost function the contours represent **isocost lines**.

As an example of a contour, suppose that we are selling two products. The profit per unit of product 1 is \$2 and the profit per unit of product 2 is \$4. Then the total profit obtained from selling x_1 units of product 1 and x_2 units of product 2 is given by a function f of two variables defined by

$$\text{profit} = f(x_1, x_2) = 2x_1 + 4x_2$$

Let us now plot all possible sales combinations of x_1 and x_2 for which we obtain \$4 of profit. To do this we plot the equation

$$2x_1 + 4x_2 = 4 \tag{5.2}$$

The plot is shown by the lowest of the three lines in Figure 5.3. This line is called the 4-contour of the function f. In reality, since negative sales do not make sense, we would be interested in only that part of the 4-contour in Figure 5.3 which lies between the two distinguished points on the axes.

Clearly, we can replace the value 4 in the right-hand side of expression (5.2) with any other constant and then plot the result to obtain a different contour of f. Figure 5.3

107

CHAPTER 5
Geometric
Representation
of the Linear
Programming
Model

Figure 5.3
4-, 6-, and 8-Contours of $2x_1 + 4x_2$

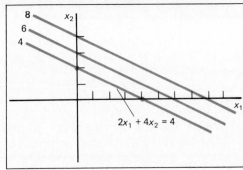

also shows two other contours of f, those corresponding to right-hand sides, in expression (5.2), with values 6 and 8. You can readily see that these contours are parallel lines (i.e., lines with the same slope) and you can deduce that in fact there are infinitely many such contours, one for each possible numerical value of the right-hand side in equation (5.2).

The two concepts reviewed in this section, plotting equalities and plotting contours, will be employed in obtaining graphical solutions of linear programming problems with two decision variables.

In summary:

Plotting contours reduces to plotting equalities. The contours of a linear function are a family of parallel lines. Plotting inequalities also reduces to plotting equalities, or contours, and then identifying the correct side.

5.3
SOLVING THE LINEAR MODEL WITH INEQUALITY CONSTRAINTS

Let us return to the PROTRAC E and F problem (Example 1 of Section 4.4). This problem can be formulated as the following linear program:

$$\text{Max} \quad 5000E + 4000F \qquad \text{(max profit)}$$

PROTRAC
Model

s.t.	$E + F \geq 5$	(minimal production requirement)	(5.3)
	$E - 3F \leq 0$	(market balance)	(5.4)
	$10E + 15F \leq 150$	(capacity in department A)	(5.5)
	$20E + 10F \leq 160$	(capacity in department B)	(5.6)
	$30E + 10F \geq 135$	(contractual labor agreement)	(5.7)
	$E, F \geq 0$	(nonnegativity conditions)	(5.8)

Recall that E and F denote, respectively, the quantities of earth-moving and forestry equipment to be produced in the next two weeks. Since there are only two decision variables (E and F) in the model, we can provide a geometric interpretation. First of all, consider the constraints:

The set of all nonnegative values of the decision variables that satisfies all the constraints is termed the constraint set, or the feasible set.

In keeping with this definition, any pair of nonnegative values for E, F that satisfies all the constraints is said to be **feasible**. These are the **allowable values** of (E, F) according to our model.

Note that it is incorrect to speak of a feasible value of E separately, or a feasible value of F separately. The term *feasible* (in this two-dimensional illustration) applies to a pair of numbers, not to a single number.

Thus, in this case, we speak of feasible pairs of values (E, F), not of feasible values for E (or F) separately. In order to illustrate these feasible pairs geometrically, you merely plot the constraint set, which is done by plotting one constraint at a time in the same picture.

Let us start by observing that since we are only interested in nonnegative values of the decision variables, we need only plot the constraints in the first (northeast) quadrant of the plane. Now consider the first constraint

$$E + F \geq 5$$

Letting E denote the horizontal axis and F the vertical the points (E, F) that satisfy the first constraint are shown in Figure 5.4. Again, we point out our convention of denoting the relevant side of the equality line with an arrow and $\leq$ or $\geq$ as appropriate. In this case, since the first constraint is $\geq$, and since for this constraint the $\geq$ side is above the line, we show an arrow labeled with $\geq$ pointing above the line.

Now consider the second constraint

$$E \leq 3F \quad \text{or} \quad E - 3F \leq 0$$

In Figure 5.5, the plot of this condition appears along with the first condition $E + F \geq 5$. The points (E, F) that simultaneously satisfy both constraints lie in the shaded region. Note that adding the second constraint to the picture has imposed more stringent conditions on the decision variables, and, as shown in Figure 5.5, has "trimmed down" the constraint set.

It will always be the case that adding more constraints either trims down the constraint set, or, possibly, leaves the set unaffected. Adding additional constraints can never enlarge the set of allowable decisions.

Adding constraints amounts to imposing tighter conditions on the decision variables, and this can never increase the number of allowable decisions. This is easily seen geometrically in Figures 5.6, 5.7, and 5.8, which show consecutive additions of the third, fourth, and fifth constraints. Figure 5.8, with all five constraints plotted, illustrates the entire **constraint set**. In two dimensions, a problem with only linear constraints will always have a set of feasible points that is a flat-sided figure called a **polygon**. A generalization of this fact also holds for problems with only linear constraints in any dimension, and the

109

CHAPTER 5
Geometric
Representation
of the Linear
Programming
Model

Figure 5.4
PROTRAC E and F Problem: The First Constraint

Figure 5.5
PROTRAC E and F Problem: The Second Constraint Added

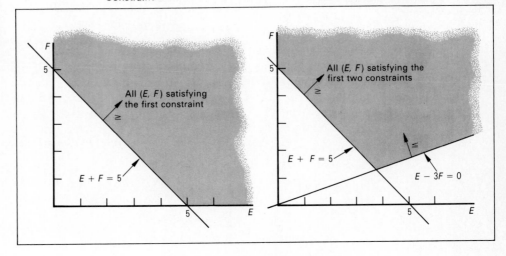

Figure 5.6
PROTRAC E and F Problem: The Third Constraint Added

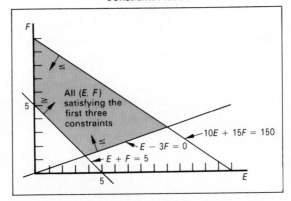

Figure 5.7
PROTRAC E and F Problem: The Fourth Constraint Added

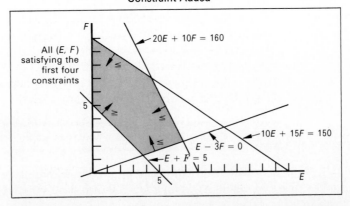

110

CHAPTER 5
Geometric
Representation
of the Linear
Programming
Model

Figure 5.8
PROTRAC *E* and *F* Problem: The Entire
Constraint Set

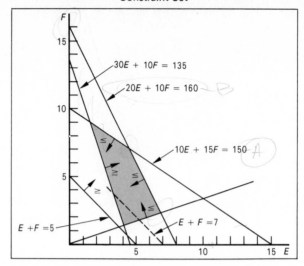

resulting figure is called a **convex polytope**. Figure 5.9 suggests the latitude of the possible shapes for these constraint sets in two dimensions. Figure 5.10 shows what LP constraint sets cannot look like. With pencil and paper and a few examples, you will be able to convince yourself that none of the shapes in Figure 5.10 can be produced by a system of linear inequalities. The shape of an LP constraint set is important, and later we shall investigate how it endows the model with many of its exceptional properties.

Figure 5.9
Possible LP Constraint Sets

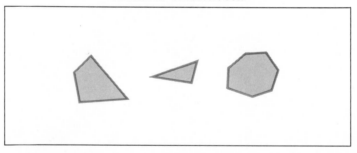

Redundant Returning to Figure 5.8, notice that although the problem has five constraints, only
Constraints four of them are required to define the feasible set. This is because, as the picture clearly indicates, any point that satisfies constraints 2 through 5 will also, automatically, satisfy the first constraint, $E + F \geq 5$, as well. In the sense that the first constraint is superfluous for the given set of data, it is termed **redundant**. You have just seen a picture of the precise meaning of the term **redundant**. Here is a verbal definition.

A redundant constraint is one whose removal does not change the feasible region.

Since a redundant constraint could, by definition, be discarded without changing the feasible region, its elimination will also have no effect on the optimal solution to the

111

CHAPTER 5
Geometric
Representation
of the Linear
Programming
Model

Figure 5.10
Sets That Cannot Be LP Constraint Sets

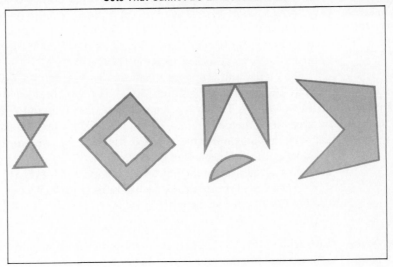

problem, and you may well ask: "Why bother including such a constraint in the model?" There are two important responses to this question:

1. Redundant constraints are not generally very easy to recognize. Even in the simple case of problems with two decision variables, if you are looking only at the algebraic form of the mathematical model, the redundant constraints are not immediately spotted.

2. A constraint that is redundant today may not be redundant tomorrow. For example, suppose that the management of PROTRAC, Inc. decides to explore the effects of a new policy decision to produce at least seven, rather than five, units of E and F in total. Then the RHS of the first constraint changes to 7 instead of 5. The modified first constraint is plotted as a dashed line in Figure 5.8, and it is seen that the new constraint is no longer redundant. In other words, *tightening* the requirement from 5 to 7 forces us to cut off some previously allowable decisions. This illustrates the important concept that

> **It is quite possible that a constraint that is redundant for a given set of data may no longer be redundant when some of the data are changed.**

It is often for this reason that a redundant constraint is in a model. It is common practice to solve planning models many times with different sets of data in order to gain insight into possible future scenarios. The model builder may intuitively know that there are conditions of interest (values of the data) for which this constraint *may become important*, and that is why she included this constraint in her model.

The Problem Restated   Now that a clear representation of the allowable decisions has been obtained, we can state the essence of a constrained optimization model as follows:

> **Find a feasible point that, relative to all other feasible points, produces an optimum value of the objective function.**

112

CHAPTER 5
Geometric
Representation
of the Linear
Programming
Model

The optimum value will be a maximum or minimum value, depending on the particular model. It is important to understand the displayed key concept completely. It does *not* say, "Find a point that, first of all, optimizes the objective function, and, second, also lies in the feasible set." It says, "Find a point that, first of all, lies in the feasible set, and second, find such a point that yields an optimal value for the objective function when compared *only* to all other points in the feasible set."

The Optimal Solution and the OV

To clarify this, suppose that we are working in a max context and that f is the objective function. Let f be a function of two variables, which we shall denote as (x_1, x_2) instead of (x, y). Thus we are considering the function $f(x_1, x_2)$. If the point (x_1, x_2) satisfies all of the constraints, (x_1, x_2) is called a **feasible point**. The feasible point, say (x_1^*, x_2^*), that maximizes the objective function over the constraint set is called an **optimal solution** to the problem. The values $x_1 = x_1^*$, $x_2 = x_2^*$ are called **optimal values of the decision variables**. If f is the objective function and if (x_1^*, x_2^*) is an optimal solution, then $f(x_1^*, x_2^*)$ is called the **optimal objective value or optimal value**. In this text we often use the symbol **OV** to refer to the optimal value.

Alternative Optima

You will ultimately learn that a given problem may or may not have an optimal solution and if it does there may be more than one. If there is a single (one and only one) optimal solution, it is said to be **unique**. Otherwise, we say that the problem has **multiple or alternative optima**.

Geometric Analysis of PROTRAC E and F Model

We now return to analyze geometrically the PROTRAC E and F model. In Figure 5.8 we see that there are many feasible points. To find an optimal solution we need to get the objective function values into the picture. One way to do this would be to attempt to plot the graph of the objective function over the constraint set. Unfortunately, to do so requires a two-dimensional rendering of a three-dimensional phenomenon; in other words, we would have to represent E, F, and $f(E, F)$ with a picture on a two-dimensional sheet of paper. Such drawings are usually meaningful only to the artist. A much simpler and more direct approach is to use the contours of the objective function. Here's how that is done.

Including the Objective Function in the Picture

For the model above, the objective function $f(E, F)$ is defined by

$$f(E, F) = 5000E + 4000F = \text{profit}$$

Contours of this function are sets of points (E, F) for which the profit has some fixed, preassigned value. It is easy to plot such sets of points. For example, three contours are shown in Figure 5.11. We obtained these contours by plotting the three straight lines

$$5000E + 4000F = 8,000$$
$$5000E + 4000F = 20,000$$
$$5000E + 4000F = 32,000$$

As you have already seen, these contours of a linear function are parallel lines. Of course, we have plotted only three. There are, as already observed, an infinite number of contours. A given contour has the equation

$$5000E + 4000F = C$$

113

CHAPTER 5
Geometric
Representation
of the Linear
Programming
Model

Figure 5.11

Three Contours of f Where

$f(E, F) = 5000E + 4000F$

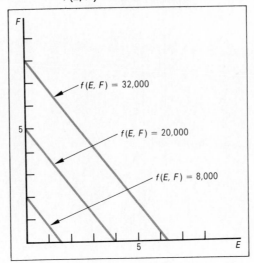

for some prescribed value of C. There are as many contours of this function as there are possible values for C. We cannot plot very many, but we do not need to. If we plot only two contours we gain most of the important information we need: namely, the shape of the contours and the uphill direction. One contour of f shows the shape (in this case, a straight line with a particular tilt). The contours of f are enough to indicate that in this particular example the contour values increase as the line moves to the northeast, which is thus the "uphill" direction. Now we can illustrate the complete model by placing the objective function contours in the same picture with the constraint set. This is done in Figure 5.12.

Here is what Figure 5.12 reveals. First, the circled numbers label the constraints. Thus, the line labeled ① is the first constraint, ② is the second constraint, and so on. The dashed lines represent three contours of the objective function $f(E, F) = 5000E + 4000F$.

*Finding
an Optimal
Solution*

Since we are considering a max problem, we want to identify the position of the highest-valued contour that touches the constraint set in at least one point.

To help locate this contour, you can plot one contour, such as $f(E, F) = 8000$. Then you must identify the uphill direction. You can do this by plotting a second contour, as in Figure 5.11 or you can simply use a trial point, just as we did when plotting inequalities. For example, since $f(0, 0) = 0 < 8000$, it is clear that for this problem the uphill direction is to the northeast. Identify this direction with an arrow, as in Figure 5.12. Then, in your mind's eye, imagine translating the plotted contour uphill, always parallel to itself, into the constraint set, and finally stopping at the point just before you leave the constraint set behind. In this way you can see that the highest-valued contour is the one that touches the constraint set at the point labeled (E^*, F^*). The point (E^*, F^*) is the optimal solution. The value of the objective function at (E^*, F^*) is the OV, or maximum profit, in our model. You can see that the solution in this case is **unique**. Reading from the graph, it looks like E^* is about 4.5 and F^* is about 7. However, this technique of graphical analysis really **does not demand much accuracy in your plotting**, for you can find the exact solution

114

CHAPTER 5
Geometric
Representation
of the Linear
Programming
Model

Figure 5.12
The Complete Model
(Inequality-Constraint Representation)

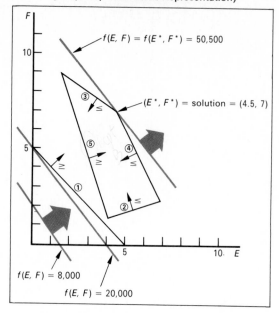

Solving for
the Optimal
Solution

as follows. The point (E^*, F^*) lies on the intersection of line ③ and line ④. This means that (E^*, F^*) satisfies the third and fourth constraints as equalities. That is, it must be true that

$$10E^* + 15F^* = 150$$
$$20E^* + 10F^* = 160$$

If you solve this system of equations, you will find that

$$E^* = 4.5, \qquad F^* = 7$$

Thus the optimal objective value (i.e., the maximum attainable profit) is

$$\text{profit} = 5000E^* + 4000F^* = 5000(4.5) + 4000(7) = 50,500 = \text{OV}$$

Thus, with the help of the picture we have been able to conclude that the optimal solution to the problem (the optimal production levels) is the point (4.5, 7), and the OV (the maximum profit) is 50,500.[1]

5.4

ACTIVE AND INACTIVE CONSTRAINTS

In addition to the optimal production plan and the optimal profit, the management of PROTRAC, Inc. may want additional information about the solution. For example, management may ask:

[1] For now, we are ignoring the fact that fractional quantities such as 4.5 may be meaningless in the E and F context. This complication will be treated in Chapter 11.

115

CHAPTER 5
Geometric
Representation
of the Linear
Programming
Model

1. How many labor hours will the optimal solution use in department A?
2. How many labor hours will the optimal solution use in department B?
3. How many hours will the optimal solution use in testing?

The labor hours used in department A are given by the left-hand side of the inequality (5.5). That is, referring back to the model, we see that

$$\text{hours used in department A} = 10E + 15F$$

Evaluating
a Constraint
Function

Since we are going to assign the optimal values $E = E^* = 4.5$, and $F = F^* = 7$, the expression above is evaluated as follows:

$$\text{hours used (at optimality) in department A} = 10E^* + 15F^* = 150$$

This means that the answer to question 1 is 150, and we say that "**at optimality**, 150 hours are used in department A." In order to answer question 2 we note that the labor hours in department B are given by the left-hand side of inequality (5.6). Hence, **at optimality**

$$\text{hours used in department B} = 20E^* + 10F^* = 160$$

Finally, to answer question 3 we employ the left-hand side of inequality (5.7) to discover that, at optimality

$$\text{hours used in testing} = 30E^* + 10F^* = 205$$

Let us now pursue these elaborations a bit further to introduce some important new terminology. We have just seen that the optimal production plan will consume 150 hours in department A. But we also recall from the model that 150 hours is the total amount of labor *available* in department A. Hence, for the optimal policy we see that

$$\text{hours of labor used} = \text{hours of labor available}$$

and the constraint is satisfied with *equality*.

Labor in Dept.
A Is an
Active
Constraint

For this constraint, since there is no labor left unused, the constraint is said to be **active**, or equivalently, **binding**, or **tight**. Note that from management's point of view an active constraint plays a role of considerable importance. For example, if there were any further production of E-9s or F-9s, this active constraint would be violated. In this sense *the active constraint prevents the earning of additional profits.*

By applying analogous reasoning to the constraint on labor hours in department B you can easily verify that this constraint is also active.

In Chapter 4 we saw that the constraints in a linear programming model are always of the form $=$, $\leq$, or $\geq$.

An equality constraint is always active. An inequality constraint, of either $\leq$ or $\geq$ type, is active only if, when evaluated at optimality, equality holds between the left-hand side and the right-hand side.

Let us now consider the constraint on testing. Recall that this constraint requires, by a union agreement, that *at least* 135 hours be used, whereas the answer to question 3 has shown that 205 hours will actually be used. Since we are using 70 hours in **excess** of what is required, there is said to be, at optimality, a **surplus** of 70 hours in this constraint. Here we have an example of an *inequality* constraint which is *not* active at optimality. As you might guess, such a constraint is said to be **inactive**.

The Market Balance Constraint Is Inactive

The terms "active" and "inactive" are applicable to each constraint in the model. For example, if we evaluate, *at optimality*, the left-hand side of the constraint labeled (5.4), we see that

$$E - 3F = 4.5 - 3(7) = 4.5 - 21 = -16.5$$

Since constraint (5.4) stipulates that

$$E - 3F \leq 0$$

and since the actual value of the left-hand side is -16.5, we see that the left-hand side falls 16.5 units *below* the right-hand side. This constraint is said to have a **slack** of 16.5 units, and is also **inactive**.

Summary

Summarizing this terminology, we see that:

1. If, at optimality (i.e., when evaluated at the optimal solution), the left-hand side of a constraint equals the right-hand side, that constraint is said to be **active**, or **tight**, or **binding. Thus, an *equality* constraint is always active.** An inequality constraint may or may not be active.

2. If a constraint is not active, it is said to be **inactive**. For a constraint of $\geq$ type, the difference between the left-hand side and the right-hand side (the excess) is called **surplus**. For a constraint of $\leq$ type, the difference between the right-hand side and the left-hand side (the amount unused) is called **slack**.

3. At optimality, each *inequality* constraint in a model has a slack or surplus value and for feasible decisions this value is always nonnegative. For a given constraint the slack or surplus value is zero if and only if that constraint is active.

We have seen how to identify algebraically those constraints which are active and those which are inactive, and hence have positive surplus or slack. We obtained this information by "plugging" the optimal values of the decision variables into the constraints. It will be useful to understand how the active and inactive constraints can also be easily identified from the graphical solution. To see this, let us again present the statement of the model:

$$\text{Max} \quad 5000E + 4000F$$

$$
\begin{array}{llll}
\text{s.t.} & E + F \geq 5 & \text{①} \\
& E - 3F \leq 0 & \text{②} \\
& 10E + 15F \leq 150 & \text{③} \\
& 20E + 10F \leq 160 & \text{④} \\
& 30E + 10F \geq 135 & \text{⑤} \\
& E, F \geq 0 & \text{⑥}
\end{array}
$$

and let us again graph the constraints. This is shown in Figure 5.13. We have just seen that

116

Figure 5.13
Active and Inactive Constraints

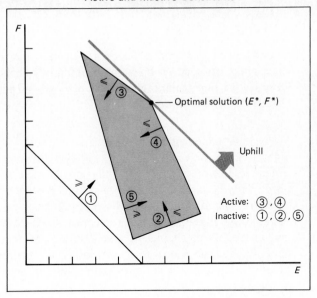

the third and fourth constraints, which represent labor capacity in departments A and B, are active in this model. From Figure 5.13 you can see that these constraints "pass through" the optimal solution. Stated equivalently, the optimal solution "lies on" these constraints. Although we did not use the term "active," we indeed solved for the values of E^* and F^* by implicitly recognizing that constraints ③ and ④ are active.

Geometrically, an active constraint is one that passes through the optimal solution.

We have seen that constraints ② and ⑤ are inactive. A quick check also shows that constraint ① is inactive. That is,

$$E + F = 4.5 + 7 = 11.5 > 5$$

Thus, Figure 5.13 illustrates that

Geometrically, an inactive constraint is one that does not pass through the optimal solution.

The active and inactive constraints are easy to spot in the process of applying the graphical solution method. Indeed, that is the very goal of the graphical method, *for once the active constraints are identified*, as you have seen, *we then solve simultaneous equations to obtain the optimal solution*. Each inactive constraint will have surplus or slack, depending upon whether the corresponding inequality is $\geq$ or $\leq$. However, the numerical value of the surplus or slack cannot be read from the picture. It must be determined algebraically, as in the foregoing illustrations.

5.5

EXTREME POINTS AND OPTIMAL SOLUTIONS

As you have seen, the solution to the PROTRAC, Inc. problem occurs at a corner of the feasible region—namely, at the corner where (what we have called) the third and fourth constraints intersect. In linear programming jargon the corners of the feasible region are called **extreme points**. The two terms, **extreme points** and **corners**, will be used interchangeably in our discussion.

Changing the Objective Function
To begin to understand the importance of the extreme points, let us imagine taking a different linear objective function, with the same constraint set, and solving the problem again. For example, suppose that we change the price of F-9s in such a way that the profitability is raised from $4000 to $10,000 per unit. Let us see how this change in the objective function affects the solution to the problem. First, since we have changed only the objective function, leaving the constraints as they were, the feasible region remains unchanged. All that is new is that the contours of the objective function will assume a new tilt. A profit line of this new objective function (the 25,000-contour) is shown in Figure 5.14. Sliding the new profit line uphill, the new optimal solution is found, as shown in Figure 5.14.

Figure 5.14
New Optimal Solution When the Objective Function is
$5000E + 10,000F$

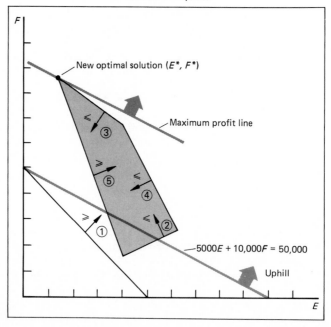

Note from Figure 5.14 that at the new optimal point the **active** constraints have changed. Now the third and fifth constraints are active, whereas previously the third and fourth were active. Thus, you can see that the change in the slope of the objective function has moved the optimal solution away from the previous corner, but it has moved to another **corner**, or extreme point. As before, we can obtain the exact value of the new

119

CHAPTER 5
Geometric
Representation
of the Linear
Programming
Model

optimal policy by simultaneously solving the third and fifth constraint equations. Thus we have

$$10E^* + 15F^* = 150 \qquad \text{(third constraint)}$$

$$30E^* + 10F^* = 135 \qquad \text{(fifth constraint)}$$

Solving these equations yields $E^* = 1.5$ and $F^* = 9$. This is the new optimal policy. As you might have predicted, the new price structure, which has increased the relative profitability of F-9s, leads to an optimal production plan which specifies a cutback in E-9s and an increase in F-9s. You can also note from Figure 5.14 that at the new optimal solution there is now positive slack in labor in department B (constraint ④).

What we have seen is that with each of two different objective functions for PROTRAC's problem we obtained an optimal corner solution. In fact, you can experiment for yourself to see that no matter how much you change the objective function, as long as it remains linear, there will always be an optimal corner solution. You can even change the constraint set and there will still always be an optimal corner solution, as long as everything is kept linear.

In Figure 5.15 you see a hypothetical six-sided constraint set and contours of three *different* (hypothetical) objective functions, denoted *f*, *g*, and *h*. For each objective function the arrow indicates the direction to slide the plotted contour to optimize the objective function. Note that in each case there is an optimal solution at a corner.

*Any Linear
Objective
Function
Gives a
Corner
Solution*

Figure 5.15

You Always Get a Corner Solution

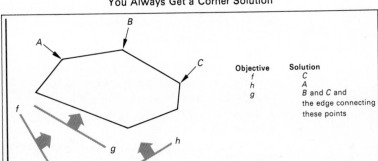

Objective	Solution
f	*C*
h	*A*
g	*B* and *C* and the edge connecting these points

*Illustration of
Alternative
Optima*

The objective function *g* in Figure 5.15 illustrates the interesting case in which *the optimal objective contour coincides with one of the constraint lines on the boundary of the feasible region. In this case there will be many optimal solutions, namely the corners B and C and all the boundary points in between.* This illustrates what we have previously called **multiple optima**, or **alternative optima**. However, even in this case when there is not a **unique** optimal solution, it is still true that there is a corner solution which is optimal (in fact, there are two). Thus, the geometry illustrates an important fact about any LP problem with any number of decision variables:

> In an LP problem, if there is an optimal solution, there is always *at least one* optimal corner solution.

This result has a powerful implication in terms of using the graphical method for solving an LP. It means that you need not be overly meticulous in your plotting. Your diagram need only be sufficiently accurate to identify an optimal corner. This is equivalent to identifying what we earlier called the active constraints. You then solve two equations in two unknowns to determine the exact optimal values of the decision variables.

In our study of the computer output, we will see other important implications of the fact that **if there is an optimal solution, there will always be at least one at a corner.**

5.6
SUMMARY OF THE GRAPHICAL SOLUTION METHOD FOR A MAX MODEL

Our discussion thus far has presented the following procedure for solving a linear programming problem in two decision variables:

1. Superimpose the graph of each constraint on the same nonnegative quadrant. The nonnegative values of the decision variables which simultaneously satisfy (lie on the correct side of) **all** the constraints form the **feasible region**, also called the **constraint set**.
2. Draw an arbitrary **profit line**, also called a **contour**, of the objective function to obtain the slope of the objective function **contours**.
3. Determine the uphill direction by, for example, evaluating the objective function at any trial point that is not on the profit line you have just constructed.
4. Now, given the slope of the profit line from step 2, and the uphill direction from step 3, determine visually the corner of the constraint set which lies on the highest possible profit line that still intersects this set.
5. The values of the decision variables at this corner (i.e., the coordinates of the corner) give the solution to the problem. These values are found by identifying the active constraints and then simultaneously solving two linear equations in two unknowns. Thus, in order to implement the graphical method, your drawing need only be accurate enough to identify the active constraints.
6. The optimal value of the objective function (i.e., the OV) is obtained by "plugging in" the optimal values for the decision variables and evaluating the objective function.
7. You have already identified the active constraints. The inactive constraints can also be read from your graph. They are those that do not pass through the solution.

5.7
THE GRAPHICAL METHOD APPLIED TO A MIN MODEL

As we saw in Chapter 4, many real-world problems occur in a minimization context, and this was illustrated with the Crawler Tread problem. Thus far we have dealt only with the graphical representation of a max model. The method applied to a min model is quite similar, the only difference being that **the optimizing direction of the objective function** is now "downhill" rather than "uphill." Recall that in a max model the objective function contours are often isoprofit lines or, more simply, profit lines. In a min model, the objective function contours are often isocost lines or, more simply, cost lines. Our goal, in a min model, is to determine a corner of the feasible region that lies on the *lowest-valued* objective function contour which still intersects the feasible region. As an example, let us apply the graphical method to the following simple minimization model in two-decision variables which we denote as x_1 and x_2.

120

121

CHAPTER 5
Geometric
Representation
of the Linear
Programming
Model

$$\text{Min} \quad x_1 + 2x_2$$

$$\text{s.t.} \quad -3x_1 + 2x_2 \leq 6 \qquad ①$$

$$x_1 + x_2 \leq 10.5 \qquad ②$$

$$-x_1 + 3x_2 \geq 6 \qquad ③$$

$$x_1, x_2 \geq 0$$

The feasible region and the optimal solution for this problem are shown in Figure 5.16.

Figure 5.16

Feasible Region for the Min Model

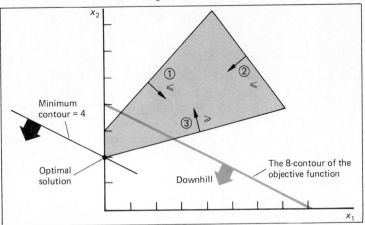

The example above shows that the graphical analysis for a min problem is exactly the same as that for a max problem, as long as it is understood that the objective contours are always moved in the **optimizing direction**. We shall always represent this direction with an arrow and it is understood that the direction of the arrow is uphill in a max model, downhill in a min model. We issue one caveat here which deserves emphasis. Students on occasion fall into the trap of thinking that in a max model the solution will always be the corner "farthest away" from the origin. And for a min model, they instinctively feel that if the origin is feasible, it must be optimal. Otherwise, if the origin is not feasible, they feel that the corner "closest to" the origin will be optimal. Such reasoning may be false. The incorrect logic has to do with the false impression that the uphill direction is always outward from the origin (the northeast), and the downhill direction always inward toward the origin. This is analogous to the fact, discussed in Section 5.2, that there is no general relationship between the sense of an inequality ($\leq$ or $\geq$) and the above or below side of the equality plot in our graphical representation.

5.8

UNBOUNDED AND INFEASIBLE PROBLEMS

Thus far we have developed a geometric portrayal of LP problems in two decision variables. This portrayal has provided the basis for solving such problems and has also illustrated the important conclusion that "*if* there is an optimal solution, there will always be at least one at a corner." But how can an LP fail to have an optimal solution? In this section we use the geometric representation to show how that can occur.

Unbounded Problems

Recall the graphical display of the PROTRAC, Inc. model as shown in Figure 5.13, but let us now change the model by supposing that the constraints which we labeled as ③ and ④ have been inadvertently omitted. Thus, we obtain the model

$$\text{Max} \quad 5000E + 4000F$$

$$\text{s.t.} \quad E + \quad F \geq \quad 5 \quad ①$$

$$E - \quad 3F \leq \quad 0 \quad ②$$

$$30E + 10F \geq 135 \quad ⑤$$

$$E, F \geq \quad 0$$

The graphical analysis for this new problem is shown in Figure 5.17. You can see that the constraint set now extends indefinitely to the northeast and it is possible to slide the profit line arbitrarily far in this direction. Since for this particular problem the northeast is the optimizing direction, we can find allowable decisions which give *arbitrarily large* values to the objective function. In other words, we can obtain profits approaching infinity. Such a problem has no solution, because for any set of allowable values for the decision variables we can always find other allowable values that improve the objective value. Problems of this type are termed **unbounded**. Unbounded problems are "pathological." They can arise as in Figure 5.17 when one or more important constraints have been left out of the model, or possibly because of typing errors when entering a problem into the computer for solution. In real life no one has yet discovered how to obtain an infinite profit, and you can be assured that *when a model is correctly formulated and correctly entered into the computer it will not be unbounded.*

Figure 5.17

Unbounded Problem

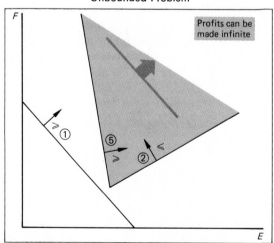

Unbounded
Constraint Set

122

Students sometimes confuse the term "**unbounded problem**" with the concept of an "**unbounded constraint set**." The latter terminology refers to a feasible region in which at least one *decision variable* can be made arbitrarily large in value. If an LP is unbounded, the constraint set must also be unbounded, as illustrated by Figure 5.17. However, it is

123

CHAPTER 5
Geometric
Representation
of the Linear
Programming
Model

possible to have an unbounded constraint set without having an unbounded problem. This is illustrated graphically in Figure 5.18, which shows a hypothetical LP model in two decision variables, x_1 and x_2. The model has three constraints and an unbounded constraint set, but there is an optimal solution.

Figure 5.18
Unbounded Constraint Set but a Solution

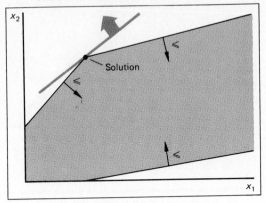

Infeasible Problems

There is one other type of pathology to be aware of in linear programming. It is called **infeasibility** or, alternatively, **inconsistency**. This term refers to a problem with an empty constraint set; that is, there is no combination of values for the decision variables which simultaneously satisfies all the constraints. A graphical illustration of an infeasible problem is obtained by changing the first constraint in the PROTRAC, Inc. model to $E + F \leq 5$ instead of $E + F \geq 5$. This gives us the new model

$$\text{Max} \quad 5000E + 4000F$$

$$
\begin{aligned}
\text{s.t.} \quad & E + F \leq 5 && \text{①} \\
& E - 3E \leq 0 && \text{②} \\
& 10E + 15F \leq 150 && \text{③} \\
& 20E + 10F \leq 160 && \text{④} \\
& 30E + 10F \geq 135 && \text{⑤} \\
& E, F \geq 0
\end{aligned}
$$

The constraint set for this LP is graphically represented in Figure 5.19 and you can see that there is no pair of values (E, F) that satisfies *all* the constraints.

As Figure 5.19 illustrates, **infeasibility depends solely on the constraints and has nothing to do with the objective function.** Obviously, an infeasible LP has no solution, but this pathology will not appear if the problem has been formulated correctly. In other words, in well-posed real problems, infeasibility always means that the model has been incorrectly specified, either because of logical errors or because of typing errors when entering the problem into the computer. Logical errors may mean either too many constraints, or the wrong constraints, have been included.

124

CHAPTER 5
Geometric
Representation
of the Linear
Programming
Model

Figure 5.19
Infeasible Model

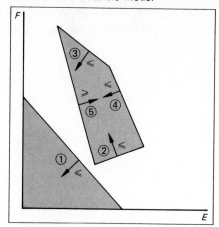

In summary:

Every linear program will fall into one of the following three nonoverlapping states:

    1. The problem has at least one optimal solution.
    2. There is no optimal solution because the problem is unbounded.
    3. There is no optimal solution because the problem is infeasible.

In practice, a correctly formulated real-world LP will always have a solution. States 2 and 3 can arise only from (i) errors in model formulation, or (ii) errors in entering the problem into the computer.

5.9

INTRODUCTION TO SENSITIVITY ANALYSIS

The PROTRAC, Inc. model was formulated in Chapter 4 and solved with graphical analysis in this chapter. You may well feel that if this were a real problem, management would now have a good solution to its real-world problem and would thus be free to turn attention to other matters. In many if not most cases this simply is not true.

Often the solution to a model is only a starting point and is, in itself, the least interesting part of the analysis of the real problem.

Remember that the model is an abstraction of the real problem. Typically, a manager will need to ask numerous additional questions before she would be confident enough about the results to apply them to her real problem. For example, there may be rather significant considerations which because of their complexity have not been built into the model. To the extent that a model is a simplification of reality there will always be factors that are left out. Such factors may, for example, be of a political or ethical nature.

Such considerations are usually difficult to quantify. Having solved her simplified model, the manager may now wish to know how well the optimal solution "fits in" with other considerations which may not have been included.

Uncertain Data

There may, as another example, be inexactitudes and uncertainty in some of the data that were used in the model. In real-world problem solving, at least in the realms of business, economics, and public policy, this is the norm rather than the exception. The motto is: "Do the best with what you have." In such cases, the manager will want to know: How **sensitive** is the optimal solution to the inexact data? We may have an estimate of the absentee rate for next month's labor force, and the model has been run using this estimate. What happens to the optimal solution if we change the estimate by 5, 10, or even 15%? Will the OV (i.e., the optimal objective value) vary wildly, or will it remain more or less unchanged? Obviously, the answer to such questions will help to determine the credibility of the model's recommendations. For example, if the OV changes very little with large changes in the value of a particular parameter, we probably would not be concerned about uncertainty in that value. If on the other hand the OV varies substantially with small changes in that parameter, we might reasonably feel it would be inappropriate to tolerate much uncertainty in its value. In this case, either the model might be rejected or more resources might be committed to establishing a more precise value for the parameter in question.

Parametric Analysis

Although some of the foregoing considerations can be dealt with only informally, we fortunately do have some *rigorous and precise tools* at our disposal. These tools are in the realm of **parametric analysis,** or **sensitivity analysis,** or **postoptimality analysis.** All of these terms mean essentially the same thing, and the topic is of such significance that an entire chapter (Chapter 6) is largely devoted to understanding the sensitivity information contained in the computer solution to an LP problem. Making good use of computer analysis is, of course, a problem faced by managers in the real world. In this chapter we lay some of the groundwork for being able to understand clearly the meaning of the computer results. The graphical approach we have been working with makes it relatively easy to do this. The ability to *see*, geometrically, how changes in the model affect the solution in the special two-decision-variable case makes it much easier to understand the changes that will occur in larger realistic models. In order to introduce the topic in a very specific way, let us again refer to our illustrative PROTRAC, Inc. model:

$$\text{Max} \quad 5000E + 4000F$$

$$
\begin{array}{lrll}
\text{s.t.} & E + F \geq & 5 & \text{(minimal production requirement)} \\
& E - 3F \leq & 0 & \text{(market position balance)} \\
& 10E + 15F \leq & 150 & \text{(capacity in department A)} \\
& 20E + 10F \leq & 160 & \text{(capacity in department B)} \\
& 30E + 10F \geq & 135 & \text{(contractual labor agreement)} \\
& E, F \geq & 0 & \text{(nonnegativity conditions)}
\end{array}
$$

Let us consider that the purpose of this model is to recommend a production target for the next 2 weeks. Therefore, all the numerical data in the model are supposed to be pertinent to this period of interest, namely 2 weeks in the future.

Objective Function Changes

A major application of linear programming involves planning models such as this, where future plans and policies are to be determined, and in such models future data are naturally required. Obviously in many real-world situations such data may not be known with complete certainty.

Suppose, for example, that the stated profitabilities of $5000 per E-9 and $4000 per F-9 are only estimates based on revenues and projected costs, and that some of the costs of raw materials to be purchased are subject to change. Unfortunately, in order to achieve the lead time required in the planning process, the model must be run now, before the exact data are known. Thus, we must use the numbers above, which are our best current estimates, knowing full well that the actual profitabilities in the next 2 weeks could differ. We might have some fairly solid ideas about the possible ranges in which the true values will lie, and the profitabilities of $5000 and $4000 might be our best estimates within such ranges. But how do we deal with the fact that data are not known with complete certainty? That is one important topic covered in **sensitivity analysis**.

RHS Changes

Another possible concern may involve uncertainty in some of the constraint data. In linear programming, this type of uncertainty usually focuses on the right-hand sides of the constraints. For example, consider the number 135, which is the right-hand side of the contractual labor agreement constraint. It represents the minimal number of hours that must be spent on product testing. In a real-life application it is possible that such a number could also be uncertain. The actual minimal requirement that will be in force in the future period could be arrived at in a rather complicated way depending, for example, on the results of quality tests of this month's production, results that can only *be estimated* at the time the planning process occurs. Thus, the value of 135 is only a "best estimate." Again, management must cope with the uncertainty in such data.

These two examples reflect the major focus of sensitivity analysis, and the topics discussed in the following two sections. The first example, in which profitabilities are uncertain, illustrates what we call **changes in the objective function coefficients**. The second example illustrates **changes in the right-hand side**. In an LP model, the objective function coefficients and the right-hand sides are often called **parameters**, and for this reason the term "parametric analysis" is sometimes used for the investigation of the effects of changing the values of these parameters. In the next chapter we see how the computer can be used to provide a wealth of sensitivity information. Our present goal is to see how graphical analysis can provide conceptual insights into both the meaning and the effects of changes in parameter values.

5.10

CHANGES IN THE OBJECTIVE FUNCTION COEFFICIENTS AND ALTERNATIVE OPTIMA

Suppose that the constraint data remain unchanged and only the objective coefficients are changed. Then the only effect on the model, from the geometric viewpoint, is that the slope of the profit lines is changed. We have, in fact, already seen an illustration of this phenomenon in Section 5.5. In Figure 5.14 all data in the PROTRAC, Inc. model remained unchanged except for the fact that the profitability of F-9s was raised from $4000 to $10,000 per unit. We saw that the effect of this change was to change the tilt of the profit lines to such an extent that a new corner solution was obtained. You can also quickly see that some changes in the objective function coefficients will *not* change

Changing the Tilt

127

CHAPTER 5
Geometric
Representation
of the Linear
Programming
Model

the optimal solution, even though the profit lines will have a different slope. Moreover, some changes will be such that numerous optimal solutions are introduced (i.e., alternative optima are created). For example, let us replace the old objective function $5000E + 4000F$ with a new objective function $5000E + 6000F$. As we saw in Figure 5.12, the solution with the old objective function is $E^* = 4.5$, $F^* = 7.0$. The new objective function $5000E + 6000F$ has the same profitability for E-9s and a higher profitability for F-9s. You might therefore expect to obtain an optimal solution calling for production of more than 7.0 of the more profitable F-9s. However, Figure 5.20 presents a graphical analysis which shows that this is not the case. In this figure there are four different objective functions: $5000E + 4000F$, $5000E + 6000F$, $5000E + 7500F$, and $5000E + 10,000F$. It is shown that the negative slopes of the contours associated with each of the four functions become progressively less steep (i.e., the contours become flatter) as the profitability of F-9s increases relative to E-9s [i.e., as the ratio (coefficient of F/coefficient of E) increases]. However, although the objectives $5000E + 4000F$ and $5000E + 6000F$ have contours with different slopes, *the slopes are not sufficiently different to give us a new corner solution.* For each of these two objectives the optimal solution is the same, namely $E^* = 4.5$ and $F^* = 7.0$.

Figure 5.20
PROTRAC, Inc. Model with Contours of Four Different Profit Functions
and the Corresponding Solutions

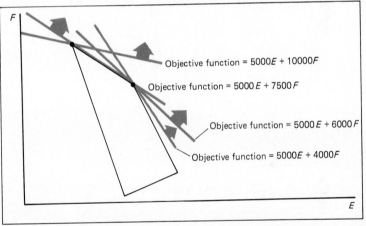

Objective function = $5000E + 10000F$

Objective function = $5000E + 7500F$

Objective function = $5000E + 6000F$

Objective function = $5000E + 4000F$

Effect on the OV   On the other hand, it is important to note that in this case, since F^* is nonzero, the optimal profits (i.e., the OVs) will differ. In the former case we have

$$\text{optimal profit} = 5000E^* + 4000F^*$$
$$= 5000(4.5) + 4000(7) = 50,500$$

whereas in the latter case,

$$\text{optimal profit} = 5000E^* + 6000F^*$$
$$= 5000(4.5) + 6000(7) = 64,500$$

As the coefficient of F continues to increase beyond 6000 (with the coefficient of E held fixed at 5000), the objective function contour continues to rotate counterclockwise until finally, with the coefficient of $F = 7500$, we obtain two optimal corner solutions.

128

CHAPTER 5
Geometric
Representation
of the Linear
Programming
Model

An infinitesimal further increase in the coefficient of F will move the corner solution from $(E^* = 4.5, F^* = 7.0)$ to the new corner to the northwest.

In summary, what we have just seen is that

Changing the objective function coefficients changes the slopes of the objective function contours. This need not change the current optimal corner solution, or it may create alternate optimal corner solutions, or it may create a new unique optimal corner solution. The result depends on the magnitude of the coefficient changes.

This geometric analysis, although conducted on a two-dimensional problem, gives you good insight into more general problems, for even in models with more than two decision variables the summary statement above is correct. In the next chapter we will see how the computer can be used to provide, for higher-dimensional models, sensitivity information on the effects of changes in the objective function coefficients. We shall also see how such information can be used to management's advantage.

5.11

CHANGES IN THE RIGHT-HAND SIDES

Let us now ignore the objective function and focus on the right-hand sides of the constraint functions. Again, graphical analysis will nicely explain the effects of changes in these parameters. As a specific example, let us suppose that the fifth constraint of the PROTRAC, Inc. model

$$30E + 10F \geq 135 \qquad \text{(contractual labor)} \tag{5.9}$$

is changed to

$$30E + 10F \geq 210 \tag{5.10}$$

and suppose that all other constraint data remain as they are given. Since 135 is a smaller number than 210, expression (5.9) is easier to satisfy than (5.10). For example, the pair $(E = 3, F = 5)$ satisfies (5.9) for

$$30E + 10F = 30(3) + 10(5) = 90 + 50 = 140$$

Shrinking the Feasible Region Since 140 is ≥ 135, (5.9) is satisfied. But 140 is less than 210 and hence the pair $(E = 3, F = 5)$ does *not* satisfy condition (5.10). Another way of saying this is that *fewer combinations of values for E and F will satisfy* (5.10). Because of this fact, it would be reasonable to expect that the change from (5.9) to (5.10) might, in some sense, "shrink" the feasible region. From the geometric point of view, you can see that changing the right-hand side of a constraint creates a parallel shift in the constraint line. In this case, then, the reasoning above suggests that, in changing the RHS from 135 to 210, the fifth constraint line [corresponding to (5.9)] will shift in such a way as to eliminate some of the feasible region. Figure 5.21 shows the original constraint set with the constraints labeled ① through ⑤. Figure 5.22 shows the new constraint set with the fifth constraint (5.9) replaced by (5.10).

129

CHAPTER 5
Geometric
Representation
of the Linear
Programming
Model

Figure 5.21
Graphical Analysis of the Original Model

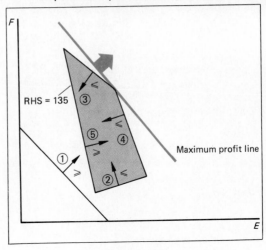

Figure 5.22
Graphical Analysis of the Model with New RHS
for the Fifth Constraint

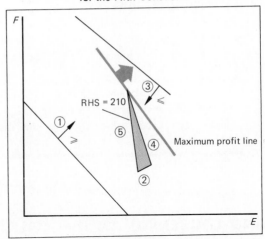

Although, geometrically speaking, the constraint set in Figure 5.22 looks quite different from the one in Figure 5.21, all that has been done is to slide the constraint labeled ⑤ farther outward from the origin to its new position. You should experiment by assigning different values to this right-hand side, and to the other right-hand sides, to see the variety of different-looking feasible regions that can arise from such simple perturbations. One particularly interesting case arises if you further increase the right-hand side of the fifth constraint to 270, leaving all the other constraint data unchanged. Such a change creates an inconsistent set of constraints. That is, the problem becomes infeasible.

A New Solution   Return now to Figure 5.22. The optimal solution is shown for the objective function $5000E + 4000F$. Comparing this with the graphical analysis for the original problem, Figure 5.21, you can see that the solution to the new problem is entirely different from the old. We have

130

CHAPTER 5
Geometric
Representation
of the Linear
Programming
Model

Old problem:

    Active constraints: ③ and ④

    Inactive constraints: ①, ②, and ⑤

    Solution (by solving active constraints): $E^* = 4.5$, $F^* = 7$

    Optimal profit $=$ OV $= 50,500$

New problem:

    Active constraints: ④ and ⑤

    Inactive constraints: ①, ②, and ③

The solution is computed by solving the two equations:

$$\text{Constraint ④:} \quad 20E + 10F = 160$$

$$\text{Constraint ⑤:} \quad 30E + 10F = 210$$

To obtain $E^* = 5$, $F^* = 6$,

$$\text{optimal profit} = \text{OV} = 5000E^* + 4000F^*$$

$$= 5000(5) + 4000(6) = 49,000$$

It should be clear from this analysis that changing even one right-hand-side value can have a profound effect on the solution. In Chapter 6 it will be shown that the computer can be used to provide precise information on the effects of such changes. For now, we summarize what we have graphically seen in this section for two-dimensional models. These results, as with the previous results for changing an objective function coefficient, are also valid for problems with more than two decision variables.

Changing a right-hand-side value results in a parallel shift of the changed constraint. This *may* affect both the optimal solution and the OV. The effect will depend on exactly which and by how much the right-hand-side values are changed.

5.12

TIGHTENING AND LOOSENING AN INEQUALITY CONSTRAINT

We conclude this discussion on parametric changes by making some general observations on the effects of right-hand-side changes for **inequality constraints**. This will lead us to several useful new terms.

Tightening   In the discussion above we compared the two constraints

$$30E + 10F \geq 135 \tag{5.9}$$

and

$$30E + 10F \geq 210 \tag{5.10}$$

and noted that since each constraint is of $\geq$ form, and since the right-hand side of (5.10) is larger than the right-hand side of (5.9), the constraint (5.10) is more difficult to satisfy. This process of increasing the RHS of a $\geq$ constraint is called **tightening the constraint**.

131

CHAPTER 5
Geometric
Representation
of the Linear
Programming
Model

The constraint (5.10) is **tighter** than (5.9). Similarly, if the RHS of a $\leq$ constraint is decreased, the constraint becomes more difficult to satisfy and hence is tighter.

Tightening an inequality constraint means making it more difficult to satisfy. For a $\geq$ constraint this means increasing the RHS. For a $\leq$ constraint this means decreasing the RHS.

Suppose that instead of increasing the RHS of (5.9) we had decreased it so that, for example, the constraint becomes

$$30E + 10F \geq 100 \tag{5.11}$$

You should be able to see that since the right-hand side has become a smaller number, and since (5.11) is a $\geq$ constraint, there are now *more* combinations of values for E and F that will satisfy the constraint. Thus, the constraint has become easier to satisfy. This *Loosening* process of decreasing the RHS of a $\geq$ constraint is called **loosening the constraint**. The constraint (5.11) is **looser** than (5.9). Similarly, if the RHS of a $\leq$ constraint is increased, the constraint becomes easier to satisfy and hence is looser.

Loosening an inequality constraint means making it easier to satisfy. For a $\geq$ constraint this means decreasing the RHS. For a $\leq$ constraint this means increasing the RHS.

The geometric effects of tightening and loosening are easily illustrated. Referring to Figures 5.21 and 5.22, we see that in moving from Figure 5.21 to Figure 5.22, constraint ⑤ has been tightened and the result was to contract the feasible region. If you move from Figure 5.22 to Figure 5.21, constraint ⑤ has been loosened and the effect is to expand the feasible region. These geometric results, that tightening contracts and loosening expands, are what you probably would have predicted, but there is another possibility that must be considered.

Consider constraint ①, $E + F \geq 5$. Note in Figure 5.21 that it currently plays no role in determining the shape of the feasible set. Also, with a suitably small change in the right-hand side, say from 5 to 5.1 or 4.9, the line will incur a small parallel displacement and still not intersect the original feasible set. Thus, in this case we see that a suitably small amount of tightening or loosening of constraint ① has no effect on the feasible set. We now summarize our observation on the geometric effects of tightening and loosening inequality constraints.

Geometric
Summary

Tightening an inequality constraint either contracts the constraint set or, possibly, leaves it unaffected. Loosening an inequality constraint either expands the constraint set or, possibly, leaves it unaffected.

These results are generally true for inequality constraints and do not depend on the dimension of the model (the number of decision variables) or on whether the constraint is of $\leq$ or $\geq$ form. It should be emphasized that in this analysis we have assumed that the RHS of one constraint is manipulated while all the other data remain fixed. The effects of tightening (loosening) several constraints at a time are also to contract (expand) or, possibly, to leave the feasible region unchanged. However, if some constraints are tightened and others simultaneously loosened, there is little that can be categorically stated about the result. We conclude this section with the observation that tightening a constraint too much can produce infeasibility. For example, we saw that this occurred when the RHS of constraint ⑤ was increased to 270.

5.13
WHAT IS AN IMPORTANT CONSTRAINT?

We have seen that, in general, an LP model may have numerous constraints. It would be of interest to know whether some of the many constraints may perhaps have special importance in the model. The management of PROTRAC, Inc. certainly has an interest in knowing which constraints are most restrictive in the sense of limiting the possibilities for greater profit.

The discussion in Section 5.3 suggests that, *for a given set of data*, the redundant constraints (if there are any) are the least important. That is, we have already observed that constraint ① in the PROTRAC model is redundant, which means that it can be ignored without changing the constraint set and hence without changing the optimal solution. Since it does not affect the solution, it is, *for the given set of data*, of little importance. But can we say more? Just in terms of what we have so far learned, can you identify other constraints in the model that seem to be "more important" than the others?

In Figure 5.23 the graphical analysis of the PROTRAC, Inc. model is reproduced. This figure shows that there are indeed other constraints in the model that can be ignored without affecting the solution, namely, constraints ② and ⑤. The graphical analysis of the model with constraints ①, ②, and ⑤ deleted is given in Figure 5.24. Although the feasible region has become greatly enlarged, the optimal solution remains unchanged. Recall that in this problem constraints ①, ②, and ⑤ are the **inactive constraints**.

The phenomenon we have just observed is generally true, even in higher-dimensional problems.

Figure 5.24
Graphical Analysis of PROTRAC, Inc. with Constraints ①, ②, and ⑤ Deleted

Figure 5.23
Graphical Analysis of PROTRAC, Inc.

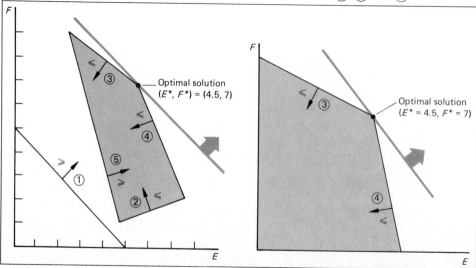

133

CHAPTER 5
Geometric
Representation
of the Linear
Programming
Model

In any LP model, *for a fixed set of data,* the inactive constraints can be removed without affecting the optimal solution. The optimal solution is determined entirely by the active constraints.

Thus, for a given set of data it is the active constraints that are the important ones in the sense that they completely determine the solution. If we could only know in advance which constraints are active, the task of solving an LP would reduce to the relatively easy problem of solving a system of simultaneous linear equations, such as the equations for the lines labeled ③ and ④ in Figure 5.24. Although we may agree that the active constraints are most important, this information becomes available only *after* the problem is solved, for unfortunately the modeler has no way of knowing, in advance, which of the inequality constraints will be active.[2]

A Logical Framework

In concluding this section, we wish to emphasize that when the data in a model change, the set of active and inactive inequality constraints can also change. *In other words, the unimportant (inactive) constraints for one set of data may become important (active) when the model is re-solved with different data.* You can think of a model as being "a logical framework or structure" that underlies the assigned numerical values of the parameters. This logical framework captures interactions among variables as well as requirements and limitations. The logical framework in a sense is independent of the actual values assigned to the parameters (i.e., the data). Different data values will give different realizations to the model. In this larger context it is not really meaningful to label some constraints as being more important than others.

The importance of the various constraints is a relative question whose answer will depend on the values assigned to the data.

5.14
ADDING OR DELETING CONSTRAINTS

There is one final general observation which the graphical analysis brings home. This concerns the effects of adding or deleting constraints. Comparing Figures 5.23 and 5.24 shows immediately what can happen when constraints are deleted. Deleting the constraint labeled ① (the redundant constraint) had no effect on the model. Deleting ② allows the feasible region to enlarge. Deleting ⑤ allows it to further enlarge, as represented in Figure 5.24. Thus, in general (i.e., for any LP problem),

Deleting constraints leaves the feasible region either unchanged or enlarged.

We have previously in Section 5.3 observed the impact of adding constraints to a model. This impact was demonstrated during the course of plotting the constraint set for the PROTRAC, Inc. model. You will recall that superimposing successive (nonredundant)

[2]Recall that an equality constraint, by definition, is always active.

constraints had the effect of "trimming down" the constraint set. Thus,

---

Adding constraints either leaves the feasible region unchanged or smaller.

Trimming Off the Previous Optimal Solution

Since adding constraints may have the effect of "trimming down" the feasible region, adding a new constraint to a complete model may happen to "trim off" a piece of the constraint set which contains the previous optimal solution. If this happens, the result will be a reduced OV for the new problem. This is shown in Figure 5.25, where a sixth

Figure 5.25
Addition of a Sixth Constraint

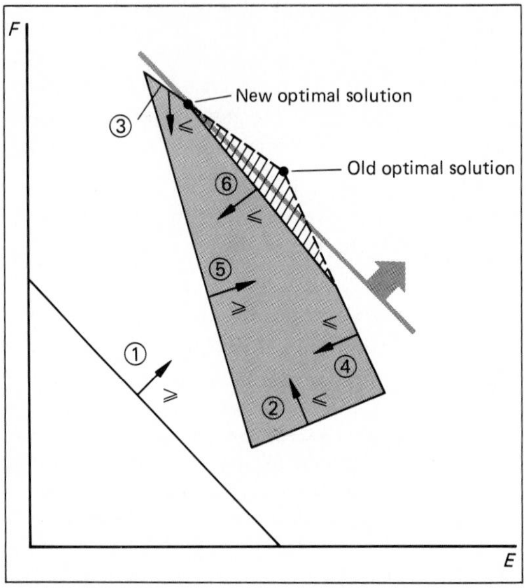

inequality constraint has been added to the PROTRAC, Inc. model. The crosshatched region in Figure 5.25 portrays that part of the constraint set which is eliminated by the addition of the constraint labeled ⑥. The "uphill" direction in this diagram is to the northeast, and the new maximum profit line is not as far "uphill" as the former maximum profit line. Hence, the imposition of a new constraint has led to a reduction in the optimal profit. This is why management often prefers to operate with as few constraints as possible. *The larger the number of constraints, the greater the chance that the optimal objective value is less desirable.* The general result is:

Adding constraints to a model will either impair the OV or leave it unchanged.
Deleting constraints will either improve the OV or leave it unchanged.

In concluding this section it should be observed that the results of adding and deleting constraints are analogous to the results of tightening and loosening inequality constraints, both in terms of effects on the feasible region and on the OV. Thus, in the above displayed result, the phrase "Tightening inequality constraints" could be substituted for "Adding constraints to a model." The phrase "Loosening inequality constraints" could be substituted for "Deleting constraints."

134

5.15
EXAMPLES AND SOLUTIONS

Example 1

Plot the set of values for x_1 and x_2 that satisfy the inequality

$$7x_1 + 6x_2 \leq 42$$

Solution to Example 1

The solution is shown in Figure 5.26.

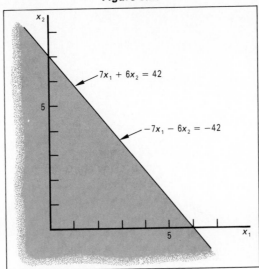

Figure 5.26

Example 2

Suppose that you have a constraint of the form $a_1x_1 + a_2x_2 \geq b$. Would you expect the set of points satisfying the constraint to be above or below the line $a_1x_1 + a_2x_2 = b$? Now, plot the set of values for x_1 and x_2 that satisfy the inequality

$$-7x_1 - 6x_2 \geq -42$$

Solution to Example 2

The set of points (x_1, x_2) that satisfy

$$7x_1 + 6x_2 \leq 42$$

also satisfy the inequality

$$-7x_1 - 6x_2 \geq -42$$

135 Thus, the required plot is the same as the one shown in Figure 5.26.

Note that although the constraint is of $\geq$ form, the points satisfying the constraint lie below, not above, the equality line. From Example 1 you can see that the points satisfying $7x_1 + 6x_2 \geq 42$ lie above the line. Thus, in general you cannot say whether the $\geq$ side of a constraint is above or below the line. The appropriate side must be determined by using a trial point and the actual data that define the constraint.

Example 3

Plot the feasible set for the following problem:

$$\text{Min}\quad 5x_1 + 2x_2$$
$$\text{s.t.}\quad 3x_1 + 6x_2 \geq 18$$
$$5x_1 + 4x_2 \geq 20$$
$$8x_1 + 2x_2 \geq 16$$
$$7x_1 + 6x_2 \leq 42$$
$$x_1, x_2 \geq 0$$

Solution to Example 3

The solution is shown in Figure 5.27.

Figure 5.27

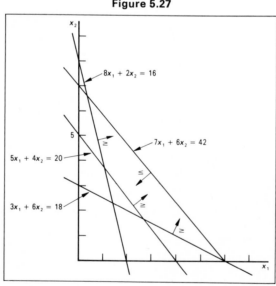

Example 4

Plot the 10- and 20-contours for the objective function in the problem given in Example 3. Indicate the downhill side of the 10-contour and the uphill side of the 20-countour.

Solution to Example 4

The solution is shown in Figure 5.28.

Figure 5.28

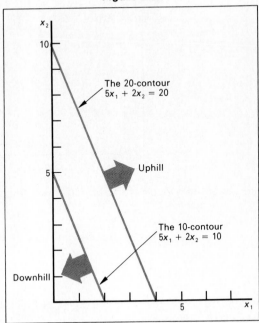

Example 5

On a plot, indicate the location of the optimal solution for the problem in Example 3. Which constraints are active? Which are inactive? Having identified the active constraints, use algebra to find the exact numerical value of the optimal solution and the optimal value of the objective function.

Solution to Example 5

The solution is shown in Figure 5.29. Here we see that the optimal solution lies on the intersection of the second and third constraints. This means that the second and third constraints are active and the first and fourth constraints are inactive. The optimal numerical value of the decision variables can be found by solving the equations for the second and third constraints simultaneously:

$$5x_1 + 4x_2 = 20$$
$$8x_1 + 2x_2 = 16$$

The solution is

$$x_1^* = 1\frac{1}{11} \quad \text{and} \quad x_2^* = 3\frac{7}{11}$$

138

CHAPTER 5
Geometric
Representation
of the Linear
Programming
Model

Figure 5.29

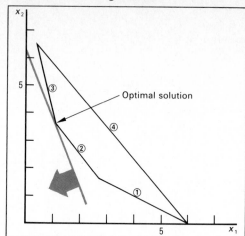

and the optimal value of the objective function is therefore

$$5\left(1\frac{1}{11}\right) + 2\left(3\frac{7}{11}\right) = \frac{140}{11} = 12\frac{8}{11}$$

Example 6

Assume that, in Figure 5.29, the objective function is $15x_1 + c_2x_2$ rather than $5x_1 + 2x_2$. First, verify that if $c_2 = 6$ the optimal solution is $x_1 = 1\frac{1}{11}$, $x_2 = 3\frac{7}{11}$ and that the optimal value of the objective function is $\frac{420}{11}$, or $38\frac{2}{11}$. Then, determine the smallest value of $c_2 \geq 6$ for which there are alternative optimal solutions to this problem.

Solution to Example 6

Note that $15x_1 + 6x_2 = 3(5x_1 + 2x_2)$. Thus, whatever values of x_1 and x_2 maximize $5x_1 + 2x_2$, these same values must also maximize $15x_1 + 6x_2$. This implies that the optimal solution must be the same as the values found in Example 5 and the optimal value of the objective function is multiplied by 3. This result can be seen geometrically by noting that the contours of $15x_1 + 6x_2$ and $5x_1 + 2x_2$ are parallel.

If $c_2 > 6$, the contours of the objective function will have less tilt than the contours of the current objective function. To illustrate this, compare the 45-contour of the function $15x_1 + 9x_2$ with the 30-contour of the function $15x_1 + 6x_2$, as shown in Figure 5.30. The effect of making $c_2 > 6$ can be thought of as rotating the contour of the objective function around the current optimal solution in a counterclockwise direction. Alternative optima occur when the contour of the objective function coincides with the side of the constraint set formed by the second constraint as you can see in Figure 5.31.

The problem thus reduces to finding a value for c_2 so that the contours for the objective function $15x_1 + c_2x_2$ are parallel to the constraint line $5x_1 + 4x_2 = 20$. Letting k denote an arbitrary constant, the contours for $15x_1 + c_2x_2$ are given by $15x_1 + c_2x_2 = k$, or equivalently,

$$x_2 = -\frac{15}{c_2}x_1 + \frac{k}{c_2}$$

139

CHAPTER 5
Geometric
Representation
of the Linear
Programming
Model

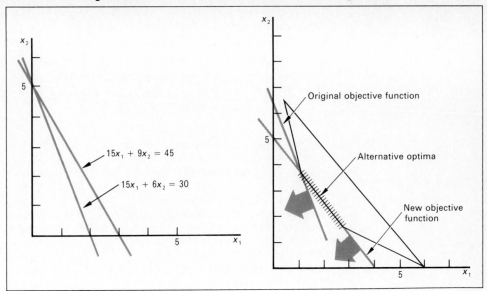

Figure 5.30   Figure 5.31

Hence, the slope is $-15/c_2$. The constraint line $5x_1 + 4x_2 = 20$ is equivalently written as $x_2 = -5x_1/4 + 5$. Thus, its slope is $-5/4$. The objective function contours will be parallel to this constraint when c_2 has a value that makes the slopes equal. Hence, $-15/c_2 = -5/4$, or $c_2 = 12$.

5.16
MAJOR CONCEPTS QUIZ

True–False

1. **T F** The feasible region is the set of all points that satisfy at least one constraint.
2. **T F** In two-dimensional problems, the intersection of any two constraints gives an extreme point of the feasible region.
3. **T F** An optimal solution uses up all of the limited resources available.
4. **T F** A well-formulated model will be neither unbounded nor infeasible.
5. **T F** Infeasibility, contrary to unboundedness, has nothing to do with the objective function.
6. **T F** If an LP is not infeasible, it will have an optimal solution.
7. **T F** Consider any point on the boundary of the feasible region. Such a point satisfies all the constraints.
8. **T F** An active inequality constraint has zero slack or surplus, which means that the optimal solution satisfies the constraint with equality.
9. **T F** Sensitivity analysis greatly increases the possibility that a model can be useful to management.
10. **T F** Consider a model in which, for some of the data, we know there is error. For example, some of the data represent estimates of future values for certain parameters. Suppose sensitivity analysis reveals that the OV is highly sensitive to these parameters. Such information provides more confidence in the recommendations of the model.
11. **T F** Changing the RHS of a constraint changes its slope.

12. **T F**   Changing a RHS cannot affect the set of inactive constraints.
13. **T F**   Loosening an inequality constraint means changing the RHS to make it easier to satisfy.
14. **T F**   A $\geq$ constraint is tightened by increasing the RHS.
15. **T F**   Tightening a redundant inequality constraint cannot affect the feasible region.
16. **T F**   For a given set of data, the inactive constraints are less important than the active ones.
17. **T F**   Adding constraints to a model may improve the OV.

_____

Multiple Choice

18. The graphical method is useful because
   a. it provides a general way to solve LP problems
   b. it gives geometric insight into the model and the meaning of optimality
   c. both a and b
19. The phrase "unbounded LP" means that
   a. at least one decision variable can be made arbitrarily large without leaving the feasible region
   b. the objective contours can be moved as far as desired, in the optimizing direction, and still touch at least one point in the constraint set
   c. not all of the constraints can be satisfied
20. Consider an optimal solution to an LP. Which of the following must be true?
   a. At least one constraint (not including nonnegativity conditions) is active at the point.
   b. Exactly one constraint (not including nonnegativity conditions) is active at the point.
   c. Neither of the above
21. Active constraints
   a. are those on which the optimal solution lies
   b. are those which, at optimality, do not use up all the available resources
   c. both a and b
22. An isoprofit contour represents
   a. an infinite number of feasible points, all of which yield the same profit
   b. an infinite number of optimal solutions
   c. an infinite number of decisions, all of which yield the same profit
23. Which of the following assertions is true of an optimal solution to an LP?
   a. Every LP has an optimal solution
   b. The optimal solution always occurs at an extreme point
   c. The optimal solution uses up all resources
   d. If an optimal solution exists, there will always be at least one at a corner
   e. All of the above.
24. Every corner of the feasible region is defined by
   a. the intersection of 2 constraint lines
   b. some subset of constraint lines and nonnegativity conditions
   c. neither of the above
25. An unbounded feasible region
   a. means the problem has no optimal solution
   b. means the objective function is unbounded
   c. neither of the above
   d. a and b
26. Sensitivity analysis
   a. allows us to more meaningfully interpret the computer solution
   b. is done after the optimal solution is obtained, and is therefore called postoptimality analysis
   c. is sometimes called parametric analysis
   d. all of the above
27. Sensitivity analysis
   a. can be done graphically in two dimensions
   b. can increase our confidence in a model
   c. can weaken our confidence in the recommendations of a model
   d. all of the above
   e. a and b

141

CHAPTER 5
Geometric
Representation
of the Linear
Programming
Model

28. The value of the geometric approach, in two dimensions, is
   a. to solve the problem quickly
   b. to understand what is happening in higher dimensions
   c. to better understand two-dimensional algebra

29. In LP, sensitivity analysis
   a. can deal with changes in the objective function coefficients
   b. can deal with changes in the RHS
   c. all of the above

30. Changing an objective function coefficient
   a. produces a new optimal solution
   b. changes the tilt of the objective function contours
   c. gives a new OV
   d. all of the above

31. Tightening an inequality constraint
   a. improves the OV
   b. cannot improve the OV
   c. hurts the OV

32. A redundant constraint
   a. may not be easy to recognize
   b. should always be dropped from the model
   c. may not be redundant if the data are changed
   d. all of the above
   e. a and c
   f. a and b
   g. b and c

Answers

1. F	12. F	23. d
2. F	13. T	24. b
3. F	14. T	25. c
4. T	15. F	26. d
5. T	16. T	27. d
6. F	17. F	28. b
7. T	18. b	29. c
8. T	19. b	30. b
9. T	20. c	31. b
10. F	21. a	32. e
11. F	22. c	

5.17

PROBLEMS

Plotting Problems

5-1. Plot the set of points (x_1, x_2) that satisfy each of the following conditions.
   (a) $2x_1 + 6x_2 = 12$
   (b) $2x_1 + 6x_2 > 12$
   (c) $2x_1 + 6x_2 \geq 12$
   (d) $2x_1 + 6x_2 < 12$
   (e) $2x_1 + 6x_2 \leq 12$

5-2. Plot the set of points (x_1, x_2) that satisfy each of the following conditions.
   (a) $6x_1 + 2x_2 = 12$
   (b) $6x_1 + 2x_2 > 12$
   (c) $6x_1 + 2x_2 \geq 12$
   (d) $6x_1 + 2x_2 < 12$
   (e) $6x_1 + 2x_2 \leq 12$

5-3. **(a)** Plot the set of points that satisfy $-2x_1 - 6x_2 > -12$.
   (b) Is this plot above or below the line $-2x_1 - 6x_2 = -12$?
   (c) The plot is the same as which of sets plotted in Problem 5–1?

142

CHAPTER 5
Geometric
Representation
of the Linear
Programming
Model

5-4. (a) Plot the set of points that satisfy $-6x_1 - 2x_2 > -12$.
(b) Is this plot above or below the line $-6x_1 - 2x_2 = -12$?
(c) The plot is the same as which of the sets plotted in Problem 5-2?

5-5. Claire Voyant, a colorful dealer in stereo equipment, puts together amps and preamps. An amp takes 12 hours to assemble and 4 hours for a high-performance check. A pre-amp takes 4 hours to assemble and 8 hours for a high-performance check. In the next month Claire will have 60 hours of assembly time available and 40 hours of high-perform-ance check time available. Plot the combinations of amps and preamps that will satisfy
(a) The constraint on assembly time
(b) The constraint on performance check time
(c) Both constraints simultaneously

5-6. Molly Bolt is a tenacious maker of cheap desks and chairs. Each desk takes 4 hours to assemble and 9 hours to paint. Each chair takes 4 hours to assemble and 3 hours to paint. For the next month Molly has allocated 32 hours for assembly and 36 hours for painting. Plot the combinations of desks and chairs which Molly can make that will satisfy
(a) Her constraint on assembly time   **(b)** Her constraint on painting time
(c) Both constraints simultaneously

Geometric Solutions

5-7. In Problem 5-5, suppose that Claire makes a profit of $10 on each amp and $5 on each preamp. Plot the 10, 20, and 60 profit contours.

5-8. In Problem 5-6, Molly makes $6 on each desk and $5 on each chair. Plot the 30 and 60 profit contours.

5-9. Consider Claire's activity as described in Problems 5-5 and 5-7. Suppose that because of limitations on transistor availability she has determined that there are two additional constraints in her model. Namely, she can produce a maximum of 4 preamps and 6 amps in the next month. Taking all constraints into account,
(a) Find Claire's optimal (profit-maximizing) production plan using graphical analysis.
(b) What is the OV?
(c) Which constraints are active?
(d) Which constraints are inactive, and what are their slack values?

5-10. Consider Molly Bolt's activity as described in Problems 5-6 and 5-8. Suppose that because of storage constraints Molly must add two additional constraints to her model. Namely, she can produce a maximum of three desks and seven chairs in the coming month. Taking all constraints into account,
(a) Find Molly's optimal (profit-maximizing) production plan using graphical analysis.
(b) What is the OV?
(c) Which constraints are active?
(d) Which constraints are inactive, and what are their slack values?

5-11. Could the omission of two constraints make Claire Voyant's problem unbounded?

5-12. Could the omission of two constraints make Molly Bolt's problem unbounded?

5-13. Suppose that Claire's constraint on amps, $A \leq 6$, is replaced by $A \geq 6$. How does this affect the problem?

5-14. Suppose that Molly's constraint on desks, $D \leq 3$, is replaced by $D \geq 5$. How does this affect the problem?

5-15. Consider the following LP.

$$\text{Max} \quad x_1 + x_2$$
$$\text{s.t.} \quad x_1 + 2x_2 \leq 6$$
$$3x_1 + 2x_2 \leq 12$$
$$x_1 \geq 0, \quad x_2 \geq 0$$

143

CHAPTER 5
Geometric
Representation
of the Linear
Programming
Model

(a) Use the graphical method to find the optimal solution and the OV.

(b) Change the objective function to $2x_1 + 6x_2$ and find the optimal solution.

(c) How many extreme points does the feasible region have? Find the values of (x_1, x_2) at each extreme point.

5-16. Consider the following LP:

$$\text{Max} \quad x_1 + 2x_2$$
$$\text{s.t.} \quad 2x_1 + 8x_2 \leq 16$$
$$x_1 + x_2 \leq 5$$
$$x_1 \geq 0, \qquad x_2 \geq 0$$

(a) Use the graphical method to find the optimal solution and the OV.

(b) Change the objective function to $x_1 + 6x_2$ and find the optimal solution.

(c) How many extreme points does the feasible region have? Find the values of (x_1, x_2) at each extreme point.

5-17. Consider the following LP:

$$\text{Max} \quad 3x_1 + 4x_2$$
$$\text{s.t.} \quad -2x_1 + 4x_2 \leq 16$$
$$2x_1 + 4x_2 \leq 24$$
$$-6x_1 - 3x_2 \geq -48$$
$$x_1, x_2 \geq 0$$

(a) Use the graphical method to find the optimal solution and the OV.

(b) Find the slack and surplus values for each constraint.

5-18. Consider the following LP:

$$\text{Min} \quad 6x_1 + 4x_2$$
$$\text{s.t.} \quad 2x_1 + 2x_2 \geq 20$$
$$-4x_1 - 2x_2 \geq -24$$
$$x_2 \leq 4$$
$$x_1, x_2 \geq 0$$

(a) Use the graphical method to find the optimal solution and the OV.

(b) Find the slack and surplus values for each constraint.

5-19. Consider the following LP:

$$\text{Min} \quad 5x_1 + 2x_2$$
$$\text{s.t.} \quad 3x_1 + 6x_2 \geq 18$$
$$5x_1 + 4x_2 \geq 20$$
$$8x_1 + 2x_2 \geq 16$$
$$7x_1 + 6x_2 \leq 42$$
$$x_1, x_2 \geq 0$$

(a) Use the graphical method to find the optimal solution and the OV.

(b) Which constraints are active? Which are inactive?

(c) What are the slack and surplus values associated with each constraint?

(d) The feasible region has how many extreme points?

(e) Change the objective function to $15x_1 + 12x_2$. What are the alternative optimal corner solutions?

Geometry of Sensitivity Analysis

5-20. In the PROTRAC, Inc. model, suppose that the objective function is changed to $5000E + 2000F$.

(a) Use graphical analysis (e.g., Figure 5-12) to determine the effect on the optimal solution.

(b) What is the effect on the OV?

144

CHAPTER 5
Geometric
Representation
of the Linear
Programming
Model

5-21. In the PROTRAC, Inc. model, suppose that the objective function is changed to $6000E + 2000F$.

(a) Use graphic analysis (e.g., Figure 5.12) to determine the effect on the optimal solution.

(b) What is the effect on the OV?

5-22. In the PROTRAC, Inc. model, replace the RHS of the fifth constraint (contractual labor agreement), which is currently 135, with the value 270. State the effect on the constraint set.

5-23. In the PROTRAC, Inc. model, how large can the RHS of the fifth constraint be made without destroying feasibility?

5-24. Consider the LP

$$\text{Max} \quad 30x_1 + 10x_2$$
$$\text{s.t.} \quad 2x_1 + x_2 \leq 4$$
$$2x_1 + 2x_2 \leq 6$$
$$x_1 \geq 0, \quad x_2 \geq 0$$

(a) Solve graphically and state the optimal solution.

(b) Keeping all other data as is, what per unit profitability should the product, whose current optimal value is zero, have in order that this product enter the optimal solution at a positive level?

(c) How many optimal corner solutions exist after making the change described in part (b)? What are they?

(d) In the original problem, how much can the RHS of the second constraint be increased (decreased) before the optimal solution is changed?

(e) Answer part (d) for the RHS of the first constraint.

(f) How do you explain the difference between parts (d) and (e)?

(g) What will be the impact of adding the constraint $4x_1 + x_2 = 4$ to the original model?

(h) What is the impact (on the optimal solution) of adding the constraint $3x_1 + 3x_2 \leq 15$ to the original model?

(i) Fill in the blanks in the following statement: "The difference between parts (g) and (h) is that the original optimal solution already _____ the constraint in part (h) but does not _____ the constraint in part (g).

5-25. Consider the LP

$$\text{Max} \quad 15x_1 + 5x_2$$
$$\text{s.t.} \quad 2x_1 + x_2 \leq 6$$
$$x_1 + x_2 \leq 6$$
$$x_1 \geq 0, \quad x_2 \geq 0$$

In terms of this model, answer all of the parts in Problem 5-24.

More Challenging Problems

5-26. Consider the following LP model:

$$\text{Max} \quad 600E + 1,000F$$
$$\text{s.t.} \quad 100E + 60F \leq 21,000$$
$$4,000E + 800F \leq 680,000$$
$$E + F \leq 290$$
$$12E + 30F \leq 6,000$$
$$E, F \geq 0$$

(a) Let E be the horizontal axis, F the vertical axis, and use graphical means to find the optimal solution to this problem and the OV. Label the corners of the constraint set as I, II, III, IV, and V, where I is on the vertical axis above the origin and you continue clockwise, ending with V at the origin.

145

CHAPTER 5
Geometric
Representation
of the Linear
Programming
Model

(b) One of the constraints is redundant in the sense that it plays no role in determining the constraint set. Which one is it?

(c) What is the minimum change in the RHS of this constraint that would cause the constraint to become active?

(d) The coefficient of E in the third constraint is currently 1. What is the minimum increase in this coefficient that would cause the constraint to become active?

(e) Suppose that the coefficient of E, say c_E, in the objective function is increased, whereas the coefficient of F, say c_F, remains fixed. At what value for the coefficient of E would alternative optima first be encountered?

5-27. Consider the following problem:

$$\text{Min} \quad 300E + 600F$$

$$
\begin{aligned}
\text{s.t.} \quad E + F &\geq 5 \\
E &\leq 3F \\
10E + 15F &\leq 150 \\
20E + 10F &\leq 160 \\
30E + 10F &\geq 135 \\
E, F &\geq 0
\end{aligned}
$$

(a) Use graphical means to find a solution and the OV.

(b) Create an objective function for a min problem with the constraints given as above so that the optimal solution lies at the intersection of the lines $20E + 10F = 160$ and $E - 3F = 0$. Find the exact value of the objective function at the solution.

(c) Create an objective function for a max problem with the constraints as above so that the optimal solution lies at the intersection of the lines $10E + 15F = 150$ and $30E + 10F = 135$. Find the optimal value of the objective function.

CHAPTER 6

Linear Programs: Computer Analysis and Interpreting Sensitivity Output

APPLICATION CAPSULE •

AN INVENTORY OF TRUCKS*

The Fleet Administration Division of North American Van Lines, Inc., has primary responsibility for planning and controlling the company's fleet of truck tractors. The task is complicated because drivers in the North American system are independent contractors. That is, they own and are responsible for the maintenance of their tractor equipment, whose service is in turn leased to North American. In particular, Fleet Administration (1) recruits and trains owner-drivers; (2) buys new tractors from manufacturers and sells used tractors; (3) sells new tractors to drivers and buys used tractors from them; and (4) provides warranty, insurance, and financing arrangements to contract truckers.

Historically, Fleet Administration used a manual system to discharge its responsibilities. This system started with a forecast of demand for shipments which was translated into a forecast for the required number of new contract owners required during each remaining week of the fiscal year. This forecast, in turn, led to recruiting and training plans as well as plans for tractor purchases and sales. This process required 120 labor hours of computational effort for each pass through the planning process. This implied both high costs and the lack of ability to evaluate alternative purchase and sales plans. In other words, the process simply evaluated the plan selected. It gave no information on what decisions could be made to improve it.

In face of this situation North American created and implemented a decision support system with two main functions:

*Dan Avramovich, Thomas M. Cook, Gary O. Langston, and Frank Sutherland, "A Decision Support System for Fleet Management: A Linear Programming Approach," *Interfaces*, Vol. 12, No. 3, June 1982, pp. 1–9.

1. It used a large-scale LP model to determine a new/used, purchase/sales plan for tractors.

2. It used the LP results to generate a series of reports that illustrate the financial impact of the suggested plan.

The model has had an important effect on three areas within the firm. First, the average inventory has been reduced by 100 tractors or approximately $3,000,000. This yields an approximate annual savings in inventory carrying costs of $600,000. Second, the ability to run up to three scenarios per day makes it possible for management to react quickly to changes in demand forecasts. Finally, the personnel used in the old manual system can be productively reassigned.

6.1
INTRODUCTION

In Chapter 5 we stated that the manager is typically interested in much more than simply the solution to an LP problem. The analysis of a real-world problem often *begins* with the solution. We stated that the process of analyzing a model after the solution has been derived is termed **sensitivity analysis**, and in Section 5.9 we dealt with some of the geometry that underlies sensitivity analysis. In this chapter we look in detail at how the manager might, in practice, use the sensitivity information contained in the computer analysis of an LP. This can be an important, even daily, problem faced by managers in the real world—the problem of making good use of computer analysis. This discussion culminates in a realistic scenario involving the manager and the management scientist.

To begin the development of this chapter, it is important to understand the form of the LP model that the computer actually solves. This is called the **standard equality constraint form**. After illustrating some relevant properties of this form, we proceed to study the computer output for a problem already seen: Crawler Tread.

6.2
THE PROBLEM THE COMPUTER SOLVES

Any linear program, regardless of the sense of the constraints (i.e., whether they are $\geq$, $=$, or $\leq$), can be transformed into an equivalent problem all of whose constraints are equalities. This step is accomplished with the use of **slack** and **surplus variables**.

Slack and Surplus Variables

Let us begin by considering a single constraint, say

$$x_1 + x_2 \leq 5 \tag{6.1}$$

This is plotted in Figure 6.1, illustrating the constraint line, the $\leq$ side, and the $\geq$ side.

148

CHAPTER 6
Linear Programs:
Computer
Analysis
and Interpreting
Sensitivity Output

Figure 6.1

$x_1 + x_2 = 5, \leq 5,$ and ≥ 5

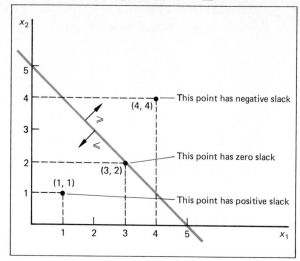

The mechanics of plotting such a constraint were presented in Chapter 5. Each point on the constraint line satisfies $x_1 + x_2 = 5$. All the points on one side of the line (in this case below the line) satisfy $x_1 + x_2 < 5$, and all the points on the other side satisfy the reverse inequality. The inequality (6.1) can be transformed to an equality constraint as follows. First, we add a new variable, say s, called a slack variable, and rewrite (6.1) as

$$x_1 + x_2 + s = 5 \tag{6.2}$$

Now note that a point will satisfy (6.1) if and only if that point along with some nonnegative value of s also satisfies (6.2). Consider, for example, the point ($x_1 = 1, x_2 = 1$). This point satisfies (6.1). It also satisfies (6.2) with $s = 3$. By trying several pairs of values, such as (3, 2) and (4, 4) as illustrated in Figure 6.1, we are led to the following observations:

1. If a point (x_1, x_2) satisfies the inequality (6.1), it will, in Figure 6.1, lie on or below the plotted line, and the value of the slack variable in the equation (6.2) is nonnegative. Thus, the inequality (6.1) is equivalent to the following two conditions:

$$\begin{aligned} x_1 + x_2 + s &= 5 \\ s &\geq 0 \end{aligned} \tag{6.3}$$

The **nonnegativity** of s ensures that the point (x_1, x_2) lies on the $\leq$ side of the line.

2. If a point (x_1, x_2) satisfies (6.1) with equality, the value of the slack variable in (6.2) is zero.

3. If the point (x_1, x_2) does not satisfy (6.1), it will lie strictly above the plotted line in Figure 6.1 [e.g., the point ($x_1 = 4, x_2 = 4$)]. In this case the value of the slack variable in (6.2) is negative, thereby violating (6.3).

We thus see that the slack variable s is the "slack," or extra amount that must be added to the left-hand side to turn the $\leq$ into $=$.

Now that we have used the notion of a slack variable to convert a single $\leq$ inequality constraint to an equality constraint, let us see what must be done to handle a *collection* of $\leq$ inequality constraints. Consider, for example, the three constraints

149

CHAPTER 6
Linear Programs:
Computer
Analysis
and Interpreting
Sensitivity Output

$$4x_1 - x_2 \leq 12$$
$$2x_1 + 6x_2 \leq 21$$
$$-3x_1 + 2x_2 \leq 6.5$$

In this case, converting to equalities requires the introduction of *three* new nonnegative slack variables, say x_3, x_4, x_5 (the three slacks could just as well be labeled as $s_1, s_2,$ and s_3). We then obtain the following equivalent system of equalities:

Adding Slack

$$4x_1 - x_2 + x_3 = 12$$
$$2x_1 + 6x_2 + x_4 = 21$$
$$-3x_1 + 2x_2 + x_5 = 6.5$$
$$x_3, x_4, x_5 \geq 0$$

Note that there is a *different* slack variable associated with each constraint.

We have now to consider the problem of converting a $\geq$ constraint into an equivalent equality. Let us take as an example

$$2x_1 + 4x_2 \geq 13$$

To convert this $\geq$ constraint to an equality, we *subtract* a nonnegative variable from the left-hand side and change the inequality to equality. This produces the two conditions

**Subtracting
Surplus**

$$2x_1 + 4x_2 - s = 13$$
$$s \geq 0$$

(6.4)

When a nonnegative variable is subtracted from a $\geq$ constraint, it is often termed a **surplus variable** (as opposed to a slack variable, which is added to a $\leq$ constraint). A surplus variable is the "surplus" that must be deducted from the left-hand side to turn the $\geq$ into $=$.

The foregoing discussion shows that

Any $\leq$ constraint can be converted to an equality by adding a new nonnegative slack variable to the left-hand side. Any $\geq$ constraint can be converted to an equality by subtracting a new nonnegative surplus variable from the left-hand side.

**Standard
Equality
Constraint
Form**

In solving linear programs, the computer uses an algorithm called the simplex method, which is designed to attack problems with only equality constraints. Given any LP, the discussion above shows how to convert it easily to the required equality constraint form. As an illustration, recall the PROTRAC, Inc. model

$$\text{Max} \quad 5000E + 4000F \tag{6.5}$$
$$\text{s.t.} \quad E + F \geq 5$$
$$E - 3F \leq 0$$
$$10E + 15F \leq 150$$
$$20E + 10F \leq 160$$
$$30E + 10F \geq 135$$
$$E, F \geq 0$$

150

CHAPTER 6
Linear Programs:
Computer
Analysis
and Interpreting
Sensitivity Output

This LP problem has two variables and five constraints, two of them $\geq$ and three of them $\leq$. To convert this problem into an equivalent problem in **standard equality constraint form**, we must add slack variables to the second, third, and fourth constraints (the $\leq$ constraints) and subtract surplus variables from the first and fifth constraints (the $\geq$ constraints). Letting s_1, s_2, s_3, s_4, and s_5 denote the five new variables, we obtain

$$\text{Max} \quad 5000E + 4000F \tag{6.6}$$

$$\begin{aligned}
\text{s.t.} \quad E + \ F - s_1 &= \ \ 5 \\
E - \ 3F + s_2 &= \ \ 0 \\
10E + 15F + s_3 &= 150 \\
20E + 10F + s_4 &= 160 \\
30E + 10F - s_5 &= 135 \\
E, F, s_1, s_2, s_3, s_4, s_5 &\geq 0
\end{aligned}$$

This is the standard equality constraint form of the PROTRAC, Inc. model. This form of the problem still has five constraints, but the addition of slack and surplus has increased the number of variables to seven instead of two. Notice that

---

When converting an LP problem into standard equality constraint form, the slack and surplus variables are never included in the objective function. Equivalently, you may think of them as being included but with zero coefficients.

In Chapter 5 we used the graphic solution method to show that $E^* = 4.5$ and $F^* = 7$ is the solution to the PROTRAC, Inc. inequality model (6.5). This means that the optimal values of the other variables (the slacks and surpluses) in the equality constraint model (6.6) are given by

*Optimal
Values of
Slack/Surplus
Variables*

$$\begin{aligned}
s_1^* &= E^* + F^* - 5 = 11.5 - 5 = 6.5 \\
s_2^* &= 0 - (E^* - 3F^*) = -(4.5 - 21) = 16.5 \\
s_3^* &= 150 - (10E^* + 15F^*) = 150 - (45 + 105) = 0 \\
s_4^* &= 160 - (20E^* + 10F^*) = 160 - (90 + 70) = 0 \\
s_5^* &= (30E^* + 10F^*) - 135 = (135 + 70) - 135 = 70
\end{aligned}$$

It would at this point be useful for you to review the material on active and inactive constraints in Section 5.4. We recall from the material: An **active** or **binding** constraint is one for which, **at optimality**, the left-hand side equals the right-hand side. From the geometric point of view, an active constraint is one on which the optimal solution lies. We saw that in the PROTRAC, Inc. model the active constraints are the third and fourth. The calculation above shows that their slack variables (s_3^* and s_4^*) are zero. On the other hand, the first, second, and fifth constraints are inactive, and their slack/surplus variables are positive. Thus, you can see that

---

Active constraints are precisely those for which *the optimal values* of the slack or surplus variables are zero. Inactive constraints are those for which *the optimal values* of the slack or surplus variables are positive.

151

CHAPTER 6
Linear Programs:
Computer
Analysis
and Interpreting
Sensitivity Output

It is not difficult to see that all of the discussion in Section 5.4 could be phrased in terms of these new entities, the slack and surplus variables. In particular, when at optimality a constraint has a zero value for the slack or surplus variable,[1] it means, geometrically speaking, that the solution to the problem lies on that constraint.

In order to check your understanding of the standard equality constraint form, try to convert the following model to one with only equality constraints.

$$
\begin{array}{llrcl}
\text{Max} & x_1 + 3x_4 \\
\text{s.t.} & 2x_1 & & + 3x_3 + & x_4 & \leq 12 \\
& x_1 + 13x_2 & + 6x_3 + 0.5x_4 & \leq 41 \\
& 0.4x_2 & + 2x_3 & & \geq 22 \\
& -3x_1 & & + 12x_4 & = 15 \\
& x_1, x_2, x_3, x_4 \geq 0
\end{array}
$$

In this example there are four constraints and four decision variables.[2] Since only three of the constraints are inequalities we need to introduce only three new variables, in this case one surplus (for the third constraint) and two slacks (for the first and second constraints). The fourth constraint is already an equality, and *we do not introduce a slack or surplus variable for this equality constraint.* Thus, the standard equality constraint form for the model above is

$$
\begin{array}{llrcl}
\text{Max} & x_1 + 3x_4 \\
\text{s.t.} & 2x_1 & & + 3x_3 + & x_4 + s_1 & = 12 \\
& x_1 + 13x_2 & + 6x_3 + 0.5x_4 + s_2 & = 41 \\
& 0.4x_2 & + 2x_3 & - s_3 & = 22 \\
& -3x_1 & & + 12x_4 & = 15 \\
& x_1, x_2, x_3, x_4, s_1, s_2, s_3 \geq 0
\end{array}
$$

To summarize the discussion above, we have shown how slack and surplus variables are used to convert any LP problem into standard equality constraint form. This is the form of the LP that the computer solves.

Geometry of
the Standard
Equality
Constraint
Problem

A brief look at the geometry of our new model will reveal a property which is important in appreciating and correctly interpreting the information contained in the computer printout. This property has to do with the number of positive variables at any corner (and in particular at an optimal corner) of the constraint set.

In the preceding section we have seen that all variables (decision variables, slack and surplus variables) in the standard equality constraint problem are required to be nonnegative (positive or zero). In this section we illustrate that at any corner (and in particular at an optimal corner) of the constraint set, the maximum number of positive (*greater than zero*) variables, counting decision variables, slacks, and surpluses, is at

---

[1]In the language of Chapter 5 we simply said that such a constraint has zero slack or surplus, without introducing the concept of a slack or surplus variable.

[2]Students are sometimes confused by a model such as this in which not all decision variables appear in the objective function and all the constraints, but this is perfectly valid. Think of the variables as being everywhere included but with zero coefficients in places.

152

CHAPTER 6
Linear Programs:
Computer
Analysis
and Interpreting
Sensitivity Output

most equal to the number of constraints in the model (not counting the "nonnegativity conditions").

To illustrate this "count property," consider the model shown in (6.7).

$$\text{Max} \quad x_1 + x_2 \tag{6.7}$$

$$\begin{array}{rrcll}
\text{s.t.} \quad 8x_1 + 7x_2 &\leq& 56 & \text{\textcircled{1}} \\
-6x_1 - 10x_2 &\geq& -60 & \text{\textcircled{2}} \\
x_1 &\leq& 6 & \text{\textcircled{3}} \\
-x_1 + x_2 &\leq& 6 & \text{\textcircled{4}}
\end{array}$$

$$x_1 \geq 0, \quad x_2 \geq 0$$

The constraint set for this model is plotted in Figure 6.2, where the appropriate constraints are labeled ① through ④. Now consider the standard equality constraint form of the same model. It is

$$\text{Max} \quad x_1 + x_2 \tag{6.8}$$

$$\begin{array}{rrcll}
\text{s.t.} \quad 8x_1 + 7x_2 + s_1 &=& 56 & \text{\textcircled{1}} \\
-6x_1 - 10x_2 \quad - s_2 &=& -60 & \text{\textcircled{2}} \\
x_1 \quad + s_3 &=& 6 & \text{\textcircled{3}} \\
-x_1 + x_2 \quad + s_4 &=& 6 & \text{\textcircled{4}}
\end{array}$$

$$x_1, x_2, s_1, s_2, s_3, s_4 \text{ all nonnegative}$$

Figure 6.2
Constraint Set for the Inequality Constrained Model (6.7)

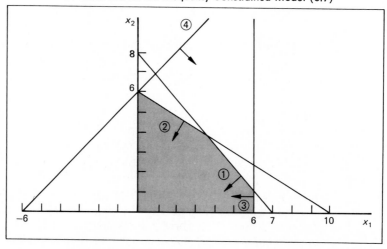

The original model had four constraints and two decision variables. The standard equality constraint form has the same number of constraints, but also has four slack/surplus variables in addition to the two decision variables, for a total of six variables. It is important to note that

153

CHAPTER 6
Linear Programs:
Computer
Analysis
and Interpreting
Sensitivity Output

When referring to the number of variables in the standard equality constraint model, we count slack and surplus as well as decision variables. Also note that in referring to the number of constraints, we do not count the nonnegativity conditions.

Our geometric representation of model (6.8) is nearly the same as for the inequality model (6.7), the only difference being that each constraint will be explicitly labeled with its slack or surplus variable. This is shown in Figure 6.3, where for convenience we have labeled the five corners (with Roman numerals) and also identified several points which will be of interest. Labeling the constraints with the slack and surplus variables allows you to make the following "visual" observations.

1. At any point interior to the feasible region, all variables are positive. This is illustrated by point P_0 in Figure 6.3. At this point you can directly read $x_1 = 1$ and $x_2 = 1$. Using these values and the constraints in (6.8) you could explicitly calculate the values for s_1, s_2, s_3, and s_4 at P_0, and you would see that these values are also positive. However, you need not perform this algebra, for the figure immediately shows us that all slacks and surpluses are positive at P_0.

Figure 6.3
Constraint Set for Standard Equality
Constraint Form (6.8)

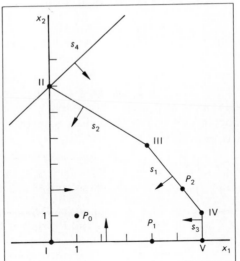

2. At any point on the boundary, at least one variable will be zero. This is illustrated at points P_1 and P_2. At P_1, you can see that $x_2 = 0$; all other variables are positive. Similarly, at P_2, which lies on the first constraint line, only s_1 is zero. Special boundary points of interest are the corners of the feasible region. For example, since the corner labeled III lies on the first and second constraint lines, the two variables s_1 and s_2 are zero at this corner, with all other variables positive. These examples show that the zero variables on the boundary could be decision variables as well as slack or surplus variables. Corner V, for example, shows that a decision variable (x_2) and a slack variable (s_3) can both be zero on the boundary.

Based on such observations, we can now illustrate the main result of this section by counting the positive variables at each of the five corners of the constraint set. The result is shown in Figure 6.4.

Figure 6.4
Counting Positive Variables at Corners

CORNER	ZERO VARIABLES	POSITIVE VARIABLES	POSITIVE COUNT
I	x_1, x_2	s_1, s_2, s_3, s_4	4
II	x_1, s_2, s_4	x_2, s_1, s_3	3
III	s_1, s_2	x_1, x_2, s_3, s_4	4
IV	s_1, s_3	x_1, x_2, s_2, s_4	4
V	x_2, s_3	x_1, s_1, s_2, s_4	4

What this figure shows, quite simply, is *which* variables are positive at each corner, and, in addition, *how many* variables are positive at each corner. Remembering that there are four constraints in the model (6.8), Figure 6.4 illustrates the important general fact that

For any LP problem in standard equality constraint form, the number of positive variables at any corner is less than or equal to the number of constraints.

This result has an important implication for the computer solution of an LP. Recall from Section 5.5 that in an LP problem, if there is an optimal solution, there is always at least one optimal corner solution (there may be noncorner optima as well). The simplex method, which is the main algorithm used by computers to solve LP problems, is illustrated in Appendix A. The important point for our purposes is that the algorithm always produces an optimal corner (assuming, of course, that the problem is neither infeasible nor unbounded). Moreover, the simplex algorithm (and the computer) solves a problem in standard equality constraint form and, for such a problem, in accord with the conclusion displayed above, the number of positive variables at *any* corner (hence at an optimal corner) is less than or equal to the number of constraints. Thus, we can now see one reason why the above "count property" is of interest.

The computer solution to an LP problem always has at most m positive variables, where m is the number of constraints.

As an illustration of this important theoretic property, let us refer to the diet problem specified in Problem 4-22. The problem is to select the quantities of each of 116 foods so as to satisfy the requirements for 16 essential nutrients at a minimum cost. There are 16 inequality constraints ($\geq$) representing nutrient requirements. Hence, in the standard equality-constraint form there are a total of 132 variables (116 decision variables and 16 surplus variables). Since there are only 16 constraints, at most 16 of these 132 variables will be positive in an optimal computer solution. This means we know ahead of time that in such a solution the minimum-cost diet can include *at most* 16 foods. *For each nutrient requirement that is inactive, there will be one less food in the optimal diet.*

A primary practical need for the "count property" displayed above is that

155

CHAPTER 6
Linear Programs:
Computer
Analysis
and Interpreting
Sensitivity Output

> **When the computer solution has less than m positive variables, the solution is called degenerate, and in this case special care will have to be taken in interpreting some of your computer output.**

Since the ramifications of degeneracy are noteworthy, let us briefly pause to define the concept formally. We will then advance to the topic of computer analysis.

Degeneracy and Nondegeneracy

A corner such as II in Figure 6.3, where the number of positive variables is *less than* the number of constraints, is termed a **degenerate corner**.[3] The remaining corners, I, III, IV, and V, where the number of positive variables is exactly equal to the number of constraints, are termed **nondegenerate corners**. If the optimal computer solution to an LP has less than m positive variables, it is termed a **degenerate solution** since it occurs at a degenerate corner. Analogously, a solution with exactly m positive variables is called a **nondegenerate solution**. The concept of degeneracy gives us the structure for additional insight into the theoretic properties of an LP model. As an illustration, let us return to the PROTRAC E and F model. Using the discussion above, we can prove that under normal conditions there will always be a solution to this problem in which *at least* three of the constraints will be inactive. By the phrase "under normal conditions," we mean "in a nondegenerate situation." In such a case, there will be exactly five positive variables in any computer solution because the problem has five constraints. Two of the five positive variables could be E and F. Thus, *at least* three of those five must be slack or surplus. This means at least three constraints are inactive, which is what we set out to prove. For any given set of data (parameter values), provided that the optimal solution is nondegenerate, at least three of the constraints can, in theory, be ignored. They do not have any effect on the problem. Unfortunately, it is not possible to tell which particular constraints will be inactive before obtaining a solution. We only know there will be at least three. Consequently, as discussed previously, in practice all constraints must be included in the model. In this case we have already seen that s_1^*, s_2^* and s_5^* are positive, meaning that the first, second, and fifth constraints are inactive at the solution ($E^* = 4.5$, $F^* = 7$).

As another, more general illustration, consider an LP problem with m stockpile constraints of the $\leq$ form. Each stockpile represents the limited availability of a particular resource. Suppose that these are the only constraints, and suppose there are two decision variables in the problem, and $m > 2$. Then, "under normal conditions" at least $m - 2$ of the stockpiles will *not* be completely consumed at optimality. By now, you

Number of Inactive Constraints, Assuming Nondegeneracy

---

[3]Here is a subtle point for those who wish to descend slightly deeper into the pits of degeneracy. Figure 6.3 shows that the degenerate corner II has a redundant constraint passing through it (namely, the fourth constraint). Although this is true of any degenerate corner in two dimensions, do not conclude that this must always be the case. As a counterexample, visualize a three-dimensional constraint set which has the shape of a great pyramid standing interior to the nonnegative orthant. This figure has four triangular sides and a base, corresponding to five inequality constraints. Thus, the original model has five inequality constraints in three variables, and the corresponding standard equality constraint

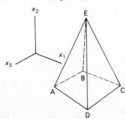

model will have five constraints and eight variables. At each of the four base corners, A, B, C, and D, three slack variables are zero and hence five variables are positive. Hence, since there are five constraints and at each of these corners five positive variables, these are nondegenerate corners. However, at the corner E, four slacks are zero and hence only four variables are positive. Thus, corner E is degenerate but there are no redundant constraints. What this illustrates is the fact that in three or more dimensions, contrary to the two-dimensional case, a degenerate corner need not have a redundant constraint passing through it.

156

CHAPTER 6
Linear Programs:
Computer
Analysis
and Interpreting
Sensitivity Output

should be able to illustrate this fact for yourself with a picture. The generalization to n decision variables is straightforward. If $m > n$, then under the nondegeneracy assumption at least $m - n$ of the stockpiles will not be completely consumed at optimality. Another way of saying this is "at most n of the original m constraints will be active at optimality." Again, you should be able to illustrate this assertion for the special case of $n = 2$.

6.3

MID-CHAPTER SUMMARY

We have seen that the process of converting a problem to standard equality-constraint form is purely mechanical. For this reason, most LP computer codes will change the inequalities to equalities for you. For example, most interactive software will allow you to input the original problem directly, from a desk console, without worrying about slack or surplus variables. Knowing the sense of each constraint ($\leq$, $=$, or $\geq$), the computer can automatically convert the model to standard equality constraint form before solving. Incidentally, the nonnegativity conditions are not explicitly entered into the computer. The simplex algorithm for solving linear programs automatically assumes that all variables are nonnegative. It would therefore be extraneous to input these conditions explicitly.

In summary, you have seen that:

1. The original model may have all sorts of constraints: $\leq$, $=$, and $\geq$. Prior to solution, the computer converts the original model to an equivalent one, all of whose constraints are equalities. This is called the **standard equality-constraint form**. The models are equivalent in the sense that if the original model can be solved, so can the new one, and any solution to the new one provides a solution to the original.

2. In the process of transforming the original model, **slack and surplus variables** are introduced as appropriate. Thus, the equality-constraint model will have more variables than the original (unless all the original constraints were equalities, in which case no conversion is required). The number of constraints in the original and transformed models is the same.

3. A $\leq$ constraint is converted to $=$ by adding a slack variable to the left-hand side. A $\geq$ constraint is converted to $=$ by subtracting a surplus variable from the left-hand side. The same slack variable never appears in more than one constraint. The same surplus variable never appears in more than one constraint. **Slack and surplus variables are always required to be nonnegative.**

4. Slack and surplus variables are never seen in the objective function (i.e., they are included with zero coefficient).

5. The constraints of a problem that is ready for solution must have all terms with variables on the left and the constant term on the right. (Note that the number zero may be the only constant term; for example, $4x_1 - 3x_2 + x_3 = 0$.)

6. Nonnegativity conditions are not explicitly input to the computer.

Handling
Variables
Unconstrained
in Sign

You may wonder what to do in the case when, for logical reasons, some of the variables in your model are *not* required to be nonnegative. This is easily treated. Suppose that in the particular model you have formulated there is a variable z that can meaningfully (i.e. in terms of the real world interpretation) be positive, negative, or zero.

157

CHAPTER 6
Linear Programs:
Computer
Analysis
and Interpreting
Sensitivity Output

In order to transform your model into the standard form (in which *all* variables must be nonnegative), introduce two new *nonnegative* variables, say z_1 and z_2, and let $z = z_1 - z_2$. Everywhere a z appears in your original model, simply replace it by $z_1 - z_2$ and rewrite the model. It can be shown that the new problem is equivalent to the old. By the way, this is a manipulation that most LP codes will not do for you; so, when not all variables are nonnegative, you must transform the model so that they are. We hasten to add that in most business or economics models, the variables in your formulation will be quantities such as price, amount of a product to be manufactured, and so on, which means that by definition these variables will satisfy the nonnegativity conditions. As a result, the difficulties associated with variables unconstrained in sign are often academic.

6.4
THE CRAWLER TREAD OUTPUT: A DIALOGUE WITH MANAGEMENT (SENSITIVITY ANALYSIS IN ACTION)

This problem was introduced in Section 4.5. Recall that the ore from four different locations is blended to make crawler tractor treads. Each ore contains three essential elements, denoted for simplicity as A, B, and C, that must appear in the final blend at minimum threshold levels. PROTRAC pays a different price per ton for the ore from each location. The cost-minimizing blend is obtained by solving the following LP model, where the decision vaciable T_i = the fraction of a ton of ore from location i in 1 ton of the blend.

$$\begin{aligned}
\text{Min}\quad & 800T_1 + 400T_2 + 600T_3 + 500T_4 && \text{(total cost)} \\
\text{s.t.}\quad & 10T_1 + 3T_2 + 8T_3 + 2T_4 \geq 5 && \text{(requirement on A)} \\
& 90T_1 + 150T_2 + 75T_3 + 175T_4 \geq 100 && \text{(requirement on B)} \\
& 45T_1 + 25T_2 + 20T_3 + 37T_4 \geq 30 && \text{(requirement on C)} \\
& T_1 + T_2 + T_3 + T_4 = 1 && \text{(blend condition)} \\
& T_i \geq 0, \quad i = 1, 2, 3, 4
\end{aligned}$$

Let us now discuss and analyze the computer output for the solution to this problem. Place yourself in the position of the manager who is responsible for planning future production. A number of questions are on the manager's mind. The modeler responds.

MANAGER: First of all, what is the solution to our problem?

I have run the problem on the computer, and here's the output [see Figure 6.5]. By "solution" I take it you mean the optimal values of the decision variables. These are printed in the section of output that I've labeled VARIABLES. The optimal values of the variables appear under the second column, headed VALUE. You can see that the rounded optimal values are

$$T1 = 0.26$$
$$T2 = 0.70$$
$$T3 = 0.04$$
$$T4 = 0.00$$

Figure 6.5
Output for Crawler Tread

```
MIN 800 T1 + 400 T2 + 600 T3 + 500 T4
SUBJECT TO
   2)   10 T1 + 3 T2 + 8 T3 + 2 T4 ≥ 5
   3)   90 T1 + 150 T2 + 75 T3 + 175 T4 ≥ 100
   4)   45 T1 + 25 T2 + 20 T3 + 37 T4 ≥ 30
   5)   T1 + T2 + T3 + T4 = 1
```

OBJECTIVE FUNCTION VALUE

1   511.111   OV

VARIABLE	VALUE	REDUCED COST	
T1	0.259	0.000	
T2	0.703	0.000	
T3	0.037	0.000	Variables
T4	0.000	91.111	

Optimal value of T1 → T1 0.259

ROW	SLACK OR SURPLUS	DUAL PRICES	
2	0.000	−44.444	
3	31.666	0.000	
4	0.000	−4.444	Constraints
5	0.000	−155.555	

SENSITIVITY ANALYSIS

OBJ COEFFICIENT RANGES

VARIABLE	CURRENT COEF.	ALLOWABLE INCREASE	ALLOWABLE DECREASE
T1	800.000	223.636	199.99
T2	400.000	66.847	299.999
T3	600.000	85.714	118.169
T4	500.000	INFINITY	91.111

RIGHTHAND SIDE RANGES

ROW	CURRENT RHS	ALLOWABLE INCREASE	ALLOWABLE DECREASE
2	5.000	2.375	0.250
3	100.000	31.666	INFINITY
4	30.000	0.714	7.000
5	1·000	0.250	0.043

MANAGER: How much does a ton of this blend cost?

The OV, which is the optimal value of the objective function, is also identified. You can see that the minimum cost is $511.11.

MANAGER: I'd like to keep my costs under $500 per ton. Isn't there any way I can do this?

It is impossible to find a lower-cost mixture that satisfies the constraints you have imposed.

MANAGER: You mean the requirements on essential elements?

Exactly.

159

CHAPTER 6
Linear Programs:
Computer
Analysis
and Interpreting
Sensitivity Output

MANAGER: Well, maybe I can modify those requirements. I really do want to keep my costs under $500 per ton.

Then you certainly will have to loosen your requirements. We can discuss how to do that.

MANAGER: All right. But first, I recall that the requirements were expressed as minimum threshold levels. Is there any way I can tell exactly how much of each essential element gets into the optimal mix?

That information is obtained from the second section of the output, which I've identified as CONSTRAINTS. The computer labels the four constraints of the problem as rows 2 to 5, respectively, since it regards the objective function as row 1. The first three constraints of the problem are the requirements on essential elements. This corresponds to the output labeled as rows 2, 3, and 4.

MANAGER: I see a column labeled SLACK or SURPLUS and one labeled DUAL PRICES, but where are the amounts of the essential elements in the optimal blend?

This has to be deduced. Remember that before the inequality problem was solved, the computer had to transform it to standard equality constraint form. For this model, the column labeled SLACK or SURPLUS is the optimal value of the surplus variable associated with each constraint in the transformed problem.

MANAGER: I think I see what you're getting at. The surplus in row 2 is zero. The first constraint is the requirement on A, which was 5 pounds. Since the original constraint is $\geq$, after conversion to equality form it must look like

$$10T1 + 3T2 + 8T3 + 2T4 - S1 = 5$$

Exactly.

MANAGER: Okay, and I understand what happens for rows 3 and 4. But the last constraint in the original model was an equality constraint. That means that it has neither a slack nor a surplus variable in standard form. Right?

Correct.

MANAGER: Then why is there a slack or surplus value of zero printed on the output for row 5? Doesn't that suggest there is a slack or surplus variable in that row?

You may be right, but the suggestion is unintended. For a constraint that was originally an equality the entry in this column is always zero. As you have correctly observed, the actual surplus variables in this problem are associated only with the first three constraints of the original model: that is, rows 2, 3, and 4.

MANAGER: Fine. Now let's return to the surplus variable on row 2. I see that its optimal value is zero. What does that have to do with the amount of essential element A in the final mix? I thought I saw the answer before, but now I'm confused.

It's easy. Since the optimal surplus value is zero, and since we know the other optimal values, it must be true that if we substitute the optimal values of all the variables into the equality form of the constraint we will obtain the following result:

$$10(0.259) + 3(0.703) + 8(0.037) + 2(0.000) - 0 = 5$$

In other words, since the optimal surplus value is zero, the optimal mix contains exactly 5 pounds of A.

MANAGER: I see. And since the surplus in row 4 is zero, the optimal mix must contain exactly 30 pounds of C. Is that right?

Precisely, and you can also figure out how much B there is.

MANAGER: Okay. For B, I have to look at row 3. Since the surplus is 31.666 it must be true that

$$90(0.259) + 150(0.703) + 75(0.037) + 175(0.0000) - 31.666 = 100$$

But where do I go from here?

Well, your equation means that in the optimal mix the minimum requirement of 100

160

CHAPTER 6
Linear Programs:
Computer
Analysis
and Interpreting
Sensitivity Output

pounds is actually exceeded by 31.666. That is, there are 131.666 pounds of B actually included.

MANAGER: Isn't that odd? You'd think I could make a cheaper blend by using less B. Why should I use more than 100 pounds if I need only 100?

That is a very good question. You see, the combination of ores that satisfies the requirements on A cand C at a minimum cost just happens to contain more than 100 pounds of B. Any combination of ores that includes less B will either not have enough of A and/or C, or, if it does have enough, it will cost more than $511.11 per ton. In other words, forcing yourself to include less of the excess amount of B while still satisfying the requirements on A and C will end up costing you more. You may have to think about that assertion, but it is exactly what the solution to the model is telling us.

MANAGER: Okay. I guess I can see your point. So how can I get my total cost down to $500 or less?

You will have to loosen your constraints. This means loosening the requirements on A or C.

MANAGER: Why not on B?

Because, in order to satisfy the requirements on A and C at minimum cost, you're already including over 100 pounds of B, which is more than your minimal threshold. In other words, the requirement on B is not active. You could loosen this requirement to a smaller number, such as 98, and the optimal mix would still contain the same composition and cost. Thus, loosening the requirement on B to a smaller number won't get us anywhere. You have to loosen one of the active requirements.

MANAGER: You mean one where there's zero surplus.

Precisely.

MANAGER: Okay. So I have to relax the requirement on A or C. But which one? And how much?

We can use the information under the DUAL PRICES heading to analyze these questions.

MANAGER: I was wondering what that column meant.

It means rate of improvement in the OV as we increase the right-hand side. Since we are interested in loosening a $\geq$ constraint, we will be decreasing the right-hand side. Now let's look at the dual price on row 2. It is −44.44. The negative sign means that as the right-hand side is *increased* the OV is "negatively improved," or hurt. Thus, as the right-hand side is loosened, or *decreased*, the OV is improved. What all of this boils down to is the commonsense idea that, as your requirement for A is loosened, your minimum cost will go down. The dual price tells us it goes down at the rate of $44.44 per pound.

MANAGER: Loosening the requirement for A must mean reducing it from 5 pounds to something less. Right?

Right.

MANAGER: And the dual price of −44.44 says that for each pound of reduction the cost goes down $44.44?

Right.

MANAGER: Great. This means if I require only 4 pounds per ton of A, instead of 5, the cost goes down to about $466.67 and I'm under $500. Right?

Well, not quite. But you're right in spirit. You have the correct rate of change, but this rate applies only to some *interval* of values around the original value of 5. The appropriate interval may not allow you to analyze the decrease of a whole unit—maybe only half a unit, for example.

MANAGER: Even so, if I cut the requirement to 4.5 pounds, I'd save (1/2)(44.44), which is over $22. My final cost would still be under $500!

True enough, but the allowable interval may not even include 4.5.

161

CHAPTER 6
Linear Programs:
Computer
Analysis
and Interpreting
Sensitivity Output

MANAGER: Obviously, we need to know that interval.

Right. And it appears on the bottom of the output under the section labeled RIGHTHAND SIDE RANGES.

MANAGER: I see. In the ALLOWABLE DECREASE column for row 2 we have 0.250. That must mean I can analyze a change from 5 down to 4.75. Right?

Right.

MANAGER: So my saving would be 0.25 (44.44), which is $11.11, and this gets me down exactly to $500. But what if I relaxed the requirement a little more, like to 4.50. Wouldn't that reduce the cost further?

Probably, but I can't tell you exactly how much because the rate of change may be different after a decrease of 0.25.

MANAGER: In technical language, that must mean the dual price may change.

Exactly.

MANAGER: Okay. Now just to see if I have it all straight, let me analyze the potential savings if I relax the requirement on C.

Go ahead.

MANAGER: The requirement on C is identified as row 4. The original right-hand side is 30. The output shows an allowable decrease of 7, so I can go down to 23. The dual price on row 4 is -4.44. This is my rate of savings as I decrease the right-hand side from 30. Hence, if I decrease the requirement to 23, I save

$$7(4.44) = \$31.08$$

This also gets me well under $500. In fact, if I cut down the requirement only 2.5 pounds, I can apply the same rate of change, and consequently I should save

$$(2.5)(4.44) = \$11.10$$

and this just about gets me down to a cost of $500. How am I doing?

Very well.

MANAGER: Okay. I see that I can get the cost per ton down to $500 if I relax the requirement on A to 4.75 pounds per ton *or* the requirement on C to 27.5 pounds per ton. But what if I relax both requirements on A and C, perhaps a little less but both at the same time? Then what?

Sorry, but again we don't have precise information on the output to answer that. The only way to tackle that question would be to rerun the model numerous times with different right-hand sides for A and C.

MANAGER: So when I use the dual price on one of the right-hand-side values, it's important to keep the others unchanged.

Correct.

MANAGER: So let me review this. I know that I can get my cost per ton down to $500 if I relax the requirement on A to 4.75 pounds per ton *or* the requirement on C to 27.5 pounds per ton. Which should I do?

The computer cannot give you a guideline on that. You might note that the required relaxation on A would be 0.25/5, or 5%, and on C it would be $2.5/30 = 8\frac{1}{3}\%$. But I don't know whether that is helpful. The point is that you, as the manager, have to decide on which change would do more harm to the properties of the blend. I think it probably boils down to an engineering question.

MANAGER: Yes, I think you are right and I know who to talk with about that.

Good.

MANAGER: By the way, I've also been noticing the column of your printout that says ALLOWABLE INCREASE. I would guess that pertains to increases in the right-hand side.

Right again.

162

CHAPTER 6
Linear Programs:
Computer
Analysis
and Interpreting
Sensitivity Output

MANAGER: Would you just run through the analysis on the increase side to make sure that I'm with you?

Let's take row 2, the requirement on A. Suppose that you want to tighten this requirement.

MANAGER: Since we are dealing with a $\geq$ constraint, tightening would mean an increase in the right-hand side, which is the required amount of A.

Correct. Tightening a requirement can never help the OV and may hurt. In this case the dual price of -44.44 tells us that increasing the right-hand side will hurt. This means that the cost will go up. The allowable increase of 2.375 tells us that if we increase the original amount, 5, by any amount up to 2.375, the increase in cost is given by 44.44 times that amount.

MANAGER: In other words, the same dual price pertains to both increases and decreases in the right-hand side. The allowable increase and decrease are provided by the computer, and the dual price is the rate of improvement in the objective value as the right-hand side increases over that entire allowable range. If this rate is negative, it hurts the OV.

Right. And loosening a constraint will always mean that the OV cannot be hurt and may be improved. Tightening means that the OV cannot be improved and may be hurt.

MANAGER: I even notice that the dual price on B is zero, which means that changes in the value of 100 don't have any effect. I guess that means we don't even need a constraint on B. Why is that?

Because, as I mentioned earlier, if you satisfy the requirements for A and C at a minimum cost, with our given set of data, the requirement for B will be satisfied automatically.

MANAGER: So am I correct? Could the constraint on B be discarded?

I would think not. If you would ever want to change some of the data and then rerun the model, the constraint on B could become important. So I don't really want to say that it can be removed from the model.

MANAGER: Could you be a little more explicit, without getting into a lot of terminology?

All right. Just as an example, last week, I heard from Mr. Shmootz that the cost of ore from location 2 might increase.

MANAGER: Mr. Shmootz?

Yes.

MANAGER: Well, I must admit that such a possibility is something I'm concerned about. But I don't see how we can take that kind of uncertainty into account.

This relates to your question. The cost of ore from location 2 is the coefficient of T2 in the objective function, namely 400. If this cost is increased, we would expect our OV to increase. If the cost of ore from location 2 goes up enough, we might even expect that less of it or maybe even none of it would be used in the optimal blend. This means more of the others must be used because the total amount used has to sum up to 1. This means that the relative importance of the constraints could change. Previous constraints that had been tight may not be, and vice versa. A lot of things can happen when you start playing with the data.

MANAGER: Tell me again what you mean by a tight constraint.

It means a constraint with an optimal slack or surplus value of zero. Such a constraint is also called *active*, or *binding*.

MANAGER: I'm glad you told me that. What about an equality constraint? Is it considered active or binding or whatever?

Yes. Always. In this terminology, although the constraint on B is currently inactive, it could become active if the data in the model are changed.

MANAGER: Fine. But I'm still confused. What does all this have to do with the cost of ore from location 2? Or is the whole thing just too complicated to explain?

163

CHAPTER 6
Linear Programs:
Computer
Analysis
and Interpreting
Sensitivity Output

Not at all. Let's look at the cost of ore from location 2. We can actually determine the range over which this cost can vary without influencing the optimal blend. In particular, look at the portion of output headed OBJ COEFFICIENT RANGES. In the row corresponding to T2 there is something called ALLOWABLE INCREASE and ALLOWABLE DECREASE. This gives the range in which the cost of T2 can vary.

MANAGER: You mean without changing the optimal mix?

Yes.

MANAGER: Okay. In other words, the cost of T2 is now $400 in our model. You mean that the output says it could be anywhere between $100 and $466.84 and the optimal mix stays the same?

Exactly.

MANAGER: I don't see how we can know that.

It's all in the mathematics.

MANAGER: I'll take your word for that. So if the cost increases from $400 to $450, we have nothing to worry about.

Well, I don't know about that. We know that the optimal mix will stay the same. This means that the optimal values of all the variables, including the slacks, stay the same. But our total cost will increase by 50 times the amount of T2 being used in the current solution.

MANAGER: I see. The OV will go from the old value, $511.11, to the new value

$$511.11 + 50(0.703) = \$546.26$$

Everything stays the same except the total cost. Did you say that even the surplus values stay the same?

Yes. If all the decision variables stay the same, you can see from either the geometry or the algebra that the surplus variables would have to also.

MANAGER: That must mean the constraints that are active also stay the same.

Good for you.

MANAGER: By the way, what happens if the cost of T2 increases by more than the allowable amount?

Well, since we have a cost minimization model I know from common sense that increasing the cost of an input cannot increase its use. Therefore, as the cost of T2 increases I know that the optimal value of T2 can never increase. In fact, since the current solution is nondegenerate I know that when the cost of T2 increases by more than the allowable amount, the optimal value of T2 will in fact surely decrease.

MANAGER: Wait a minute. Slow down. You said nondegenerate?

Yes. This simply means that in the computer output the number of variables with a positive optimal value, including both decision and slack or surplus variables, is equal to the number of constraints. Figure 6.5 shows that at optimality three decision variables and one surplus variable are positive. Thus there are four positive variables and four constraints, which means that we have a nondegenerate solution. This is a technicality but it is important in interpreting some of the output.

MANAGER: All right. Fine. So if the per unit cost of ore from mine 2 increases by more than its allowable amount, we will get an optimal solution with a smaller value of T2.

Yes. And not only that. The optimal values of some of the other variables may also change, but it isn't possible to say exactly which ones or how much. This means that a surplus that was positive could become zero, and hence a constraint that was inactive could become active, if you know what I mean.

MANAGER: Yes, I think I'm with you.

164

CHAPTER 6
Linear Programs:
Computer
Analysis
and Interpreting
Sensitivity Output

Good. And it could also mean that a constraint that previously had zero surplus could now become inactive in the sense that its surplus becomes positive. In other words, once the cost change exceeds the limit of the indicated range, all sorts of things can happen.

MANAGER: You're talking about a cost change that *exceeds* the allowable limit. What if it actually hits the limit?

Then, again since the current solution is nondegenerate, we know that there will be alternative optimal solutions, the current solution together with a new one which has less T2 in it.

MANAGER: Well, it seems to me that we have considerable information about the influence of uncertainty. That strikes me as remarkable.

I agree.

MANAGER: Okay. Thank you very much. I think I can do pretty well now on my own with the output analysis. We should really call it model analysis, shouldn't we?

I guess so.

MANAGER: Okay. Thanks again. I'm amazed at how much we can learn about the actual problem, above and beyond the solution.

Right. That is because of the relative simplicity of linear mathematics. By the way, do you mind if I ask you just one question to more or less check you out?

MANAGER: Okay. Shoot.

You have already noticed on the output that the optimal value of T4 is zero.

MANAGER: True.

I happen to know that ore from location 4 has some desirable tensile properties that haven't really been built into the model.

MANAGER: That is true.

Also, I understand from Mr. Shmootz that it isn't unreasonable to renegotiate the cost of T4 periodically.

MANAGER: Are you referring to the fact that PROTRAC has some family connections in the location 4 enterprise?

Something like that. But my point is this. How much would the cost of T4 have to decrease before you're willing to buy some?

MANAGER: Let's see. The current cost of T4 is $500 per ton. I think what you're trying to ask me is this: How much must this cost decrease before we obtain an optimal policy that uses T4? Is that your question?

Yes.

MANAGER: Okay. To find the answer I look at the SENSITIVITY ANALYSIS, where I see that if the cost of T4 decreases by less than $91.11 per ton, then, according to what you just said, the optimal value of this variable remains unchanged. That obviously means it remains at zero. Consequently, taking into account what you just said about nondegeneracy, I know that if its cost is negotiated down to 408.89 or less, there will be an optimal solution with T4 positive. Right?

Correct. Now can you tell me what happens to the optimal objective value?

MANAGER: I guess I can figure that out. If the cost decreases as much as $91.11, no change occurs in the optimal values of any of the variables. In the objective function only the cost of T4 is changing. But since the value of T4 stays at zero, the OV won't change either. I guess it stays at $511.11 as long as the reduction in cost is less than $91.11.

Correct.

MANAGER: But what happens if the reduction exactly equals 91.11? You've told me that in this case the optimal value of T4 will become positive. Is that right?

165

CHAPTER 6
Linear Programs:
Computer
Analysis
and Interpreting
Sensitivity Output

Not quite. There will be two optimal solutions: the current one, and another one which has a positive optimal value of T4 and some new values for some of the other variables. But I don't know exactly how the others will change.

MANAGER: Okay, but does this mean that when the cost of T4 is reduced by exactly $91.11, the total cost suddenly drops down from $511.11?

No, since these are alternative optima the OV equals 511.11 at each.

MANAGER: Can we tell how much of T4 will be used in the alternative optimum?

I'm afraid not. All we know is that there will be some positive value for this variable.

MANAGER: And how do you know all that?

From the mathematics. And remember that these statements about alternative optimal solutions depend on the nondegeneracy of the current solution on the printout.

MANAGER: Okay. Great. And I suppose that if the decrease in the cost of T4 exceeds the allowable amount, the OV will then begin to decrease.

Again this is true because of the nondegeneracy.

MANAGER: What if the nondegeneracy weren't satisfied?

Then we would have what is termed a degenerate solution. All we could say then is that the optimal solution will not change if the cost of T4 stays within the allowable range. Conceivably, the cost could decrease by *more than* 91.11 and we would still not get a new optimal solution. Thus you can see that in the degenerate case the output gives us somewhat less information.

MANAGER: Well, by now I think I know all that I need to about what's going on. Do you agree?

Yes. Shall we stop?

MANAGER: Really, since I'm doing so well, I have to ask one final question. What about that column in the first section of the output under the heading REDUCED COST?

It is really meaningful only for a decision variable whose optimal value is zero, and it has two possible interpretations. Let's concentrate on a min model. In its first interpretation, the reduced cost tells how much the per unit cost of that variable can be reduced before the optimal value of the variable will become positive.

MANAGER: We just answered that question about T4.

I know.

MANAGER: But we didn't use this column. We used the cost-sensitivity part of the output. In fact, I see that exactly the same value, 91.11, appears in both places.

Right.

MANAGER: So why bother with this reduced-cost column if the same value appears under the cost-sensitivity column?

Simply for convenience. The reduced cost pertains to variables whose optimal value is zero. You can easily spot these variables in the top section of the output. In the next column you can immediately read the reduced cost, which is a little easier than going down into the cost-sensitivity section. That's all there is to it.

MANAGER: That wasn't very exciting! What's the second interpretation?

The reduced cost is the initial rate at which the OV will be hurt if the variable is forced into the solution. In other words, if management insisted on using some T4 in its blend, the OV would *initially* increase at the rate of $91.11 per ton of T4.

MANAGER: What if I insist the blend includes 0.1 ton of T4? Will the new OV be 511.11 + (0.1)(91.11)?

We can't be sure. We only know that the initial rate of change is 91.11. The solution doesn't tell us if this rate holds for 0.05, 0.1, 0.2 ton or what.

166

CHAPTER 6
Linear Programs:
Computer
Analysis
and Interpreting
Sensitivity Output

MANAGER: O.K. Just one more question. Does reduced cost apply only to a min model?

Not at all. Suppose that you had a max model with an optimal value of zero for one of the decision variables. Why is it zero?

MANAGER: Because its profitability is too small.

Exactly. And the reduced cost tells us how much the per unit profitability of that variable can be increased before the optimal value of that variable will become positive.

MANAGER: Thank you. It's been very instructive!

My pleasure. And one final point. Whenever you have a degenerate output, all of your interpretations of cost sensitivity, reduced cost, and alternative optima must be slightly qualified, as we mentioned above. But let's dig into that later.

6.5
A SYNOPSIS OF THE SOLUTION OUTPUT

When a linear program is solved, the computer output contains the following information:

Optimal
Values

1. Optimal values are given for the decision variables, the slack and surplus variables, and the objective function. From the optimal value of the slack and surplus variables you can quickly deduce the values of the constraint functions (the amount of resources used, the levels of requirements satisfied, etc.) at an optimal solution. The constraints with zero slack or surplus are called **active**, or **binding**, or **tight**. Those with positive slack or surplus are called **inactive**.

Dual Price
and RHS
Ranges

2. The **dual price** on the ith constraint is the **rate of improvement in the OV** (optimal value of the objective function) as the right-hand side of that constraint *increases*, with all other data kept fixed. If the RHS is *decreased*, the dual price is the rate at which the OV is impaired. "Improvement" means increase in a max model and decrease in a min model. RIGHTHAND SIDE RANGES gives you an allowable range in right-hand-side (RHS) changes over which the dual price on the printout is valid. Outside this allowable range the dual price may change to a different value. If the units of the objective function are dollars and the units of the ith RHS are pounds, then the ith dual price is in units of dollars per pound. If the units of the jth RHS are hours, then the units of the jth dual price are dollars per hour. The **dual price** is also frequently referred to as a **shadow price**, or an **imputed price**.

2a. It follows from the foregoing interpretation of dual price that the dual price of an inactive constraint will always be zero.

2b. Note that the RHS sensitivity information tells us nothing about how the optimal solution (i.e., the optimal values of the decision variables) changes. It merely explains the way in which the OV will change as the RHS on a particular constraint changes.

2c. In a degenerate solution, some of the dual prices will have either a zero allowable increase or a zero allowable decrease. Thus, in the degenerate case, we obtain more limited information in the sense of learning only about the effect on the OV of "one-sided" changes in the RHS.

Objective
Coefficient
Ranges

3. OBJ COEFFICIENT RANGES tells you the allowable changes that can be made in the objective function coefficients without changing the optimal solution (the optimal values of the variables). In interpreting this portion of the output you must be careful to distinguish between the cases of a degenerate versus a nondegenerate solution.

Nondegenerate Solution

3a. The columns "ALLOWABLE INCREASE" and "ALLOWABLE DE-CREASE," under the "OBJ COEFFICIENT RANGES" heading, tell you how much the coefficient c_j of a given variable x_j in the objective function may be increased or decreased without changing the current optimal solution,[4] where all other data are assumed to be fixed. As the profitability varies in this range the OV values may or may not change, depending on whether or not x_j^* is positive.

3b. When the coefficient c_j is changed by less than the allowable amounts, the current optimal solution will remain optimal.

3c. When c_j is increased by its allowable amount, there will be a new alternative optimal solution with, for a max model, a larger optimal value for the variable x_j. (For a min model, increasing c_j the allowable amount will produce an alternative optimum with a lower optimal value for x_j.)

3d. When the coefficient c_j is decreased by its allowable amount, there will be a new alternative optimal solution with x_j having a lower (higher) optimal value for a max (min) model.

3e. When you see, for some variable in the "OBJ COEFFICIENT RANGES" section of the output, a zero entry under either of the columns "ALLOWABLE INCREASE" or "ALLOWABLE DECREASE," you know that there is at least one alternative optimal solution to the problem at hand. Moreover, whenever there are alternative optima such a signal will appear. *Remember that all of these statements apply to a printout showing a nondegenerate optimal solution.*

The signal for alternative optima is illustrated in Figure 6.6, a hypothetical maximization LP in two decision variables and three inequality constraints. The objective function contour is parallel to the second constraint (labeled ②) and in employing the graphic solution technique you can see that the corners labeled I and II are alternative optima for this problem. The computer, because of the algorithm it employs to solve the prob-

Illustrating Alternative Optima

Figure 6.6
Alternative Optima

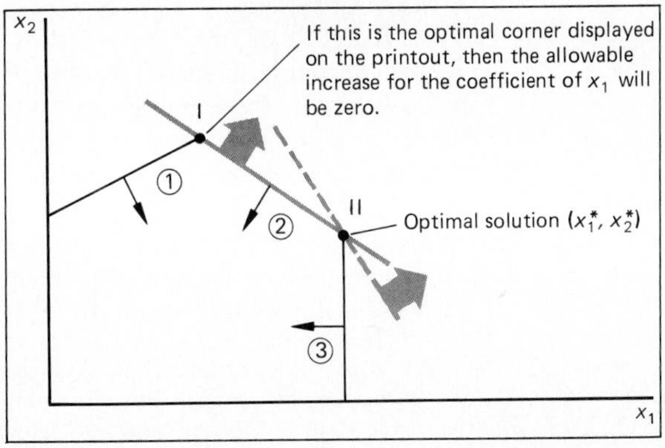

If this is the optimal corner displayed on the printout, then the allowable increase for the coefficient of x_1 will be zero.

Optimal solution (x_1^*, x_2^*)

[4]The term "current optimal solution" refers to the optimal solution presented in the computer output. If there are alternative optima, the "current optimal solution" will be one of the many optima.

167

168

CHAPTER 6
Linear Programs:
Computer
Analysis
and Interpreting
Sensitivity Output

lem, will find only one of these corners as an optimal solution and (as implied by footnote 4) the computer output applies only to that corner. Let us suppose that corner I is the solution found by the computer. The geometry in Figure 6.6 shows that any increase in the coefficient of x_1 will change the objective function contour to a tilt like that of the dashed line. Now corner I is no longer optimal, and corner II which was previously an alternative optimum now becomes a unique optimal solution. The computer output for the solution at corner I would have, as a signal for this phenomenon, a zero value next to x_1 under the "ALLOWABLE INCREASE" column.

Let us now consider the case of a printout showing a **degenerate optimal solution**. In this case there are two caveats that must be observed.

**Degenerate
Solution**

FOR A DEGENERATE SOLUTION:

3f. The signals described above for alternative optima should be ignored.

3g. As long as an objective function coefficient is varied in the indicated range the current optimal solution will remain optimal. This was also true in the nondegenerate case. In the latter case, however, new alternative optima were obtained when the coefficient was changed to the limit of its range.[5] In the degenerate case this can be no longer guaranteed. All we can say is that any objective function coefficient must be changed by **at least**, and **possibly more than**, the indicated allowable amounts in order to produce an alternative optimal solution.

**Reduced
Cost**

4. REDUCED COST output is another instance of where, in order to give a correct interpretation, you must first observe whether or not the optimal solution is nondegenerate.

**Nondegenerate
Case**

FOR A NONDEGENERATE SOLUTION:

4a. The reduced cost of any particular decision variable is defined to be *the amount the coefficient of that variable in the objective function would have changed in order to have a positive optimal value for that variable*. Thus, if a variable is already positive at optimality, its reduced cost is zero (as in the case for T1, T2, and T3 in Figure 6.5). If the optimal value of a variable is zero, then from the definition of reduced cost you can see that the reduced cost is either the "ALLOWABLE INCREASE" or "ALLOWABLE DECREASE" for the objective function coefficient of the given variable (one of these values will be infinite; the other will be the reduced cost). Whether or not the coefficient of a variable must be increased or decreased to bring that variable into the solution at a positive level depends on whether the model is "max" or "min." For

---

[5]In two dimensions, as the geometry clearly illustrates, exactly one alternative optimum corner solution will be introduced, in the nondegenerate case, when an objective function coefficient is changed to the limit of its range (e.g., when the dashed line in Figure 6.6 is rotated counterclockwise to create optima at I and II). In higher dimensions it is possible that several alternative optima corner solutions can be created simultaneously. Also, in two dimensions, it is clear that a change by more than the allowable amount (in the nondegenerate case) will produce a new optimal solution which is unique (e.g., a counterclockwise rotation of the dashed line in Figure 6.6, beyond the point at which I and II are optimal, creates a unique optimum at I). Again it should be mentioned that this reasoning does not extend to higher dimensions. In other words, in more than two dimensions a change by more than the allowable amount may retain several optimal corner solutions.

169

CHAPTER 6
Linear Programs:
Computer
Analysis
and Interpreting
Sensitivity Output

example, in Figure 6.5, T4* is zero. Since the problem is a min model, the reduced cost of 91.111 is the same as the allowable decrease for the coefficient of T4. This is the amount we would have to *decrease* the current coefficient to obtain an alternative optimal solution with a positive value for T4. And of course if the coefficient of T4 is made any amount greater than its current value of 500 (making this ore even more costly) then the optimal value of T4 would surely remain at zero. This is why the allowable increase for this coefficient is infinity. In a max model, interpretations are appropriately modified. The reduced cost would be the same as the allowable increase (i.e., increase in per unit profitability), and the allowable decrease would be infinity.

4b. Another equivalent interpretation of reduced cost, for a nondegenerate solution, can be given. In a nondegenerate solution, the reduced cost of a decision variable (whose optimal value is currently zero) is the rate (per unit amount) at which the objective value is hurt as that variable is "forced into" (i.e., is forced to assume positive values in) an optimal solution. In Figure 6.5, with T4* = 0, the OV would increase if we forced ourselves to find an optimal solution with the *additional* constraint that T4* = 0.1. (To see that the OV would increase you need merely recognize that in the current model the optimal value of T4 is zero. Forcing T4 to be 0.1, then, could not possibly give us a lower total cost.) This **rate of increase** as T4 is initially forced to be positive would be given by the reduced cost of T4.

FOR A DEGENERATE SOLUTION:

Degenerate Case

4c. Again we consider a decision variable whose optimal value is zero. In the degenerate case, the coefficient of that variable in the objective function must be changed by *at least*, and *possibly more than*, the reduced cost in order for there to be an optimal solution with that variable appearing at a positive level.

This completes our exploration of the meaning of each entry in the computer output. This discussion has been introductory, and more geometric insights will be given in Chapter 7. But if you have mastered the material presented from Chapter 4 up to this point, you are now able to use LP in a knowledgeable way in practical situations. You have learned to formulate problems, solve them on a computer, and correctly interpret the output. In concluding, it is to be noted that the format used for the solution of LP problems differs in minor details from one software package to another. However, a solid understanding of one system prepares you to deal with any system with a minimum of effort.

6.6

EXAMPLES AND SOLUTIONS

Example 1

Use slack and surplus variables as required to convert the following LP problem to standard equality-constraint form.

170

CHAPTER 6
Linear Programs:
Computer
Analysis
and Interpreting
Sensitivity Output

$$\text{Min} \quad 7x_1 + 5x_2 - 9x_3 + x_6$$

$$
\begin{aligned}
\text{s.t.} \quad & 12x_1 - 2x_4 & \geq & \quad 13x_3 - 29 \\
& -4x_2 + 5x_3 + 7x_5 \leq 6x_2 + 3x_4 + 15 \\
& x_1 + x_2 + x_3 & = & \quad x_4 + x_5 - x_6 \\
& x_4 + 7x_6 & \leq & \quad 92 \\
& x_i \geq 0 \quad i = 1, 2, 3, 4, 5, 6
\end{aligned}
$$

Solution to Example 1

$$\text{Min} \quad 7x_1 + 5x_2 - 9x_3 + x_6$$

$$
\begin{aligned}
\text{s.t.} \quad 12x_1 \quad - 13x_3 - 2x_4 \quad - s_1 &= -29 \\
- 10x_2 + 5x_3 - 3x_4 + 7x_5 + s_2 &= 15 \\
x_1 + x_2 + x_3 - x_4 - x_5 + x_6 &= 0 \\
x_4 + 7x_6 + s_3 &= 92 \\
x_i \geq 0 \quad i &= 1, \ldots, 6 \\
s_i \geq 0 \quad i &= 1, 2, 3
\end{aligned}
$$

Example 2

Consider a profit-maximizing LP problem with 100 variables, 50 constraints of the $\leq$ form, and 20 constraints of the $\geq$ form. Use slack and surplus variables as required to convert the problem to standard equality-constraint form and express the result with summation notation. Let c_j denote the objective function coefficients, b_i denote the right-hand sides, and a_{ij} the coefficients of the variables x_j in the constraints.

Solution to Example 2

$$\text{Max} \quad \sum_{j=1}^{100} c_j x_j$$

$$
\begin{aligned}
\text{s.t.} \quad \sum_{j=1}^{100} a_{ij}x_j + s_i = b_i \quad & i = 1, 2, \ldots, 50 \\
\sum_{j=1}^{100} a_{ij}x_j - s_i = b_i \quad & i = 51, \ldots, 70 \\
x_j \geq 0 \quad & j = 1, \ldots, 100 \\
s_i \geq 0 \quad & i = 1, \ldots, 70
\end{aligned}
$$

An alternative but equivalent formulation is

$$\text{Max} \quad \sum_{j=1}^{100} c_j x_j$$

$$
\begin{aligned}
\text{s.t.} \quad \sum_{j=1}^{100} a_{ij}x_j + x_{100+i} = b_i \quad & i = 1, \ldots, 50 \\
\sum_{j=1}^{100} a_{ij}x_j - x_{100+i} = b_i \quad & i = 51, \ldots, 70 \\
x_j \geq 0 \quad & j = 1, \ldots, 170
\end{aligned}
$$

Example 3

Consider the problem

$$\text{Min} \quad 5x_1 + 2x_2$$
$$\text{s.t.} \quad 3x_1 + 6x_2 \geq 18$$
$$5x_1 + 4x_2 \geq 20$$
$$8x_1 + 2x_2 \geq 16$$
$$7x_1 + 6x_2 \leq 42$$
$$x_1, x_2 \geq 0$$

Change the problem into standard equality form. Plot the feasible set and indicate which variables are nonzero at each corner.

Solution to Example 3

$$\text{Min} \quad 5x_1 + 2x_2$$
$$\text{s.t.} \quad 3x_1 + 6x_2 - s_1 \qquad\qquad = 18$$
$$5x_1 + 4x_2 \quad - s_2 \qquad\quad = 20$$
$$8x_1 + 2x_2 \qquad\quad - s_3 \quad\; = 16$$
$$7x_1 + 6x_2 \qquad\qquad\quad + s_4 = 42$$
$$x_1, x_2, s_1, s_2, s_3, s_4 \geq 0$$

The feasible set is shown in Figure 6.7. The positive variables at each corner are also indicated.

Figure 6.7

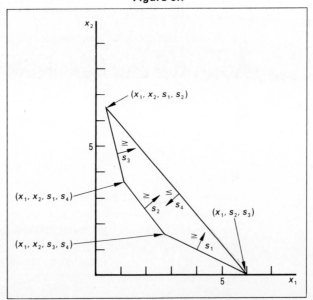

171

Example 4

Is the solution to the problem in Example 3 degenerate? Which variables are positive in the solution to the problem? Which slacks are zero?

Solution to Example 4

The optimal solution is the corner determined by the second and third constraints. Hence, the solution is *not* degenerate since there are as many positive variables in the solution (four) as there are constraints in the model. The positive variables are x_1, x_2, s_1, and s_4. Note that both decision variables are positive and two of the slack variables are positive. The zero slacks correspond to the active constraints. Hence, they are s_2 and s_3.

Example 5

Change the min to a max in Example 3, and answer the questions posed in Example 4.

Solution to Example 5

When the objective is to maximize $5x_1 + 2x_2$, the solution is $x_1 = 6$ and $x_2 = 0$. At this point there are only three positive variables in the solution, x_1, s_2, and s_3. Since there are four constraints and only three positive variables, the solution is degenerate. The zero slacks in this case are s_1 and s_4.

Example 6

Recall the Astro/Cosmo problem from Section 3.4. The situation has changed. In particular the chassis is now purchased. The new formulation and the computer solution to this problem are presented in Figure 6.8.

(a) What are the optimal values of the decision variables?

(b) What profit will be attained from the optimal solution?

(c) Does the firm have any excess capacity? If so, how much excess capacity exists, and where?

(d) How much will the optimal value of the objective function change if the capacity of the Astro line is increased from 70 to 72? Will the value of the objective function increase or decrease?

(e) How much will the value of the objective function change if the capacity of the Cosmo line is decreased from 50 to 40? Will the value of the objective function increase or decrease?

(f) If labor capacity could be expanded by 10 labor hours per day for a cost of $10 per labor hour *or* the capacity of the Astro line could be expanded by 16 sets per day at a cost of $2 per set, which alternative would you choose?

(g) What is the current rate of change in the optimal value of the objective function as the capacity of the Astro line changes? Over what set of values for the capacity of the Astro line does this rate hold?

(h) What happens to the optimal production plan if the profitability of a Cosmo set increases from $30 to $35? What happens to the optimal value of the objective function?

173

CHAPTER 6
Linear Programs:
Computer
Analysis
and Interpreting
Sensitivity Output

Figure 6.8
Computer Solution to Astro/Cosmo Production Problem

```
MAX 20A + 30C
SUBJECT TO
   2)   A ≤ 70
   3)   C ≤ 50
   4)   A + 2C ≤ 120
```

OBJECTIVE FUNCTION VALUE
2150.000

VARIABLE	VALUE	REDUCED COST
A	70.000	0.000
C	25.000	0.000

ROW	SLACK OR SURPLUS	DUAL PRICE
2	0.000	5.000
3	25.000	0.000
4	0.000	15.000

SENSITIVITY ANALYSIS

OBJ COEFFICIENT RANGES

VARIABLE	CURRENT COEF	ALLOWABLE INCREASE	ALLOWABLE DECREASE
A	20	INFINITE	5.000
C	30	10.000	30.000

RIGHTHAND SIDE RANGES

ROW	CURRENT RHS	ALLOWABLE INCREASE	ALLOWABLE DECREASE
2	70	50.000	50.000
3	50	INFINITE	25.000
4	120	50.000	50.000

(i) What happens to the optimal production plan and the optimal value of the objective function if the profitability of an Astro set decreases by $2?

Solution to Example 6

(a) The optimal values of A and C are 70 and 25, respectively.

(b) Profit equals $2150.

(c) Yes. The firm has excess capacity of 25 sets on the Cosmo line.

(d) The optimal value of the objective function will increase by 2($5) = $10.

(e) The optimal value of the objective function will not change because the dual price on row 3 is zero, and this value holds for a decrease of up to 25 units.

(f) The increase in the optimal value of the objective function from expanding labor capacity by 10 hours per day would be 10($15) = $150. The cost would be $10(10) = $100 and thus a net increase of $50 would result from this change. A net increase of 16($5) − 16($2) = $48 results from expanding the capacity of the Astro line by 16 sets per day. Thus, the correct choice is to expand labor capacity.

174

CHAPTER 6
Linear Programs:
Computer
Analysis
and Interpreting
Sensitivity Output

(g) The current rate of change is \$5 per Astro set. This rate holds for an increase or a decrease of 50 sets; thus, it holds for a line capacity of anywhere between 20 and 120 sets.

(h) The optimal production plan remains the same, but the optimal value of the objective function increases by \$125.

(i) The optimal production plan remains the same, but the optimal value of the objective function decreases by $70(\$2) = \$140$.

Example 7

A farmer who has specialized in chickens and eggs adjusts the size of her flock on a monthly basis. Let $h_t I_t$ be the *profit* of having I_t chickens on hand at the end of month t. Shortly before the end of month t, she may either buy or sell chickens for c_t dollars each. During month t she cannot sell more chickens than she had on hand at the end of the previous month. She cannot have more than 2000 chickens on hand at the end of any month. Let I_o be a constant denoting the number of chickens on hand initially (i.e., at the end of month 0). The farmer would like to know how many chickens to buy (or sell) in each month in order to maximize her profit over the next T periods.

(a) Let z_t be the number of chickens bought just before the end of month t. A negative value of z_t will indicate that chickens are sold. Formulate the farmer's problem as an LP model with variable z_t unconstrained in sign.

(b) Transform the problem in part (a) into an LP problem with all variables non-negative. How does the farmer obtain the optimal values of z_t from the solution to this transformed model?

Solution to Example 7

(a)
$$\text{Max} \sum_{t=1}^{T} (h_t I_t - c_t z_t)$$

$$
\begin{aligned}
\text{s.t.} \quad & I_t = I_{t-1} + z_t && t = 1, \ldots, T \\
& I_t \leq 2000 && t = 1, \ldots, T \\
& I_t \geq 0 && t = 1, \ldots, T
\end{aligned}
$$

(b)
$$\text{Let } z_t = x_t - y_t.$$

$$\text{Max} \sum_{t=1}^{T} (h_t I_t - c_t x_t + c_t y_t)$$

$$
\begin{aligned}
\text{s.t.} \quad & I_t = I_{t-1} + x_t - y_t && t = 1, \ldots, T \\
& I_t \leq 2000 && t = 1, \ldots, T \\
& I_t, x_t, y_t \geq 0
\end{aligned}
$$

The optimal values of z_t, say z_t^*, are obtained by computing $z_t^* = x_t^* - y_t^*$, where x_t^* and y_t^* are optimal values of x_t and y_t in the model above.

Example 8

The PROTRAC E and F production problem is:

$$\text{Max} \quad 5000E + 4000F$$

s.t.	$E + F \geq 5$	(1)
	$10E + 15F \leq 150$	(2)
	$20E + 10F \leq 160$	(3)
	$30E + 10F \geq 135$	(4)
	$E - 3F \leq 0$	(5)
	$E, F \geq 0$	

(a) Assuming the sign convention stated in the text, what can you say about the dual prices associated with constraints (1) and (2)? That is, will they be ≥ 0 or ≤ 0?

(b) Suppose that rather than maximizing profit, this problem was formulated as a cost-minimization problem. Specifically, assume that the objective is to min $2000E + 3000F$ subject to the same constraints. Now what is the answer to the questions posed in part (a)?

(c) Does "impairing" the optimal value of the objective function mean that it becomes larger or smaller?

Solution to Example 8

(a) The dual price for constraint (1) will be ≤ 0 since *increasing* the right-hand side tightens the constraint and hence cannot help the optimal value of the objective function. The dual price for constraint (2) will be ≥ 0 since *increasing* the right-hand side loosens the constraint and hence cannot hurt the optimal value of the objective function.

(b) The answers remain the same. The sign of the dual prices is not influenced by whether the model is a maximization or a minimization problem.

(c) The answer to this question depends upon whether the problem is max or min. If the objective is max, then impairing means making it smaller. If the objective is min, then impairing means making it larger.

6.7
MAJOR CONCEPTS QUIZ

True–False

1. **T F** Any inequality constraint can be converted to an equivalent equality constraint by properly introducing slack or surplus variables which are unconstrained in sign.

2. **T F** Suppose that a $\leq$ constraint is converted to an equality. If a point does not satisfy the $\leq$ constraint, the associated slack value is negative.

176

CHAPTER 6
Linear Programs:
Computer
Analysis
and Interpreting
Sensitivity Output

3. **T F** We have an LP in n decision variables with $m > n$ inequality constraints (no equality constraints). The optimal solution is nondegenerate. Then the number of active constraints is at most n.

4. **T F** Degeneracy is important because we must give more restrictive interpretations to the computer output when the optimal solution is degenerate.

5. **T F** Dual price, for a given constraint, is the rate of "change" in OV as the RHS increases.

6. **T F** The dual price on the ith constraint is a nonconstant linear function of b_i over the range given by allowable decrease and allowable increase.

7. **T F** The manager says, "I have a profit-maximizing LP model. The current optimal solution says to make 7.6 super-widgets, whose per unit profitability is $210.20. If we can reduce costs so as to increase per unit profitability, the new optimal solution will obviously have us producing more than 7.6."

8. **T F** Consider the standard equality constraint form of the model. At any point on the boundary of the constraint set at least 1 variable in the problem has the value zero.

9. **T F** Before submitting your problem to the computer, you must change it to standard equality constraint form.

10. **T F** Positive slack variables at optimality indicate redundant constraints.

11. **T F** A $\leq$ constraint with positive optimal slack will always have an infinite allowable increase for the RHS.

The following questions refer to the computer output shown in Figure 6.5.

12. **T F** If the requirements on A and C are each increased by 0.5 pound, sensitivity analysis tells us that the optimal cost will increase by $24.44.

13. **T F** The fact that the dual prices are all ≤ 0 is explained by the fact that we are dealing with a min model.

Multiple Choice

14. Conversion to the standard equality constraint form
    a. is entirely automatic and hence can be done by the computer
    b. must be performed before the problem can be solved because this is the form of the problem solved by the simplex algorithm
    c. leads to an important observation about the number of positive variables in the computer solution
    d. all of the above

15. A degenerate optimal solution
    a. has less than m positive variables (where m is the number of constraints)
    b. provides no information on alternative optima
    c. may not provide information on the full range of allowable increase and allowable decrease in objective coefficients
    d. all of the above

16. "Improvement" means
    a. the OV is increased for a max model
    b. the OV is decreased for a min model
    c. both a and b

17. For a nondegenerate optimal solution to a max model, if the objective function coefficient c_1 increases by (exactly) the allowable increase,
    a. the OV may change
    b. the previous optimal solution remains optimal
    c. there will be a new optimal solution with a larger optimal value of x_1
    d. all of the above

18. We have just solved a cost min model, the solution is nondegenerate and $x_1^* = 0$. Management wants to know: "How much does the cost of x_1 have to be reduced before we will begin to use it at a positive level in an optimal solution?" The answer appears in which portion of the printout?
    a. values of variables
    b. allowable changes in RHS of first constraint
    c. allowable increase in the coefficient of x_1
    d. reduced cost

177

CHAPTER 6
Linear Programs:
Computer
Analysis
and Interpreting
Sensitivity Output

19. We have an optimal solution to a nondegenerate model with $x_3^* = 0$. Change the objective function coefficient of x_3 by the reduced cost.
    a. There will be a new unique optimal solution with $x_3^* > 0$.
    b. The OV will not change.
    c. The OV will change.
    d. There will be a new solution with $x_3^* = 0$.

20. We have an LP in n decision variables with $m > n$ inequality constraints (no equality constraints). The optimal solution is nondegenerate. The number of inactive constraints is
    a. $m - n$
    b. at most $m - n$
    c. at least $m - n$
    d. m

21. We have a cost min problem with a degenerate solution and $x_1^* = 0$.
    a. If we decrease the objective function coefficient of x_1 by the allowable decrease, there will be an alternative optimal solution with $x_1^* > 0$.
    b. If we decrease the objective function coefficient of x_1 by the reduced cost, there will be an alternative optimal solution with $x_1^* > 0$.
    c. The allowable increase on the objective function of x_1 is infinite.
    d. All of the above.

22. Consider the standard equality constraint form. Suppose that the first constraint, evaluated at a given point P_0, has a zero value for the slack variable. Then
    a. P_0 lies on the boundary of the feasible region
    b. P_0 lies on the first constraint line
    c. both a and b

23. A correct relationship is:
    a. a constraint with zero dual price must be inactive
    b. a constraint with positive dual price must be active
    c. both a and b

The following questions refer to the computer output shown in Figure 6.5.

24. If the requirement on A is changed from 5 to 6.5,
    a. the OV will decrease by $66.66
    b. the OV will improve by $66.66
    c. the OV will increase by $66.66
    d. the OV will not change

25. If the requirement on C is reduced from 30 to 20,
    a. the OV will decrease by $44.44
    b. the OV will increase by $44.44
    c. the OV will improve

26. If the cost of ore from location 2 is decreased to $300 per ton,
    a. the OV will not change
    b. the optimal solution will not change
    c. neither a nor b
    d. both a and b

27. If the cost of ore from location 1 is reduced to $680 per ton,
    a. there will be a new optimal solution with T.1* > 0.259
    b. there will be alternative optima
    c. the current optimal solution remains optimal
    d. all of the above

Answers

1. F	10. F	19. b
2. T	11. T	20. c
3. T	12. F	21. c
4. T	13. F	22. b
5. F	14. d	23. b
6. F	15. d	24. c
7. F	16. c	25. c
8. T	17. d	26. b
9. F	18. d	27. d

6-1. Use slack and surplus variables as required to convert the following LP problem to standard equality-constraint form.

$$\text{Max} \quad 2x_1 - x_3 + 14x_6$$
$$\text{s.t.} \quad 3x_1 - 2.4x_2 + 12x_3 - 10 \leq \qquad\qquad -29x_4$$
$$-x_1 + x_5 + 41x_6 \geq \qquad\quad 22 + 6x_5$$
$$-12 + x_2 + 33x_4 + 16x_5 = 8 - 13x_3 - x_6$$
$$3x_2 - 24x_6 \leq \qquad\qquad 18$$
$$x_i \geq \qquad\qquad 0 \qquad i = 1, 2, 3, 4, 5, 6$$

6-2. Consider a linear program with m inequality constraints and n variables, where $m > n$. Show that when this problem is transformed to standard equality-constraint form, the number of variables will exceed the number of constraints; that is, there will be more than m variables.

6-3. Use summation notation to write a cost-minimizing LP problem with 200 variables, 160 constraints of the form $\leq$, and 60 constraints of the form $\geq$. Let c_j denote the objective function coefficients, b_i denote the right-hand sides, and a_{ij} the coefficients of the variables x_j in the constraints. Use slack and surplus variables as required to convert to standard equality-constraint form and express the result with summation notation.

6-4. Consider the following problem:

$$\text{Max} \quad 4x_1 + x_2$$
$$\text{s.t.} \quad 3x_1 + 2x_2 - x_3 \leq 0$$
$$x_1 - 3x_2 \qquad \geq 14$$
$$x_1, x_3 \geq 0$$

Thus, the variable x_2 is unconstrained in sign. Replace x_2 with $y_1 - y_2$, $y_1 \geq 0$, $y_2 \geq 0$ to convert this problem to an equivalent form in which all variables are nonnegative. Then convert the latter model to a problem in standard equality-constraint form, with all variables denoted by the symbol z_j (replace x's, y's, and so on, with z's).

6-5. Consider the following problem:

$$\text{Min} \quad 3y + 4x$$
$$\text{s.t.} \quad 2x + 6y \geq 12$$
$$5x + 2y \leq 25$$
$$7x + 7y \leq 49$$
$$21x + 3y \geq 42$$
$$x, y \geq 0$$

(a) Let s_i be the slack or surplus variable in constraint i and write the problem in standard equality-constraint form.

(b) Plot the equality constraint representation of the model.

(c) Starting with the corner that has the largest value of y and moving in a clockwise direction, label the corners with roman numerals.

(d) Identify the variables that are zero and those that are positive at each corner.

(e) Is there a degenerate corner in the problem? Why?

(f) Find the values for *all variables* (including surplus and slacks) in the optimal solution.

(g) Use the geometric representation (not algebra) obtained in part (b) to specify the appropriate sign for the variables s_1, s_2, s_3 and s_4 if $x = y = 5$.

(h) Find the value for s_1 if $x = 3$ and $y = 1$. Explain why s_1 assumes this particular value.

179

CHAPTER 6
Linear Programs:
Computer
Analysis
and Interpreting
Sensitivity Output

6-6. Add the constraint

$$3x + 2y \leq 17\frac{2}{3}$$

to the model in Problem 6-5. Verify that it passes through corner II.
(a) Where is the new optimal solution?
(b) How many variables (including surplus and slacks) will be positive at the optimal solution?
(c) Indicate which variables will be zero and which will be positive at the optimal solution.
(d) Is there a degenerate corner in this problem?
(e) Is the optimal solution degenerate?
(f) Is there a redundant constraint? If so, which one?

6-7. Consider adding the constraint $x + y \geq 3.2$ to the model in Problem 6-5.
(a) How many variables (including surplus and slacks) will be positive at the optimal solution?
(b) Indicate which variables will be zero and which will be positive.
(c) Is there a degenerate corner in this problem?
(d) Are there alternative optima?

Interpreting
the Computer
Solution

6-8. The solution to the first formulation of the Diablo/Red Baron problem (Example 13 of Section 4.9) is shown in Figure 6.9. Use this solution to answer the following questions.
(a) How many quarts of Diablo are produced?

Figure 6.9

Diablo/Red Baron

```
MAX      3.35 D + 2.85 R − 1.6 A1 − 1.6 A2 − 2.05 B1 − 2.05 B2
SUBJECT TO
         2)  −D + A1 + B1 = 0
         3)  −R + A2 + B2 = 0
         4)   A1 + A2 ≤ 40
         5)   B1 + B2 ≤ 30
         6)  −0.25 D + A1 ≥ 0
         7)  −0.5 D + B1 ≥ 0
         8)  −0.75 R + A2 ≤ 0

              OBJECTIVE FUNCTION VALUE
         1)          99.000

VARIABLE           VALUE          REDUCED COST
       D          50.000             0.000
       R          20.000             0.000
      A1          25.000             0.000
      A2          15.000             0.000
      B1          25.000             0.000
      B2           5.000             0.000

   ROW       SLACK OR SURPLUS      DUAL PRICES
       2)          0.000             −2.350
       3)          0.000             −4.350
       4)          0.000              0.750
       5)          0.000              2.300
       6)         12.500              0.000
       7)          0.000             −2.000
       8)          0.000              2.000
```

180

CHAPTER 6
Linear Programs:
Computer
Analysis
and Interpreting
Sensitivity Output

Figure 6.9 (Cont.)

```
                    SENSITIVITY ANALYSIS

                 OBJ COEFFICIENT RANGES
               CURRENT      ALLOWABLE      ALLOWABLE
 VARIABLE       COEF        INCREASE       DECREASE
      D         3.350        0.750          0.500
      R         2.850        0.500          0.375
     A1        -1.600        1.500          0.667
     A2        -1.600        0.667          0.500
     B1        -2.050        1.500          1.000
     B2        -2.050        1.000          1.500

                 RIGHTHAND SIDE RANGES
               CURRENT      ALLOWABLE      ALLOWABLE
  ROW           RHS         INCREASE       DECREASE
      2         0.000       10.000         10.000
      3         0.000       16.667          3.333
      4        40.000       50.000         10.000
      5        30.000       10.000         16.667
      6         0.000       12.500         INFINITY
      7         0.000        6.250          5.000
      8         0.000        2.500         12.500
```

(b) How much profit does the firm make on these two products?

(c) Will the dual price on row 4 be ≥ 0, or ≤ 0? Why? Answer the same question about row 6.

(d) What *additional* amount should the firm be willing to pay to have another quart of ingredient B available? What is the *total* amount the firm should be willing to pay for one additional quart of B?

(e) How much can the price of Diablo increase before the composition of the current optimal blend changes?

(f) How would you explain to your nonmathematical boss the purpose of row 6 and how well the current solution satisfies the condition imposed in this constraint?

6-9. The solution to Example 15 of Section 4.9 is shown in Figure 6.10. Use this solution to answer the following questions.

(a) How many units of model B are produced?

(b) What is the total profit obtained from the optimal plan?

(c) Will the sign of the dual price associated with row 3 be ≥ 0 or ≤ 0? Explain your answer.

(d) How much per unit does the firm pay for its decision to satisfy the minimum weekly production requirement for model C? Over how large a decrease would this cost hold?

Figure 6.10

Producing Tape Recorders

```
MAX       15 A + 40 B + 60 C
SUBJECT TO
       2)     A ≥ 25
       3)     B ≥ 130
       4)     C ≥ 55
       5)    0.333 A + 0.208 B + 0.5 C ≤ 130
       6)    0.25 A + 0.333 B + 0.75 C ≤ 170
       7)    0.083 A + 0.167 B + 0.333 C ≤ 52
```

181

CHAPTER 6
Linear Programs:
Computer
Analysis
and Interpreting
Sensitivity Output

Figure 6.10 (Cont.)

```
              OBJECTIVE FUNCTION VALUE
     1)              11246.257

VARIABLE         VALUE         REDUCED COST
    A            25.000           0.000
    B           189.281           0.000
    C            55.000           0.000

  ROW        SLACK OR SURPLUS     DUAL PRICES
    2)            0.000             -4.880
    3)           59.281             0.000
    4)            0.000            -19.760
    5)           54.804             0.000
    6)           59.469             0.000
    7)            0.000            239.521


              SENSITIVITY ANALYSIS

            OBJ COEFFICIENT RANGES
              CURRENT     ALLOWABLE     ALLOWABLE
VARIABLE       COEF       INCREASE      DECREASE
    A         15.000       4.880        INFINITY
    B         40.000      INFINITY       9.819
    C         60.000      19.760        INFINITY

            RIGHTHAND SIDE RANGES
              CURRENT     ALLOWABLE     ALLOWABLE
  ROW          RHS        INCREASE      DECREASE
    2         25.000      119.277       25.000
    3        130.000       59.281       INFINITY
    4         55.000       29.730       55.000
    5        130.000      INFINITY      54.804
    6        170.000      INFINITY      59.469
    7         52.000       29.824        9.900
```

(e) How much can the profitability of model B decrease before the optimal production plan would change?

(f) What are the units of the dual price on row 5?

6-10. Consider the Buster Sod problem: Buster Sod operates a 1200-acre irrigated farm in the Red River Valley of Arizona. Sod's principal activities are raising wheat, alfalfa, and beef. The Red Valley Water Authority has just given its water allotments for next year (Sod was alloted 2000 acre-feet) and Sod is busy preparing his production plan for next year. He figures that beef prices will hold at around $600 per ton and wheat will sell at $1.60 per bushel. Best guesses are that he will be able to sell alfalfa at $34 per ton, but if he needs more alfalfa to feed his beef than he can raise, he will have to pay $36 per ton to get the alfalfa to his feedlot.

Some technological features of Sod's operation are as follows: wheat yield, 50 bushels per acre; alfalfa yield, 3 tons per acre. Other features are given in Figure 6.11. Define the variables:

$$W = \text{wheat raised and sold (acres)}$$
$$A = \text{alfalfa raised (tons)}$$
$$B = \text{beef raised and sold (tons)}$$
$$A3 = \text{alfalfa bought (tons)}$$
$$A5 = \text{alfalfa sold (tons)}$$

182

CHAPTER 6
Linear Programs:
Computer
Analysis
and Interpreting
Sensitivity Output

Figure 6.11

Data for Buster Sod Problem

ACTIVITY	LABOR, MACHINERY, AND OTHER COSTS	WATER REQUIREMENTS (acre-ft)	LAND REQUIREMENTS (acres)	ALFALFA REQUIREMENTS (tons)
1 acre of wheat	$ 8	1.5	1	
1 acre of alfalfa	30	2.5	1	
1 ton of beef	40	0.1	0.05	4

An LP formulation and solution to Buster Sod's problem are shown in Figure 6.12.

(a) Show calculations that explain the values of the coefficient of W in the objective function and the coefficients of A in the first and second constraints.

Figure 6.12

Solution for Buster Sod Problem

```
MAX       72 W − 10 A + 560 B − 36 A3 + 34 A5
SUBJECT TO
      2)      W + 0.333 A + 0.05 B ≤ 1200
      3)      1.5 W + 0.833 A + 0.1 B ≤ 2000
      4)      −A + 4 B − A3 + A5 = 0

            OBJECTIVE FUNCTION VALUE
      1)            8320000.00

VARIABLE          VALUE           REDUCED COST
      W           0.000            6168.000
      A           0.000            3439.280
      B       20000.000               0.000
      A3      80000.000               0.000
      A5          0.000               2.000

  ROW       SLACK OR SURPLUS        DUAL PRICES
      2)         200.000               0.000
      3)           0.000            4160.000
      4)           0.000              36.000


            SENSITIVITY ANALYSIS

            OBJ COEFFICIENT RANGES
                CURRENT        ALLOWABLE        ALLOWABLE
VARIABLE         COEF          INCREASE         DECREASE
      W         72.000         6168.000         INFINITY
      A        −10.000         3439.280         INFINITY
      B        560.000         INFINITY          411.200
      A3       −36.000            2.000          100.212
      A5        34.000            2.000         INFINITY

            RIGHTHAND SIDE RANGES
                CURRENT        ALLOWABLE        ALLOWABLE
  ROW            RHS           INCREASE         DECREASE
      2        1200.000        INFINITY          200.000
      3        2000.000         400.000         2000.000
      4           0.000       80000.000         INFINITY
```

183

CHAPTER 6
Linear Programs:
Computer
Analysis
and Interpreting
Sensitivity Output

(b) How much water is being used?
(c) How much beef is being produced?
(d) Does Sod buy or sell alfalfa?
(e) How much should Sod pay to acquire another acre of land?
(f) Interpret the dual price on row 3.
(g) What happens to the optimal planting policy if the price of wheat triples?
(h) How much profit will Sod receive from the optimal operation of his farm?
(i) What happens to the optimal value of the objective function if the cost of alfalfa purchased increases from $36 to $37? (*Note:* The coefficient of $A3$ is currently—$36 and it will become —$37. Thus the coefficient has *decreased* by $1.)
(j) How much can the cost of buying alfalfa decrease before the current optimal planting policy will change?

6-11. Recall the nut-blending scenario in Problem 4-20. The Party Nut Company has on hand 550 pounds of peanuts, 150 pounds of cashews, 90 pounds of brazil nuts, and 70 pounds of hazelnuts. It packages and sells four varieties of mixed nuts in standard 8-ounce (half-pound) cans. The mix requirements and net wholesale prices are shown in Figure 6.13. The firm can sell all that it can produce at these prices. What mixes of products should it produce?

Figure 6.13
Nut Mix Data

MIX	CONTENTS	PRICE PER CAN
1 (peanuts)	Peanuts only	$0.26
2 (party mix)	No more than 50% peanuts; at least 15% cashews; at least 10% brazil nuts	0.40
3 (cashews)	Cashews only	0.51
4 (luxury mix)	At least 30% cashews; at least 20% brazil nuts; at least 30% hazelnuts	0.52

The problem can be formulated as the linear program shown in Figure 6.14, where

Pi = pounds of peanuts used in mix i
Ci = pounds of cashews used in mix i
Bi = pounds of brazil nuts used in mix i
Hi = pounds of hazelnuts used in mix i

Note that in the model given in Figure 6.14:

1. The coefficient of $P1$ in the objective function is 52 rather than 26 because there are two 8-ounce cans for each pound of peanuts sold as peanuts only.
2. Row 6 is a rewritten version of the constraint $P2/(P2 + C2 + B2 + H2) \leq 0.5$. A similar comment applies to each of the rows 7 through 11.

In the output in Figure 6.14 we have purposely deleted several of the dual prices. Use this output to answer the questions. If it is impossible to answer the question, state why.

(a) What can you say about the dual price associated with row 2? In other words, will it be ≥ 0, or ≤ 0?

184

CHAPTER 6
Linear Programs:
Computer
Analysis
and Interpreting
Sensitivity Output

Figure 6.14

Solution for the Party Nut Problem

```
MAX     52 P1 + 80 P2 + 80 C2 + 80 B2 + 80 H2 + 102 C3 + 104 P4
        + 104 C4 + 104 B4 + 104 H4
SUBJECT TO
        2)      P1 + P2 + P4 ≤ 550
        3)      C2 + C3 + C4 ≤ 150
        4)      B2 + B4 ≤ 90
        5)      H2 + H4 ≤ 70
        6)      0.5 P2 − 0.5 C2 − 0.5 B2 − 0.5 H2 ≤ 0
        7)      −0.15 P2 + 0.85 C2 − 0.15 B2 − 0.15 H2 ≥ 0
        8)      −0.1 P2 − 0.1 C2 + 0.9 B2 − 0.1 H2 ≥ 0
        9)      −0.3 P4 + 0.7 C4 − 0.3 B4 − 0.3 H4 ≥ 0
        10)     −0.2 P4 − 0.2 C4 + 0.8 B4 − 0.2 H4 ≥ 0
        11)     −0.3 P4 − 0.3 C4 − 0.3 B4 + 0.7 H4 ≥ 0
```

OBJECTIVE FUNCTION VALUE

1)   63760.0000

VARIABLE	VALUE	REDUCED COST
P1	380.000	0.000
P2	123.333	0.000
C2	80.000	0.000
B2	43.333	0.000
H2	0.000	24.000
C3	0.000	6.000
P4	46.667	0.000
C4	70.000	0.000
B4	46.666	0.000
H4	70.000	0.000

ROW	SLACK OR SURPLUS	DUAL PRICES
2)	0.000	
3)	0.000	
4)	0.000	108.000
5)	0.000	132.000
6)	0.000	56.000
7)	43.000	0.000
8)	18.667	
9)	0.000	−56.000
10)	0.000	−56.000
11)	0.000	−80.000

SENSITIVITY ANALYSIS

OBJ COEFFICIENT RANGES

VARIABLE	CURRENT COEF	ALLOWABLE INCREASE	ALLOWABLE DECREASE
P1	52.000	6.000	12.000
P2	80.000	9.000	6.000
C2	80.000	24.000	6.000
B2	80.000	36.000	56.000
H2	80.000	24.000	INFINITY
C3	102.000	6.000	INFINITY
P4	104.000	INFINITY	36.000
C4	104.000	56.000	24.000
B4	104.000	56.000	36.000
H4	104.000	INFINITY	24.000

185

CHAPTER 6
Linear Programs:
Computer
Analysis
and Interpreting
Sensitivity Output

Figure 6.14 (Cont.)

RIGHTHAND SIDE RANGES

ROW	CURRENT RHS	ALLOWABLE INCREASE	ALLOWABLE DECREASE
2	550.000	INFINITY	380.000
3	150.000	93.333	61.428
4	90.000	143.333	23.333
5	70.000	56.000	70.000
6	0.000	93.333	61.667
7	0.000	43.000	INFINITY
8	0.000	18.667	INFINITY
9	0.000	46.667	70.000
10	0.000	23.333	46.667
11	0.000	28.000	56.000

(b) Noting the economic meaning of row 2, can you give a lower bound (not zero) for the dual price associated with row 2?

(c) How many 8-ounce cans of party mix (mix 2) will be produced at optimality?

(d) Analyze the effect of changing the price of mix 1 to $0.27 per can; $0.30 per can.

6-12. Recall Example 2 of Section 4.4. A plant can manufacture five different products in any combination. Each product requires time on each of three machines, as shown in Figure 6.15. All figures are in minutes per pound of product. Each machine is available 128 hours

Figure 6.15
Machine-Time Data (min)

PRODUCT	MACHINE 1	2	3
A	12	8	5
B	7	9	10
C	8	4	7
D	10	0	3
E	7	11	2

per week. Products A, B, C, D, and E are purely competitive, and any amounts made may be sold at respective per pound prices of $5, $4, $5, $4, and $4. Variable labor costs are $4 per hour for machines 1 and 2, and $3 per hour for machine 3. Material costs for each pound of products A and C are $2, and $1 for each pound of products B, D, and E. You wish to maximize profit to the firm. The *LP* formulation and solution are shown in Figure 6.16.

(a) How many hours are used on each of the three machines?

wrong **(b)** What are the units of the dual prices on the constraints that control machine capacity?

(c) How much should the firm be willing to spend to obtain another hour of time on machine 2?

(d) How much can the sales price of product A increase before the optimal production plan changes? State your answer in the proper units.

186

CHAPTER 6
Linear Programs:
Computer
Analysis
and Interpreting
Sensitivity Output

Figure 6.16

Solution for Five-Product, Three-Machine Problem

```
MAX      1.417 A + 1.43 B + 1.85 C + 2.183 D + 1.7 E
SUBJECT TO
      2)    12 A + 7 B + 8 C + 10 D + 7 E ≤ 7680
      3)     8 A + 9 B + 4 C + 11 E ≤ 7680
      4)     5 A + 10 B + 7 C + 3 D + 2 E ≤ 7680

         OBJECTIVE FUNCTION VALUE
      1)          1817.59999

VARIABLE          VALUE          REDUCED COST
      A           0.000              1.380
      B           0.000              0.248
      C         512.000              0.000
      D           0.000              0.075
      E         512.000              0.000

ROW          SLACK OR SURPLUS      DUAL PRICES
      2)          0.000              0.226
      3)          0.000              0.011
      4)       3072.000              0.000


              SENSITIVITY ANALYSIS

              OBJ COEFFICIENT RANGES
                 CURRENT     ALLOWABLE      ALLOWABLE
VARIABLE          COEF       INCREASE       DECREASE
      A          1.417        1.380         INFINITY
      B          1.430        0.248         INFINITY
      C          1.850        0.093          0.041
      D          2.183        0.075         INFINITY
      E          1.700        0.113          0.081

              RIGHTHAND SIDE RANGES
                 CURRENT     ALLOWABLE      ALLOWABLE
ROW               RHS        INCREASE       DECREASE
      2        7680.000      2671.304       2792.727
      3        7680.000      4388.571       3840.000
      4        7680.000      INFINITY       3072.000
```

6-13. Problem 6-12 can be reformulated with definitional variables as suggested in Problem 4-19. This formulation and solution are shown in Figure 6.17. Use this new solution and reanswer parts (a) through (d) of Problem 6-12. In addition, answer parts (a) and (b), which follow.

(a) How much can the variable labor cost of machine 2 increase before the optimal production plan changes?

● (b) Why is it impossible to find the answer to part (a) of Problem 6-13, with the techniques currently at your disposal if you use the formulation in Problem 6.12?

6-14. Give a geometric example of an LP problem where the RHS of an active constraint can be changed, in a degenerate setting, and the optimal solution will not change.

6-15. Give a geometric example of an LP problem where the RHS of an active constraint can be changed, in an alternative optima setting, and the optimal objective value will not change.

187

CHAPTER 6
Linear Programs:
Computer
Analysis
and Interpreting
Sensitivity Output

Figure 6.17
Reformulation with Definitional Variables

```
MAX     3 A + 3 B + 3 C + 3 D + 3 E − 4 M1 − 4 M2 − 3 M3
SUBJECT TO
        2)    12 A + 7 B + 8 C + 10 D + 7 E − 60 M1 = 0
        3)     8 A + 9 B + 4 C + 11 E − 60 M2 = 0
        4)     5 A + 10 B + 7 C + 3 D + 2 E − 60 M3 = 0
        5)    M1 ≤ 128
        6)    M2 ≤ 128
        7)    M3 ≤ 128

              OBJECTIVE FUNCTION VALUE
        1)        1817.60001

     VARIABLE         VALUE         REDUCED CUST
          A           0.000             1.380
          B           0.000             0.245
          C         512.000             0.000
          D           0.000             0.075
          E         512.000             0.000
          M1        128.000             0.000
          M2        128.000             0.000
          M3         76.800             0.000

     ROW        SLACK OR SURPLUS      DUAL PRICES
        2)           0.000              0.292
        3)           0.000              0.077
        4)           0.000              0.050
        5)           0.000             13.550
        6)           0.000              0.650
        7)          51.200              0.000

                  SENSITIVITY ANALYSIS

              OBJ COEFFICIENT RANGES

                      CURRENT      ALLOWABLE      ALLOWABLE
     VARIABLE          COEF        INCREASE       DECREASE
          A           3.000         1.380         INFINITY
          B           3.000         0.245         INFINITY
          C           3.000         0.093           0.041
          D           3.000         0.075         INFINITY
          E           3.000         0.113           0.081
          M1         −4.000        INFINITY        13.550
          M2         −4.000        INFINITY         0.650
          M3         −3.000         1.182           0.529

              RIGHTHAND SIDE RANGES

                      CURRENT      ALLOWABLE      ALLOWABLE
     ROW               RHS         INCREASE       DECREASE
        2            0.000        2671.304       2792.727
        3            0.000        4388.571       3840.000
        4            0.000        4608.000       3072.000
        5          128.000          44.522         46.545
        6          128.000          73.143         64.000
        7          128.000        INFINITY         51.200
```

188

CHAPTER 6
Linear Programs:
Computer
Analysis
and Interpreting
Sensitivity Output

6-16. Assume $(\hat{x}_1, \hat{x}_2)$ and (x_1^*, x_2^*) are alternative optimal solutions for an LP problem. Consider a new solution

$$\alpha(\hat{x}_1, \hat{x}_2) + (1 - \alpha)(x_1^*, x_2^*)$$

where α is some specified number with the property that $0 < \alpha < 1$. Geometrically, this new solution happens to lie on the straight line connecting the two points $(\hat{x}_1, \hat{x}_2)$ and (x_1^*, x_2^*). Use algebra to show that the new point is an alternative optimal solution. That is, show that the new point is feasible (satisfies each constraint) and that the objective value at the new point is the same as at the previous solutions.

6.1 APPENDIX

QUESTIONS BASED ON THE RED BRAND CANNERS CASE

We first saw the Red Brand Canners case in Chapter 4 where the model was formulated and assumptions were discussed. In the following questions, the analysis continues. You are asked to solve several formulations on the computer and then analyze the outputs.

1. Run on your own computer your LP formulation of the Red Brand Canners production problem. Do not include the option of purchasing up to 80,000 additional pounds of grade A tomatoes.

2. What is the net profit obtained after netting out the cost of the crop?

3. Myers has proposed that the net profit obtained from his policy would be $48,000. Is this true? If not, what is his net profit (taking into account, as in question 2, the cost of the crop).

4. Suppose Cooper suggests that, in keeping with his accounting scheme as advanced in Exhibit 2 on page 102, the crop cost of 6 cents per pound should be subtracted from each coefficient in the objective function. Change your formulation accordingly, and again solve the problem. You should obtain an optimal objective value which is greater than that obtained in question 2. Explain this apparent discrepancy (assume that unused tomatoes will spoil).

5. Suppose that unused tomatoes could be resold at 6 cents per pound. Which solution would be preferred under these conditions? How much can the resale price be lowered without affecting this preference?

6. Use the sensitivity output from question 1 to determine whether or not the additional purchase of up to 80,000 pounds of grade A tomatoes should be undertaken. Can you tell how much should be purchased?

7. Use a reformulated model to obtain an optimal product mix using the additional purchase option. The solution to your reformulated model should explicitly show how the additional purchase should be used.

8. Suppose that in question 1 the Market Research Department feels they could increase the demand for juice by 25,000 cases by means of an advertising campaign. How much should Red Brand be willing to pay for such a campaign?

9. Suppose in question 1 that the price of juice is increased by $0.10 per case. Does your computer output tell you whether or not the optimal production plan will change?

10. Suppose that RBC is forced to reduce the size of the product line in tomato-based products to two. Would additional computer runs be required to tell which product should be dropped from the line?

11. Suppose that in question 1 an additional lot of grade B tomatoes is available. The lot is 50,000 pounds. How much should RBC be willing to pay for this lot of grade B tomatoes?

SAW MILL RIVER FEED AND GRAIN COMPANY

The purpose of this case is to exercise both judgmental and technical skills. You will have to decide, based on Mr. Overton's objectives, just what information you should provide him with. You will then have to formulate an LP model (or models), run it (or them) on the computer, and present, in a summary report, the relevant results.

On Monday, August 28, 1978, Mr. Overton called in his sales manager and purchasing manager to discuss the company's policy for the coming month. Saw Mill had accepted orders from Turnbull Co. and McClean Bros. and had the option of accepting an order from Blue River, Inc. They also had the option of buying some additional grain from Cochrane Farm. Mr. Overton, managing director of Saw Mill, had to decide by the end of the week what action to take.

Usually, all purchases of grain were completed by the end of August. However, Saw Mill still had the possibility of buying an extra purchase of grain from Cochrane Farm. This commitment had to be made by September 1. The grain would be delivered to the Midwest Grain Elevator by the 15th of the month. This elevator acts simply as a storage facility for Saw Mill.

It is immutable company policy to charge a markup of 15% on the cost of the grain supplied to customers. Payments to the Midwest Grain Elevator are treated as an overhead and this is not to be challenged. Turnbull, McClean, and Blue River have agreed to pay, for their current orders, whatever price Saw Mill charges. However, Saw Mill realizes that if its price becomes too high, future business will be lost.

The details of the Turnbull, McClean, and Blue River orders are presented in Exhibit 1. The quantity, as well as the maximum moisture content, minimum weight per bushel, maximum percentage damaged, and maximum percentage foreign material are presented.

Exhibit 1
Data on Grain Orders

ORDERING COMPANY	QUANTITY (BUSHELS)	MAXIMUM PERCENT MOISTURE (per lb.)	MINIMUM WEIGHT PER BUSHEL (LB)	MAXIMUM PERCENT DAMAGE (per lb.)	MAXIMUM PERCENT FOREIGN MATERIAL (per lb.)	DELIVERY DATE
Turnbull	40,000–45,000	13	56	2	2	9/20
McClean	32,000–36,000	15.5	54	5	3	9/22
Blue River	50,000–54,000	15	56	2	4	9/26

The company had the option to supply any amount of grain that it wished, within the specified range. It must, of course, satisfy the requirements. By September 4, Saw Mill must inform Turnbull and McClean how much grain they will receive. By the same date it must inform Blue River if it will accept its order and how much grain will be delivered if it accepts.

Saw Mill blends the grains that it owns to satisfy customer orders. On August 28 the company had 326,000 bushels of corn stored in the elevator. Obviously, it would be impossible to identify the exact composition of each kernel of corn that the Saw Mill River Feed and Grain Company delivered to the elevator. Hence, Exhibit 2 represents aggregated amounts and characteristics of different types of corn credited to Saw Mill River's account with the elevator. The 326,000 bushels are segregated into 11 different types of corn, which differ according to (1) quantity available, (2) cost per bushel, (3) percentage moisture content, (4) weight per bushel, (5) percentage damaged, and (6) percentage foreign material.

Exhibit 2
Characteristics of Corn Types

TYPE OF CORN	QUANTITY (BUSHELS)	COST PER BUSHEL	PERCENT MOISTURE CONTENT	WEIGHT PER BUSHEL (LB)	PERCENT TOTAL DAMAGE	PERCENT FOREIGN MATERIAL
1	30,000	$1.45	12	57	2	1.5
2	45,000	1.44	15	57	2	1
3	25,000	1.45	12	58	3	3
4	40,000	1.42	13	56	4	2
5	20,000	1.38	15	54	4	2
6	30,000	1.37	15	55	5	3
7	75,000	1.37	18	57	5	1
8	15,000	1.39	14	58	2	4
9	16,000	1.27	17	53	7	5
10	20,000	1.28	15	55	8	3
11	10,000	1.17	22	56	9	5

The grain on offer from Cochrane Farm was one load of up to 50,000 bushels, with an average of 15% moisture, 3% damage, and 2% foreign material. The load has a density of 57 pounds per bushel, and Straddle (the purchasing manager) was convinced that the order could be obtained at a cost of $1.41 per bushel.

Use linear programming to help analyze Mr. Overton's problem. (Use notation T_i = bushels of corn type i to be sent to Turnbull. Similarly for B_i and M_i. Also let corn type 12 denote the corn from Cochrane Farm.) In no more than one page labeled "Executive Summary," provide as concisely as possible information that will help Overton answer his questions. His main objectives are to maximize profit and to keep prices to the customers sufficiently low to attract future business. He can be expected to use his judgment to make the eventual decision; your job is to provide information that will enable him to look at the important trade-offs. You should also make your own recommendations.

Your presentation will be judged on the economy of your formulation (i.e., formulate your model, or models, *for the given set of data* as efficiently as possible) as well as on your recommendations concerning:

(a) to buy or not to buy from Cochrane;

(b) to accept or not to accept the Blue River option;

(c) how much corn to supply to Blue River, Turnbull, and McClean.

DIAGNOSTIC ASSIGNMENT

CRAWLER TREAD AND A NEW ANGLE

In important respects, some of a manager's task invokes analysis and evaluation of the work of others as opposed to producing "from rock bottom" his own formulation and analysis. In this diagnostic role the manager will judge someone else's model. Have the correct questions been asked? Has a correct analysis been performed? The following vignette captures the spirit of such a situation. You are asked to comment on the analysis of a new opportunity.

Ralph Hanson has been the chief metallurgist at PROTRAC's cast iron foundry for the last five years. He brings several important qualities to this position. First, he has an excellent technical background. He graduated from Case Western with an MMS (Master of Material Science) and had five years' experience with U.S. Steel before joining PROTRAC. He has used this training and experience to implement several changes that have contributed to product quality and process efficiency. In addition, he has become an effective manager. Through a combination of formal course work and self-education, he has become familiar with many modern management techniques and approaches and has worked to see that these new methods are exploited whenever it is appropriate. Indeed, Ralph is responsible for introducing the use of LP models into the ore-blending and scrap-recycling activities at PROTRAC.

Ralph was the chief metallurgist when Crawler Tread, the first ore-blending application, was completed. By now both Ralph and Sam Togas, the plant manager, are comfortable with the use of LP models in the ore-blending area. Ralph typically formulates, solves, and interprets the output himself. Currently, Ralph is facing a new problem. The recession has seriously affected the demand for heavy equipment and PROTRAC has excess capacity in most departments, including the foundry. However, the defense industries are booming. A manufacturer of tanks requires a high-grade ore for producing tank treads. Indeed, the requirements are exactly the same as PROTRAC used in the Crawler Tread problem (see Section 6.4). The tank manufacturer is willing to pay PROTRAC $850 per ton of ore for up to 150,000 tons to be delivered within the next month. Ralph learns that he can have up to 98,000 tons of ore available. This is made up of 21,000 tons from mine 1; 40,000 from mine 2; 15,000 from mine 3; and 22,000 from mine 4.

Based on these data, Ralph formulates a new LP model. In this model, T_i is the number of tons of ore from mine i (for $i = 1, \ldots, 4$) that are used in the blend and B is the number of tons of blended ore. He carefully annotates the formulation so that he can easily explain his analysis to Sam, the plant manager. The formulation and solution that Ralph used in his presentation are shown in Figure 6.18.

Sam was delighted with the project. It yielded a contribution margin of 30,500,000 and occupied resources (labor and machinery) that otherwise would have been idle.

He immediately had the legal department draw up a contract for the sale of 98,000 tons of ore.

When Ralph arrived the next morning. Sam was waiting for him. The following discussion took place:

Figure 6.18
Ralph's Formulation

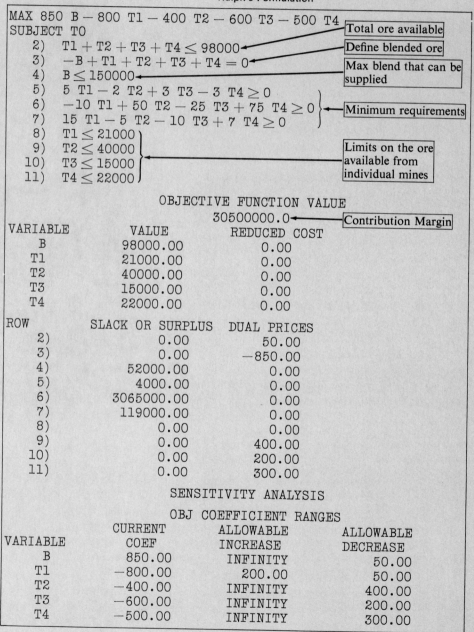

```
MAX 850 B — 800 T1 — 400 T2 — 600 T3 — 500 T4
SUBJECT TO
   2)   T1 + T2 + T3 + T4 ≤ 98000          Total ore available
   3)   −B + T1 + T2 + T3 + T4 = 0         Define blended ore
   4)   B ≤ 150000                          Max blend that can be
                                            supplied
   5)   5 T1 − 2 T2 + 3 T3 − 3 T4 ≥ 0
   6)   −10 T1 + 50 T2 − 25 T3 + 75 T4 ≥ 0   Minimum requirements
   7)   15 T1 − 5 T2 − 10 T3 + 7 T4 ≥ 0
   8)   T1 ≤ 21000
   9)   T2 ≤ 40000                          Limits on the ore
  10)   T3 ≤ 15000                          available from
  11)   T4 ≤ 22000                          individual mines
```

OBJECTIVE FUNCTION VALUE

        30500000.0   Contribution Margin

VARIABLE	VALUE	REDUCED COST
B	98000.00	0.00
T1	21000.00	0.00
T2	40000.00	0.00
T3	15000.00	0.00
T4	22000.00	0.00

ROW	SLACK OR SURPLUS	DUAL PRICES
2)	0.00	50.00
3)	0.00	−850.00
4)	52000.00	0.00
5)	4000.00	0.00
6)	3065000.00	0.00
7)	119000.00	0.00
8)	0.00	0.00
9)	0.00	400.00
10)	0.00	200.00
11)	0.00	300.00

SENSITIVITY ANALYSIS

OBJ COEFFICIENT RANGES

VARIABLE	CURRENT COEF	ALLOWABLE INCREASE	ALLOWABLE DECREASE
B	850.00	INFINITY	50.00
T1	−800.00	200.00	50.00
T2	−400.00	INFINITY	400.00
T3	−600.00	INFINITY	200.00
T4	−500.00	INFINITY	300.00

Figure 6.18 (Cont.)

		RIGHTHAND SIDE RANGES	
ROW	CURRENT RHS	ALLOWABLE INCREASE	ALLOWABLE DECREASE
2	98000.00	0.00	800.00
3	0.00	98000.00	52000.00
4	150000.00	INFINITY	52000.00
5	0.00	4000.00	INFINITY
6	0.00	3065000.00	INFINITY
7	0.00	119000.00	INFINITY
8	21000.00	INFINITY	0.00
9	40000.00	571.42	0.00
10	15000.00	2000.00	0.00
11	22000.00	500.00	0.00

SAM: The contract is ready and I was about to call and confirm the arrangement, but there is a new development. We've just received a telex from mine 1. Due to the cancellation of another order, we can have up to another 3000 tons of ore at the standard price of $800 per ton if we want it. What should we do? Why don't you go back and re-solve your problem including the possibility of the additional 3000 tons from mine 1 and draw up a new contract if the new solution is better. Obviously, we can't do worse than we are doing now, and that's not bad.

RALPH: Actually, we don't have to do that. One of the great things about LP is that we can answer many questions involving changes from the original problem. In particular, the dual price on the amount of T_1 available (row 8) provides an upper bound on how much more we should pay to have the opportunity of buying an additional ton of ore from mine 1. If the dual price is positive, say $10, we should be willing to pay up to $10 more for the opportunity to buy another ton of ore (i.e., up to $810 for a ton of ore from mine 1). If it is zero, increasing the amount of ore that is available from mine 1 will not enable us to increase our profit.

A quick inspection of the solution reveals that the dual price on row 8 is zero.

RALPH continues: Since we can't increase our contribution margin, let's just leave the contract as it is and get back to work.

SAM: Damn it, Ralph, I don't understand this. We can buy the ore for $800 a ton and sell it for $850 a ton and you tell me we shouldn't do it.

RALPH: I know it's hard to see, but I know that if the right-hand side of row 8 is increased, the optimal value of the objective function will remain the same. This implies that additional tons of ore from mine 1 won't help us. I suppose it's because we can't add this additional ore to our blend and still satisfy the minimum elements requirements. Remember that the ore from mine 1 has only 90 pounds of element B per ton and the blend must have at least 100.

SAM: Look, Ralph, I have to meet with the grievance committee now. I just can't spend any more time on this project. I can't say I understand your answer, but you're the expert. Let's go with the current contract.

Questions

1. Is Ralph's interpretation of the numbers on the printout correct?

2. Is Ralph's response to the additional purchase opportunity correct? If you believe he has erred, where is the flaw?

3. Suppose row 2 were dropped from the model. What would be the dual price on row 8? On row 9?

4. Can you figure out what will happen to the OV if the RHS of row 9 is changed to 39,999?

5. Suppose the RHS of row 9 is increased to 40,001. What are the new optimal values of T_1, T_2, T_3, and T_4?

6. Figure out why the Allowable Increase on row 9 is 571.42.

7. Can you tell which constraint causes the degeneracy in Ralph's model?

DIAGNOSTIC ASSIGNMENT

WINSTON-SALEM DEVELOPMENT MANAGEMENT

This problem is based on the Winston-Salem Development Management problem which was originally presented as Example 11 of Section 4.7 and will be repeated along with the computer solution in Example 3 of Chapter 9. Read these two examples in order to obtain the necessary background.

Richard Ruckhaus, the treasurer for WSDM, was contacted by James French, a senior VP at National City Bank (NCB) and informed that due to WSDM's outstanding credit rating, NCB was expanding the line of credit available to WSDM. In particular, in addition to being able to borrow funds for 6 months at a rate of 3.5% for 6 months, WSDM would now have the opportunity to borrow funds for 1 year at the rate of 7.5% per year. Otherwise, WSDM's problem remains exactly what is was. In particular, the total outstanding principal can never exceed $2 million.

In order to incorporate this new borrowing option into the decision-making process, Richard modifies the original LP into the form shown in Figure 6.19. He is

Figure 6.19

```
MAX    Z
SUBJECT TO
   2)  −3000 F − 2000 M − 2000 D + BB1 + B1 − L1 ≥ −2000
   3)  −1000 F − 500 M − 2000 D − 1.035 B1 + 1.03 L1 + B2
       + BB2 − L2 ≥ −500
   4)  −1800 F + 1500 M − 1800 D − 1.075 BB1 − 1.035 B2
       + 1.03 L2 − L3 + B3 + BB3 ≥ −400
   5)   400 F + 1500 M + 1000 D − 1.075 BB2 + 1.03 L3
       − 1.035 B3 + B4 + BB4 − L4 ≥ −380
   6)  1800 F + 1500 M + 1000 D − 1.075 BB3 − 1.035 B4
       + 1.03 L4 + B5 + BB5 − L5 ≥ −360
   7)  1800 F + 200 M + 1000 D − 1.075 BB4 − 1.035 B5
       + 1.03 L5 + B6 − L6 ≥ −340
   8)   −Z + 5500 F − 1000 M + 6000 D − 1.075 BB5 − 1.035 B6
       + 1.03 L6 ≥ −300
   9)  BB1 + B1 ≤ 2000
```

Figure 6.19 (Cont.)

```
        10)   BB1 + B2 + BB2 ≤ 2000
        11)   BB2 + B3 + BB3 ≤ 2000
        12)   BB3 + B4 + BB4 ≤ 2000
        13)   BB4 + B5 + BB5 ≤ 2000
        14)   BB5 + B6 ≤ 2000
        15)   F ≤ 1
        16)   M ≤ 1
        17)   D ≤ 1
END
: GO
    LP OPTIMUM FOUND AT STEP     13
          OBJECTIVE FUNCTION VALUE
    1)        7676.68933
VARIABLE          VALUE          REDUCED COST
        Z      7676.689             0.000
        F         0.712             0.000
        M         0.661             0.000
        D         0.000           454.184
      BB1      1457.587             0.000
       B1         0.000             0.002
       L1         0.000             0.007
       B2         0.000             0.004
      BB2       542.413             0.000
       L2         0.000             0.336
       L3         0.000             0.251
       B3      1457.587             0.000
      BB3         0.000             0.004
       B4       435.830             0.000
      BB4         0.000             0.009
       L4         0.000             0.005
       B5         0.000             0.005
      BB5         0.000             0.014
       L5      2181.675             0.000
       B6         0.000             0.005
       L6      4000.985             0.000
      ROW     SLACK OR SURPLUS    DUAL PRICES
        2)        0.000             −1.819
        3)        0.000             −1.759
        4)        0.000             −1.382
        5)        0.000             −1.098
        6)        0.000             −1.061
        7)        0.000             −1.030
        8)        0.000             −1.000
        9)      542.413             0.000
       10)        0.000             0.333
       11)        0.000             0.245
       12)     1564.170             0.000
       13)     2000.000             0.000
```

Figure 6.19   (Cont.)

14)	2000.000	0.000
15)	0.288	0.000
16)	0.339	0.000
17)	1.000	0.000

OBJ COEFFICIENT RANGES

VARIABLE	CURRENT COEF	ALLOWABLE INCREASE	ALLOWABLE DECREASE
Z	1.000	INFINITY	1.000
F	0.000	138.101	462.472
M	0.000	201.397	52.224
D	0.000	454.184	INFINITY
BB1	0.000	0.007	0.001
B1	0.000	0.001	INFINITY
L1	0.000	0.007	INFINITY
B2	0.000	0.004	INFINITY
BB2	0.000	0.001	0.004
L2	0.000	0.336	INFINITY
L3	0.000	0.251	INFINITY
B3	0.000	0.004	0.002
BB3	0.000	0.004	INFINITY
B4	0.000	0.005	0.004
BB4	0.000	0.009	INFINITY
L4	0.000	0.005	INFINITY
B5	0.000	0.005	INFININY
BB5	0.000	0.014	INFINITY
L5	0.000	0.005	0.015
B6	0.000	0.005	INFINITY
L6	0.000	0.005	0.017

RIGHTHAND SIDE RANGES

ROW	CURRENT RHS	ALLOWABLE INCREASE	ALLOWABLE DECREASE
2	−2000.000	2364.583	1467.850
3	−500.000	1882.716	700.617
4	−400.000	887.500	1205.000
5	−380.000	1564.170	435.830
6	−360.000	2181.675	INFINITY
7	−340.000	4000.985	INFINITY
8	−300.000	7676.689	INFINITY
9	2000.000	INFINITY	542.413
10	2000.000	536.267	1147.303
11	2000.000	1032.585	287.713
12	2000.000	INFINITY	1564.170
13	2000.000	INFINITY	2000.000
14	2000.000	INFINITY	2000.000
15	1.000	INFINITY	0.288
16	1.000	INFINITY	0.339
17	1.000	INFINITY	1.000

delighted to observe that the value of the objective function has increased from its previous value of $7,665,180 (see Example 3 of Chapter 9) to its current value of $8,429,670.

During lunch Richard begins discussing the new solution with Susan Hirst from the real estate investment staff. Susan says, "Richard, you know that I don't know anything about LP, but I don't see that the new loan offering from NCB is any advantage to us. The six-month rate compounded over two periods is $(1.035) \times (1.035) = 1.071$, whereas the annual rate is 1.075. Why in the ever-loving world would you take out a 1-year loan when you could take out two consecutive 6-month loans?"

Richard replies, "Listen Susan, no one ever accused me of being Milton Friedman. All I know is that we were well satisfied with the solution to the original problem. I simply let *BBi* be the amount borrowed for 1 year at the beginning of year i and made a straightforward extension of the original model. This is the answer it produced."

Questions

1. Is Susan correct?
2. Is the model constructed by Richard correct? If not, why not?
3. If the answer to Question 2 is no, and Susan is correct, then since according to Susan's argument the new borrowing opportunities will never be used, the optimal solution in the text must still be optimal under the new conditions. Is this logic correct? Can you specify the optimal solution to the new problem by inspection?
4. If the answer to Question 2 is no, can you specify a correct model?
5. If you have computing facilities available, run the model from Question 4. Use your results, if appropriate, to rethink your answer to Question 1. Explain any insight that you have obtained.

CHAPTER 7

Special LP Topics: Duality, V(b) and V(c)

7.1
INTRODUCTION

We wrote this chapter especially for those of you who want to dig deeper into some of the theoretical and technical specifics of LP. Chapter 7 is not a prerequisite for any of the succeeding material in the book, but its coverage will give you valuable insight toward becoming more expert in the use of LP.

7.2
THE DUAL PROBLEM

Given any set of data for an LP model, we can use the same data to form a *different* LP model. The resulting problem is called the **dual** of the original problem. The dual has theoretic, computational, and economic importance, all of which we shall discuss.

Transformation Rules First, let us see exactly how the dual problem is formed. In order to discuss duality theory in a satisfactory way it is convenient to drop the restriction that all variables in an LP model are nonnegative. For example, let us consider the following problem.

Problem (E1)

$$
\begin{array}{llll}
\text{Max} & 3x_1 + 4x_2 - 2x_3 & \text{dual variables} & \text{(E1)} \\
\text{s.t.} & 4x_1 - 12x_2 + 3x_3 \leq 12 & y_1 \\
& -2x_1 + 3x_2 + x_3 \leq 6 & y_2 \\
& -5x_1 + x_2 - 6x_3 \geq -40 & y_3 \\
& 3x_1 + 4x_2 - 2x_3 = 10 & y_4 \\
& x_1 \geq 0, \quad x_2 \leq 0, \quad x_3 \text{ unconstrained in sign}
\end{array}
$$

In this problem we see the appearance of each type of constraint ($\leq$, $\geq$, and $=$). Moreover, we have dropped the requirement that all variables must be nonnegative. In this example we have required that only the variable x_1 be nonnegative. The variable x_2 is required to be nonpositive and x_3 is unconstrained in sign. (That is, the optimal value of x_3 can be positive, negative, or zero.) The dual of problem (E1) is created by applying the following rules.

■ **Rule 1:** The number of variables in the dual problem is equal to the number of constraints in the original problem. The number of constraints in the dual problem is equal to the number of variables in the original problem.

Since (E1) has four constraints and three variables, the dual to (E1) will have three constraints and four variables. We shall see that each of the four variables in the dual to (E1) will correspond to one of the constraints in (E1). For this reason we show the column of dual variables y_1, y_2, y_3, y_4, to the right of (E1).

■ **Rule 2:** Coefficients of the objective function in the dual problem come from the righthand side of the original problem.

Thus, according to Rule 2, the objective function for the dual problem is

$$12y_1 + 6y_2 - 40y_3 + 10y_4$$

■ **Rule 3:** If the original problem is a max model, the dual is a min model. If the original problem is a min model, the dual is a max model.

Thus, since (E1) is a max model the complete objective function for the dual problem is

$$\text{Min} \quad 12y_1 + 6y_2 - 40y_3 + 10y_4$$

■ **Rule 4:** The coefficients for the first constraint function for the dual problem are the coefficients of the first variable in the constraints for the original problem, and similarly for the other constraints.

Thus, the first constraint function for the dual is

$$4y_1 - 2y_2 - 5y_3 + 3y_4$$

The second constraint function is

$$-12y_1 + 3y_2 + y_3 + 4y_4$$

Note that these constraints are obtained by reading "down" the rows of (E1). Using the same pattern, try to write out the third constraint function. (By Rule 1, there are only three constraints in the dual.) You should get

$$3y_1 + y_2 - 6y_3 - 2y_4$$

■ **Rule 5:** The right-hand sides of the dual constraints come from the objective function coefficients in the original problem.

Thus, by applying Rules 4 and 5 we have obtained the following constraint functions and respective right-hand sides for the dual

constraint function	RHS
$4y_1 - 2y_2 - 5y_3 + 3y_4$	3
$-12y_1 + 3y_2 + y_3 + 4y_4$	4
$3y_1 + y_2 - 6y_3 - 2y_4$	-2

■ **Rule 6:** The sense of the *i*th dual constraint is $=$ if and only if the *i*th variable in the original problem is unconstrained in sign.

Thus, since the third variable in the original problem (E1) is unconstrained in sign, the third dual constraint is an equality:

$$3y_1 + y_2 - 6y_3 - 2y_4 = -2$$

■ **Rule 7:** If the original problem is a max (min) model, then after applying Rule 6, assign to the remaining dual constraints a sense the same as (opposite to) the corresponding variable in the original problem.

To apply Rule 7, note that the first variable in the original (max) model is ≥ 0 and the second is ≤ 0. This means that the first dual constraint is $\geq$ and the second dual constraint is $\leq$:

$$4y_1 - 2y_2 - 5y_3 + 3y_4 \geq 3$$
$$-12y_1 + 3y_2 + y_3 + 4y_4 \leq 4$$

Also, Rule 7 means that if (E1) had been written as a min model the inequalities above would be written as ≤ 3 and ≥ 4, respectively.

■ **Rule 8:** The *i*th variable in the dual problem is unconstrained in sign if and only if the *i*th constraint in the original problem is an equality.

Since the fourth constraint in the original problem is $=$, Rule 8 dictates that the fourth dual variable, y_4, must be unconstrained in sign.

■ **Rule 9:** If the original problem is a max (min) model, then after applying Rule 8, assign to the remaining dual variables a sense opposite to (the same as) the corresponding constraint in the original problem.

Since the first and second constraints in the original max problem are $\leq$, Rule 9 dictates that $y_1 \geq 0, y_2 \geq 0$. Since the third constraint in the original problem is $\geq$, we must have $y_3 \leq 0$.

Dual of Problem (E1)

Application to (E1) of the nine rules above has created the following dual problem:

$$\text{Min} \quad 12y_1 + 6y_2 - 40y_3 + 10y_4 \qquad \text{(E2)}$$
$$\text{s.t.} \quad 4y_1 - 2y_2 - 5y_3 + 3y_4 \geq \quad 3$$
$$-12y_1 + 3y_2 + y_3 + 4y_4 \leq \quad 4$$
$$3y_1 + y_2 - 6y_3 - 2y_4 = -2$$
$$y_1 \geq 0, \quad y_2 \geq 0, \quad y_3 \leq 0, \quad y_4 \text{ unconstrained in sign}$$

You could now imagine that (E2) is the original problem. Let x_1, x_2, and x_3 be the variables in the problem that is dual to (E2), and you can verify that an application of the foregoing rules to (E2) will return us to (E1). This means that **taking the dual of the dual gives back the original problem.** We have called (E2) the dual of (E1), but it would be equally correct to call (E1) the dual of (E2). It just depends on which problem is considered the original one.

The rules above may at first seem like a lot to remember. However, compare Rules 6 and 8 and note that they are symmetric, merely stipulating that in *either* problem a variable that is unconstrained in sign corresponds to an equality constraint in the other problem. Similarly, Rules 7 and 9 are nearly symmetric. In schematic representation they say:

max model		min model
$x_i \geq 0$	$\Longleftrightarrow$	*i*th constraint is $\geq$
$x_i \leq 0$	$\Longleftrightarrow$	*i*th constraint is $\leq$
*i*th constraint is $\leq$	$\Longleftrightarrow$	$y_i \geq 0$
*i*th constraint is $\geq$	$\Longleftrightarrow$	$y_i \leq 0$

Here, now, are several examples of these rules.

Examples of Dual Problems

Example 1:

$$\text{Max} \quad 3x_1 + 4x_2 \qquad \qquad \textit{dual variables}$$
$$\text{s.t.} \quad -2x_1 + 3x_2 \leq 6 \qquad \qquad y_1$$
$$5x_1 - x_2 \leq 40 \qquad \qquad y_2$$
$$x_1 + x_2 \leq 7 \qquad \qquad y_3$$
$$x_1 \geq 0, \quad x_2 \geq 0$$

The dual is

$$\text{Min} \quad 6y_1 + 40y_2 + 7y_3$$
$$\text{s.t.} \quad -2y_1 + 5y_2 + y_3 \geq 3$$
$$3y_1 - y_2 + y_3 \geq 4$$
$$y_1 \geq 0, \quad y_2 \geq 0, \quad y_3 \geq 0$$

Notice how the dual constraint functions are formed by reading "down" the data in the original constraints. Incidentally, when as in this example the max model has all constraints $\leq$ with all variables nonnegative (and hence the min model has all constraints $\geq$ with all variables nonnegative) the pair of problems carries the label **symmetric dual problems.**

Example 2:

$$\text{Max} \quad 19x_1 - 22x_2 \qquad \qquad \textit{dual variables}$$
$$\text{s.t.} \quad 4x_1 + 5x_2 = 12 \qquad \qquad y_1$$
$$x_1 \geq 0, \quad x_2 \geq 0$$

The dual is

$$\text{Min} \quad 12y_1$$
$$\text{s.t.} \quad 4y_1 \geq \quad 19$$
$$5y_1 \geq -22$$

y_1 unconstrained in sign

Example 3:

$$\text{Min} \quad x_1 + 12x_2 - 2x_3 \qquad \qquad \textit{dual variables}$$
$$\text{s.t.} \quad 4x_1 + 2x_2 + 12x_3 \leq \quad 10 \qquad \qquad y_1$$
$$2x_1 - \quad x_2 + 11x_3 \geq -2 \qquad \qquad y_2$$
$$x_1 \geq 0, \quad x_2 \text{ unconstrained in sign}, \quad x_3 \geq 0$$

The dual is

$$\text{Max} \quad 10y_1 - 2y_2$$
$$\text{s.t.} \quad 4y_1 + \quad 2y_2 \geq \quad 1$$
$$2y_1 - \quad y_2 = \quad 12$$
$$12y_1 + 11y_2 \leq -2$$
$$y_1 \leq 0, \quad y_2 \geq 0$$

Relations
between
Primal and
Dual

In referring to a pair of dual problems it is often said that one of them (usually the original model) is the **primal** problem and the other is the **dual** problem. From an historical point of view, the term "primal" was invented by the mathematician Tobias Dantzig to denote the problem whose dual is a particular problem. The point to stress, however, is that duality is what is called a **symmetric** and **reflexive** relationship. This means that either problem may be considered to be the dual of the other, and whichever of the problems is designated as the primal,

---

The dual of the dual problem is again the primal problem.

For convenience, in this section let us adopt the convention that the max model with, in general, m constraints and n variables is the *primal*, and the min model with n constraints and m variables is the *dual*.

The theoretic relationships between the primal and the dual are very simply stated, yet these relations have considerable importance in the theory of linear problems.

Let us say that a set of decision variable values is **feasible** for a given model if the set of values satisfies the constraints and sign requirements that are specified by the model. Moreover, we shall say that a specific set of decision variable values $(x_1, \ldots, x_n)$ is **primal feasible** if these values are feasible in the max model, and similarly that a specific set of values $(y_1, \ldots, y_m)$ is **dual feasible** if these values are feasible in the min model. The following result is important.

If $(x_1, \ldots, x_n)$ is any set of primal feasible values and $(y_1, \ldots, y_m)$ is any set of dual feasible values, the primal objective function (i.e., the function to be maximized) evaluated at x cannot exceed the dual objective function (the function to be minimized) evaluated at y.

As an illustration of this fact, let us refer to Example 1. The max model is the primal and the min model is the dual. Verify that the values (3, 2) are primal feasible (i.e., $x_1 = 3$, $x_2 = 2$) since they satisfy all the primal constraints and sign conditions. The associated primal objective value is

$$3x_1 + 4x_2 = 17$$

The values (0, 1, 6) are dual feasible (i.e., $y_1 = 0$, $y_2 = 1$, $y_3 = 6$) since they satisfy all the constraints and sign conditions of the dual problem. The associated objective value is

$$6y_1 + 40y_2 + 7y_3 = 82$$

and since $82 > 17$, the dual objective value exceeds the primal value. You may wish to select other sets of primal feasible values and other dual feasible values. No matter what values are selected, as long as they are primal and dual feasible, the primal objective value will not exceed the dual value.

Now suppose that primal and dual feasible values are found that produce equal objective function values. If there were a different primal feasible value that produced a larger value for the primal objective function, it would also be larger than the above mentioned dual objective value and this would contradict the foregoing result. Hence, there can be no primal feasible values for the decision variables that produce a larger value of the primal objective function. This means that the originally found primal feasible values are optimal. Similar reasoning applies to the dual. In other words, **if primal and dual feasible values are found that produce equal objective function values, those decision variable values are optimal in their respective problems.** In fact, an even stronger result links the primal and dual problems. Namely,

---

1. Either of the two problems has an optimal solution if and only if the other does.
2. When there is an optimal solution, the optimal value of the objective function in the primal is the same as the optimal value of the objective function in the dual.

This elegant result says that solving either problem yields the same optimal objective value. It does *not* say that the *optimal solution* to each problem (i.e., the optimal values of the decision variables) is the same. Such a result would not be reasonable since the two problems are in spaces of different dimension. That is, there are n of the x variables (the primal variables) and m of the y variables (the dual variables). As an illustration of this, refer back to Example 1. There the primal variables are in two-dimensional space and the dual variables in three-dimensional space.

To explain the relations between the primal and dual problems more fully, it is necessary to recall the technical terms **infeasible (*or* inconsistent)** and **unbounded**. An LP problem is said to be *infeasible, or inconsistent*, if the constraints (including the sign conditions on the variables) cannot all be (simultaneously) satisfied. This means that the set of points described by the constraints is an empty set. An LP problem is said to be *unbounded* if the objective contour can be translated arbitrarily far in the optimizing direction without leaving the constraint set behind. This means that in a max problem there are allowable decision variable values that make the value of the objective function arbitrarily large. The reverse interpretation holds for a min problem.

It turns out that any linear program falls into one of the following three categories:

1. The problem has an optimal solution. (This implies a finite optimal objective value.)
2. The problem is unbounded. (This means consistent constraints but, if you like, an infinite—or negatively infinite, for a min model—optimal objective value.)
3. The problem is infeasible. (This means that there is no allowable choice for the decision variables.)

Although perfectly respectable as mathematical possibilities, the second and third phenomena are, in terms of applied problems, abnormal. Infinite profits do not exist, and a sensible real-world problem, correctly formulated, cannot lead to an infeasible model.

Using the foregoing terminology, we can now more completely characterize the relations between any pair of dual linear programs. These relations are known as the **dual theorem of linear programming**. This is the most important theoretic result in the study of LP problems. The dual theorem says that of the nine possible states for a pair of dual problems (e.g., one optimal, the other optimal; one optimal, the other unbounded; one optimal, the other infeasible; etc.), only four possibilities can actually occur.

**Dual
Theorem of
LP**

1. In any pair of dual linear programs, both may have optimal solutions, in which case the optimal objective values will be the same.
2. In any pair of dual linear programs, both may be inconsistent.
3. In any pair of dual linear programs, one may be unbounded and the other inconsistent.

The dual theorem states that these combinations are mutually exclusive and exhaustive. For example, the possibility that both the primal and the dual are unbounded is ruled out. The possibility is also ruled out that one problem can be unbounded while the other has an optimal solution. Thus, the dual theorem implies that if it is known that either problem is unbounded, the other *must* be inconsistent.

There is a final theoretic relationship between the primal and dual problem of considerable importance in applications. This is called the **principle of complementary slackness**, which can be stated as follows:

> **Consider an inequality constraint in any LP problem. If that constraint is inactive for any optimal solution to the problem, the corresponding dual variable will be zero in any optimal solution to the dual of that problem.**

We have now presented essentially all the important theoretic relationships between pairs of dual linear programs. This theory is of considerable mathematical interest in its own right. In addition, the theory of duality has economic and computational significance. This will become apparent in the following sections.

**Economic
Significance
of the Dual
Variables**

From the point of view of applied analysis, the most important aspect of dual variables is probably the associated economic interpretation. The fact is established by the following relationships:

> **In a Max problem,**
>
> | ith dual price on printout $=$ optimal value of the ith dual variable |

In a Min problem,

> *i*th dual price on printout $= -$ optimal value of the *i*th dual variable

Thus, all of the economic analysis in Chapter 6 concerning changes in the RHS could have been presented in terms of **dual variables** rather than the **dual prices** in the printout. Indeed, the theory on which this analysis is based was historically developed in the context of the dual problem.

Rather than now dwelling on how the change in the sign convention requires a somewhat different interpretation, we shall simply state that

1. The optimal value of the *i*th dual variable is the rate at which the primal optimal objective value will **increase** as b_i increases, assuming that all other data are unchanged; that is,

2. If an increase in the RHS increases (decreases) the OV, the dual variable is positive (negative), regardless of whether the primal is a max or a min problem.

Note that in discussing **dual prices** we used the term **rate of improvement**. In talking about **dual variables** we use the term **rate of increase**. These are the same for a max model, opposite in sign for a min model. The geometric relations between dual price and dual variable will be explored in depth in Section 7.7.

Evaluating a Resource

To illustrate the interpretation of the dual variables, let us imagine ourselves in a profit-maximization production context with constraints on the input resources. Suppose that aluminum is one of our resources and that the first constraint of our models is of $\leq$ form and represents a limitation on the availability of aluminum. Imagine that 8000 pounds of aluminum is currently in our stockpile, so we solve the model using the value 8000 for the first RHS, b_1. Let us suppose that in reading the computer output we find that the dual price for the first constraint is $16.50, which is the optimal value of y_1 in the dual problem. This means that the *marginal* contribution of aluminum (the value of the last, or the next, unit consumed) to the total profit is $16.50. Suppose the sensitivity information shows that this value of $16.50 holds for b_1 values between 7500 and 9000, and suppose the market price of aluminum is $20 per pound. Using the lower limit of 7500, and the fact that we have 8000 pounds in the stockpile, we can infer that each of our last 500 pounds of aluminum is yielding us less than the market value (the OV increases only 16.50 per unit, the market value is 20 per unit). In theory, then, we might sell 500 pounds on the market for a return of $(20)(500) = \$10,000$, whereas the cost, in terms of the output profit, would be $(16.50)(500) = \$8250$. This transaction would net us an additional $1750 above current profits.[1]

On the other hand, suppose that the market value of aluminum is only $14 per pound. In this case, the dual price of $16.50 indicates that we may want to consider purchasing an additional 1000 pounds of aluminum, for this would net us $16.50 - 14.00 = \$2.50$ per pound, or $2500 above and beyond the current profit.

The discussion above assumes the existence of a market for resources, and illustrates how the dual variables enable the planner to compare the market values with the value obtained from the consumption of those resources in his own operations. Although this discussion illustrates one possible economic interpretation of dual vari-

---

[1] In a realistic situation the manager may not wish to exercise this option because he "may not be in the business of selling aluminum."

ables, one caveat should be issued. When a model includes constraints on resources, it generally implies that these resources are genuinely scarce over the planning period under consideration. This could occur, for example, because of bottlenecks, lead times to delivery, and so on, as discussed at length in Chapter 3. In such a situation, there is, in essence, no market for the scarce resource.

Economic Significance of the Dual Problem

Let us now focus on the economic interpretation, at least in one particular context, of the dual problem as a whole. Often, for example, the primal problem has the interpretation of finding profit-maximizing levels of production subject to constraints on scarce resources. How might we interpret the dual to this problem? Since the dual will be a min model, we could say that it is a cost-minimization model. But it minimizes the cost of doing what? The following scenario will provide an answer to this question.

Suppose that a firm owns two factories in two different marketing districts. For simplicity, assume that each factory uses the same three scarce raw materials. Factory 1 makes two products, such as lawn mowers and sprinklers, in quantities x_1 and x_2. Factory 2 makes three different products, doorknobs, refrigerator handles, and cowbells, in quantities z_1, z_2, and z_3, and factory 2 uses precisely the same raw materials as factory 1. Let us imagine that the factory 1 data are as given in Figure 7.1. Then we obtain

Factory 1 Production Model

$$\text{Max} \quad 4x_1 + 3x_2 \qquad \qquad (\text{F1})$$
$$\text{s.t.} \quad 6x_1 + 4x_2 \le 38$$
$$x_1 + 3x_2 \le 34$$
$$10x_1 + 7x_2 \le 44$$
$$x_1 \ge 0, \quad x_2 \ge 0$$

The analogous data for factory 2 are presented in Figure 7.2. From Figure 7.2 we obtain

Figure 7.1
Factory 1 Data

RAW MATERIAL	INPUT PER LAWN MOWER	INPUT PER SPRINKLER	TOTAL AVAILABILITY
1	6	4	38
2	1	3	34
3	10	7	44
Per unit profitability	4	3	

Figure 7.2
Factory 2 Data

RAW MATERIAL	INPUT PER DOORKNOB	INPUT PER REFRIGERATOR HANDLE	INPUT PER COWBELL	TOTAL AVAILABILITY
1	4	2	7	54
2	3	9	8	126
3	6	5	2	33
Per unit profitability	6	2	1	

$$\text{Max} \quad 6z_1 + 2z_2 + z_3 \qquad\qquad\qquad\qquad (\text{F2})$$
$$\text{s.t.} \quad 4z_1 + 2z_2 + 7z_3 \le 54$$
$$3z_1 + 9z_2 + 8z_3 \le 126$$
$$6z_1 + 5z_2 + 2z_3 \le 33$$
$$z_1 \ge 0, \quad z_2 \ge 0, \quad z_3 \ge 0$$

Now recall our assumption that the same firm owns both of these factories and that the factories are located in different marketing districts. We also assume that the three raw materials are scarce in the sense of long lead times to delivery. Now we suppose that management obtains information indicating that for various economic reasons the prices (i.e., the profitabilities) in the factory 2 marketing district are going to increase drastically. It is not known exactly how much the prices will increase, but management is confident that the increase will be so large that it will be desirable for factory 2 to take over all production. Thus, all of the factory 1 stockpile of raw materials should be transferred to factory 2. However, management decides that factory 2 should pay factory 1 a "fair price" for the transfer of these raw materials. What is such a "fair price?" It seems intuitively clear that, at least from factory 1's point of view, a fair total price would be one that is equal to the maximum possible profit factory 1 would make if it retained use of its resources that may now be shifted to factory 2. This is the factory 1 OV, and it would be a fair overall "lump-sum payment" for the three raw materials. Let us suppose that the firm, however, needs to know more than the lump-sum payment. For accounting reasons, it must have per unit prices for each material. These prices are required for financial reporting (i.e., tax) purposes. All accounting for individual products is carried out on a per item basis. The firm thus must find "fair" unit prices that can stand the scrutiny of a careful review. In order to obtain "fair" per unit prices, we make the following observations. If factory 2 pays per unit prices of y_1, y_2, and y_3 for the three raw materials, then since factory 1 possesses 38, 34, and 44 units, respectively, of each raw material,

$$\text{amount factory 2 pays} = 38y_1 + 34y_2 + 44y_3$$

Factory 2 wants to look as profitable as possible; thus, its goal is to minimize its total payment, that is,

$$\text{Min} \quad 38y_1 + 34y_2 + 44y_3$$

Factory 1, however, wants to make sure that it makes as much profit as it would if it remained in business for itself. From Figure 7.1 we see that if factory 1 had 6 units of raw material 1, 1 unit of raw material 2, and 10 units of raw material 3, it could produce one lawn mower for a profit of \$4. Recall that y_i is the sales price of raw material i. Thus, factory 1 will insist that

$$6y_1 + y_2 + 10y_3 \ge 4$$

If this condition does not hold, factory 1 will choose not to sell its raw materials to factory 2. Making use of the raw materials to produce lawn mowers will be more profitable.

Similarly, factory 1 will insist that

$$4y_1 + 3y_2 + 7y_3 \ge 3$$

Otherwise, it is more profitable to make sprinklers than to sell the raw materials to factory 2.

The Factory 1
Liquidation
Model
In summary, then, the problem of determining fair prices is

$$\text{Min} \quad 38y_1 + 34y_2 + 44y_3$$
$$\text{s.t.} \quad 6y_1 + \ \ y_2 + 10y_3 \geq 4$$
$$4y_1 + 3y_2 + \ \ 7y_3 \geq 3$$
$$y_1, y_2 \geq 0$$

and this problem is the dual of (F1). Thus we have shown that the dual to the production problem has the following interpretation.

It provides "fair prices" in the sense of prices that yield the minimum acceptable liquidation payment.

Computational
Significance
of the Dual
When the simplex algorithm is used to solve an LP problem, it turns out that optimal solutions to both the original problem (which may be either a max or min model) and its dual are obtained. We have already seen this fact on the printout (subject to a possible sign change).[2] Thus, if you want to solve a particular problem, you can, of course, go about it by solving the problem directly. Alternatively, you can take the dual of the original problem and then solve the dual problem on the computer.[3] This will also provide an optimal solution to the dual of the dual, which is the original problem. Since each of these possible routes leads to the same result, it is of interest, from the computational point of view, to inquire as to which procedure is more efficient.

To shed light on this question, we take note of the empirical fact that the amount of time required to solve a linear program depends more critically on the number of constraints than on the number of variables. If the original problem has m constraints and n variables, the dual problem has n constraints and m variables. It is then apparent that, *all other things being equal*, you should choose to solve the problem with fewer constraints.

Although the foregoing rule of thumb is a reasonably good general prescription, when you get into fairly large and structured models it may well break down, for in such cases, all other things may not be equal. Possible reasons for departure from this rule of thumb tend to become quite technical in nature. In some cases, irrespective of the number of constraints, one of the two problems, because of its form, may be solvable with a special code, such as what we call a *network code*, as opposed to a general-purpose LP code. The other problem, however, may not have the required special structure and hence may have to be solved with the general-purpose code. Since special structure codes tend to be computationally more efficient than a general-purpose code, this is an important consideration.

[2]It is also true that when properly interpreted, the same sensitivity information is produced on the output, whether one solves the primal or the dual.

[3]If the problem you wish to solve has a variable which is unconstrained in sign, we have already explained in Chapter 6 that such a variable is everywhere replaced by the difference of two nonnegative variables (see conclusion of Section 6.3 as well as Example 7 of Chapter 6). Suppose that the problem you wish to solve contains a variable z with the sign condition $z \leq 0$. Then to solve this on the computer, introduce a new nonnegative variable $w \geq 0$, and throughout the model replace z with $-w$.

Other technical considerations have to do with the fact that even with a general LP code it may be easier to "get started" with one problem rather than the other. This technically has to do with what is sometimes called *phase I of the simplex method*, and is discussed further in AppendixA, where the simplex method is briefly described.

The choice between solving the original problem or its dual does not have much computational significance for small problems, say when either model has no more than several hundred constraints, since such problems can be handled with great speed on modern computing equipment. As the problems grow larger, into the ballpark of several thousand constraints, the choice between the original problem and its dual can become very important. On such occasions, technical consultation with a professional linear programmer may well be worthwhile.

This concludes our formal discussion of the dual problem, per se. We now continue with ramifications of the topic, related to **sensitivity analysis**, with an emphasis on some of the underlying geometric structure.

7.3

SENSITIVITY ANALYSIS

Before proceeding, let us review the notion of sensitivity analysis. In the context of mathematical programming (linear or nonlinear), the terms **sensitivity analysis** and **parametric analysis** refer to the analysis of changes in the optimal solution and the OV as changes are made in the numerical value assigned to a parameter. This type of analysis occurs after one has already found an optimal solution to an initial problem, and that is why the term **postoptimality analysis** is also employed.

The sensitivity topic is one where the art and some of the technicalities of modeling come together. It is based on theory, but it has great practical importance. In order to appreciate this importance, let us suppose that a constrained optimization model (linear or nonlinear) has been formulated and solved. The manager now has an optimal solution to the problem, and this obviously provides him with information not previously at his disposal. However, he knows that his model is only an approximation of his real decision problem. In order to simplify his problem, and to construct a usable model, some logical considerations and interactions have not been included. This is one sense in which the model is an approximation. But there is another quite different and equally important sense in which the model is an approximation. Obviously, every model has parameters, and the values assigned to the parameters constitute the data of the model for a given execution. These data appear in both the objective function and the constraints. For example, in the PROTRAC *E* and *F* model, the RHS of the fifth constraint is 135. You will recall that this value comes from a formula based upon an existing contractual agreement with the union. But this value is renegotiated every six months with the union.

*A Typical
Sensitivity
Question*

Management believes that a value of 135 will be agreed upon for the next 6-month period, but this is far from certain. A look at historical data reveals that the figure has changed a number of times during the last 10 years. Even though the manager feels that 135 is the current best estimate, he cannot help wondering, "What if it turns out to be 130 or 140 instead?" When he solves the problem he uses the value 135, but he wonders, "How valid is this solution if the true parameter value turns out to differ from my estimate?" This is a **sensitivity question**. In the face of uncertainty, the manager wants to know how sensitive his solution is to the data he has provided.

If a sensitivity analysis reveals that the optimal policies are rather insensitive to the particular parameter values employed and if the decision maker "believes in" the logical structure of the model, then he will have more confidence in the results in spite of the uncertainty in the data. If small changes in parameter values can lead to large changes in the results (a high degree of sensitivity), then the manager must exercise more caution in obtaining good data and in transforming model output into real-world decisions.

In general, the term *sensitivity analysis* can apply to any of the data in a problem. One possible way to answer sensitivity questions is simply to solve the model again and again, using different parameter values. In fact, for nonlinear problems this is usually the only way to address such questions. As you might imagine, this can be expensive.

Because of the special structure of LP problems, a good deal of useful sensitivity information is easily produced along with a solution to the problem. Thus, although the topic is of importance for all constrained optimization models, *because of both practical and theoretic obstacles one rarely sees a sensitivity study outside the realm of LP.*

Changing the RHS Outside the Allowable Range   In Chapter 5, the topic of sensitivity analysis on the RHS was briefly introduced and motivated from a geometric point of view. In Chapter 6 it was seen that when a particular RHS value was perturbed **within a given allowable range**, precise statements about the resulting OV can be made. In this chapter, we focus on the way in which dual prices change as the RHS is perturbed by **more than** these allowable amounts.

7.4

ILLUSTRATING DUAL-PRICE OUTPUT

Let us illustrate this discussion with the PROTRAC E and F problem. The computer output is shown in Figure 7.3. The output is annotated in a way that reviews relevant material from Chapter 6.

Reviewing Rate of Change versus Rate of Improvement versus Sign of Dual Price   Recall from Chapter 6 that the dual price is interpreted as the rate of improvement in the OV as the RHS *increases*. This means that

The dual price is positive if increasing the RHS helps (improves) the optimal objective value (OV).

The dual price is negative if increasing the RHS hurts (impairs) the optimal objective value (OV).

For a max model, help means "increase" and hurt means "decrease."

For a min model, help means "decrease" and hurt means "increase."

Now, concerning Figure 7.3, consider the dual price on the availability of labor hours in department B, which is the RHS of the fourth constraint (row 5). We shall let b_4

Figure 7.3
Computer Output for PROTRAC

```
MAX 5000E + 4000F
SUBJECT TO
  2)   E + F ≥ 5
  3)   E − 3F ≤ 0
  4)   10E + 15F ≤ 150
  5)   20E + 10F ≤ 160
  6)   30E + 10F ≥ 135
```

OBJECTIVE FUNCTION VALUE

50500.00

OV = 50,500

VARIABLE	VALUE	REDUCED COST
E	4.50	0.00
F	7.00	

The optimal solution is $E^* = 4.5$, $F^* = 7.0$

ROW	SLACK OR SURPLUS	DUAL PRICES
2	6.50	0.00
3	16.50	0.00
4	0.00	150.00
5	0.00	175.00
6	70.00	0.00

Additional profit obtained if an additional hour of labor is available in department B

s_1^*

Designates active constraints

SENSITIVITY ANALYSIS

OBJ COEFFICIENT RANGES

VARIABLE	CURRENT COEF	ALLOWABLE INCREASE	ALLOWABLE DECREASE
E	5000	3000.00	2333.33
F	4000	3500.00	1500.00

Allowable increase and decrease in profitability of F without changing E^* or F^*

RIGHTHAND SIDE RANGES

ROW	CURRENT RHS	ALLOWABLE INCREASE	ALLOWABLE DECREASE
2	5	6.50	INFINITY
3	0	INFINITY	16.50
4	150	90.00	47.14
5	160	73.33	40.00
6	135	70.00	INFINITY

Reflects valid range for dual price of 175

denote possible values for this parameter. Since the dual price (175) is positive, a unit *increase* in the RHS will help the OV. This also means that a unit *decrease* in the RHS will hurt the OV. Since the units of the objective function are dollars and the units of b_4 are hours, the units of the dual price are dollars per hour. Specifically, if one additional hour of labor were available in department B and the resulting 161 units were *optimally used*, then the increase in revenue would be $175. (In the language of economics, one would say that in the context of this model the marginal return to labor is 175.) It is important to note that in order to obtain this $175 of incremental return, the 161 units of labor must be used *optimally*. This does not mean the same thing as "the extra unit of labor must be used optimally." What it does mean is this. If you were to change b_4 to 161, leaving all other data unchanged, and again solve the problem, the computer output for the new problem would indicate the new optimal values for the decision variables, and producing these quantities would *optimally* employ the 161 units of labor. The resulting OV would be 175 units larger than before, i.e.

$$\text{new OV} = 50,500 + 175 = 50,675$$

In general, the new optimal production policy will *not* be obtained by taking the former optimal production policy and "adding to it" the "optimal employment of another hour of labor." For example, Figure 7.4 shows that as b_4 increases from 160 to 161 the optimal solution moves to the southeast down the line $10E + 15F = 150$. An additional hour of labor leads to the production of more E and **less** F.

Geometric Interpretation

Figure 7.4
Changing the Value of b_4

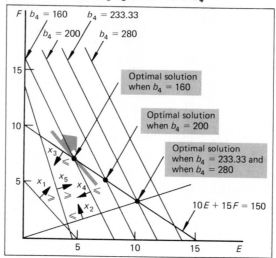

Figure 7.4 provides a geometric interpretation of several possible changes in b_4. Referring to this figure, let us consider the following cases.

Case 1: $b_4 = 160$ This is the original problem. As shown in Figures 7.3 and 7.4, $E^* = 4.5$ and $F^* = 7.0$. The optimal objective value is 50,500, and constraints 3 and 4 are active.

Case 2: $b_4 = 200$ The increase in b_4 of 40 hours $(200 - 160)$ is well within the allowable increase of 73.333 which appears in Figure 7.3. Thus

$$\text{new OV} = 50,500 + 40(175) = 57,500$$

Case 3: $b_4 = 233.3$ Now b_4 has been increased by exactly its allowable amount. As Figure 7.4 shows, at this value for b_4, the fourth constraint passes through the intersection of the second and third constraints. This intersection point is the optimal solution. Thus constraints 2, 3, and 4 are all active and, as a result, the optimal solution is now **degenerate**. The OV now equals

$$\text{new OV} = 50,500 + 73.33(175)$$
$$= 63,333.33$$

The optimal solution is (10, 3.33).

Case 4: $b_4 = 280$ As soon as b_4 becomes larger than 233.33, the fourth contraint becomes redundant. The optimal solution remains at the same corner as when $b_4 = 233.33$. However, this corner is no longer degenerate since the second and third constraints are the only ones active at the solution.

In summary, then, Cases 1 through 4 have helped to demonstrate the following facts:

---

1. For changes in the RHS *less than* the allowable increase, the dual price at the new solution is the same as at the old. The change in the OV between the new solution and the old is obtained by multiplying this dual price by the change in the RHS.

2. For a change in the RHS *exactly equal to* the allowable increase, the new solution is degenerate. The change in the OV between the new solution and the old is obtained by multiplying the dual price at the old solution by the change in the RHS.

3. For a change in the RHS *greater than* the allowable increase, the dual price can be expected to change.[4] The change in the OV between the new solution and the old can *not*, in general, be obtained by multiplying the dual price at the old solution by the change in the RHS.

Although all of the discussion and the illustrations have been for increases in the RHS, the same type of analysis holds for decreases as well.

7.5
THE V(b) FUNCTION

Determining V(b₄)

In Figure 7.4 we saw that for changes in b_4 between the allowable increase and the allowable decrease the optimal values of E and F are determined by the point of intersection of the third and fourth constraints. Thus, if b_4 is a specific value between 120 and 233.33 then the optimal values, say E^* and F^*, must satisfy the algebraic conditions

$$10E^* + 15F^* = 150 \qquad \text{(third constraint line)}$$
$$20E^* + 10F^* = b_4 \qquad \text{(fourth constraint line)}$$

Solving this system of simultaneous equations for E^* and F^*, in terms of b_4, it must be true that

$$E^* = \left(\frac{3}{40}\right)b_4 - 7\frac{1}{2}$$

$$F^* = 15 - \frac{b_4}{20}$$

The corresponding optimal objective value is

$$OV = 5000E^* + 4000F^*$$
$$= 5000\left(\frac{3b_4}{40} - 7.5\right) + 4000\left(15 - \frac{b_4}{20}\right)$$
$$= 175b_4 + 22{,}500$$

---

[4] Under unusual circumstances, the dual price before and after the allowable increase could be the same. This phenomenon is illustrated in Example 7 of Section 7.12.

This equation tells us that as b_4 moves from 120 to 233.33, the OV is produced by a new linear function. Let us use the symbol $V(b_4)$ to denote this function. More generally, we use the notation $V(b)$ to refer to the same construction without specifying a particular constraint. In this specific case, dealing with the fourth constraint, we have seen that if

$$120 < b_4 < 233.33 \qquad \text{then} \qquad V(b_4) = 175b_4 + 22{,}500$$

The slope of the graph of this function is 175. Thus, we have demonstrated algebraically that for $120 < b_4 < 233.33$ the slope of the graph of $V(b_4)$, which is by definition the rate of change (i.e., increase) in the OV as the RHS increases, is the same as the dual price that has appeared in the computer printout (Figure 7.4). Since the active constraints change at 120 and 233.33, the foregoing simultaneous equations that determine E^* and F^* will change, and hence the equation for the values $V(b_4)$ will generally be expected to change. That is why the dual price of 175 can be expected to change as b_4 falls below 120 or rises above 233.33.

The analysis above has led to the notion of a new and important function, $V(b)$, whose values are precisely the OV as the RHS b changes, with all other data remaining the same. For this reason $V(b)$ is also called the OV function. It is a function of a single variable, and you can associate such a function with the RHS of each constraint in any LP problem. Thus, if an LP problem has m constraints, with some given values for the RHS parameters, say $\bar{b}_1, \bar{b}_2, \ldots, \bar{b}_m$, then associated with this problem are m different OV functions, one for each constraint. This means you think of the ith RHS as a variable b_i and keep the other parameters fixed at the assigned values $\bar{b}_j, j \neq i$. The number $V(\bar{b}_i)$ is the OV of the original linear program, and $V(b_i)$ is the OV of a new linear program, with $\bar{b}_i$ replaced by some other value b_i and all other data unchanged. The domain of the function $V(b_i)$ is all values of b_i for which the constraint set is nonempty. In the E and F model, the domain of the function $V(b_4)$ is all values of $b_4 \geq 94.50$, because when b_4 is less than 94.50 there is no point (E, F) satisfying *all* the inequalities. (This is easily seen from Figure 7.5.)

Figure 7.5
Geometric Interpretation as b_4 Varies

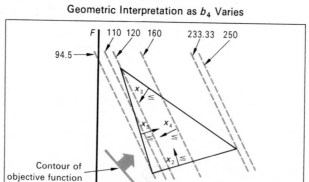

Figures 7.5 and 7.6 show the relation between the OV function and the geometry of the underlying model. These figures should be carefully compared. Note that the graph of $V(b_4)$ is **piecewise linear**; that is, it consists of pieces that are linear between points at which the slope changes. The slopes change at the following two values for b_4:

Figure 7.6
Graph of the Optimal Value Function $V(b_4)$

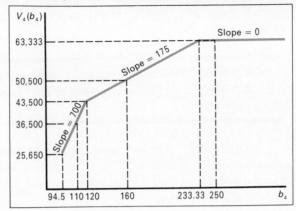

$$b_4 = 120$$
$$b_4 = 233.33$$

**The Slopes
of $V(b_4)$**

These values correspond to two of the points of degeneracy shown in Figure 7.5. The third point of degeneracy ($b_4 = 94.50$) is the point where the domain of $V(b_4)$ begins. Suppose that $(\bar{b}_4, V(\bar{b}_4))$ is any point where the graph of $V(b_4)$ is smooth (i.e., is not a point where the slope changes). Then the slope at $(\bar{b}_4, V(\bar{b}_4))$ is unambiguously defined. It is by definition the rate of change in the optimal objective value at $b_4 = \bar{b}_4$, which for a max model is the same as the dual price corresponding to the RHS b_4. Thus we see that the slopes of $V(b_4)$ are the optimal values of the dual variable on the fourth constraint.

**Degeneracy
and One-Sided
Slopes**

At RHS values that produce a degenerate solution ($b_4 = 94.5, 120, 233.33$), it will generally, though not always, be the case that the slope of the OV graph will differ to the right and to the left of that RHS value. (Or it may not be defined in one direction, as at $b_4 = 94.5$.) This typically means that the dual price (or dual variable) is not unambiguously defined at such a point. There are two values. The computer will print out only one value, and this value will represent either a slope to the left or a slope to the right, but there is no simple way of describing, in advance, which of these will be chosen. However, in any given case the computer printout will provide this information in the following way. **Either the allowable increase or the allowable decrease will be zero.** If the increase is zero, the dual price printed out is the slope to the left, and if the decrease is zero it is the slope to the right.

7.6
RHS CHANGES OUTSIDE THE ALLOWABLE RANGE

In Figure 7.6 we saw that the slopes of the $V(b_4)$ function (defined at all noncorner points) are **nonincreasing**. It is this type of observation that will allow us to obtain at least a limited amount of sensitivity information for RHS changes which exceed allowable limits. First, however, we need to characterize the $V(b)$ slopes more generally. The nonincreasing slopes in Figure 7.6 are related to the fact that the underlying model is a "max" model and the fourth constraint is $\leq$. The general shape of a $V(b)$ function is derived from the following important concepts about inequality constraints in an LP context:

---

1. Loosening an inequality constraint can't hurt, and when it helps it helps less and less.
2. Tightening an inequality constraint can't help, and when it hurts it hurts more and more.

Although this may be a rather pessimistic view of a world hurling faster and faster toward doom, it is a correct view, *if* you believe in constraints and linearity. On a more mundane level, we now immediately have the machinery to talk about RHS changes outside allowable ranges.

Loosening   Let us begin with the concept of loosening an inequality constraint. We know that this can't hurt the OV and may help it (e.g., if the constraint is active). And of course helping means that the rate of improvement in OV, *as you loosen*, is positive. The first concept in the display above means that, when you loosen beyond the allowable range, the rate of improvement either remains the same or decreases.

Example of   To illustrate the above, suppose that you have just solved an LP. Suppose that the first
Loosening   constraint is an inequality constraint with the dual price $d_1 \neq 0$ ($d_1 > 0$ if the constraint is $\leq$, $d_1 < 0$ if the constraint is $\geq$). You wish to loosen the first constraint by an amount Δ that exceeds the allowable range. Here is how your analysis should proceed.

1. If the first constraint is $\leq$, then you are changing b_1 to $b_1 + \Delta$, where Δ exceeds the *allowable increase*, AI, in b_1.
2. If the first constraint is $\geq$, then loosening means you are changing b_1 to $b_1 - \Delta$, where Δ exceeds the *allowable decrease*, AD, in b_1.
3. When we exceed the allowable range the rate of improvement either remains the same or decreases, and it could conceivably decrease to zero (as in Figure 7.6 when $b_4 = 250$). It never becomes negative because loosening can't hurt. This implies that

---

In case 1, OV improvement is at least $d_1 \cdot (\text{AI})$, and at most $d_1 \cdot (\Delta)$. That is, the actual change will be between these two extremes.

In case 2, OV improvement is at least $|d_1| \cdot (\text{AD})$, at most $|d_1| \cdot (\Delta)$.

Note that everything that we have said is independent of whether the problem is max or min.

Tightening   We now consider tightening an inequality constraint. Tightening can't help and may hurt the OV, in which case the rate of improvement, as you tighten, is negative. The second concept in the display above means that, when you tighten beyond the allowable range (assuming that the problem remains feasible) the negative rate of improvement either stays the same or becomes more negative.

Using the examples above, we now tighten by an amount Δ which exceeds the allowable range. You should be able to verify that:

If the constraint is $\leq$, OV is impaired by at least $d_1 \cdot (\Delta)$.

If the constraint is $\geq$, OV is impaired by at least $|d_1| \cdot (\Delta)$.

Note that in the case of tightening outside the allowable limit it is not possible to establish an upper bound on the total impairment of the OV; that is, it is not possible to say that the OV will be impaired by "at most something." Indeed, in the case of tightening, there is one strong caveat to be issued:

Tightening in excess of the allowable amount may create an infeasible problem.

This fact is illustrated in Figure 7.5. There we saw that if b_4 is tightened to a level less than 94.5, the problem became infeasible. Unfortunately, there is nothing on the computer printout to indicate whether this is the case.

7.7

GEOMETRY OF THE $V(b)$ FUNCTION IN GENERAL

We shall now present the general shapes of the $V(b)$ function corresponding to any type of constraint ($\leq$, $\geq$, or $=$) in any type of LP problem (max or min). In order to deduce these general shapes we again make use of the displayed concepts at the beginning of the preceding section. In any given situation, one must also deduce whether the terms **help** or **hurt** imply **increases** or **decreases** in the OV. With these simple concepts, the OV shape can be easily determined, as follows.

Max Problem, $\leq$ Constraint   In this case, increasing the RHS means to loosen. This can't hurt and may help. Since we are maximizing, *help* means "increase." But since loosening helps less and less, the rates of increase become smaller and smaller. Hence, the $V(b)$ shape as shown in Figure 7.7 is the same as the one presented earlier in Figure 7.6.

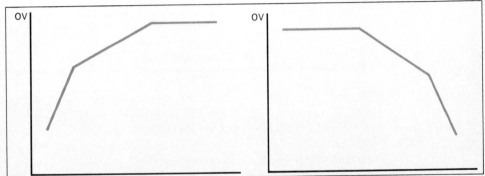

Figure 7.7

$V(b)$ Function for a $\leq$ Constraint in a Max LP Problem

Figure 7.8

$V(b)$ Function for a $\geq$ Constraint in a Max LP Problem

Max Problem, ≥ Constraint   In this case, increasing the RHS means to tighten. This can't help and may hurt. Since we are maximizing, *hurt* means "decrease." But since tightening hurts more and more, the rates of decrease become more severe. This implies the shape shown in Figure 7.8.

Min Problem, ≤ Constraint   In this case, increasing the RHS means to loosen. This can't hurt and may help. Since we are minimizing, *help* means "decrease." But since loosening helps less and less, the rates of decrease become less severe. This implies the shape shown in the leftmost graph in Figure 7.9.

Min Problem, ≥ Constraint   In this case, increasing the RHS means to tighten. This can't help and may hurt. Since we are minimizing, *hurt* means "increase." But since tightening hurts more and more, the rates of increase will become larger and larger. This implies the shape shown in the rightmost graph in Figure 7.9.

Thus, whether we have a max model or a min model, we know that a ≤ constraint can be tightened (decrease the RHS) or loosened (increase the RHS). A ≥ constraint can

Figure 7.9
V(*b*) Function for Inequality Constraints in a Min LP Problem

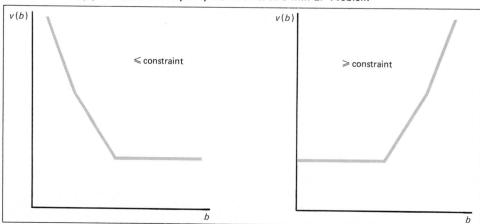

be tightened (increase the RHS) or loosened (decrease the RHS). With either type of constraint, regardless of whether the model is max or min, the *V*(*b*) shapes reflect the following phenomena:

Tightening hurts more and more.

Loosening helps less and less.

The *logo* in Figure 7.10 gives a convenient summary of the four possibilities described above.

One additional observation about tightening and loosening can be made. *The fact that "loosening helps less and less" is a manifestation of diminishing marginal returns. The fact that "tightening hurts more and more" is a manifestation of increasing marginal cost.* That is, for a ≥ constraint, as the numerical value of the RHS increases, stronger

Figure 7.10

V(b) Shapes for Inequality Constraints

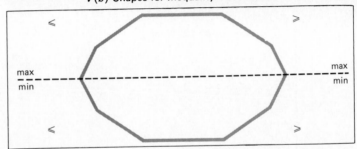

requirements are being imposed. As this occurs, a greater and greater price must be paid to satisfy **incremental** increases in these requirements.

V(b) Slopes for Equality Constraints

In concluding this section, we will consider the OV function associated with a constraint that, in original form, is an *equality* as opposed to an *inequality*. The cases for max and min must be treated separately. Figure 7.11 shows the geometric representation of a hypothetical max model that, in standard equality format, has the following form:

$$
\begin{aligned}
\text{Max} \quad & c_1 x_1 + c_2 x_2 \\
\text{s.t.} \quad & a_{11} x_1 + a_{12} x_2 + y_1 && = b_1 \\
& a_{21} x_1 + a_{22} x_2 && + y_2 && = b_2 \\
& a_{31} x_1 + a_{32} x_2 && && + y_3 && = b_3 \\
& a_{41} x_1 + a_{42} x_2 && && && = b_4 \\
& a_{51} x_1 + a_{52} x_2 && && && + y_5 = b_5 \\
& x_1, x_2, y_1, y_2, y_3, y_5 \geq 0
\end{aligned}
$$

The Max Model

Since the fourth constraint in original form is an equality, there is no slack or surplus variable associated with it (or, if you prefer, the associated slack or surplus must always be zero), and the constraint set consists of the points **on** the fourth constraint line that also satisfy the other four inequalities. In Figure 7.11, the optimal objective contour is also drawn, and the solution is shown when $b_4 = 70$. The dotted lines represent alternative positions of the fourth constraint for other values of b_4. The graph of the corresponding OV function $V(b_4)$ is shown in Figure 7.12. It should be clear to you that the positive and negative slopes of the graph are a direct consequence of the geometry shown in Figure 7.11. Note that the problem is infeasible if either $b_4 < 30$ or $b_4 > 150$.

Since this is a max problem, a positive slope on the graph in Figure 7.12 means that the objective is being improved, which also means that the dual price is positive and hence the same as the slope of the graph. The fact that the slopes of the graph of $V(b_4)$ are both positive and negative shows that the dual price associated with an equality constraint can be positive or negative. (It could also be zero.) It is also possible that the OV graph for an equality constraint in a max problem could have the shape displayed either in Figure 7.7 or 7.8. You may wish to verify this by constructing an appropriate geometric rationale (for example, analogous to Figure 7.11).

The Min Model

Now consider a min problem with an equality constraint. We shall simply state that in this case the OV function corresponding to the equality constraint can have any of the

Figure 7.11
Hypothetical Max LP Model with
an Equality Constraint

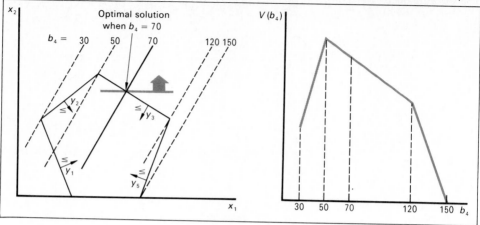

Figure 7.12
Graph of $V(b_4)$ (an OV Function for an
Equality Constraint in a Max LP Model)

Figure 7.13
OV Function for an Equality Constraint in
a Min LP Problem

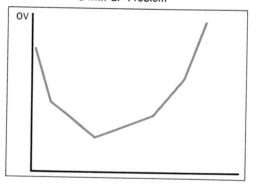

shapes shown in Figure 7.9 or 7.13. Since we are considering a min problem, a negative slope on the OV graph means the objective is being improved. Hence, at such a point the dual price would be positive. Reverse statements hold for positive slopes on the OV graph. Thus, *for the min problem, we see that for an equality constraint as well as for an inequality constraint, it is true that the dual price is the negative of the slope of the OV function.*

In summary, for an *equality constraint*, changing the RHS in a given direction may hurt or help, and

Moving the RHS in a direction of hurt hurts more and more.

Moving the RHS in a direction of help helps less and less and may eventually even hurt.

The observations in this section concerning the general shape of the OV function can be presented more concisely by resorting to more mathematical language. For a max problem the OV functions are always **concave**, and for a min problem the OV functions are always **convex**. It is convenient to employ these facts without proof, and we have implicitly done so in the diagrams used in the previous development. These facts are a mathematical statement of the economic concepts of **diminishing marginal returns** and **increasing marginal costs,** respectively.

7.8
SENSITIVITY ANALYSIS AND $V(c)$

At the outset, let us review some of what we learned in Chapter 6. Consider the PRO-TRAC E and F problem again. The computer output (which includes the problem statement) is shown in Figure 7.14 (which is a reproduction of Figure 7.3). Information for

Figure 7.14
Computer Output for PROTRAC

```
MAX 5000E + 4000F
SUBJECT TO
  2)    E + F ≥ 5
  3)    E - 3F ≤ 0
  4)   10E + 15F ≤ 150
  5)   20E + 10F ≤ 160
  6)   30E + 10F ≥ 135
              OBJECTIVE FUNCTION VALUE
                  50500.00
```

VARIABLE	VALUE	REDUCED COST
E	4.50	0.00
F	7.00	0.00

ROW	SLACK OR SURPLUS	DUAL PRICES
2	6.50	0.00
3	16.50	0.00
4	0.00	150.00
5	0.00	175.00
6	70.00	0.00

SENSITIVITY ANALYSIS

OBJ COEFFICIENT RANGES

VARIABLE	CURRENT COEF	ALLOWABLE INCREASE	ALLOWABLE DECREASE
E	5000	3000.00	2333.33
F	4000	3500.00	1500.00

The current solution remains optimal for changes in this range

RIGHTHAND SIDE RANGES

ROW	CURRENT RHS	ALLOWABLE INCREASE	ALLOWABLE DECREASE
2	5	6.50	INFINITY
3	0	INFINITY	16.50
4	150	90.00	47.14
5	160	73.33	40.00
6	135	70.00	INFINITY

performing sensitivity analysis on the coefficients in the objective function is presented in the section identified as OBJ COEFFICIENT RANGES. In Chapter 6, the interpretation of this information was tersely presented without discussion. We will now illustrate the use of this information by focusing on the per unit revenue for E-9s. This is one of the input parameters for the problem. For the current computer run (Figure 7.14) we have used a value of 5000 for this parameter. Now consider the question: What happens to the number of E-9s in the optimal solution as the per unit revenue of E-9s is increased? In providing a partial answer to this question, it might first be observed that if the per unit revenue of E-9s were to increase, *with all other data unchanged*, we would then expect to produce more, rather than less, E-9s. In the current solution the optimal level of E-9 production is 4.5. The per unit revenue is $5000. If we were to increase the per unit revenue, say to 5010 or to 6000, and then resubmit the problem for solution, it would surely defy intuition if the resulting solution were to specify a production level of **less** than 4.5 E-9s. Recall that all other data have remained the same. The only change has been to make E-9s more profitable. How could this ever persuade us to make a smaller number of E-9s? It cannot, and this illustrates a first important principle in the realm of sensitivity analysis on objective function coefficients:

Intuitive
Observations

> **In a max model, increasing the profitability of an activity, keeping all other data unchanged, cannot reduce the optimal level of that activity.**

Alternatively, suppose that you are working in a min context. You would expect that increasing the per unit cost of an activity, keeping all other data unchanged, could certainly **not** lead to an increase in its level at optimality. On the other hand, as the cost contribution becomes smaller, that activity becomes more attractive. Thus, we have the following counterpart to the preceding key concept:

> **In a min model, lowering the cost of an activity, keeping all other data unchanged, cannot reduce the optimal level of that activity.**

Now then, let us return to the question raised above. Suppose the per unit revenue of E-9s is only *slightly* increased. Does this mean there will be more E-9s produced at optimality? Although your intuition may say yes, we have already learned that the correct answer is no. In optimization models, it is important to pay careful attention to the logical difference between the phrases such as "cannot reduce" and "must increase." It turns out that, in the E and F problem, as the per unit revenue is gradually and continuously increased from 5000, the optimal production remains **unchanged** at the value 4.5— **until the profitability increase is sufficiently large.** With this in mind, let us refine the earlier question to, "*How much* would the per unit revenue of E-9s have to increase before the number of E-9s in the optimal solution would increase?" The discussion in Chapter 6 provided the following analysis. The entry in the ALLOWABLE INCREASE column is 3000. This tells us the amount that the coefficient of E in the objective function could be increased *without* changing the optimal solution, where it is understood that all other data in the problem remain unchanged. In this problem, if the change is more than 3000 the optimal solution *will* change. The objective function for the E and F model is

$$5000E + 4000F$$

The optimal solution is $E^* = 4.5$, $F^* = 7$, and the optimal objective value is 50,500. We have just stated that if the objective function is changed to

$$cE + 4000F$$

where c is any specific number between 5000 and 8000, and if the new problem is then solved, the optimal solution will still be $E^* = 4.5$, $F^* = 7$. Of course, you can see that the new optimal objective value will be

$$\text{New OV} = c(4.5) + 4000(7) = 4.5c + 28{,}000$$

The V(c) Function

That is, as our choice for the number c varies between 5000 and 8000, the OV is given by a linear function of c. Letting $V(c)$ denote the values of this function,[5] we see that

$$\boxed{V(c) = 4.5c + 28{,}000 \qquad \text{for } 5000 \leq c \leq 8000}$$

Thus, if the coefficient of E is increased the maximum amount, by 3000, c will be 8000, and we have

$$V(8000) = 64{,}000$$

It is quite simple to represent the foregoing facts geometrically. Let us refer to the interpretation in Figure 7.15. Considering our new objective function (i.e., letting c

Figure 7.15
Effects of Increasing c in the Equation
$cE + 4000F = K$

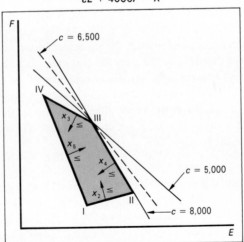

denote the per unit revenue for E-9s), the general isorevenue contour is given by

$$cE + 4000F = K \qquad \text{or} \qquad F = -\left(\frac{c}{4000}\right)E + \frac{K}{4000}$$

[5]Do not confuse this $V(c)$ function with the $V(b)$ function discussed earlier. The latter is a function of an RHS value. The former is a function of an objective function coefficient. Since the argument explicitly appears, there should be no confusion in using the same symbol, V.

where K is a constant representing the revenue at each point on the K-contour. (Recall that K is fixed on a given contour, and K differs on different contours.)

As c, the coefficient of E, is increased, the slope of the contour becomes more negative (that is, the contour tilts downward more steeply). When the coefficient c is 8000, the slope of the contour is

$$-\frac{8000}{4000} = -2$$

But, referring again to Figure 7.15, -2 is also the slope of the fourth constraint line, whose equation is

$$20E + 10F = 160 \quad \text{or} \quad F = -\frac{20}{10}E + \frac{160}{10} = -2E + 16$$

Now you can see in Figure 7.15 exactly what is happening. As the coefficient (c) of E slightly increases, the tilt of the objective contour changes, becoming more steep. The optimal solution, however, remains at the same corner, **although the optimal objective value $V(c)$ changes.** As the coefficient of E continues to increase, this same state of affairs persists until the coefficient hits the value 8000. When this occurs, the objective function contours are parallel to the fourth constraint line, and both of the corners II and III are optimal solutions. In this case the problem has **alternative**, *or* **multiple, optima.** Thus, at a per-unit revenue of 8000 for E, the model is indifferent between using the production policy prescribed by corner II or the one associated with corner III. At corner II, the optimal value of E is larger. Thus, at the point when the per unit revenue for E is 8000, you would be willing to produce more than 4.5 E-9s, and this is the answer to the question posed above. Of course, you do not know exactly *how many* more without obtaining the values of the variables at the newly introduced optimal corner.

Note in Figure 7.15 that as the coefficient of E increases slightly beyond 8000, then corner II becomes the unique solution. Further increases in the coefficient of E will have no effect on the solution since the objective contour will merely become increasingly steep approaching, but never reaching, a vertical line (i.e., the slope approaches $-\infty$).

By similar reasoning, a *decrease* in the coefficient of E will give the objective contours a less negative tilt. Verify that when the coefficient is decreased by 2,333.33, the slope of the contour is -0.67, which is the same as the slope of the third constraint line

$$10E + 15F = 150.$$

When this occurs, the corners III and IV are optimal, and you should be willing to produce fewer E-9s and more F-9s. As the price decreases by more than 2,333.33, corner IV becomes the unique solution. This is true even when $c = 0$. Note, however, that at corner IV the value of E is still positive. Does it surprise you that the optimal value of E is positive even when the per unit revenue is zero?

General
Review of
Sensitivity
Analysis on
Objective
Function
Coefficients

Let us now turn from the analysis of the PROTRAC E and F model to the general case. It will be seen that, with one exception concerning degeneracy, the analysis is analogous. Suppose that x_j is one of the decision variables in a max LP model. Let x^* denote an optimal solution to the current problem. Thus, x^* is the vector $(x_1^*, x_2^*, \ldots, x_n^*)$, and x_j^* is the optimal value of x_j in this solution. Suppose that c_j denotes the coefficient of x_j in the objective function and that $c_j = \bar{c}_j$ in the problem that has just been solved. Unfortunately, in order to discuss the general case it is necessary to use this more general and more abstract notation. If the abstraction seems to interfere with your understanding, you should substitute specific numbers for the symbols. For example, you might let $n = 2, j = 1$, and let x_1^* have the value of E^* in the E and F discussion above. That is, we could let $\bar{c}_1 = 5000$, and then, following the E and F context, x_1^* would be 4.5. Substituting specific values in this way should help you to understand the abstraction.

We shall now quickly review the information provided on the computer output for sensitivity analysis on *increases* in c_j. Let I be the number in the column ALLOWABLE INCREASE. (In Figure 7.14, I has the value 3000.)

1. If the coefficient c_j increases by an amount less than I (which can be true only if $I > 0$), then x^* remains an optimal solution to the problem. (Of course, the OV will change if $x_j^* > 0$.) This does not imply that x^* is a unique optimal solution for $\bar{c}_j \leq \bar{c}_j < \bar{c}_j + I$. It is possible to have alternative optima. (To see this, one must consider a problem with more than two decision variables.) However, if alternative optima do exist, then in any such solution the optimal value of x_j is x_j^*.

2. If c_j increases by an amount equal to I or by an amount greater than I, there are two cases to consider:

    a. Suppose that x^* is a **nondegenerate** optimal solution. In this case, if I is zero, then there are multiple optimal corner solutions and in one of these it will be true that $x_j > x_j^*$. For an increase in c_j beyond $\bar{c}_j$, any optimal solution will have $x_j > x_j^*$. If I is positive rather than zero, then we are assured that when c_j is increased by *exactly* this amount (from $\bar{c}_j$, to $\bar{c}_j + I$) there will be multiple optimal corner solutions. One of these will be the previous solution, x^*, and another of these will have an optimal value of x_j larger than x_j^*. Thus, we would be willing to increase the optimal level of x_j when the profitability is increased to $\bar{c}_j + I$. For values of c_j greater than $\bar{c}_j + I$ (keeping all other data fixed), any optimal solution will have $x_j > x_j^*$. Again, in problems with more than two decision variables, it may be possible to have alternative optima when c_j is slightly larger than $\bar{c}_j + I$.

    b. Suppose that x^* is a **degenerate** optimal solution. In this case we *cannot* be assured that there will be a solution with an increased level of x_j when c_j is given the value $\bar{c}_j + I$ (regardless of whether I is positive or zero). In addition, it could be possible that, even when c_j is greater than $\bar{c}_j + I$, the former solution x^* remains optimal.

The two cases in items a and b cover the interactions for an increase in c_j in a max model. Analogous statements can be made for decreases in c_j in a max model or for increases and decreases in c_j in a min model. All of the considerations above can be graphically illustrated and amplified by further emphasis on the $V(c)$ function. This is accomplished in the next section.

7.9

GEOMETRY OF THE V(c) FUNCTION

Earlier in this chapter, we made extensive use of $V(b)$, the OV function, whose argument is the RHS of a particular constraint. We suggested in the preceding section that it is possible to define a similar function whose argument is the coefficient of a particular variable in the objective function. For example, we saw that for the PROTRAC E and F model displayed in the computer output (Figure 7.14) it was possible to express the OV as a function

$$V(c) = 4.5c + 28{,}000$$

for values of c between 2666.67 and 8000. When $c = 8000$, we saw that there were two alternative optimal solutions, namely corners II and III in Figure 7.15. Moreover, as the coefficient c takes on values larger than 8000, corner II becomes the unique solution. This corner is determined by the intersection of the second and fourth constraint lines, namely the equalities corresponding to rows 3 and 5 in the model. Solving these equations

$$\text{(row 3)} \qquad E - 3F = 0$$
$$\text{(row 5)} \qquad 20E + 10F = 160$$

simultaneously, one obtains the optimal values of the decision variables $E^* = 6\frac{6}{7}$, $F^* = 2\frac{2}{7}$.

Constructing
V(c)

Consequently, for values of $c \geq 8000$ one can obtain the OV from the expression

$$V(c) = cE^* + 4000F^* = 6\frac{6}{7}c + 9142.86$$

Also, for a value of c equal to $5000 - 2333.33 = 2666.67$ we saw that corners III and IV are optimal, and for $0 \leq c < 2666.67$ corner IV becomes the unique solution. (Since c denotes a revenue, we assume that its value must remain nonnegative.) Corner IV is determined by the intersection of the third and fifth constraint lines, namely the equalities corresponding to rows 4 and 6 in the model. Solving these equations

$$\text{(row 4)} \qquad 10E + 15F = 150$$
$$\text{(row 6)} \qquad 30E + 10F = 135$$

simultaneously, one obtains the optimal decision variable values $E^* = 1.5$, $F^* = 9$. Consequently, for $0 \leq c \leq 2666.67$ one obtains the OV from the expression

$$V(c) = cE^* + 4000F^* = 1.5c + 36{,}000$$

We can now put this together by plotting the graph of the $V(c)$ function for *all* values of $c \geq 0$. This is done in Figure 7.16. This function $V(c)$ gives the OV corresponding to all nonnegative values of c, with all other data in the original model unchanged.

Figure 7.16
OV as a Function of c, the Per Unit
Revenue of E

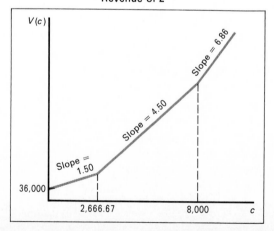

It is important to note the following fact:

The slope of the $V(c)$ graph, for a given value of c, is precisely the optimal value of E when the per unit revenue is c.

Shape of V(c) for a Max Model

Also note that the slopes of the graph in Figure 7.16 are increasing. Since these slopes are the optimal values of E, the shape reflects the fact that increasing the profitability of E-9s cannot reduce the optimal level of production of E-9s.

Alternative Optima and the Corners of V(c)

Note that when $c = 2666.67$ there are two optimal corner solutions. In one of these solutions, the optimal level of production is the old value, 1.5 (the slope to the left of 2666.67). In the other corner solution, the optimal level of production has increased to 4.5, which is the slope to the right of 2666.67. You can see from this analysis that the following statement is true:

Each corner on the $V(c)$ graph corresponds to a c value for which there is more than one optimal corner solution, and the values of E differ at these solutions.

It is of interest to contrast the facts that

The corners on the $V(b)$ graph correspond to values of b for which there is a degenerate optimal solution, whereas the corners on the $V(c)$ graph correspond to values of c for which there are multiple optima.

Recall that the coefficients in the objective function of an LP problem correspond to the RHS for the dual of that problem. This observation suggests that $V(c)$ for the primal corresponds to a $V(b)$ for the dual, and hence that if the primal has alternative optimal solutions, the optimal solution to the dual of that problem will be degenerate. This suggestion is indeed correct and can be rigorously established by other means. This is explored further in Example 10 of Section 7.12.

The discussion above has been couched in terms of the specific E and F model. In the general max model, consider the current solution (for, say, $c_j = \bar{c}_j$) and let I be the number on the output under ALLOWABLE INCREASE and let D denote the number under ALLOWABLE DECREASE. Then, as discussed under items 1 and 2 at the end of Section 7.8, several observations can be made:

1. In all cases, the slope of $V(c)$ surely will not change for values of c_j greater than $\bar{c}_j - D$ and less than $\bar{c}_j + I$.
2. If the solution is **nondegenerate**, then corners in $V(c_j)$ will occur when c_j equals $\bar{c}_j - D$ and $\bar{c}_j + I$. (This case is illustrated in Figure 7.16.)
3. If the solution is **degenerate**, the nearest corners in each direction may be at (one or the other or both of) the end points of the above interval, or they may lie beyond the interval in either direction.

For a min problem, the general shape of the $V(c)$ graph can be easily inferred. In this case, increasing the cost (c) of an activity can only hurt the OV. For a min problem, hurting the objective value means that it must increase. Consequently, $V(c)$ is again an increasing function. However, as we have already observed, increasing the cost of an activity while everything else remains constant *cannot* increase the level of that activity in an optimal solution. Thus, just as for a max problem, since the optimal level of the activity in any optimal solution is the slope of $V(c)$, the slopes cannot increase for a min problem. They must either decrease or remain the same. (Of course the slopes will always be nonnegative, because the optimal values of the decision variables are always nonnegative.) Figure 7.17 shows the general concave shape of the $V(c)$ graph for a min problem. Again, the corners to the left and to the right of a current solution are given by the computer output, **provided that the current solution is nondegenerate.**

Shape of V(c) for a Min Model

Figure 7.17
$V(c)$ Function for a Min Problem

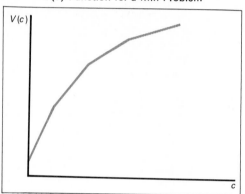

7.10

ESTIMATING CHANGES IN $V(c)$

Consider a linear program in which $\sum_{j=1}^{n} \bar{c}_j x_j$ is the objective function and $x^* = (x_1^*, x_2^*, \ldots, x_n^*)$ is an optimal solution. Let us focus on the effects of perturbations in a particular coefficient, c_j, with all other data in the model held fixed. In the previous discussion, we have defined $V(c_j)$ as the OV as a function of c_j. Thus, $V(\bar{c}_j)$ is the OV for the initial problem. That is, $V(\bar{c}_j) = \sum_{j=1}^{n} \bar{c}_j x_j^*$.

In order to plot the general shape of the $V(c_j)$ graph for a max model, one need only remember that increasing c_j (the profitability) cannot hurt and cannot reduce the optimal level of x_j, which is the slope.

Thus, the graph must have the shape shown in Figure 7.18. The shaded regions show where the $V(c_j)$ graph must lie to the right of $\bar{c}_j + I$ and to the left of $\bar{c}_j - D$.

In order to plot the general shape of the $V(c_j)$ graph for a min model, one need only remember that increasing c_j (the cost) cannot help and cannot increase the optimal level of x_j, which is the slope.

---

228   Thus, the graph must have the shape shown in Figure 7.19, where the shaded regions are interpreted as in Figure 7.18. The distances D and I in these figures are the allowable decrease and increase, respectively, that appear on the computer printout. The corners on the $V(c_j)$ graphs correspond to values of c_j at which there are alternative optimal corner solutions with different values for x_j.

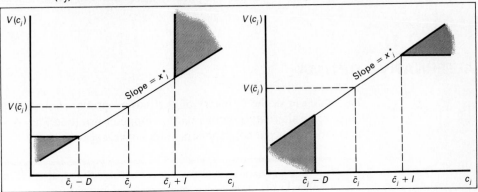

Figure 7.18
$V(c_j)$ for a General Max Model

Figure 7.19
$V(c_j)$ for a General Min Model

Using Figures 7.18 and 7.19, you can easily see how to determine limits on the change in OV when c_j is perturbed to a value larger than $\bar{c}_j + I$ or smaller than $\bar{c}_j - D$. In particular, the following facts can be deduced from Figures 7.18 and 7.19:

1. For a max problem, two-sided estimates can be obtained for decreases in c_J, and one-sided estimates can be obtained for increases.
2. For a min problem, two-sided estimates can be obtained for increases in c_J, and one-sided estimates can be obtained for decreases.

Let us illustrate these ideas with a particular example. Consider the output in Figure 7.14. We shall estimate the change in the OV if the per unit price of E is decreased from 5000 to 2500. (Of course, the exact value $V(2500)$ could be obtained from Figure 7.16 but we are assuming here that the entire $V(c)$ function has not been generated. We are acting as if we have at our disposal only the output from the single computer run shown in Figure 7.14.) Since the allowable decrease is only 2333.33, the desired decrease of 2500 takes us outside the range for making exact inferences. The estimation is illustrated in Figure 7.20.

Figure 7.20
Using $V(c)$ to Estimate OV Changes

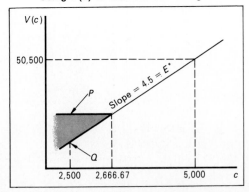

When $c = 2500$ the $V(c)$ graph lies between the points P and Q. Thus the OV would decrease by at least $(2333.33)(4.5) = 10,500$ to the value $50,500 - 10,500 = 40,000$. Similarly, the decrease would be at most $(2500)(4.5) = 11,250$ to the value $50,500 - 11,250 = 39,250$. In this way the $V(c)$ graph makes it quite simple to estimate changes in the OV when c_j is assigned a value outside the allowable range.

As a final point, we note that this entire discussion on use of the $V(c)$ graph for the estimation of OV changes is applicable whether or not the current solution is degenerate.

7.11

ALTERNATIVE OPTIMA

This section links the geometry of alternative optimal corner solutions with the signals that indicate alternative optima on the computer printout. Suppose that you are reading the computer output corresponding to a **nondegenerate solution**.

> **In a nondegenerate solution, the basic signal for alternative optima is the presence in the output of a zero allowable increase or zero allowable decrease in one of the objective function coefficients.**

This fact should be clear from the geometric interpretations presented in the earlier discussions. In particular, if there is a unique nondegenerate optimal corner solution, it must be possible to change each coefficient in the objective function at least a small amount in either the positive or negative direction without changing the current optimal corner. Therefore, if there is no allowable change for some coefficient in either direction, there must be multiple solutions. It should also be clear from the geometry that whenever there are alternative optimal corners, it must be the case that every feasible point on the line segment between the two corners is also optimal. However, since such solutions are not corner solutions, they would never be produced by the computer.

It is worth pointing out there are two special cases of the foregoing displayed signal for alternative optima. First, consider the max model with the geometry shown in Figure 7.21. There are two decision variables, x_1 and x_2, and three inequality constraints

Figure 7.21
Alternative Optima Signals

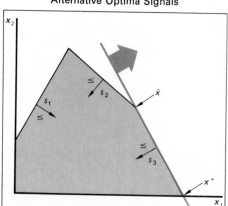

with slacks s_1, s_2, and s_3. The alternative optimal solutions are x^* and $\bar{x}$. Each solution is nondegenerate. Suppose the computer has produced x^*. You can see that x_2^* is zero and the reduced cost of x_2 is also zero. This is true because it is possible to find a solution in which $x_2 > 0$ that does not decrease the OV. In other words, there is already an alternative optimal solution with $x_2 > 0$.

In a nondegenerate solution, a zero decision variable with zero reduced cost signals alternative optima.

In the case above, the zero reduced cost on a decision variable with zero optimal value shows that you are already at the point of indifference between a positive and a zero optimal value for that variable. This can only be true if there are alternative optima.

The second special case is seen by supposing that for Figure 7.21 the computer has produced the solution $\bar{x}$ rather than x^*. (There is no way in general to tell which one would actually be obtained.) You can see that the optimal slack value on the second constraint is zero, namely $\bar{s}_2 = 0$. You can also see that the dual price associated with this constraint must be zero. That is because an increase in b_2 will slide the second constraint line to the northeast and the new solution will produce the same OV as before. Thus,

---

In a nondegenerate solution, the appearance of a zero dual price on an active inequality constraint signals alternative optima.

You may be wondering whether this applies to an equality constraint. That is, if you discover an equality constraint with a zero dual price, does this signal alternative optima? A negative answer can be quickly obtained with a geometric analysis. Consider Figure 7.22, in which there are three inequality constraints and one equality constraint. The constraint set is the hatched line, and there is a unique solution. It is nondegenerate. The objective function contours are parallel to the first constraint line. As the RHS on the equality constraint is perturbed, the solution will slide along the first constraint line. Hence, the optimal objective value will not change. This means the dual price on the equality constraint is zero. But there are *not* alternative optima.

Figure 7.22
Equality Constraint with Zero Dual Price

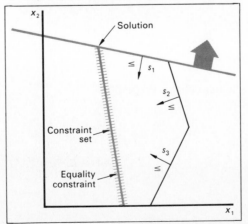

EXAMPLES AND SOLUTIONS

Example 1

Use summation notation to write the primal problem as a max model with n nonnegative variables and m inequality ($\leq$) constraints. Let c_j, a_{ij}, and b_i denote the parameters for the objective function, the constraint functions, and the RHS, respectively. Then write out the dual of this problem.

Solution to Example 1

Primal

$$\text{Max} \quad \sum_{j=1}^{n} c_j x_j$$

$$\text{s.t.} \quad \sum_{j=1}^{n} a_{ij} x_j \leq b_i \qquad i = 1, \ldots, m$$

$$x_j \geq 0 \qquad j = 1, \ldots, n$$

Dual

$$\text{Min} \quad \sum_{i=1}^{m} b_i y_i$$

$$\text{s.t.} \quad \sum_{i=1}^{m} a_{ij} y_i \geq c_j \qquad j = 1, \ldots, n$$

$$y_i \geq 0 \qquad i = 1, \ldots, m$$

Example 2

Find the dual to the following problem:

$$\text{Min} \quad \sum_{j=1}^{n} c_j x_j$$

$$\text{s.t.} \quad \sum_{j=1}^{n} a_{ij} x_j \leq b_i \qquad i = 1, \ldots, m$$

$$x_j \geq 0 \qquad j = 1, \ldots, n$$

Solution to Example 2

The dual of this problem is

$$\text{Max} \quad \sum_{i=1}^{m} b_i y_i$$

$$\text{s.t.} \quad \sum_{i=1}^{m} a_{ij} y_i \leq c_j \qquad j = 1, \ldots, n$$

$$y_i \leq 0 \qquad i = 1, \ldots, m$$

The dual variables for the original problem are negative since, in this case, a per unit increase in each RHS value b_i will help and, hence, decrease the optimal objective value. This negative sign is consistent with the fact that **the dual variable is the rate of change in the optimal (primal) objective value as the RHS increases.** Note that in this instance the **dual prices** that appear on the computer printout will be positive.

Example 3

Suppose that the primal problem

$$\text{Max} \quad \sum_{j=1}^{n} c_j x_j$$

$$\text{s.t.} \quad \sum_{i=1}^{n} a_{ij} x_i \le b_i \qquad i = 1, \ldots, m \tag{P}$$

$$x_j \ge 0 \qquad j = 1, \ldots, n$$

is unbounded for some set of RHS parameters b_i, $i = 1, \ldots, m$. Use the dual theorem to show that this implies (P) is either unbounded or inconsistent for every choice of b_is.

Solution to Example 3

If (P) is unbounded for some choice of b_is, say $b_i = \hat{b}_i$, $i = 1, \ldots, m$, then by the dual theorem the following dual problem must be inconsistent:

$$\text{Min} \quad \sum_{i=1}^{m} \hat{b}_i y_i$$

$$\text{s.t.} \quad \sum_{i=1}^{m} a_{ij} y_i \ge c_j \qquad j = 1, \ldots, n \tag{D}$$

$$y_i \ge 0 \qquad i = 1, \ldots, m$$

The fact that (D) is inconsistent depends only on the constraints of (D), not on the objective function. Changing the b_i values in (P) will not affect the constraints in (D). Consequently, (D) will remain inconsistent for all choices of the parameters b_i. It follows then from the dual theorem that, for any set of right-hand sides, (P) will be either unbounded or inconsistent.

Example 4

Recall the Astro/Cosmo TV production problem:

$$\text{Max} \quad 20A + 30C$$

$$\text{s.t.} \quad A \qquad\quad \le 70$$

$$C \le 50$$

$$A + 2C \le 120$$

$$A, C \ge 0$$

Assume that the RHS of the third constraint is b_3 rather than 120. Use a combination of geometric and algebraic techniques to plot the $V(b_3)$ function.

233

Solution to Example 4

Figure 7.23 shows four values for b_3 and the associated location of the optimal solution. As b_3 increases, the location of the optimal solution moves from the origin along the A axis to the corner (70, 0) and then along the line $A = 70$. It follows the path indicated by the roman numerals I, II, III, IV. We observe that since corner II is given by $A = 70$, $C = 0$, it clearly lies on the line $A + 2C = 70$. Similarly, corner IV with coordinates (70, 50) lies on the line $A + 2C = 170$.

Figure 7.23

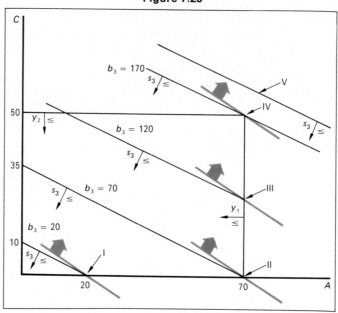

For $0 \leq b_3 \leq 70$, the location of the optimal solution is determined by the intersection of the lines

$$C = 0$$
$$A + 2C = b_3$$

The solution is $A = b_3$, $C = 0$. Thus, the OV function is

$$20A + 30C = 20(b_3) + 30(0) = 20b_3$$

For $70 \leq b_3 \leq 170$, the location of the optimal solution is determined by the intersection of the lines

$$A = 70$$
$$A + 2C = b_3$$

The solution is $A = 70$, $C = (b_3 - 70)/2$. Thus, the OV function is

$$20A + 30C = 20(70) + 30\left(\frac{b_3 - 70}{2}\right) = 350 + 15b_3$$

For $b_3 > 170$, the third constraint becomes redundant, as indicated by roman numeral V. The optimal solution remains at the point (70, 50). Thus, for $b_3 > 170$ the OV function is

$$20(70) + 30(50) = 2900$$

Figure 7.24 shows the plot of the $V(b_3)$ function.

Figure 7.24

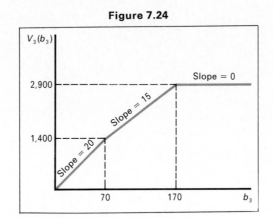

Example 5

Recall the Crawler Tread ore-blending problem from Chapter 6. The output for this problem (including the formulation) is shown in Figure 7.25.
   Specify the tightest bounds possible for the OV function if
   (a) The RHS of the first constraint (row 2) becomes 4 and all other parameters remain as shown.
   (b) The RHS of the third constraint (row 4) becomes 32 and all other parameters remain as shown. (Assume that the constraint set is not empty when $b_3 = 32$.)

Solution to Example 5

   (a) The allowable decrease is 0.25. Hence the constraint is being loosened beyond the allowable decrease. The dual price is -44.44. Hence, according to the discussion in Section 7.6, the OV will be improved by at least $0.25(44.44) = 11.11$ and by at most 44.44. That is, the new OV will satisfy $466.67 \le$ NEW OV ≤ 500.00.
   (b) The allowable increase is 0.714. Hence the constraint is being tightened beyond the allowable range. This means the OV will be hurt by at least $2|$dual price$| = 2(4.44) = 8.88$. That is,

$$\text{NEW OV} \ge 519.99$$

Figure 7.25
Output for Crawler Tread

```
MIN 800 T1 + 400 T2 + 600 T3 + 500 T4
SUBJECT TO
  2) 10 T1 + 3 T2 + 8 T3 + 2 T4 ≥ 5
  3) 90 T1 + 150 T2 + 75 T3 + 175 T4 ≥ 100
  4) 45 T1 + 25 T2 + 20 T3 + 37 T4 ≥ 30
  5) T1 + T2 + T3 + T4 = 1
```

OBJECTIVE FUNCTION VALUE

1   511.111   OV

VARIABLE	VALUE	REDUCED COST
T1	0.259	0.000
T2	0.703	0.000
T3	0.037	0.000
T4	0.000	91.111

Optimal Value of T1 → (points to T1 0.259)

Variables

ROW	SLACK OR SURPLUS	DUAL PRICES
2	0.000	−44.444
3	31.666	0.000
4	0.000	−4.444
5	0.000	−155.555

Constraints

SENSITIVITY ANALYSIS

OBJ COEFFICIENT RANGES

VARIABLE	CURRENT COEF	ALLOWABLE INCREASE	ALLOWABLE DECREASE
T1	800.000	223.636	119.999
T2	400.000	66.847	299.999
T3	600.000	85.714	118.169
T4	500.000	INFINITY	91.111

RIGHTHAND SIDE RANGES

ROW	CURRENT RHS	ALLOWABLE INCREASE	ALLOWABLE DECREASE
2	5.000	2.375	0.250
3	100.000	31.666	INFINITY
4	30.000	0.714	7.000
5	1.000	0.250	0.043

Example 6

Use a hypothetical constraint set diagram to illustrate that in a max problem the slope of the graph of the $V(b)$ function *need not always* become zero as the constraint continues to loosen.

Solution to Example 6

An illustrative constraint set diagram is shown in Figure 7.26. Assume that constraint 3 is a $\leq$ inequality. As b_3 increases, constraint 3 continues to loosen, and the plot of con-

Figure 7.26

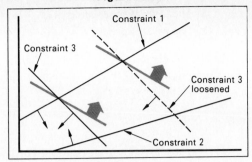

straint 3 will move to the northeast, parallel to its initial position. The optimal solution will move along constraint 1 indefinitely, and the increase in the OV per unit increase in b_3 remains constant and is not zero.

Example 7

Construct a hypothetical example that illustrates the fact the slope of the $V(b)$ function does not always change when the RHS has been perturbed by the allowable amount. Note that in such a situation there are alternative optimal solutions.

Solution to Example 7

The secret to success in this example is to make the contours of the objective function parallel to the constraint whose RHS is being manipulated. Such a situation is shown in Figure 7.27. Suppose that you are constructing the $V(b_1)$ function. Note that when $b_1 = b_1^{(1)}$, there are alternative optimal solutions, one at A and one at B. For the solution at A, the computer would indicate an allowable increase of $b_1^{(2)} - b_1^{(1)}$. At B the allowable increase would be $b_1^{(3)} - b_1^{(1)}$. Hence, $V(b_1)$ must increase at a constant rate between $b_1^{(1)}$ and $b_1^{(3)}$, as shown in Figure 7.28.

Figure 7.27   **Figure 7.28**

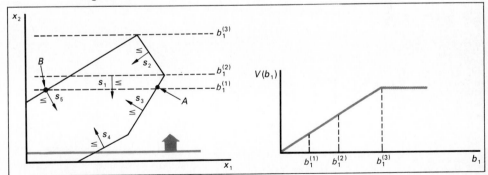

Example 8

Consider again the Crawler Tread problem and the computer output in Figure 7.25.
    (a) For each of the changes suggested below, first, specify the exact value of the OV or the tightest possible bounds. Then, state as precisely as possible what happens to the optimal solution.

1. The price of ore from location 1 increases by $100.
2. The price of ore from location 2 increases by $100.
3. The price of ore from location 1 decreases by $150.

(b) At what rate and in what direction does the optimal value of the objective function change if the ore from location 4 is introduced into the solution?

Solution to Example 8

(a) 1. The allowable increase in the coefficient $T1$ is 223.636. The suggested increase is 100. Therefore, the optimal solution remains the same. The OV will increase by 100(0.259) to the value 537.011.

2. The allowable increase in the coefficient of $T2$ is 66.84. The suggested increase is 100. Since the current solution is nondegenerate, we know for sure that the increase of 100 will produce a new optimal solution. Moreover, in this new solution the optimal value of $T2$ will be smaller. Bounds on the new value of the OV function can be found by using Figure 7.29.

$$\text{(lower bound)} \quad 511.111 + 66.84(0.703) = 558.09$$
$$\text{(upper bound)} \quad 511.111 + 100(0.703) = 581.41$$

3. The allowable decrease is 120. The suggested decrease is 150. Again, since the current solution is nondegenerate, we know for sure that a change beyond the allowable amount will produce a new optimal solution with a new value for $T1$. In this case, since the price is decreasing, the new optimal value of $T1$ will be larger. Bounds on the value of the OV function can be found by using Figure 7.30.

Figure 7.29   **Figure 7.30**

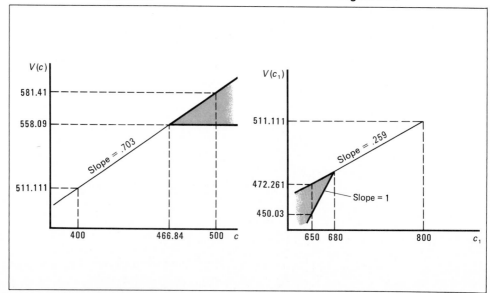

upper bound $= 511.111 - 150(0.259) = 472.261$

In general, it is impossible to specify a lower bound other than zero. In this case, however, we know from the fourth constraint that $T1^* \leq 1$. It thus follows that lower bound $= 511.111 - 120(0.259) - 30(1) = 450.03$.

(b) The OV function will *increase* at the rate of $91.111 per ton.

Example 9

Consider again the Astro/Cosmo problem (Example 4). The LP formulation is:

$$\text{Max} \quad 20A + 30C$$
$$\text{s.t.} \quad A \qquad \leq 70$$
$$C \leq 50$$
$$A + 2C \leq 120$$
$$A, C \geq 0$$

Use geometry and algebra to plot the graph of the $V(C_A)$ function for all values of $C_A \geq 0$, where C_A is the coefficient of A in the objective function. Specify the value of C_A and $V(C_A)$ for all corners on the graph and indicate the slope of the graph on each linear segment.

Solution to Example 9

The constraint set is plotted as shown in Figure 7.31. We then determine the values of A and C at the corners of the feasible set. Corners I, II, and V can be read directly from the constraints. Corner III occurs at the intersection of the two lines

$$A + 2C = 120 \qquad C = 50$$

or $A = 20$, $C = 50$. Corner IV occurs at the intersection of the two lines

$$A + 2C = 120 \qquad A = 120$$

or $A = 70$, $C = 25$.

Now we determine the $V(C_A)$ function. When $C_A = 0$, the objective function is simply $30C$ and the contours of the objective function are parallel to the A axis. Thus, the optimal solutions lie on the line between corners II and III. The value of the objective function is $30(50) = 1,500$. We can thus plot the point $(0, 1,500)$ on the $V(C_A)$ graph, Figure 7.32.

As C_A increases, the optimal solution remains at point III, with $A^* = 20$, until the contour of the objective function becomes parallel to the line $A + 2C = 120$. Rewriting the equation of this line as $C = 60 - 0.5A$ shows that the slope of the line is -0.5. The slope of the contours of the objective function equals -0.5 when $C_A = 15$. At this point the value of the objective function is $15(20) + 30(50) = 1800 = 15(70) + 30(25)$. We can thus plot the point $(15, 1,800)$ on the $V(C_A)$ graph.

For values of $C_A > 15$, the optimal solution will remain at corner IV with A^*

Figure 7.31

Figure 7.32

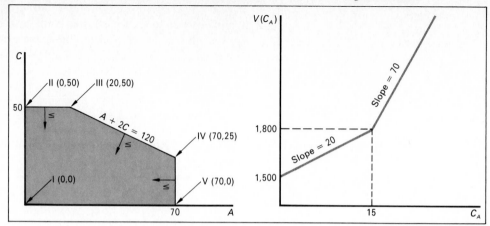

$= 70$. The slope of the contour of the objective function will become arbitrarily close to $-\infty$.

The previous information has given us the graph for the $V(C_A)$ function shown in Figure 7.32.

___

Example 10

Consider the following *dual problems*:

$$\text{Max} \quad \sum_{j=1}^{n} c_j x_j$$

$$\text{s.t.} \quad \sum_{j=1}^{n} a_{ij} x_j \leq b_i \qquad i = 1, \ldots, m \qquad \qquad \text{(I)}$$

$$x_j \geq 0 \qquad j = 1, \ldots, n$$

$$\text{Min} \quad \sum_{i=1}^{m} b_i y_i$$

$$\text{s.t.} \quad \sum_{i=1}^{m} a_{ij} y_i \geq c_j \qquad j = 1, \ldots, n \qquad \qquad \text{(II)}$$

$$y_i \geq 0 \qquad i = 1, \ldots, m$$

Let $V(c_k)$ denote the OV for model (I) as a function of the objective function coefficient c_k, for some fixed index k. Let $\hat{V}(c_k)$ denote the OV for model (II) as a function of the RHS parameter c_k. Important relations between (I) and (II) include the following fact: if either of the problems has a solution, then so does the other, and the respective optimal objective values are equal. In this case, then,

$$V(c_k) = \hat{V}(c_k)$$

In other words, for all values of c_k for which (I) has an optimal solution, the $V(c_k)$ function for (I) is equal to the $\hat{V}(c_k)$ function for (II).

    (a) Use your knowledge of the shape of the $V(b)$ function to deduce the shape and slopes of the $V(c_k)$ graph for (I).

(b) Consider the OV function corresponding to an objective coefficient b_k in (II). Use the relationship between (I) and (II) above to deduce the shape of this graph.

(c) If (I) has alternative optimal solutions, then argue that the dual must have a degenerate solution.

Solution to Example 10

(a) For (II) we know from properties of $V(b)$ that the graph of $\hat{V}(c_k)$ is increasing, piecewise linear, and has increasing slopes, since tightening the RHS in (II) hurts more and more. Since $V(c_k) = \hat{V}(c_k)$, the graph of $V(c_k)$ must have the same properties.

(b) Increasing an objective function coefficient in (II) is equivalent to loosening the RHS of a $\leq$ constraint in (I). This produces a piecewise linear increasing function with decreasing slopes.

(c) Suppose (I) has alternative optimal solutions when $c_k = \bar{c}_k$, in which the x_k^* values differ. Then the $V(c_k)$ graph must have a corner when $c_k = \bar{c}_k$. Since the $V(c_k)$ graph is the same as the $\hat{V}(c_k)$ graph, it follows that $\hat{V}(c_k)$, the RHS OV function from (II), also has a corner at $\bar{c}_k$. This means that the dual problem must have a degenerate solution corresponding to the RHS value $\bar{c}_k$.

7.13

MAJOR CONCEPTS QUIZ

True–False

1. T F The optimal value of the ith dual variable is defined as rate of improvement in OV as the ith RHS increases.

2. T F Assuming that an optimal solution exists, the simplex method for a max model produces optimal values for the variables in both the primal and the dual problem.

3. T F In most cases it is more efficient to solve the primal as opposed to the dual.

4. T F Optimal dual variables give optimal liquidation prices for the dual problem.

5. T F The dual variable corresponding to a $\geq$ constraint in a primal max problem is restricted to nonpositive values.

6. T F Suppose that the dual is a max model and the ith primal variable has a ≤ 0 sign condition. Then the ith dual constraint is $\geq$.

7. T F Dual variables are the slopes of the $V(b)$ function.

8. T F Corners on the $V(b)$ function correspond to alternative optima.

9. T F You have just obtained a nondegenerate optimal solution to an LP. The ith constraint is an active $\geq$ constraint and there is no alternative optima. Then the ith dual price is negative.

10. T F Corners on the $V(c)$ function indicate degeneracy.

11. T F The $V(c)$ function shows where alternative optima occur, regardless of whether or not the problem is degenerate.

12. T F The domain of the $V(b)$ function is all values of b for which the problem is feasible.

13. T F A zero dual price on an equality constraint indicates alternative optima.

14. T F In a nondegenerate case, increasing a c_j by slightly more than the "allowable increase" will produce a new optimal solution which is unique.

15. The primal is a max model in m equality constraints and n nonnegative variables. The dual
   a. has n constraints and m nonnegative variables
   b. is a min model
   c. both a and b
   d. neither a nor b

16. Consider any primal problem (P) and its dual (D).
   a. The OVs in (P) and (D) will be the same.
   b. (P) will have an optimal solution if and only if (D) does also.
   c. Both (P) and (D) cannot be infeasible.
   d. All of the above.

17. Let x be a nonoptimal feasible point in a maximization primal model. Let y be a dual feasible point. Then
   a. the primal objective value at x is greater than the dual objective value at y
   b. the primal objective value at x is less than the OV for the dual
   c. the primal objective value at x could equal the dual objective value at y
   d. the dual could be unbounded

18. You have just solved an LP. The ith constraint is an active $\leq$ constraint with a positive dual price. Increasing b_i by more than the allowable amount
   a. may change the dual price
   b. will decrease the dual price
   c. may increase the dual price
   d. will change the dual price if the current optimal solution is nondegenerate

19. The $V(c_j)$ function for a min model
   a. shows increasing marginal returns
   b. shows nonincreasing slopes
   c. can be used to estimate RHS changes outside the allowable ranges
   d. none of the above

20. Concerning $V(c_j)$
   a. the shape depends on whether the problem is max or min
   b. the shape can be used to estimate the effect of c_j changes outside the allowable ranges
   c. the slopes are determined by x_j^* as a function of c_j
   d. all of the above

21. When you tighten a constraint beyond the allowable range
   a. you get a two-sided estimate of the possible effect
   b. you get a lower bound (an "at least" statement) on how much it will hurt
   c. you may improve the OV
   d. you are certain to hurt the OV

22. You have just solved an LP. The ith constraint is an inequality constraint with a dual price of -10. Then
   a. the ith constraint has to be $\geq$
   b. the ith constraint is active
   c. if you tighten this constraint by the allowable amount, without making the problem infeasible, and the dual price changes, then it must become more negative
   d. all of the above

Answers

1. F	9. T	16. b
2. T	10. F	17. b
3. F	11. F	18. a
4. F	12. T	19. b
5. T	13. F	20. d
6. T	14. F	21. b
7. T	15. b	22. d
8. F		

7.14
PROBLEMS

7-1. Find the dual to the following LP.

$$\text{Min} \quad 4y_1 + 13y_2$$
$$\text{s.t.} \quad 18y_1 + 12y_2 \leq 3$$
$$6y_1 + 2y_2 = 17$$
$$y_1 \geq 0, \qquad y_2 \geq 0$$

7-2. Find the dual to the following LP.

$$\text{Max} \quad 3x_1 - 11x_2$$
$$\text{s.t.} \quad 2x_1 + 13x_2 \geq 5$$
$$3x_1 - 4x_2 \leq 16$$
$$x_1 \leq 0, \qquad x_2 \text{ unconstrained in sign}$$

7-3. Suppose that the primal problem has 120 variables and 1500 constraints.
(a) How many variables are in the dual problem?
(b) How many constraints are in the dual problem?
(c) All other things equal, which problem should you prefer to solve (the primal or the dual)?

7-4. Change the data in Problem 7-3 to a primal problem with 1500 variables and 120 constraints and answer the same three questions.

7-5. Regarding Problem 7-3(c), give a reason why "all other things may not be equal."

7-6. "Except for a possible sign difference, the dual prices on the computer output are the same as the optimal values of the variables in the dual of the problem being solved." Answer True or False.

7-7. Employing the words "rate" and "OV," give the correct interpretation of
(a) dual price on computer output
(b) optimal dual variable

7-8. Let $c_1x_1 + c_2x_2 + \cdots + c_kx_k$ denote the primal objective function (a max model) and $b_1y_1 + b_2y_2 + \cdots + b_Ly_L$ the dual objective function.
(a) How many constraints are in the primal problem?
(b) How many constraints are in the dual problem?
(c) If $(u_1, \ldots, u_k)$ is primal feasible and $(v_1, \ldots, v_L)$ is dual feasible, what can you say about the two objective values?

7-9. Consider the following problem:

$$\text{Max} \quad 4x_1 + x_2$$
$$\text{s.t.} \quad 3x_1 + 2x_2 - x_3 \leq 0$$
$$x_1 - 3x_2 \qquad \geq 14$$
$$x_1, x_3 \geq 0$$

Thus, the variable x_2 is unconstrained in sign. Take the dual of this problem. Call it D_1. Replace x_2 with $y_1 - y_2$, $y_1 \geq 0$, and $y_2 \geq 0$ to convert this problem to an equivalent form in which all variables are nonnegative. Call this new problem P_2. Now take the dual of P_2. Call it D_2. Show that D_1 and D_2 are equivalent. Now convert P_2 to a problem in standard equality constraint form, with all variables denoted by the symbol z_j (replace x's, y's, and so on, with z's). Call this new problem P_3. Take its dual and call it D_3. Show that D_3 is equivalent to D_1 and D_2.

7-10. Consider the LP

$$\text{Max } x_1$$
$$\begin{aligned}
\text{s.t. } 5x_1 + 3x_2 &\geq 15 \\
-x_1 + x_2 &\leq 3 \\
-x_1 + 3x_2 &\geq 0 \\
4x_1 + x_2 &\leq b_4 \\
-3x_1 + 2x_2 &\geq -15 \\
x_1, x_2 &\geq 0
\end{aligned}$$

where b_4 is a parameter.

(a) Plot the constraint set and the OV function, $V(b_4)$.

(b) Does the slope of the graph of $V(b_4)$ eventually become zero (for b_4 sufficiently large)? Explain the value of the eventual slope.

(c) Use algebraic means to find an expression for the first segment of $V(b_4)$.

7-11. Picture a hypothetical situation with a zero dual price on an equality constraint.

7-12. Picture a hypothetical inequality-constraint problem with a nondegenerate solution and a constraint with both a zero slack and a zero dual price.

7-13. Consider the output reproduced in Figure 7.3. The dual price on labor hours in department B is 175.

(a) Does this mean that if we (1) use the original 160 hours in the optimal way (namely, make 4.5 E-9s and 7.0 F-9s) and then (2) use an additional hour to make some small additional amounts of E or F or both in some appropriate mix that then $175 of additional revenue would be obtained? Use the geometric interpretation of this model (Figure 7.4) for guidance.

(b) Use Figure 7.4 and the appropriate algebra to determine *exactly* what the optimal values of E and F would be if $b_4 = 161$. Verify that the change from the previous optimal policy ($E = 4.5$, $F = 7.0$) does in fact generate $175 of additional revenue.

7-14. Consider the output reproduced in Figure 7-3. For parts (a)–(c), specify either the exact value or the best possible bounds on the OV given the stated changes.

(a) Management decides to cut back the labor supply in department A (row 4) by 40 hours.

(b) Management decides to cut back the labor supply in department A by 60 hours. (Assume that the problem remains feasible.)

(c) Management decides to increase the labor supply in department A by 100 hours.

(d) What would happen to the OV if the RHS of the first constraint is changed from 5 to 12? (HINT: Use Figure 7.4.)

(e) The current labor contract specifies that at least 135 hours must be used in testing the finished product. This is expressed by the fifth constraint. The union wishes to renegotiate this contract in such a way as to increase the testing time. How much would management be able to increase the 135 figure before it would begin to cut into current revenues?

7-15. Consider the solution to the ore-blending problem shown in Figure 7.25. Specify the tightest bounds possible for the OV if the RHS of the third constraint becomes 20 and all other parameters remain as shown.

7-16. Consider the tape recorder production problem originally presented in Example 15 of Section 4.9. The solution (including the formulation) is shown in Figure 7.33. Specify the best possible bounds on the OV in the following cases:

(a) The RHS of the first constraint increases by 125. (Although this may destroy feasibility, assume that it does not.)

(b) The RHS of the first constraint decreases by 30.

7-17. Recall the transportation problem presented in Problem 4-24. Let Ai (or Bi or Ci), $i = 1, 2, 3, 4$ be the number of gallons of jet fuel sent from oil company A (or B or C) to airport i. The LP solution to this problem (including the formulation) is shown in Figure 7.34. Specify the tightest bounds possible for the OV in the following cases:

Figure 7.33

```
MAX 15A + 40B + 60C
SUBJECT TO
   2)   A ≥ 25
   3)   B ≥ 130
   4)   C ≥ 55
   5)   4A + 2.5B + 6C ≤ 1560
   6)   3A + 4B + 9C ≤ 2040
   7)   A + 2B + 4C ≤ 624
```

VARIABLE	VALUE	REDUCED COST
A	25.000	0.000
B	189.500	0.000
C	55.000	0.000
OBJ FCTN	11255	

ROW	SLACK OR SURPLUS	DUAL PRICES
2	0	−5
3	59.5	0
4	0	−20
5	656.25	0
6	712	0
7	0	20

SENSITIVITY ANALYSIS

OBJ COEFFICIENT RANGES

VARIABLE	CURRENT COEF	ALLOWABLE INCREASE	ALLOWABLE DECREASE
A	15.00	5.000	INFINITE
B	40.00	INFINITE	10.000
C	60.00	20.000	INFINITE

RIGHTHAND SIDE RANGES

ROW	CURRENT RHS	ALLOWABLE INCREASE	ALLOWABLE DECREASE
2	25.00	119.000	25.000
3	130.00	59.500	INFINITE
4	55.00	29.750	55.000
5	1560.00	INFINITE	656.250
6	2040.00	INFINITE	712.000
7	624.00	356.000	119.000

Figure 7.34

```
MIN 12A1 + 11A2 + 11A3 + 11A4 + 9B1 + 10B2 + 8B3 + 13B4 + 15C1
      + 12C2 + 12C3 + 14C4
SUBJECT TO
   2)   A1 + B1 + C1 ≥ 100000
   3)   A2 + B2 + C2 ≥ 200000
   4)   A3 + B3 + C3 ≥ 300000
   5)   A4 + B4 + C4 ≥ 400000
   6)   A1 + A2 + A3 + A4 ≤ 250000
   7)   B1 + B2 + B3 + B4 ≤ 500000
   8)   C1 + C2 + C3 + C4 ≤ 600000
```

Figure 7.34 (Cont.)

VARIABLE	VALUE	REDUCED COST
A1	0.000	4.000
A2	0.000	2.000
A3	0.000	4.000
A4	249999.997	0.000
B1	99999.999	0.000
B2	99999.999	0.000
B3	299999.996	0.000
B4	0.000	1.000
C1	0.000	4.000
C2	99999.999	0.000
C3	0.000	2.000
C4	149999.998	0.000
OBJ FCTN	1.03500E + 07	

ROW	SLACK OR SURPLUS	DUAL PRICES
2	0	—11
3	0	—12
4	0	—10
5	0	—14
6	0	3
7	0	2
8	350000.	0

SENSITIVITY ANALYSIS

VARIABLE	CURRENT COEF	ALLOWABLE INCREASE	ALLOWABLE DECREASE
A1	12	INFINITE	4.000
A2	11	INFINITE	2.000
A3	11	INFINITE	4.000
A4	11	2.000	INFINITE
B1	9	4.000	11.000
B2	10	1.000	2.000
B3	8	2.000	10.000
B4	13	INFINITE	1.000
C1	15	INFINITE	4.000
C2	12	2.000	1.000
C3	12	INFINITE	2.000
C4	14	1.000	2.000

RIGHTHAND SIDE RANGES

ROW	CURRENT RHS	ALLOWABLE INCREASE	ALLOWABLE DECREASE
2	100000	99999.999	99999.999
3	200000	349999.996	99999.999
4	300000	99999.999	99999.999
5	400000	349999.996	149999.998
6	250000	149999.998	24999.997
7	500000	99999.999	99999.999
8	600000	INFINITE	349999.996

(a) The RHS of the sixth constraint increases by 140,000 gallons, and all other parameters remain as shown.

(b) The RHS of the sixth constraint decreases by 150,000 gallons, and all other parameters remain as shown.

7-18. Consider the output in Figure 7.14. Assume the coefficient of F in the objective function decreases from 4000 to 2800. What is the optimal solution? What is the OV?

7-19. Consider the E, F model displayed at the top of Figure 7.14. Suppose the per unit revenue of E-9s is changed to zero. Will the optimal production of E-9s go to zero? Explain the reason for your answer.
(HINT: Refer to Figure 7.15).

7-20. Recall the LP formulation of the Astro/Cosmo TV production model discussed in Examples 4 and 9 of this chapter.

$$\text{Max} \quad 20A + 30C$$
$$\text{s.t.} \quad A \qquad \leq 70$$
$$C \leq 50$$
$$A + 2C \leq 120$$
$$A, C \geq 0$$

Use geometry and algebra to plot the graph of the $V(c_C)$ function for all values of $c_C > 0$, where c_C is the coefficient of C in the objective function. Specify the values of c_C and $V(c_C)$ for all corners on the graph and indicate the slope of the graph on each linear segment.

7-21. Consider the output in Figure 7.14. For each of the changes suggested below, either specify the exact value or provide the best possible bounds for the new OV.
(a) Suppose that the per unit price of E is increased to 9000 and all other parameters remain the same.
(b) Suppose that the per unit price of F is decreased to 2000 and all other parameters remain the same.

7-22. Let $cE + 4000F$ be the objective function in the PROTRAC E and F problem.
(a) Try to provide a rigorous logical argument to support the fact that the values $V(c)$ are increasing.
(b) What is the slope of the $V(c)$ graph wher $c = 5000$?

DIAGNOSTIC ASSIGNMENT

PALM OIL REFINING

Fred Chung is the production manager for KL Oils, a Malaysian firm that produces palm oil products. KL owns a palm oil fractionating plant and a refinery. The prices of the inputs and outputs of these two facilities vary. Fred is responsible for approving production plans 4 weeks in advance. At that time the purchase contracts for inputs must be signed. The eventual sales price remains uncertain. The corporate economic analysis group provides Fred with price estimates. His responsibility is to assume that the estimates are accurate and to operate the plants as efficiently as possible.

For the week under consideration, the economic analysis group estimates the following market prices in dollars per ton:

Crude palm oil	640
Crude palm olein	700
Crude palm stearin	800

In this market, transportation costs are paid by the buyer. The prices above are "at origin." In addition to these prices, KL must pay transportation costs of $20 for each ton delivered to the fractionating plant and $30 for each ton delivered to the refinery.

The following chart summarizes the performance of the fractionating plant and the current price estimates.

INPUT		OUTPUT		
Commodity	Purchase Price	Commodity	Proportion	Sales Price
Crude palm oil	$660	Crude palm olein	0.75	$700
		Crude palm stearin	0.24	800
		Waste	0.01	0

This plant has an input capacity of 100 tons per week.

The refinery produces refined palm oil, refined palm olein, or refined palm stearin. The fatty acid, which is a by-product of the refining process, is also sold. The performance characteristic and market prices relevant to refinery operation appear in the following table.

COMMODITY	INPUT PRICE	OUTPUT OF REFINERY		SALES PRICE
		Commodity	Proportion	
Crude palm oil	$670	Refined palm oil	0.94	$740
		Fatty acid	0.05	570
		Waste	0.01	0
Crude palm olein	730	Refined palm olein	0.94	800
		Fatty acid	0.06	570
Crude palm stearin	830	Refined palm stearin	0.96	910
		Fatty acid	0.04	570

The refinery has an input capacity of 120 tons per week.

To obtain input for the refinery Fred has the option of using products from his own fractionating plant, for which he pays only the transportation cost, or buying them on the open market at the input price. The economic analysis group estimates transportation costs of $40 per ton for material shipped from the fractionating plant to the refinery.

The corporate economic analysis group has constructed an LP model of the palm products problem. This model was built by first using a computerized editor to define the variables and create the constraints and then solving the model with LINDO. The outputs from the editor and from LINDO are shown in Figures 7.35 and 7.36, respectively.

Figure 7.35

Editor Version

```
GO:*
00100    !VARIABLE DEFINITION
00200    !CPOF CRUDE PALM OIL INPUT TO FRACTIONATING PLANT
00300    !CPL CRUDE PALM OLEIN OUTPUT FRAC
00400    !CPS CRUDE PALM STEARIN OUTPUT FROM FRAC
00500    !RPO REFINED PALM OIL OUTPUT FROM REFIN
00600    !RPL REFINED PALM OLEIN OUTPUT FROM REFIN
00700    !RPS REFINED PALM STEARIN OUTPUT FROM REFIN
00800    !FAL FATTY ACID FROM OLEIN FROM REFIN
00900    !FAS FATTY ACID FROM STEARIN FROM REFIN
01000    !FAO FATTY ACID FROM OIL FROM REFIN
01100    !FA TOTAL FATTY ACID FROM REFIN
01200    !CPLR CPL FROM FRAC TO REFIN
01300    !CPSR CPS FROM FRAC TO REFIN
01400    !CPSM CPS FROM FRAC TO MARKET
01500    !CPLM CPL FROM FRAC TO MARKET
01600    !CPOR CRUDE OIL PURCHASED FOR REFIN
01700    !CPLP CRUDE PALM OLEIN PURCHASED FOR REFIN
01800    !CPSP CRUDE PALM STEARIN PURCHASED FOR REFIN
01900    !W WASTE FROM FRAC
02000    !WR WASTE FROM REFINED PALM OIL
02100    !NOW THE FORMULATION
02200    !OBJECTIVE FUNCTION
02300    MAX 740RPO + 800RPL + 910RPS + 570FA + 700CPLM + 800CPSM
           − 660CPOF
02400      −730CPLP − 830CPSP − 670CPOR
02500      −40CPLR − 40CPSR
02600    ST
02700    !OUTPUT FROM FRAC
02800    CPL − .75CPOF = 0
02900    CPS − .24CPOF = 0
03000    W − .01CPOF = 0
03100    !SPLIT PRODUCT FROM FRAC
03200    CPL − CPLR − CPLM = 0
03300    CPS − CPSR − CPSM = 0
03400    !CAPACITY ON FRAC
03500    CPOF < 100
03600    !REFIN OUTPUT OLEIN
03700    RPL − .94CPLR − .94CPLP = 0
```

Figure 7.35 (Cont.)

```
03800    FAL — .06CPLR — .06CPLP = 0
03900    !REFIN OUTPUT STEARIN
04000    RPS — .96CPSR — .96CPSP = 0
04100    FAS — .04CPSR — .04CPSP = 0
04200    !REFIN OUTPUT OIL
04300    RPO — .94CPOR = 0
04400    FAO — .05CPOR = 0
04500    WR — .01CPOR = 0
04600    !TOTAL FATTY ACID OUTPUT
04700    FA — FAL — FAS — FAO = 0
04800    !CAPACITY CONSTRAINT ON REFIN
04900    CPLR + CPLP + CPSR — CPSP + CPOR < 120
05000    END
05100    LEAVE
*EU
```

Jacob Tony, the vice-president of operations, is planning to visit the KL facilities next week and Fred will have to explain his production plans to him. Fred knows that Mr. Tony will critically evaluate the plan with standard economic analysis (i.e., marginal analysis). He is determined to analyze and understand the solution so that he can answer any question Jacob might raise. Indeed, this process has caused Fred some real problems. The LP solution shows that the fractionating plant sells its product to the market and the refinery buys crude palm stearin on the market. Fred's analysis, however, shows that the refinery should buy some crude palm stearin from the fractionating plant rather than on the market as the LP solution indicates. His calculations show that the cost of a ton of crude palm stearin from the fractionating plant is substantially less than the cost of purchasing a ton on the market. In particular, since a ton of crude palm oil yields 0.24 ton of crude palm stearin, it takes $1/0.24 = 4.17$ tons of crude palm oil to produce 1 ton of crude palm stearin. However, these 4.17 tons of crude palm oil also yield $(4.17) \times (0.75) = 3.13$ tons of crude palm olein. Fred thus estimates the cost of a ton of crude palm stearin as follows:

Cost = 4.17 tons at 660 =	2752.20
Recovery from = 3.13 tons at 700 =	2191.00
Olein	561.20
Transportation	40.00
Cost per ton	601.20

Since a ton of crude palm stearin purchased on the market and delivered to the refinery costs $830, it seems clear that KL Oils should use the crude palm stearin it produces from the fractionating plant as input to the refinery.

Is Fred's argument correct? If so, formulate an LP model that will yield the correct solution.

Is the LP formulation correct? If so, present a marginal cost analysis that shows that it does not pay for the refinery to buy crude palm stearin from the fractionating plant.

Figure 7.36
Computer Output

```
MAX    740 RPO + 800 RPL + 910 RPS  + 570 FA + 700 CPLM
     + 800 CPSM − 660 CPOF − 730 CPLP − 830 CPSP − 670 CPOR
     − 40 CPLR − 40 CPSR
SUBJECT TO
     2)      −0.75 CPOF + CPL = 0
     3)      −0.24 CPOF + CPS = 0
     4)      −0.01 CPOF + W = 0
     5)      −CPLM − CPLR + CPL = 0
     6)      −CPSM − CPSR + CPS = 0
     7)      CPOF ≤ 100
     8)      RPL − 0.94 CPLP − 0.94 CPLR = 0
     9)      −0.06 CPLP − 0.06 CPLR + FAL = 0
     10)     RPS − 0.96 CPSP − 0.96 CPSR = 0
     11)     −0.04 CPSP − 0.04 CPSR + FAS = 0
     12)     RPO − 0.94 CPOR = 0
     13)     −0.05 CPOR + FAO = 0
     14)     −0.01 CPOR + WR = 0
     15)     FA − FAL − FAS − FAO = 0
     16)     CPLP + CPSP + CPOR + CPLR + CPSR ≤ 120

 1)                13668.0001


VARIABLE          VALUE          REDUCED COST
   RPO          0.000000          0.000000
   RPL          0.000000          0.000000
   RPS        115.200000          0.000000
    FA          4.800000          0.000000
  CPLM         75.000000          0.000000
  CPSM         24.000000          0.000000
  CPOF        100.000000          0.000000
  CPLP          0.000000         10.199999
  CPSP        120.000000          0.000000
  CPOR          0.000000         12.300000
  CPLR          0.000000         20.199999
  CPSR          0.000000         10.000000
   CPL         75.000000          0.000000
   CPS         24.000000          0.000000
     W          1.000000          0.000000
   FAL          0.000000          0.000000
   FAS          4.800000          0.000000
   FAO          0.000000          0.000000
    WR          0.000000          0.000000
```

251

CHAPTER 8

Management Science in Action: Optimizing Production, Marketing, and Distribution at PROTRAC

8.1
INTRODUCTION

The following verbal description gives a fairly structured but not overly detailed portrayal of some of the important interactions involved in production and marketing at PROTRAC. Our goal is to construct a formal constrained optimization model as an aid for decision making in this environment.

The problem centers around the production and marketing of the large E-9 crawler tractor. The planning of production and marketing for this particular product is centralized at corporate headquarters.

Assumptions Behind the Model

Facilities Seven of the plants in the midwest tractor division are geographically located in two clusters. In regard to the production of E-9s, each cluster of plants has similar operating characteristics. As a result, the seven plants have been aggregated into two groups, identified as plant 1 and plant 2. The *individual* plants within each group have no separate identity in the model.

Time The questions to be answered concern the next *two* planning periods.

Inputs The thousands of individual items and processes that go into the production of an E-9 are aggregated into three major categories. Iron (I), which includes all the iron castings used in an E-9, transmissions (T), which includes all the material associated with the power train except the engine, and, finally, labor hours (L), which is an aggregated measure of human and machine hours. This measure combines the inputs of both the work-force and the machinery in the manufacturing and assembly-line facilities.

Production Processes A unit of *finished product* consists of a *tractor body* and a *transmission*. The components of the transmissions are fabricated in a different division and are then shipped to the midwest tractor division where they are assembled in the two PROTRAC plants. The tractor bodies are entirely produced and assembled in the

253

CHAPTER 8
Management
Science in Action:
Optimizing
Production,
Marketing,
and Distribution
at PROTRAC

two plants. Units of *finished* product and units of *transmissions* can be carried in inventory from period 1 into period 2. Because of the assembly-line design and established union procedures, as soon as a complete body is assembled, the transmission is immediately installed. This means that a tractor body without a transmission cannot be carried in inventory. In computing costs, a specified charge is assessed at each plant for each unit of finished product in inventory at the end of each period and for each transmission in inventory at the end of each period. The per unit carrying costs will differ for finished product and transmissions.

Cross-Shipment of Transmissions The plants can cross-ship the assembled transmissions from one plant to another at a specified cost per unit. Transmissions cross-shipped from either plant 1 or 2 in either period are assumed to leave the plant during the period and arrive at the other plant at the beginning of the next period. Transmissions that are eligible for installation in the tractor bodies produced in a specific plant in a specific period come from one of three sources: those that arrive at the beginning of the period via cross-shipment from the other plant; those that are assembled in the specific plant in the specific period; and those that are carried in inventory in the specific plant into the specific period.

Labor-Hour Utilization The *assembly* of transmissions and the production and assembly of tractor bodies requires the utilization of labor hours. The labor required for *installing* a transmission is negligible and therefore is not directly measured.

The Supply of Iron The firm owns a foundry, which produces a limited amount of iron available for purchase by the individual plants. The firm uses a transfer-pricing scheme under which the manufacturing plants are charged for iron purchased from the foundry. In calculating each plant's costs, these transfer prices are treated the same as the prices paid for other items purchased by the plant. Additional iron can be purchased from outside sources (in any quantity) on the open market at the market price. Currently, the exogenously purchased iron has a higher price than the transfer price. Iron cannot be stored in inventory at either plant. That is, iron taken from the company's foundry or purchased from outside sources can be used only in the same period in which it is purchased. Obviously, this requirement is not dictated by the physical properties of the materials being purchased. It results from the fact that management has discovered that it can, in this way, force the supplying firms to absorb part of the inventory carrying cost. However, since this policy might imply underutilization of the PROTRAC foundry, it may not be optimal in an overall sense. Iron is used only in producing the tractor bodies. Iron is not used for transmissions since they are prefabricated elsewhere.

Marketing The two plants serve dealers in the midwest regional marketing district. There is a known demand (called **existing demand**) for the finished product that, according to the firm's goodwill policy, must be satisfied. The marketing department can expend dollars to cultivate additional demand (called **new demand**). Finished product can be shipped to the marketing district in the period in which it is produced. Alternatively, finished product produced in one period can be held in inventory and shipped to the marketing district in the next period.

Transportation Costs There is an "average" transportation cost associated with the shipment of each unit of finished product from each plant to the marketing district. The cost depends on the plant of origin. **No finished product can be stored at the district**.

Cost and Price Assumptions Linearity is assumed throughout. There are revenues from the sale of finished product. Costs are associated with the use of iron, the transpor-

254

CHAPTER 8
Management
Science in Action:
Optimizing
Production,
Marketing,
and Distribution
at PROTRAC

tation of finished product, the holding of inventories, the cross-shipping of transmissions, and the creation of new demand. The size of the labor force is assumed *not* to be a decision variable, and its cost is part of the fixed overhead. This assumption is reasonable if the planning periods are not too long. Union agreements and lack of experience in working with alternative sources of capacity make it economically impossible for PROTRAC to expand capacity in the short run. It is not unusual for management to consider short-run capacity and labor costs as fixed. As a result of this assumption, labor costs are not included in the model.

Management's Goal

A schematic diagram of these interactions is shown in Figure 8.1. Centralized management intends to use the previous assumptions in developing a planning model to use as an input to their deliberations to determine a production plan, a distribution plan, and a marketing plan that will *maximize total profit*.

Figure 8.1
Schematic Diagram of the PROTRAC Interactions

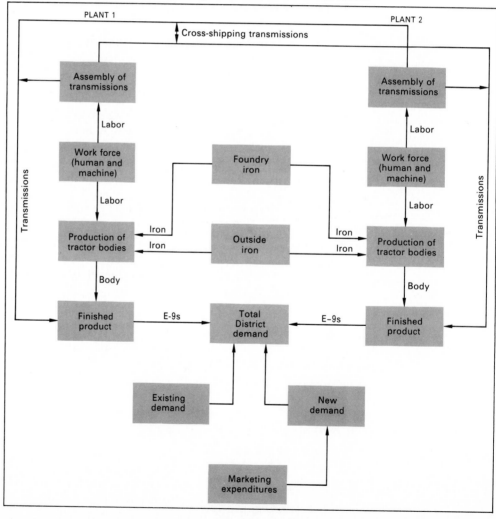

255

CHAPTER 8
Management
Science in Action:
Optimizing
Production,
Marketing,
and Distribution
at PROTRAC

A **production plan** specifies:

1. The number of bodies that should be produced in each plant in each period
2. The number of transmissions to be assembled in each plant in each period
3. The number of transmissions to be cross-shipped from each plant to the other in each period
4. The number of tons of iron purchased by each plant in each period from the company owned foundry
5. The number of tons of iron purchased by each plant in each period from outside sources
6. The amount of finished product and the number of transmissions to be carried in inventory in each plant

A **distribution plan** specifies the amount of finished product to be sent from each plant to the marketing district in each period.

The **marketing plan** specifies how many dollars to invest in creating new demand in each period.

8.2

THE FORMAL MODEL

The decision variables used in creating a formal model for this problem are defined in Figure 8.2. It is seen that there are 34 variables in the model. The following mnemonic abbreviations are employed: FP for finished product, TR for transmissions, FI for

Figure 8.2

Decision Variables for PROTRAC Production and Marketing Model

DECISION VARIABLES	PLANT	NOTATION Time Period 1	Time Period 2
Number of BOD produced in	1	BODP1T1	BODP1T2
	2	BODP2T1	BODP2T2
Amount of FP shipped from	1	FPP1T1	FPP1T2
	2	FPP2T1	FPP2T2
TR assembled in	1	TRP1T1	TRP1T2
	2	TRP2T1	TRP2T2
TR cross-shipped	1 → 2	CSTRP1T1	CSTRP1T2
	2 → 1	CSTRP2T1	CSTRP2T2
Tons of FI purchased in	1	FIP1T1	FIP1T2
	2	FIP2T1	FIP2T2
Tons of OI purchased in	1	OIP1T1	OIP1T2
	2	OIP2T1	OIP2T2
Amount of ND created		NDT1	NDT2
FP inventory in	1	INFPP1T1	INFPP1T2
	2	INFPP2T1	INFPP2T2
TR inventory in	1	INTRP1T1	INTRP1T2
	2	INTRP2T1	INTRP2T2

foundry iron, OI for outside iron, ND for new demand, BOD for bodies, and INFP, INTR for inventories of finished product and transmissions, respectively.

The Constraints

There are six sets of constraints in the model.

Demand The goodwill policy requires that existing demand be satisfied. The existing demand (the orders on hand for finished product) is 130 in time period 1 and 190 in time period 2. Thus, a demand constraint for period t will say

$$\left.\begin{array}{c} \text{FP shipped from plant 1 in time } t \\ + \\ \text{FP shipped from plant 2 in time } t \end{array}\right\} = \text{total demand (existing + new) in time } t$$

The symbolic formulation is

First Set

$$\text{FPP1T1} + \text{FPP2T1} - \text{NDT1} = 130 \qquad \text{(Time 1)}$$
$$\text{FPP1T2} + \text{FPP2T2} - \text{NDT2} = 190 \qquad \text{(Time 2)}$$

Note that NDT1 and NDT2 have been moved to the left-hand side of the equations since they are variables, and in the standard LP format, the right-hand side must be a specified number.

Labor Capacity In plant 1, there are 80,000 hours of labor available in each time period. It requires 90 hours of labor to assemble each transmission and 900 hours to produce and assemble each tractor body. Thus, in plant 1 a total of 990 labor hours goes into each unit of finished product. In the more modern plant 2, there are only 70,000 hours of labor available in each time period. It takes 60 hours to assemble each transmission and 600 hours to produce and assemble each tractor body. Thus, in plant 2 a total of 660 hours goes into each unit of finished product. The symbolic formulation of the labor constraints is

Second Set

$$\left.\begin{array}{c} 900\text{BODP1T1} + 90\text{TRP1T1} \leq 80,000 \\ 900\text{BODP1T2} + 90\text{TRP1T2} \leq 80,000 \end{array}\right\} \quad \text{(plant 1)}$$

$$\left.\begin{array}{c} 600\text{BODP2T1} + 60\text{TRP2T1} \leq 70,000 \\ 600\text{BODP2T2} + 60\text{TRP2T2} \leq 70,000 \end{array}\right\} \quad \text{(plant 2)}$$

Foundry Capacity In each time period, the foundry capacity is 1000 tons. The symbolic form of the relevant constraints is

Third Set

$$\text{FIP1T1} + \text{FIP2T1} \leq 1000 \qquad \text{(time 1)}$$
$$\text{FIP1T2} + \text{FIP2T2} \leq 1000 \qquad \text{(time 2)}$$

Iron Consumption In each plant and each time period, the production of a single tractor body requires 6 tons of iron. Since iron cannot be stored in inventory, we can say that in each plant and each time period

256

total iron purchased = total iron used

Thus, the symbolic formulation of the iron consumption constraints is

Fourth Set

$$6BODP1T1 - FIP1T1 - OIP1T1 = 0 \quad \text{(plant 1, time 1)}$$
$$6BODP2T1 - FIP2T1 - OIP2T1 = 0 \quad \text{(plant 2, time 1)}$$
$$6BODP1T2 - FIP1T2 - OIP1T2 = 0 \quad \text{(plant 1, time 2)}$$
$$6BODP2T2 - FIP2T2 - OIP2T2 = 0 \quad \text{(plant 2, time 2)}$$

Finished-Product Inventory   In plant 1, the initial inventory of finished product is 5 units. The amount of finished product held in inventory in plant 1 at the end of time period 1 is determined as follows:

$$\text{FP inventory at end of time 1} = \begin{cases} \text{FP inventory at beginning of time 1} \\ + \\ \text{FP produced in time 1} \\ - \\ \text{FP delivered in time 1} \end{cases}$$

To obtain the appropriate symbolic expression, we must use the fact that after each tractor body is produced, a transmission is immediately installed. This means that the number of units of finished product produced in each time period is synonymous with the number of bodies produced in that period. Hence the symbolic representation of the condition above is

Fifth Set

$$INFPP1T1 - BODP1T1 + FPP1T1 = 5 \quad \text{(plant 1, end of time 1)}$$

Similarly for plant 1, at the end of time 2

$$\text{FP inventory at end of time 2} = \begin{cases} \text{FP inventory at beginning of time 2} \\ + \\ \text{FP produced in time 2} \\ - \\ \text{FP delivered in time 2} \end{cases}$$

The symbolic formulation is

$$INFPP1T2 - INFPP1T1 - BODP1T2 + FPP1T2 = 0 \quad \text{(plant 1, end of time 2)}$$

In plant 2, the initial inventory of finished product is 2 units. The relevant constraints are

$$INFPP2T1 - BODP2T1 + FPP2T1 \quad\quad\quad = 2 \quad \text{(plant 2, end of time 1)}$$
$$INFPP2T2 - INFPP2T1 - BODP2T2 + FPP2T2 = 0 \quad \text{(plant 2, end of time 2)}$$

Transmissions Inventory   In plant 1, the initial inventory of transmissions is 6 units. The number of transmissions held in inventory in plant 1 at the end of time period 1 is determined as follows:

258

CHAPTER 8
Management
Science in Action:
Optimizing
Production,
Marketing,
and Distribution
at PROTRAC

$$\text{TR inventory at end of time 1} = \begin{cases} \text{TR inventory at beginning of time 1} \\ \quad + \\ \text{TR assembled in time 1} \\ \quad - \\ \text{number of TR installed in time 1} \\ \quad - \\ \text{number of TR cross-shipped out in time 1} \end{cases}$$

We now use the fact that the number of transmissions installed in plant 1, time 1, is equal to the number of bodies produced in plant 1, time 1. Hence, the symbolic representation of the constraint above is

Sixth Set $\text{INTRP1T1} - \text{TRP1T1} + \text{BODP1T1} + \text{CSTRP1T1} = 6$ (plant 1, end of time 1)

In order to determine the transmissions inventory at the end of time 2 in plant 1, it is necessary to add in the transmissions *received* at the beginning of time period 2 via cross-shipment from plant 2. Recall that these transmissions are sent out from plant 2 during time period 1, and they arrive at plant 1 at the beginning of time period 2. Thus, the relevant constraint is

$$\text{INTRP1T2} - \text{INTRP1T1} - \text{TRP1T2} + \text{BODP1T2}$$
$$+ \text{CSTRP1T2} - \text{CSTRP2T1} = 0 \quad \text{(plant 1, end of time 2)}$$

In an analogous way, the transmission inventory constraints in plant 2 are as follows. (Note that the initial inventory is 4 transmissions.)

$$\text{INTRP2T1} - \text{TRP2T1} + \text{BODP2T1} + \text{CSTRP2T1} = 4 \quad \text{(plant 2, end of time 1)}$$
$$\text{INTRP2T2} - \text{INTRP2T1} - \text{TRP2T2} + \text{BODP2T2}$$
$$+ \text{CSTRP2T2} - \text{CSTRP1T1} \qquad = 0 \quad \text{(plant 2, end of time 2)}$$

Thus, there are a total of 20 constraints in the model.

The Objective Function

The revenue for finished product is 30,000 per unit in each period. The costs are

shipping finished product from plant 1	= 30 per unit
shipping finished product from plant 2	= 90 per unit
foundry iron	= 1000 per ton
outside iron	= 1200 per ton
cross-shipping transmissions	= 20 per unit
transmission inventories	= 20 per unit
finished-product inventories	= 300 per unit
marketing cost of creating new demand	= 3000 per unit

259

CHAPTER 8
Management
Science in Action:
Optimizing
Production,
Marketing,
and Distribution
at PROTRAC

The objective function is

$$\text{revenue} - \text{cost} = \begin{cases} 30{,}000(\text{FPP1T1} + \text{FPP1T2} + \text{FPP2T1} + \text{FPP2T2}) \\ -30(\text{FPP1T1} + \text{FPP1T2}) - 90(\text{FPP2T1} + \text{FPP2T2}) \\ -1{,}000(\text{FIP1T1} + \text{FIP1T2} + \text{FIP2T1} + \text{FIP2T2}) \\ -1{,}200(\text{OIP1T1} + \text{OIP1T2} + \text{OIP2T1} + \text{OIP2T2}) \\ -20(\text{CSTRP1T1} + \text{CSTRP1T2} + \text{CSTRP2T1} + \text{CSTRP2T2}) \\ -20(\text{INTRP1T1} + \text{INTRP1T2} + \text{INTRP2T1} + \text{INTRP2T2}) \\ -300(\text{INFPP1T1} + \text{INFPP1T2} + \text{INFPP2T1} + \text{INFPP2T2}) \\ -3{,}000(\text{NDT1} + \text{NDT2}) \end{cases}$$

The Complete Model

Maximize the objective function above subject to the 20 constraints above (sets 1, 2, 3, 4, 5, 6) and nonnegativity of all 34 variables.

8.3
EXAMPLES AND SOLUTIONS

The model specified above is simple enough for textbook use and yet sufficiently complex as to provide a useful paradigm for the type of analysis the manager may be confronted with in real-world problem solving. In Chapter 9, the complete computer solution for this problem will be presented and several policy issues of concern to management will be studied. As a prelude, however, let us be sure that we understand the model as formulated thus far. This would be the obvious first step in any real-would scenario—to understand the model before attempting to understand the solution. "Understanding the model" means raising questions such as:

1. What are some of the properties? Could it be infeasible or unbounded?
2. What are alternative, perhaps equally plausible, formulations?
3. Is the formulation correct for all possible changes in the data? (The model, in the future, may be run with quite different sets of data. Thus, if the correctness of the given formulation is data dependent, the manager had better understand that.)
4. What will the sensitivity analysis tell us?

The following examples and solutions are designed to help us better understand the given formulation, as are the problems at the end of this chapter. Once again we remind the student that the following examples should be pondered and answered before reading the solution.

Example 1

Is this model solvable? Could it be unbounded or infeasible?

Solution to Example 1

The capacity constraints on labor eliminate the possibility of having an unbounded solution. To see this, we note that the objective function (the profit) is limited by the amount of finished product shipped. From the fifth set of constraints, this is directly tied to the number of bodies assembled, which in turn is limited by labor capacity (the second set of constraints). Consequently, the OV must be bounded. On the other hand,

Implication of the Goodwill Policy the problem could be infeasible. If existing demand were very large and labor capacity too small, it would simply be impossible to produce enough to meet demand. It is interesting to note that *the relation between existing demand and labor capacity is the only phenomenon in the model which could cause infeasibility.* Even when costs are relatively higher than revenues, so that losses will be incurred, the model forces the firm to produce. This characteristic is due to the goodwill policy (namely, all existing demand must be satisfied) as captured in the demand constraints.

Example 2

Does PROTRAC have sufficient capacity to satisfy existing demand in each of the two time periods considered separately? If not, does this imply that the problem is infeasible?

Solution to Example 2

The following computation shows that the combined labor capacity of both plants *in time period* 2 is insufficient to satisfy the existing demand in time period 2.

Plant 1

labor available	=	80,000 hours
required labor per unit of finished product	=	990 hours
maximum possible production of finished product	$= \dfrac{80,000}{990} =$	80.808 units

Plant 2

labor available	=	70,000 hours
required labor per unit of finished product	=	660 hours
maximum possible production of finished product	$= \dfrac{70,000}{660} =$	106.06 units

Demand and Combined Production

existing demand in time period 2 = 190 units

maximum total production in time period 2 = $80.808 + 106.06 = 186.868$ units

Capacity Is Tight in Period 2 The total production potential is 3.132 units *short* of the required amount. This does not cause infeasibility because there is considerably more than enough labor capacity to satisfy the 130 units of existing demand in time period 1. Thus, the necessary 3.132 units of finished product could be produced in time 1 and carried over in inventory into time 2. We note, however, that *if existing demand were to exceed capacity in time 1, then the problem would be infeasible.*

260

Example 3

What is the meaning of the dual price on a demand constraint? Consider, for example, the equation from the first time period:

$$FPP1T1 + FPP2T1 - NDT1 = 130$$

Solution to Example 3

Note that the RHS represents units of **existing demand**. Hence, the dual price for the equation above would be interpreted as the improvement in the optimal objective value per unit increase in existing demand in period 1. It is the maximum amount the manager should be willing to pay for the creation of one additional unit of demand, in period 1, assuming the allowable increase in this RHS is not less than 1. It follows, then, that if NDT1 (new demand created by advertising expenditures) is positive, its per unit soct, which is 3000, will be $\le$ the dual price on the constraint above. Conversely, if in either period the dual price on the demand constraint is *less than* 3000, there will be no new demand created in that period.

Example 4

What is the meaning of the dual price on an inventory constraint? Consider, for example, the equations for finished product in plant 1 in each time period:

$$INFPP1T1 - BODP1T1 + FPP1T1 \qquad\qquad = 5 \qquad \text{(time 1)}$$
$$INFPP1T2 - INFPP1T1 - BODP1T2 + FPP1T2 = 0 \qquad \text{(time 2)}$$

Solution to Example 4

Value of an Additional Unit of Inventory

Clearly, increasing the RHS of the equation for time period 1 can be interpreted as increasing the inventory on hand at the beginning of time 1. Similarly, increasing the RHS of the equation for time period 2 by a unit can be thought of as increasing the value of INFPP1T1, the inventory on hand at the beginning of time 2, by a unit. The dual price then can be interpreted as *the maximum amount a manager would be willing to pay to have an additional unit on hand in the appropriate plant at the beginning of that time period.*

Example 5

The actual decision variables (the number of bodies to be produced, transmissions to be assembled, etc.) are, in reality, integral quantities, but our LP formulation may well yield fractional answers. Does this seriously impair the usefulness of the model?

Solution to Example 5

Forcing the variables to satisfy "integrality conditions" would take the model out of the LP framework and would consequently make it considerably more difficult to solve. There is, therefore, a substantial advantage to following the common approach of allowing fractional optimal values for the variables and then rounding the solutions to integers before implementation. This approach is usually justified by the fact that there is almost always a good deal of noise and error both in the model logic and in the data. In this case, that is certainly true. Seven plants are coalesced into two aggregates, transportation costs to the district are "averages," and "labor hours" is a composite measure of man and machine time. *In such an instance, it seems clear that the process of rounding will not detract from the overall role of the model as only one of possibly many inputs to the decision-making process.*

8.4
PROBLEMS

8-1. Can you think of a rationale for the policy to "satisfy existing demand"? Is it possible that in so doing, the firm could make negative profits? If so, under what conditions?

8-2. What, if anything, could make the model infeasible?

8-3. Suppose that it pays to create as much new demand as possible and to buy on the market as much outside iron as needed. What prevents the occurrence of infinite policies?

8-4. Suppose it is known in advance that it pays to create new demand, but only until all foundry iron is consumed. What type of investment should be considered in order to increase overall profits?

8-5. What, in general, would be the effect on the feasible set and the optimal value of the objective function if the second group of constraints were changed to $=$?

8-6. In Section 8.2, in the paragraph discussing iron consumption, the text states that since iron cannot be stored in inventory, we can say that in each plant and in each time period, total iron purchased equals total iron used. Provide an economic rationale for this statement. In this context, discuss whether or not the fourth group of constraints could just as well have been written as $\leq$ instead of $=$. That is, in general we know that an equality constraint is more restrictive than an inequality. Is that true in this particular instance?

8-7. Could the first group of constraints just as well be written as $\geq$ instead of $=$?

8-8. Is it possible for some set of parameters to have an optimal solution with slack in the foundry in both time periods and slack in labor in both time periods in both plants? Under what conditions? Could this phenomenon occur in an optimal solution that also calls for positive new demand? Explain your answer.

8-9. What is the economic interpretation of the dual variable of an iron-consumption constraint? For example, consider the constraint for plant 1, time period 1:

$$6BODP1T1 - FIP1T1 - OIP1T1 = 0$$

8-10. Suppose the dual price corresponding to one of the labor constraints is 21 and the cost of labor is $4 per hour. Is this enough information to know whether all available labor hours are being used? Discuss the logic of the following statement: "Since each additional hour of labor will gain me 21 additional dollars, and each hour costs only $4, there is a net gain of $17, and consequently I should hire an unlimited amount of labor. That is, I should get all that I can."

8-11. Suppose the cost of outside iron is so expensive, and all other costs sufficiently reasonable, that an optimal solution consists of producing and selling as much as possible in each time period (and creating new demand as required) until the foundry capacity is exhausted. Suppose it turns out that an optimal policy has the property that it also completely exhausts the labor supply in both plants in time period 1. In reality, how likely would it be that the foundry capacity in a given time period is exhausted by exactly the same amount of production that completely exhausts the labor capacity? What term would be used to describe this situation?

263

CHAPTER 8
Management
Science in Action:
Optimizing
Production,
Marketing,
and Distribution
at PROTRAC

8-12. Suppose it is known in advance that it is simply too expensive to create new demand in either time period. How might the model be rewritten? Is this new formulation preferable?

8-13. Suppose it is known in advance that it never pays to buy outside iron. How might this be incorporated in the original model?

8-14. Suppose that existing demand can be satisfied with slack in all labor constraints and in the foundry constraint in both periods. Set up a model for determining how to satisfy this demand most economically (that is, at minimum cost).

8-15. What in the model specifies that finished product can be produced only if enough transmissions are available?

8-16. What specifies that the number of transmissions cross-shipped from a given plant cannot exceed the number available?

8-17. What in the model specifies that the amount of finished product shipped to the marketing district cannot exceed the amount of finished product actually produced?

8-18. Suppose that in a given optimal solution all of the labor force in plant 1, time period 1 is used. However, the union contract is about to expire. This introduces speculation in management about the effects of inadvertently establishing potentially dangerous precedents on utilization of work force. For political reasons, management is contemplating underutilization of labor by 10,000 hours in plant 1, time period 1. What would this do to profits? Discuss how the dual prices might be used to estimate the *minimum* change in profit that would be incurred. Graph the optimal objective value as a function of the RHS of the appropriate constraint, and show why the actual profit change could be more than the estimate.

8-19. **(a)** Reformulate the constraints of the model so that bodies (without transmissions), transmissions, and finished product can all be separately carried in inventory. Only finished product can be shipped to the marketing district. Assume zero initial inventory of bodies and initial inventories of transmissions and finished product as stated in the text. Define any new decision variables that are required in your reformulation. Discuss the appropriate modifications to the objective function. Show how your reformulation assures that (1) the amount of finished product assembled in a given plant in a given time period will not exceed either the number of available bodies or the number of available transmissions; and (2) the amount of finished product shipped from a given plant in a given time period will not exceed the amount on hand.

(b) Reformulate the constraints of the model so that only bodies and transmissions can be carried in inventory, not finished product. Take initial inventories of transmissions and bodies as in part (a). Assume that only finished product can be shipped to the marketing district. Discuss the appropriate modifications to the objective function.

(c) Reformulate the model so that only finished product can be carried in inventory, though it is still possible to cross-ship transmissions.

8-20. Consider the demand constraint for time period 1 and the corresponding dual price.

(a) Suppose that the dual price is negative in a nondegenerate optimal solution. Could the optimal value of the "new demand" variable be positive? What is the interpretation of the dual price in this case? What can you conclude about the profitability of the goodwill policy?

(b) Suppose that at optimality the "new demand" variable is positive. What can you say about the dual price?

(c) Suppose that the dual price is positive. What can you say about the optimal value of the new demand variable? Discuss whether or not it would be possible to have, at optimality, a positive dual price and a zero value for new demand.

(d) Graph the possible shapes of the maximum profit curve (the optimal objective value) as a function of the existing demand RHS. Give possible interpretations to the points at which the slope changes.

CHAPTER 9

Two Case Studies at PROTRAC Based on Computer Analysis of the Model

9.1
INTRODUCTION

Motives for Modeling

This chapter provides fairly realistic illustrations of an important theme in this text. *Often, the solution to a problem is only a starting point and is, in itself, the least interesting part of the analysis to follow.* In Chapters 1 and 3 we discussed a variety of reasons that models are employed. By now, you yourself have the technical know-how to be a user of LP models. This know-how will allow you to better appreciate why models can be important tools to managers in competitive firms. In this chapter we provide two illustrations of important motives for modeling.

The first motive is to *learn as much as possible about the real-world problem at hand.* Of course, the solution provides optimal decisions, but looking at the solution alone provides about as much insight into the logical interactions in a complex problem as the hands on a fine Swiss watch reveal about the underlying mechanism.

Learning from the Model

Let us be more specific. One of the great advantages of LP is that one is able to solve problems with many constraints and an even greater number of variables. In such problems, it is typically impossible for a person to trace through the many interactions between the decision variables to get a measure of the effect of changing this or that decision or to determine the effect on the operating policies of changing a parameter. For example, in a manufacturing and distribution system that involves a number of products, more than one manufacturing location, several marketing districts, and alternative means of transportation, it is extremely difficult to "cost-out" the effect of increasing the production of a given product in a specific plant. Analysis of such problems might progress somewhat as follows: "If I expand production of product A in plant 1, then since I am already at full capacity I must reduce the amount of B, C, and/or D that I make in plant 1. This implies that I'll have less of at least one of these products to distribute unless I change my production plans in some other location. In a way, I'd like to decrease the amount of product B I make in plant 1 because it takes the most time per unit in the heat-treat department, where we're really short of capacity. But our largest

264

265

CHAPTER 9
Two Case Studies
at PROTRAC
Based on
Computer
Analysis
of the Model

demand for product B is in the district closest to plant 1, so that would have a negative effect on our transportation costs. Maybe we should decrease product C instead, since. . . ."

The number of possible alternatives, each with its own advantages and disadvantages, is, for practical purposes, endless. Without the help of a model, management must often settle for a feasible (as opposed to optimal) solution, justified on the basis of intuitive arguments that, though plausible, may be far from optimal.

In previous chapters we have seen that formulating a problem as a linear program and solving it on a computer provides not only an optimal set of decisions but also a wealth of sensitivity information. This type of information reveals the effect on the objective of changing various parameters, like an RHS or a coefficient in the objective function, or of introducing a new variable into the solution. Although this is extremely useful, it still leaves many questions unanswered. For example, suppose that the dual variable associated with a particular constraint equals $2000. What changes in the decision variables must one make to achieve this increase? Or, suppose that the reduced cost of a particular variable is $72. What adjustments in the other decision variables must one make in order to introduce the new variable into the solution at the cost of $72 per unit?

Activity Analysis

It is, of course, always possible to answer these questions by appropriately modifying the LP problem (e.g., changing a parameter value) and solving it again. This limits the analyst's involvement, but it also limits the amount of thinking he has to do about his real-world problem and hence the amount he can learn about important interactions and relations between activities. In the first part of this chapter, we shall see that the analyst or manager can obtain a deeper understanding by using the information provided in the computer output and then "working backward" with marginal cost and marginal revenue arguments. This is a process that we call **activity analysis**, which involves *determining the sequence of actions or activities that produce a particular dual price or reduced cost*.

An unstructured process, activity analysis can be frustrating. But it is potentially rewarding, for it provides a method for determining how the model is operating at optimality and what costs are associated with particular activities. In more technical jargon, this is called looking at the **optimal technology** for the problem at hand. The insight as to how the model is operating at optimality gives the analyst or manager a deeper understanding of the logical structure and the important tradeoffs in the decision-making environment. An activity analysis will show that certain interactions and cost assumptions are essential to the fact that the current optimal solution is in fact optimal. A constraint or coefficient that was initially easy to agree to as 1 of 1000 or 1 of 10,000 may seem to merit change, or at least further consideration, when one understands the way in which the optimal decisions would change if that particular constraint or coefficient were to be changed. What all of this means is that activity analysis is really applied economics at work. The implications that are uncovered by activity analysis may clash with a manager's intuition or prior judgments. This presents another situation where the manager must either adjust her concept of reality or modify the logic of the model.

Activity analysis forces a manager or analyst to think critically about the model being used.

In the second part of this chapter, we illustrate an application of the PROTRAC model to a specific planning problem. This desire to answer *specific questions*, as opposed to learning as much as possible about the general interactions for the problem at hand, provides our second important motive for modeling. In other words, *models can be used as tools to perform studies aimed at answering specific questions.*

9.2

ACTIVITY ANALYSIS

The manager for centralized planning in the Midwest tractor division has been recently transferred to this job from marketing and sales. This move is intended to give him manufacturing experience as a step toward broader responsibilities. He has set aside several hours to discuss some operational policies with one of the articulate members of the operations analysis group. The modeler arrives, lugging a printout that shows the current operating plan for the two-plant, two-period PROTRAC problem discussed in the previous chapter, and some schematic diagrams concerning the model. The decision variables used in the model are shown in Figure 9.1. The printout and a diagram of the model are displayed in Figures 9.2 and 9.3, respectively.

Figure 9.1

Decision Variables for the PROTRAC Production and Marketing Model

		NOTATION	
DECISION VARIABLES	**PLANT**	**Time Period 1**	**Time Period 2**
Number of BOD produced in	1	BODP1T1	BODP1T2
	2	BODP2T1	BODP2T2
Amount of FP shipped from	1	FPP1T1	FPP1T2
	2	FPP2T1	FPP2T2
TR assembled in	1	TRP1T1	TRP1T2
	2	TRP2T1	TRP2T2
TR cross-shipped	1 → 2	CSTRP1T1	CSTRP1T2
	2 → 1	CSTRP2T1	CSTRP2T2
Tons of FI purchased in	1	FIP1T1	FIP1T2
	2	FIP2T1	FIP2T2
Tons of OI purchased in	1	OIP1T1	OIP1T2
	2	OIP2T1	OIP2T2
Amount of ND created		NDT1	NDT2
FP inventory in	1	INFPP1T1	INFPP1T2
	2	INFPP2T1	INFPP2T2
TR inventory in	1	INTRP1T1	INTRP1T2
	2	INTRP2T1	INTRP2T2

MANAGER: I assume you have the optimal two-period operating plan with you.

Yes, I have the printout, and it includes both the solution and the sensitivity analysis. Do you want to look it over?

MANAGER: No, not yet. Let me first explain what I need. There are two pressing matters at the moment. Let's begin with the first. As you may know, we've received orders from upstairs to improve our methods for inventory handling.

266   What do you mean by "improve our methods?"

267

CHAPTER 9
Two Case Studies
at PROTRAC
Based on
Computer
Analysis
of the Model

MANAGER: I can't go into all that detail right now. But what I basically mean is that we've got to have lower per-unit carrying charges. This means that the industrial engineers are going to step in and analyze how things are currently being done and then make recommendations to reduce costs. One of my difficulties is that I'm in a new position and I am already in the middle of a dispute. I want your help in providing a solid quantitative basis for settling this thing.

I see. Can you give me any details?

MANAGER: The supervisors at the plant 1 complex are telling me that I should worry about plant 2 because that's where the inefficiencies are. But the plant 2 people are telling me that their operations are optimal and I should be looking at plant 1. So that's where I am. Do you have an opinion from what your model tells you?

If I understand you correctly, you want to know where an improvement in inventory handling would give the most return. Is that correct?

MANAGER: Yes, and I'd like you to give me some quantitative support for taking one side or the other in this dispute.

To be honest with you, it looks to me like a toss-up.

MANAGER: Why is that?

Because neither side is right. Or, maybe I should say both sides are right.

MANAGER: That's what your output tells you?

Yes.

MANAGER: Well, I'm not really sure what you mean. Let's have a look at it.

Okay. I'll show it to you in a minute. But first, I want to mention something relevant. You may recall that the combined labor capacity of both plants in period 2 is insufficient to satisfy the current figure of 190 units of existing demand in period 2.

MANAGER: Hmmm . . . would you take a second to review your thinking on that?

Insufficient Capacity in Period 2

We have 80,000 hours of labor in the plant 1 complex. Using the estimated requirement of 990 hours of labor per unit of finished product, we can obtain an estimated maximum total production of 80.808 units of finished product from plant 1. In the plant 2 complex, we have 70,000 hours of labor. At 660 hours of labor per unit of finished product, we get a maximum output of 106.06 units. Thus, maximum total production is about 3.13 units short, and we must somehow carry inventories into period 2. There are three options for doing that, right?

MANAGER: Right. We can carry forward finished product in inventory, or carry forward transmissions in inventory, or we can cross-ship transmissions. Of course, any combination of these activities could be employed and I would guess that we're probably doing some of each.

If you don't mind my saying so, that is where you're wrong.

MANAGER: Really?

Let's look at the computer output. The inventory variables are denoted by INFPPiTj and INTRPiTj where i and j indicate the appropriate plant and period, respectively. You can see that they're all zero, but that CRTRP2T1, which represents the transmissions cross-shipped from plant 2 to plant 1 in period 1, is positive. Remember, these transmissions leave plant 2 in period 1 and cannot be used in plant 1 until period 2.

MANAGER: I see. So the model claims that we cross-ship and do nothing else. But I thought we usually carry inventories also. I'm not sure the model's policy seems right.

Perhaps I can explain the reason.

MANAGER: You mean you can tell me why the solution turns out this way?

I think so.

MANAGER: Well, okay. But I don't see how you can do that. Do you solve the whole model in your head?

Figure 9.2
PROTRAC Computer Analysis

```
MAX    29970 FPP1T1 + 29970 FPP1T2  + 29910 FPP2T1 + 29910 FPP2T2 − 1000 FIP1T1
       − 1000 FIP1T2 − 1000 FIP2T1 − 1000 FIP2T2  − 1200 OIP1T1 − 1200 OIP1T2
       − 1200 OIP2T1 − 1200 OIP2T2 − 20 CSTRP1T1 − 20 CSTRP1T2 − 20 CSTRP2T1
       − 20 CSTRP2T2  − 3000 NDT1 − 3000 NDT2 − 20 INTRP1T1 − 20 INTRP1T2
       − 20 INTRP2T1 − 20 INTRP2T2 − 300 INFPP1T1 − 300 INFPP1T2 − 300 INFPP2T1
       − 300 INFPP2T2
SUBJECT TO
   2)    FPP1T1 + FPP2T1 − NDT1 =         130
   3)    FPP1T2 + FPP2T2 − NDT2 =         190
   4)    900 BODP1T1 + 90 TRP1T1 ≤    80000
   5)    900 BODP1T2 + 90 TRP1T2 ≤    80000
   6)    600 BODP2T1 + 60 TRP2T1 ≤    70000
   7)    600 BODP2T2 + 60 TRP2T2 ≤    70000
   8)    FIP1T1 + FIP2T1 ≤    1000
   9)    FIP1T2 + FIP2T2 ≤    1000
  10)    −FIP1T1 − OIP1T1 + 6 BODP1T1 =   0
  11)    −FIP2T1 − OIP2T1 + 6 BODP1T1 =   0
  12)    −FIP1T2 − OIP1T2 + 6 BODP1T2 =   0
  13)    −FIP2T2 − OIP2T2 + 6 BODP2T2 =   0
  14)    FPP1T1 − BODP1T1 + INFPP1T1 =     5
  15)    FPP1T2 − BODP1T2 − INFPP1T1 + INFPP1T2 =     0
  16)    FPP2T1 − BODP2T1 + INFPP2T1 =     2
  17)    FPP2T2 − BODP2T2 − INFPP2T1 + INFPP2T2 =     0
  18)    CSTRP1T1 + INTRP1T1 + BODP1T1 − TRP1T1 =     6
  19)    CSTRP1T2 − CSTRP2T1 + INTRP1T1 + INTRP1T2 + BODP1T2 − TRP1T2 =     0
  20)    CSTRP2T1 + INTRP2T1 + BODP2T1 − TRP2T1 =     4
  21)    −CSTRP1T1 + CSTRP2T2 − INTRP2T1 + INTRP2T2 + BODP2T2 − TRP2T2 =     0


          OBJECTIVE FUNCTION VALUE

   1)        8942181.
```

VARIARLE	VALUE	REDUCED COST		ROW	SLACK OR SURPLUS
FPP1T1	86.353537	0.000000			
FPP1T2	83.939392	0.000000			
FPP2T1	105.292932	0.000000			
FPP2T2	106.060608	0.000000			
FIP1T1	380.242416	−0.000031			
FIP1T2	363.636360	0.000000			
FIP2T1	619.757591	−0.000031			
FIP2T2	636.363640	0.000000			
OIP1T1	107.878805	0.000000			
OIP1T2	140.000000	0.000000			
OIP2T1	0.000000	0.000000			
OIP2T2	0.000000	0.000000			
CSTRP1T1	0.000000	10.909225			
CSTRP1T2	0.000000	1831.818220		2)	0.000000
CSTRP2T1	34.444434	0.000000		3)	0.000000
CSTRP2T2	0.000000	1826.363660		4)	0.000000
NDT1	61.646467	0.000000		5)	0.000000
NDT2	0.000000	160.000000		6)	0.000000
INTRP1T1	0.000000	5.454666		7)	0.000000
INTRP1T2	0.000000	1831.818220		8)	0.000000
INTRP2T1	0.000000	5.454559		9)	0.000000
INTRP2T2	0.000000	1826.363660		10)	0.000000
BODP1T1	81.353537	0.000671		11)	0.000000
TRP1T1	75.353537	−0.000122		12)	0.000000
BODP1T2	83.939392	0.000351		13)	0.000000
TRP1T2	49.494958	0.000000		14)	0.000000
BODP2T1	103.292932	0.000351		15)	0.000000
TRP2T1	133.737366	−0.000015		16)	0.000000
BODP2T2	106.060608	0.000381		17)	0.000000
TRP2T2	106.060608	0.000015		18)	0.000000
INFPP1T1	0.000000	140.000000		19)	0.000000
INFPP1T2	0.000000	27430.000000		20)	0.000000
INFPP2T1	0.000000	140.000000		21)	0.000000
INFPP2T2	0.000000	27370.000000			

SENSITIVITY ANALYSIS
COST COEFFICIENT RANGES

VARIABLE	CURRENT COEF	ALLOWABLE INCREASE	ALLOWABLE DECREASE
FPP1T1	29970.000000	INFINITY	60.001326
FPP1T2	29970.000000	159.999998	60.000152
FPP2T1	29910.000000	60.001327	159.999998
FPP2T2	29910.000000	60.000152	19870.000500
FIP1T1	−1000.000000	0.000000	10.000221
FIP1T2	−1000.000000	0.000000	9.999999
FIP2T1	−1000.000000	10.000221	0.000000
FIP2T2	−1000.000000	9.999999	0.000000
OIP1T1	−1200.000000	23.333333	0.000000
OIP1T2	−1200.000000	26.668400	INFINITY
OIP2T1	−1200.000000	0.000000	INFINITY
OIP2T2	−1200.000000	0.000000	INFINITY
CSTRP1T1	−20.000000	10.909225	INFINITY
CSTRP1T2	−20.000000	1831.818220	INFINITY
CSTRP2T1	−20.000000	14.545454	5.454559
CSTRP2T2	−20.000000	1826.363660	INFINITY
NDT1	−3000.000000	INFINITY	160.000000
NDT2	−3000.000000	160.000000	INFINITY
INTRP1T1	−20.000000	5.454666	INFINITY
INTRP1T2	−20.000000	1831.818220	INFINITY
INTRP2T1	−20.000000	5.454559	INFINITY
INTRP2T2	−20.000000	1826.363660	INFINITY
BODP1T1	0.000000	INFINITY	60.001326
TRP1T1	0.000000	6.000133	19770.000500
BODP1T2	0.000000	159.999998	60.000152
TRP1T2	0.000000	6.000015	16.000000
BODP2T1	0.000000	60.001327	159.999998
TRP2T1	0.000000	16.000000	6.000133
BODP2T2	0.000000	60.000152	19870.000500
TRP2T2	0.000000	2008.999990	6.000015
INFPP1T1	−300.000000	140.000000	INFINITY
INFPP1T2	−300.000000	27430.000000	INFINITY
INFPP2T1	−300.000000	140.000000	INFINITY
INFPP2T2	−300.000000	27370.000000	INFINITY

RIGHTHAND SIDE RANGES

DUAL PRICES	ROW	CURRENT RHS	ALLOWABLE INCREASE	ALLOWABLE DECREASE
3000.000000	2	130.000000	61.646467	INFINITY
2840.000000	3	190.000000	4.949496	3.131312
19.969697	4	80000.000000	INFINITY	17800.002700
20.131314	5	80000.000000	3099.998990	4454.546200
29.863637	6	70000.000000	41826.665500	11866.668500
30.106061	7	70000.000000	2066.665990	3266.667240
199.999970	8	1000.000000	107.878805	380.242416
200.000000	9	1000.000000	139.999996	363.636360
1200.000000	10	0.000000	107.878805	INFINITY
1200.000000	11	0.000000	107.878805	380.242416
1200.000000	12	0.000000	139.999996	INFINITY
1200.000000	13	0.000000	139.999996	363.636360
26970.000000	14	5.000000	INFINITY	61.646467
27130.000000	15	0.000000	3.131312	4.949496
26910.000000	16	2.000000	INFINITY	61.646467
27070.000000	17	0.000000	3.131312	4.949496
1797.272890	18	6.000000	82.888890	197.777803
1811.818220	19	0.000000	34.444433	197.777805
1791.818220	20	4.000000	147.111101	197.777805
1806.363660	21	0.000000	34.444433	54.444453

270

CHAPTER 9
Two Case Studies
at PROTRAC
Based on
Computer
Analysis
of the Model

Figure 9.3
Schematic Diagram of the
PROTRAC Model

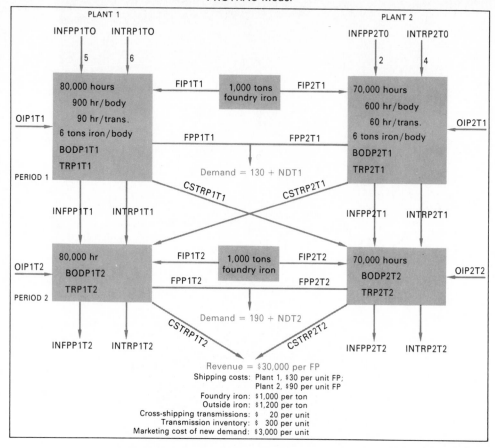

No. I can't duplicate what the computer does, but I can use the computer results as a starting point to figure out some of the trade-offs the computer analysis must be taking into account. Can I show you what I mean?

Carrying
Finished
Product
Inventory

MANAGER: Go ahead.

Well, we've already observed that we have to get 3.13 additional units of finished product into period 2. One way to do this would be to carry forward finished product inventory at a cost of $300 per unit.

MANAGER: Right. So in that case it would cost $939 to make up the 3.13-unit deficit. That seems to be the obvious way to do it. In fact, I'm not sure that I clearly understand how to do it any other way.

Let me explain another possibility. Suppose that in one of the plants we carry 11 transmissions in inventory into period 2. That means that in this plant we could assemble 10 fewer transmissions in period 2 than we did previously.

MANAGER: Wait a minute. Why are you carrying 11 transmissions into period 2? I don't get it.

You'll see in a minute. For now, let's just accept the fact that we are using all labor in both plants in period 2 and still we cannot make enough finished product to satisfy the period 2 demand. And also, we know that I have excess labor in period 1 relative to the existing demand. Certainly then I have enough resources in period 1 to allow me to carry forward 11 transmissions into period 2. You'll grant that I can do that?

271

CHAPTER 9
Two Case Studies
at PROTRAC
Based on
Computer
Analysis
of the Model

MANAGER: Yes, I don't see why not. But I still don't see the point.

And you'll also grant that I can assemble 10 fewer transmissions in period 2 and replace those with 10 of the 11 that are carried in?

MANAGER: Yes. But since you're carrying 11 in, why don't you assemble 11 fewer?

It is also true that I could assemble 11 fewer. In fact, there are many different adjustments we could pursue, but I've done my homework and I want to show you what I've learned. So let's say that we assemble exactly 10 fewer in period 2 and replace these with 10 of the 11 that are carried forward.

MANAGER: Okay. Then what?

Since we now assemble 10 fewer in period 2, we have released enough labor to make an additional body, because in either plant the amount of labor required to make a body is the same as the amount required to assemble 10 transmissions.

MANAGER: Okay. Go on.

*Carrying
TR Allows
for Creation
of More FP
in Period 2*

Now we're sitting here with an extra body and an eleventh transmission. We slap the eleventh transmission into the body, and we have an additional unit of finished product. So the 11 transmissions that are carried forward have a final net effect of allowing us to create an additional unit of finished product.

MANAGER: I see. Pretty neat! What you are really saying is that the transmissions release enough labor to make another finished product, and that is true in either plant. And for each 11 carried into period 2, only 10 fewer will be assembled in period 2. Since an extra body is made with the released labor, the new policy continues to use all labor in period 2 but now we have an additional unit of output.

Right. Now let's see what these adjustments would cost in additional inventory charges.

MANAGER: Since the inventory charge on a transmission is $20, it must cost 20(11), or $220. So that would be (3.13)(220), or $688.60 to make up our total shortage of finished product. That's clearly better than the $939-cost of carrying finished product forward. So holding transmissions is preferred to holding finished product?

*Carrying TR
Is an Implicit
Way to Carry
the Tight
Resource*

Right. One way to look at it is like this. The tight resource in period 2 is labor. So what we would like to do is carry labor in inventory from period 1 into period 2. But we cannot do that. So what we do instead is carry forward something that consumes labor, and that is an implicit way of carrying forward labor.

MANAGER: Sure. The labor is already in the transmission. That's clear enough. But let's get back to the optimal solution in your printout. We just figured out that carrying forward transmissions is preferable to carrying finished product. But the optimal solution says to cross-ship transmissions. Since the per-unit charge for cross-shipping is $20, and that is the same as the carrying charge for transmissions, I can't see why cross-shipping would be preferred to holding transmissions in inventory. I would guess that it's probably a situation involving—oh heck, what is that phrase?—optimal alternatives. You know what I mean.

Are you referring to the existence of alternative optima?

MANAGER: Yes, that's it. Since it costs $20 both to cross-ship and to carry forward in either plant, we must clearly be indifferent. Right?

*Cross-Shipping
Is Cheaper*

No. There is a good reason for the fact that cross-shipping is preferred. Recall that cross-shipping involves a transfer from one plant to the other. Now the important fact that you've overlooked is that the charge for shipping finished product is $60 less in plant 1 than in plant 2. When we cross-ship 11 transmissions from plant 2 to plant 1, the net final effect over the two periods is to ship one less unit of finished product from plant 2 in period 1 and one additional unit of finished product from plant 1 in period 2. The net saving on shipping charges is $60. This means that the cross-shipment policy has a net cost of 220 − 60 or $160 for each batch of 11 transmissions.

MANAGER: I'm sorry, but you lost me on that one. I understand the $220-cross-shipping charge, and I see that it costs $90 to ship finished product from plant 2 and only $30 from plant 1. But it seems to me that the total cost of the cross-shipping policy should be 220 + 30, or

272

CHAPTER 9
Two Case Studies
at PROTRAC
Based on
Computer
Analysis
of the Model

$250, and this is the same as what it would cost to carry forward 11 transmissions in plant 1 and then send out the finished product. Again, it looks to me like we should be indifferent between the two policies.

Okay, I can explain it very clearly. The idea is this. Suppose that we're producing at full capacity in both plants in each period, and everything produced is being sold. Now we want to produce and sell one less in period 1 and one more in period 2 in the cheapest possible way, right?

MANAGER: Absolutely. No problem so far.

Good. Now look at this diagram (see Figure 9.4). The left and center panels show what happens costwise if we carry transmissions forward in plant 1 or plant 2, respectively. In each case, the net cost is 220. But in the right panel you can see the effects of cross-shipping from plant 2 to plant 1. Can you now see that the net cost is only 160?

Figure 9.4
Comparing the Cost of Alternative Policies

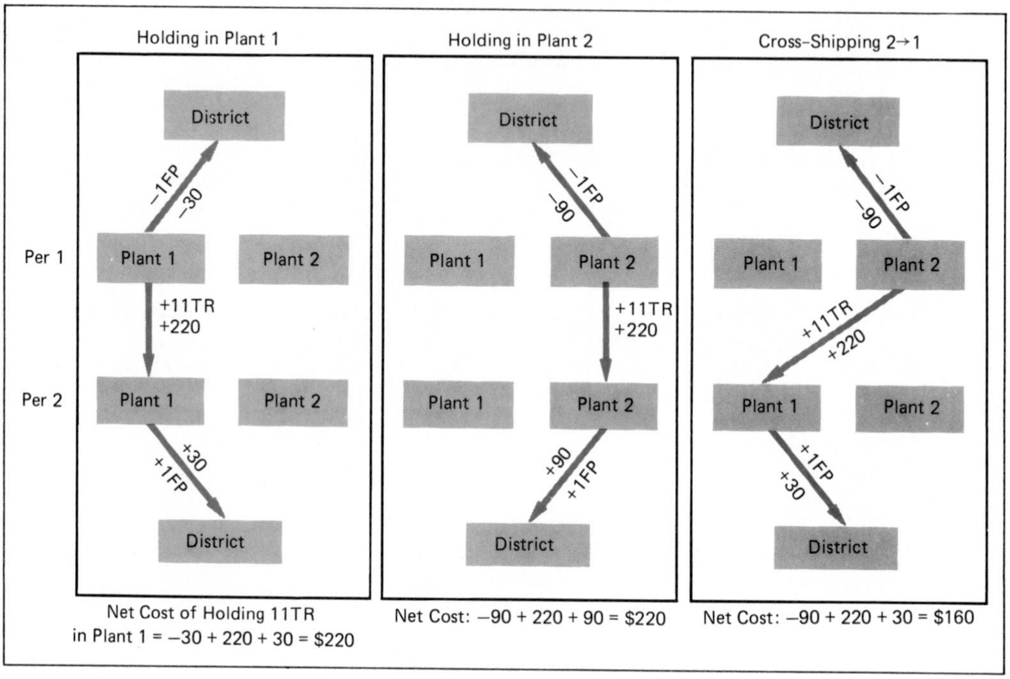

Net Cost of Holding 11TR in Plant 1 = −30 + 220 + 30 = $220

Net Cost: −90 + 220 + 90 = $220

Net Cost: −90 + 220 + 30 = $160

MANAGER: Yes, I can. How long does it take you to figure all that out?

It isn't bad once you've done it a few times.

MANAGER: I see. So in this case it looks like the total cost of the cross-shipping policy is (3.13)160, or $500.80. I agree that this is the cheapest way to do things. So I assume this is our current recommended operating policy.

Correct. By the way, you can also see why the optimal value of CSTRP2T1 is 34.44.

MANAGER: I can? Let's see, that is the number of transmissions cross-shipped, so 34.44 must equal (3.13)11, and indeed that is true. So now let's figure out what this has to do with our dispute. I can see why you said it's a toss-up. Since neither plant should currently be planning to carry inventories, there doesn't seem to be much room for improvement in that respect. Since neither of the plants' management knows what the other is doing, it is clear why each one thinks I should look at the other.

That seems to be what's happening.

MANAGER: Even though this is an interesting analysis, I am not very sure how helpful it is.

273

CHAPTER 9
Two Case Studies
at PROTRAC
Based on
Computer
Analysis
of the Model

After all, the upstairs wants to improve inventory handling, and they have their own reasons for wanting to do so. So suppose I just say, the heck with optimality. I want to make the old man upstairs happy, so I'm going to adjust our current activities and start carrying inventories even though we'll pay a price to do so. How much would it cost?

Look at the reduced costs of INTRP1T1 and INTRP2T1. The value is 5.45. That is the initial per-unit cost of forcing yourself to carry an inventory of transmissions. As you can see, it's independent of the plant in this case.

MANAGER: Yes, and I see that the reduced cost of finished product inventory is 140. That seems much too costly, so let's concentrate on the transmissions. Now suppose we tell one of the plant managers to start holding transmissions in inventory. How do I know that he'll adjust in an optimal way so that the cost doesn't go up by more than the 5.45 per unit?

We could tell him not only what to do but also how to do it.

MANAGER: You mean we have to rerun the problem, or what?

*Activity
Analysis and
Reduced Cost*

No. We can see what's going on from the output we already have, but it requires some coordination of activities. Suppose that you decide to carry forward 11 transmissions in plant 1. This means that in period 1 the manager of plant 1 will produce 1 less body and instead he will assemble 10 additional transmissions. He will ship one less unit of finished product to the district. In period 1, the plant 2 manager must cross-ship 11 less transmissions over to plant 1. He will assemble 10 fewer transmissions and 1 additional body. An additional unit of finished product goes to the district to replace the one withdrawn by plant 1. The policies in period 2 will all be the same as they are now planned.

MANAGER: How do you know that's the optimal adjustment?

Let's figure out the cost. If it turns out to be 5.45 per transmission it will be optimal. Do you agree?

MANAGER: Of course.

In plant 1 there will be a holding cost of 220 and a period 1 shipping saving of 30. In plant 2 there will be a cross-shipping saving of 220 and an added period 1 shipping cost of 90. The net added cost is 60. There will also be six tons of iron that had been purchased in plant 1 and must now be purchased in plant 2. So that cost nets out to 0. In summary, the added cost is $60 for carrying the 11 transmissions forward in plant 1. That figures to be 60/11, or $5.45 per transmission. Since that is the value of the reduced cost, the adjustment must be optimal.

MANAGER: Very good. Now suppose that instead I decide to carry the transmissions in plant 2. Let's see if I can figure out how to do it optimally. All I have to do is find some adjustments that lead to the number 5.45, right?

Right you are.

MANAGER: Okay, here we go. If I carry forward 11 transmissions in plant 2, I will cross-ship 11 less. The saving in cross-shipment costs will equal the added holding costs. In period 2, plant 2 will make 1 additional body and plant 1 will make 1 less body. The adjustments in iron charges cancel. In period 2, plant 1 assembles 10 more transmissions and plant 2 assembles 10 less. Plant 1 satisfies one less unit of demand in period 2, and plant 2 satisfies one more. Thus there is an added cost for shipping of $(90 - 30)/11$, or 60/11, which again gives $5.45. It looks like I've got it. Do you agree?

Absolutely. Of course, you remember that we can't be sure how long that figure of 5.45 will remain valid.

MANAGER: I understand. The incremental cost will probably change as we force more and more of these transmissions to be carried forward.

In fact, it will increase.

MANAGER: How can you tell?

Look at it this way. When you force F transmissions in plant 2 to be carried forward, you are implicitly imposing a constraint

As you increase F, you are tightening the constraint, and we know that tightening a constraint can't help and when it hurts, it hurts more and more.

MANAGER: I see. So the penalty of satisfying the upstairs is incrementally increasing—or, more correctly, nondecreasing. Right?

Yes.

MANAGER: By the way, I recall that we can reinterpret this current reduced cost of 5.45 somewhat differently. Isn't it correct to say that this is the amount the carrying charge would have to be reduced before the activity of carrying transmissions will actually be as good as cross-shipping?

Exactly.

MANAGER: Very interesting. That means about a 25% reduction would be required, which seems an unlikely possibility in either plant.

Perhaps you could persuade the upstairs to focus on the cross-shipping charges, since any reduction there will result in immediate added profits.

MANAGER: I see what you mean. We could reduce carrying costs 10 or 15% and still obtain no payoff. Even a 1% reduction in cross-shipping charges will give some added profits. Well, I can now see much more clearly into some of these interactions, but I still have the feeling that some of our past optimal policies have involved carrying inventories.

You mean historically?

MANAGER: Yes.

That could well have been the case at different levels of demand.

MANAGER: I see. Maybe we should analyze some of those interactions.

Which ones?

**Changing
Existing
Demand**

MANAGER: The interactions related to increases in the level of demand. I haven't told you this, but that seems to be the underlying motive for the upstairs interest in reducing our inventory costs. I guess there is some reason to believe that there may be a windfall of demand in period 2. It has something to do with an anticipated change in the farm subsidy program.

When would this become apparent?

MANAGER: I'm not sure. Maybe by the middle of period 1.

How do they know that?

MANAGER: Because the old man has a son-in-law on one of the congressional committees, a man by the name of Shmootz. Anyway, if they can give us the right signals by the middle of period 1, I would assume that we could react appropriately. But what I am wondering is this: how much additional demand would there have to be before the optimal activities change?

I think what you're asking me is this: if existing demand increases enough, will the optimal inventory activities change?

MANAGER: Right, but not just inventory. Let's look at all of the activities.

Fine, let's first take a look at the allowable increase in existing demand in period 1. That is 61.45 units, which is the optimal value of the new demand variable for period 1.

MANAGER: I can see how to interpret that. For each additional unit of existing demand in period 1, we simply create one less unit of new demand in that same period. This would save $3000 of marketing expense. All other decision variables remain unchanged in value. After adding on 61.64 additional units of existing demand, there will be 0 new demand. At that point, I can see that any additional existing demand would make the problem infeasible.

Very good. And you've also explained why the dual price on row 2 is $3000.

MANAGER: You mean because the only change in cost would be the $3000-saving in the marketing cost.

Yes.

MANAGER: All right. That much is clear. But I see on your printout that the allowable change in period 2 existing demand is only 4.94. Frankly, that puzzles me.

In what particular way?

MANAGER: For each additional unit of existing demand in period 2, we should create one less unit of new demand in period 1 and cross-ship 11 transmissions from plant 2 to plant 1. This should save 3000 and cost 160, giving a net saving of $2840. The dual price on row 3 is indeed 2840, which shows that my analysis is correct. I don't see why we can't continue doing this until 61.45 units of existing demand have been added in period 2, with a new demand of 0 in period 1, just as we did in the other case.

Because the cost structure will change after you've increased existing demand by only 4.94.

MANAGER: I understand that's what the output means. But I don't see the reason. Do you?

Yes, I believe so. Here is what happens. Your analysis begins correctly, but you've overlooked an important fact. At optimality, plant 1 currently assembles 49.49 transmissions in period 2. This is the optimal value of TRP1T2. If we continue to use the optimal cross-shipping scheme, plant 1 will be producing only bodies and assembling no transmissions after 4.949 additional units of existing demand are satisfied in period 2. This is because the assembly of transmissions is reduced by 10 for each additional unit of demand, and $10(4.949) = 49.49$. At this point, sending additional transmissions into plant 1 does nothing for you. Worse than that, it's wasteful because they cannot be used. The cost structure will therefore change at this point because a new optimal inventory activity will go into effect. In fact, the new activity will be to begin carrying forward transmissions in inventory in plant 2.

MANAGER: I see. Since plant 2 is still assembling transmissions, 106.06 of them, in fact, it is possible for them to cut back on transmission assembly in period 2 and make more bodies. Well, it looks to me like we've arrived at some interesting ideas.

Yes, but we haven't really settled your dispute.

MANAGER: Nevertheless, if I understand you correctly, we have good support for the following two recommendations. First of all, we should continue to operate optimally if possible, and that means we should have the industrial engineers examine the cross-shipping activity. Any increased efficiency in that area will be realized in immediate returns. Second, if it is true that we may have a significant increase in existing demand in period 2, then we should look at the inventory handling in plant 2. Of course, I am assuming that what you said is correct.

In particular?

MANAGER: That after an increase of 4.94 units of demand in period 2, we will see inventories of transmissions in plant 2.

I can assure you that's correct. In fact, we could use precisely this type of analysis to construct the entire $V(b)$ curve for demand in period 2. Doing that would allow us to determine the optimal inventory policy for any level of existing demand in period 2. In fact, that is precisely what Problem 9-15 asks you to do.

MANAGER: Good. I may have a look at that later.

By the way, if you are really expecting a surge in period 2 demand, why not increase the labor supply?

MANAGER: I'm glad you asked, because that leads me to the second thing I wanted to discuss, and this is a more detailed study. It involves capacity expansion.

I thought so.

MANAGER: I'd like you to take notes on this and prepare an analysis. No, better yet, I'll send you a memo. You can do the study and send me your analysis. I don't think you will need my help.

9.3

AN INVESTMENT ANALYSIS

The Cost Functions and the Plan of Analysis

The board of directors has approved a recommendation to modernize and expand the company foundry. The new capacity will be 1400 tons in each period. A revised transfer-pricing policy will set the cost of foundry iron at $900 per ton. It is clear to management that the availability of labor hours is going to be the single binding constraint in future operations. Therefore, in order to make the most of the new foundry, the capacity of *one* (and only one) of the plants, as indirectly measured in the model by available labor hours, is going to be expanded. The management science department has been asked for recommendations on the following questions:

1. Which plant should be expanded?
2. What is the optimal capacity in the chosen plant?

In order to answer these questions, a study has been performed using the PRO-TRAC model discussed above as a starting point. Management has requested that the recommendations be based on a two-period problem with estimated existing demands as follows:

160 units (period 1)

210 units (period 2)

Because of union agreements and lead-time requirements, the plant capacity expansion will not be effective until period 2. In other words, the study should assume that the period 1 availability of labor is the same as it is currently (80,000 hours in plant 1, 70,000 hours in plant 2). However, it should be assumed that the new foundry and the new costs of iron will be operative and effective in both periods. Moreover, all initial inventories should be taken as in the foregoing model (refer to Figure 9.2).

Cost of Expansion Unfortunately, the cost of capacity expansion is not linear. As the scale of the effort increases, the basic construction plans become more elaborate. Increasing amounts of architectural and design time are required, and material specifications become more rigid and more costly. Management has solicited bids for potential expansion in each plant, and cost curves have been constructed. These are shown in Figures 9.5 and 9.6. For plant i, the function $C_i(b_i)$ denotes the cost of expanding capacity from the current level (80,000 in plant 1, 70,000 in plant 2) up to the level b_i.[1] All costs are expressed in

---

[1] Hence the symbol b_1 now represents the RHS of the fourth constraint in the PROTRAC model, and b_2 is the RHS of the sixth constraint. In Chapter 7 these quantities were denoted as b_4 and b_6. The somewhat different notation is introduced here to stress the distinction between plants 1 and 2.

277

CHAPTER 9
Two Case Studies
at PROTRAC
Based on
Computer
Analysis
of the Model

Figure 9.5

Cost of Expansion to b_1 Hours in Plant 1

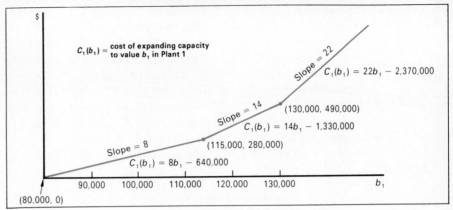

Figure 9.6

Cost of Expansion to b_2 Hours in Plant 2

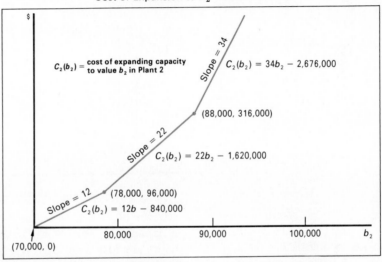

equivalent value at the end of period 2; that is, appropriate discounting has been per-formed. As you can see, each function is increasing, and the functions are *convex* (the rates of change are increasing). You will recall that the plant 2 facilities are more advanced and more efficient than plant 1. They require only 660 hours to produce a unit of finished product, as opposed to 990 in plant 1. As a result, the facilities and equipment in plant 2 are also more expensive, and that is reflected in the C_2 function.

***Determining
Optimal
Capacity***
Since the costs of expansion are nonlinear, they cannot be incorporated per se in the existing model. One approach for handling this problem, and the one we shall pursue, is now described. Another useful approach is shown in Problem 9-14.

First of all, each plant is considered separately. Let us use plant 1 as an illustration. We know that the OV function for labor hours in period 2 is an increasing concave function (the rate of change is decreasing). This is true because we are considering a max problem and a $\leq$ constraint, and relaxing a constraint helps less and less. As already noted, the cost-of-expansion curve is convex. For the moment, assume that

278

CHAPTER 9
Two Case Studies
at PROTRAC
Based on
Computer
Analysis
of the Model

each of these curves is smooth, as shown in Figure 9.7. This figure reveals that the number b_1^* is the optimal capacity. To demonstrate this, suppose that the capacity is at a value of b_1 to the left of b_1^*, such as $\hat{b}_1$ in Figure 9.7. Now consider a small increase in b_1, to $\hat{b}_1 + \Delta$. The associated increase in the OV function is $V_1(\hat{b}_1 + \Delta) - V_1(\hat{b}_1)$.[2] The associated increase in the expansion cost is $C_1(\hat{b}_1 + \Delta) - C_1(\hat{b}_1)$. Clearly, the increase in OV exceeds the increase in expansion cost, and hence the net increase in profit is positive. This means that $\hat{b}_1$ cannot be optimal. The same argument applies to all values of the capacity that are smaller than b_1^*. You can also convince yourself that if b_1 is larger than b_1^*, a small decrease will cut the expansion cost by more than the cut in the optimal objective value. Consequently, the optimal capacity must be b_1^*; that is, current capacity should be expanded to b_1^*. As shown in Figure 9.7, b_1^* is the point at which the tangent to each of the graphs has the same slope.

Figure 9.7
Hypothetical Smooth Functions for the OV and the Cost of Expansion

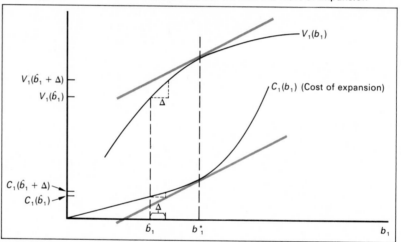

Assuming that the curves for plant 2 are also smooth, the same method can be followed to obtain an optimal capacity b_2^*. The plant to be chosen is obtained as follows. Recall that the current capacities are 80,000 and 70,000 in plants 1 and 2, respectively. The number $V_1(b_1^*) - V_1(80,000) - C_1(b_1^*)$ denotes the net gain associated with the optimal expansion in plant 1, since $V_1(b_1^*) - V_1(80,000)$ is the increase in profits, and $C_1(b_1^*)$ is the cost of obtaining this increase. Similarly, $V_2(b_2^*) - V_2(70,000) - C_2(b_2^*)$ is the net gain for the optimal plant 2 expansion. The plant with the largest net gain will be selected, since this is the one that yields the greatest net return from the proposed investment.

Basically, this is the approach to be employed. The optimal value functions for each plant, as a function of labor hours in period 2, will be generated. Each OV function will be compared with the cost of expansion function to determine the optimal capacity for each plant. The only departure from the above analysis involves the fact that the OV functions and the cost functions are not everywhere smooth. Each curve is piecewise linear and has corners at several points. However, this is only a minor complication. Figure 9.8 shows an illustration for this hypothetical situation at plant 1 with the optimal value b_1^*.

---

[2]In the notation of Chapter 7, $V_1(b_1)$ is $V(b_4)$, and $V_2(b_2)$ is $V(b_6)$. Here, since we are dealing with two different OV functions, we opt for a slightly more cumbersome but more correct notation.

279

CHAPTER 9
Two Case Studies
at PROTRAC
Based on
Computer
Analysis
of the Model

Figure 9.8

Hypothetical Functions for the OV and the Cost
of Expansion

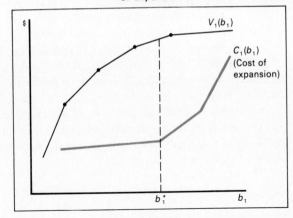

The point b_1^* is the unique capacity with the property that a change in either direction will diminish the net profit. This point b_1^* is characterized by the fact that the slope of the graph of C_1 to the right of b_1^* is greater than the slope of the graph of V_1, whereas to the left of b_1^* the situation is reversed.

Following the approach above, we shall now

1. Present the OV function for each plant
2. Determine the optimal investment

The OV Function for Each Plant and the Optimal Investment

The model is shown in Figure 9.9. Row 5 represents the capacity constraint on labor in plant 1, period 2. The right-hand side of 80,000 was increased in successive steps to generate the OV function for plant 1. This is called a **parametric analysis** on b_1. Specifically, the following calculations were performed:

1. The model in Figure 9.9 is run.
   a. The optimal objective value V_1 (80,000), is recorded, and we thus have obtained the point (80,000, V_1 (80,000)), which lies on the graph of V_1.
   b. The allowable increase is 4000.01. From this, we know that the first corner on the OV graph will occur when $b_1 = 80,000 + 4000.01 = 84,000.01$.
   c. The dual price is 22.105. Using this value, we can calculate that

$$V_1(84,000.01) = V_1(80,000) + [4000.01(22.105)] = V_1(80,000) + 88,420$$

2. The model in Figure 9.9 is modified so that b_1 takes on a value slightly larger than 84,000.01 (in this case 84,005), and the model is run again. The same procedure as in item 1 above is followed to find the value of b_1 at the next corner and the optimal objective value at that point.
3. The process in item 2 is repeated until the allowable increase becomes infinite. At this point, we have the entire OV function for values of $b_1 \geq 80,000$.

The table in Figure 9.10 shows the successive right-hand sides with the associated data and summarizes the important changes in the optimal activities and the cost structure that occur at each corner of the OV graph (i.e., at each degenerate solution). The

280

CHAPTER 9
Two Case Studies
at PROTRAC
Based on
Computer
Analysis
of the Model

notation used in this table is FP = finished product; TR = transmissions; CSTR = cross-ship transmissions; FI = foundry iron; OI = outside iron; ND = new demand; and the plants are referred to as 1 and 2. *For our investment analysis, the differences $V_1(b_1) - V_1(80,000)$ are of more interest than $V_1(b_1)$, because these are the added returns, and so it is these differences that are recorded.*

The sequence of computer runs reveals that, for each value of b_1, all labor is used in each period. There is always slack in the foundry in period 1 since the labor constraint is binding before the foundry capacity is exhausted, and iron cannot be carried in inventory. Initially, there is also foundry slack in period 2. The *initial* labor supply in period 2 is insufficient to satisfy all 210 units of existing demand. In order to make up the deficit (in the initial solution), transmissions are cross-shipped from plant 2 to plant 1, transmissions are carried forward in inventory in plant 2, and finished product is carried forward in inventory in plant 1.

Figure 9.9

PROTRAC Model

```
MAX     29970 FPP1T1 + 29970 FPP1T2 + 29910 FPP2T1 + 29910 FPP2T2
        − 900 FIP1T1 − 900 FIP1T2 − 900 FIP2T1 − 900 FIP2T2
        − 1200 OIP1T1 − 1200 OIP1T2 − 1200 OIP2T1 − 1200 OIP2T2
        − 20 CSTRP1T1 − 20 CSTRP1T2 − 20 CSTRP2T1 − 20 CSTRP2T2
        − 3000 NDT1 − 3000 NDT2 − 20 INTRP1T1 − 20 INTRP1T2
        − 20 INTRP2T1 − 20 INTRP2T2 − 300 INFPP1T1 − 300 INFPP1T2
        − 300 INFPP2T1 − 300 INFPP2T2

SUBJECT TO
  2)    FPP1T1 + FPP2T1 + NDT1 = 160
  3)    FPP1T2 + FPP2T2 − NDT2 = 210
  4)    900 BODP1T1 + 90 TRP1T1 ≤ 80000
  5)    900 BODP1T2 + 90 TRP1T2 ≤ 80000 (Labor in plant 1, period 2)
  6)    600 BODP2T1 + 60 TRP2T1 ≤ 70000
  7)    600 BODP2T2 + 60 TRP2T2 ≤ 70000 (Labor in plant 2, period 2)
  8)    FIP1T1 + FIP2T1 ≤ 1400
  9)    FIP1T2 + FIP2T2 ≤ 1400
 10)    FIP1T1 + OIP1T1 − 6 BODP1T1 = 0
 11)    FIP2T1 + OIP2T1 − 6 BODP2T1 = 0
 12)    FIP1T2 + OIP1T2 − 6 BODP1T2 = 0
 13)    FIP2T2 + OIP2T2 − 6 BODP2T2 = 0
 14)    FPP1T1 − BODP1T1 + INFPP1T1 = 5
 15)    FPP1T2 − BODP1T2 − INFPP1T1 + INFPP1T2 = 0
 16)    FPP2T1 − BODP2T1 + INFPP2T1 = 2
 17)    FPP2T2 − BODP2T2 − INFPP2T1 + INFPP2T2 = 0
 18)    CSTRP1T1 + INTRP1T1 + BODP1T1 − TRP1T1 = 6
 19)    CSTRP1T2 − CSTRP2T1 − INTRP1T1 + INTRP1T2 + BODP1T2
        − TRP1T2 = 0
 20)    CSTRP2T1 + INTRP2T1 + BODP2T1 − TRP2T1 = 4
 21)    − CSTRP1T1 + CSTRP2T2 − INTRP2T1 + INTRP2T2 + BODP2T2
        − TRP2T2   = 0
```

Operating
Implications of
Increased
Capacity

You can see from the changes in the activities that as the labor supply in plant 1, period 2 increases (that is, as the constraint is loosened), the possibilities for greater economy are increased. In earlier chapters, we saw that loosening a ≤ constraint in a max problem leads to improvement in the optimal objective value and that the improvement occurs at

281

CHAPTER 9
Two Case Studies
at PROTRAC
Based on
Computer
Analysis
of the Model

Figure 9.10

Analysis for Capacity Expansion in Plant 1, Period 2

b_1	$V_1(b_1) -$ $V_1(80,000)$	DUAL	ALLOWABLE INCREASE	DEGENERATE SOLUTION?	CHANGES IN ACTIVITIES AND COST STRUCTURE
80,000	0	22.105	4,000.01	No	
84,000.01	88,420			Yes	Holding of FP in 1 goes to zero
84,005		22.0162	9,540.45	No	
93,545.45	298,574			Yes	Holding of TR in 2 goes to zero
93,565		21.9495	9,335.01	No	
102,900.01	503,902			Yes	CSTR goes to zero and begin to create ND in period 2
103,000		21.7879	23,000.019	No	
126,000.019	1,007,202			Yes	Foundry slack goes to zero in period 2, hence begin to buy OI
127,000		19.97	140,000	No	
231,000				Yes	
232,000		19.97	Infinite	No	

a decreasing rate. In this problem, we have a specific demonstration of the interactions that yield this result. We note in Figure 9.10 that as the labor supply in period 2 (b_1) increases, PROTRAC first stops holding finished product inventory, since this is the most costly way of using capacity in period 1 to satisfy demand in period 2. As b_1 is further increased, the carrying of transmissions inventory is eliminated, since this is the next most expensive way to satisfy period 2 demand. Finally, when b_1 becomes large enough, the cross-shipping of transmissions is terminated, since this is the least expensive way of satisfying period 2 demand. At this point, there is enough labor in period 2 to satisfy all 210 units of demand. PROTRAC then begins creating new demand in period 2. At the point the firm begins to buy outside iron in period 2 (i.e., as soon as the foundry capacity is completely exhausted), the optimal activities and the cost structure stabilize, and the dual price on the labor constraint remains at 19.97 from that point. It is interest-ing to note that there is an allowable increase of 104,000 at $b_1 = 127,000$, but the dual price does not change at $b_1 = 231,000$. This phenomenon was discussed in Example 7 of Section 7.12. It is taken up again in Problem 9-13.

In Figure 9.11, the graph of $V_1(b_1) - V_1(80,000)$ appears, with the graph of $C_1(b_1)$. It is apparent from the graphic representation that the optimal capacity is given by $b_1^* = 130,000$. This is the value of b_1 that maximizes $V_1(b_1) - V_1(80,000) - C_1(b_1)$. If the capacity is, in fact, expanded from 80,000 to 130,000, the net return will be

$$V_1(130,000) - V_1(80,000) - C_1(130,000) = 1,087,080 - 490,000 = 597,080$$

The analysis for plant 2 parallels that for plant 1. The graph of $V_2(b_2) - V_2(70,000)$ appears with the graph of $C_2(b_2)$ in Figure 9.12. The parametric analysis for generating $V_2(b_2)$ is left as an exercise for the student (see problem 9). The graphic representation shows that the optimal capacity is given by $b_2^* = 88,000$. This is the value of b_2 that

282

CHAPTER 9
Two Case Studies
at PROTRAC
Based on
Computer
Analysis
of the Model

Figure 9.11
The Functions $V_1(b_1) - V_1(80,000)$ and $C_1(b_1)$

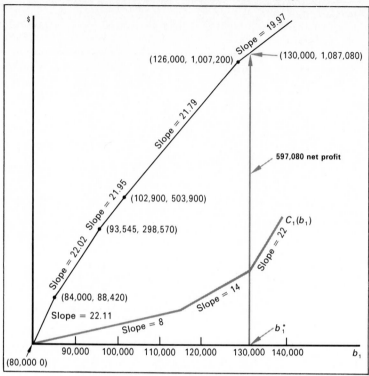

Figure 9.12
The Functions $V_2(b_2) - V_2(70,000)$ and $C_2(b_2)$

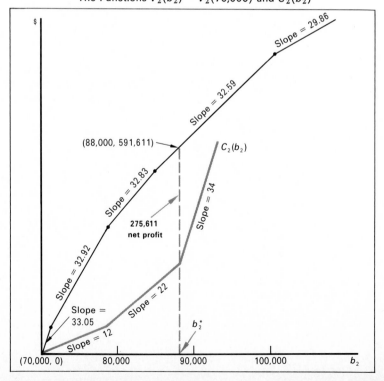

283

CHAPTER 9
Two Case Studies
at PROTRAC
Based on
Computer
Analysis
of the Model

maximizes $V_2(b_2) - V_2(70,000) - C_2(b_2)$. The associated net return will be

$$V_2(88,000) - V_2(70,000) - C_2(88,000) = 591,611 - 316,000 = 275,611$$

Comparing the results from the two plants, the analysis indicates that the optimal investment is to expand the capacity in plant 1 to 130,000.

This example provides a good illustration of how the parametric dual-pricing analysis can be used to deal with nonlinear conditions. The process of plotting the graphs of the OV function and the cost function on the same axis allows management to see what the return would be for any particular decision. Such data could be of considerable help in the decision-making process. As we have pointed out, any real decision problem is likely to involve factors not included in the model, and thus the question of optimality is often less important than giving management an opportunity to accurately assess at least some of the quantitative effects of the chosen decision.

9.4

EXAMPLES AND SOLUTIONS

Example 1

This example involves activity analysis in the PROTRAC scenario. Consider the computer output shown in Figure 9.2. Suppose another unit of labor is available in plant 2 in period 2. How would this extra unit affect the optimal levels of all activities?

Solution to Example 1

A preliminary analysis of the relevant production and shipping changes is indicated by Figure 9.13. Note that *the extra hour of labor in period 2 leads to the shipping of additional finished product in period 1, not in period 2*. The interactions work as follows. The extra hour of labor in plant 2 (period 2) permits production of $\frac{1}{660}$ more finished product, and hence $\frac{1}{660}$ less finished product will be required from plant 1 in satisfying the period 2 existing demand. This means that, in period 2, plant 1 produces $\frac{1}{660}$ fewer bodies. With the released labor $\frac{10}{660}$ transmissions are assembled. Thus fewer transmissions need to be cross-shipped from plant 2 to plant 1, and this in turn releases the resources in plant 2 (period 1) to create the additional finished product. Using Figure 9.13, it is not difficult to verify the optimality of these proposed changes. To do this, however, it will be useful to more completely specify all of the activity changes. These are enumerated in the table in Figure 9.14. In order to demonstrate the optimality of these changes, we first observe that they are feasible and then must show that the associated net return is equal to the dual price on the relevant labor constraint (row 7). The net return is computed as follows:

284

CHAPTER 9
Two Case Studies
at PROTRAC
Based on
Computer
Analysis
of the Model

Figure 9.13
Relevant Production and Shipping Changes

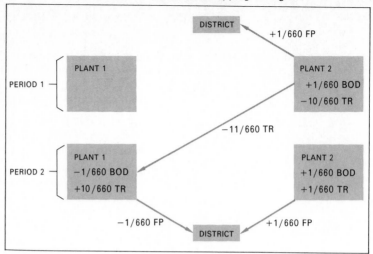

Figure 9.14
Activity Changes

PERIOD	PLANT	FP SHIPPED	BOD	TR	INTR	CSTR	ND	OI	FI	INFP
1	1							$+\dfrac{6}{660}$	$-\dfrac{6}{660}$	
	2	$+\dfrac{1}{660}$	$+\dfrac{1}{660}$	$-\dfrac{10}{600}$		$-\dfrac{11}{660}$	$+\dfrac{1}{600}$		$+\dfrac{6}{660}$	
2	1	$-\dfrac{1}{660}$	$-\dfrac{1}{660}$	$+\dfrac{10}{660}$					$-\dfrac{6}{660}$	
	2	$+\dfrac{1}{660}$	$+\dfrac{1}{660}$	$+\dfrac{1}{660}$					$+\dfrac{6}{660}$	

Additional revenue

Sales	$\dfrac{30,000}{660}$
Savings on cross-shipping	$\dfrac{220}{660}$
Savings on shipping	$\dfrac{30}{660}$
Total	$\dfrac{30,250}{660}$

Additional cost

New demand	$\dfrac{3,000}{660}$
Shipping	$\dfrac{180}{660}$
Outside iron	$\dfrac{7,200}{660}$
Total	$\dfrac{10,380}{660}$

$$\text{Net} = \frac{30,250 - 10,380}{660} = \frac{19,870}{660} = 30.106$$

Since the dual price on row 7 is also 30.106, the proposed changes are optimal. We note in passing that we have not claimed uniqueness for these optimal changes. In some situations, there may be more than one way to adjust optimally.

Example 2

The Party Nut Company has on hand 550 pounds of peanuts, 150 pounds of cashews, 90 pounds of brazil nuts, and 70 pounds of hazelnuts. It packages and sells four varieties of mixed nuts in 8-ounce (half-pound) cans. The mix requirements and net wholesale prices are indicated in Figure 9.15. The firm can sell all that it can produce at these prices. When addressing the issue of what quantities of the various mixes should be produced, a consulting firm formulated the problem as follows: Let

$$Pi = \text{pounds of peanuts used in mix } i$$
$$Ci = \text{pounds of cashews used in mix } i$$
$$Bi = \text{pounds of brazil nuts used in mix } i$$
$$Hi = \text{pounds of hazelnuts used in mix } i$$

Figure 9.15
Product Data for Party Nut Company

MIX	CONTENTS	PRICE PER CAN
1 (peanuts)	Peanuts only	$0.26
2 (party mix)	No more than 50% peanuts; at least 15% cashews; at least 10% brazil nuts	0.40
3 (cashews)	Cashews only	0.51
4 (luxury mix)	At least 30% cashews; at least 20% brazil nuts; at least 30% hazelnuts	0.52

The computer solution is shown in Figure 9.16.

(a) What is the meaning of the dual price for the second row (availability of pea-

Figure 9.16
Computer Solution to the Party Nut Company Problem

```
MAX    52P1 + 80P2 + 80C2 + 80B2 + 80H2 + 102C3 + 104P4 + 104C4
       + 104B4 + 104H4
SUBJECT TO
   2)    P1 + P2 + P4 ≤ 550
   3)    C2 + C3 + C4 ≤ 150
   4)    B2 + B4 ≤ 90
   5)    H2 + H4 ≤ 70
   6)    .5P2 − .5C2 − .5B2 − .5H2 ≤ 0
   7)   −.15P2 + .85C2 − .15B2 − .15H2 ≥ 0
   8)   −.1P2 − .1C2 + .9B2 − .1H2 ≥ 0
   9)   −.3P4 + .7C4 − .3B4 − .3H4 ≥ 0
  10)   −.2P4 − .2C4 + .8B4 − .2H4 ≥ 0
  11)   −.3P4 − .3C4 − .3B4 + .7H4 ≥ 0
```

286

CHAPTER 9
Two Case Studies
at PROTRAC
Based on
Computer
Analysis
of the Model

Figure 9.16 (Cont.)

VARIABLE	VALUE	REDUCED COST
P1	380.00000	0.00000
P2	123.33337	0.00000
C2	80.00000	0.00000
B2	43.33333	0.00000
H2	0.00000	23.99997
C3	0.00000	6.00002
P4	46.66667	0.00000
C4	70.00000	0.00000
B4	46.66667	0.00000
H4	70.00000	0.00000

OBJ FCTN   63760.

ROW	SLACK OR SURPLUS	DUAL PRICES
2	0	52
3	0	108.
4	0	108
5	0	132
6	0	56
7	43.	0
8	18.6667	0
9	0	−56.
10	0	−56
11	0	−80.

SENSITIVITY ANALYSIS

COST SENSITIVITY

VARIABLE	INCREASE IN C(J)	DECREASE IN C(J)
P1	6.00001	11.99998
P2	8.99999	6.00001
C2	23.99997	6.00002
B2	35.99995	56.00000
H2	23.99997	INFINITE
C3	6.00002	INFINITE
P4	INFINITE	35.99995
C4	55.99998	23.99997
B4	56.00000	35.99995
H4	INFINITE	23.99997

RIGHT HAND SENSITIVITY

ROW	ALLOWABLE INCREASE	ALLOWABLE DECREASE
2	INFINITE	380.00000
3	93.33365	61.42858
4	143.33334	23.33337
5	56.00001	70.00000
6	93.33337	61.66669
7	43.0000	INFINITE
8	18.6667	INFINITE
9	46.66669	70.00000
10	23.33337	46.66667
11	28.00000	56.00001

nuts)? Suppose that an additional pound of peanuts is available. What changes in the optimal solution would occur?

(b) Answer part (a) for the third row.

Solution to Example 2

(a) The dual price for the second row implies that the optimal value of the objective function would increase at the rate of 52 cents per additional pound of peanuts available. Since mix 1, peanuts (only) sells for 52 cents per pound (26 cents per 8-ounce can), it seems clear that each additional pound of peanuts that becomes available would be sold as mix 1. This solution is consistent with the facts that: (1) in the current optimal solution peanuts are being sold in their least profitable employment (as mix 1), and (2) the allowable increase in the RHS of the second row is infinite. Under the assumptions of the model, Party Nut can use as many peanuts as are available and sell them as mix 1 for 52 cents per pound.

(b) The dual price for the third row states that the optimal value of the objective function will increase at the rate of 108 cents per pound of additional cashews available. Since mix 3, cashews (only), sells for 102 cents per pound, it is clear that one cannot obtain an additional return of 108 cents by selling an additional pound of cashews as mix 3. The cashews must be mixed to obtain a higher return. The clue that suggests how to best use an additional pound of cashews is provided by the coefficients in the objective function. Note that if the additional pound of cashews was added to mix 2 and one pound of peanuts currently sold as mix 1 was also added to mix 2, the increase in revenue would be 108 cents. Two additional pounds of mix 2 yield an increase of 160 cents, but one less pound of mix 1 yields a decrease of 52 cents for a net increase of 108 cents. Although this change provides the proper increase in the objective function, we cannot be sure that this is the correct answer until we verify its feasibility. That is, we must verify that the proposed change satisfies the constraints.

If a pound of cashews and a pound of peanuts are added to mix 2, its composition would be 124.33 pounds of peanuts, 81 pounds of cashews, and 43.33 pounds of brazil nuts. The percentage of each nut in the mix is as follows:

$$\text{peanuts} = 124.33/248.66 = 50\%$$
$$\text{cashews} = 81/248.66 = 33\%$$
$$\text{brazil nuts} = 43.33/248.66 = 17\%$$

Since this blend satisfies the constraints, the suggested answer is correct.

Example 3

Winston-Salem Development Management (WSDM) is trying to complete its investment plans for the next 3 years. Currently, WSDM has $2 million available for investment. At 6-month intervals over the next 3 years, WSDM expects the following income stream from previous investments: $500,000 (6 months from now); $400,000; $380,000; $360,000; $340,000; and $300,000 (at end of third year). There are three development projects in which WSDM is considering participating. The Foster City Development

288

CHAPTER 9
Two Case Studies
at PROTRAC
Based on
Computer
Analysis
of the Model

would, if WSDM participated fully, have the following projected cash-flow stream at 6-month intervals over the next 3 years (negative numbers represent investments, positive numbers represent income): −\$3,000,000 (beginning of period 1); −\$1,000,000; −\$1,800,000; \$400,000; \$1,800,000; \$1,800,000; \$5,500,000. The last figure is its estimated value at the end of 3 years. A second project involves taking over the operation of some old, lower-middle-income housing on the condition that certain initial repairs to it be made and that it be demolished at the end of 3 years. The cash-flow stream for this project, if participated in fully, would be: −\$2,000,000 (beginning of period 1); −\$500,000; \$1,500,000; \$1,500,000; \$1,500,000; \$200,000; −\$1,000,000. The third project, the Disney-Universe Hotel, would have the following cash-flow stream (6-month intervals) if WSDM participated fully. Again, the last figure is the estimated value at the end of the 3 years: −\$2,000,000 (beginning of period 1); −\$2,000,000; −\$1,800,000; \$1,000,000; \$1,000,000; \$1,000,000; \$6,000,000. WSDM can borrow money for half-year intervals at 3.5% interest per half-year. At most, \$2 million can be borrowed at one time; that is, the total outstanding principal can never exceed \$2 million. WSDM can invest surplus funds at 3% per half-year.

Consider the problem of maximizing WSDM's net worth at the end of 3 years. Disregard taxes, and assume that if WSDM participates in a project at less than 100%, all the cash flows of that project are reduced proportionately. Then this problem can be formulated as an LP model. In order to do this, let

$$F = \text{fractional participation in Foster City}$$
$$M = \text{fractional participation in Lower-Middle}$$
$$D = \text{participation in Disney}$$
$$B_i = \text{amount borrowed in period } i, i = 1, \ldots, 6$$
$$L_i = \text{amount lent in period } i, i = 1, \ldots, 6$$
$$Z = \text{net worth } after \text{ the six periods}$$

The formulation and computer solution are shown in Figure 9.17. (*Note:* All numbers

Figure 9.17

WSDM Problem

```
MAX Z
SUBJECT TO
   2)    −3000F − 2000M − 2000D + B1 − L1 ≥ −2000
   3)    −1000F − 500M − 2000D − 1.035B1 + 1.03L1 + B2 − L2 ≥ −500
   4)    −1800F + 1500M − 1800D − 1.035B2 + 1.03L2 − L3 + B3 ≥ −400
   5)    400F + 1500M + 1000D + B4 − L4 + 1.03L3 − 1.035B3 ≥ −380
   6)    1800F + 1500M + 1000D − 1.035B4 + 1.03L4 + B5 − L5 ≥ −360
   7)    1800F + 200M + 1000D − 1.035B5 + 1.03L5 + B6 − L6 ≥ −340
   8)    −Z + 5500F − 1000M + 6000D − 1.035B6 + 1.03L6 ≥ 300
   9)    B1 ≤ 2000
  10)    B2 ≤ 2000
  11)    B3 ≤ 2000
  12)    B4 ≤ 2000
  13)    B5 ≤ 2000
  14)    B6 ≤ 2000
  15)    F ≤ 1
  16)    M ≤ 1
  17)    D ≤ 1
```

289

CHAPTER 9
Two Case Studies
at PROTRAC
Based on
Computer
Analysis
of the Model

Figure 9.17   (Cont.)

VARIABLE	VALUE	REDUCED COST
Z	7665.17866	0.00000
F	0.71533	0.00000
M	0.63840	0.00000
D	0.00000	452.37945
B1	1417.44335	0.00000
L1	0.00000	0.00879
B2	1999.99999	0.00000
L2	0.00000	0.33317
B4	448.44958	0.00000
L4	0.00000	0.00530
L3	0.00000	0.25052
B3	2000.00047	0.00000
B5	0.00000	0.00515
L5	2137.48338	0.00000
B6	0.00000	0.00500
L6	3954.86375	0.00000

OBJ FCTN   7665.18

ROW	SLACK OR SURPLUS	DUAL PRICES
2	0	−1.81922
3	0	−1.7577
4	0	−1.38193
5	0	−1.09803
6	0	−1.0609
7	0	−1.03
8	0	−1
9	582.557	0
10	0	.327403
11	0	.245466
12	1551.55	0
13	2000	0
14	2000	0
15	.284669	0
16	.361603	0
17	1.	0

are measured in units of 1000.) Row 2 imposes the condition that at the beginning of period 1, WSDM can spend only the money that is available at that time. Rows 3–7 impose a similar condition on periods 2–6, respectively. Row 8 defines the profit variable, Z. Rows 9–14 are borrowing constraints. Rows 15–17 limit the participation in each of the projects to no more than 100 percent.

(a) Is the solution degenerate?

(b) Can there ever be slack in rows 2–8 (if, for example, the RHS is changed)?

(c) What is the meaning of the dual price associated with row 6 (the beginning of period 5)? Assuming the allowable increase in the RHS of row 6 is at least 1, what changes in the optimal solution would occur from such an increase?

(d) Perform activity analysis for an *extra* dollar of availability at the beginning of periods 6 and 4.

Solution to Example 3

(a) The problem has 16 constraints. The solution shows that nine variables and seven slack variables are positive. The solution is nondegenerate.

(b) There cannot be slack in rows 2–8. If there were, lending could always be increased, or borrowing decreased, to the benefit of the company. Therefore, rows 2–8 will always be satisfied with equality.

(c) The dual price for row 6 is -1.0609. This implies that the optimal value of the objective function would *decrease* \$1.0609 if the RHS of the fifth constraint is increased by a unit. Note that a unit increase in the RHS of the fifth constraint, from -360 to -359, implies that Winston-Salem has \$1000 less income at the beginning of year 3, and so the fact that the net worth, Z, decreases is intuitively appealing. To see what changes in the current optimal solution will yield a decrease of \$1.0609, we note that Winston-Salem is currently lending money in period 5; that is, $L_5 = 2137.48$. Since the company now has one less dollar at its disposal, it seems reasonable that one less dollar will be lent. The loss of \$1 lent at 3% per period for two periods yields a total loss of $(1.03)^2$, or \$1.0609. In terms of the variables, let $\hat{}$ (e.g., $\hat{L}_5$) indicate the changed variables. All variables remain the same except those shown below.

$$\hat{L}_5 = L_5 - 1$$
$$\hat{L}_6 = L_6 - 1.03$$
$$\hat{Z} = Z - 1.0609$$

It is intuitive and easily checked that this new policy is feasible. We merely note that if the right-hand side of row 6 is -359, then the new values above for the variables will maintain equality in rows 6–8.

(d) For row 7 (beginning of period 6), the dual is -1.03. Thus, an extra dollar available should produce an additional 1.03 return. This is obtained by lending one more dollar in period 6, to produce 1.03 at the end of period 6. Variables are redefined in the obvious way.

For row 5 (beginning of period 4), the dual is -1.09803. An additional return of 1.09803 is obtained from an extra dollar available in period 4 by borrowing one less dollar at the beginning of period 4. We will then have 1.035 extra on hand at the beginning of period 5. Lend this amount and lend the accrued amount at the beginning of period 6 to obtain

$$(1.035)(1.03)(1.03) = 1.09803$$

Variables are redefined in the obvious way.

9.5
PROBLEMS

9-1. Refer to Figure 9.2.

(a) Due to forecasting errors, PROTRAC's Australian plant has some excess units of final product in inventory. What is the maximum amount that the midwest tractor division manager should pay to obtain a unit from Australia? Where and when should it be delivered, that is, to which plant and at the beginning of which period?

291

CHAPTER 9
Two Case Studies
at PROTRAC
Based on
Computer
Analysis
of the Model

(b) Rather than using conventional methods for creating new demand, PROTRAC is considering hiring a consultant who will accept payment on the basis of the number of units of new demand that he generates. What is the maximum amount PROTRAC should be willing to pay him for the first unit of new demand that he generates in period 2?

(c) How many units would management be willing to have him create at this price? Assume that, all other things equal, we prefer more production to less.

● (d) How much should management be willing to pay to have demand increased by an additional unit if it had already been increased by the amount specified in part (c)? Give an exact answer (see Problem 9-15).

(e) A private contractor feels that he can help increase the existing demand by using his contacts in the construction industry. What is the most you would be willing to pay him to obtain another unit of demand in period 1?

(f) Explain any difference between this figure and the answer to part (b).

(g) What is the maximum number of units you would have this contractor increase the existing demand at the price specified in part (e)? (Again, assume that, all other things equal, you prefer more production to less.)

(h) How much would you be willing to pay to have existing demand increased beyond the answer you found in part (g)? Why?

(i) Suppose that a competitor offers to supply you with iron at less than the foundry price of $1000 per ton because he has excess capacity. How many tons should you purchase from him in each period?

9-2. Note that the reduced cost on transmission inventory in plant 1 at the end of period 2 (INTRP1T2) is 1831.82. The dual price on labor in plant 1, period 2 is 20.1313. It takes 90 hours of labor to assemble a single transmission in plant 1. Carrying a single transmission in inventory at the end of period 2, in plant 1, might thus be interpreted as being equivalent to "throwing away" 90 hours of the labor supply. But $90(20.1313) = 1811.82 < 1831.82$. How do you explain this discrepancy of $20?

9-3. The dual price on an iron consumption constraint can be interpreted as the maximum amount a manager should be willing to pay to have a ton of iron on hand in the appropriate plant at the beginning of the period. The computer output shows that outside iron is purchased in plant 1 in each period. The dual price on the iron consumption constraints for plant 1 would therefore be expected to equal the price of outside iron, which is 1200. Indeed, this is the case. For plant 2 there is no purchase of outside iron in either period. Why then is the dual price on the plant 2 iron consumption constraints also 1200?

9-4. *The Parsimony of Corner Solutions.* Figure 9.2 reveals that outside iron is purchased only in plant 1. Why couldn't a little less be purchased in plant 1 and have this amount purchased in plant 2, with a corresponding change in the levels of foundry iron purchased? (That is, let plant 1 purchases Δ fewer units of OI in period 1, and Δ more units of FI. Let plant 2 purchase Δ fewer units of FI and Δ more units of OI.) Would such a policy be optimal? Could it be produced by the computer? Comment on what this reveals about the "parsimony" of optimal basic solutions.

9-5. Refer to Figure 9.2. Is there any way a solution could be produced with outside iron purchased in plant 2 in period 1? Support your answer.

9-6. Refer to Figure 9.2. In period 2, all labor is used and no new demand is created. Thus, it appears that existing demand is satisfied at just the point that all labor is used. Is this improbable phenomenon a correct interpretation?

9-7. Refer to the Party Nut problem presented in Example 2.

(a) The dual price on row 4 (brazil nuts available) is 108. Suppose that an extra pound of brazil nuts is available. What changes in the optimal solution would occur that would cause the optimal value to increase by 108?

(b) The dual price on row 5 (hazelnuts available) is 132. Suppose that an additional pound

292

CHAPTER 9
Two Case Studies
at PROTRAC
Based on
Computer
Analysis
of the Model

of hazelnuts is available. What changes in the optimal solution would occur that would cause the optimal value to increase by 132?

[HINT: Be guided by the fact that no currently active (inactive) constraint should become inactive (active). No currently positive (zero) variable should become zero (positive).]

9-8. Refer to the Winston-Salem Development Management problem presented in Example 3. A summary of the solution is presented in Figure 9.18.

Figure 9.18
WSDM Solution Summarized

VARIABLE	VALUE	ROW	DUAL PRICE
Z	7665.18	2	−1.81922
F	.71533	3	−1.7577
M	.6384	4	−1.38193
D	0	5	−1.09803
B1	1417.44	6	−1.0609
B2	2000	7	−1.03
B3	2000	8	−1
B4	448.45	9	0
B5	0	10	0.327403
B6	0	11	0.245466
L1	0	12	0
L2	0	13	0
L3	0	14	0
L4	0	15	0
L5	2137.48	16	0
L6	3954.86375	17	0

(a) Explain the algebraic relation between the dual prices on rows 2 and 3.

(b) The dual price on borrowing at the beginning of period 2 is 0.327403; that is, the ability to borrow an additional unit at the beginning of period 2 would increase the net worth at the end by 0.327403 unit. Explain the relation

$$0.327403 = 1.7577 - 1.035(1.38193)$$

What is the maximum interest rate we would be willing to pay to borrow an additional unit at the beginning of period 2?

9-9. Use your own computer to generate the OV function for plant 2. Produce (for plant 2) the analogue of Figure 9.10.

9-10. Refer to Figure 9.2. Consider the values and allowable increases for the dual prices on labor capacity in plants 1 and 2, period 1. Use this information to analyze the optimal change in activities and costs that would result from an additional hour of labor in each plant (separately) in period 1. Explain why the allowable increase has the indicated value.

9-11. Refer to Figure 9.2. Suppose that the labor supply in plant 2, period 1, is increased by the allowable amount, 41,826.66 hours. The associated activity changes were analyzed in Problem 9-10. Based on this analysis, do you expect the dual price to change at this point? Present a rationale to defend your answer.

9-12. Consider Figure 9.2. Explain the costs and the activities associated with the following deviations from optimality. Pay attention to all adjustments in both plants in both periods on: the purchases of iron (both from the foundry and outside), the assembly of transmissions, the production of bodies, the shipment of finished product, the creation of new demand, the inventory of finished product and transmission, and the cross-shipment of transmissions.

(a) Holding a unit of finished product in inventory at the end of period 1 in plant 1.

(b) Holding a unit of finished product in inventory at the end of period 1 in plant 2.

(c) Holding a transmission in inventory at the end of period 2 in plant 1.

(d) Holding a transmission in inventory at the end of period 1 in plant 1.

(e) Holding a transmission in inventory at the end of period 2 in plant 2.

9-13. Refer to Figure 9.10. At $b_1 = 231{,}000$ the dual price does not change, which means that although the activities change, the cost structure does not. Analyze why. The information in Figure 9.19 on iron activities in period 2 should be used. (The symbol $+FI$ means the optimal solution involves the purchase of foundry iron; similarly for $+OI$.)

Figure 9.19

Iron Activities in Period 2

FOR $b_1 = 127{,}000$		FOR $b_1 = 231{,}000$		FOR $b_1 = 232{,}000$	
Plant 1	Plant 2	Plant 1	Plant 2	Plant 1	Plant 2
+FI	+FI	+FI(1400)	FI = 0	+FI(1400)	FI = 0
OI = 0	+OI	OI = 0	+OI	+OI	+OI

9-14. *An Alternative Approach to the Investment Problem.* Recall that there are three "pieces" to the cost of expansion function for plant 1. That is, letting $C(b_1)$ denote the cost of expanding the capacity to b_1, we have

$$C(b_1) = \begin{cases} 8b_1 - 640{,}000 & \text{if } 80{,}000 \le b_1 \le 115{,}000 \\ 14b_1 - 1{,}330{,}000 & \text{if } 115{,}000 \le b_1 \le 130{,}000 \\ 22b_1 - 2{,}370{,}000 & \text{if } 130{,}000 \le b_1 \end{cases}$$

The model in Figure 9.9 is modified by introducing two new variables. Let

$$B = \text{capacity in plant 1}$$
$$C = \text{cost of obtaining that capacity}$$

The following changes are then required:

1. C is subtracted from the current expression for the objective function

2. Row 5 becomes

$$900 \text{ BODP1T2} + 90 \text{ TRP1T2} - B \le 0$$

3. Three new constraints are added:

$$\begin{aligned} C &\ge 8B - 640{,}000, & \text{i.e., } C - 8B &\ge -640{,}000 \\ C &\ge 14B - 1{,}330{,}000, & \text{i.e., } C - 14B &\ge -1{,}330{,}000 \\ C &\ge 22B - 2{,}370{,}000, & \text{i.e., } C - 22B &\ge -2{,}370{,}000 \end{aligned}$$

The complete formulation and solution of this problem is shown in Figure 9.20. You can see that the optimal value of B is 130,000, just as obtained from the analysis in the text. Try to analyze why this approach works. Would the approach work for any nonlinear C that is convex? What about the approach in the text?

9-15. Consider the PROTRAC model shown in Figure 9.2. Use activity analysis arguments (and *not* the computer!) to construct the OV function corresponding to the constraint on existing demand in period 2. Show the *entire* OV function, with all corners and all slopes.

Figure 9.20

```
MAX    29970 FPP1T1 + 29970 FPP1T2 + 29910 FPP2T1 + 29910 FPP2T2 − 900 FIP1T1
       − 900 FIP1T2 − 900 FIP2T1 − 900 FIP2T2 − 1200 OIP1T1 − 1200 OIP1T2
       − 1200 OIP2T1 − 1200 OIP2T2 − 20 CSTRP1T1 − 20 CSTRP1T2 − 20 CSTRP2T1
       − 20 CSTRP2T2 − 3000 NDT1 − 3000 NDT2 − 20 INTRP1T1 − 20 INTRP1T2
       − 20 INTRP2T1 − 20 INTRP2T2 − 300 INFPP1T1 − 300 INFPP1T2 − 300 INFPP2T1
       − 300 INFPP2T2 − C

SUBJECT TO
  2)      FPP1T1 + FPP2T1 − NDT1 = 160
  3)      FPP1T2 + FPP2T2 − NDT2 = 210
  4)      900 BODP1T1 + 90 TRP1T1 ≤ 80000
  5)      900 BODP1T2 + 90 TRP1T2 − B ≤ 0
  6)      600 BODP2T1 + 60 TRP2T1 ≤ 70000
  7)      600 BODP2T2 + 60 TRP2T2 ≤ 70000
  8)      FIP1T1 + FIP2T1 ≤ 1400
  9)      FIP1T2 − FIP2T2 ≤ 1400
 10)      −FIP1T1 − OIP1T1 + 6 BODP1T1 = 0
 11)      −FIP2T1 − OIP2T1 + 6 BODP2T1 = 0
 12)      −FIP1T2 − OIP1T2 + 6 BODP1T2 = 0
 13)      −FIP2T2 − OIP2T2 + 6 BODP2T2 = 0
 14)      FPP1T1 − BODP1T1 + INFPP1T1 = 5
 15)      FPP1T2 − BODP1T2 − INFPP1T1 + INFPP1T2 = 0
 16)      FPP2T1 − BODP2T1 + INFPP2T1 = 2
 17)      FPP2T2 − BODP2T2 − INFPP2T1 + INFPP2T2 = 0
 18)      CSTRP1T1 + INTRP1T1 + BODP1T1 − TRP1T1 = 6
 19)      CSTRP1T2 − CSTRP2T1 − INTRP1T1 + INTRP1T2 + BODP1T2 − TRP1T2 = 0
 20)      CSTRP2T1 + INTRP2T1 + BODP2T1 − TRP2T1 = 4
 21)      −CSTRP1T1 + CSTRP2T2 − INTRP2T1 + INTRP2T2 + BODP2T2 − TRP2T2 = 0
 22)      C − 8 B ≥ −640000
 23)      C − 14 B ≥ −1330000
 24)      C − 22 B ≥ −2370000
OBJECTIVE FUNCTION VALUE

  1)        9959167.
```

VARIABLE	VALUE	REDUCED COST	ROW	SLACK OR SURPLUS	DUAL PRICES
FPP1T1	86.353538	0.000000	2)	0.000000	3000.000000
FPP1T2	131.313131	0.000000	3)	0.000000	3000.000000
FPP2T1	108.424244	0.000000	4)	0.000000	21.787880
FPP2T2	106.060607	0.000000	5)	0.000000	19.969698
FIP1T1	488.121216	0.000000	6)	0.000000	32.590909
FIP1T2	763.636375	0.000000	7)	0.000000	29.863637
FIP2T1	638.545479	0.000000	8)	273.333317	0.000000
FIP2T2	636.363640	0.000000	9)	0.000000	300.000000
OIP1T1	0.000000	300.000000	10)	0.000000	900.000000
OIP1T2	24.242417	0.000000	11)	0.000000	900.000000
OIP2T1	0.000000	300.000000	12)	0.000000	1200.000000
OIP2T2	0.000000	0.000000	13)	0.000000	1200.000000
CSTRP1T1	0.000000	189.090988	14)	0.000000	26970.000000
CSTRP1T2	0.000000	1817.272810	15)	0.000000	26970.000000
CSTRP2T1	0.000000	178.181732	16)	0.000000	26910.000000
CSTRP2T2	0.000000	1811.818220	17)	0.000000	26910.000000

Figure 9.20 (Cont.)

NDT1	34.777780	0.000000	18)	0.000000	1960.909210
NDT2	27.373738	0.000000	19)	0.000000	1797.272810
INTRP1T1	0.000000	183.636398	20)	0.000000	1955.454540
INTRP1T2	0.000000	1817.272810	21)	0.000000	1791.818220
INTRP2T1	0.000000	183.636322	22)	89999.996100	0.000000
INTRP2T2	0.000000	1811.818220	23)	0.000000	−0.253788
BODP1T1	81.353537	0.001007	24)	0.000000	−0.746212
TRP1T1	75.353536	−0.000031			
BODP1T2	131.313131	0.000839			
TRP1T2	131.313137	−0.000015			
BODP2T1	106.424244	0.000198			
TRP2T1	102.424245	0.000031			
BODP2T2	106.060607	0.000351			
TRP2T2	106.060608	−0.000015			
INFPP1T1	0.000000	300.000000			
INFPP1T2	0.000000	27270.000000			
INFPP2T1	0.000000	300.000000			
INFPP2T2	0.000000	27210.000000			
C	490000.008000	0.000000			
B	130000.001000	0.000000			

DIAGNOSTIC ASSIGNMENT

NEW CONDITIONS AT PROTRAC

Jack Martin has just been promoted to manager of plant 2 for PROTRAC. That's the good news! The bad news is that life has changed significantly and most of the changes have been bad news for PROTRAC. In particular:

1. Kawanooki, the Japanese heavy machinery manufacturing firm has entered the U.S. market with strong price competition and thus PROTRAC has been forced to lower the price of E-9's from $30,000 to $17,000.

2. Strict pollution controls have greatly increased the cost of outside iron. Indeed, PROTRAC must now pay $2,000 per ton for outside iron.

3. Finally, increased energy prices and taxes have increased transportation costs. The cost accountants at PROTRAC now estimate that the cost of supplying finished product is $1500 and $2500 for plants 1 and 2, respectively.

In view of these changes, PROTRAC revises the LP that it has used to determine its production plan for E-9s and runs it again. The new formulation and the solution are shown in Figure 9-21.

Figure 9.21

```
MAX    15500 FPP1T1 + 15500 FPP1T2 + 14500 FPP2T1 + 14500 FPP2T2
       — 1000 FIP1T1 — 1000 FIP1T2 — 1000 FIP2T1 — 1000 FIP2T2 — 2000 OIP1T1
       — 2000 OIP1T2 — 2000 OIP2T1 — 2000 OIP2T2 — 20 CSTRP1T1 — 20 CSTRP1T2
       — 20 CSTRP2T1 — 20 CSTRP2T2 — 3000 NDT1 — 30CO NDT2 — 20 INTRP1T1
       — 20 INTRP1T2 — 20 INTRP2T1 — 20 INTRP2T2 — 300 INFPP1T1
       — 300 1NFPP1T2 — 300 INFPP2T1 — 300 INFPP2T2

SUBJECT TO
   2)     FPP1T1 + FPP2T1 — NDT1 = 130
   3)     FPP1T2 + FPP2T2 — NDT2 = 190
   4)     900 BODP1T1 + 90 TRP1T1 ≤ 80000
   5)     900 BODP1T2 + 90 TRP1T2 ≤ 80000
   6)     600 BODP2T1 + 60 TRP2T1 ≤ 70000
   7)     600 BODP2T2 + 60 TRP2T2 ≤ 70000
   8)     FIP1T1 + FIP2T1 ≤ 1000
   9)     FIP1T2 + FIP2T2 ≤ 1000
  10)     —FIP1T1 — OIP1T1 + 6 BODP1T1 = 0
  11)     —FIP2T1 — OIP2T1 + 6 BODP2T1 = 0
  12)     —FIP1T2 — OIP1T2 + 6 BODP1T2 = 0
  13)     —FIP2T2 — OIP2T2 + 6 BODP2T2 = 0
  14)     FPP1T1 + INFPP1T1 — BODP1T1 = .5
  15)     FPP1T2 — INFPP1T1 + INFPP1T2 — BODP1T2 = 0
  16)     FPP2T1 + INFPP2T1 — BODP2T1 = 2
  17)     FPP2T2 — INFPP2T1 + INFPP2T2 — BODP2T2 = 0
  18)     CSTRP1T1 + INTRP1T1 + BODP1T1 — TRP1T1 = 6
  19)     CSTRP1T2 — CSTRP2T1 — INTRP1T1 + INTRP1T2 + BODP1T2 — TRP1T2 = 0
  20)     CSTRP2T1 + INTRP2T1 + BODP2T1 — TRP2T1 = 4
  21)     —CSTRP1T1 + CSTRP2T2 — INTRP2T1 + INTRP2T2 + BODP2T2 — TRP2T2 = 0
END
:GO
    LP OPTIMUM FOUND AT STEP    29

OBJECTIVE FUNCTION VALUE
  1)        3040297.97

VARIABLE        VALUE      REDUCED COST    ROW   SLACK OR SURPLUS    DUAL PRICES
  FPP1T1     86.353536       0.000000      2)        0.000000       3000.000000
  FPP1T2     88.888889       0.000000      3)        0.000000       2700.000000
  FPP2T1     63.979798       0.000000      4)        0.000000          1.010101
  FPP2T2    101.111111       0.000000      5)        0.000000          1.088889
  FIP1T1    488.121212       0.000000      6)     8600.000000          0.000000
  FIP1T2    533.333336       0.000000      7)    18666.666748          0.000000
  FIP2T1    511.878788       0.000000      8)        0.000000        916.666672
  FIP2T2    466.666668       0.000000      9)        0.000000        966.666672
  OIP1T1      0.000000      83.333328     10)        0.000000       1916.666672
  OIP1T2      0.000000      33.333328     11)        0.000000       1916.666672
  OIP2T1      0.000000      83.333328     12)        0.000000       1966.666672
  OIP2T2      0.000000      33.333328     13)        0.000000       1966.666672
  CSTRP1T1    0.000000     110.909091     14)        0.000000      12500.000000
  CSTRP1T2    0.000000      40.000000     15)        0.000000      12800.000000
```

Figure 9.21 (Cont.)

CSTRP2T1	88.888889	0.000000	16)	0.000000	11500.000000
CSTRP2T2	0.000000	20.000000	17)	0.000000	11800.000000
NDT1	20.333333	0.000000	18)	0.000000	90.909091
NDT2	0.000000	300.000000	19)	0.000000	20.000000
INTRP1T1	0.000000	90.909091	20)	0.000000	0.000000
INTRP1T2	0.000000	40.000000	21)	0.000000	0.000000
INTRP2T1	0.000000	20.000000			
INTRP2T2	0.000000	20.000000			
INFPP1T1	0.000000	0.000000			
INFPP1T2	0.000000	13100.000000			
INFPP2T1	23.333333	0.000000			
INFPP2T2	0.000000	12100.000000			
BODP1T1	81.353536	0.000000			
TRP1T1	75.353536	0.000000			
BODP1T2	88.888889	0.000000			
TRP1T2	0.000000	78.000000			
BODP2T1	85.313131	0.000000			
TRP2T1	170.202021	0.000000			
BODP2T2	77.777778	0.000000			
TRP2T2	77.777778	0.000000			

When Jack sees the new production plan he is apoplectic. He immediately gets Tom Trammel, the manager of production planning, on the phone. The following conversation ensues:

JACK: "Tom, as I recall, when I was the assistant manager and the plant was operating at full capacity, you and I reviewed the results from the production planning model and I found them to be both interesting and useful. This new result is another story. It's ridiculous! It seems as if you have forgotten that we just spent a bundle to build this plant with the latest in production processes. Now you are going to cut our production down to less than 75% in period 2 and run the old inefficient plant at full capacity. What kind of sense can that make?"

TOM: "You know, Jack, these problems are rather complicated. There are many interactions. As you recall, in the previous model the difference in the cost of sending finished product to the market is what led us to transship about 34 transmissions from your plant to plant 1 in order to save transportation costs. Sometimes your intuition turns out to be wrong. Besides, the costs spent to modernize your plant are sunk."

JACK: "Now that you mention it, I suppose that the transportation costs are at the root of the current solution as well. We are better than plant 1 on all dimensions except transportation costs and they are operating at full capacity. Frankly, I think that's a lot of crap. Think for a minute about how the new transportation costs were calculated. Ours include an $850 allocation for the shipping facility that was built at this plant last spring. Talk about sunk costs! What, pray tell, does that have to do with the way we should produce?"

TOM: "You've got me there. I wasn't aware that the transportation costs included allocated costs, and so I guess we should change those coefficients appropriately and solve the model again. Unfortunately, I don't think that you will like the new result. Consider two facts: First, in the new solution it is the high cost of outside iron that stops you from using all of your capacity. Total production is terminated as soon as the supply of foundry iron is exhausted. Second, if we reduce the coefficients of FPP2T1 and FPP2T2 by $850 and solve again, you still won't produce at capacity. The high cost of outside iron will stop us short of

297

total capacity, and since plant 1 will continue to have lower transportation costs, we will use up all of that capacity first. I agree that I find it hard to believe that we shouldn't use the capacity in our most efficient plant, but that is the way it will work out."

JACK: "I still don't believe it. In fact I am sure there must be a problem with your formulation. We previously learned that transshipping was the cheapest way to bring product forward into period 2, but your solution shows us also carrying forward finished product into inventory. That just can't be correct. I'm going to get one of my people to run the model with our costs reduced by $850. Then I'll get back to you. I'm simply unwilling to take this as the last word."

Questions

1. Is Tom correct in his analysis of the solution shown in Figure 9-21? If not, why not?

2. Is Tom correct in his analysis of the solution that will arise if the coefficients are reduced by $850 in plant 2? If you, why not?

3. Comment on Jack's observation about finished product being carried forward in inventory.

CHAPTER 10

Multiple Objectives and Goal Programming

APPLICATION CAPSULE •

NATIONAL CENTER FOR DRUG ANALYSIS*

The National Center for Drug Analysis is a division of the Bureau of Drugs at FDA (the U.S. Food and Drug Administration). A major responsibility of the National Center for Drug Analysis is the analysis of drug samples in order that the FDA can perform its market surveillance function. A new recent responsibility is implementation of the Good Laboratory Practice Program. This program ensures accuracy and reliability of analytical data which the FDA obtains. Implementation of the latter program requires the allocation of employees' time to numerous activities (e.g., follow-up on quality control stipulations, etc.). The Center has only 44 person-years of staff to allocate to its total responsibilities. The need to implement the Good Laboratory Practice Program implied that not all of the Center's goals could be completely achieved. For example, a goal of analyzing 1600 drug samples per year requires about 20 person-years. A complete implementation of the Good Laboratory Practice Program would leave only 4.9 person-years for drug sample analysis. In order to deal with these competing demands on the limited resources, a goal programming approach was adopted. A formulation with 11 preemptive priorities, 25 constraints, and 11 decision variables has been implemented as a decision-making tool to evaluate outcomes and costs associated with implementing the Good Laboratory Practice Program. The code is interactive so that priority rankings can be adjusted, allowing management to evaluate the effects of the resource allocations obtained from different priority assignments.

*Lawrence Jones and K. K. Kwak, "A Goal Programming Model for Allocating Human Resources for the Good Laboratory Practice Regulations," *Decision Sciences*, Vol. 13, No. 1, January 1982, pp. 156–166.

MANAGEMENT OF COLLEGE STUDENT RECRUITING ACTIVITIES*

Declining enrollments can be costly. A drop in enrollment of 50 students in a single freshman class may result in a 4-year revenue loss of nearly a million dollars. But due to a decrease in the birthrate, as well as the high cost of education, college enrollments are falling. This creates a requirement for improved strategies in the recruiting of college freshmen. Since resources are limited, the recruiting effort must be efficient as well as effective.

One approach using the goal programming technique was developed and implemented to manage recruiting activities at a small college in Nebraska. The two major recruiting activities are (1) candidate identification, and (2) follow-up work. Since early in the season the emphasis is on generating a candidate list, three separate models were developed. One model, for the first two quarters, emphasizes candidate identification. Variables include numbers of local high school visits, numbers of long-distance visits, numbers of phone calls made, form letters mailed, personal letters written, and so on. The coefficients needed in the model are estimated from the college's historical data. For the first two quarters, the goal program had 9 priorities and fewer than 28 decision variables. The third quarter model gives equal emphasis to candidate identification and follow-up, and in the fourth quarter, follow-up and budget balancing become more important. The overall objective is to identify the type and number of activities that must be completed each quarter in order to reach an enrollment goal for a given year. Use of the model enables recruiters to meet enrollment requirements while managing recruiting resources in order to remain within the budget. The model and its results can also be used as a tool in lobbying for more funds.

*Kenneth E. Kendall and Richard L. Luebbe, "Management of College Student Recruiting Activities Using Goal Programming," *Decision Sciences,* Vol. 12, No. 2, April 1981, pp. 193–205.

10.1

INTRODUCTION

The president of a firm wants high profits but also wants to maintain low prices in order to keep from losing clients. An executive with a fixed budget wants to invest in R & D but also wants to purchase raw materials to use as inputs for production to obtain near-term profits. In business applications, the existence of multiple objectives is commonplace.

In such cases, these different objectives may all be of equal importance or, at the very least, it may be difficult for the planner to compare the importance of one objective as opposed to another. The presence of multiple objectives is frequently referred to as the problem of "combining apples and oranges." As another example, consider the corporate planner whose long-range goals are to (1) maximize discounted profits, (2) maximize market share at the end of the planning period, and (3) maximize existing physical capital at the end of the planning period. These goals are not commensurate,

301

CHAPTER 10
Multiple
Objectives
and Goal
Programming

which means that they cannot be *directly* combined or compared. It is also clear that the goals are *conflicting*. That is, there are *trade-offs* in the sense that sacrificing the requirements on any one goal will tend to produce greater returns on the others. For example, fewer dollars spent on advertising (less marketing) allows for the building of new plants (more physical capital) and the purchase of more raw materials (more production). The treatment of multiple objectives is a young but important area in applications, and several approaches to multiple objective problems (also called multicriteria decision making) have been developed. They are: use of multiattribute utility theory, search for Pareto optimal solutions via multicriteria linear programming, heuristic search methods, and goal programming. Our discussion is limited to goal programming, a concept introduced by A. Charnes and W. W. Cooper,[1] and which is in essence an extension of linear programming. It is an area that is now experiencing considerable interest and development and is potentially an important topic for future managers.

10.2
GOAL PROGRAMMING

Goal programming is generally applied to linear problems; it is an extension of LP that enables the planner to come as close as possible to satisfying various goals and constraints. It allows the decision maker to incorporate his or her preference system in dealing with multiple conflicting goals. It is sometimes considered to be an attempt to

Satisficing   put into a mathematical programming context the concept of *satisficing. This term was coined to communicate the idea that individuals often do not seek optimal solutions, but rather, they seek solutions that are "good enough" or "close enough."* We shall illustrate the method of goal programming with several examples.

Example: Designing an Education Program

Suppose that we have an educational program design model with decision variables x_1 and x_2, where x_1 is the hours of classroom work and x_2 is the hours of laboratory work. Assume that we have the following constraint on total program hours:

$$x_1 + x_2 \leq 100 \text{ (total program hours)}$$

In the goal programming approach there are two kinds of constraints:

1. *System constraints* (so-called "hard constraints") that cannot be violated
2. *Goal constraints* (so-called "soft constraints") that may be violated if necessary

The above constraint on total program hours is an example of a system constraint.

Now, in the program we are designing, suppose that each hour of classroom work involves 12 minutes of small-group experience and 19 minutes of individual problem solving, whereas each hour of laboratory work involves 29 minutes of small-group experience and 11 minutes of individual problem solving. Note that the total program time is at most 60(100) or 6000 minutes. The designers have the following two *goals*.

[1] *Management Models and Industrial Applications of Linear Programming* (New York: John Wiley & Sons, Inc., 1961.)

302

CHAPTER 10
Multiple
Objectives
and Goal
Programming

1. Each student should spend as close as possible to one-fourth of the maximum program time working in small groups.

2. Each student should, if possible, spend one-third of the time on problem solving.

These conditions are written as

$$12x_1 + 29x_2 \cong 1500 \qquad \text{(small-group experience)}$$
$$19x_1 + 11x_2 \cong 2000 \qquad \text{(individual problem solving)}$$

where the symbol $\cong$ means that the left-hand side is desired to be "as close as possible" to the RHS. If it were possible to find a policy that exactly satisfies the small-group and problem-solving goals (that is, exactly achieve both right-hand sides), *without violating the system constraint on total program hours*, then this policy would solve the problem. The simple geometric analysis in Figure 10.1 shows that no such policy exists. Clearly then, in order to satisfy the system constraint, at least one of the two goals will be violated.

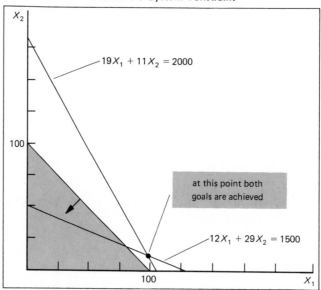

Figure 10.1
The Point That Exactly Satisfies the Two Goals Happens to
Violate the System Constraint

To implement the goal programming approach, the small-group condition is rewritten as the **goal constraint**

$$12x_1 + 29x_2 + u_1 - v_1 = 1500 \qquad (u_1 \geq 0, v_1 \geq 0)$$

where u_1 = the amount by which total small-group experience falls short of 1500
v_1 = the amount by which total small-group experience exceeds 1500

Deviation Variables   The variables u_1 and v_1 are called **deviation variables**. We note that by definition we must have a zero value for either u_1 or v_1 (or both) because it is impossible simultaneously to exceed and fall short of 1500. In order to make $12x_1 + 29x_2$ as close as possible to 1500, it suffices to make the sum $u_1 + v_1$ as small as possible.

303

CHAPTER 10
Multiple
Objectives
and Goal
Programming

In a similar way, the problem-solving condition is written as the **goal constraint**

$$19x_1 + 11x_2 + u_2 - v_2 = 2000 \qquad (u_2 \geq 0, v_2 \geq 0)$$

and in this case we want the sum of the two deviation variables $u_2 + v_2$ to be small. In order to satisfy **both** goals as closely as possible, our procedure will be to make the sum $u_1 + v_1 + u_2 + v_2$ as small as possible. Thus, the complete (illustrative) model is written as follows:

The Goal

Programming

Model

$$
\begin{aligned}
\text{Min} \quad & u_1 + v_1 + u_2 + v_2 \\
\text{s.t.} \quad & x_1 + x_2 && \leq 100 && \text{(total program hours)} \\
& 12x_1 + 29x_2 + u_1 - v_1 && = 1500 && \text{(small group experience)} \\
& 19x_1 + 11x_2 + u_2 - v_2 && = 2000 && \text{(problem solving)} \\
& x_1, x_2, u_1, v_1, u_2, v_2 \geq 0
\end{aligned}
$$

This is an ordinary LP problem and can now be easily solved on the computer. The optimal decision variables will satisfy the system constraint (total program hours). Also, it turns out that the simplex method (for technical reasons that we shall not dwell on) will guarantee that either u_1 or v_1 (or both) will be zero and thus these variables automatically satisfy this desired condition. The same statement holds for u_2 and v_2 and in general for any pair of deviation variables.

Note that we have chosen to express the objective function as the sum of the deviation variables. This choice of an objective function implies that we have no preference among the various deviations from the stated goals. For example, we are indifferent between the following three decisions: (1) a decision that overachieves the group experience goal by 5 minutes and hits the problem solving goal exactly, (2) a decision that hits the group experience goal exactly and underachieves the problem solving goal by 5 minutes, and (3) a decision that underachieves each goal by 2.5 minutes. In other words, we are indifferent between the three solutions

(1) $u_1 = 0$	(2) $u_1 = 0$	(3) $u_1 = 2.5$
$v_1 = 5$	$v_1 = 0$	$v_1 = 0$
$u_2 = 0$	$u_2 = 5$	$u_2 = 2.5$
$v_2 = 0$	$v_2 = 0$	$v_2 = 0$

We must be indifferent because each of these three decisions yield the same value (5) for the objective function. This condition may be appropriate for this particular problem, but in general this sort of indifference would not hold for many goal programming problems. Differences in units alone could produce a preference among the deviation variables. Suppose, for example, that the individual problem solving constraint had been written in hours; that is,

$$\frac{19}{60}x_1 + \frac{11}{60}x_2 + u_2 - v_2 = \frac{2000}{60}$$

It is hard to believe that the program designers would be indifferent between a 1-minute excess of small-group experience ($v_1 = 1$) and 1-hour shortfall of individual problem solving ($u_2 = 1$). Of course in this case you could say, "Write both constraints in hours."

But one goal could be in units of time, another in units of money, and another in units of weight. Now how do you put the three goals in comparable units?

Weighting the Deviation Variables One way of expressing a preference among the various goals is to assign different coefficients to the deviation variables in the objective function. In the program planning example one might select

$$\text{min} \quad 2u_1 + 10v_1 + u_2 + 20v_2$$

as the objective function. Since u_2 (underachievement of problem solving) has the smallest coefficient, the program designers would prefer to have u_2 positive than any of the other deviation variables (positive u_2 is penalized the least). Indeed, with this objective function it is better to be 9 minutes under the problem-solving goal than to overachieve by 1 minute the small-group experience goal. To see this, note that for any solution in which $v_1 \geq 1$, decreasing v_1 by 1 and increasing u_2 by 9 would yield a smaller value for the objective function.

Goal Interval Constraints Another type of goal constraint is called a **goal interval constraint**. Suppose, for example, that in the above illustration the designers were indifferent among programs for which

$$1800 \leq [\text{minutes of individual problem solving}] \leq 2100$$
$$\text{i.e., } 1800 \leq 19x_1 + 11x_2 \leq 2100$$

In this situation the interval goal is captured with two goal constraints:

$$19x_1 + 11x_2 - v_1 \leq 2100 \qquad (v_1 \geq 0)$$
$$19x_1 + 11x_2 + u_1 \geq 1800 \qquad (u_1 \geq 0)$$

When the terms u_1 and v_1 are included in the objective function, the LP code will attempt to minimize them. We note that when, at optimality, $u_1^* = 0$ and $v_1^* = 0$ (their minimum possible values), the total minutes of problem solving ($19x_1 + 11x_2$) falls within the desired range (i.e., $1800 \leq 19x_1 + 11x_2 \leq 2100$). Otherwise it will turn out that, at optimality, one of the two variables will be positive and the other zero, which means that only one side of the two-sided inequality can be satisfied.

In some cases managers do not wish to express their preferences among various goals in terms of weighted deviation variables, for the process of assigning weights may seem too arbitrary or subjective. In such cases it may be more acceptable to state pref- **Absolute Priorities** erences in terms of an **absolute priority** of the goals. Before turning to this approach, it will be useful to summarize the various ways in which goal constraints can be formulated and employed.

10.3
SUMMARY ON THE USE OF GOAL CONSTRAINTS

Each goal constraint consists of a left-hand side, say $g_i(x_1, \ldots, x_n)$, and a right-hand side, b_i. Goal constraints are written by using nonnegative **deviational variables** u_i, v_i. At optimality at least one of the pair u_i, v_i will always be zero. The variable u_i represents underachievement; v_i represents **overachievement**. Whenever u_i is used it is **added** to

305

CHAPTER 10
Multiple
Objectives
and Goal
Programming

$g_i(x_1, \ldots, x_n)$. Whenever v_i is used it is **subtracted** from $g_i(x_i, \ldots, x_n)$. Only deviational variables (or a subset of deviational variables) appear in the objective function and the objective is always "**minimize**." The decision variables x_i, $i = 1, \ldots, n$ do not appear in the objective. We have discussed four types of goals.

1. *Target:* Make $g_i(x_1, \ldots, x_n)$ as close as possible to b_i. To do this we write the goal constraint as

$$g_i(x_1, \ldots, x_n) + u_i - v_i = b_i \qquad (u_i \geq 0, v_i \geq 0)$$

and in the objective we minimize $u_i + v_i$. At optimality, at least one of the variables u_i, v_i will be zero.

2. *Minimize underachievement:* To do this, we can write

$$g_i(x_1, \ldots, x_n) + u_i - v_i = b_i \qquad (u_i \geq 0, v_i \geq 0)$$

and in the objective we minimize u_i, the **underachievement**. Since v_i does not appear in the objective function, and is in only this constraint, it plays the same role as a **surplus variable**, and hence the constraint can be equivalently written as

$$g_i(x_1, \ldots, x_n) + u_i \geq b_i \qquad (u_i \geq 0)$$

If the optimal u_i is positive, this constraint will be **active**. Otherwise, u_i^* could be made smaller without violating the constraint, thereby contradicting the fact that u_i^* is optimal (i.e., at a minimum value subject to the constraint). This is also clear from the equality form of the constraint. That is, if $u_i^* > 0$ then, since v_i^* must equal zero, it must be true that $g_i(x_1, \ldots, x_n) + u_i^* = b_i$.

3. *Minimize overachievement:* To do this, we can write

$$g_i(x_1, \ldots, x_n) + u_i - v_i = b_i \qquad (u_i \geq 0, v_i \geq 0)$$

and in the objective we minimize v_i, the **overachievement**. Since in this case u_i plays the same role as a **slack variable**, the constraint can be equivalently written as

$$g_i(x_1, \ldots, x_n) - v_i \leq b_i \qquad (v_i \geq 0)$$

If the optimal v_i is positive, this constraint will be **active**. The argument for this is analogous to that in item 2 above.

4. *Goal interval constraint:* In this instance, the goal is to come as close as possible to satisfying

$$a_i \leq g_i(x_1, \ldots x_n) \leq b_i$$

In order to write this as a goal, we first "stretch out" the interval by writing

$$a_i - u_i \leq g_i(x_1, \ldots, x_n) \leq b_i + v_i \qquad (u_i \geq 0, v_i \geq 0)$$

which is equivalent to the two constraints

$$\left.\begin{array}{l} g_i(x_1, \ldots, x_n) + u_i \geq a_i \\ g_i(x_1, \ldots, x_n) - v_i \leq b_i \end{array}\right\} \longleftrightarrow \left\{\begin{array}{ll} g_i(x_1, \ldots, x_n) + u_i - \hat{v}_i = a_i & (u_i \geq 0, \hat{v}_i \geq 0) \\ g_i(x_1, \ldots, x_n) + \hat{u}_i - v_i = b_i & (\hat{u}_i \geq 0, v_i \geq 0) \end{array}\right.$$

306

CHAPTER 10
Multiple
Objectives
and Goal
Programming

In the case of a goal interval constraint we minimize $u_t + v_t$ in the objective function. The variables $\hat{v}_t$ and $\hat{u}_t$ are merely surplus and slack, respectively (not deviational variables). As usual, at optimality, at least one of the deviational variables u_t, v_t will be zero. *In dealing with two constraints representing a goal interval, the constraint with the nonzero deviational variable (if there is one) will be active.*

In general, goal constraints are most often expressed in the appropriate equality form using deviational variables, surplus, and slack as required. The equivalent inequality forms which we have displayed will allow us, for problems in two decision variables, to obtain some geometric insight into the solution procedure. We now turn to what is probably the most useful type of goal programming model.

10.4
GOAL PROGRAMMING WITH ABSOLUTE PRIORITIES

In this approach, **absolute priorities**, as opposed to relative weights are assigned to goals. That is, goals must be **ranked** in order of importance. Let us illustrate with an example.

***Media
Selection
Problem (A
Minicase
Involving
Absolute
Priorities)***
Tom Swenson, a senior partner at J. R. Swenson, his father's advertising agency, has just completed an agreement with a pharmaceutical manufacturer to mount a radio and television campaign to introduce a new product, Mylonal. The total expenditures for the campaign are not to exceed $120,000. The client is interested in reaching several audiences with this campaign. To determine how well a particular campaign meets this client's needs, the agency estimates the impact of the advertisements on the audiences of interest. The impact is measured in *rated exposures*, a term that means "people reached per month." Radio and television, the two media the agency is considering using, are not equally effective in reaching all audiences. Data relevant to the Mylonal campaign are shown in Figure 10.2.

Figure 10.2

Exposures per $1000 Expenditure

	TV	RADIO
Total	14,000	6,000
Upper income	1,200	1,200

After lengthy discussions with the client, Tom accepts the following goals for this campaign. Tom feels that the order in which he has listed his goals reflects the absolute priority among them.

1. He hopes total exposures will be at least 840,000.
2. In order to maintain effective contact with the leading radio station, he hopes to spend no more than $90,000 on TV advertising.
3. He feels that they should achieve at least 168,000 upper-income exposures.
4. Finally, if all other goals are satisfied, he would like to come as close as possible to maximizing the total number of exposures. He notes that if he spends all of the

307

CHAPTER 10
Multiple
Objectives
and Goal
Programming

$120,000 on TV advertising he would obtain 120 × 14,000 or 1,680,000 exposures and this is the maximum obtainable.

This is clearly a problem with a number of constraints. It is not quite a typical mathematical programming problem, however, since Tom has a number of objectives. Nevertheless, he feels that a mathematical programming approach will help him understand and solve the problem. He thus proceeds in the typical manner. To model the problem, he introduces the notation

$$x_1 = \text{dollars spent on TV} \quad \text{(in thousands)}$$

$$x_2 = \text{dollars spent on radio (in thousands)}$$

Since his highest-priority goal is total exposures, he feels that a reasonable way to model the problem is to use total exposures as the objective function and to treat the other goals as constraints. The formulation and computer solution of this problem are shown in Figure 10.3. Each constraint and the objective function are labeled to indicate the purpose they serve. We see that the problem is infeasible.

Figure 10.3
Maximizing Total Exposures

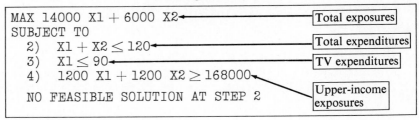

```
MAX 14000 X1 + 6000 X2                              Total exposures
SUBJECT TO
    2)   X1 + X2 ≤ 120                              Total expenditures
    3)   X1 ≤ 90                                    TV expenditures
    4)   1200 X1 + 1200 X2 ≥ 168000                 Upper-income
                                                    exposures
NO FEASIBLE SOLUTION AT STEP 2
```

An Infeasible
Problem

Clearly, since it is infeasible, there is no way to satisfy simultaneously the three goals (total expenditures, TV expenditure, and upper income exposures) that Tom has stated as constraints. Since there are only two decision variables in this problem, the graphical approach can be used to investigate this initial formulation. The analysis in Figure 10.4 clearly shows that there are no points that satisfy both the first (total

Figure 10.4
Maximizing Total Exposures: A Graphical Approach

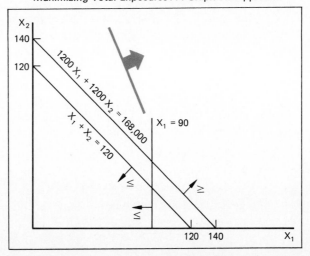

308

CHAPTER 10
Multiple
Objectives
and Goal
Programming

expenditures) and the third (upper income exposures) constraints. At this point, Tom could attempt to approach the problem somewhat differently. He might change one or more of his goals or perhaps the objective function and start again. In general, however, this is not a satisfactory systematic approach. In problems with many decision variables and several conflicting goals, restructuring the problem to create a new problem that has a feasible solution could prove a difficult task. More important, in this restructuring process, the essence of the real problem could be lost.

Recall that Tom is not indifferent about the various goals; indeed, he has stated an absolute priority among them. Goal programming with absolute priorities is designed to handle exactly the type of decision process Tom Swenson wants. It is a sequential process in which goals are added one at a time (in the order of decreasing priority) to an LP problem. A description of the general procedure, illustrated by the advertising campaign problem above, follows.

10.5

SWENSON'S GOAL PROGRAMMING MODEL

In order to set up his problem as a goal program, Tom notes that the first goal, if violated will be underachieved. The second goal, if violated, will be overachieved, and so on. Employing this reasoning, he restates his goals, in descending priority, as

Goals as
Inequalities

1. Minimize the underachievement of 840,000 total exposures (i.e., min u_1, subject to the condition $14{,}000x_1 + 6000x_2 + u_1 \geq 840{,}000$, $u_1 \geq 0$).
2. Minimize expenditures in excess of $90,000 on TV (i.e., min v_2, subject to the condition $x_1 - v_2 \leq 90$, $v_2 \geq 0$).
3. Minimize underachievement of 168,000 upper-income exposures (i.e., min u_3, subject to the condition $1200x_1 + 1200x_2 + u_3 \geq 168{,}000$, $u_3 \geq 0$).
4. Minimize underachievement of 1,680,000 total exposures—the maximum possible (i.e., min u_4, where $14{,}000x_1 + 6000x_2 + u_4 \geq 1{,}680{,}000$, $u_4 \geq 0$).

Note that Tom's priorities are now clearly stated in terms of either minimizing underachievement (i.e., minimizing a u_i), or minimizing overachievement (i.e., minimizing a v_i). His goals, as stated above, have been expressed as inequalities in accord with our previous discussion. This will facilitate a graphical analysis.

Given that he has correctly formulated his priorities, Tom must distinguish between (1) **system constraints** (all constraints which may not be violated) and (2) **goal constraints**. In his problem, the only system constraint is that total expenditures will be no greater than $120,000. Thus (since the units of x_1 and x_2 are thousands), we have

$$x_1 + x_2 \leq 120 \tag{S}$$

In goal programming notation, Tom's problem can now be expressed as follows:

309

CHAPTER 10
Multiple
Objectives
and Goal
Programming

$$\min \quad P_1u_1 + P_2v_2 + P_3u_3 + P_4u_4 \qquad \text{(P)}$$

$$\text{s.t.} \qquad\qquad x_1 + x_2 \le 120 \qquad\qquad\qquad \text{(S)}$$

$$14{,}000x_1 + 6000x_2 + u_1 \ge \quad 840{,}000 \qquad \text{(1)}$$

$$x_1 + \qquad\quad - v_2 \le \qquad\quad 90 \qquad \text{(2)}$$

$$1200x_1 + 1200x_2 + u_3 \ge \quad 168{,}000 \qquad \text{(3)}$$

$$14{,}000x_1 + 6000x_2 + u_4 \ge 1{,}680{,}000 \qquad \text{(4)}$$

$$x_1, x_2, u_1, v_2, u_3, u_4 \ge 0$$

Note that the objective function consists only of deviational variables and is of the **min** form. As already stated, *this is true of every goal programming formulation.* In the objective function, the terms P_k serve merely to indicate priorities, with P_1 denoting highest priority, and so on. What the problem statement above means precisely is:

Sequential Feasible Regions

I. Find the set of decision variables that satisfy the system constraint (S) and which also give the min possible value to u_1 subject to constraint (1) and $x_1, x_2, u_1 \ge 0$. Call this set of decisions FR I (i.e., "feasible region I.") Considering *only the highest priority goal*, all of the points in FR I are "optimal" (i.e., the best that Tom can do) and (again considering only the highest priority goal) he is indifferent between which of these points he selects.

II. Find the subset of points in FR I that gives the min possible value to v_2, subject to constraint (2) and $v_2 \ge 0$. Call this subset FR II. Considering only the ordinal ranking of the two highest-priority goals, all of the points in FR II are "optimal," and in terms of these two highest-priority goals he is indifferent between which of these points he selects.

III. Let FR III be the subset of points in FR II that minimize u_3, subject to constraint (3) and $u_3 \ge 0$.

IV. FR IV is the subset of points in FR III that minimize u_4, subject to constraint (4) and $u_4 \ge 0$. Any point in FR IV is an optimal solution to Tom's overall problem.

Since Tom's marketing problem has only two decision variables, the solution method above can be accomplished with graphical analysis. In general, the computer would be required. In the next section we show how this can be done using LP.

10.6
GRAPHICAL ANALYSIS AND COMPUTER IMPLEMENTATION OF THE SOLUTION PROCEDURE

I. In Figures 10.5 and 10.6, the computer output and the geometry respectively reveal that the min of u_1 s.t. (S), (1), and $x_1, x_2, u_1 \ge 0$ is $u_1^* = 0$. Although the computer prints out optimal values for x_1^* and x_2^* these values are not of interest. The important information is that $u_1^* = 0$, which tells us that the first goal can be completely attained. Alternative optima for the current problem are provided by all values of (x_1, x_2) that satisfy the conditions

310

CHAPTER 10
Multiple
Objectives
and Goal
Programming

Figure 10.5

First Goal

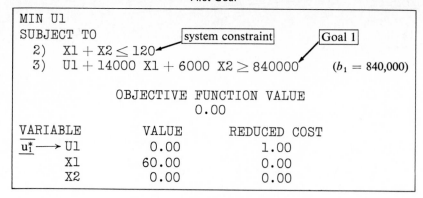

Figure 10.6

Geometric Analysis of First Goal (FR I)

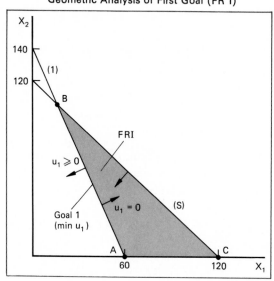

$$\text{FR I} \begin{cases} x_1 + x_2 \leq 120 \\ 14{,}000x_1 + 6000x_2 \geq 840{,}000 \\ x_1 \geq 0, \ x_2 \geq 0 \end{cases}$$

At any such point Tom's first goal is attained ($u_1^* = 0$) so that, in terms of only the first goal, these decisions are equally preferable. Thus FR I is the shaded area ABC. The line labeled (1) represents goal 1. The arrow marked $u_1 = 0$ indicates that at all points to the right of line (1) goal 1 is achieved.

II. In the computer formulation in Figure 10.7, we have entered the constraints defining FR I (rows 2 and 3), together with the new goal constraint, row 4. Figure 10.8 shows the geometric analysis, with the new goal labeled as (2). We see that

$$\min \quad v_2$$

$$\text{s.t.} \quad x \text{ in FR I, goal (2), and } v_2 \geq 0$$

311

CHAPTER 10
Multiple
Objectives
and Goal
Programming

Figure 10.7

Goal 2

```
MIN V2
SUBJECT TO
   2)    X1 + X2 ≤ 120                          b₁ − u₁*
   3)    14000 X1 + 6000 X2 ≥ 840000
   4)    −V2 + X1 ≤ 90                     Goal 2      (b₂ = 90)

              OBJECTIVE FUNCTION VALUE
                         0.00

   VARIABLE          VALUE        REDUCED COST
   v₂* ──→V2          0.00           1.00
          X1         60.00           0.00
          X2          0.00           0.00
```

Figure 10.8

Geometric Analysis of Second Goal (FR II)

*The Feasible
Region Is
Smaller*

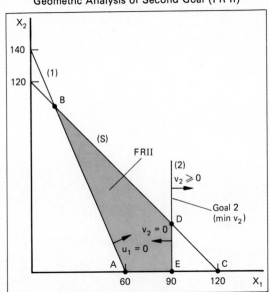

is $v_2^* = 0$. Thus, FR II is defined by

$$\text{FR II}\begin{cases} x_1 + x_2 \leq 120 \\ 14{,}000x_1 + 6000x_2 \geq 840{,}000 \\ x_1 \leq 90 \\ x_1, x_2 \geq 0 \end{cases}$$

which is the shaded area ABDE in Figure 10.8. This shaded region is clearly a subset of FR I in Figure 10.6.

   III. Continuing in this way, Figure 10.9 gives the next computer output. The corresponding geometric analysis, Figure 10.10, shows that FR III is the line segment BD. In this case $u_3^* = 24{,}000$. Although the first two goals were completely attained (since

Figure 10.9
Goal 3

**Goal 3 Is Not
Attained**

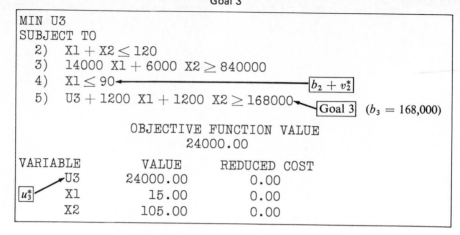

```
MIN U3
SUBJECT TO
   2)   X1 + X2 ≤ 120
   3)   14000 X1 + 6000 X2 ≥ 840000
   4)   X1 ≤ 90                                    b₂ + v₂*
   5)   U3 + 1200 X1 + 1200 X2 ≥ 168000      Goal 3  (b₃ = 168,000)

              OBJECTIVE FUNCTION VALUE
                    24000.00

VARIABLE          VALUE          REDUCED COST
       U3        24000.00            0.00
u₃*    X1           15.00            0.00
       X2          105.00            0.00
```

Figure 10.10
Geometric Analysis of Third Goal (FR III)

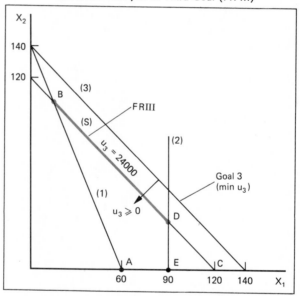

$u_1^* = v_2^* = 0$), the third goal cannot be completely attained because $u_3^* > 0$. At this stage, Tom is indifferent about any decision satisfying

$$\text{FR III} \begin{cases} x_1 + x_2 \leq 120 \\ 14{,}000x_1 + 6000x_2 \geq 840{,}000 \\ x_1 \leq 90 \\ 1200x_1 + 1200x_2 \geq 168{,}000 - 24{,}000 = 144{,}000 \end{cases}$$

which defines the line segment BD.

IV. Finally, Figure 10.11 shows the optimal solution which, in Figure 10.12, is at point D. Recall that the fourth goal is to minimize underachievement of the maximum possible number of exposures, which is 1,680,000. Thus, we wish to minimize u_4 where

Figure 10.11

Optimal Solution

The Optimal Solution

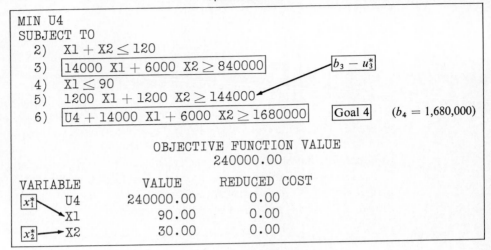

```
MIN U4
SUBJECT TO
  2)   X1 + X2 ≤ 120
  3)   14000 X1 + 6000 X2 ≥ 840000          b₃ − u₃*
  4)   X1 ≤ 90
  5)   1200 X1 + 1200 X2 ≥ 144000
  6)   U4 + 14000 X1 + 6000 X2 ≥ 1680000    Goal 4   (b₄ = 1,680,000)
```

$$\text{OBJECTIVE FUNCTION VALUE}$$
$$240000.00$$

VARIABLE	VALUE	REDUCED COST
x_1^* U4	240000.00	0.00
X1	90.00	0.00
x_2^* ➤ X2	30.00	0.00

Figure 10.12

Geometric Analysis of Fourth Goal

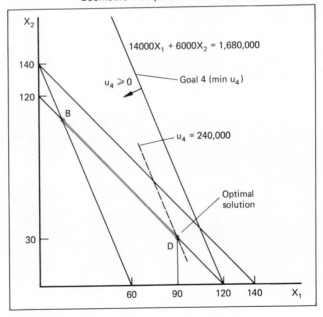

$$14{,}000x_1 + 6000x_2 + u_4 \geq 1{,}680{,}000$$

In Figure 10.11, we find the unique optimum $x_1^* = 90$ and $x_2^* = 30$; that is, Tom should spend \$90,000 on TV advertising and \$30,000 on radio advertising. This fact is verified in the geometric analysis, where it is clear that point D ($x_1 = 90$, $x_2 = 30$) is closer to the line that describes goal 4 ($14{,}000x_1 + 6000x_2 = 1{,}680{,}000$) than any other point in FR III (i.e., than any other point on the line BD). We also note that $u_4^* = 240{,}000$. Thus, Tom only achieves $1{,}680{,}000 - 240{,}000 = 1{,}440{,}000$ exposures.

313   We see, then, that goal programming with absolute priorities allows a manager (like Tom) to solve a problem in which there is no solution that achieves all the goals, but where he is willing to specify an absolute ranking among the goals and successively restrict his attention to those points that come as close as possible to each goal.

10.7
COMBINING WEIGHTS AND ABSOLUTE PRIORITIES

It is possible to combine, to some extent, the concepts of weighted and absolute priority goals. To illustrate this fact, we return to Tom Swenson's advertising problem.

In reviewing the results of the absolute priority study, Tom and his client begin to discuss the importance of the older members of the Mylonal market. In particular, they focus on the number of exposures to individuals 50 years or older. Again, they see that radio and TV are not equally effective in generating exposures in this segment of the population. The exposures per $1000 of advertising are as follows:

	TV	RADIO
50 and over	3000	8000

A New Goal If there were no other considerations, Tom would like as many 50-and-over exposures as possible. Since radio yields such exposures at a higher rate than TV (8000 > 3000), Tom sees that the maximum possible number of "50-and-over" exposures would be achieved by allocating all of the $120,000 available to radio. Thus, the maximum number of "50-and-over" exposures is $120 \times 8000 = 960,000$. Tom and his client would like to be as close as possible to this goal (minimize underachievement) once the first three goals are satisfied. Recall, however, that they also wanted to be as close as possible to the goal of 1,680,000 total exposures (minimize underachievement) once the first three goals are satisfied. To resolve this conflict of goals, they decide to use a weighted sum of the deviation variables as the objective in the final phase of the absolute priorities approach. It is their judgment that underachievement in the fifth goal (960,000 exposures to the 50-and-over group) is three times as serious as underachievement in the fourth goal (1,680,000 total exposures). The formulation, solution, and graphical analysis are presented in Figures 10.13 and 10.14.

From the computer solution we see that the optimal solution to this problem is point B ($x_1^* = 15$, $x_2^* = 105$). Recall that when the objective function was to minimize u_4, the optimal decision was point D ($x_1^* = 90$, $x_2^* = 30$). Thus, in the computer analysis, we see that the new objective function has moved the optimal solution from one end of FR III to the other. In order to see this graphically note from the geometry in Figure 10.14 that u_4 and u_5 will be positive at optimality. This means that rows 6) and 7) of the model must, at optimality, be active. One can then solve these two equations for u_4 and u_5 as functions of x_1 and x_2. Then the objective function, $3u_5 + u_4$, can be written in terms of x_1 and x_2. Once this is accomplished the geometric analysis can proceed in the usual fashion.

This, then, completes the analysis of Tom Swenson's advertising campaign problem. It is important to note that the general sequential LP procedure described above for goal programming with absolute priorities holds for any problem in which the system constraints and the goal constraints are formulated with linear functions. For each new

315

CHAPTER 10
Multiple
Objectives
and Goal
Programming

Figure 10.13
Weighting the Final Step

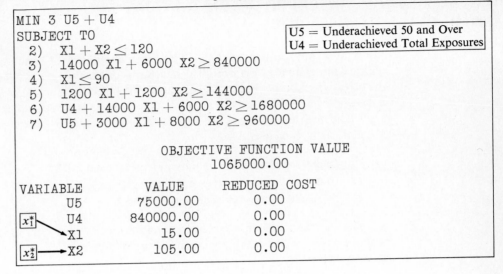

```
MIN 3 U5 + U4
SUBJECT TO
  2)    X1 + X2 ≤ 120
  3)    14000 X1 + 6000 X2 ≥ 840000
  4)    X1 ≤ 90
  5)    1200 X1 + 1200 X2 ≥ 144000
  6)    U4 + 14000 X1 + 6000 X2 ≥ 1680000
  7)    U5 + 3000 X1 + 8000 X2 ≥ 960000
```

| | U5 = Underachieved 50 and Over |
| | U4 = Underachieved Total Exposures |

```
              OBJECTIVE FUNCTION VALUE
                   1065000.00

VARIABLE          VALUE        REDUCED COST
     U5        75000.00           0.00
     U4       840000.00           0.00
     X1           15.00           0.00
     X2          105.00           0.00
```

x_1^* → X1
x_2^* → X2

Figure 10.14
Geometric Analysis of Weighted Sum

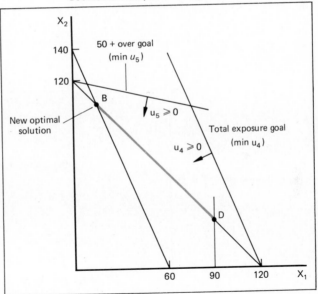

problem a single constraint is added to the previous model and the objective function is slightly modified. Generally speaking, a fairly large number of decision variables can be involved. The example with two variables was useful since it made it possible to present, in tandem with the computer output, geometric interpretations. This adds insight to the solution technique.

The foregoing problem is useful in indicating how conflicting and noncommensurate goals (i.e., apples and oranges) can be simultaneously considered via goal programming. Thus, it gives some insight into why goal programming is a promising and increasingly useful tool in analyzing public policy questions.

AN ALTERNATIVE INTERPRETATION OF GOAL PROGRAMS
WITH ABSOLUTE PRIORITIES

One reason for the importance of goal programming with absolute priorities is the difficulty, in complex organizational structures, of obtaining any consensus as to what the objective might be. For example, what is the objective function of a large university-affiliated hospital? For such an organization it may be possible to obtain a consensus on goals, and then on priorities for those goals. For example, it may be agreed that the hospital has three goals:

1. To become a recognized tertiary care center (goal 1)
2. To deliver quality health care to the student population (goal 2)
3. To upgrade emergency room service (goal 3)

Suppose that each goal is represented by an inequality constraint. Specifically, suppose that we wish, in each case, to minimize the underachievement of specified levels of services delivered.

Figure 10.15 shows a hypothetical "hard" constraint set defined by five system constraints (the shaded region). Superimposed on this figure are the foregoing three goal constraints, labeled G_1, G_2, and G_3. For each constraint, all points on the side designated by the arrow are points that satisfy the goal. Points on the other side violate the goal.

Figure 10.15
Superimposing Goals in Different Orders

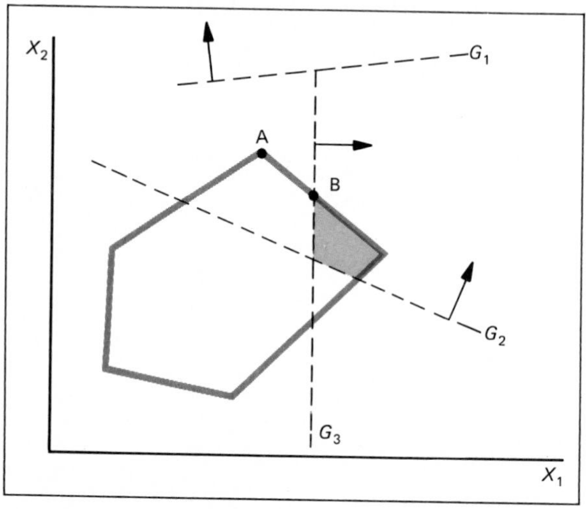

We now make the following observations:

1. If the priority order is G_1, G_2, G_3, point A is the solution and goals 1 and 3 are violated.
2. If the priority is G_2, G_3, G_1, point B is the solution and only goal 1 is violated.

This simple two-dimensional illustration suggests the following general interpretation. As each goal is successively imposed, either

Case 1: It can be satisfied, in which case the previous feasible region is trimmed down (as in the G_2, G_3, G_1 ordering, which trims the original "hard set" down to the darkly shaded region).

Case 2: It cannot be satisfied, in which case, under fairly general assumptions, there will be a *unique point* that minimizes the violation of the goal. Any further imposition of goals has no effect (as illustrated by the G_1, G_2, G_3 ordering).

Of course if all goals can be satisfied simultaneously (by some subset of points in the "hard set"), the order of imposition is irrelevant. (The same set of final points will be achieved regardless of order.) If all goals cannot be simultaneously satisfied, the order determines when the infeasibility will occur. Upon the occurrence of the first infeasibility, a unique point will then be identified.

This interpretation provides some insight into how the results can be significantly different when either priorities are changed (in terms of ordering) or even when levels of desired attainment are adjusted. In essence, the user of this technique is ranking his objectives, treating them one after another as constraints, until encountering one which, when so treated, creates infeasibility. Note that in the G_2, G_3, G_1 ordering, point B is the one that maximized G_1, the first goal violated, over the most recent feasible region.

10.9
MAJOR CONCEPTS QUIZ

True–False

1. **T F** Goal programming is the only quantitative technique designed for use on problems with multiple objectives.

2. **T F** Each step in goal programming with absolute priorities introduces a new goal and eliminates from further consideration all points in the current feasible region that do not satisfy this new goal as well as possible.

3. **T F** Consider the goal constraint $12x_1 + 3x_2 + u_1 - v_1 = 100$. Suppose that, because of other constraints in the model, the goal cannot be achieved. If u_1 is positive the goal is overachieved.

4. **T F** One way to state priorities among goals is to place weights on deviational variables.

5. **T F** Consider the goal interval constraint $180 \leq 4x_1 + 12x_2 \leq 250$. A correct goal formulation is

$$4x_1 + 12x_2 - v_1 \leq 250$$
$$4x_1 + 12x_2 - u_1 \geq 180$$

6. **T F** If a goal interval constraint cannot be achieved (exactly satisfied) then one deviational variable will be positive and the constraint in which that variable appears will be active.

7. **T F** In goal programming a system constraint may never be violated.

8. **T F** A goal programming problem cannot be infeasible.

Multiple Choice

9. If a goal programming problem includes the constraint $g_1(x_1, \ldots, x_n) + u_1 - v_1 = b_1$ and the term $6u_1 + 2v_1$ in the objective function, the decision maker
   a. prefers $g_1(x_1, \ldots, x_n)$ to be greater than, rather than smaller than, b_1
   b. prefers $g_1(x_1, \ldots, x_n)$ to be smaller than, rather than larger than, b_1
   c. is indifferent as to whether $g_1(x_1, \ldots, x_n)$ is larger than or smaller than b_1

10. Problems with multiple objectives
    a. are difficult because it is often true that improving one objective will hurt another
    b. are difficult because the objectives may be in incommensurate units (i.e., the problem of "combining apples and oranges")
    c. can sometimes be treated with the goal programming approach
    d. all of the above

Questions 11, 12, and 13 apply to the following problem:

    1. $g_1(x_1, x_2) \leq b_1$ is a system constraint.
    2. Minimizing underachievement of $g_2(x_1, x_2) = b_2$ is top priority.
    3. Minimizing overachievement of $g_3(x_1, x_2) = b_3$ is next in priority.

11. The first step of the solution procedure is
    a. min u_2, s.t. $g_1(x_1, x_2) \leq b_1, g_2 - u_2 = b_2, x_1, x_2, u_2 \geq 0$
    b. min u_2, s.t. $g_1(x_1, x_2) \leq b_1, g_2 + u_2 \geq b_2, x_1, x_2, u_2 \geq 0$
    c. min u_2, s.t. $g_1(x_1, x_2) \leq b_1, g_2 - u_2 \leq b_2, x_1, x_2, u_2 \geq 0$

12. Let FR I denote the points (x_1, x_2) obtained in the first step of the solution procedure. The second step is
    a. min $u_3 + v_3$, s.t. (x_1, x_2) in FR I and $g_3(x_1, x_2) + u_3 - v_3 = b_3$
    b. min u_3, s.t. (x_1, x_2) in FR I and $g_3(x_1, x_2) + u_3 \leq b_3$
    c. min v_3, s.t. (x_1, x_2) in FR I and $g_3 - v_3 \leq b_3$

13. In this model
    a. at least one goal will be achieved
    b. the first goal will not be overachieved and the second will not be underachieved
    c. none of the above

14. Consider a goal program with the constraint

$$g_1(x_1, \ldots, x_n) - v_1 \leq b_1, v_1 \geq 0$$

with v_1 in the objective function. Then
    a. the goal is to minimize overachievement
    b. if $v_1^* > 0$, then the constraint will be active
    c. neither of the above
    d. both a and b

15. In goal programming with absolute priorities
    a. objectives are ranked and treated sequentially as constraints
    b. the order will generally affect when a violation occurs
    c. the unique point that minimizes the violation can be obtained by optimizing the violated goal over the feasible region obtained last
    d. all of the above

Answers

1. F	6. T	11. b
2. T	7. T	12. c
3. F	8. F	13. c
4. T	9. a	14. d
5. F	10. d	15. d

10-1. Erma McZeal is in charge of quality control for the city of Chicago's water supply. There are currently three test stations located in Lake Michigan. Letting (x_1, x_2) denote coordinates, the three existing locations are placed as follows:

$$\text{station 1:} \quad x_1 = 2, x_2 = 10$$
$$\text{station 2:} \quad x_1 = 6, x_2 = 6$$
$$\text{station 3:} \quad x_1 = 1, x_2 = 3$$

Erma's job is to locate the new station in such a way as to minimize the total distance of the new station from the three existing stations. Assume that because of existing channel marker locations, distance is measured rectangularly. In other words, if the new station is located at $(x_1 = 3, x_2 = 4)$, then it is a distance of $(3 - 2) + (10 - 4)$ or 7 units from station 1; and so on. Let (x_1, x_2) denote the coordinates of the new station and formulate a goal programming model to solve Erma's problem.

10-2. In Problem 10-1, suppose that station 1 handles twice the work load of station 3 and station 2 handles four times the work load of station 3. Suppose it is felt that the importance of locating the new station near an existing station is proportional to its work load. Reformulate the model with weights on the deviations that reflect this importance.

10-3. *Product Mix*   A firm produces two products. Each product must be processed through two machines each of which has available 240 minutes of capacity per day. Each unit of product 1 requires 20 minutes on machine 1 and 12 minutes on machine 2. Each unit of product 2 requires 12 minutes on machine 1 and 20 minutes on machine 2. In determining the daily product mix, management would like to achieve the following goals:

1. Joint total production of 12 units
2. Produce 9 units of product 2
3. Produce 10 units of product 1

Suppose that management wishes to minimize the underachievement of each of these goals and that predetermined priority weights w_1, w_2, and w_3 are to be assigned to the three goals, respectively. Formulate this as a goal programming problem.

10-4. In Problem 10-3 suppose that the three goals are in order of descending absolute priority.
   (a) Use graphical analysis to find an optimal product mix.
   (b) Suppose that the marginal profits associated with each unit of products 1 and 2 are, respectively, $6, and $12. Replace the third goal with "attain a daily profit of $192," where you wish to minimize underachievement. Use graphical analysis to find the new solution.

10-5. Consider the goal programming model:

$$\min \quad P_1 v_1 + P_2 v_2 + P_3 u_3 + P_4 (u_4 + v_4)$$
$$\text{s.t.} \qquad\qquad x_2 + u_1 - v_1 = 100$$
$$x_1 + x_2 + u_2 - v_2 = 80$$
$$x_2 + u_3 \qquad\quad = 40$$
$$x_1 + 2x_2 + u_4 - v_4 = 160$$
$$x_1, x_2, u_1, u_2, u_3, u_4, v_1, v_2, v_3, v_4 \geq 0$$

   (a) Use the graphical method to solve the problem.
   (b) Interpret the third goal $x_2 + u_3 = 40$.
   (c) Replace $x_2 + u_3 = 40$ with $x_2 + u_3 \geq 40$. What is the new interpretation?

320

CHAPTER 10
Multiple
Objectives
and Goal
Programming

(d) Use the graphical method to solve the problem with the replacement prescribed in part (c).

10-6. Consider the goal programming model:

$$\min \quad P_1v_1 + P_2v_2 + P_3v_3 + P_4(u_4 + v_4)$$

$$\text{s.t.} \quad x_1 + u_1 - v_1 = 100$$
$$x_1 + x_2 + u_2 - v_2 = 80$$
$$x_1 - v_3 = 40$$
$$x_1 + 2x_2 + u_4 - v_4 = 160$$
$$x_1, x_2, u_1, u_2, u_3, u_4, v_1, v_2, v_3, v_4 \ge 0$$

(a) Use the graphical method to solve the problem.
(b) Interpret the third goal $x_1 - v_3 = 40$.
(c) Replace $x_1 - v_3 = 40$ with $x_1 - v_3 \le 40$. What is the new interpretation?
(d) Use the graphical method to solve the problem with the replacement prescribed in part (c).

10-7. Consider the following goal program:

$$\min \quad P_1u_2 + P_2v_1 + P_3u_3$$
$$\text{s.t.} \quad x_1 + x_2 + u_1 - v_1 = 80$$
$$x_1 + u_2 - v_2 = 100$$
$$x_2 + u_3 \ge 45$$
$$x_1, x_2, u_1, v_1, u_2, v_2, u_3 \ge 0$$

(a) Solve by the graphical method.
(b) Is the first priority goal achieved? What about the second and third? In case of under-achievement or overachievement state actual numerical amounts of the violations.

10-8. An electronics firm produces two types of tape recorders: reel-to-reel and cassette. Production of either type requires an average of three hours. The plant has a normal production capacity of 150 hours per week. According to the marketing department, in each week 30 cassette recorders can be sold and 25 reel-to-reel recorders can be sold. The reel-to-reel models are twice as profitable as the cassettes. Management has set the following goals, in order of decreasing importance:

1. Minimize underutilization of production capacity
2. Produce at least as many items of each type as the sales estimated by the marketing department. Production of the more profitable reel-to-reel models is twice as desirable as production of the cassette models.
3. Minimize overtime (production in excess of capacity) as much as possible.

Formulate the goal programming model.

CHAPTER 11

Integer Programming and Network Models

A NETWORK MODEL AT AIR PRODUCTS AND CHEMICALS, INC.

Air Products and Chemicals, Inc., of Allentown, Pennsylvania, has developed and implemented a large mathematical model to control deliveries of liquid oxygen and nitrogen to customers at minimum cost and with improved reliability. It is estimated that the system saves Air Products over $2 million annually.

With annual sales exceeding $1.5 billion, Air Products is one of the three largest manufacturers and distributors of industrial gases in North America. In particular, oxygen and nitrogen are manufactured in highly automated plants and transported as liquids at a temperature of −320°F using a fleet of more than 500 tractor-trailer trucks. Storage tanks at customer sites are provided by Air Products under long-term contracts, and inventories are monitored and replenished.

Air Products has made a quantum leap from manual order generation and scheduling to the use of an advanced state-of-the-art on-line constrained optimization model. The computer solves daily a mathematical problem involving 800,000 variables and 200,000 constraints.

The first implementation was at Wharton, New Jersey, in October 1981. The system has since been implemented in nine additional depots and continues to be expanded. It has been saving the company between 6 and 10% of operating costs. Other benefits are its significant impact on the management of the distribution function and the opportunities it has created to piggyback other applications onto the on-line network. It has changed decision making from a reactive to an active mode. The system is being presented to customers as a competitive advantage in providing better service.

11.1

INTRODUCTION TO INTEGER PROGRAMMING

Integer programming deals with problems that could be formulated and solved as linear programming problems except for the complicating factor that some or all of the variables are required to assume integer values. You will recall from previous chapters that in a linear programming problem the variables are permitted to take on fractional values such as 6.394, and in keeping with the principle that "whatever is allowed will occur," fractional answers must be expected.[1] In spite of this, actual (real-world) decision variables often must be integers. For example, a firm produces bags of cattle feed. A solution that requires them to make 3000.472 bags does not make sense. In such situations a noninteger

A Practical Approach

solution is often adapted to the integer requirement by simply rounding the results to a neighboring integer. This produces what we call "a rounded solution." Using such a solution is acceptable to management in those situations where, in a significant practical sense, the rounding simply does not matter. For example, there is no significant difference either in the objective function or in the constraints between producing 19,283.64 and

[1]An exception to this is described in the discussion of network models in Section 11.8.

19,283 bags of Big Bull cattle feed. Indeed, there are probably enough approximations used in assembling the data for the model that management would be content with any production figure near the 19,000-bag level.

When Integer Solutions Matter There are, however, a number of important problems where this rather cavalier attitude toward the integer requirements of the real problem just does not work. This complication can be caused by the scale of the variables under consideration. For example, if the solution to an LP model suggested that Boeing should build 11.6 747's and 6.8 727's, management probably would not be comfortable just going ahead and deciding to build 11 747's and 6 727's or, for that matter, any other rounded combination. The magnitude of the return and the commitment of resources associated with each unit of this problem makes it advisable to determine the best possible **integer solution**. As another example, it will be seen that many models use integer variables to indicate logical decisions. For example, we will see problems where we want X_7 to equal 1 if we should build a warehouse in Kansas City and X_7 to equal 0 if we should not. Suppose that the solution to an LP version of this problem yielded a noninteger value (e.g., $X_7 = 0.38$). This value contains no useful information about the solution to the real problem. Clearly, we cannot build 0.38 of a warehouse. We certainly could select warehouses of different sizes, but nevertheless, either we have a warehouse in Kansas City or we do not. You might guess that, in a case such as this, rounding to the nearest integer (0 in this case) would be a way to approach this difficulty. Unfortunately, that is not guaranteed to give a good (to say nothing of optimal) solution. Indeed, we shall see that rounding may not even lead to a feasible solution in cases such as these.

Management scientists have been aware of the importance of integer linear programming problems for years, and a great deal of time and effort has been devoted to research on the solution of these problems. These efforts have returned some dividends and marked progress has been made in this area over the last 10 years. It should be also noted that the great strides in computer technology have made a crucial contribution to the increased ability to solve integer linear programming problems.

LP vs. IP In spite of the impressive improvement in our ability to solve integer programming problems, the technology is still quite different from what we have available to attack programming problems in which the decision variables need not be integer. Some problems that can be solved easily as LP problems become unsolvable for practical purposes if the decision variables are required to be integers (i.e., the time and cost needed to compute a solution is too large).

In this chapter we first describe two general classes of integer linear programming models and use **graphical analysis** to illustrate the relationship between linear programming, integer linear programming, and the process of rounding LP solutions to obtain a possible solution to the IP. This graphical approach will provide an intuitive feeling for the nature of the problem we are confronting. We then turn our attention to a special variety of integer linear programs in which the integer variables are restricted to the values of 0 or 1. Using such "indicator" or "Boolean" variables allows us to *formulate* a variety of logical conditions which are not otherwise easily captured. A number of important practical problems involve such conditions, and several of these formulations are discussed.

In real applications, integer programs are never solved by hand. In order to convey the context of how you would, in practice, deal with such problems we have provided in this chapter, as in others, several computer printouts. Some of these are annotated in order to highlight the interpretation of various numbers. In looking over these printouts, review the problem and the formulation; ask yourself whether the solution is intuitively plausible and, if not, try to explain why. This type of analytic thinking can be developmental; it plays a useful role in the management function.

The First Type of Integer Program The first subclass is illustrated by the PROTRAC E and F model, or by the two-period production, inventory, distribution, and marketing application of Chapters 8 and 9. These are problems in which many of the decision variables, in the most ideal sense, should be constrained to integer values, for fractional levels of production do not have much physical meaning in the case of large crawler tractors.

In practice, there are two ways to approach this difficulty. The easiest and most common approach is to ignore the ideal integrality conditions and solve the problem as though it were truly a continuous model. The second approach is to use a more costly algorithm that does not ignore the integer constraints and that is designed to find the true solution to the integer program.

In the first case, for the purpose of implementation, the continuous solution would be rounded to integer values.

The usual justification for rounding is that the error introduced by rounding is minor compared to other errors in the model introduced by approximation, averaging, aggregation, and so on.

For this first type of IP problem the procedure of rounding the variables is frequently adopted. However, there may be applications when it is not justified, because:

1. The rounded solution may violate critical constraints. For example, suppose that three of the decision variables, say E, F, and G, have optimal values 2.3, 2.4, and 5.3, respectively, in the continuous model, which includes a constraint

$$E + F + G = 10$$

Then feasibility of the current solution is lost in applying any uniform rounding rule to the variables. That is, feasibility of the current solution is destroyed when all three variables are simultaneously rounded to the nearest integer, simultaneously rounded down, or simultaneously rounded up. In the next section, it will become clear that, in fact, there may be no way to round a solution and preserve feasibility (with respect to several constraints), even when some variables are rounded up and others rounded down.

2. The rounding approach may be unjustifiable because even when a rounded solution preserves feasibility, the objective value produced by that solution may be unacceptably far from the true optimal value. That is, the potential error introduced may not be acceptable. Unfortunately, we can never tell exactly how much error is introduced by rounding, because to know this would require advance knowledge of the optimal value for the integer program. The best we can do is place a bound on the maximum error that could occur. For example, consider a max model. One way to measure the potential error is as follows. Let T denote the true integer optimal value, C denote the continuous optimal value, and R denote the objective value produced by rounded variables. Since the integer model is *more constrained* than the continuous problem, we know that its optimal value can be no larger. Hence

$$T \leq C$$

325

CHAPTER 11
Integer
Programming
and Network
Models

If the rounded integer solution is feasible (satisfies all constraints), then we also know that

$$R \leq T \leq C$$

Consequently, the difference

$$C - R$$

is an upper bound on the absolute error $(C - T)$ that rounding could introduce. Also, since

$$\frac{T - R}{T} \leq \frac{C - R}{T} \leq \frac{C - R}{R}$$

it must be true that

$$\frac{C - R}{R}$$

is an upper bound on the relative error $(T - R)/T$ that rounding could introduce.

It is often stated that the bound on relative error tends to be small when the optimal continuous variables are large in value.[2] For example, rounding 968.21 down to 968 will typically introduce less error than rounding 6.21 down to 6, or even more drastically, 1.21 down to 1. This is perhaps intuitively plausible, since it may be interpreted as stating that small percentage deviations from optimality in the decision variables should lead to a small percentage deviation in the objective value. In practice, the number $(C - R)/R$ is a possible and not uncommon criterion for determining whether or not the rounded solution is acceptable. If this bound on relative error is too large, then it may be considered important to have more confidence in the solution and to use a more costly algorithm designed to find the true integer solution. In practice, then, in this first subclass of integer programs, integrality conditions are frequently ignored and solutions are rounded.

The Second Type of Integer Program   There is a second subclass of IP problems in which the integer variables are constrained to take on only the values 0 or 1 (denoted 0/1). *In this class of problems, the process of rounding is almost never justifiable because the potential error introduced can be very large.* For example, a decision variable x_i may have the following interpretation in the model:

$x_i = 1$ means build a new warehouse in city i

$x_i = 0$ means do not build a new warehouse in city i

As another example, a variable x_{ij} may have the following interpretation in the model:

$x_{ij} = 1$ means assign individual i to task j

$x_{ij} = 0$ means do not assign individual i to task j

These variables are allowed to take on only the values 0 or 1. In a continuous version of such a model the variable may be constrained to lie between 0 and 1. When the continuous

[2]To see the facts more precisely, consider an LP max model in which all variables x_j are rounded from optimal (in the continuous problem) noninteger values x_j^* to $\hat{x}_j$ to obtain a feasible integer solution. Also, let I be the set of subscripts of the positive values x_j^*, and suppose that $\sum_I c_j \hat{x}_j > 0$.

$$\frac{C - R}{R} = \frac{\sum_I c_j x_j^* - \sum_I c_j \hat{x}_j}{\sum_I c_j \hat{x}_j} \leq \frac{\sum_I |c_j| |x_j^* - \hat{x}_j|}{\sum_I c_j \hat{x}_j} \leq \frac{\sum_I |c_j|}{\sum_I c_j \hat{x}_j}$$

As a special case, suppose that for j in I the c_j values are all positive. Then the right side of the expression above will be $\leq 1/\min_{j \text{ in } I} \hat{x}_j$. For example, if $\min_{j \text{ in } I} \hat{x}_j \geq 100$, then $(C - R)/R \leq 1\%$.

version is solved, a fractional value such as 0.6 could be produced. If the fractional values are rounded to produce a feasible 0/1 solution, it is clear that the possibility of introducing large errors exists. This is especially true when the coefficients of the variables in the objective function are large (see footnote 2). Thus, it is almost always the case that problems with 0/1 variables must be attacked with algorithms particularly designed to handle these constraints. Such problems, though sometimes difficult and costly to solve, are prominent in applications, as will be illustrated in later sections of this chapter. At the end of the chapter, the **case** in **municipal bond underwriting** provides another excellent illustration.

Role of Special Algorithms

In concluding this section, we remark that numerous special types of models will be formulated in the following pages. It should be kept in mind that our main motive in converting linguistic descriptions into the symbolic model is to give you additional training in problem formulation and additional insight into the real-world applicability of constrained optimization models. In some instances, it will be true that an alternative formulation which is logically equivalent will be computationally more efficient because of the nature of the particular algorithms that exist for solving the model in question. Such considerations may become important when one is solving integer programming problems, but they also become more involved with the theory and mechanics of specific algorithms. Limitations of space and purpose preclude a detailed discussion of such matters.

11.2

THE LINEAR IP MODEL: GRAPHICAL INTERPRETATIONS

In IP, the problems usually considered are linear except for the dramatic corruption of the added **integrality conditions**. These integrality conditions essentially annihilate the applicability of linear algebra to this model, and this helps to explain the difficulty of the problem. If *all* variables are required to be integers, the problem is called a **pure integer program**. If some but not all of the variables are required to be integers, the problem is called a **mixed integer program**. In Chapter 5 we saw that it was possible to gain substantial insight into the nature and the solution of LP problems by examining the graphical analysis of a problem with two decision variables. The same approach is useful for an IP problem and we now turn our attention to that topic.

Solving the IP Problem: A Modification of PROTRAC, Inc.

Consider a modified version of the PROTRAC E and F problem discussed in Chapters 4 through 7. In particular, consider the problem

$$
\begin{array}{lrl}
\text{Max} & 18E + 6F & \\
\text{s.t.} & E + F \geq 5 & (1) \\
& 42.8E + 100F \leq 800 & (2) \\
& 20E + 6F \leq 142 & (3) \\
& 30E + 10F \geq 135 & (4) \\
& E - 3F \leq 0 & (5) \\
& E, F \geq 0 \text{ and integer} &
\end{array}
$$

326

327

CHAPTER 11
Integer
Programming
and Network
Models

Recall that E is the number of E-9s and F is the number of F-9s that PROTRAC decides to produce. The objective function is the profit as a function of the production decision. Constraint (1) reflects a need to meet previous commitments. Constraints (2) and (3) are production time restrictions in departments A and B, respectively. Constraint (4) represents part of a union agreement and constraint (5) is imposed because of management's attitude about the appropriate product mix. The only important change between this model and the previously studied LP problem is the word "integer." The linear problem obtained by dropping the integrality conditions is called the **LP relaxation** of the IP.

To solve the IP above with a graphical approach, we prescribe three steps:

1. Find the feasible set for the LP relaxation of the IP problem.
2. Identify the integer points inside the set determined in step 1.
3. Find, among those points determined in step 2, one that optimizes the objective function.

The first two steps have been accomplished in Figure 11.1. The shaded region is the feasible set for the LP relaxation and the dark dots are the integer points contained in this set. This set of integer points is the set of feasible solutions to the IP. In other words, there are only 13 feasible solutions to the IP problem. They are the points (3, 6), (4, 6), (3, 5), (4, 5), (5, 5), (4, 4), (5, 4), (4, 3), (5, 3), (6, 3), (4, 2), (5, 2), and (6, 2).

To solve the problem, we must now determine which of the feasible points yields the largest value of the objective function. We proceed as in an LP problem, that is, by moving a contour of the objective function in an *uphill direction* (since we are dealing

Figure 11.1
Feasible Set for PROTRAC ILP

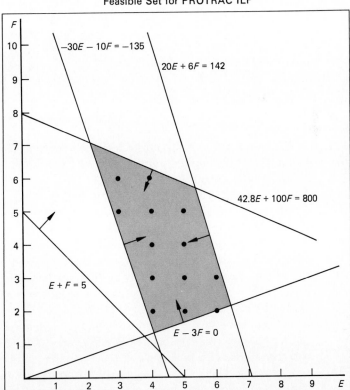

328

CHAPTER 11
Integer
Programming
and Network
Models

with a max model) until it is not possible to move it further and still intersect a feasible point.

The result of this process is shown in Figure 11.2. We see that the optimal solution to the IP is the point $E = 6$ and $F = 3$. Since the objective function is $18E + 6F$, this solution yields an optimal value of the objective function of $18(6) + 6(3) = 126$.

Figure 11.2
Graphical Solution to PROTRAC IP

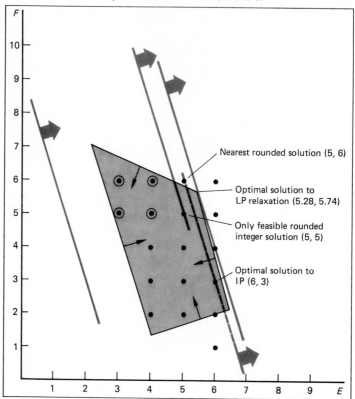

The LP Relaxation

We can use Figure 11.2 to illustrate some important facts about the LP relaxation. We first note that the optimal solution to the LP relaxation occurs at the intersection of lines $42.8E + 100F = 800$, $20E + 6F = 142$.

This result is obtained by pushing, uphill, the contour of the objective function as far as possible and still have it intersect the feasible set for the LP relaxation. Since the intersection of the two constraints does not occur at an integer point, the optimal solution to the LP relaxation is not feasible for the IP. To find the optimal solution (i.e., the optimal values of the decision variables) for the LP relaxation, we solve for the intersection of the two binding constraints. Solving these two equations in two unknowns yields $E^* = 5.28$, $F^* = 5.74$. Thus, the optimal value of the objective function, *termed the OV*, for the LP relaxation is $18(5.28) + 6(5.74) = 129.48$.

Comparing these two optimal values (126 for the IP and 129.48 for the LP relaxation), we see that the OV for the LP relaxation is larger than for the original IP. This fact is a special case of a phenomenon that we observed in our earlier discussions of linear programming. Think of creating an IP by starting with the LP relaxation and adding the integer restrictions. We know that **in any mathematical programming problem, adding**

329

CHAPTER 11
Integer
Programming
and Network
Models

constraints cannot help and may hurt the optimal value of the objective function. Thus, our optimal value decreases with the addition of the integer constraints. With this observation we are prepared to make the following comments:

1. In a **max** problem the OV of the LP relaxation always provides an **upper bound** on the OV of the original IP. Adding the integer constraints either hurts, or leaves unchanged, the OV for the LP. In a max problem, hurting the OV means making it smaller.

2. In a **min** problem the OV of the LP relaxation always provides a **lower bound** on the OV of the original IP. Again, adding the integer constraints either hurts, or leaves unchanged, the OV for the LP. In a min problem, hurting the OV means making it larger.

Rounded Solutions

We have observed that the optimal solution to the LP relaxation is $E^* = 5.28$, $F^* = 5.74$. Each of these variables could be rounded up or down and hence there are four rounded solutions [(5, 5), (5, 6), (6, 5), (6, 6)] that neighbor the optimal solution to the LP relaxation. The general fact is that with two decision variables there are four rounded neighbor solutions; with n decision variables there could be 2^n such points.

Let us now examine in more detail some of the potential problems that can arise when using a rounded solution. Refer once again to Figure 11.2. If we solve the LP relaxation and round each variable to the nearest integer, we obtain (5, 6), which is infeasible. In this case the point (5, 5) is the *only* feasible point that can be obtained by rounding (5.28, 5.74). The other candidates, (5, 6), (6, 6), and (6, 5), are all infeasible.

This geometric analysis illustrates two important facts about rounded solutions.

1. **A feasible rounded solution need not be optimal.** In this case the value of the objective function at the only feasible rounded solution is

$$18(5) + 6(5) = 120$$

This compares to a value of 126 for the optimal value of the IP. We see, then, that a proportional loss of 6/126 or almost 5% is incurred by using this rounded solution rather than the optimal solution.

2. **A feasible rounded solution need not be near the optimal IP solution.** Students often have an intuitive idea that even though a rounded solution may not be optimal, it should be "near" the optimal IP solution. Referring again to Figure 11.2, we see that the rounded solution is not one of the immediate integer neighbors of the optimal IP solution. Indeed, only the four circled points in the feasible set [(3, 6), (4, 6), (3, 5), and (4,5)] are more distant from the optimal solution than the rounded solution. It seems hard to claim that in this example the rounded solution is "near" the optimal IP solution.

In Figure 11.3 we introduce another IP that illustrates an additional and even more drastic problem associated with rounded solutions. In this figure the shaded area is the feasible set for the LP relaxation, the dots are integer points, and the circled dot is the only feasible solution to the IP. The optimal solution to the LP relaxation is indicated at the tip of the wedge-shaped feasible set. Notice that if we start with the optimal solution to the LP [roughly (3.3, 4.7)] and then round this to any of the four neighboring integer points, we obtain an infeasible point. That is, for this example, *no manner of rounding can produce feasibility.*

330

CHAPTER 11
Integer
Programming
and Network
Models

Figure 11.3
All Rounded Solutions Are Infeasible

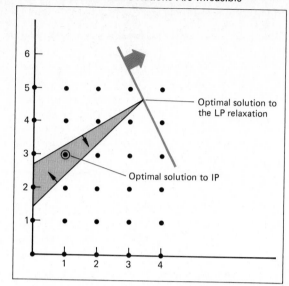

In summary, we have noted that an intuitively appealing way of attacking an IP is to solve the LP relaxation of the original problem and then round the solution to a neighboring integer point. We have seen that this approach can have certain problems. In particular:

1. None of the neighboring integer points may be feasible.
2. Even if one or more of the neighboring integer points is feasible,
   a. Such a point need not be optimal for the IP.
   b. Such a point need not be even "near" the optimal IP solution.

Complete Enumeration

The graphical approach is used to illustrate some important ideas about integer programming. However, sometimes a figure like Figure 11.1 gives students the wrong perspective about the difficulty of solving an IP. Since there are only 13 feasible points for the PROTRAC IP, a student may get the impression that one can reasonably list all the feasible points, evaluate the objective function at each of them, and select the best one, that is, solve the problem by **complete enumeration**. In this case, one could do that. Unfortunately, however, complete enumeration is not a reasonable solution procedure for most IPs. Suppose, for example, that we had an IP with one hundred 0/1 variables. In this case there could be up to 2^{100}, which is 1.27×10^{30}, feasible points. The time required to enumerate all of these points would exceed a lifetime, even with the fastest computer. Some of the most useful algorithms for solving IP problems are actually modified types of enumeration techniques. These techniques are quite refined and are much more intelligent than complete enumeration. In technical jargon, such techniques are formally referred to as **partial enumeration**. They are designed to examine only a "few" of the feasible points but in such a way as to be assured of obtaining an optimal solution. For example, consider a 0/1 IP model. In the optimal solution, some subset of the decision variables will have the value 1, while the remaining variables have the value 0. The partial enumeration algorithms consist of rules for searching certain combinations and

Partial Enumeration

331

CHAPTER 11
Integer
Programming
and Network
Models

for eliminating numerous other combinations without having to explicitly "look" at them. For example, suppose the algorithm "learns" that the variable x_4 cannot have an optimal value of 1 (the basis for such an insight could be the discovery that there is no feasible point for which $x_4 = 1$). Then we can eliminate from consideration *all* combinations of decision variables in which $x_4 = 1$. Solution techniques based on this type of underlying rationale are also referred to as **combinatorial algorithms**.

Local
Optima

The mathematical complexity of integer programs is reflected in the following pathological phenomenon. In Figure 11.2, the objective value at (5, 5) is 32. This is larger than the objective value at any of the neighboring feasible points, (4, 5), (4, 6), (4, 4), and (5, 4). Thus, the problem has what is called a **local optimal solution** at one of the feasible points. This local optimal solution is not the **global** (true) **solution**. This phenomenon cannot occur with a continuous LP problem, *in which case any local optimum is also global.*

    This type of mathematical complexity, along with the limited power of the available algorithms, makes the state of the art in IP inferior to that in continuous LP. In Chapter 7 we saw that as a general rule of thumb the amount of time required to solve an LP varies linearly with the number of constraints. For IP, the difficulty is usually measured in terms of the number of variables, as opposed to the number of constraints. In fact, with some of the IP algorithms, the constraints are actually an asset because they help to eliminate combinations. In any case, one does not often encounter applications with more than several thousand variables, and even in such cases execution times can be long and costly. For these reasons, and because of the importance of the applications, IP is currently an active area of research. As a final comment, it should be noted that much of this research is in the area of **heuristic algorithms**. These are algorithms designed to efficiently produce "good," although not necessarily optimal, solutions. It should be clear by now that

> **From the viewpoint of the manager, a heuristic procedure may certainly be as acceptable as, and possible even preferable to, a "more exact" algorithm that produces an optimal solution. The dominant considerations should be the amount of insight and guidance the model can provide, and the cost of obtaining these.**

11.3
APPLICATIONS OF 0/1 VARIABLES

Binary or 0/1 variables play an especially important role in the applications of integer programming. These variables make it possible to incorporate "yes or no decisions," sometimes called "dichotomous decisions," into a mathematical programming format. Two quick examples will illustrate what we mean.

1. In a plant location problem we let $x_j = 1$ if we choose to have a plant at location j and $x_j = 0$ if we do not.
2. In a routing problem we let $x_{ijk} = 1$ if truck k goes from city i to city j and $x_{ijk} = 0$ if it does not.

Thus, you can see from these examples that the use of 0/1 variables provides us with a new tool for formulating models. In this section we will see some examples of how 0/1 variables are used to make dichotomous decisions in several different applications. We will also see how they can be manipulated to enforce various types of logical conditions.

Capital Budgeting: An Expansion Decision

Many firms make decisions on capital investments on an annual basis. In large firms the decisions are often the culmination of a long process that starts with recommendations from individual departments and continues through various firm-wide and division-wide competitions. It is not unusual to have the final selection among major alternatives rest with the board of directors. In smaller firms the process is not so elaborate, but the capital budgeting decision is still a fundamental part of an annual evaluation of the firm's future.

In its simplest form, the capital budgeting decision is a matter of choosing among n alternatives in order to maximize the return subject to constraints on the amount of capital invested over time. As a particular example, suppose that PROTRAC's board of directors faces the problem summarized in Figure 11.4. The dollar amounts in this figure are in thousands. The board must select one or more of the alternatives. If they decide to expand the Belgian plant, the present value of the net return to the firm is $40,000. This project requires $10,000 of capital in the first year, $5000 in the second, and so on. The board has previously budgeted up to $50,000 for all capital investments in year 1, up to $45,000 in year 2, and so on.

Figure 11.4
PROTRAC's Capital Budgeting Problem

ALTERNATIVE, j	PRESENT VALUE OF NET RETURN	CAPITAL REQUIRED IN YEAR i BY ALTERNATIVE j				
		1	2	3	4	5
Expand Belgian plant	40	10	5	20	10	0
Expand small machine capacity in U.S.	70	30	20	10	10	10
Establish new plant in Chile	80	10	20	27	20	10
Expand large machine capacity in U.S.	100	20	10	40	20	20
Capital available in year i	b_i	50	45	70	40	30

IP Model for Capital Budgeting at PROTRAC

This problem can be modeled as an IP in which all the variables are 0/1 variables. This is called a pure 0/1 IP. In particular, let $x_i = 1$ if project i is accepted and $x_i = 0$ if project i is not accepted. The problem then becomes

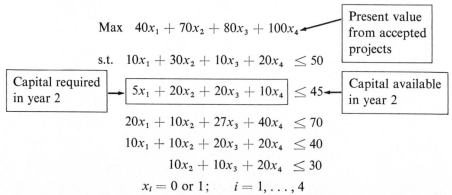

$$\text{Max} \quad 40x_1 + 70x_2 + 80x_3 + 100x_4 \longleftarrow$$

Present value from accepted projects

$$\text{s.t.} \quad 10x_1 + 30x_2 + 10x_3 + 20x_4 \leq 50$$

Capital required in year 2 $\longrightarrow$ $5x_1 + 20x_2 + 20x_3 + 10x_4 \leq 45 \longleftarrow$ Capital available in year 2

$$20x_1 + 10x_2 + 27x_3 + 40x_4 \leq 70$$
$$10x_1 + 10x_2 + 20x_3 + 20x_4 \leq 40$$
$$10x_2 + 10x_3 + 20x_4 \leq 30$$
$$x_i = 0 \text{ or } 1; \quad i = 1, \ldots, 4$$

Here the objective function is the total present value of the net returns and each constraint controls the amount of capital used in each of the five periods.

The LP Relaxation

Let us approach this problem by first solving the LP relaxation. The formulation and solution are shown in Figure 11.5. Note that in working with the LP relaxation to a 0/1 IP, we ignore the constraints $x_i = 0$ or 1. Instead, we add the constraints $x_i \leq 1, i = 1, 2, 3, 4$ (as shown in Figure 11.5). Of course, in an LP, each x_i is always nonnegative. Thus, in the relaxation, instead of $x_i = 0$ or 1, we have x_i constrained to an interval (i.e., $0 \leq x_i \leq 1$). It would be nice if in the optimal solution, each x_i were, fortuitously, to take one extreme or the other of these allowable values (either 0 or 1) for then the original IP would be solved. Unfortunately, as Figure 11.5 shows, this happened only with x_4; the values of x_1, x_2, and x_3 are fractional. Since x_3 should equal 1 if PROTRAC establishes a plant in Chile and 0 if it does not, the result $x_3 = 0.33$ is not meaningful. We also note that attempting to find a solution to the IP problem by solving the LP relaxation and then rounding does not work very well. Standard "nearest integer" rounding rules (i.e., round numbers ≤ 0.499 to 0 and numbers ≥ 0.500 to 1) yield the solution $x_1 = 1, x_2 = 1, x_3 = 0, x_4 = 1$. A quick check reveals that this solution is infeasible since it grossly violates the first constraint.

Figure 11.5

LP Relaxation of PROTRAC's Capital Budgeting Problem

```
MAX 40 XI + 70 X2 + 80 X3 + 100 X4
SUBJECT TO
    2)      10 X1 + 30 X2 + 10 X3 + 20 X4 ≤ 50
    3)       5 X1 + 20 X2 + 20 X3 + 10 X4 ≤ 45
    4)      20 X1 + 10 X2 + 27 X3 + 40 X4 ≤ 70
    5)      10 X1 + 10 X2 + 20 X3 + 20 X4 ≤ 40
    6)              10 X2 + 10 X3 + 20 X4 ≤ 30
    7)      X1 ≤ 1⎫  ┌─────────────────────┐
    8)      X2 ≤ 1⎪  │ Constraints associated
    9)      X3 ≤ 1⎬  │ with the relaxation
   10)      X4 ≤ 1⎭  │ of 0/1 conditions
                     └─────────────────────┘

          OBJECTIVE FUNCTION VALUE

                  200.00

VARIABLE        VALUE        REDUCED COST
   X1           0.67            0.00
   X2           0.67            0.00
   X3           0.33            0.00
   X4           1.00            0.00
```

The Optimal IP Solution

To obtain the optimal IP solution for the PROTRAC capital budgeting problem, we must turn to *an integer programming code*—in this case, a computer program that employs an algorithm specifically designed to solve the 0/1 integer program. The formulation and solution of the IP are shown in Figure 11.6.

Note that the four constraints that require the x_i's to be ≤ 1 have been dropped. In this particular program (LINDO), the phrase "integer variables = 4" indicates that all four of the variables are 0/1 variables.

333

334

CHAPTER 11
Integer
Programming
and Network
Models

Figure 11.6

IP Model of PROTRAC's Capital Budgeting Problem

```
MAX 40 X1 + 70 X2 + 80 X3 + 100 X4
SUBJECT TO
    2)    10 X1 + 30 X2 + 10 X3 + 20 X4 ≤ 50
    3)     5 X1 + 20 X2 + 20 X3 + 10 X4 ≤ 45
    4)    20 X1 + 10 X2 + 27 X3 + 40 X4 ≤ 70
    5)    10 X1 + 10 X2 + 20 X3 + 20 X4 ≤ 40
    6)          10 X2 + 10 X3 + 20 X4 ≤ 30
INTEGER VARIABLES = 4

          OBJECTIVE FUNCTION VALUE

                  190.00

VARIABLE        VALUE        REDUCED COST

    X1          1.00            50.00
    X2          1.00             0.00
    X3          1.00             0.00
    X4          0.00            50.00
```

The solution shows that management should accept the first three alternatives; x_4 is now zero, whereas in the LP relaxation it was 1. Note also that the objective function is now 190. This is a reduction of 10 (5%) from the optimal value of the objective function for the LP relaxation. In practice, one may well be interested in solving integer programs with hundreds or even thousands of 0/1 variables. After seeing the analysis of this small example and the problems associated with using the LP relaxation as a basis for solving an IP problem, you can well appreciate the even greater importance, in larger and more complex applications, of having special algorithms to solve the IP problem.

Logical Conditions   An important use of 0/1 variables is to impose constraints which arise from logical conditions. Several examples are cited below.

No More Than k of n Alternatives   Suppose that $x_i = 0$ or 1, for $i = 1, \ldots, n$. The constraint

$$x_1 + x_2 + \cdots + x_n \leq k$$

implies that at most k alternatives of n possibilities can be selected. That is, since each x_i can be only 0 or 1, the above constraint says that not more than k of them can equal 1. For the data in Figure 11.4, assume that PROTRAC feels that not more than one foreign project can be accepted. For this reason, the Board wants to rule out a decision that includes the Belgian expansion and a new plant in Chile. Adding the constraint

$$x_1 + x_3 \leq 1$$

to the IP in Figure 11.6 implies that the solution can contain at most one of the overseas alternatives.

Dependent Decisions   You can use 0/1 variables to force a dependent relationship on two or more decisions. Suppose, for example, that management does not want to select alternative k unless it first selects alternative m. The constraint

335

CHAPTER 11
Integer
Programming
and Network
Models

$$x_k \leq x_m \qquad (11.1)$$

or

$$x_k - x_m \leq 0$$

enforces this condition. Note that if *m is not* selected, then $x_m = 0$. Equation (11.1) then forces x_k to be 0 (i.e., alternative k is not selected). Alternatively, if *m* is selected, $x_m = 1$; then equation (11.1) becomes $x_k \leq 1$. This leaves the program free to select $x_k = 1$ or $x_k = 0$.

As an example, again consider Figure 11.4, and suppose that PROTRAC's management feels that, if they are going to expand within the United States, their competitive position implies that they must definitely expand the large machine capacity. Adding the constraint

$$x_2 - x_4 \leq 0$$

to the IP in Figure 11.6 assures that the model cannot select "expand small machine capacity" unless "expand large machine capacity" is also selected.

Similarly, suppose the board decided: "If we're going to expand our domestic capacity, we're going to expand both lines." Adding the constraint

$$x_4 - x_2 = 0$$

to the IP in Figure 11.6 would enforce this condition since it implies that x_4 and x_2 must take the same values.

Lot Size Constraints Consider a portfolio manager with the following constraints: (1) if he purchases security j, he must purchase at least 20 shares; and (2) he may not purchase more than 100 shares of security j. Let x_j be the number of shares of security j purchased. The constraint that **IF** j is purchased, then at least 20 shares must be purchased, is called a "minimum lot size" or "batch size" constraint. Note that we cannot create such a constraint in an LP model. The constraints

$$20 \leq x_j \leq 100$$

do not do the job since they insist that x_j always be at least 20. We want the conditions either $x_j = 0$ or $20 \leq x_j \leq 100$. To achieve this we will make use of a 0/1 variable, say y_j, for security j. The variable y_j has the following interpretation:

- ■ If $y_j = 1$, then purchase security j.
- ■ If $y_j = 0$, do not purchase security j.

Now consider the two constraints

$$x_j \leq 100 y_j \qquad (11.2)$$
$$x_j \geq 20 y_j \qquad (11.3)$$

We see that if $y_j = 1$, then (11.2) and (11.3) imply that $20 \leq x_j \leq 100$. On the other hand, if $y_j = 0$, then (11.2) implies that $x_j \leq 0$. Similarly, (11.3) implies that $x_j \geq 0$. These two inequalities together imply that $x_j = 0$. Thus, if $y_j = 1$ when we purchase j, and 0 when we do not, we have the proper conditions on x_j.

How can we be sure that $y_j = 1$ if we purchase security j? The inequality (11.2) $(x_j \leq 100y_j)$ guarantees it. We see that in this inequality you cannot have both $x_j > 0$ and $y_j = 0$. Thus, if $x_j > 0$, y_j must equal 1. We see then that inequalities (11.2) and (11.3) together guarantee the "minimum lot size" constraint.

Fixed-Charge Problems   In this type of problem, there is a fixed startup cost associated with some particular activity. There is an inexhaustible list of specific examples of this phenomenon in the production and inventory control area alone. Consider, for example, the utilization of an open-hearth furnace or an ice-cream machine. If the activity is not being used (there is no production), then there is no associated cost. If the activity is used, even at a minute level, then there is a significant associated startup cost (e.g., to reline and heat the furnace or to clean and cool the ice-cream machine). A fixed cost associated with the variable x_j is shown in Figure 11.7. It is seen that if $x_j = 0$, then the cost is zero, but if $x_j > 0$, then there is a fixed cost F_j as well as a marginal cost c_j. It is the discontinuity of this cost function at $x_j = 0$ that is responsible for the mathematical complexity of this problem. Let us denote the cost function in Figure 11.7 as $C_j(x_j)$. Thus

$$C_j(x_j) = \begin{cases} x_j & \text{if } x_j = 0 \\ c_j x_j + F_j & \text{if } x_j > 0 \end{cases}$$

Figure 11.7
Fixed Cost Associated with x_j

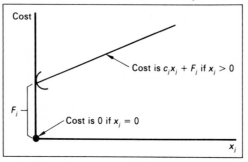

A typical fixed-charge model can then be formulated as:

$$\text{Min} \quad \sum_{j=1}^{n} C_j(x_j)$$

$$\text{s.t.} \quad \sum_{j=1}^{n} a_{ij}x_j = b_i \qquad i = 1, \ldots, m \tag{I}$$

$$x_j \geq 0, \text{ all } j$$

The difficulty with this formulation is that there is no algorithm for attacking problems in the form above. (Note that the objective function is not linear; in fact, it is badly nonlinear, because of the behavior at $x_j = 0$.) The problem is cast into a mixed integer program as follows:

$$\text{Min} \quad \sum_{j=1}^{n} (c_j x_j + z_j F_j)$$

$$\text{s.t.} \quad \sum_{j=1}^{n} a_{ij}x_j = b_i \qquad i = 1, \ldots, m \tag{II}$$

$$x_j - z_j U \leq 0 \qquad j = 1, \ldots, n$$

$$x_j \geq 0, \text{ all } j; \ z_j = 0 \text{ or } 1, \text{ all } j$$

337

CHAPTER 11
Integer
Programming
and Network
Models

The symbol U denotes a number that is so large that whenever x is feasible in model (I), it is true that $x_j \leq U$ for all j. (We will assume that such a value can be assigned to U; that is, the constraint set in the original model (I) is assumed bounded.) Note that the group of constraints

$$x_j - z_j U \leq 0$$

force x_j to be zero if z_j is 0. In the problems, you are asked to prove that if x^* is a solution to (I), then x^*, z^* is a solution to (II), where

$$z_j^* = \begin{cases} 1 & \text{if } x_j^* > 0 \\ 0 & \text{if } x_j^* = 0 \end{cases}$$

and if x^*, z^* is a solution to (II), then x^* is a solution to (I). That is, if (I) has a solution then so does (II), and any solution to (II) provides a solution to (I). The advantage of casting the problem into form (II) is that an algorithm for attacking problems with 0/1 variables can then be applied.

Plant
Location

In Chapter 4 the following **transportation model** was described. A single product is considered. There are m plants and n marketing districts, with limited supply at each plant and known demand at each district. There is a per unit cost c_{ij} associated with a shipment from plant i to district j. The problem is to determine how much to ship from each plant to each district, in such a way as to minimize total shipping cost while satisfying all demands and not exceeding available supplies. This model can be formulated as follows. Let x_{ij} be a decision variable denoting the quantity to be shipped from plant i to district j. The transportation model is

$$\text{Min} \quad \sum_{i=1}^{m} \sum_{j=1}^{n} c_{ij} x_{ij}$$

$$\text{s.t.} \quad \sum_{j=1}^{n} x_{ij} \leq S_i \quad i = 1, \ldots, m \tag{I}$$

$$\sum_{i=1}^{m} x_{ij} \geq D_j \quad j = 1, \ldots, n$$

$$x_{ij} \geq 0, \text{ all } i, j$$

Now let us complicate the model above as follows. Suppose that a fixed cost of F_i dollars is associated with the use of plant i. That is, if any amount of material is shipped out of plant i, then a fixed charge of F_i dollars is incurred. If nothing is shipped from plant i, then there is no associated cost. This is often called a plant location model, since it can be used to determine which of m possible locations should be selected for the construction of plants. In this interpretation, the charge F_i would be the cost of constructing a plant in location i. To formulate this model, introduce new 0/1 decision variables y_i, defined as

$$y_i = \begin{cases} 1 & \text{means use location } i \\ 0 & \text{means do not use location } i \end{cases}$$

Now the complete model is

338

CHAPTER 11
Integer
Programming
and Network
Models

$$\text{Min } \sum_{i=1}^{m} y_i F_i + \sum_{i=1}^{m} \sum_{j=1}^{n} c_{ij} x_{ij}$$

$$\text{s.t. } \sum_{j=1}^{n} x_{ij} - y_i S_i \le 0 \qquad i = 1, \dots, m$$

$$\sum_{i=1}^{m} x_{ij} \qquad \ge D_j \qquad j = 1, \dots, n \tag{II}$$

$$x_{ij} \ge 0, \text{ all } i, j; \; y_i = 0 \text{ or } 1; i = 1, \dots, m$$

The constraints assure that if plant i is not used ($y_i = 0$), then nothing can be sent out of plant i, since in this case

$$\sum_{j=1}^{n} x_{ij} \le 0$$

Also note that if $y_i = 0$, then the fixed charge F_i in the objective function is not incurred for plant i.

Fixed Cost on a Route As another complication, suppose there is a fixed overhead cost F_{ij} associated with the maintenance of a shipping route between location i and district j. The problem is now to select the plant locations, routings, and shipping schedule so as to minimize total cost. The new model is formulated by introducing 0/1 variables z_{ij} defined as

$$z_{ij} = \begin{cases} 1 & \text{if the route between } i \text{ and } j \text{ is used} \\ 0 & \text{if not} \end{cases}$$

The complete model is

$$\text{Min } \sum_{i=1}^{m} y_i F_i + \sum_{i=1}^{m} \sum_{j=1}^{n} c_{ij} x_{ij} + \sum_{i=1}^{m} \sum_{j=1}^{n} F_{ij} z_{ij}$$

$$\text{s.t. } \sum_{j=1}^{n} x_{ij} - y_i S_i \le 0 \qquad i = 1, \dots, m$$

$$\sum_{i=1}^{m} x_{ij} \qquad \ge D_j \qquad j = 1, \dots, n \tag{III}$$

$$x_{ij} - z_{ij} U \le 0, \text{ all } i, j$$

$$x_{ij} \ge 0, \text{ all } i, j; \; y_i = 0 \text{ or } 1, \text{ all } i; \; z_{ij} = 0 \text{ or } 1, \text{ all } i, j$$

In this model, the number U is chosen so large that any point that is feasible in model (II) has the property that $x_{ij} \le U$, all i, j. This number U could be taken as the maximum of the supplies $S_1, S_2, \dots, S_m$.

k of m Constraints Suppose we have a model requiring that *at least* k of the following conditions are satisfied:

$$g_i(x_1, \dots, x_n) \le b_i \qquad i = 1, \dots, m$$

To express this requirement, introduce m new 0/1 variables y_i and let U be chosen so large that for each i, $g_i(x_1, \dots, x_n) \le U$ for every x satisfying any set of k inequalities taken from the m above. Then the following $m + 1$ constraints express the desired condition:

$$\sum_{i=1}^{m} y_i \ge k$$

$$g_i(x_1, \dots, x_n) \le b_i y_i + (1 - y_i) U \qquad i = 1, \dots, m$$

339

CHAPTER 11
Integer
Programming
and Network
Models

Note that

$$\sum_{i=1}^{m} y_i \geq k$$

forces at least k of the y_i variables to have the value 1. This means that at least k of the last m inequalities are equivalent to $g_i(x_1, \ldots, x_n) \leq b_i$. The remaining inequalities are equivalent to $g_i(x_1, \ldots, x_n) \leq U$, and by the foregoing assumption on the choice of U, these conditions are innocuous.

The Knapsack Problem

This is an important problem that arises in different contexts, such as loading containers in box cars or aircraft or satisfying the demand for various lengths of cloth which must be cut from fixed-length bolts of fabric that are held in stock. The generic statement is quite simple. Consider a set of indivisible items that differ in weight and value. We are given a knapsack that holds a maximum allowable weight. The problem is to load the knapsack in such a way as to maximize the value it holds.

As an example, suppose a knapsack holds 91 pounds. Assume that there is one unit of each of five items that can be placed in the knapsack. The weight and value of each item is given in Figure 11.8. Suppose the items are divisible, so that less than one unit of each is allowed to be loaded. Then the problem is one in continuous variables and the solution is easy. Simply rerank the items in the order of decreasing value per unit weight, as shown in Figure 11.9. Then place items in the knapsack in the order of decreasing value per unit weight, as shown in Figure 11.10.

For the discrete (indivisible) case, one might use the ranking approach to conjecture the following solution. Load 3 and 1 to get 66 pounds, then 2 to add 24 pounds, using 90 pounds of total capacity and obtaining a value of 132. Though this, in fact, is a solution to the example above, this technique will not, in general, be valid. Perhaps you can construct an example to illustrate this fact. You are asked to do so in Problem 11-17.

The above intuitive approach (i.e., ranking items according to value per unit weight and then selecting from this list from top down) is an example of a **heuristic**

Figure 11.8
Weight/Value Data for the Knapsack Problem

ITEM NUMBER	WEIGHT	VALUE
1	36	54
2	24	18
3	30	60
4	32	32
5	26	13

Figure 11.9
Ranking When Items in Knapsack Are Divisible

ITEM NUMBER	WEIGHT	VALUE	VALUE/WEIGHT
3	30	60	2
1	36	54	$1\frac{1}{2}$
4	32	32	1
2	24	18	$\frac{3}{4}$
5	26	13	$\frac{1}{2}$

340

CHAPTER 11
Integer
Programming
and Network
Models

Figure 11.10
Solution to the Knapsack Problem
with Divisible Items

LOAD	WEIGHT	VALUE
All of item 3	30	60
All of item 1	36	54
$\frac{25}{32}$ of item 4	25	25
Total	91	139

algorithm for solving a combinatorial problem. *In many applications, heuristic algorithms work quite well in the sense of efficiently producing solutions that, though not optimal, are good enough to enable management to improve current operations*, and, after all, that is the name of the game. Moreover, heuristic algorithms are often able to produce bounds on the "goodness" of a candidate solution so that the manager can, for example, have assurance that he is within such and such a percentage of optimality.

The formal IP formulation of the knapsack problem is extremely simple. Suppose that there are n distinct items for potential inclusion. Let

$$x_i = \begin{cases} 1 & \text{if item } i \text{ is to be included in the knapsack} \\ 0 & \text{otherwise} \end{cases}$$

Let

$$w_i = \text{weight of item } i$$
$$v_i = \text{value of item } i$$
$$W = \text{capacity of the knapsack}$$

Then the formulation is

$$\text{Max} \quad \sum_{i=1}^{n} v_i x_i$$

$$\text{s.t.} \quad \sum_{i=1}^{n} w_i x_i \le W$$

$$x_i = 0 \text{ or } 1, \text{ all } i$$

Any integer program with *one* constraint and *nonnegative data* is called a knapsack problem. If unlimited numbers of each item i can be selected, subject only to the capacity constraint, then the 0/1 condition is replaced by the requirement that each x_i is integer valued.

***Sequencing,
Scheduling,
and Routing
Problems***

These problems tend to be quite large, involving many combinations to be scanned, and consequently they tend to be difficult to solve. In practice, heuristic algorithms are often applied with considerable success. A generic routing problem is the so-called **traveling salesman problem**. It is a good example of a problem that is easy to state but hard to solve. There are n cities. A **tour** is a route that begins at city 1, visits each city once and only once, and returns to city 1. The problem is to find the shortest tour. The data of the

341

CHAPTER 11
Integer
Programming
and Network
Models

problem consist of the terms c_{ij}, the distance between city i and city j. Some of the c_{ij} could be infinity (you cannot go from i to j), and c_{ij} need not equal c_{ji}. Note that when one starts in city 1, he can choose any of the remaining $(n - 1)$ cities to visit first. Having chosen this city, he can now select any of the remaining $(n - 2)$ cities, and so on. There are thus a total of $(n - 1)(n - 2) \ldots (2)(1)$ possible tours. This product is written as $(n - 1)!$. You may be surprised that $29! = 8.84 \times 10^{30}$; thus, the notion of solving a 30-city problem by total enumeration is clearly out of the question. To state a formal mathematical model of this problem, let

$$x_{ij} = \begin{cases} 1 & \text{if a tour includes traveling from } i \text{ to } j \\ 0 & \text{otherwise} \end{cases}$$

Then the model can be written as

$$\text{Min} \quad \sum_{i=1}^{n} \sum_{j=1}^{n} c_{ij} x_{ij}$$

s.t. $\quad \sum_{j=1}^{n} x_{ij} = 1 \quad i = 1, \ldots, n \quad$ (leave each city exactly once)

$\quad \sum_{i=1}^{n} x_{ij} = 1 \quad j = 1, \ldots, n \quad$ (enter each city exactly once)

$\quad x_{ij} \geq 0$, integer, all $i, j \quad$ (with the constraints above, this ensures $x_{ij} = 0$ or 1)

In this formulation, $c_{jj} = \infty; j = 1, \ldots, n$ because $x_{jj} = 1$ is meaningless.[3] The formulation above is not complete, for a feasible solution to the problem stated above may contain disconnected **subtours**, which are not allowed. A solution with two subtours is presented in Figure 11.11. Since such a solution does not provide an answer to the real problem, subtours must be ruled out. We shall merely state that this can be done formally by introducing additional constraints into the formulation.

One of the most intuitive ways to approach sequential decision problems is to follow a policy that "does the best at each stage." The costs shown in the four-city example in Figure 11.12 can be used to illustrate the fallacy of such an approach. Suppose you select the cheapest alternative at each stage, while maintaining a tour. The tour obtained would

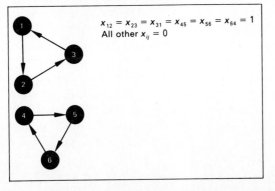

| **Figure 11.11** | **Figure 11.12** |
| Solution with Subtours | Four-City Tour Costs |

$x_{12} = x_{23} = x_{31} = x_{45} = x_{56} = x_{64} = 1$
All other $x_{ij} = 0$

	To			
From	**1**	**2**	**3**	**4**
1	∞	6	4	5
2	2	∞	5	4
3	5	30	∞	20
4	7	3	6	∞

[3] When the model is input to the computer for solution, a very large number is input for the c_{jj} values, or the variables x_{jj} are eliminated from the formulation.

be $1 \rightarrow 3 \rightarrow 4 \rightarrow 2 \rightarrow 1$, with a cost of 29. The tour $1 \rightarrow 4 \rightarrow 2 \rightarrow 3 \rightarrow 1$ is better, with a cost of 18.

Applications of the Traveling Salesman Model The traveling salesman model is actually applicable to numerous diverse problems in real life; it is probably rarely applied to abate the dilemmas of a traveling salesman. A more meaningful application might involve drawing up routes for delivery trucks. As an example of the diversity of the scheduling problems that are actually traveling salesman models, consider the problem of scheduling the flavors of ice cream to run through a manufacturer's equipment.

Let

c_{ij} = time spent setting up (cleaning and preparing equipment) for j when flavor j follows i

These c_{ij}s vary considerably, since many flavors are near variants (chocolate ripple and chocolate fudge almond) and others require significant cleanup time (chocolate followed by vanilla). The problem of scheduling production to minimize total setup time is a traveling salesman problem, where

$$x_{ij} = \begin{cases} 1 & \text{if flavor } j \text{ follows flavor } i \\ 0 & \text{if not} \end{cases}$$

In addition to the traveling salesman model, there are numerous other types of problems that involve sequencing decisions. Many of these are discussed in the standard reference texts on IP.

11.4
AN IP VIGNETTE: STECO'S WAREHOUSE LOCATION PROBLEM—FORMULATION AND COMPUTER ANALYSIS

In order to conserve capital, STECO, the steel wholesaler, leases its regional warehouses. It currently has a list of three warehouses it can lease. The cost per month to lease warehouse i is F_i. Also, warehouse i can handle a maximum of T_i trucks per month.

There are four sales districts and the typical monthly demand in district j is d_j truckloads. The average cost of sending a truck from warehouse i to district j is c_{ij}. STECO wants to know which warehouses to lease and how many trucks to send from each warehouse to each district. A schematic representation of the problem is illustrated in Figure 11.13. The data for this problem are presented in Figure 11.14.

In this table we see, for example, that it costs $7750 to lease warehouse A for a month and that up to 200 trucks can be dispatched from this warehouse. Also, the monthly demand in sales district 1 is 100 trucks. The numbers in the body of the table are the costs of sending a truck from warehouse i to sales district j (e.g., the cost of sending a truck from B to 3 is $100).

Modeling Considerations If you want to attack this problem with a mathematical programming model, you must first decide which variables (if any) you will treat as integers and which (if any) you will **342** treat as continuous variables.

343

CHAPTER 11
Integer
Programming
and Network
Models

Figure 11.13
STECO's Warehouse Location Problem

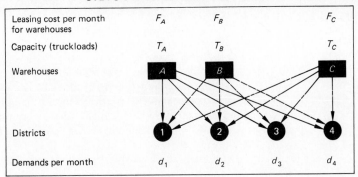

Figure 11.14
Warehouse Location Data

| | COST PER TRUCK, (c_{ij}) SALES DISTRICT | | | | MONTHLY CAPACITY | MONTHLY LEASING |
WAREHOUSE	1	2	3	4	(NUMBER OF TRUCKS)	COST
A	$170	$ 40	$ 70	$160	200	$7750
B	150	195	100	10	250	4000
C	100	240	140	60	300	5500
Monthly demand (truck loads)	100	90	110	60		

From the previous discussion of the plant location model in Section 11.3 we know that the decision to lease a particular warehouse or not requires a 0/1 variable. We will thus let

$$y_i = 1 \quad \text{if we lease warehouse } i, \qquad y_i = 0 \quad \text{if we do not}$$

At first glance it also seems appropriate to treat the number of trucks sent from a warehouse to a district as an integer variable. Trucks are, after all, integer entities and it does not make sense to talk about sending one-third of a truck from here to there. There are, however, several factors that could persuade us to treat the number of trucks as a continuous variable. In particular:

1. This is a planning model, not a detailed operating system. In actual operation the demands in the districts will vary. Management will have to devise methods of handling this uncertainty. Trucks assigned to a specific warehouse might be allocated among adjacent districts on a daily-as-needed basis or STECO might use common carriers to satisfy excess demand. At any rate, the number of trucks that the solution to our mathematical programming problem says should go from warehouse i to district j is only an *approximation* of what will actually happen on any given day. Thus, treating these entities as continuous variables and rounding to the nearest integer to determine how many trucks to assign to each warehouse could provide a useful answer and a good approximation of the *average* monthly operating cost.

344

CHAPTER 11
Integer
Programming
and Network
Models

2. Treating the number of trucks as integer variables may make the problem much more difficult to solve. This is simply a reflection of the general fact that the more the number of integer variables, the more difficult it is to solve an IP.

3. It certainly costs much more to lease one of the warehouses than to send a truck from a warehouse to a sales district. The relative magnituof these costs deaga in implies that it is relatively more important to treat the "lease or not lease" decision as an integer variable, as opposed to the trucks. To illustrate this point, note that it costs $5500 per month to lease warehouse C and $60 to send a truck from warehouse C to sales district 4. Suppose that we modeled the problem as an LP. If $y_3 = 0.4$ in the optimal solution, rounding to 0 causes a $2200 change in the OV (optimal value of the objective function), whereas if $x_{C4} = 57.8$, rounding either up or down has less than a $60 effect.

In summary, there are, in this example, arguments that suggest little advantage to treating the number of trucks as integers. We thus proceed to formulate STECO's warehouse location problem as a mixed integer program, and we will have a pleasant surprise.

The Mixed Let
IP Model

$$y_i = 1 \quad \text{if lease warehouse } i, \qquad y_i = 0 \quad \text{if not;} \qquad i = \text{A, B, C}$$

$$x_{ij} = \text{the number of trucks sent from warehouse } i \text{ to district } j;$$

$$i = \text{A, B, C}; \quad j = 1, \dots, 4$$

We shall now construct the model by developing each of its component parts. First consider the objective function. The expression

$$170x_{A1} + 40x_{A2} + 70x_{A3} + \cdots + 60x_{C4}$$

is the total cost associated with the trucks and

$$7750y_A + 4000y_B + 5500y_C$$

is the total leasing cost. Thus, the objective function is

$$\min \quad 7750y_A + 4000y_B + 5500y_C + 170x_{A1} + \cdots + 60x_{C4}$$

Now consider the constraints. We must consider both demand and capacity. The following constraint guarantees that demand will be satisfied at sales district 1:

$$x_{A1} + x_{B1} + x_{C1} = 100$$

Four constraints like this (one for each district) are required to guarantee that demand is satisfied.

The constraint

$$x_{A1} + x_{A2} + x_{A3} + x_{A4} \le 200y_A \quad \text{or} \quad x_{A1} + x_{A2} + x_{A3} + x_{A4} - 200y_A \le 0$$

serves two purposes. It guarantees that capacity at warehouse A is not exceeded and it forces us to lease warehouse A (i.e., forces $y_A = 1$) if we want to send anything out of this warehouse. Also note when $y_A = 1$, the term $7750y_A$ in the objective function equals 7750. Thus, we see that nothing is sent out of warehouse A unless we incur the monthly leasing cost for that particular warehouse. Three such constraints, one for each warehouse, are needed in the model.

The complete model and the computer solution are shown in Figure 11.15.

Figure 11.15
STECO's Warehouse Location Problem

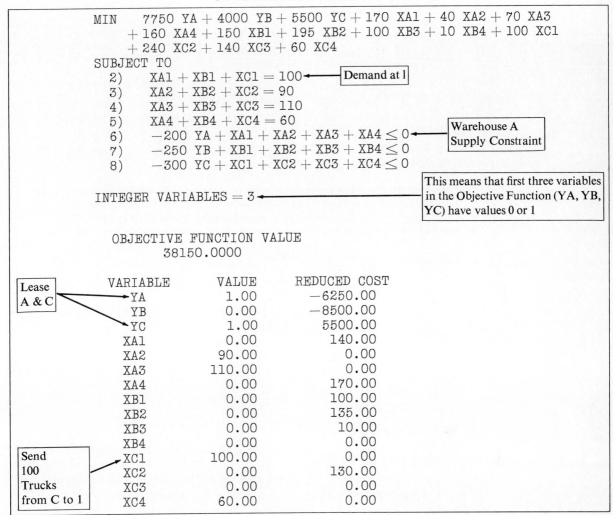

MIN   7750 YA + 4000 YB + 5500 YC + 170 XA1 + 40 XA2 + 70 XA3
       + 160 XA4 + 150 XB1 + 195 XB2 + 100 XB3 + 10 XB4 + 100 XC1
       + 240 XC2 + 140 XC3 + 60 XC4
SUBJECT TO
   2)   XA1 + XB1 + XC1 = 100 ←── Demand at 1
   3)   XA2 + XB2 + XC2 = 90
   4)   XA3 + XB3 + XC3 = 110
   5)   XA4 + XB4 + XC4 = 60
   6)   −200 YA + XA1 + XA2 + XA3 + XA4 ≤ 0 ←── Warehouse A Supply Constraint
   7)   −250 YB + XB1 + XB2 + XB3 + XB4 ≤ 0
   8)   −300 YC + XC1 + XC2 + XC3 + XC4 ≤ 0

INTEGER VARIABLES = 3 ←── This means that first three variables in the Objective Function (YA, YB, YC) have values 0 or 1

       OBJECTIVE FUNCTION VALUE
            38150.0000

            VARIABLE   VALUE   REDUCED COST
Lease   YA   1.00   −6250.00
A & C   YB   0.00   −8500.00
            YC   1.00   5500.00
            XA1   0.00   140.00
            XA2   90.00   0.00
            XA3   110.00   0.00
            XA4   0.00   170.00
            XB1   0.00   100.00
            XB2   0.00   135.00
            XB3   0.00   10.00
            XB4   0.00   0.00
Send   XC1   100.00   0.00
100   XC2   0.00   130.00
Trucks   XC3   0.00   0.00
from C to 1 XC4   60.00   0.00

Output Analysis A quick glance at the output shows that the optimal values of all truck allocations are integer, even though we decided in the formulation to allow these variables to be continuous. Was this just fortuitous? The answer is no. Here is the reason. We started with a warehouse location problem. Note that once we have decided which warehouse to lease, the problem of finding the optimal allocation of trucks is an LP problem called *the transportation problem*. In the next section you will learn that the occurrence of integer solutions is a remarkable property of transportation models which have integral supplies and demands. We can therefore conclude that the optimal solution to the above warehouse location problem with integer supplies and demands will always include an integer allocation of trucks. The argument involves two steps: (1) the optimal solution must lease some set of warehouses and (2) every possible set of leased warehouses yields an integer allocation of trucks.

345

For this problem, then, we now see that it would have been naive and costly to require additional constraints that the x_{ij}'s be integer. The word is: "Never pay for a free good."

1.15

SENSITIVITY ANALYSIS IN IP

Many IP codes use repeated applications of the simplex method to obtain an optimal solution to the IP. The technicality of how this is done is not within our scope. We do, however, wish to point out that care must be taken in interpreting the computer output associated with the solution. In particular, any sensitivity information on the printout must be ignored. For the most part it is meaningless, although in special cases it may provide limited information for highly expert users. In other words,

> **It is generally true that in integer programming we cannot obtain information that is equivalent to the dual price and cost sensitivity information in an LP.**

RHS Sensitivity   This does not imply that changes in the RHS, or in a cost coefficient, do not affect the solution to an IP. They do. Indeed, the solution to integer programs can be extremely sensitive to changes in parameter values.

The following somewhat unrealistic but for the present purpose illustrative capital budgeting example will illustrate these points:

$$\text{Max} \quad 10x_1 + 100x_2 + 1000x_3$$

$$\text{s.t.} \quad 29x_1 + 30x_2 + 31x_3 \le b_1$$

$$x_1, x_2, x_3 \text{ are 0 or 1}$$

The problem is easily solved by inspection. The table in Figure 11.16 shows the optimal solution and the OV for various values of the parameter b_1. From the data in Figure 11.16 we note that a change in 1 unit in the right-hand side of the constraint (say from 29 to 30) increases the OV by a factor of 10 (from 10 to 100). Clearly, if the manager were aware of such an opportunity, she would be anxious to make such a change.

Figure 11.16
Sensitivity Data

| | OPTIMAL SOLUTION | | | |
b_1	x_1	x_2	x_3	OV
29	1	0	0	10
30	0	1	0	100
31	0	0	1	1000

This sort of sensitivity information can generally be achieved only by repeatedly solving the model with new parameter values. When the model has a number of constraints, using this approach to generate useful sensitivity data for an IP can require the

347

CHAPTER 11
Integer
Programming
and Network
Models

analyst to run a large number of alternative programs. This can be an expensive and time-consuming activity.

A major difference between IP and LP is revealed by the data shown in Figure 11.16. In Chapter 7 we learned that, in an LP, loosening the RHS helps less and less. Figure 11.16 shows that

---

In integer programming, loosening can help more and more.

Thus, integer programs can show increasing returns to scale. This is a difficult phenomenon to deal with quantitatively, and helps to explain why integer programming is a more difficult topic than LP.

11.6
NOTES ON IMPLEMENTATION OF INTEGER PROGRAMMING

Integer solutions are an important, indeed essential, condition for the application of mathematical programming models to many important real-world problems. Recent advances in research and computer technology have made it possible to make real progress on problems that involve variables that must be treated as integers. Several examples appeared in the Applications Capsules at the beginning of this chapter. Other examples follow.

Kelly-Springfield The Kelly-Springfield Tire Company has a model-based system to coordinate sales forecasting, inventory control, production planning, and distribution decisions. One crucial link in this system is the production planning model. Central to this problem is the effect of setup time. In the manufacture of each particular line of tires a machine is "set up" by installing a piece of equipment (called a die) particular to that line. It takes a fixed amount of time (and thus a fixed cost) to remove one die from a machine and insert another. In other words, there is a fixed "changeover" or "setup" cost of moving from the production of one line of tires to another, no matter how many tires you decide to produce after the machine is set up. The decision to set up (i.e., to produce a particular line or not, in a given production period), or not, is treated as a 0/1 variable in the mixed-integer program used to attack this problem. The total integrated system (including the production planning system) is credited with impressive results. The system implemented in 1970 is estimated to have yielded savings of $500,000 a year. Since an improved system was installed in 1976, average unit inventory decreased by 19%, customer service improved, productivity increased, and additional savings totaling $7.9 million annually resulted. For more details, see "Coordinated Decisions for Increased Profits," *Interfaces*, Vol. 10, December 1980.

Flying Tiger Line Another interesting application concerns the use of integer programming by Flying Tiger Line (an all-cargo airline) in approaching two strategic questions: the design of their service network, and the selection and deployment of their aircraft fleet. The size of the IP used to attack this problem and the cost of solving it are staggering when your primary exposure has been to classroom problems. One model for 33 cities, 8 hubs (locations where cargo can be interchanged), and 10 aircraft types included 843 constraints, 3807 continuous variables, and 156 integer (aircraft selector) variables. No explicit cost savings are included in the presentation of this application. Management's satisfaction with the project, however, is obvious from the ongoing nature of the investigation. For a detailed account, see "A Mixed-Integer Programming Approach to Air Cargo Fleet Planning," *Management Science*, November 1980.

Hunt-Wesson Foods A third application is a major distribution system study for Hunt-Wesson Foods, Inc. The problem is to select sites for regional distribution centers and to determine what customer zones each distribution center should serve, as well as which of several plants should supply the distribution centers. The problem is an IP with two types of integer variables:

$y_k = 1$ if site k is used for a distribution center and 0 if it is not

$y_{kl} = 1$ if customer district l is served by the warehouse at site k and 0 if it is not

The quantities of material shipped are continuous variables.

The problem involved 17 commodity classes, 14 plants, 45 possible distribution center sites, and 121 customer zones. The IP model used to attack it had 11,854 rows, 727 0 or 1 integer variables, and 23,513 continuous variables. A special algorithm was constructed to solve the problem. In the article describing this problem the authors state that the realizable annual cost savings produced by the study are estimated to be in the low-seven figures. For more details, see "Multicommodity Distribution System Design by Benders Decomposition," *Management Science*, January 1974.

The three studies cited here have a number of features in common:

1. Each attacked a major problem of strategic importance to a firm.
2. Each made a significant contribution to successfully dealing with the problem.
3. Each included a large-scale mixed-integer program.
4. Clever modeling and/or special algorithms were required in each application.
5. Each project required a major commitment of funds and managerial talent.

The examples illustrate that a good model may enable management to achieve a level of analysis and performance that might otherwise be impossible, but such models are costly to develop, and often require an ongoing and time-consuming input from management. In all of the examples the authors (of the articles) stressed a close working relationship between the analysts (modelers) and management. In the case of Kelly-Springfield, the current model has evolved over a 15-year horizon with two major efforts. We see, then, that the use of quantitative models to solve important problems may well entail a serious commitment to a long process. Small tactical problems may be successfully subdued with a quick "off the shelf" treatment. Fundamental strategic problems are seldom that obliging.

11.7

NETWORK MODELS

Network problems constitute a large and special class of LP models. These problems have a special mathematical form, called a **special structure**, that endows the model with two
powerful properties:

349

CHAPTER 11
Integer
Programming
and Network
Models

Property 1: Very efficient solution algorithms have been developed.

Property 2: Under quite general assumptions, there will be an optimal solution for which the decision variables have integer values. Moreover, such a solution (as opposed to an alternative optimal fractional solution) is always produced by the existing algorithms.

Property 2 is of great interest since, as we have seen, integrality conditions may be important. Models *requiring* fractional (as opposed to integer) solutions simply do not exist. Thus, it is entirely advantageous that an integer solution is always produced. We shall introduce network models with the following example.

11.8
AN EXAMPLE: SEYMOUR MILES (A CAPACITATED TRANSSHIPMENT MODEL)

Seymour Miles is the distribution manager for Zigwell Inc., PROTRAC's largest midwestern distributor. Zigwell distributes its crawler tractors in five midwestern states. Currently, Seymour has 10 E-9s *in situ* at what we shall designate as site ①. These crawlers must be delivered to two major construction sites denoted as sites ③ and ④. Three E-9s are required at site ③ and seven are required at site ④. Because of prearranged schedules concerning driver availability, these crawlers may be distributed only according to any of the alternative routes shown in Figure 11.17, called a **network diagram**.

The Arcs In Figure 11.17, each of the arrows between sites is termed an **arc**, or **branch**, of the network. The arc from ② to ④ is sometimes denoted symbolically by the pair (2, 4).

Figure 11.17
Diagram for Seymour's Problem

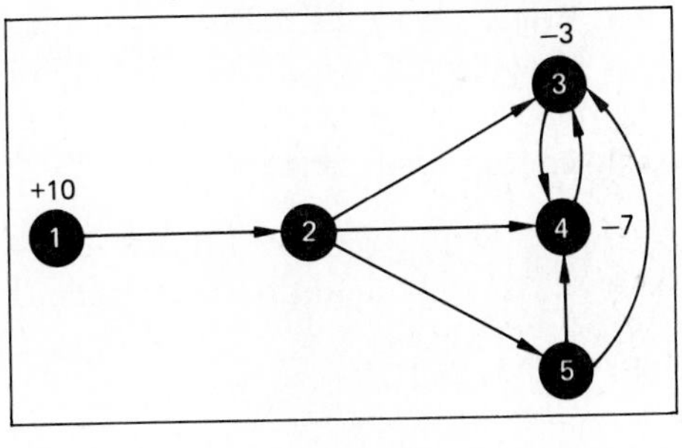

The Nodes Each site is termed a **node** of the network. The figure shows a +10 identified with site ①. This means that 10 E-9s (items of **supply**) are available at this site. The identifiers -3 and -7 attached to sites ③ and ④, respectively, denote the **requirements** or **demands** at these two sites. The figure also indicates that E-9s may be delivered to site ③ via any of the alternative routings ① → ② → ③, ① → ② → ④ → ③, ① → ② → ⑤ → ④ → ③, or ① → ② → ⑤ → ③. Which of the allowable routes is ultimately selected will be determined by the associated **costs** of traversing the routes and **capacities** along the routes. These additional data are shown in Figure 11.18. For convenience the costs and capacities are represented in symbolic (i.e., parametric) notation. The costs c_{ij} are *per unit costs*. For example, the cost of traversing arc (5, 3) is c_{53} per crawler. These costs are primarily due to fuel, tolls, and the cost of the driver for the average time it takes

Capacities and Costs

350

CHAPTER 11
Integer
Programming
and Network
Models

to traverse the arc. Because of preestablished agreements with the Teamsters, Zigwell must change drivers at each site it encounters on a route. Because of limitations on the current availability of drivers, there is an upper bound on the number of crawlers that may traverse any given arc. Thus, as an example, u_{53} is the upper bound or *capacity* on arc (5, 3).

Figure 11.18
Capacities and Cost Appended

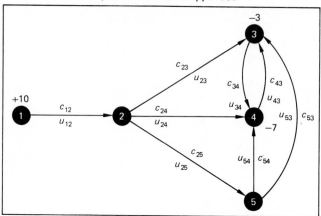

Seymour's problem is to find a shipment plan that satisfies the demands at minimum cost subject to the capacity constraints. You can now appreciate the trade-offs facing Seymour. For example, if $c_{25} + c_{53}$ is less than c_{23}, the route ① → ② → ⑤ → ③ will have a total cost which is less than the total cost of route ① → ② → ③, and hence ① → ② → ⑤ → ③ is preferred to ① → ② → ③. However, the maximum number of E-9s that can be sent across the preferred route is min $\{u_{12}, u_{25}, u_{53}\}$. If this number is less than three, the number of E-9s required at 3, all of the shipment cannot be accomplished via ① → ② → ⑤ → ③. This is a problem in only five nodes and eight arcs and even in a simplified example such as this the optimal solution may not be obvious. Imagine such a problem with 30 or 40 nodes and many more arcs.

Seymour's problem is called a **capacitated transshipment model**. We now show that this problem can easily be expressed as an LP. First, define the decision variables

$$x_{ij} = \text{total number of E-9s sent on arc } (i, j)$$
$$= \text{flow from node } i \text{ to node } j$$

Then the problem is

Min $c_{12}x_{12} + c_{23}x_{23} + c_{24}x_{24} + c_{25}x_{25} + c_{34}x_{34} + c_{43}x_{43} + c_{53}x_{53} + c_{54}x_{54}$

s.t. $+x_{12}$ $= 10$

$-x_{12} + x_{23} + x_{24} + x_{25}$ $= 0$

$-x_{23}$ $- x_{43} - x_{53} + x_{34}$ $= -3$

$- x_{24}$ $+ x_{43}$ $- x_{34} - x_{54} = -7$

$- x_{25}$ $+ x_{53}$ $+ x_{54} = 0$

$0 \le x_{ij} \le u_{ij}, \quad \text{all arcs } (i, j) \text{ in the network}$

There are now a number of observations to be made about this model.

351

CHAPTER 11
Integer
Programming
and Network
Models

1. The problem is indeed an LP. There is one variable x_{ij} associated with each arc in the network (Figure 11.17). There are eight arcs in this network and thus eight corresponding variables, $x_{12}, x_{23}, x_{24}, x_{25}, x_{43}, x_{53}, x_{34},$ and x_{54}. The objective is to minimize total cost.

2. There is one equation associated with each node in the network. The first equation says that the total flow *out of* node ① is 10 units. Recall that this is the total supply at node ①. The second equation says that the total flow *out of* node ② (namely, x_{32}

Flow Balance
Equations

$+ x_{24} + x_{25}$) minus the total flow *into* node ② (namely, x_{12}) is zero. In other words, the total flow out of node ② must equal the total flow into node ②. The third equation says that the total flow *out of* node ③ (namely, x_{34}) must be 3 units less than the total flow *into* node ③ (namely, $x_{23} + x_{43} + x_{53}$). This is the mathematical way of expressing the requirement for a *net delivery* of 3 units to node ③. The equations for nodes ④ and ⑤, respectively, have similar interpretations. Thus, the equation for each node expresses a **flow balance** and takes into account the fact that the node may be either a **supply point** or a **demand point** or neither. Intermediate nodes (such as 2 and 5 in Figure 11.17) which are neither supply points nor demand points are often termed **transshipment nodes**.

3. The *positive* right-hand sides correspond to nodes that are net suppliers (*origins*). The *negative* right-hand sides correspond to nodes that are net destinations (*demand points*). The *zero* right-hand sides correspond to nodes that have neither supply nor demand (*transshipment nodes*). The sum of all right-hand-side terms is zero, which means that *the total supply in the network equals the total demand.*

4. The **special structure** of this network model is revealed by placing the data of the constraints in the tableau format shown in Figure 11.19 called a **node-arc incidence**

Node Arc
Incidence
Matrix

matrix. Each row of Figure 11.19 corresponds to a node and contains the data of the corresponding constraint in the LP. Each column of Figure 11.19 corresponds to an arc (or a variable). Since there are eight arcs in the model, there are eight corresponding columns in the tableau. The key to the *special structure* of this network model is the fact that in each column of the node–arc incidence matrix there is a $+1$ and a -1 and the remaining terms are zero. The $+1$ is in the row corresponding to the node at which the arc originates. The -1 is in the row corresponding to the node at which the arc terminates. In Figure 11.19, consider the column under arc (2, 5). Since this arc originates at node 2, there is a $+1$ in row 2. Since the arc terminates at node 5, there is a -1 in row 5. All other entries in this column are zero. It should be noted that the node–arc incidence matrix can be created directly from Figure 11.17 without first writing down the LP. Similarly, Figure 11.17 could be constructed from the data in Figure 11.19 (or from the LP). In other words, Figures 11.17 and 11.19 are equivalent ways of communicating

Figure 11.19
Node–Arc Incidence Matrix

NODE	(1, 2)	(2, 3)	(2, 4)	(2, 5)	(4, 3)	(5, 3)	(3, 4)	(5, 4)	RHS
				ARC					
1	+1	0	0	0	0	0	0	0	10
2	-1	+1	+1	+1	0	0	0	0	0
3	0	-1	0	0	-1	-1	+1	0	-3
4	0	0	-1	0	+1	0	-1	-1	-7
5	0	0	0	-1	0	+1	0	+1	0

the network structure of Seymour's problem. In large real-world problems it may not be evident whether your model is, in fact, a network model. That is why the node–arc incidence matrix is useful. It provides a convenient way to tell whether on not you are in fact dealing with a network problem.

11.9

A GENERAL FORMULATION OF THE CAPACITATED TRANSSHIPMENT MODEL

The Model   Seymour's problem is a special case of the following symbolic form of a general network model. Again, the decision variables x_{ij} will denote the "flow" from node i to node j across the arc connecting these two nodes.

$$
\begin{aligned}
\text{Min} \quad & \sum_{(i,j)} c_{ij} x_{ij} \\
\text{s.t.} \quad & \sum_{k} x_{jk} - \sum_{k} x_{kj} = L_j, \qquad j = 1, \ldots, n \\
& 0 \leq x_{ij} \leq u_{ij}, \qquad \text{all } (i, j) \text{ in the network}
\end{aligned}
$$

Let us observe that

1. The sum $\sum_{(i,j)} c_{ij} x_{ij}$ in the objective function is understood to be over all arcs in the network. Thus, the objective is to minimize the total cost of the flow.

2. Consider the jth constraint, for some fixed value of j. The sum $\sum_{k} x_{jk}$ is understood to be over all k for which arc (j, k), with j fixed, is in the network. Thus, $\sum_{k} x_{jk}$ is the total flow **out of** the specified node j. Similarly, $\sum_{k} x_{kj}$ is over all k for which arc (k, j), with j fixed, is in the network. Thus $\sum_{k} x_{kj}$ is the total flow **into** node j. Thus, the jth constraint says

$$\text{total flow out of node } j - \text{total flow into node } j = \text{supply at } j$$

where negative supply (i.e., $L_j < 0$) represents a requirement. Nodes with negative supply are called *destinations, sinks,* or *demand points.* Nodes with positive supply (i.e., $L_j > 0$) are called *origins, sources,* or *supply points.* Nodes with zero supply are called *transshipment points.*

3. Note that $\sum_{j=1}^{n} L_j = 0$ (i.e., total supply = total demand) and all $c_{ij} \geq 0$.

4. The last set of constraints places *capacities* on the flows x_{ij}. As a special case some of the u_{ij} could be infinitely large, meaning that these are arcs with no capacity constraints. Setting a zero value for a u_{ij} would be equivalent to eliminating arc (i, j) from the network.

5. The given data for the model are the c_{ij}'s, the L_j's, and the u_{ij}'s.

Its Importance   One reason that the *capacitated transshipment model* (often called *the network model,* or the *general network model*) is of interest is that several important management decision problems are special cases. In particular the *transportation problem, assignment problem,* and *shortest-route problem* are special cases of the capacitated transshipment model and

353

CHAPTER 11
Integer
Programming
and Network
Models

the *maximal flow problem* is closely related. These special problems are also referred to as *network models*.

There are two advantages in being able to identify a problem as a special case of the general network (or capacitated transshipment) model. First, theoretical results that are established for the general model apply automatically to the specific cases. The outstanding example of this phenomenon is the integer property which we alluded to at the beginning of Section 11.7. We now can state this property more precisely.

If all terms L_j and u_{ij} are integers in the capacitated transshipment model, there will always be an integer-valued optimal solution to this problem. Moreover, such an optimal solution will be produced by the simplex algorithm as well as by the special modifications of this algorithm which specifically attack the various network problems.

From earlier chapters you know that LP models do not in general yield optimal solutions that have integer-valued variables. The network model with integer values for all L_j and u_{ij} does. This has an important implication on the usefulness of the various special versions of the network model.

The second reason it is useful to identify a problem as a special case of the capacitated transshipment model is that the *special structure* of this model typically makes it possible to find a special algorithm that solves the problem more easily than applying the general simplex algorithm. The impact of some of the superefficient codes derived from the special structure of the network model is rather amazing. Recently, the Internal Revenue Service constructed a network model with 50,000 constraints and 60 million variables. Only 1 hour of high-speed computer time was required to solve the problem. It turns out that in such a problem it can require less time to obtain the optimal solution than to read the output. The remainder of this chapter is devoted to a presentation of important special cases of the general network model.

11.10

THE TRANSPORTATION AND ASSIGNMENT MODELS

There are m origins or supply points (plants, for example), and n destinations (warehouses, marketing areas, and so on) for a single product. Each destination has a demand, D_j, and each origin has a supply, S_i. It costs c_{ij} to ship a unit from origin i to destination j. The problem is to find a shipping schedule that does not violate the supply constraints and satisfies the demand constraints at a minimum cost.

Transportation Problem

We have previously presented this model with inequality constraints. However, it can always be written with equality constraints instead, by making the following observations. The demand constraints will always be active. Hence, they can be written as either $\geq$ or $=$. If total supply is equal to total demand, then since all supply must be used, the $\leq$ constraints may be written as $=$. If total supply exceeds total demand, then each $\leq$ supply constraint can be converted to an equality by introducing a slack variable. (Each such slack, say $x_{i,n+1}$, can be interpreted as the amount shipped from origin i to some artificial destination called $n + 1$, to which the shipping cost is zero.) Hence, without loss of generality, the formal **transportation model** can be stated in equality form as

354

CHAPTER 11
Integer
Programming
and Network
Models

$$\text{Min} \ \sum_{i=1}^{m} \sum_{j=1}^{n} c_{ij} x_{ij}$$

$$\text{s.t.} \ \sum_{j=1}^{n} x_{ij} = S_i \qquad i = 1, \ldots, m$$

$$\sum_{i=1}^{m} x_{ij} = D_j \qquad j = 1, \ldots, n$$

$$x_{ij} \geq 0, \text{ all } i, j$$

We now note that this is a special case of the general network model, given in Section 11.9. In particular, it is a problem with m sources, n sinks, and mn possible arcs. It follows that if the S_i and D_j are positive integers, then at least one optimal corner solution will be integer-valued, and the simplex method will lead to such a solution. We also note that the c_{ij} terms can incorporate per-unit production costs as well as the cost for shipping.

As a special case of the transportation problem, let each $S_i = 1$, each $D_j = 1$, and $m = n$. Then we obtain

$$\text{Min} \ \sum_{i=1}^{n} \sum_{j=1}^{n} c_{ij} x_{ij}$$

$$\text{s.t.} \ \sum_{j=1}^{n} x_{ij} = 1 \qquad i = 1, \ldots, n$$

$$\sum_{i=1}^{n} x_{ij} = 1 \qquad j = 1, \ldots, n$$

$$x_{ij} \geq 0$$

Assignment Problem This special form of the transportation model is called the **assignment problem**. Note that since there is always an integer solution, the constraints imply there is always a solution in which each x_{ij} is zero or one. The variables are often interpreted as follows:

$$x_{ij} = \begin{cases} 1 & \text{means assign agent } i \text{ to task } j \\ 0 & \text{means do not assign agent } i \text{ to task } j \end{cases}$$

In accordance with these definitions, the assignment model can be given the following meaning. There are n agents and n tasks. Each agent must be assigned to a single task, and each task must have a single agent assigned to it. The cost of assigning agent i to task j is c_{ij}. Find a minimum-cost assignment that satisfies all of the constraints. Of course, the literal problem underlying such a model may have nothing to do with the assignment of people to tasks. The same model can arise in allocating weapons to targets and, as in Section 11.3, to attack sequence and routing problems (c.f. the **travelling salesman** discussion).

11.11

THE SHORTEST-ROUTE PROBLEM

The shortest-route problem refers to a network for which each arc (i, j) has an associated number c_{ij} which is interpreted as the distance (or possibly the cost, or time) from node i to node j. A **route**, or a **path**, between two nodes is any sequence of arcs connecting the two nodes. The objective is to find the *shortest* (or *least cost* or *least time*) routes from a specific node to *each* of the other nodes in the network.

Aaron's Delivery Service

As an illustration, Aaron Drunner makes frequent wine deliveries to seven different sites. Figure 11.20 shows the seven sites together with the possible travel routes between sites. Note that here, unlike the transshipment model, the arcs are *nondirected*. That is, on each arc, flow is permitted in either direction. Each arc in Figure 11.20 has been labeled with the distance between the nodes the arc connects. The home base is denoted H. Aaron feels that his overall costs will be minimized by making sure that any future delivery to any given site is made along the shortest route to that site. Thus, his objective is to specify the seven shortest routes from node H to each of the other seven nodes. Note that in this problem, as stated, the task is not to find optimal x_{ij}'s. The task is to find an optimal set of routes.

Figure 11.20
Aaron's Network of Sites

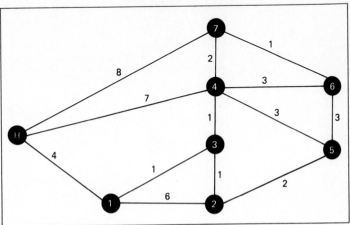

Given the source H, and any particular sink, G, a formal statement of the model is

$$\text{Min} \quad \sum_i \sum_{j \neq i} c_{ij} x_{ij}$$

$$\text{s.t.} \quad \sum_{k \neq j} x_{jk} - \sum_{k \neq j} x_{kj} = \begin{cases} 1 & \text{if } j = \text{source} = \text{H} \\ 0 & \text{if } j \neq \text{source, sink} \\ -1 & \text{if } j = \text{sink} = \text{G} \end{cases}$$

$$x_{ij} \geq 0$$

The solution to this problem will reveal the optimal (the shortest) route from source to sink.

An Application: Equipment Replacement

Lisa Carr is responsible for obtaining reproduction equipment (Xerox-like machines) for PROTRAC's secretarial service. She must choose between leasing newer equipment at high rental cost but low maintenance cost or more used equipment with lower rental costs but higher maintenance costs. Lisa has a four-period time horizon to consider. Let c_{ij} denote the cost of *leasing* new equipment at the beginning of period i, $i = 1, 2, 3, 4$, and *maintaining* it to the beginning of period j, where j can take on the values $i + 1, \ldots, 5$. If the equipment is maintained only to the beginning of period j, for $j < 5$, new equipment must again be leased at the beginning of j. For example, several alternative feasible policies are:

355

356

CHAPTER 11
Integer
Programming
and Network
Models

1. Lease new equipment at the beginning of each time period. Presumably, such a policy would involve the highest leasing charges and the minimum maintenance charges. The total (leasing + maintenance) cost of this policy would be $c_{12} + c_{23} + c_{34} + c_{45}$.

2. Lease new equipment only at the beginning of period 1 and maintain it through all successive periods. This would undoubtedly be a policy of minimum rental cost but maximum maintenance. The total (leasing + maintenance) cost of this policy would be c_{15}.

3. Lease new equipment at the beginning of periods 1 and 3. The total cost would be $c_{13} + c_{35}$.

Of all feasible policies, Lisa desires one with a minimum cost. The solution to this problem is obtained by finding the shortest (i.e., in this case, minimum cost) route from node 1 to node 5 of the network shown in Figure 11.21. Each node on the shortest route denotes a replacement, that is, a period at which new equipment should be leased.

Figure 11.21
Network for Lisa's Decision

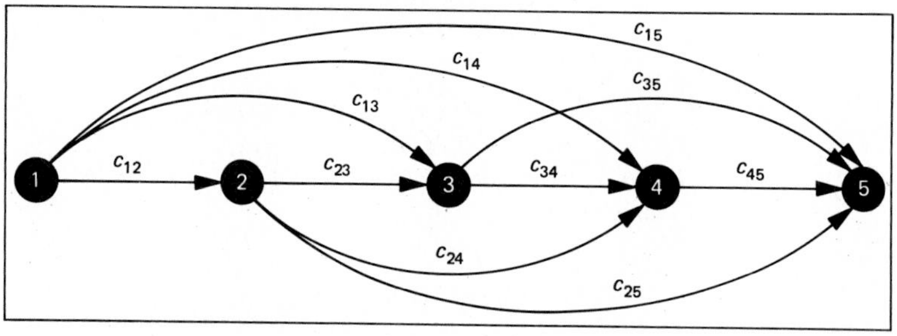

11.12

THE MIN-COST-FLOW PROBLEM

This is a generalization of the shortest-route model. Consider a network with n nodes and m arcs. Associated with every arc there is an arc capacity b_{ij} that indicates the maximum amount of flow that is allowed to traverse the arc from node i to node j. If x_{ij} is the arc flow, then $0 \le x_{ij} \le b_{ij}$. As before, c_{ij} is the cost of shipping one unit of flow along (i, j). The objective is to find the min-cost path of sending v units of flow from source to sink. Note that if for all (i, j) on the shortest path from source to sink, we have $v \le b_{ij}$, then the arc capacities are not constraining and the shortest path will give the solution. In general, however, this will not be the case. Formally, the min-cost-flow problem can be stated as

$$\text{Min} \ \sum_i \sum_{j \ne i} c_{ij} x_{ij}$$

$$\text{s.t.} \ \sum_{k \ne j} x_{jk} - \sum_{k \ne j} x_{kj} = \begin{cases} v & \text{if } j = \text{source} \\ 0 & \text{if } j \ne \text{source, sink} \\ -v & \text{if } j = \text{sink} \end{cases}$$

$$0 \le x_{ij} \le b_{ij}$$

THE MAX-FLOW PROBLEM

The problem is to find the maximum amount of flow that can be routed from a single source to a single sink in a network that has capacities on the arcs. Formally, the problem is

$$\text{Max} \quad v$$

$$\text{s.t.} \quad \sum_{k \neq j} x_{jk} - \sum_{k \neq j} x_{kj} = \begin{cases} v & \text{if } j = \text{source} \\ -v & \text{if } j = \text{sink} \\ 0 & \text{otherwise} \end{cases}$$

$$0 \leq x_{ij} \leq b_{ij}$$

where the summations above are over the nodes for which x_{ij} is defined.

This problem, together with the shortest-path problem, is of interest in its own right. It also appears as a subproblem in solving other more complicated models. For such reasons, as well as because of some of the theoretic underpinnings (which go beyond our present scope of interest), it is sometimes stated that these two problems (shortest path and max flow) are of central importance in network theory.

The Urban Development Planning Commission

Here is an example of the maximal-flow problem. Gloria Stime is in charge of the UDPC (Urban Development Planning Commission) ad hoc special interest study group. This group's current responsibility is to coordinate the construction of the new subway system with the highway maintenance department. Due to the construction of the new subway system in the proximity of the city's beltway, the eastbound traffic on the beltway must be detoured. The planned detour actually involves a network of alternative routes which have been proposed by the highway maintenance department. Different speed limits and traffic patterns produce different flow capacities on the various arcs of the proposed network. This is shown in Figure 11.22.

Figure 11.22

Proposed Network and Flow Capacities (Thousands of Vehicles per Hour)

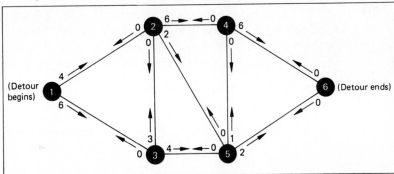

Node ① denotes the beginning of the detour, that is, the point at which the eastbound traffic leaves the beltway. Node ⑥ is the point at which the detoured traffic reenters the beltway. Also, in Figure 11.22, the flow capacities depend on the direction of the flow. The symbol 6 on arc (1, 3) denotes a capacity of 6000 vehicles per hour in the $1 \rightarrow 3$ direction. The symbol 0 on the same arc means that a zero capacity exists in the $3 \rightarrow 1$ direction. This is because the indicated arc (1, 3) denotes a one-way street from ① to ③. In this example it is seen that each of the other arcs denotes one-way travel.

The Max Flow/
Min Cut Result

One of the key theoretic results in network theory relates to the maximal-flow problem. The result, called the **max flow/min cut theorem**, is very simple to state. We first define the notion of a *cut* and a *cut capacity*.

- ■ *Cut:* A partition of the entire collection of nodes into two disjoint classes, say C_1 and C_n, where the source is in C_1 and the sink is in C_n.
- ■ *Cut capacity:* Consider all individual arcs that directly connect a node in C_1 to a node in C_n. The sum of the capacities on these arcs, in the $C_1 \rightarrow C_n$ direction, is called *the cut capacity*.

In Gloria's network, Figure 11.22, there are many possible cuts. Several are shown in Figure 11.23.

Figure 11.23
Illustrative Cuts and Cut Capacities

C_1	C_n	CUT CAPACITY
1, 2, 3, 5	4, 6	9
1, 2, 3	4, 5, 6	12
1	2, 3, 4, 5, 6	10
1, 2, 3, 4, 5	6	8
1, 2	3, 4, 5, 6	14

To calculate the cut capacity of the first cut in Figure 11.23 we must sum up the capacities on each of the arcs connecting a node in C_1 with a node in C_n. In this case we must sum the capacities on arcs (2, 4), (5, 4), and (5, 6). Since these capacities are 6, 1, and 2, respectively, the cut capacity is 9. Other cut capacities are calculated in a similar manner.

You can see in Figure 11.23 that the smallest of the cut capacities is 8, which turns out to be the maximal flow in Gloria's network. The *max flow/min cut theorem* states that this equality will always be true. Intuitively, it generalizes the concept that the maximal flow on any *path* is equal to the min of the capacities on the path. Thus, we have

---

MAX FLOW/MIN CUT THEOREM: **The maximal flow in any network is equal to the minimal-cut capacity.**

11.14

NOTES ON IMPLEMENTATION OF NETWORK MODELS

Network models and integer programming often go hand in hand. Also, network models are among the most important applications of management science, and specialization in this topic has become a career path in the field. Along this line, in recent years one has

359

CHAPTER 11
Integer
Programming
and Network
Models

seen the appearance of a number of consulting firms that deal exclusively with network applications. The main emphasis of such firms is often on strategic planning problems from the point of view of "distribution" studies, where the term "distribution" is taken in a quite general sense: flow of physical product, information, vehicles, cash, and so on.

The software libraries for most of the large computer systems include packages for solving various network problems. Some of the "state of the art" software for very large scale applications must be purchased from private vendors.

The application of network models to real problems involves considerable skill and experience in casting problems, which initially may not appear to be network models, into a network representation. For example, an LP model for a problem of interest may not be a network problem, but its dual may in fact have a network structure; or the network structure may emerge in the dual only after some clever manipulation of the original problem. To capitalize on the advantages of the network structure, it is often worth the price of "straining" the initial formulation to cast it (or its dual) into a network representation.

As a final note, it is worth emphasizing that many real problems contain subproblems which may have a network form.

11.15
EXAMPLES AND SOLUTIONS

Example 1

Consider model (III) of the plant location problem in Section 11.3. Suppose we wish to impose the additional constraint that at least three plant locations must be used, and a route from plant 1 to the first marketing district can be used only if plant 2 is also used. How can these conditions be imposed?

Solution to Example 1

Add the following constraints to the model:

$$\sum_{i=1}^{m} y_i \geq 3 \qquad \text{(at least three plants)}$$
$$z_{11} \leq y_2 \qquad \text{(route 1–1 is used only if plant 2 is used)}$$

Example 2

Consider the following linear constraints. Construct the corresponding node-arc incidence matrix and the associated network diagram, labeling each arc with the flow variable and each node with its supply.

$$
\begin{array}{rcll}
x_1 + x_2 \qquad\qquad + x_5 \qquad\qquad\qquad\qquad & = & 2 & ① \\
- x_2 + x_3 \qquad\qquad\qquad\qquad\qquad & = & 1 & ② \\
-x_1 \qquad\qquad + x_4 \qquad\qquad\qquad\qquad & = & 0 & ③ \\
- x_3 \qquad - x_5 + x_6 \qquad + x_8 & = & 0 & ④ \\
- x_4 \qquad\qquad + x_7 - x_8 & = & 0 & ⑤ \\
- x_6 - x_7 \qquad & = & -3 & ⑥ \\
\end{array}
$$
$$x_j \geq 0, j = 1, \ldots, 8$$

Solution to Example 2

The node–arc incidence matrix will have eight columns (equal to the number of variables) and six rows (equal to the number of constraints), as shown in Figure 11.24. We recall that each variable corresponds to an arc, with $+1$ denoting the node of origin and -1 the termination. The network diagram is shown in Figure 11.25.

Figure 11.24

NODES	x_1	x_2	x_3	x_4	x_5	x_6	x_7	x_8	SUPPLIES
1	1	1			1				2
2		-1	1						1
3	-1			1					0
4			-1		-1	1		1	0
5				-1			1	-1	0
6						-1	-1		-3

Figure 11.25

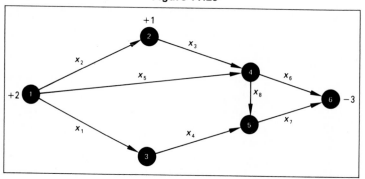

Example 3

Write the linear constraints corresponding to the network in Figure 11.26. Use double-subscript notation.

Figure 11.26

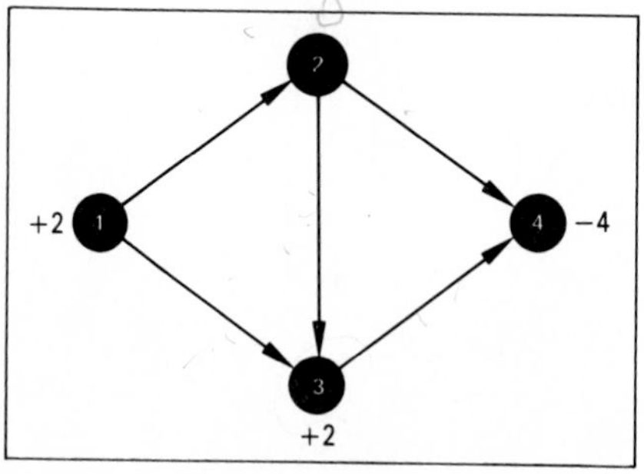

Solution to Example 3

$$
\begin{aligned}
\text{Node 1:} \quad & x_{12} + x_{13} && = 2 \\
\text{Node 2:} \quad & x_{24} + x_{23} - x_{12} && = 0 \\
\text{Node 3:} \quad & x_{34} - x_{13} - x_{23} && = 2 \\
\text{Node 4:} \quad & -x_{24} - x_{34} && = -4
\end{aligned}
$$

Example 4

Consider the following four-period production model:

x_t = amount to be produced
in period t
(Decision variable)

d_t = demand in period t (known data)

I_t = inventory at end of period t

h_t = per unit cost of holding inventory at end of period t

Assume demand in each period must be satisfied, so that

$$
\left.\begin{array}{l}
I_t = I_{t-1} + x_t - d_t \\
I_t \geq 0
\end{array}\right\} \quad t = 1, 2, 3, 4
$$

where $I_0 = 0$. Let the cost of producing in period t be given by

$$
C_t(x_t) = \begin{cases}
x_t & \text{if } x_t = 0 \\
C_t x_t + F_t & \text{if } x_t > 0
\end{cases}
$$

Formulate the problem of determining a four-period production policy that satisfies demand at a minimum cost. (*Hint*: Use 0/1 variables.)

Solution to Example 4

$$
\text{Min} \quad \sum_{t=1}^{4} (C_t x_t + z_t F_t + h_t I_t)
$$

$$
\begin{aligned}
\text{s.t.} \quad & I_t = I_{t-1} + x_t - d_t && t = 1, 2, 3, 4 \\
& x_t - z_t U \leq 0 && t = 1, 2, 3, 4 \\
& x_t, I_t \geq 0 && t = 1, 2, 3, 4 \\
& z_t = 0 \text{ or } 1 && t = 1, 2, 3, 4
\end{aligned}
$$

where $I_0 = 0$ and U is very large.

MAJOR CONCEPTS QUIZ

True–False

1. T F Rounding LP solutions to meet the real-world requirement for integer decision variables is a common practice.

2. T F In general, it is no more difficult to solve an IP than an LP.

3. T F The binary variable in an IP may be used to represent dichotomous decisions.

4. T F In a *max* problem, the OV of the LP relaxation always provides a *lower bound* on the OV of the original IP.

5. T F The first step in obtaining a rounded solution to an IP is to solve its LP relaxation.

6. T F Solving a two-dimensional IP by complete enumeration involves evaluating the objective function at all corners of the feasible set of the LP relaxation.

7. T F In the LP relaxation of the IP capital budgeting problem there are as many constraints as there are periods.

8. T F In an IP with n binary decision variables, x_i, $i = 1, \ldots, n$, each of which indicates the selection (or not) of an alternative, the condition that no more than k alternatives be selected can be imposed with the constraint $x_1 + x_2 + \cdots x_n \leq k$.

9. T F In STECO's warehouse location problem, the optimal number of trucks to send from each warehouse to each plant was an integer because after the warehouses are selected the problem is a transportation problem with integer supplies and demands.

10. T F Suppose x_1 and x_2 are both binary variables where $x_i = 1$ has the interpretation of building a plant in location i. The condition "a plant can be built in location 2 only if the plant in location 1 is also built" is captured with the constraint $x_1 \leq x_2$.

11. T F Consider a transportation model with integer supplies and demands and where, in addition, integrality conditions are imposed on the x_{ij}'s. Since this makes the problem an integer program, it must be solved with special IP codes.

12. T F A capacitated transshipment problem has one variable for each node.

13. T F A node–arc incidence matrix for the network problem has a +1, a −1, and all other entries 0 in each column.

14. T F If the right-hand side of any arc capacity inequality in a capacitated transshipment problem is zero, the problem is infeasible.

15. T F The maximal flow through any path in a network is equal to the minimum arc capacity on that path.

16. T F In the maximal-flow problem a cut is *any* two disjoint sets of nodes.

Multiple Choice

17. A positive right-hand side in a flow balance equation of a capacitated transshipment problem indicates that
   a. the node is an origin
   b. the node is a destination
   c. the node is a transshipment node
   d. both a and b

18. To be sure that there is an optimal integer solution to a capacitated transshipment problem, it must be required that
   a. the right-hand side of all flow equations (the L_j's) be integer
   b. the arc capacities (the u_{ij}'s) be integer
   c. either a or b
   d. both a and b

363

CHAPTER 11
Integer
Programming
and Network
Models

19. In the maximal-flow problem the maximixed flow is equal to
  a. the flow over an arbitrary cut
  b. the maximal capacity over all cuts
  c. the minimal cut capacity
  d. none of the above

20. In a pure integer linear program
  a. ignoring integrality restrictions, all constraints are linear
  b. all decision variables must be integers
  c. all decision variables must be nonnegative
  d. all of the above

21. In a mixed integer linear program
  a. the objective function is linear
  b. all decision variables must be integers
  c. some coefficients are restricted to be integers, others are not
  d. all of the above

22. The LP relaxation of an IP
  a. permits a nonlinear objective function
  b. ignores the integrality restrictions on the decision variables
  c. relaxes the nonnegativity restrictions on the decision variables
  d. all of the above

23. A rounded solution to a max IP may not be feasible because
  a. it violates the integrality constraints
  b. it violates the nonnegativity constraints
  c. its OV is smaller than the OV of the LP relaxation
  d. none of the above

24. If x_k and x_m are 0/1 variables indicating the selection of projects k and m, respectively, the constraint $x_k + x_m \leq 0$ implies that
  a. k cannot be selected unless m is selected
  b. k must be selected if m is selected
  c. m cannot be selected unless k is selected
  d. none of the above

25. Suppose a product can be manufactured either not at all or else in lot sizes $\geq L$ and let x be the quantity of the product produced. The following two constraints are appropriate:
  a. $x + Uy \leq 0; x - Ly \geq 0$
  b. $x - Uy \geq 0; x - Ly \geq 0$
  c. $x - Uy \leq 0; x - Ly \geq 0$
  d. $x - Uy \leq 0; x - Ly \leq 0$
  where U is an arbitrarily large number and y is a 0/1 variable.

26. In solving a max IP a lower bound for the OV of the original problem can always be found by
  a. solving the LP relaxation and using the OV of the LP
  b. finding a feasible solution to the IP by any available means and evaluating the objective function
  c. solving the LP relaxation and then rounding fractions < 0.5 down, those ≥ 0.5 up, and evaluating the objective function at this point
  d. none of the above

27. The computer solution to a mixed-integer linear program
  a. contains no generally useful sensitivity information
  b. contains sensitivity information on only the noninteger variables
  c. contains sensitivity information only on right-hand sides
  d. contains sensitivity information only on the objective function

28. The biggest advantage to knowing whether or not a complex IP model is in fact a network model is
  a. you can draw a network diagram and then interpret it
  b. the flow interpretations may lend new insights
  c. you don't need to use an IP code to solve the problem
  d. the computer output will have different interpretations

364 *Answers*

CHAPTER 11
Integer
Programming
and Network
Models

1. T
2. F
3. T
4. F
5. T
6. F
7. F
8. T
9. T
10. F

11. F
12. F
13. T
14. F
15. T
16. F
17. a
18. d
19. c

20. d
21. a
22. b
23. d
24. d
25. c
26. b
27. a
28. c

11.17
PROBLEMS

IP Problems

11-1. A firm produces two products, A and C. Capacity on the A line is 7 units per day. Each unit of C requires 4 hours of drying time and a total of 22 drying hours per day is available. Also, each unit of A requires 2 hours of polishing and each unit of C requires 3 hours of polishing. A total of 19 hours of polishing time is available each day. Each unit of A yields a profit of $1, whereas each unit of C yields a profit of $3. The firm wants to determine a daily production schedule to maximize profits. A and C can only be produced in integer amounts.

(a) Formulate this problem as an IP.
(b) Use a graphical approach to find the optimal solution to the LP relaxation.
(c) Find the optimal solution to the IP.
(d) Find an integer solution by rounding each value in the answer to part b to *its integer part*. Is this solution feasible?
(e) How much profit would the firm lose by adopting the latter rounded solution?

11-2. Consider the following IP.

$$\text{Min} \quad 4x_1 + 5x_2$$
$$\text{s.t.} \quad 3x_1 + 6x_2 \geq 18$$
$$5x_1 + 4x_2 \geq 20$$
$$8x_1 + 2x_2 \geq 16$$
$$7x_1 + 6x_2 \leq 42$$
$$x_1 \geq 0 \text{ and integer}, \qquad x_2 \geq 0 \text{ and integer}$$

(a) Find the optimal solution to the LP relaxation.
(b) List all the feasible points.
(c) Find the optimal solution to the IP.
(d) Find a feasible rounded solution.
(e) Is the latter optimal?
(f) How large is the cost of using the rounded solution identified above relative to the optimal solution?

11-3. (a) Consider a minimization IP. Does the optimal value for the LP relaxation provide an upper or a lower bound for the optimal value of the IP?
(b) Consider a minimization IP. Does the value of the objective function at a feasible rounded solution provide an upper or a lower bound for the optimal value of the IP?

365

CHAPTER 11
Integer
Programming
and Network
Models

(c) Consider a maximization IP. Does the optimal value of the LP erlaxation of this problem provide an upper or a lower bound for the optimal value of the IP?

(d) Consider a maximization IP. Does the value of the objective function at a feasible rounded solution provide an upper or a lower bound for the optimal value of the IP?

11-4. A portfolio manager has just been given $100,000 to invest. She will choose her investments from among a list of 20 stocks. She knows that the net return from investing one dollar in stock i is r_i. (Thus, if she invests x_i dollars in stock i, she will end up with $(1 + r_i)x_i$ dollars.) In order to maintain a balanced portfolio, she adopts the following two rules of thumb:

1. She will not invest more than $20,000 in a single stock.

2. *If* she invests anything in a stock, she will invest at least $5000 in it.

The manager would like to maximize her return subject to these rules of thumb. Formulate this problem as a mixed-integer linear program. Define your decision variables carefully.

11-5. You are the scheduling coordinator for a small but growing airline. You must schedule *exactly one* flight out of Chicago to each of the following cities: Atlanta, Los Angeles, New York, and Peoria. The available departure slots are 8 A.M., 10 A.M., and 12 noon. Your airline has only two departure lounges, so at most two flights can be scheduled per slot. Demand suggests the expected profit contribution per flight as a function of departure time that is shown in Figure 11.27. Formulate a model for solving this problem. Define your decision variables carefully.

Figure 11.27
Expected Profit Contribution (thousands)

DESTINATION	TIME		
	8	10	12
Atlanta	10	9	8.5
Los Angeles	11	10.5	9.5
New York	17	16	15
Peoria	6.4	2.5	−1

11-6. A problem faced by an electrical utility each day is that of deciding which generators to start up. The utility in question has three generators with the characteristics shown in Figure 11.28. There are two periods in a day and the number of megawatts needed in the first period is 2900. The second period requires 3900 megawatts. A generator started in the first period may be used in the second period without incurring an additional startup cost. All major generators (e.g., A, B, and C above) are turned off at the end of each day. Formulate this problem as a mixed-integer program.

Figure 11.28

GENERATOR	FIXED STARTUP COST	COST PER PERIOD PER MEGAWATT USED	MAXIMUM CAPACITY IN EACH PERIOD (mW)
A	$3000	$5	2100
B	2000	4	1800
C	1000	7	3000

366

CHAPTER 11
Integer
Programming
and Network
Models

11-7. A certain production line makes two products. Relevant data are given in Figure 11.29. Total time available (for production and set up) each week is 40 hours. The firm has 10 units or product B and 0 units of product A in inventory before the start of week 1. The cost of carrying a unit of inventory from one week to the next is $3 for each product. Management policy is that all demand must be satisfied. Demand data are given in Figure 11.30. The line is torn down and cleaned each weekend. As a result, if either product is produced in a week the appropriate setup time cost is incurred. Note that it is possible to produce both products in the same week. If both are produced, both setup times and costs are incurred. No production can take place during the time that the line is being set up. Formulate this 3-week planning problem as a mixed-integer program. Define your notation carefully and use summation notation in your formulation.

11-8. The board of directors of a large manufacturing firm is considering the set of investments shown in Figure 11.31. Let R_i be the total revenue from investment i and C_i be the cost to make investment i. The board wishes to maximize total revenue and invest no more than a total of M dollars. Formulate this problem as an IP. Define your decision variables.

Figure 11.29

	PRODUCT	
	A	**B**
Setup time	6 hours	8 hours
Per unit production time	0.5 hour	0.75 hour
Setup cost	$120.00	$160.00
Per unit production cost	$6.00	$8.00

Figure 11.30

	WEEK		
PRODUCT	**1**	**2**	**3**
A	28	34	10
B	6	8	16

Figure 11.31

INVESTMENT	CONDITION
1	None
2	Only if 1
3	Only if 2
4	Must if 1 *and* 2
5	Not if 1 *or* 2
6	Not if 2 *and* 3
7	Only if 2 *and not* 3

11-9. A real estate developer is considering the set of investments described in Figure 11.32. Let R_i be the total revenue from investment i and C_i be the cost to make investment i. The developer wishes to maximize total revenue and invest no more than a total of M dollars. Formulate this problem as an IP. Define your decision variables.

367

CHAPTER 11
Integer
Programming
and Network
Models

Figure 11.32

INVESTMENT	CONDITION
1	None
2	Only if 1
3	Only if 1
4	Only if 2 *and* 3
5	None
6	Only if 5
7	Only if 5
8	Only if 6 *or* 7
9	None
10	Not if 11
11	Not if 10

11-10. Consider the following formulation of Problem 11-1.

$$\text{Max} \quad A + 3C$$
$$\text{s.t.} \qquad A \le 7$$
$$4C \le 22$$
$$2A + 3C \le 19$$
$$A \ge 0 \text{ and integer}, \qquad C \ge 0 \text{ and integer}$$

Plot the optimal objective value as a function of the RHS of the second constraint as the value of the RHS ranges between 0 and 24 [i.e., plot $V(b_2)$ for $0 \le b_2 \le 24$].
Use the graphical approach and the analysis performed in Problem 11-1.

11-11. Consider the IP presented in Problem 11-2.
Plot the optimal objective value as a function of the RHS of the constraint

$$3x_1 + 6x_2 \ge \text{RHS}$$

for $0 \le \text{RHS} \le 40$.

11-12. Consider the printout shown in Figure 11.15. Given the optimal values of YA, YB, and YC, write out the transportation model that could be used to determine the optimal truck allocations.

11-13. Consider the fixed-charge problem in Section 11.3.
(a) Suppose that x^* is a solution to (I). Show that x^*, z^* must be a solution to (II), where, for each j

$$z_j^* = \begin{cases} 1 & \text{if } x_j^* > 0 \\ 0 & \text{if } x_j^* = 0 \end{cases}$$

(b) Suppose that x^*, z^* is a solution to (II). Show that x^* must be a solution to (I).

11-14. Consider model (III) in the description of the plant location problem is Section 11.3.
(a) If there is a shipment from i to j, how do we know the route from i to j is paid for?
(b) How is it assured that if no routes are used from plant i, then plant i is not used?
(c) How do we know that if plant i is not used, then no routes from plant i will be used?
(d) How can you add to the model the specification that, at most, k plants and, at most, p routes can be used, where k is a known integer less than m, and p is a known integer between n and mn?

11-15. A method for satisfying at least k of m constraints was presented in Section 11.3. It included the constraints

$$\sum_{i=1}^{m} y_i \ge k$$
$$g_i(x_1, \ldots, x_n) \le b_i y_i + (1 - y_i)U \qquad i = 1, \ldots, m$$

368

CHAPTER 11
Integer
Programming
and Network
Models

We know that, in general, if we replace an inequality constraint with an equality constraint, it may turn out that the optimal objective value will be impaired. Argue that the constraint

$$\sum_{i=1}^{m} y_i \geq k$$

in the conditions above can always be assumed to be active, and hence, in this situation it is harmless to replace the inequality with an equality.

11-16. Suppose that the function $f(x_1, \ldots, x_n)$ is required to take on one of the values $v_1, \ldots, v_k$. Show how k 0/1 variables can be used to formulate this condition.

11.17. Consider the knapsack problem discussed in Section 11.3. Construct an example for which the method of ranking items according to value/weight will not lead to an optimal solution for the indivisible case.

11-18. Refer back to Problem 4-24. Use a 0/1 variable to formulate the discount modification of part (c).

11-19. Refer back to Problem 4-19(b). Modify the problem as follows. Products A, B, and C are purely competitive, and any amounts made may be sold at respective per-pound prices of $5, $4, and $5. The first 20 pounds of products D and E produced per week can be sold at $4 each, and all made in excess of 20 can be sold at $6 each. Reformulate the model as modified, using the variables $M1$, $M2$, and $M3$, and two new 0/1 variables y and z, and new variables:

$$D20 = \text{quantity of product } D \text{ produced in excess of 20}$$
$$E20 = \text{quantity of product } E \text{ produced in excess of 20}$$

11-20. This question focuses on one particular aspect of the production process in one of the PROTRAC plants, namely the soaking of frames for units of E and F, called E-frames and F-frames, in a heat-treatment facility. In reality, the plant has four heat-treatment facilities. Two were constructed when the plant was built, and two were recently added. These latter facilities differ from the former in both capacity and effectiveness. In general, there is a difference in the heat-treatment requirements (in temperature and in hours of soaking) for E-frames and F-frames. Also, because the E-frames and F-frames differ in volume and shape, the capacity of a facility depends on which type of frame is being treated. Since requirements differ, not both E- and F-frames can be treated in the same facility at the same time. All four facilities are run off a central fuel supply system that provides only A_4 soaking hours each quarter. In the coming quarter, it has been determined that the total number of batches to be heat-treated is β, and each batch will consist of N_E E-frames and N_F F-frames (where β, N_E, and N_F are given). These frames are prepared for treatment and then simultaneously delivered in a batch to the heat-treatment plant. These batches of fixed size must always be treated immediately upon arrival, and, in particular, all the frames are treated simultaneously. For this reason, deliveries are staggered in such a way that the facilities are empty when each new batch arrives. The problem is to divide each batch among the four facilities in such a way as to minimize quarterly fuel costs. Note that this will be equivalent to minimizing the fuel cost per batch. Figure 11.33 gives data on fuel costs, capacities, and soaking times (heating hours) required for the various facility/frame combinations. (For example, the fuel cost of using facility 1 for E-frames is $700, the capacity of facility 1 if used for E-frames is 6, the soaking time of an E-frame in facility 1 is 13 hours, and so on.) Note that although the soaking times for E-frames are less than for F-frames, the fuel cost is more because higher temperatures are required.

(a) State the optimization problem that is implicit in the above discussion in the form of a mathematical program, expressing the objective function and each constraint in prose, not symbols.

369

CHAPTER 11
Integer
Programming
and Network
Models

Figure 11.33

FRAME	FAC 1	FAC 2	FAC 3	FAC 4
		Fuel Cost ($)		
E	700	700	1,200	1,200
F	600	600	1,000	1,000
		Capacities (frames)		
E	6	6	4	4
F	9	9	5	5
		Soaking Times (hr)		
E	13	13	10	10
F	16	16	12	12

(b) For each batch, let E_i and F_i denote the number of E-frames and F-frames, respectively, treated in facility i. Let y_i be a variable that has the value 1 if facility i is to be used for E-frames. Otherwise, the value of the variable is 0. Let z_i be similarly defined for F-frames. For each facility, write three constraints that express the capacity conditions for that facility. One such constraint should say that if y_i is zero, then E_i must also be zero. Another should make a similar statement for z_i and F_i. The third constraint should say that if facility i is used for either type of frame, then it cannot be used for the other.

(c) Suppose that, at most, three facilities can be used on a given batch. Write a constraint that says this.

(d) Write constraints that say that N_E E-frames and N_F F-frames must be heat-treated.

(e) Write a constraint that says the total number of soaking hours per batch does not exceed A_4/β.

(f) Write the total cost of treating a batch with the policy E_i, F_i, $i = 1, 2, 3, 4$.

(g) Write out the complete mathematical program as developed in parts b through d in the form of a cost-min model. Note the relationship between the problem as now stated in symbols and your answer to part (a). How would you classify this model?

(h) Suppose that if facilities 1 and 2 are to be used at all, they must be prepared in advance and then relined at the end of the treatment. The combined cost of these operations is $1000 per facility. Include this in the model.

(i) Suppose that no fewer than four E-frames can be soaked in facility 1. Express this constraint.

(j) Suppose that F-frames in facility 1 can be soaked only in multiples of three. Express this constraint.

(k) Suppose that because of temporary equipment alterations, facility 1 can be used only if facility 2 is used. Express this constraint.

(l) What is the total number of hours the soaking facilities are used for treating the batch with the plan E_i, F_i, $i = 1, 2, 3, 4$ in the model from part (g)? How would you determine the average hourly cost of heat treating the batch (in this same model)?

Network Problems

11-21. Consider the following linear constraints of a transshipment model. Construct the corresponding node-arc incidence matrix and the associated network diagram, labeling each node with its supply or demand.

370

CHAPTER 11
Integer
Programming
and Network
Models

$$x_{13} + x_{12} + x_{14} = 2$$
$$-x_{12} + x_{24} = 1$$
$$-x_{13} + x_{35} = 0$$
$$-x_{24} - x_{14} + x_{46} + x_{45} = 0$$
$$-x_{35} + x_{56} - x_{45} = 0$$
$$-x_{46} - x_{56} = -3$$
$$x_{ij} \geq 0, \quad \text{all } (i, j)$$

11-22. Consider the following constraints.

$$x_{12} + x_{13} + x_{14} = 1$$
$$-x_{12} + x_{23} = 0$$
$$-x_{13} - x_{23} + x_{34} = 0$$
$$-x_{14} - x_{34} = -1$$

Construct the corresponding incidence matrix and network diagram.

11-23. Write the linear constraints corresponding to the transshipment network of Figure 11.34. Use double-subscript notation.

11-24. Write the linear constraints corresponding to the transshipment network of Figure 11.35. Use double-subscript notation.

11-25. Construct the incidence matrix for the network shown in Figure 11.35.

11-26. Consider the network shown in Figure 11.36 where ① is the source and ⑦ is the sink. The indicated cut partitions the network into the disjoint sets of nodes {①, ②} and {③, ④, ⑤, ⑥, ⑦}. The capacity of this cut is 55. What is the minimum-cut capacity?

11-27. Demonstrate that the transportation problem with S origins and D destinations is a special case of the capacitated transshipment model.

Figure 11.34   **Figure 11.35**

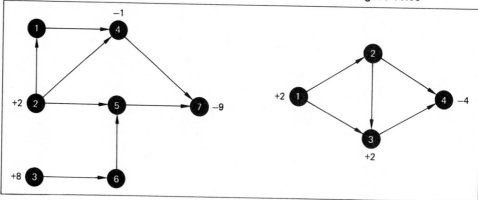

Figure 11.36

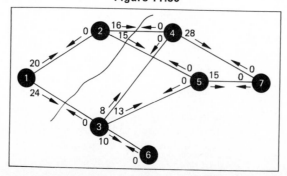

11-28. Demonstrate that the assignment problem is a special case of the capacitated transshipment model.

DIAGNOSTIC ASSIGNMENT

ASSIGNING SALES REPRESENTATIVES

One of the important themes in the text is that the manager plays the role of the intermediary between the real problem and the model. The manager must decide if the assumptions are appropriate and if the solution produced by the model makes sense in the context of the real problem.

Sally Erickson is midwest sales director for Lady Lynn Cosmetics. Lady Lynn is a rapidly expanding company that sells cosmetics through representatives. These representatives originally contact most of their customers through house parties. At these parties, the representative demonstrates the products and takes orders. The guests have an opportunity to win some samples of the products and to order products. The hostess receives "gifts" depending on the volume of orders.

Sally is in the process of assigning representatives to the seven eastern Iowa counties shown in Figure 11.37. Actually, she only has two trained representatives to assign at this time. The policy at Lady Lynn is to assign a representative to a base county and one adjacent county. Actual practice is based on a *heuristic* which assigns representatives sequentially. The county with the largest population is selected as the base for the first representative and the adjacent county with the largest population

Figure 11.37

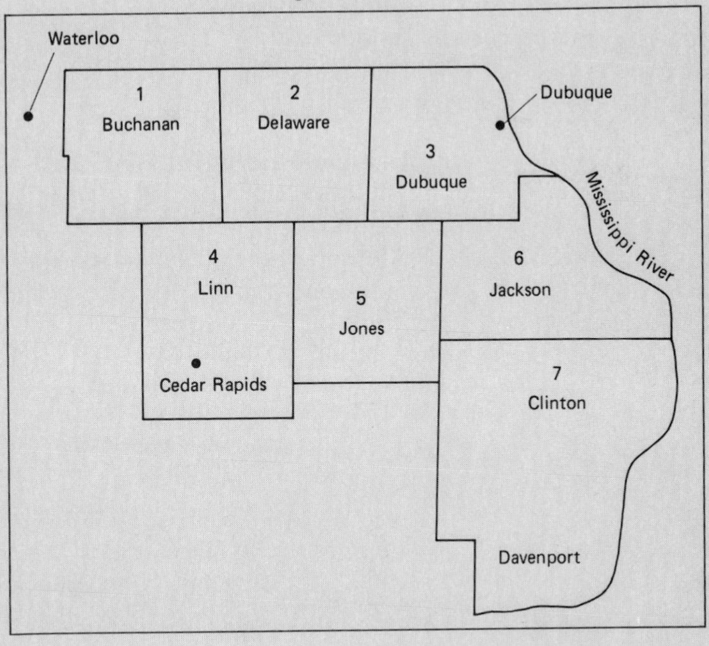

is also assigned to her. The unassigned county with the largest population is assigned as the next base and so on. The populations of the counties are shown below.

1. Buchanan   16,000
2. Delaware   15,000
3. Dubuque   98,000
4. Linn   109,000
5. Jones   4,000
6. Jackson   6,000
7. Clinton   100,000

Using this scheme, the first representative would be assigned to Linn County as a base. As the map shows, Buchanan, Delaware, and Jones are the adjacent counties. Since Buchanan has the largest population of these three counties it would be the assigned adjacent county. The second representative would be based in Clinton with Jackson as the assigned adjacent county. Sally realizes that the goal is to maximize the total population assigned to representatives. She is concerned that, since Dubuque County is nearly as large as Clinton, the proposed solution may not be optimal, and after a moment's thought she can see that it clearly is not. The pair Dubuque and Delaware beat Clinton and Jackson. She decides to abandon the traditional heuristic approach and to model the problem as an IP. Although the particular problem is quite simple, she believes that if she can create a successful model it could then be appropriately modified to assign the company's 60 midwest representatives to well over 300 counties. In formulating the problem, she lets

$$y_i = \begin{cases} 1 & \text{if county } i \text{ is a base} \\ 0 & \text{if not} \end{cases}$$

$$x_{ji} = \begin{cases} 1 & \text{if adjacent county } j \text{ is assigned to base } i \\ 0 & \text{if not} \end{cases}$$

The complete formulation and solution are shown in Figure 11.38. She has used an IP code to solve the problem.

The solution shows that y_4 and $y_1 = 1$; thus, Linn and Buchanan counties are selected as the base counties. It also shows that the optimal value of the objective function is 250, which implies that 250,000 people will be served by the two representatives. Sally thus is pleased to discover that the solution suggested by the traditional heuristic is incorrect before she implemented that solution. She is a bit surprised that the optimal solution does not involve either Dubuque or Clinton Counties, but she

Figure 11.38

```
MAX    16 Y1 + 15 Y2 + 98 Y3 + 109 Y4 + 4 Y5 + 6 Y6 + 100 Y7
      + 15 X21 + 109 X41 + 16 X12 + 98 X32
      + 109 X42 + 4 X52 + 15 X23 + 4 X53 + 6 X63 + 16 X14 + 15 X24
      + 4 X54 + 15 X25 + 98 X35 + 109 X45 + 6 X65 + 100 X75
      + 4 X56 + 98 X36 + 100 X76 + 4 X57 + 6 X67
```

Figure 11.38 (Cont.)

```
SUBJECT TO
  2)     −Y1 + X21 + X41 = 0
  3)     −Y2 + X12 + X32 + X42 + X52 = 0
  4)     −Y3 + X23 + X53 + X63 = 0
  5)     −Y4 + X14 + X24 + X54 = 0
  6)     −Y5 + X25 + X35 + X45 + X65 + X75 = 0
  7)     −Y6 + X56 + X36 + X76 = 0
  8)     −Y7 + X57 + X67 = 0
  9)     Y1 + Y2 + Y3 + Y4 + Y5 + Y6 + Y7 = 2

INTEGER VARIABLES = 29

      OBJECTIVE FUNCTION VALUE
            250.000000


VARIABLE      VALUE      REDUCED COST
   Y1          1.00          0.00
   Y2          0.00          0.00
   Y3          0.00          0.00
   Y4          1.00          0.00
   Y5          0.00          0.00
   Y6          0.00          0.00
   Y7          0.00          0.00
  X21          0.00         94.00
  X41          1.00          0.00
  X12          0.00         94.00
  X32          0.00         12.00
  X42          0.00          1.00
  X52          0.00        106.00
  X23          0.00         12.00
  X53          0.00         23.00
  X63          0.00         21.00
  X14          1.00          0.00
  X24          0.00          1.00
  X54          0.00         12.00
  X25          0.00        106.00
  X35          0.00         23.00
  X45          0.00         12.00
  X65          0.00        115.00
  X75          0.00         21.00
  X56          0.00        115.00
  X36          0.00         21.00
  X76          0.00         19.00
  X57          0.00         21.00
  X67          0.00         19.00
```

feels sure that the IP code provides the optimal solution to her model and thus she is determined to implement it.

1. Sally's solution is obviously wrong. Find, by inspection of the data, a correct optimal solution. How many alternative optima are there?

2. What is wrong with Sally's model? Write out seven additional constraints which will give a correct formulation.

3. Is this problem a network model? How can you tell?

CASE

MUNICIPAL BOND UNDERWRITING*

The municipal bond market is tough and aggressive, which means that a successful underwriter must be at the state-of-the-art in terms of competitive bidding. Bond markets often change from hour to hour. An active underwriter may bid on several issues each day with as little as 15 to 20 minutes to prepare a bid. This case has two objectives: (1) The student is familiarized with some of the mechanics of an important financial market; (2) The student will develop an IP model with real world importance. A variant of this model is actually used by several banks and investment bankers. In practice, bids are routinely prepared in a minute of CPU time on an IBM 370/168 for problems involving as many as 100 maturities and 35 coupon rates.

---

1. Basic Scenario

Each year billions of dollars of tax-exempt debt securities are offered for sale to the public. This is usually done through an underwriter acting as a broker between the issuer of the security and the public. The issuing of the securities to the underwriter is usually done through a competitive bid process. The issuer will notify prospective underwriters in advance of the proposed sale and invite bids which meet constraints set forth by the issuer. In constructing a proposed sale, the issuer divides the total amount to be raised (say $10,000) into bonds of various maturities. For example, to raise $10,000, the issuer might offer a one year bond with face value of $2,000, a two year bond with face value of $3,000, and a three year bond with face value of $5,000. At maturity, the face value of these bonds would be paid to the buyer. Thus in this example, the issuers would pay the buyers $2,000 in principal at the end of year one, and so on.

A bid by an underwriter (to the issuer) has three components:

1. An agreement to pay the issuer the face value of all of the bonds at the issue date. ($10,000 in our example).

2. A premium paid to the issuer at the issue date. (More on this later).

*This modeling approach was derived from the discussion in Nauss and Keeler, *Management Science*, Vol. 27, No. 4, April 1981, pp. 365–376. This CASE was initially formulated by Professor K. Martin.

3. An annual interest rate for each of the bonds cited in the proposal. These rates are called the coupon rates and determine the amount of interest the issuer must pay the buyers each year. Suppose that the underwriter proposed the following coupon rates for our example.

Maturity date	Rate %
1 year	3
2 years	4
3 years	5

The interest to be paid by the issuer would then be calculated as follows:

$$\text{Year 1} = 2{,}000(.03) + 3{,}000(.04) + 5{,}000(.05) = 430$$
$$\text{Year 2} = \qquad\qquad 3{,}000(.04) + 5{,}000(.05) = 370$$
$$\text{Year 3} = \qquad\qquad\qquad\qquad 5000(.05) = 250$$

Historically, the net interest cost (NIC) is the criterion most often employed by the issuer in evaluating bids. The NIC is the sum of interest payments over all years for all maturities minus any premium offered by the underwriter. The winning bid is the one with the minimum NIC. The time value of money is ignored in calculating the NIC.

The profit of the underwriter is the difference between what the buyer pays him and what he (the underwriter) pays the issuer. That is,

Profit = [Total Selling Price to Public] — [Total Face Value + Premium].

Thus, in preparing a bid the underwriter must

(1) determine the coupon (interest) amounts the issuer will pay on each maturity,
(2) for each maturity, estimate the selling price (i.e., the underwriter's selling price to the public) for bonds of each coupon rate. (The selling price for bonds need not be the same as the face value of the bond.)

The underwriter has two conflicting objectives. Higher coupon rates imply the bonds will have a higher selling price to the public and hence more money to the underwriter which can be used both as premium and profit. Thus the coupon rates must be set large enough so that if the bid is accepted the underwriter makes a reasonable profit. But higher coupon rates affect the interest the issuer will have to pay (higher coupon rates imply more interest) as well as the premium which the underwriter can offer the issuer. This tradeoff between premium and interest may imply that lower coupon rates will decrease the cost to the issuer and hence increase the chances of winning the bid.

The approach we take is to incorporate the underwriter's profit as a constraint and then minimize NIC (the cost to the issuer) in order to maximize the chances of winning the bid.

2. Data for a Specific Scenario

The city of Dogpatch is going to issue municipal bonds in order to raise revenue for civic improvements. Sealed bids will be received until 5:00 p.m. on February 7, 1973 for $5,000,000 in bonds dated March 1, 1973. The bid represents an offer from the underwriter to (i) pay $5,000,000 to Dogpatch, (ii) pay an additional (specified) premium to Dogpatch, (iii) an interest schedule which Dogpatch will pay to the bond holders. The interest is payable on March 1, 1974 and annually thereafter. The bonds become due (i.e. Dogpatch must pay off the face value, without option for prior payment) on March 1 in each of the maturity years in Table 1 below and in the amounts indicated. That is, Table 1 indicates Dogpatch's obligation (in terms of principal) to the bondholders.

Table 1

Year (Maturity)	Amount (× $1000)
1975	$250
1976	425
1977	1025
1978	1050
1979	1100
1980	1150

The bonds will be awarded to the bidder on the basis of the minimum NIC. No bid will be considered with an interest rate greater than 5% or less than 3% per annum. Bidders must specify interest rates in multiples of one-quarter of one percent per annum. Not more than three different interest rates will be considered (a repeated rate will not be considered a different rate). The same rate must apply to all bonds of the same maturity.

Estimating selling prices of various maturities as a function of coupon rates is a complicated process depending upon available markets and various parameters. For the sake of this example, take the data in Table 2 as given. Note that the underwriter may sell bonds to the public at more or less than the face value.

Table 2
Estimated Selling Price (×1000)

FACE VALUE	250	425	1025	1050	1100	1150
Percent	1975	1976	1977	1978	1979	1980
3	245	418	1015	1040	1080	1130
3 1/4	248	422	1016	1042	1084	1135
3 1/2	250	423	1017	1044	1085	1140
3 3/4	251	424	1025	1046	1090	1150
4	253	430	1029	1050	1095	1155
4 1/4	255	435	1035	1055	1096	1160
4 1/2	256	437	1037	1060	1105	1165
4 3/4	257	440	1038	1062	1110	1170
5	258	441	1040	1065	1115	1175

3. Example (A sample bid)

Assume an underwriter establishes the following coupon rates for each maturity.

Table 3

MATURITY	COUPON RATE	TOTAL INTEREST ($\times$ $1000)
1975	3%	$ 15.00
1976	4 1/2%	57.375
1977	4 3/4%	194.75
1978	4 1/2%	236.25
1979	4 1/2%	297.00
1980	4 1/2%	362.25

Given these coupon rates the bonds would be sold to the public (see estimates in Table 2) for $5,050,000. Assume the underwriter's spread or profit requirement is $8.00 per $1,000 of face amount of bonds. For a $5,000,000 issue this will be $40,000. Thus the premium paid to Dogpatch by the underwriter for this bid is

$$\text{premium} = \$5,050,000 - \$5,000,000 - \$40,000$$
$$= \$10,000.$$

4. Questions

1. Calculate Dogpatch's NIC for the example given in Section 3.
2. Suppose, as in Table 2, the underwriter has a choice between selling a 1975 bond at 4 1/4 percent for $255,000 or a 1975 bond at 4 1/2 percent for $256,000. Just in terms of minimizing NIC (ignoring other possible constraints), which would the underwriter prefer to offer. Suppose that in either case the underwriter's profit is the same.
3. In Table 2, consider the 1975 maturity at 5%. Suppose that you as an investor can with certainty receive 5% interest on money invested on March 1, 1974. What compounded yearly rate of interest would you be receiving if you pay $258,000 for the 1975 bond and use the above investment opportunity with your first receipt of interest?
4. Formulate a constrained optimization model for solving the underwriter's problem. This formulation should minimize the NIC of the underwriter's bid subject to the underwriter receiving an $8 margin per $1000 of face amount and the other constraints given in Section 2. Be very clear and concise in defining any notation you use and indicate the purpose of each constraint in your formulation.
5. Solve your constrained optimization model using LINDO.
6. Bid requests often include additional constraints. Assume that one such additional restriction is that coupon rates must be nondecreasing with maturity. Add the necessary constraint(s) to enforce this condition. You do not need to resolve with LINDO.

7. Next assume that the maximum allowed difference between the highest and lowest coupon rates is one percent. Add the necessary constraint(s) to enforce this condition. You do not need to resolve with LINDO.

8. Refer to your formulation in question 4. If the bonds (regardless of maturity and coupon value) could never be sold in excess of face value will your formulation have a feasible solution? Why or why not?

9. Assume your formulation in question 4 has a feasible solution. Is it possible that the addition of the constraint(s) from question 6 or the constraint(s) from question 7 (or both taken together) make the formulation infeasible?

A word of advice: One danger of misformulating a rather large integer programming model, and then attempting to run it on a computer, is that you may waste a great deal of computer time (this of course could be true of any large model). Your solution to question 5 above, using a correctly formulated model, should take no more than one minute of *CPU time* on any machine as fast as a DEC 2050. Your model, although rather large, should take no more than an hour to correctly type-in at a console.

CHAPTER 12

Project Management: PERT and CPM

12.1

INTRODUCTION

The task of managing major projects is an ancient and honorable art. In about 2600 B.C., the Egyptians built the Great Pyramid for King Khufu. The Greek historian Herodotus claimed that 400,000 men worked for 20 years to build this structure. Although these figures are now in doubt, there is no question about the enormity of the project. The Book of Genesis reports that the Tower of Babel was not completed because God made it impossible for the builders to communicate. This project is especially important, since it establishes an historical precedent for the ever-popular practice of citing divine intervention as a rationale of failure.[1]

Modern projects ranging from building a suburban shopping center to putting a man on the moon are amazingly large, complex, and costly. Completing such projects on time and within the budget is not an easy task. In particular, we shall see that the complicated problems of scheduling such projects are often structured by the interdependence of activities. Typically, certain of the activities may not be initiated before others have been completed. In dealing with projects possibly involving thousands of such dependency relations, it is no wonder that managers seek effective methods of analysis. Some of the key questions to be answered in this chapter are:

Key Questions

1. What is the expected project completion date?
2. What is the potential "variability" in this date?
3. What is the scheduled start and completion date for each specific activity?
4. What activities are *critical* in the sense that they must be completed exactly as scheduled in order to meet the target for overall project completion?
5. How long can *noncritical* activities be delayed before a delay in the overall completion date is incurred?

[1] The *Chicago Tribune* (August 5, 1977) noted the following comment concerning the blackout in New York in July of that year: "Con Ed called the disaster an act of God."

6. How might I effectively concentrate resources on activities in order to speed up project completion?

7. What controls can be exercised on the flows of expenditures on the various activities throughout the duration of the project in order that the overall budget can be adhered to?

PERT and CPM, acronyms for Program Evaluation Review Technique and Critical Path Method, respectively, will provide answers to these questions. Each of these approaches to scheduling represents a project as a network, and hence the material in this chapter, although self-contained, can be viewed as a natural extension of the network approach as discussed in Chapter 11.

Brief History

PERT was developed in the late 1950s by the Navy Special Projects Office in cooperation with the management consulting firm of Booz, Allen, and Hamilton. The technique received substantial favorable publicity for its use in the engineering and development program of the Polaris missile, a complicated project that had 250 prime contractors and over 9000 subcontractors. Since that time, it has been widely adopted in other branches of government and in industry and has been applied to such diverse projects as construction of factories, buildings, and highways, research management, product development, the installation of new computer systems, and so on. Today, many firms and government agencies require all contractors to use PERT.

CPM was developed in 1957 by J. E. Kelly of Remington Rand and M. R. Walker of DuPont. It differs from PERT primarily in the details of how time and cost are treated. Indeed, in actual implementation, the distinctions between PERT and CPM have become blurred as firms have integrated the best features of both systems into their own efforts to manage projects effectively.

In keeping with our philosophy throughout the text, we approach the topic of project management on two levels. First, the essential techniques will be developed on an easily grasped illustrative example. Second, the use of the computer will be illustrated to indicate how one would handle the techniques in a large-scale, real-world application.

12.2

THE GLOBAL OIL CREDIT CARD OPERATION

Planning a Move

No one would claim that it is like building the Great Pyramid, but the impending move of the credit card operation to Des Moines, Iowa, from the home office in Dallas is an important project for Rebecca Goldstein and Global Oil. The Board of Directors of Global has set a firm deadline of 22 weeks for the move to be accomplished. Becky is a manager in the Operations Analysis Group. She is in charge of planning the move, seeing that everything comes off according to plan and that the deadline is met.

The move is difficult to coordinate because it involves many different divisions within the company. Real estate must select one of three available office sites. Personnel has to determine which employees from Dallas will move, how many new employees to hire, and who will train them. The systems group and the treasurer's office must organize and implement the operating procedures and the financial arrangements for the new operation. The architects will have to design the interior space and oversee needed structural improvements. Each of the sites that Global is considering is an existing building with the appropriate amount of open space. However, office partitions, computer facilities, furnishings, and so on, must all be provided.

A second complicating factor is that there is an interdependence of activities. In other words, some parts of the project cannot be started until other parts are completed. Consider two obvious examples: Global cannot construct the interior of an office before it has been designed. Neither can they hire new employees until they have determined their personnel requirements.

The Activity List for Global Oil

Becky knows that PERT and CPM are specifically designed for projects of this sort and she wastes no time in getting started. The first step in the process is to define the activities in the project and to establish the proper precedence relationships. This is an important first step since errors or omissions at this stage can lead to a disastrously inaccurate schedule. Figure 12.1 shows the first **activity list** that Becky prepares for the move (the columns labeled "Time" and "Resources" are indications of things to come).

Figure 12.1
First Activity List

ACTIVITY	DESCRIPTION	IMMEDIATE PREDECESSORS	TIME	RESOURCES
A	Select office site	—		
B	Create the organizational and financial plan	—		
C	Determine personnel requirements	B		
D	Design facility	A, C		
E	Construct the interior	D		
F	Select personnel to move	C		
G	Hire new employees	F		
H	Move records, key personnel, etc.	F		
I	Make financial arrangements with institutions in Des Moines	B		
J	Train new personnel	H, E, G		

Immediate Predecessors

Conceptually, Figure 12.1 is straightforward. Each activity is placed on a separate line and its **immediate predecessors** are recorded on the same line. The immediate predecessors of an activity are those activities that must be completed prior to the start of the activity in question. For example, in Figure 12.1 we see that Global cannot start activity C, determine personnel requirements, until activity B, create the organization and financial plan, is completed. Similarly, activity G, hire new employees, cannot begin until activity F, select the Global personnel that will move from Texas to Des Moines, is completed. This activity, F, in turn, cannot start until activity C, determine personnel requirements, is completed.

The activity list with immediate predecessors, and the yet to be obtained time estimates will provide the essential ingredients to answer the first five questions posed in Section 12.1 and we shall shortly see how PERT and CPM are used to produce these answers. In practice, however, another graphical approach, the Gantt chart, also is used commonly to attack such problems. We thus make a slight detour to consider this precursor of the network approaches (PERT and CPM) before returning to the main thrust of the chapter.

The Gantt chart was developed by Henry L. Gantt in 1918 and remains a popular tool in production and project scheduling. Its simplicity and clear graphical display have established it as a popular device for simple scheduling problems. The Gantt chart for Becky's problem is shown in Figure 12.2. Each activity is listed on the vertical axis. The horizontal axis is time and the anticipated as well as actual duration of each activity is represented by a bar of the appropriate length. The chart also indicates **the earliest possible starting time** for each activity. For example, activity C cannot start before time 5 since, according to Figure 12.1, activity B must be completed before activity C can begin. As each activity (or part thereof) is completed the appropriate bar is shaded. At any point in time, then, it is clear which activities are "on schedule" and which are not. The Gantt chart in Figure 12.2 shows that as of week 13 activities D, E and H are "behind schedule," while G has actually been entirely completed (because it is all shaded) and hence is "ahead of schedule."

Figure 12.2

A Gantt Chart

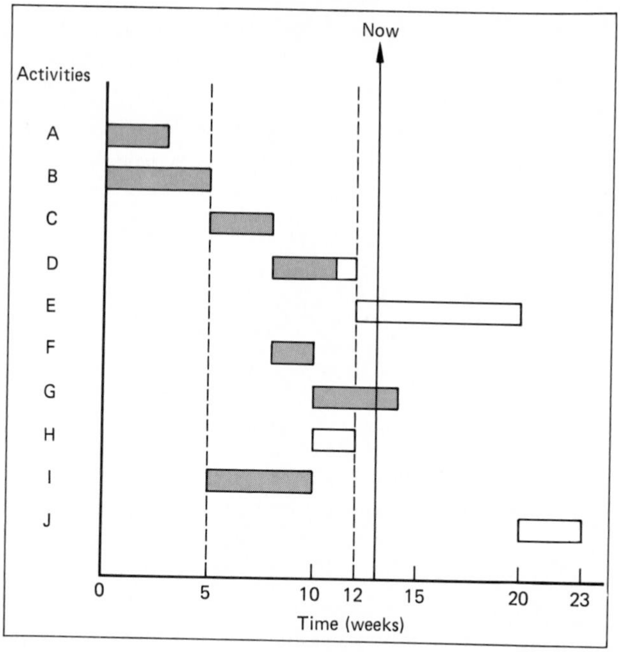

This simple example shows how the Gantt chart is mainly used as a record keeping device for following the progression in time of the subtasks of a project. As Figure 12.2 shows, we can see which individual tasks are "on or behind schedule." It seems important to note at this point that in the Gantt chart context the phrase "on schedule" means "it has been completed no later than the earliest possible completion time." Thus Figure 12.2 shows that D and H could have been completed, **at the earliest,** by week 12. Since they are not completed by week 13 they are, in this sense, "behind schedule." As we shall see, this is too simple a concept for whether or not an activity is "on schedule." The appropriate point of view should be whether or not **the overall project** is being delayed in terms of a target completion date. The Gantt chart fails to reveal some of the important information needed to attack this question. For example, the Gantt chart fails to reveal which activities are **immediate predecessors** of other activities. In Figure 12.2 it may appear that F and I are immediate predecessors of G since G can start at

10 and F and I can each finish at 10. In fact, however, Figure 12.1 tells us that only F is an immediate predecessor of G. A delay in I would **not** affect the potential starting time of G, or for that matter of any other activity. It is this type of "immediate predecessor" information that must be used to deduce the impact on completion time for the overall project. This latter type of information is of obvious importance to the manager. The overall weakness of Gantt charts is reflected by their impotence in making such inferences. We shall now see that the network representation contains the immediate predecessor information that we need.

The Network Diagram

In a PERT network diagram each activity is represented by an arrow that is called a **branch** or an **arc**: The beginning and end of each activity is indicated by a circle that is called a **node**. The term **event** is also used in conjunction with the nodes. An event represents the completion of the activities that lead into a node. Referring to the activity list in Figure 12.1, we see that "select office site" is termed activity A. When this **activity** is completed, the **event** "office site selected" occurs.

Constructing the Diagram

Figure 12.3 shows a network diagram for activities A through C. We emphasize at the outset that the numbers assigned to the nodes are arbitrary. They are simply used to identify events and do not imply anything about precedence relationships. Indeed, we shall renumber the node that terminates activity C several times as we develop the network diagram for this project, but correct precedence relationships will always be preserved. In the network diagram each activity must start at the node in which its immediate predecessors ended. For example, in Figure 12.3, activity C starts at node ③ because its immediate predecessor, activity B, ended there. We see, however, that complications arise as we attempt to add activity D to the network diagram. Since both A and C are immediate predecessors to D, and since we want to show any activity such as D only once in our diagram, nodes ② and ④ in Figure 12.3 must be combined and D should start from this new node. This is shown in Figure 12.4. Node ③ now represents the event that both activities A and C have been completed. Note that activity E, which has only D as an immediate predecessor, can be added with no difficulty. However, as we attempt to add activity F, a new problem arises. Since F has C as an immediate predecessor, it would emanate from node ③ (of Figure 12.4). We see, however, that this would imply that F also has A as an immediate predecessor, which is incorrect.

Figure 12.3

Network Diagram for Activities
A through C

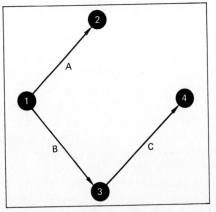

Figure 12.4

Partial Network Diagram

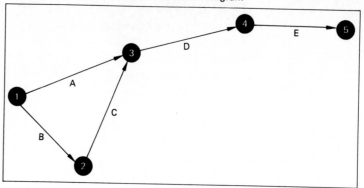

A Dummy Activity This diagramming dilemma is solved by introducing a **dummy activity** which is represented by a dashed line in the network diagram in Figure 12.5. This dummy activity is fictitious in the sense that it requires no time or resources. It merely provides a pedagogical device that enables us to draw a network representation that correctly maintains the appropriate precedence relationships. Thus, Figure 12.5 indicates that activity D can begin only after both of the activities A and C have been completed. Similarly, activity F can occur only after activity C is completed.

Figure 12.5

Introducing a Dummy Activity

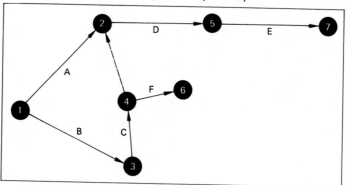

Figure 12.6 shows the network diagram for the first activity list as presented in Figure 12.1. We note that activities G and H both start at node ⑥ and terminate at node ⑦. This does not present a problem in portraying the appropriate precedence relationships, since only activity J satrts at node ⑦. This might, however, create a problem for certain computer programs used to solve PERT and CPM problems. In some of these programs, each activity is identified by the number of its *starting and ending* note. If such a program is to be used, the representation of G and H in Figure 12.6 would lead the computer to regard them as the same activity. This would be incorrect, since in fact activities G and H are not the same. Once again, a dummy activity can be used to cure this condition. Figure 12.7 illustrates the procedure. Since the dummy activity requires no time the correct time and precedent relationships are maintained. This new representation has been introduced into Figure 12.9. The computer code which we will employ does not require that these dummy activities be used. Thus, for our

Figure 12.6
Network Diagram for the First Activity List for the Move to Des Moines

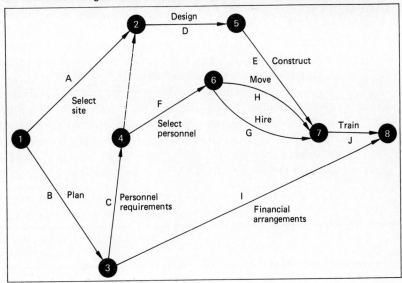

purposes, they serve mainly the pedagogical goal of correctly portraying the precedence relations (i.e., as used in Figure 12.5).

Figure 12.7
Introducing a Second Dummy Activity

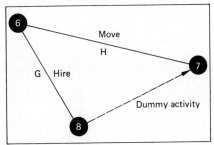

12.3
THE CRITICAL PATH: MEETING THE BOARD'S DEADLINE

The activity list and an appropriate network diagram are useful devices for representing the precedence relationships among the activities in a project. Recall that the board has set a firm goal of 22 weeks for the overall project to be completed. Before Becky can tell if she can meet this goal, she will have to incorporate time estimates into the process.

Time Assignments   The PERT–CPM procedure requires management to produce an estimate of the expected time it will take to complete each activity on the activity list. Let us assume that Becky has worked with the appropriate departments at Global to arrive at the expected time estimates (in weeks) shown in Figure 12.8. (In Section 12.4 we shall discuss in more detail the way in which these time estimates were produced.) Figure 12.9 shows the network diagram with the expected activity times appended in brackets.

From Figure 12.8 you can see (i.e., by adding up the separate expected activity times) that the total working time required to complete all the individual activities would be 39 hours. However, the total calendar time required to complete the entire project can clearly be less than 39 hours, for many activities can be performed simultaneously. For example, Figure 12.9 shows that activities A and B can be initiated at the same time. Activity A takes 3 hours and B takes 5 hours. If management arranges to begin both activities at the same time (at calendar time = 0), both will be completed at calendar time = 5. To obtain a prediction of the minimum calendar time required for overall project duration, we must find what is referred to as a **critical path** in the network. A **path** can be defined as a sequence of connected activities that leads from the starting node ① to the completion node ⑨. For example, the sequence of activities B–I requiring 10 hours to complete, is a path. So is the sequence B–C–D–E–J requiring 23 hours to complete. You can identify numerous other paths in Figure 12.9. To complete the project,

Figure 12.8

First Activity List with Expected Activity Times in Weeks

ACTIVITY	DESCRIPTION	IMMEDIATE PREDECESSORS	EXPECTED ACTIVITY TIME (weeks)	RESOURCES
A	Select office site	—	3	
B	Create the organization and financial plan	—	5	
C	Determine personnel requirements	B	3	
D	Design facility	A, C	4	
E	Construct the interior	D	8	
F	Select personnel to move	C	2	
G	Hire new employees	F	4	
H	Move records, key personnel, etc.	F	2	
I	Make financial arrangements with institutions in Des Moines	B	5	
J	Train new personnel	H, E, G	3	

Figure 12.9

Network Diagram with Expected Activity Times

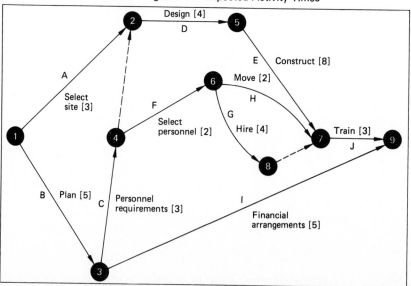

386

the activities **on all paths** must be completed. In this sense we might say that "all paths must be traversed." Thus, we have just seen that our project will take **at least** 23 hours to complete, for the path B–C–D–E–J must be traversed. However, numerous other paths must also be traversed, and some of these may require even more time. Our task will be to analyze the total amount of calendar time required in order that all paths should be traversed. Thus, we wish to determine the **longest path** from start to finish. This path, called the **critical path,** will determine the overall project duration, because no other path will be longer. If activities on the longest path are delayed, then, since these activities must be completed, the entire project will be delayed. For this reason the activities on the critical path are called the **critical activities** of the project. It is this subset of activities that must be kept "on schedule."

*Earliest
Start Time*

We now specify the steps employed in finding a critical path. Fundamental in this process will be the **earliest start time** for each activity. To illustrate this idea, consider activity D, "design the facility." Now assume that the project starts at time zero and ask yourself: "What is the earliest time at which activity D can start?" Clearly, it cannot start until activity A is complete. It, thus, cannot start before time = 3. However, it also cannot start before the dummy activity (that requires 0 time) is complete. Since the dummy cannot start until B and C are complete (a total of 8 weeks), we see that D cannot start until 8 weeks have passed. In this calculation, it is crucial to note that activities A and B both start at time 0. After 3 weeks A is complete, but B still requires another 2 weeks. After a total of 5 weeks, B is complete and C can start. After another 3 weeks, a total of 8 from the start, C is completed. Thus, after 8 weeks, both A and C are complete and D can start. In other words,

$$\text{earliest start time for activity D} = 8 \text{ weeks}$$

Another important concept is **earliest finish time** for each activity. If we let

$$ES = \text{earliest start time for a given activity}$$

$$EF = \text{earliest finish time for a given activity}$$

$$t = \text{expected activity time for the given activity}$$

then, for a given activity, the relation between earliest start time and earliest finish time is

$$EF = ES + t$$

For example, we have just shown that for activity D we have $ES = 8$. Thus, for activity D,

$$EF = ES + t = 8 + 4 = 12$$

We now recall that each activity begins at a node. We know that a given activity leaving a node cannot be started until *all* activities leading into that node have been finished. This observation gives the following

*Earliest Start
Time Rule*

EARLIEST START TIME RULE: The ES time for an activity leaving a particular node is the largest of the EF times for all activities entering the node.

Let us apply this rule to nodes ①, ②, ③, and ④ of Becky's network, Figure 12.9.

The result is shown in Figure 12.10. We write in brackets the earliest start and earliest finish times for each activity next to the letter of the activity, as shown in Figure 12.10. Note that the earliest start time rule applied to activity D says that ES for activity D is equal to the largest value of the EF times for the two precedent activities C (via the dummy) and A. Thus, the ES for D is the larger of the two values [8, 3], which is 8.

Figure 12.10
Earliest Start Time Rule

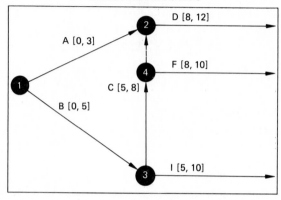

The Forward
Pass

Continuing to each node in a **forward pass** through the entire network, the values [ES, EF] are computed for each activity. The result is shown in Figure 12.11. Note that the earliest finish time for J is 23 weeks. This means that the earliest completion time for the entire project is 23 weeks. This answers the first of the questions itemized in Section 12.1. "What is the expected project completion date?" In order to answer the third, fourth, and fifth questions, we now proceed with the algorithm for finding the critical path. Having gone through the above **forward pass,** the next step is to make a **backward pass** calculation.

Figure 12.11
Global Oil Network with Earliest Start and Earliest Finish Times Shown

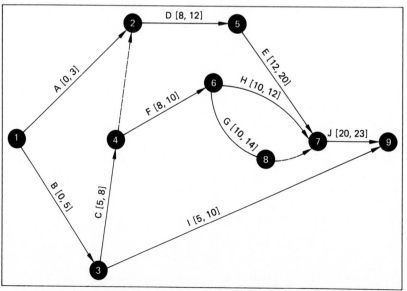

The **backward pass** begins at the completion node, node ⑨. We then trace back through the network computing what is termed a latest start and latest finish time for each activity. In symbols,

$$LS = \text{latest starting time for a particular activity}$$
$$LF = \text{latest finish time for a particular activity}$$

The relation between these quantities is

$$LS = LF - t$$

For activity J we define the latest finish time to be the same as its earliest finish time, which is 23. Hence, for activity J,

$$LS = LF - t = 23 - 3 = 20$$

To determine the latest finish time for activity H, as well as for all other activities in the network, the following rule is applied:

LATEST FINISH TIME RULE: The LF time for an activity entering a particular node is the smallest of the LS times for all activities leaving that node.

Thus, for activity H, which enters node ⑦, we apply the rule to see that LF = 20 because J is the only activity leaving node ⑦ and we have already stated that LS = 20 for activity J. Also, for activity H we can then compute

$$LS = LF - t = 20 - 2 = 18$$

The complete network with the LS and LF entries is shown in Figure 12.12. These

Figure 12.12
Global Oil Network with ES, EF, LS and LF Times Shown

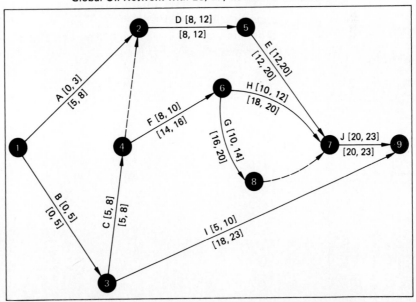

entries appear in brackets on the arc for each activity, directly under the ES and EF times.

Slack Based on Figure 12.12, the next step of the algorithm is to identify another important value, the amount of slack or free time associated with each activity. **Slack** is defined to be the amount of time an activity can be delayed without affecting the completion date for the overall project. For each activity, the slack value is computed as

$$\text{slack} = LS - ES = LF - EF$$

For example, the slack for activity G is given by

$$\text{slack for G} = LS \text{ for G} - ES \text{ for G}$$
$$= 16 - 10 = 6$$

and the same value is given by

$$LF \text{ for G} - EF \text{ for G} = 20 - 14 = 6$$

This means that activity G could be delayed up to 6 weeks beyond its earliest start time without delaying the overall project. On the other hand, the slack associated with activity C is

$$\text{slack for C} = LS \text{ for C} - ES \text{ for C}$$
$$= 5 - 5 = 0$$

The Critical Path Thus, activity C has no slack and must begin as scheduled at week 5. **Since this activity cannot be delayed without affecting the entire project, it is a critical activity and is on the critical path.**

The critical path activities are those with zero slack.

A computer printout of relevant data for this project is shown in Figure 12.13. This is the type of output you would be likely to see in a real study. Note that asterisks are printed for those activities with zero slack. Thus, we can see from this computer output that the critical path for Becky's project is B–C–D–E–J. The minimum overall completion

Figure 12.13
Summary Scheduling

ACTIVITY	EARLIEST START	EARLIEST FINISH	LATEST START	LATEST FINISH	SLACK
A	0	3	5	8	5
B	0	5	0	5	*****
C	5	8	5	8	*****
D	8	12	8	12	*****
E	12	20	12	20	*****
F	8	10	14	16	6
G	10	14	16	20	6
H	10	12	18	20	8
I	5	10	18	23	13
J	20	23	20	23	*****

time is 23 weeks, which is the sum of the times on the critical path, as well as the earliest finish time for the last activity (J). Figure 12.13 also provides the answers to questions 3, 4, and 5 raised in Section 12.1. In other words, we have, up to this point, answered the following questions from that section.

---

1. What is the expected project completion date?

   Answer: 23 weeks.

3. What is the scheduled start and completion date for each specific activity?

   Answer: An activity may be scheduled to start at any date between "earliest start" and "latest start." The scheduled completion date will be "start date + expected activity time." For example, activity G can be scheduled to start anywhere between time = 10 and time = 16. As shown in Figure 12.8, the expected activity time is 4 weeks. Hence, the scheduled completion date will be "start date + 4."

4. What activities are *critical* in the sense that they must be completed exactly as scheduled in order to meet the target for overall project completion?

   Answer: The activities on the critical path: namely, B, C, D, E, J.

5. How long can *noncritical* activities be delayed before a delay in the overall completion date is incurred?

   Answer: Any activity may be started as late as the "latest start" date without delaying the overall project completion.

Shortening the Critical Path

Three questions, namely 2, 6, and 7, remain to be answered. But first, before proceeding further, let us take an overview of what we have learned. It is clear from the critical path analysis that Becky has a problem. The Board of Directors wants the credit-card operation to start operating in Des Moines in 22 weeks, and with the current plan 23 weeks are required. Obviously, something must change if this goal is to be met. There are two basic ways to proceed:

1. *A strategic analysis:*   Here the analyst asks: "Does this project have to be done the way it is currently diagrammed?" In particular, "Do all of the activities on the critical path have to be done in the specified order?" Can we make arrangements to accomplish some of these activities in a different way not on the critical path?

2. *A tactical approach:*   In this approach the analyst assumes that the current diagram is appropriate and works at reducing the time of certain activities on the critical path by devoting more resources to them. The current expected times assume a certain allocation of resources. For example, the 8 weeks for construction (activity E) assumes a regular 8-hour workday. The contractor can complete the job more rapidly by working overtime, but at increased costs.

The tactical approach will get us more into CPM considerations, to be discussed in Section 12.6. For now, let us deal with the so-called strategic questions.

A Strategic Analysis

Becky starts with a strategic analysis, since she is anxious to keep the cost of the move as low as possible. After some study she suddenly realizes that the current network **assumes** that activity J, the training of new employees, must be carried out in the new building (after E is complete), and after records and key personnel have been moved (after H is complete). After reconsidering, she believes that these requirements can be changed. First of all, J can be accomplished independently of H. The previous specification that H should be an immediate predecessor of J was simply incorrect. Moreover, she believes that she can secure an alternative training facility by arranging to use surplus classroom space in Des Moines at a minimal cost. She can then have the new employees trained and ready to start the moment that construction ends. On the other hand, she has to add another activity: secure a training facility (to be denoted as activity K) to the activity list. Although she feels that such a rearrangement may be helpful, it is possible that in this redefined network she may have created a new critical path with a still unsatisfactory minimum time (i.e., one greater than 22 weeks).

Computer
Output for the
Redefined
Network

Figure 12.14 shows the redefined activity list in the form in which Becky submits the problem to her on-line computer. In the input which she is required to provide, the dummy activities are never employed. Line 100 specifies the total number of activities, 11. To understand the rest of the format, consider line 600. This tells us that the activity D (design facility) has an expected completion time of four weeks and that it has two immediate predecessors. The next line, 700 shows that these two predecessors are A (select office site) and C (determine personnel requirements). In lines 2000 and 2100 we see that the new activity, K (secure training facility) takes 3 weeks and has one immediate predecessor, F (select personnel). Also note how the input for activity J (line 1800) shows that activity H is no longer one of its immediate predecessors. Figure 12.15 shows the network diagram for the redefined project.

Although this diagram is useful for pedagogical reasons, it is not an important part of solving the problem. Indeed, Becky skips this step and asks the computer to solve the

Figure 12.14
Computer Input for Redefined Activity List

Input: PERT. DAT. 8

	Total Number of Activities	Activity Time	Number of Immediate Predecessors
00100	11		
00200	A	3	0
00300	B	5	0
00400	C	3	1
00500	B		
00600	D	4	2
00700	A	C	
00800	E	8	1
00900	D		
01000	F	2	1
01100	C		
01200	G	4	1
01300	F		
01400	H	2	1
01500	F		
01600	I	5	1
01700	B		
01800	J	3	2
01900	G	K	
02000	K	3	1
02100	F		

Figure 12.15

Network Diagram for the Redefined Project

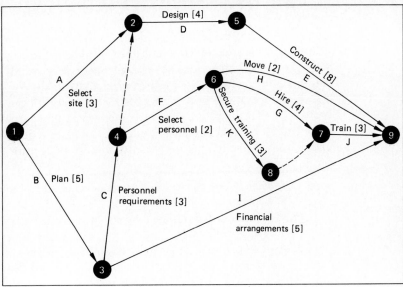

problem. The computer solution is shown in Figure 12.16. Here we see that the redefined project can be completed in 20 weeks (the sum of the times on the critical path) and hence the board's deadline can be met. It is also seen that the activity "train" (J) is no longer on the critical path. In spite of the fact that 3 weeks is needed to secure a training facility, activity J has a slack of 3 weeks. The computer solution shows that the critical path for the redefined project is B–C–D–E. (Recall that ***** in the SLACK column indicates that an activity is on the critical path.)

Figure 12.16

Computer Solution for the Redefined Project

NAME OF INPUT FILE =
PERT. DAT

PROJECT LENGTH = 20.00

ACTIVITY	TIME	EARLIEST START	LATEST START	EARLIEST FINISH	LATEST FINISH	SLACK
B	5.00	0.00	0.00	5.00	5.00	********
A	3.00	0.00	5.00	3.00	8.00	5.00
C	3.00	5.00	5.00	8.00	8.00	********
I	5.00	5.00	15.00	10.00	20.00	10.00
F	2.00	8.00	11.00	10.00	13.00	3.00
D	4.00	8.00	8.00	12.00	12.00	********
K	3.00	10.00	14.00	13.00	17.00	4.00
G	4.00	10.00	13.00	14.00	17.00	3.00
H	2.00	10.00	18.00	12.00	20.00	8.00
E	8.00	12.00	12.00	20.00	20.00	********
J	3.00	14.00	17.00	17.00	20.00	3.00

Let us now consider the second question raised in the introduction: "What is the potential variability in the expected project completion date?"

VARIABILITY IN ACTIVITY TIMES

So far, we have been acting as though the activity times and the derived values for ES, LS, EF, and LF were all deterministic. This may not be strictly correct, for in reality the activity times are often not known in advance with certainty. In view of this fact, PERT employs a special formula for estimating activity times. We shall now present the details, and in so doing it will be seen that the PERT approach can also be used to calculate the probability that the project will be completed by any particular time.

The PERT system of estimating activity times requires someone who well enough understands the activity in question to produce three estimates of the activity time:

1. **Optimistic time** (denoted by a): the minimum time. Everything has to go perfectly to achieve this time.
2. **Most probable time** (denoted by m): the most likely time. The time required under normal circumstances.
3. **Pessimistic time** (denoted by b): the maximum time. One version of Murphy's Law is that if something can go wrong, it will. The pessimistic time is the time required when Murphy's Law is in effect.

Consider, for example, activity E, construct the interior. Becky and the general contractor carefully examine each phase of the construction project and arrive at the following estimates:

$$a = 4 \qquad m = 7 \qquad b = 16$$

The relatively large value for b is caused by the possibility of a delay in the delivery of the air-conditioning unit for the computer. If this unit is delayed, the entire activity is delayed. Moreover, in this case, since E is on the critical path, a delay in this unit will delay overall project completion.

Estimating the Expected Activity Time

The estimate of the expected activity time is based on the assumption that activity time is a random variable which has a unimodal beta probability distribution. It is not useful to dwell on the details of this distribution; instead, we will concentrate on the estimation procedure. A typical beta probability distribution is shown in Figure 12.17. Indeed, this

Figure 12.17

Unimodal Beta Distribution

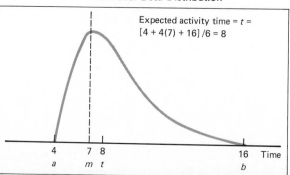

Expected activity time = t =
$[4 + 4(7) + 16]/6 = 8$

is the distribution of completion time for activity E. This figure illustrates the assumptions that

1. a, the optimistic estimate, is the lower limit for the activity time.
2. b, the pessimistic estimate, is the upper limit for the activity time.
3. m, the most likely estimate, is the mode of this distribution; that is, in rough terms, m is the time that has the largest probability of occurring.

When the activity time has a beta probability distribution the expected activity time can be calculated as follows:

$$\text{expected activity time} = \frac{a + 4m + b}{6} \qquad (12.1)$$

Thus, for activity E,

$$\text{expected activity time} = \frac{4 + 4(7) + 16}{6} = 8$$

By working with the appropriate individuals in Global Oil, Becky used (12.1) to estimate each of the expected activity times that were presented in Figure 12.8 and subsequently used in the critical path analysis.

This is the way the activity times would be estimated in most applications of PERT. Of course, if they are known with certainty, this estimation technique would be circumvented.

Estimating the Standard Deviation of an Activity Time

The standard deviation of an activity time is estimated by assuming that there are 6 standard deviations between the optimistic and pessimistic times:

$$\text{standard deviation of activity time} = \frac{b - a}{6} \qquad (12.2)$$

For the beta distribution shown in Figure 12.17 all activity times will occur between a and b and the distance $b - a$ is 6 standard deviations. Thus, for activity E,

$$\text{standard deviation} = \frac{16 - 4}{6} = 2$$

Figure 12.18 shows the three estimates (a, m, b), the expected activity times, the standard deviation of the activity times, and the variance of the activity times for the redefined activity list. The variance is simply the square of the standard deviation. It is useful to record the variance of each activity since these values will be used in making statements about the probability of completing the overall project by a specific date.

The Probability of Completing the Project on Time

The fact that activity times are random variables implies that the completion time for the project is also a random variable. That is, there is a potential variability in the overall completion time. Even though the redefined project has an **expected** completion time of 20 weeks, there is no guarantee that it will actually be completed within 20 weeks. If **by chance** various activities take longer than their expected time, the project might not be

Figure 12.18

Time Estimates

ACTIVITY	a	m	b	$(a + 4m + b)/6$ (EXPECTED VALUE)	$(b - a)/6$ (STD. DEV.)	$[(b - a)/6]^2$ (VARIANCE)
A	1	3	5	3	2/3	4/9
B	3	4.5	9	5	1	1
C	2	3	4	3	1/3	1/9
D	2	4	6	4	2/3	4/9
E	4	7	16	8	2	4
F	1	1.5	5	2	2/3	4/9
G	2.5	3.5	7.5	4	5/6	25/36
H	1	2	3	2	1/3	1/9
I	4	5	6	5	1/3	1/9
J	1.5	3	4.5	3	1/2	1/4
K	1	3	5	3	2/3	4/9

completed within the desired 22-week schedule. In general, it would be useful to know the probability that the project will be completed within a specified time. In particular, Becky would like to know the probability that the move will be completed within 22 weeks.

The analysis proceeds as follows:

1. Let T equal the total time that will be taken by the activities on the critical path.
2. Find the probability that the value of T will turn out to be less than or equal to any specified value of interest. In particular, for Becky's project we would find Prob $\{T \leq 22\}$. A good approximation for this probability is easily found if two assumptions hold.
   a. *The activity times are independent random variables.* This is a valid assumption for most **PERT** networks and seems reasonable for Becky's problem. There is no reason to believe that the time to construct the interior should depend on the design time, etc.
   b. *The random variable T has an approximately normal distribution.* This assumption relies on the *central limit theorem*, which in broad terms states that the sum of independent random variables is approximately normally distributed.

Now recalling that our goal is to find $P\{T \leq 22\}$, where T is the time along the critical path, we will want to convert T to a standard normal random variable and use Table T.1 at the end of the text to find $P\{T \leq 22\}$. The first step in this process is to find the standard deviation of T. To do this we need the variance of T. When the activity times are independent, we know that the variance of the total time along the critical path equals the sum of the variances of the activity times on the critical path. Thus, for Becky's problem,

$$\text{var } T = \begin{pmatrix} \text{variance for} \\ \text{activity B} \end{pmatrix} + \begin{pmatrix} \text{variance for} \\ \text{activity C} \end{pmatrix} + \begin{pmatrix} \text{variance for} \\ \text{activity D} \end{pmatrix} + \begin{pmatrix} \text{variance for} \\ \text{activity E} \end{pmatrix}$$

Using the numerical values in Figure 12.18 yields

$$\text{var } T = 1 + 1/9 + 4/9 + 4 = 50/9$$

Finally,

$$\text{std. dev. } T = \sqrt{(var\ T)} = \sqrt{50}/3 = 2.357$$

We now proceed to convert T to a standard normal random variable in the usual way. Recalling that 20 weeks is the mean (i.e., the expected completion time), we see that the distance from the mean to 22 weeks is

$$(22 - 20)/2.357 = 0.8485$$

standard deviations. If we consult Table T.1 at the end of the text for the area under a normal curve from the left-hand tail to a point 0.8485 standard deviations above the mean, we find that the answer is about 0.80. Thus, there is about an 80% chance the critical path will be completed in less than 22 weeks.

The Probability the Critical Path Will Be Completed on Time

This analysis shows how to shed light on the second of the questions asked in the introduction. In particular, it shows how to find the probability that the **critical path** will be finished by *any* given time. It illustrates the importance of considering the variability in individual activity times when considering overall project completion times. The analysis for Becky's problem incicates that, using expected time as our "real-world forecast," the expected project duration will be 20 weeks and, if so, it will be completed 2 weeks ahead of the desired date. The analysis of uncertainty above sheds additional light on this estimate. It shows a significant probability (i.e., $0.2 = 1 - 0.8$) that **the critical path** will not be completed by the desired completion date of 22 weeks. The implication of this analysis is that there is **at least** a probability of 0.2 that the **overall project** may not be completed by the desired date. The modifier "at least" has been employed because of the following complicating factor. Because of randomness, some other path, estimated as being noncritical, may in reality take longer to complete than the purported critical path.

12.5

A MID-CHAPTER SUMMARY

Using the PERT approach the analyst must provide the following inputs:

1. A list of the activities that make up the project
2. The immediate predecessors for each activity
3. The expected value for each activity time [using $t = (a + 4m + b)/6$]
4. The standard deviation for each activity time [using $t = (b - a)/6$]

The PERT estimation procedure uses pessimistic, most likely, and optimistic estimates of the activity time to obtain the expected value and the standard deviation for each activity. The standard deviation is required only if the analyst wishes to make probability statements about completing the project by a certain date.

The analysis uses the inputs listed above to

1. Calculate the critical path.
2. Calculate the minimum expected time in which the project can be completed.
3. Show slack values for each activity, together with the latest expected time that any activity can start (or finish) without delaying the project.
4. If estimates of the standard deviation are provided, the analyst can calculate the probability that the current critical path will be completed by a specified date.

If the project cannot (or is unlikely to) be completed by a desired date, the project must be redefined either by

1. Strategic analysis, in which the project network is modified by introducing new activities or changing the relationships between existing activities, or
2. Tactical analysis, in which activity times are changed by the application of additional resources.

Using PERT as a Monitor

Finally, we can observe that PERT is not only a planning system. You can now see that it can also be used to monitor the progress of a project. Management can compare the actual activity times as they occur with those that were used in the planning process. If, for example, activity B takes 6 or 7 weeks, rather than the 5 weeks used in the network diagram, Becky would know that the project is behind schedule. This would give her the opportunity to arrange to assign more resources to some other activity on the critical path in an effort to shorten that activity and hopefully meet the desired overall due date.

Identification of the critical path and prompt reporting give management a powerful tool to deal with the difficult problem of bringing a complicated project in on schedule.

12.6

CPM AND TIME–COST TRADE-OFFS

As we have just seen, PERT provides a useful approach to the analysis of scheduling problems in the face of *uncertainty about activity times*. Such uncertainty will often be the case with new or unique projects where there is little previous time and cost experience to draw upon. In other types of projects there may be considerable historical data with which one may make good estimates of time and resource requirements. In such cases it may be of interest to deal more explicitly with costs in the sense of analyzing possibilities to shift resources in order to reduce completion time. The concept that there is a trade-off between the time that it takes to complete an activity and the cost of the resources devoted to that activity is the basis of a model that was originally part of the CPM method.

Cost as a Linear Function of Time

The model assumes that cost is a linear function of time. Consider, for example, Figure 12.19. This figure illustrates that management has the opportunity to aim at an activity time anywhere between a minimum value and a maximum value. The choice of an activity time implies an activity cost as specified by the diagram.

Given the availability of such a time–cost trade-off function for each activity in the project, management has the opportunity to select each activity time (within limits) and

Figure 12.19
Time–Cost Trade-Off Function

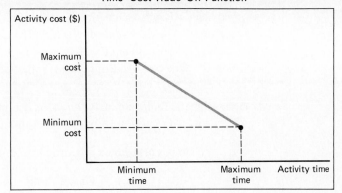

incur the associated cost. Clearly, the choice of individual activity times affects the project completion time. The question becomes: "What activity times should be selected to yield the desired project completion time at minimum cost?" The CPM approach to answering this question will be presented in the context of the creation of a financial analysis package by the Operations Analysis Group at Global.

A Financial Analysis Project for Retail Marketing

In addition to the move to Des Moines, Becky is responsible for a new financial analysis package that will be used in the retail marketing section of Global. The program is used in evaluating potential outlets (gas stations) in terms of location and other characteristics. The systems design is complete. The computer programming must still be done and the package must be introduced to the retail marketing section.

Figure 12.20 shows the activity list and network diagram for this project. The time shown is termed the **normal time.** This corresponds to the maximum time shown in Figure 12.19. Recall that we are here assuming that activity times can be estimated with good accuracy, and hence "normal time" is a known quantity. From Figure 12.20 it is clear that the longest path through the network is DAP–WAP–INT and hence this is the critical path. The earliest completion time for the project is 194 hours.

Figure 12.20
Activity List and Network Diagram for the Financial Analysis Project

ACTIVITY	IMMEDIATE PREDECESSOR	NORMAL TIME (hr)
DIP (design information processor)	—	32
WIP (write information processor)	DIP	40
DAP (design analysis package)	—	50
WAP (write analysis package)	DAP	24
INT (introduce system)	WIP, WAP	120

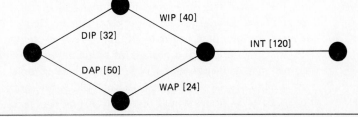

The CPM system is based on four pieces of input data for each activity:

1. *Normal time:* The maximum time for the activity
2. *Normal cost:* The cost required to achieve the normal time
3. *Crash time:* The minimum time for the activity
4. *Crash cost:* The cost required to achieve the crash time

These data for the financial analysis project are presented in the first four columns of Figure 12.21. The fifth column shows the maximum crash hours, defined by

$$\text{max crash hours} = \text{normal time} - \text{crash time}$$

Figure 12.21
Time–Cost Data for the Financial Analysis Project

ACTIVITY	(1) NORMAL TIME	(2) NORMAL COST	(3) CRASH TIME	(4) CRASH COST	(5) MAXIMUM CRASH HOURS	(6) COST PER CRASH HOUR
DIP	32	$ 640	20	$ 800	12	$13.33
WIP	40	480	30	720	10	24.00
DAP	50	1000	30	1200	20	10.00
WAP	24	288	15	360	9	8.00
INT	120	4800	70	5600	50	16.00
Total		$7208				

Figure 12.22 shows how these data are used to create the time–cost trade-off function for activity DIP, design the information processor.

Figure 12.22
Time–Cost Trade-Off Function for DIP

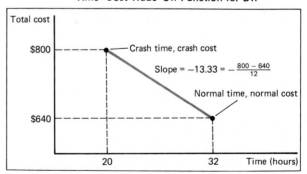

Crashing   Note that, according to Figure 12.21, using all normal times leads to a total project cost of $7208. Also note that the last column in Figure 12.21 shows how much it costs per hour (as computed in Figure 12.22) to reduce each activity time beneath its normal time. In CPM jargon, the process of reducing an activity time is called **crashing**. For example, management could choose to have DIP completed in 31 hours, rather than the normal 32 hours, for a marginal cost of $13.33. The normal time of 32 hours costs $640 and a time of 31 hours would therefore cost $640 + 13.33 = $653.33.

Crashing the Project

We have noted that, using only the normal time for each activity, the earliest completion time for this project is 194 hours (along the critical path DAP–WAP–INT). Management is now in a position to determine the minimum-cost method of reducing this time to specified levels. To reduce the project time to 193 Becky would crash an activity on the critical path by 1 hour. Since it costs less per hour to crash WAP than either of the other activities on the critical path ($8.00 < $10.00 and $8.00 < $16.00), Becky would first crash WAP by 1 hour. This decision yields a project time of 193 hours, a critical path of DAP–WAP–INT, and a total project cost of $7216 = $7208 + $8. If Becky wants to achieve a time of 192 hours, exactly the same analysis would apply and she would crash WAP by another hour and incur a marginal cost of $8.00.

If Becky has crashed WAP by 2 hours to achieve a project time of 192 hours, and still wants to crash the project by another hour (to achieve 191), the analysis becomes more complicated. Figure 12.23 shows the situation. The dollar figure in the diagram is the marginal cost of crashing. Note that there are now two critical paths, DIP–WIP–INT and DAP–WAP–INT, and that both require 192: Crashing one of the four activities (DIP, WAP, DAP, or WAP) by 1 hour would bring one path down to 191 hours, but would still leave the project time at 192, since there would still be a critical path of 192 hours. A time of 191 could only be obtained by crashing activities on both paths. If Becky crashed DIP and WAP by 1 hour each it would reduce both paths to 191 hours and it would cost her $13.33 + $8.00 = $21.33. Alternatively, INT could be crashed by 1 hour for a cost of $16.00. Can you see that there are other alternatives to consider?

Figure 12.23
Marginal Costs of Crashing the Financial Analysis Project

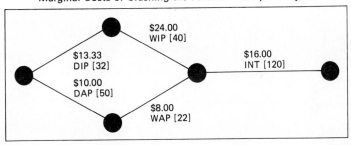

Although it is possible to do this sort of marginal cost analysis in any CPM network, it is clear that it would be difficult and tedious to carry it out in a complicated network. This consideration leads us to an LP formulation of the problem.

A Linear Programming Model The problem of obtaining a specific project time at minimum cost can be formulated as a linear programming problem. Figure 12.24 shows the formulation of the financial analysis problem with a limit of 184 hours on the project time. To understand this formulation, let

$$CWIP = \text{hours crashed on activity WIP}$$

$$ESWIP = \text{earliest start time for activity WIP}$$

$$EFINT = \text{earliest finish time for activity INT}$$

Figure 12.24
LP Solution of the Financial Analysis Problem

```
MIN 13.33 CDIP + 24 CWIP + 10 CDAP + 8 CWAP + 16 CINT
SUBJECT TO
  2)  CDIP + ESWIP ≥ 32
  3)  CDAP + ESWAP ≥ 50
  4)  CWIP − ESWIP + ESINT ≥ 40
  5)  CWAP − ESWAP + ESINT ≥ 24
  6)  CINT − ESINT + EFINT = 120
  7)  CDIP ≤ 12
  8)  CWIP ≤ 10
  9)  CDAP ≤ 20
 10)  CWAP ≤ 9
 11)  CINT ≤ 50
 12)  EFINT ≤ 184

              OBJECTIVE FUNCTION VALUE

                   144.000000

 VARIABLE         VALUE        REDUCED COST

    CDIP          0.00             5.33
    CWIP          0.00            16.00
    CDAP          0.00             2.00
    CWAP          2.00             0.00
    CINT          8.00             0.00
   ESWIP         32.00             0.00
   ESWAP         50.00             0.00
   ESINT         72.00             0.00
   EFINT        184.00             0.00

 ROW             SLACK         DUAL PRICES

    2             0.00            −8.00
    3             0.00            −8.00
    4             0.00            −8.00
    5             0.00            −8.00
    6             0.00           −16.00
    7            12.00             0.00
    8            10.00             0.00
    9            20.00             0.00
   10             7.00             0.00
   11            42.00             0.00
   12             0.00            16.00
```

The other decision variables follow this same pattern. From these definitions it follows that

1. The objective function is the total cost of crashing the network. This is the appropriate objective. The cost of completing the project on normal time is already determined. You can think of management's problem as deciding how much (and where) to crash to obtain the desired earliest finish time at minimum additional cost.

Establishing
Earliest Start
Times

2. Rows 2 through 5 establish limits for the earliest start time for activities WIP, WAP, and INT. For example, rewriting row 2 yields

$$\text{ESWIP} \geq 32 - \text{CDIP}$$

Figure 12.24
LP Solution of the Financial Analysis Problem (cont.)

```
              SENSITIVITY ANALYSIS
             OBJ COEFFICIENT RANGES

              CURRENT    ALLOWABLE    ALLOWABLE
   VARIABLE     COEF      INCREASE     DECREASE

    CDIP       13.33     INFINITY       5.33
    CWIP       24.00     INFINITY      16.00
    CDAP       10.00     INFINITY       2.00
    CWAP        8.00        2.00        5.33
    CINT       16.00        5.33        8.00
    ESWIP       0.00        5.33        8.00
    ESWAP       0.00        2.00        8.00
    ESINT       0.00        5.33        8.00
    EFINT       0.00       16.00      INFINITY


            RIGHT HAND SIDE RANGES

              CURRENT    ALLOWABLE    ALLOWABLE
    ROW         RHS       INCREASE     DECREASE

     2         32.00        2.00        7.00
     3         50.00        7.00        2.00
     4         40.00        2.00        7.00
     5         24.00        7.00        2.00
     6        120.00       42.00        8.00
     7         12.00     INFINITY      12.00
     8         10.00     INFINITY      10.00
     9         20.00     INFINITY      20.00
    10          9.00     INFINITY       7.00
    11         50.00     INFINITY      42.00
    12        184.00        8.00       42.00
```

We note that since 32 is the normal time for DIP and CDIP is the amount that DIP is crashed, the right-hand side is the time that activity DIP will take after it is crashed. Thus, this constraint states that the earliest start time for WIP must be $\geq$ the modified activity time for DIP. Since DIP is *the only* predecessor for WIP, we know that the earliest start time for WIP is exactly this modified activity time of DIP. You will thus expect to see

$$\text{ESWIP} = 32 - \text{CDIP}$$

A $\geq$ constraint is used rather than an $=$ constraint because, in general, there could be several paths leading into a node and the earliest start time of an activity leaving that node is determined by the entering path that takes the longest time. This is illustrated by rows 4 and 5. Rewriting these constraints yields

$$\text{row 4} \quad \text{ESINT} \geq 40 - \text{CWIP} + \text{ESWIP}$$
$$\text{row 5} \quad \text{ESINT} \geq 24 - \text{CWAP} + \text{ESWAP}$$

Row 4 states that INT cannot start until WIP is complete and row 5 makes a similar statement for WAP. It will often be the case that only one of these will be active in an optimal solution.

3. Row 6 is the definition of earliest finish time for activity INT:

$$EFINT = ESINT + \underbrace{120 - CINT}_{\substack{\text{activity time for} \\ \text{INT after crashing}}}$$

4. Rows 7 through 11 limit the amount of crashing on each activity. The limit is given by column (5) in Figure 12.21 "Maximum Crash Hours."

5. Row 12 sets an upper limit on the project time we want to achieve. This constraint depends on the fact that the finish time for activity INT determines the finish time for the overall project. In general, a similar constraint would be required for each activity leading into the terminal node. Here we have only one such activity, INT.

Sensitivity Analysis

The solution shows that WAP should be crashed by 2 hours and INT by 8 hours to achieve a minimum cost reduction of 10 hours in the project completion time (i.e., the optimal value of EFINT is 184 and this is the project completion time). As usual with LP output, however, this is only a samll part of the information available. For example, the dual price on row 12 tells us that it will cost $16 to crash the network for 1 additional hour. The right-hand-side ranges show that this rate of $16 per hour holds for another 42 hours. In this simple problem you can see that this next 42 hours of crashing (beyond the first 10) should be done on INT. In general this type of LP sensitivity information can provide useful guidance to management in the attempt to control the progress of large projects.

In concluding this section, we recall the sixth of the questions raised in Section 12.1: "How might I effectively concentrate resources on activities in order to speed up project completion?" In this section we have seen that in a context where time and costs are suitably defined, as in the CPM model, **project crashing** allows management to answer this question.

We now proceed to discuss the final question raised in Section 12.1: "What controls can be exercised on the flows of expenditures of the various activities throughout the duration of the project in order that the overall budget can be adhered to?"

12.7
PROJECT COST MANAGEMENT: PERT/COST

The desirability of a project typically depends on its total costs and revenues. (Discounting may be necessary to express costs and/or returns in current dollars if the project is of long duration.) Once a project has been selected, effective cost management includes two important functions: planning and control.

Planning Costs for the Credit Card Project: The PERT/Cost System

Large projects can strongly influence the financial situation within a firm. The need to pay for the various activities creates a demand on both the firm's overall budget and the daily cash flow. Obviously, the times at which activities are scheduled determines when budget demands occur.

It is important for a firm to be able to anticipate budget demands in order to be able to handle them economically and effectively. The PERT/Cost system is specifically designed to help management anticipate such demands in a clear and consistent manner. PERT/Cost is essentially an alternative approach to cost accounting. Typically, cost accounting systems are organized on a cost center basis (e.g., by departments). The PERT/Cost system is organized on a project basis, where the basic elements of control are the activities.

In order to apply the PERT/Cost system to the project of moving the credit-card operation to Des Moines, Becky must now complete Figure 12.8 by filling in the final column, titled "Resources." This is an estimated or "expected" total cost of completing each activity. These expected activity costs, together with the expected activity times, the earliest start time, and the latest start time are presented in Figure 12.25 for the redefined credit-card project. The earliest start and latest start data are taken from the computer solution, Figure 12.16.

Figure 12.25
Resource Requirements for the Redesigned Project

ACTIVITY	EXPECTED TIME	EARLIEST START	LATEST START	TOTAL RESOURCES REQUIRED
A	3	0	5	$ 2,100
B	5	0	0	5,000
C	3	5	5	1,800
D	4	8	8	4,800
E	8	12	12	32,000
F	2	8	11	1,000
G	4	10	13	2,800
H	2	10	18	7,000
I	5	5	15	4,000
J	3	14	17	30,000
K	3	10	14	1,500
Total				$92,000

Pattern of Expenditures

The goal of the PERT/Cost system is to construct a graph of budget demands over time. This requires knowledge of how funds will be spent throughout the life of an activity. For example, the demands on the budget are different if the $32,000 for activity E, construct the interior, is due at the beginning of the 8-week activity time or at the end of it. PERT/Cost makes the assumption that expenditures occur uniformly throughout the life of the activity; that is, for E a budget demand of $4000 occurs during each of the 8 weeks.

Figure 12.26 shows the budget demands by time if all activities start at their **earliest start time**. This table is constructed by assigning a row to each activity and recording the budget demands for that activity in the appropriate column (week) as determined by the earliest start time. In forming this table, "earliest start" times are interpreted as referring to the end of the appropriate week. Thus activity B starts at time 0 (the end of week 0 = beginning of week 1) and requires 5 weeks to complete. This means that activity C, as shown in Figure 12.26, cannot start until the end of week 5. It lasts 3 weeks and makes a budget demand of $600 per week. All of this information is summarized in the third row of Figure 12.26.

The total weekly cost is determined by adding down a column, that is, by adding the budget demands during the week from all the activities. For example, the budget demand during the thirteenth week is $5200, the sum of $4000 from E, $700 from G, and $500 from K.

Figure 12.26

Budget Demands: Earliest Start Time

ACTIVITY	1	2	3	4	5	6	7	8	9	10	11	12	13	14	15	16	17	18	19	20
A	700	700	700																	
B		1,000	1,000	1,000	1,000															
C						600	600	600												
D									1,200	1,200	1,200	1,200								
E													4,000	4,000	4,000	4,000	4,000	4,000	4,000	4,000
F									500	500										
G											700	700	700	700						
H											3,500	3,500								
I						800	800	800	800	800										
J															10,000	10,000	10,000			
K											500	500	500							
Weekly cost	1,700	1,700	1,700	1,000	1,000	1,400	1,400	1,400	2,500	2,500	5,900	5,900	5,200	4,700	14,000	14,000	14,000	4,000	4,000	4,000
Cumulative project cost	1,700	3,400	5,100	6,100	7,100	8,500	9,900	11,300	13,800	16,300	22,200	28,100	33,500	38,000	52,000	66,000	80,000	84,000	88,000	92,000

WEEK

Figure 12.27

Budget Demands: Latest Start Time

ACTIVITY									WEEK											
	1	2	3	4	5	6	7	8	9	10	11	12	13	14	15	16	17	18	19	20
A						700	700	700												
B	1,000	1,000	1,000	1,000	1,000															
C						600	600	600												
D									1,200	1,200	1,200	1,200								
E													4,000	4,000	4,000	4,000	4,000	4,000	4,000	4,000
F												500	500							
G														700	700	700	700			
H																			3,500	3,500
I																800	800	800	800	800
J																		10,000	10,000	10,000
Weekly cost	1,000	1,000	1,000	1,000	1,000	1,300	1,300	1,300	1,200	1,200	1,200	1,700	4,500	4,700	5,200	6,000	6,000	14,800	18,300	18,300
Cumulative project cost	1,000	2,000	3,000	4,000	5,000	6,300	7,600	8,900	10,100	11,300	12,500	14,200	18,700	23,400	28,600	34,600	40,600	55,400	73,700	92,000

The total project cost is found by cumulating the weekly costs from the beginning of the project. For example, note that the weekly cost is $1700 for each of the first 3 weeks. The total project cost after 3 weeks is therefore $5100. The total cost at the end of the project (week 20) must, of course, be the total cost for the entire project.

Figure 12.27 creates the profile of budget demands over time if each activity starts at its **latest start time**.

Plot of
Cumulative
Budget
Demands

The information from Figures 12.26 and 12.27 is combined in Figure 12.28. The upper line is a plot of the earliest start time costs from Figure 12.26 and the lower line is a plot of the latest start time costs from Figure 12.27. The shaded area between the lines shows the area of feasible cumulative budgets for total project costs if the project is completed on time. The fact that the actual budget demands must fall within the envelope created by the earliest start time and the latest start time makes it easy for management to anticipate its cumulative expenditures. For example, Becky can see that by the end of week 11 Global Oil will have to have spent between $12,500 and $22,200.

We have progressed step-by-step through the budget calculations for the PERT/ Cost planning system because this is a useful exercise from the pedagogical point of

Figure 12.28
Cumulative Budget Demands versus Time

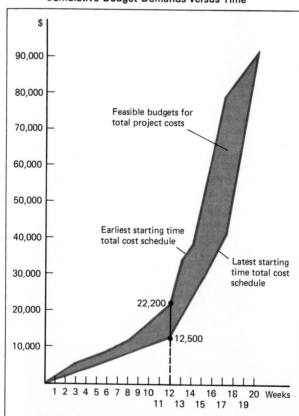

view. In practice these calculations are typically done on a computer. Figure 12.29 shows the computer output that corresponds to Figures 12.26 and 12.27.

Figure 12.29

Computer Analysis of Budget Demands

```
RESOURCE USAGE PROFILE ACCORDING TO EARLIEST START TIME
       TIME INTERVAL                RESOURCE USAGE

   FROM END      TO END
   OF WEEK       OF WEEK         WEEKLY       CUMULATIVE

     0.00→        3.00          1700.00        5100.00
     3.00→        5.00          1000.00        7100.00
     5.00→        8.00          1400.00       11300.00
     8.00→       10.00          2500.00       16300.00
    10.00→       12.00          5900.00       28100.00
    12.00→       13.00          5200.00       33300.00
    13.00→       14.00          4700.00       38000.00
    14.00→       17.00         14000.00       80000.00
    17.00→       20.00          4000.00       92000.00


RESOURCE USAGE PROFILE ACCORDING TO LATEST START TIME
       TIME INTERVAL                RESOURCE USAGE

   FROM END      TO END
   OF WEEK       OF WEEK         WEEKLY       CUMULATIVE

     0.00→        5.00          1000.00        5000.00
     5.00→        8.00          1300.00        8900.00
     8.00→       11.00          1200.00       12500.00
    11.00→       12.00          1700.00       14200.00
    12.00→       13.00          4500.00       18700.00
    13.00→       14.00          4700.00       23400.00
    14.00→       15.00          5200.00       28600.00
    15.00→       17.00          6000.00       40600.00
    17.00→       18.00         14800.00       55400.00
    18.00→       20.00         18300.00       92000.00
```

Controlling Project Costs The concept behind any control system is to compare the *actual performance* with *planned performance* and to take remedial action if it is necessary. The thermostat in your house is a control system that operates continuously in time by comparing the actual temperature to the desired temperature and turning the furnace (air conditioner) off or on as necessary.

The PERT/Cost system compares actual project costs to budgeted project costs at regular intervals so that management has an early indication if the project is not proceeding according to plan. Management is then in a position to take appropriate action.

PERT/Cost Control Report Figure 12.30 is a PERT/Cost *control report* prepared 11 weeks after the start of the redefined project to move the credit-card operation to Des Moines. The labels on the columns indicate how the report is prepared. Column (4), the actual cost, and column (3),

Figure 12.30
Project Costs after 11 Weeks

ACTIVITY	(1) PERCENT COMPLETE	(2) BUDGET	(3) [(1)/100] × (2) BUDGETED COST TO DATE	(4) ACTUAL COST TO DATE	(5) (4) − (3) COST OVERRUN TO DATE
A	100	2,100	2,100	2,300	200
B	100	5,000	5,000	4,900	(100)
C	100	1,800	1,800	1,800	0
D	75	4,800	3,600	4,600	1,000
E	0	32,000	0	0	0
F	100	1,000	1,000	1,200	200
G	25	2,800	700	1,400	700
H	50	7,000	3,500	5,400	1,900
I	20	4,000	800	500	(300)
J	0	30,000	0	0	0
K	0	1,500	0	0	0
Total		92,000	18,500	22,100	3,600

the budgeted cost, provide the basic information used in the control function. The actual cost, column (4), is self-explanatory. *The budgeted cost, column (3), is calculated on the assumption that the percentage of budget used up by an activity is the same as the percentage of that activity that is completed.* Thus, when an activity is 50% complete, its budgeted cost is 50% of the entire budget [column (2)] for that activity. Note that if an activity is completed, the entry in column (1) is 100 and this means the entry in column (3) will be the same as the entry in column (2). Consider, for example, activity A, "select office site." We see from column (1) of Figure 12.30 that this activity, by the end of week (11), is 100% complete. Thus, its budgeted cost, column (3), is equal to its entire budget [column (2)] of $2100. Since its actual cost is $2300, there is a cost overrun of $200. This number is recorded in the last column. A similar interpretation applies to activity I, "make financial arrangements." It is 20% complete and has a budget of $4000; thus, its budgeted cost is $800 ($800 = 0.20 × $4000). Since only $500 has been spent, there is a budget surplus of $300. The parentheses in the last column indicate a budget surplus.

In this situation, since activities A and F are already completed, their cost overruns cannot be corrected. However, activities D, G, and H, none of which are yet complete, are showing significant overruns to date and these activities should be promptly reviewed. This type of periodic managerial intervention is often required to keep the total project cost within the budget.

Although PERT/Cost can provide an effective control procedure, it is well to be aware of potential implementation problems. For example, the required recording of data can involve significant clerical effort, especially when many projects with many activities are underway. Moreover, some costs such as overhead may be common to several activities. The allocation of such common costs can be problematic. Finally, as we mentioned at the beginning of Section 12.7, the PERT/Cost system differs in organization from typical cost accounting systems. The typical departmental cost center orientation needs to be substantially revised to handle the PERT/Cost activity oriented system. Such redesign may be politically as well as materially expensive.

12.8

MAJOR CONCEPTS QUIZ

True–False

1. **T F** In a PERT network diagram, each activity is represented by a circle called a node.
2. **T F** The term "event" is used to refer to nodes in a PERT network.
3. **T F** A dummy activity is required in a correct network representation of the following activity list.

ACTIVITY	IMMEDIATE PREDECESSORS
1	—
2	—
3	1
4	2, 3
5	2
6	5

4. **T F** The earliest finish time for an activity depends on the earliest finish time for the project.
5. **T F** The latest finish time for an activity depends on the earliest finish time for the project.
6. **T F** All activities on the critical path have their latest finish time equal to their earliest start time.
7. **T F** A strategic analysis of a PERT network concentrates on the allocation of resources to reduce the time on the critical path.
8. **T F** The probability of completing the project by time T is equal to the probability of completing the critical path by time T.
9. **T F** The standard deviation of an activity time is estimated as $(b - a)/6$, where b is the pessimistic and a is the optimistic time.
10. **T F** The CPM approach to time–cost trade-offs assumes that cost is a linear function of time.
11. **T F** The LP formulation of the network crashing problem minimizes total (cost of) crashing subject to an upper bound on project duration.
12. **T F** In the PERT/Cost model the earliest starting time total cost schedule always is less than or equal to the latest starting time total cost schedule.
13. **T F** Time variabilities leading to a longer than expected total time for the critical path will always extend the project completion date.
14. **T F** If a noncritical activity is delayed more than its slack time, all other factors unchanged, then the project completion date will be extended.
15. **T F** Gantt charts provide useful immediate predecessor information.

Multiple Choice

16. Of all paths through the network, the critical path
    a. has the maximum expected time
    b. has the minimum expected time
    c. has the maximum actual time
    d. has the minimum actual time
17. The earliest start time (ES) for an activity leaving node C
    a. is the max of the earliest finish times for all activities entering node C

b. equals the earliest finish time for the same activity minus its expected activity time
c. depends on all paths leading from the start through node C
d. all of the above

18. The latest finish time for an activity entering node H
a. equals the max of the latest start times for all activities leaving node H
b. depends on the latest finish time for the project
c. equals the latest start time minus the activity time for the same activity
d. none of the above

19. The slack for activity G
a. equals EF for G − ES for G
b. equals LF for G − ES for G
c. equals LS for G − ES for G
d. none of the above

20. Estimating expected activity times in a PERT network
a. makes use of three estimates
b. puts the greatest weight on the most likely time estimate
c. is motivated by a beta distribution
d. all of the above

21. The calculation that the critical path will be completed by time T
a. assumes that activity times are statistically independent
b. assumes that total time of the critical path has approximately a beta distribution
c. requires knowledge of the standard deviation for all activities in the network
d. all of the above

22. In the CPM time—cost trade-off function,
a. the cost at normal time is 0
b. within the range of feasible times, the activity cost increases linearly as time increases
c. cost decreases linearly as time increases
d. none of the above

23. The marginal cost of crashing a network could change when
a. the activity being crashed reaches its crash time
b. the activity being crashed reaches a point where another path is also critical
c. both a and b

24. Fundamental ideas in the LP network crashing models are
a. activity time equals normal time + crash time
b. earliest start time for an activity leaving a node equals the max of the earliest finish times for activities leaving that node
c. earliest finish time equals latest finish time minus activity time
d. none of the above

25. The PERT/Cost model assumes that
a. each activity achieves its optimistic time
b. the costs are uniformly distributed over the life of the activity
c. that activity times are statistically independent
d. none of the above

26. The PERT/Cost control report
a. requires a budget for each activity
b. requires a report on the percentage of completion of each activity
c. calculates cost overruns
d. all of the above

Answers

1. F	10. T	19. c
2. T	11. T	20. d
3. T	12. F	21. a
4. F	13. T	22. c
5. T	14. T	23. c
6. F	15. F	24. d
7. F	16. a	25. b
8. F	17. d	26. d
9. T	18. b	

12-1. The Build-Rite Construction Company has identified 10 activities that take place in building a house. They are:

1. Walls and ceiling (erect the wall frames and ceiling joists).
2. Foundation (pour the foundation slab).
3. Roof timbers (put up the roof timbers).
4. Roof sheathing (install roof sheathing over the timbers).
5. Electrical wiring (install the electrical wiring).
6. Roof shingles (shingle the roof).
7. Exterior siding (put on the exterior siding).
8. Windows (install the window units).
9. Paint (paint the interior and exterior).
10. Inside wall board (hang the inside wall board).

In addition, the following customs are typically observed:

1. Wiring is done from the interior side of the wall, while the window unit is mounted after the wall frame has been erected.
2. Inside wall board and exterior siding are installed over the window unit.
3. Painting is not begun until the house is watertight.

Make a list showing each activity and its immediate predecessors.

12-2. Quacker Mills hires engineering undergraduates and moves them through six management experiences (activities) to prepare them to be plant managers. There are three disciplines and two positions (starting and advanced) in each discipline. These six activities are shown in Figure 12.31. Further, one cannot be a department head unless he has been a production line engineer, nor can he be a product line scheduler unless he has been a foreman. Make an activity list showing each activity and its immediate predecessors.

Figure 12.31

| | DISCIPLINE | | |
	Plant Engineering	Line Supervision	Production Planning
Starting	Production Line Engineer 1	Foreman 2	Assistant Product Line Scheduler 3
Advanced	Plant Engineer 4	Department Head 5	Product Line Scheduler 6

12-3. Construct the network diagram for the house construction system used by Build-Rite Construction Company in Problem 12-1.

12-4. Given the activity list in Figure 12.32, construct a network diagram.

Figure 12.32

ACTIVITY	IMMEDIATE PREDECESSORS
1	—
2	—
3	—
4	1, 2
5	3
6	1
7	4, 5, 6
8	3
9	8
10	4, 5
11	10, 9
12	7
13	11, 12

12-5. Build-Rite has estimated the times given in Figure 12.33 as necessary to complete each of the tasks involved in building a house.

Figure 12.33

ACTIVITY NUMBER	ACTIVITY	IMMEDIATE PREDECESSORS	EXPECTED TIME (DAYS)
1	Walls and ceiling	2	5
2	Foundation	—	3
3	Roof timbers	1	2
4	Roof sheathing	3	3
5	Electrical wiring	1	4
6	Roof shingles	4	8
7	Exterior siding	8	5
8	Windows	1	2
9	Paint	6, 7, 10	2
10	Inside wall board	8, 5	3

For each activity, define:
(a) Earliest start time
(b) Earliest finish time
(c) Latest start time
(d) Latest finish time
(e) Slack
In addition, identify the critical path.

12-6. As a project manager, you are faced with the activity network and estimated activity times shown in Figure 12.34. For each activity, define
(a) Earliest start time
(b) Earliest finish time
(c) Latest start time
(d) Latest finish time
(e) Slack
In addition, identify the critical path.

Figure 12.34

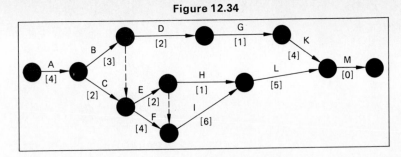

12-7. You are called in as a production consultant. The plant currently uses a PERT–CPM approach to a production run described by the activity network of Figure 12.35.

Figure 12.35

Based on your evaluation, however, the immediate predecessors of each activity are as follows:

ACTIVITY	IMMEDIATE PREDECESSORS
A	—
B	—
C	A
D	B
E	B
F	C
G	D
H	E
I	G
J	E
K	H
L	F
M	L, I, K, J

(a) Draw the revised activity network.

(b) Compute earliest and latest start and finish times for the revised network based on the assumption that each activity takes 1 hour longer than its alphabetic predecessor (i.e., A = 1 hour, B = 2 hours, etc.). Find the slack of each activity. Identify the critical path. How much less time does the production run take under this revised activity network than it did with the original network?

12-8. Consider the network and activity times shown in Figure 12.36. You would like to reduce the minimum time to complete the project. Suppose that you can reduce an activity time as much as you like as long as you increase some other activity or activities by the same amount. For example, you can reduce G by 1 hour if you increase C and D by $\frac{1}{2}$ hour each. Assume that activity times of zero are permissible.

Figure 12.36

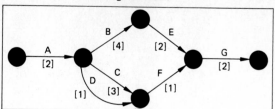

(a) Find the current critical path and the minimum time required to complete the project.

(b) Reallocate times to achieve the minimum possible time to complete the project. Note that in this network, the total of all activity times must equal the current total which is 15 hours.

12-9. Based on company history, Build-Rite's management has determined that the optimistic, most probable, and pessimistic times for each activity are as follows:

ACTIVITY NUMBER	ACTIVITY	OPTIMISTIC TIME (DAYS) *a*	MOST PROBABLE TIME (DAYS) *m*	PESSIMISTIC TIME (DAYS) *b*
1	Walls and ceiling	3	5	7
2	Foundation	2	3	4
3	Roof timbers	1	2	3
4	Roof sheathing	1	2	9
5	Electrical wiring	4	4	4
6	Roof shingles	4	8	12
7	Exterior siding	1	3	17
8	Windows	1	2	3
9	Paint	2	2	2
10	Inside wall board	2	3	4

Compute the expected activity time and the standard deviation for each activity.

12-10. Based on the activity network and the associated activity times shown in Figure 12.37,

Figure 12.37

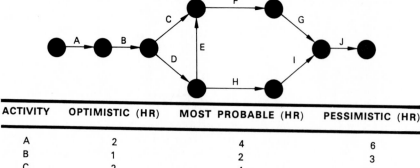

ACTIVITY	OPTIMISTIC (HR)	MOST PROBABLE (HR)	PESSIMISTIC (HR)
A	2	4	6
B	1	2	3
C	2	4	12
D	1	4	7
E	1	1	1
F	1	3	5
G	2	4	6
H	1	6	11
I	2	2	2
J	2	3	4

compute the expected value and the standard deviation for each activity time. Find the earliest start times, earliest finish times, latest start times, latest finish times, and slack for each activity. Specify the critical path.

12-11. Assume that activity times in Build-Rite's activity network (see Problem 12-9) are independent of each other and that the sum of any combination of activity times is normally distributed. What is the probability that all the activities on the current critical path will be completed within 12 days? Within 25 days? Is this the same as the probability that a house will be completed within 25 days? Comment.

12-12. As a project manager, you are faced with the activity network of Figure 12.38 and the associated estimates of optimistic, most probable, and pessimistic activity times shown below.

Figure 12.38

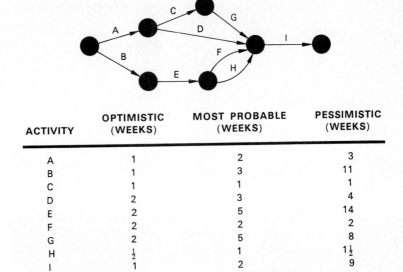

ACTIVITY	OPTIMISTIC (WEEKS)	MOST PROBABLE (WEEKS)	PESSIMISTIC (WEEKS)
A	1	2	3
B	1	3	11
C	1	1	1
D	2	3	4
E	2	5	14
F	2	2	2
G	2	5	8
H	$\frac{1}{2}$	1	$1\frac{1}{2}$
I	1	2	9

(a) Compute the expected activity time and standard deviation for each activity time, assuming a unimodal beta probability distribution for each activity time. Identify the critical path and expected time for completion of the project.

(b) Under the usual assumptions find the probability that the activities on the critical path will be completed within 17 weeks.

(c) How many weeks should be allowed to give a 95% probability of completing the critical path on time?

12-13. Build-Rite's engineers have calculated the cost of completing each activity in both normal time and crash time, where the values for normal time and crash time respectively correspond to the estimates of expected time and optimistic time from Problem 12-9. Their results follow:

(a) Specify the normal time, normal cost, crash time, crash cost, maximum crash days, and cost per crash day for each activity. Assume linear cost relationships.

(b) Compute the expected cost of the project (based on normal time).

(c) Suppose that the company has to reduce the completion time by 7 days. How much would this reduction cost? How much would it cost to reduce the completion time by 11 days?

ACTIVITY	ACTIVITY	NORMAL COST	CRASH COST
1	Walls and ceiling	$50	$72
2	Foundation	20	30
3	Roof timbers	15	30
4	Roof sheathing	8	20
5	Electrical wiring	30	30
6	Roof shingles	13	21
7	Exterior siding	65	45
8	Windows	45	52
9	Paint	40	40
10	Inside wall board	22	34

12-14. Consider the activity network in Problem 12-10. The following are estimates of costs for completion in crash time and normal time, where the times correspond to the optimistic and expected time, respectively.

ACTIVITY	CRASH COST	NORMAL COST
A	$60	$40
B	19	12
C	60	48
D	30	24
E	10	10
F	39	25
G	28	18
H	71	46
I	30	30
J	34	25

(a) Prepare a table showing the normal time, normal cost, crash time, crash cost, maximum crash hours, and cost per crash hour for each activity.
(b) What would be the cost of the project if it were to be completed in
   (i) 18 hours?
   (ii) 15 hours?
   (iii) 10 hours?

12-15. Refer to Problem 12-13 and formulate a linear programming model that would allow Build-Rite to assess the cost of crashing its activity network by x hours.

12-16. Consider the activity network and normal activity times shown in Figure 12.39, as well as the following data. Formulate a linear programming model that will assess the additional cost of reducing the completion time to 45 units.

Figure 12.39

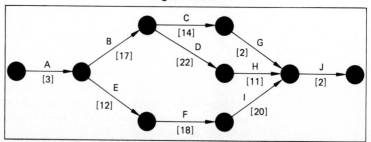

ACTIVITY	COST/CRASH UNIT	MAXIMUM CRASH UNITS
A	12	1
B	15	4
C	25	10
D	16	8
E	4	2
F	9	3
G	21	1
H	18	5
I	7	6
J	19	1

12-17. Use the normal costs from Problem 12-13 and the time data from Problem 12-5 to construct early-start and late-start cost tables and the graph of cumulative expenditures versus time for Build-Rite.

12-18. Figure 12.40 shows the activity network for the Molotov Explosives Company (activity times shown in brackets). Activity costs for Molotov Explosives' production process follow:

Figure 12.40

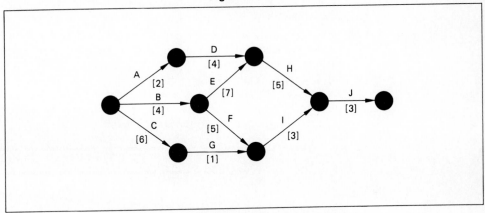

ACTIVITY	COST
A	40
B	60
C	72
D	28
E	56
F	25
G	13
H	55
I	27
J	39
Total cost	$415

Construct early-start and late-start cost tables and a graph of cumulative expenditures versus time for a production run. Assume that costs are incurred linearly for each activity.

12-19. Build-Rite's record of historical expenditures at the end of day 15 is as follows:

ACTIVITY NUMBER	ACTIVITY	COST INCURRED TO DATE
2	Foundation	$22
1	Walls and ceiling	46
3	Roof timbers	15
4	Roof sheathing	10
6	Roof shingles	4.50
5	Electrical wiring	20
8	Windows	22.50
10	Inside wall board	20
7	Exterior siding	40
9	Paint	0

Evaluate the current project costs based on the assumption that:
(a) All activities begin on the earliest possible date and that the expected value is the time required.
(b) All activities begin on the latest possible start date and that the expected value is the time required.
In both cases, assume that budgeted cost is equal to the budget for the completed activity multiplied by the proportion of the activity that is complete.

12-20. Review the data for Molotov Explosives (Problem 12-18). Prepare an analysis of the current production costs if the figures below represent costs incurred at the end of
(a) The tenth unit of time.
(b) The eleventh unit of time.
Assume that the budgeted cost is equal to the budget for the completed activity multiplied by the proportion of the activity that is complete. Assume further that all activities are proceeding along the earliest start schedule.

ACTIVITY	COST INCURRED TO DATE
A	$45
B	55
C	70
D	32
E	53
F	27
G	13
H	0
I	15
J	15

12-21. This is a more complex version of Problem 12-8. As the Production Foreman for the Hurricane Fan Company, you have used PERT–CPM techniques to schedule your production runs. Your current activity network and activity times are shown in Figure 12.41. The production consultant from Problem 12-8 has pointed out that, due to the similarity in job skills needed for each activity, resources are perfectly transferable between activities (i.e., the time required to do an activity can be reduced by any amount by increasing the time required for another job by the same amount). If the consultant is correct, how much can the time needed for each production run be reduced?

Figure 12.41

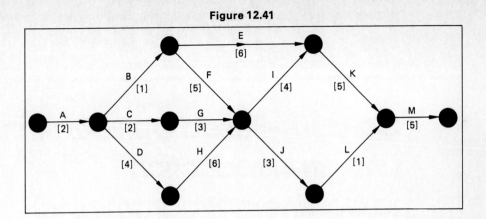

CHAPTER 13

Calculus-Based Optimization and an Introduction to Nonlinear Programming

13.1

INTRODUCTION

There are many problems in business and economics where the functions or mathematical relationships involved are not all linear. In fact, it is probably true that the real-world problems which fit the strict mold of linearity are the exception rather than the rule. As a simple illustration:

In a linear model price is usually assumed to be a given constant, say p, and quantity to be sold is a variable x which is assumed to be independent of price. Hence, revenue is given by px, and we say that revenue is proportional to price. In reality, however, price may be a variable and quantity of sales (demand) might be dependent on price. This dependency is expressed by writing sales $= f(p)$, where f is some specified (nonconstant) function of p. Thus, revenue would be given by

$$\text{revenue} = \text{price} \cdot \text{sales} = pf(p)$$

which is nonlinear in the variable p. In this case a model to find the price level that maximizes revenue would be a nonlinear model.

In general, some of the prominent (and not necessarily distinct) reasons for nonlinearity are (1) nonproportional relationships [in the example above, revenue is not proportional to price, for, depending on the specific form of $f(p)$, price may increase and revenue decrease]; (2) nonadditive relationships (e.g., when two chemicals are added together the resulting volume need not be the sum of the two added volumes); and (3) efficiencies or inefficiencies of scale (e.g., when too many workers try to plant beans on the same acre of ground they begin to get into each other's way and the yield per worker will decrease, as opposed to remaining constant[1]). In short, any number of physical, structural, biological, economic, and logical relationships may be responsible for the appearance of nonlinearity in a model.

It must be stated at the outset that, although nonlinear phenomena are common, nonlinear models are considerably more difficult to solve than linear models. Combine

[1]Note that this leads to a nonproportional relationship between total yield and number of workers.

423

CHAPTER 13
Calculus-Based
Optimization and
an Introduction
to Nonlinear
Programming

this with the fact that linear models, in many contexts, provide *good approximations* to nonlinear models, and you can understand the popularity of linear models, such as LP.

As we know, a model is not the real world. It is an abstract representation of reality. The important point for the modeler is to know when a linearized version provides an *adequate* representation of the nonlinear world. The answer to such a judgmental question comes with experimentation and much experience, and even then only imperfectly and often without consensus. In this chapter we want to address those situations where nonlinear programming models are deemed to be required. Our objective is to provide some understanding of the tools and concepts necessary to deal with nonlinear programming models.

The chapter is organized as follows. The first two sections review the facts concerning *unconstrained* optimization in several decision variables. Then we give a descriptive and geometric introduction to constrained nonlinear optimization. We then focus on problems with equality constraints, emphasizing the role of Lagrange multipliers and their interpretation in a pricing context. Following this, we loosely define the concept of concave and convex programs and discuss in a qualitative way the kinds of nonlinear problems that can be routinely solved. The chapter concludes with some notes on implementation of NLP (nonlinear programming), including a brief discussion of the nature of some of the algorithms used to solve NLP problems.

13.2

UNCONSTRAINED OPTIMIZATION
IN TWO DECISION VARIABLES

Let us first consider the case of two decision variables, x_1 and x_2. Thus, we consider a function $f(x_1, x_2)$. For the case of two decision variables (that is, two independent variables) we must use partial derivatives to describe local or global optima. We shall use the notation f_{x_i} for first partial derivative, $f_{x_i x_i}$ for second partial derivative, and so on. Any point at which all first partial derivatives vanish is called a **stationary point**. We have the following **necessary condition** for optimality.

> At a local max or min both partial derivatives must equal zero (i.e., $f_{x_1} = f_{x_2} = 0$). That is, a local maximizer or a local minimizer is always a stationary point.

However, not all stationary points provide maxima and minima. Thus, we may wish to employ the so-called second-order (meaning that second derivatives are involved) sufficient condition for optimality, which is somewhat more complicated than the necessary condition. The rule is:

> Suppose that $x^* = (x_1^*, x_2^*)$ is a stationary point of f. Define
>
> $$D = D(x_1^*, x_2^*) = [f_{x_1 x_1}(x_1^*, x_2^*)][f_{x_1 x_1}(x_1^*, x_2^*)] - [f_{x_1 x_2}(x_1^*, x_2^*)]^2$$

Case 1: If $f_{x_1 x_1}(x_1^*, x_2^*) > 0$ and $D > 0$, then (x_1^*, x_2^*) is a local **minimizer**.
Case 2: If $f_{x_1 x_1}(x_1^*, x_2^*) < 0$ and $D > 0$, then (x_1^*, x_2^*) is a local **maximizer**.

424

CHAPTER 13
Calculus-Based
Optimization and
an Introduction
to Nonlinear
Programming

Case 3: If $D < 0$ then (x_1^*, x_2^*) is a so-called saddle point, which is neither a local minimizer or maximizer. Indeed, at such a point the function will attain a local max with respect to one of the variables and a local min with respect to the other, thereby having a saddle shape at that point.

Case 4: If $D = 0$, further analysis (beyond the scope of the present discussion) is required to determine the nature of the stationary point.

Note, in the above conditions, that if $f_{x_1 x_1}(x_1^*, x_2^*) = 0$ then $D \leq 0$ and we are in either Case 3 or Case 4.

Importing Coconut Oil: Profit Maximization

Hoot Spa imports coconut oil from his home town in Jamaica. He uses this oil to produce two kinds of tanning creme: Sear and Char. The price per pound at which he will be able to sell these products depends on how much of each he produces. In particular, if Hoot produces x_1 pounds of Sear and x_2 pounds of Char, he will be able to sell all he produces at the following prices (in dollars):

$$\text{price per pound of Sear} = 80 - 3x_1$$

and

$$\text{price per pound of Char} = 60 - 2x_2$$

The cost of manufacturing x_1 pounds of Sear and x_2 pounds of Char is

$$\text{cost of manufacturing the two cremes} = 12x_1 + 8x_2 + 4x_1 x_2$$

Assuming that he can sell all he produces, Hoot wishes to determine how many pounds of each creme he should schedule for production so as to maximize his profit.

We observe that

$$\text{revenue received for Sear} = x_1(80 - 3x_1)$$
$$\text{revenue received for Char} = x_2(60 - 2x_2)$$
$$\text{total revenue received} = x_1(80 - 3x_1) + x_2(60 - 2x_2)$$
$$\text{profit received} = x_1(80 - 3x_1) + x_2(60 - 2x_2) - (12x_1 + 8x_2 + 4x_1 x_2)$$
$$= 80x_1 - 3x_1^2 + 60x_2 - 2x_2^2 - 12x_1 - 8x_2 - 4x_1 x_2$$
$$= P(x_1 x_2)$$
$$= \text{profit function}$$

To find the optimal production schedule we first locate the stationary points of the profit function. Taking first partial derivatives of $P(x_1, x_2)$ yields

$$P_{x_1} = 80 - 6x_1 - 12 - 4x_2$$
$$P_{x_2} = 60 - 4x_2 - 8 - 4x_1$$

Hence, solving the **necessary** optimality conditions $P_{x_1} = 0$ and $P_{x_2} = 0$ gives

$$6x_1 + 4x_2 = 68$$
$$4x_1 + 4x_2 = 52$$

425

CHAPTER 13
Calculus-Based
Optimization and
an Introduction
to Nonlinear
Programming

The solution to these simultaneous equations is

$$x_1^* = 8 \text{ pounds} \quad \text{and} \quad x_2^* = 5 \text{ pounds}$$

To see whether this solution actually gives a local maximum, we check the second-order conditions. The second partials of $P(x_1, x_2)$ are

$$P_{x_1 x_1} = -6, \quad P_{x_2 x_2} = -4, \quad P_{x_1 x_2} = -4$$

Hence,

$$D = P_{x_1 x_1} P_{x_2 x_2} - P_{x_1 x_2}^2 = (-6)(-4) - (-4)^2 = 8 > 0$$

Since $P_{x_1 x_1} = -6 < 0$ and $D > 0$, it follows from Case 2 above that we have a local maximum. In fact (using methods beyond our scope), it can be demonstrated that $P(x_1 x_2)$ is a strictly concave function and hence the solution $(x_1^* = 8, x_2^* = 5)$ is in fact a unique global maximizer of the profit. Thus, Hoot should produce 8 pounds of Sear and 5 pounds of Char in order to maximize his profit.

Let us now exercise these tools on the following problem.

Example 1   Define

$$f(x_1, x_2) = 5x_1^2 + 10x_2^2 + 10x_1 x_2 - 22x_1 - 32x_2 + 20$$

Let us find all local maximizers and minimizers of this function. To achieve this, we first set both first partials equal to zero and find all solutions. This gives all stationary points of the function, and among these points will be the points we are seeking. Proceeding, then, we obtain

$$f_{x_1} = 10x_1 + 10x_2 - 22 = 0$$
$$f_{x_2} = 20x_2 + 10x_1 - 32 = 0$$

Solving these two equations in two unknowns yields

$$x_1^* = 1.2, \quad x_2^* = 1.0$$

Thus, there is only one stationary point. To determine its nature we first compute the second partials at (x_1^*, x_2^*):

$$f_{x_1 x_1} = 10, \quad f_{x_2 x_2} = 20, \quad f_{x_1 x_2} = 10$$

Since

$$f_{x_1 x_1} = 10 > 0$$

and

$$D = (f_{x_1 x_1})(f_{x_2 x_2}) - (f_{x_1 x_2})^2 = (10)(20) - 10^2 = 100 > 0$$

Case 1 applies and the point (1.2, 1.0) is a local minimizer of the function.

Thus, we have seen that (just as for functions of a single variable) there is a first-order (first derivative) and second-order (involving second derivatives) test that can be applied to locate unconstrained local optima. These tests are called **first-order optimality conditions** and **second-order optimality conditions**. Note that the first-order conditions

426

CHAPTER 13
Calculus-Based
Optimization and
an Introduction
to Nonlinear
Programming

are necessary; the second-order conditions are sufficient. Also note that the second-order conditions subsume the first-order ones (that is, the second order conditions assume that x_1^*, x_2^* is a stationary point).

In the absence of knowledge that the function is either concave or convex, a local (as opposed to global) optimizer is the most that one can generally hope to find. The first derivative test (the necessary condition) says that the local optima are contained among the stationary points of the function. The second derivative test (the sufficient condition) allows us to distinguish between local maximizers and minimizers, and points which are neither.

Let us now move on to the most general case, a function of n variables.

13.3

UNCONSTRAINED OPTIMIZATION
IN n DECISION VARIABLES: THE COMPUTER APPROACH

For a differentiable function of n variables, each local optimizer is a stationary point. In order to guarantee that a stationary point is, for example, a local maximizer, second-order sufficiency conditions must be invoked. Although these two types of optimality conditions have theoretic interest they have, for many nonlinear problems in more than two variables, limited *practical relevance*. The reasons are:

1. Setting the first partial derivatives equal to zero gives a system of n equations in n unknowns. Unless this system is linear (i.e., the original function was quadratic) it is not easy to find solutions. It may well be impossible to do by hand.
2. The second-order sufficiency conditions are quite complicated, requiring the evaluation of determinants of certain entries in the matrix of second partial derivatives. Indeed, even in the case of one or two decision variables, if the function f is sufficiently complicated, it may not be possible to hand-solve the optimality conditions, and hence this approach is not generally viable.

For these reasons, computer codes have been developed to find local optima of nonlinear functions of n variables (where n is any integer ≥ 1). Often such codes are based on hill-climbing (or hill-descent) behavior. That is, for a maximization problem, an initial point is chosen, and then an uphill direction is determined. Intuitively, the algorithm moves from the initial point, along a straight line in an uphill direction, to the highest point that can be attained on that line. Then a new uphill direction is defined and the procedure is continued. The algorithm terminates when the first partials are sufficiently close to zero. Such a point, then, will always be a "local peak." Other local maxima are searched for by initiating the computer code at a different point.

The description above reveals the main role of the first-order necessary conditions in applications. They are used indirectly, in the sense that they serve as a **termination criterion** for the "hill-climbing" computer codes which search for local optima. The second-order sufficiency conditions, for the general problem in n variables, are mainly of theoretic interest, and go beyond the introductory nature of this chapter.

In concluding this section we mention one other practical approach that one sometimes takes in maximizing a *concave function*. For a concave function, any stationary point is a global maximizer (for a convex function, any stationary point is a global minimizer). Thus, if one can write out the first derivatives, we can then try to solve the n equations in n unknowns. Special computer codes exist to solve such systems. Whereas in the general case a solution could be a local maximizer or minimizer or neither, in the concave case we are guaranteed that any solution is a global maximizer. This approach is generally limited to the case of a concave or convex function. Moreover, it is limited by the requirement that the first order partial derivatives can be explicitly written. For some problems this may not be possible.

13.4
NONLINEAR OPTIMIZATION WITH CONSTRAINTS: A DESCRIPTIVE GEOMETRIC INTRODUCTION

This chapter, up to this point, has focused on *unconstrained* optimization. More typically, in a management-oriented decision-making setting, we are interested in optimizing an objective function subject to constraints. These constraints are in the form of mathematical equalities and/or inequalities, just as in the case of linear programming, except that in this chapter linearity is not assumed. Thus, the **general mathematical programming model**, in symbolic terms, can be written as:

$$\text{Max} \quad f(x_1, x_2, \ldots, x_n) \quad \text{(objective)} \qquad (P_0)$$

$$\text{s.t.} \quad \left.\begin{array}{l} g_1(x_1, \ldots, x_n) = b_1 \\ g_2(x_1, \ldots, x_n) = b_2 \\ \qquad \cdot \qquad \qquad \cdot \\ \qquad \cdot \qquad \qquad \cdot \\ g_m(x_1, \ldots, x_n) = b_m \end{array}\right\} m \text{ equality constraints}$$

$$\left.\begin{array}{l} h_1(x_1, \ldots, x_n) \leq r_1 \\ h_2(x_1, \ldots, x_n) \leq r_2 \\ \qquad \cdot \qquad \qquad \cdot \\ \qquad \cdot \qquad \qquad \cdot \\ h_k(x_1, \ldots, x_n) \leq r_k \end{array}\right\} k \text{ inequality constraints}$$

Graphical Just as with LP, we can use two-dimensional geometry to gain insight into this problem.
Analysis For example, let us use graphical analysis to solve the specific problem

$$\text{Max} \quad x_1 - x_2$$

$$\text{s.t.} \quad -x_1^2 + x_2 \geq 1$$
$$x_1 + x_2 \leq 3$$
$$-x_1 + x_2 \leq 2$$
$$x_1 \geq 0, \qquad x_2 \geq 0$$

Note that everything in this model is linear except for the first constraint. A model is called nonlinear if at least one of the constraint functions, or the objective function, or both are nonlinear. Therefore, the model above is properly termed a **nonlinear program**. In order to use the graphic approach to solve this problem, we proceed just as we did in LP. First we plot the set of points that simultaneously satisfy *all* the constraints.

The Feasible Region

This is called, just as in LP, the *constraint set*, or the *feasible region*. This set represents the allowable decisions. In order to find an allowable decision that maximizes the objective function, we find the "most uphill" (i.e., highest-valued) *contour* of the objective function that still touches the constraint set. The point at which it touches will be an optimal solution (often more simply referred to as a solution) to the problem. Figure 13.1 shows the graphical solution to the problem presented above.

You can see in Figure 13.1 that the nonlinear constraint puts curvature into the boundary of the constraint set. The feasible set is no longer a polyhedron (i.e., a flat-sided figure defined by linear inequalities) as is the case with LP, and the optimal solution does not lie on a corner. Recall that in the LP case the graphical analysis allowed us to identify the active constraints at an optimal corner and then the *exact solution* was obtained by solving two equations in two unknowns. In general this does not work in the nonlinear case. As shown in Figure 13.1, there is only one active constraint. We defer to Section 13.5 a discussion of what can be done, in a case like this, to obtain the exact solution algebraically.

Figure 13.1
Graphical Solution to the Nonlinear Model

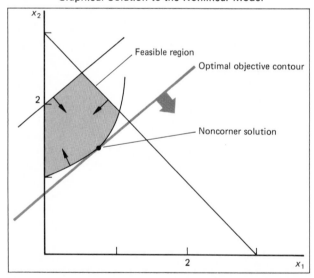

Noncorner Optima

Another example of an NLP is shown in Figure 13.2, which shows a *hypothetical* nonlinear inequality constrained maximization model. In this figure the constraints are all linear, and hence the constraint set is a polyhedron. The objective function, however, is nonlinear and again it is seen that the solution does not occur at a corner. Of course, a solution *could* appear at a corner, but the important point is that this property is not guaranteed, as it is in the linear model.

This fact has significant algorithmic implications. It means that in the nonlinear case, we cannot use a "corner-searching" method such as the simplex algorithm for finding a solution. This enormously complicates the solution procedure. The topic of solution procedures will be taken up in Sections 13.5, 13.6, and 13.7.

429

CHAPTER 13
Calculus-Based
Optimization and
an Introduction
to Nonlinear
Programming

Figure 13.2
Noncorner Solution

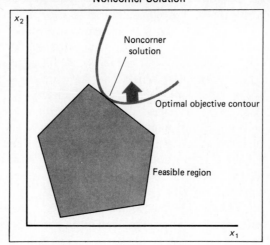

**Comparisons
between LP
and NLP**

There are several instructive parallels between LP and NLP. For example, the following four statements hold *in either type of model.*

1. Increasing (decreasing) the RHS on a $\leq$ ($\geq$) constraint loosens the constraint. This cannot contract and may expand the constraint set.
2. Increasing (decreasing) the RHS on a $\geq$ ($\leq$) constraint tightens the constraint. This cannot expand and may contract the constraint set.
3. Loosening a constraint cannot hurt and may help the optimal objective value.
4. Tightening a constraint cannot help and may hurt the optimal objective value.

Another concept that is common to both LP and NLP is the notion of changes in the OV as a right-hand side changes, with all other data held fixed. In LP we defined (see Chapter 7) the *dual variable* on a specified constraint to be *the rate of change in OV as the RHS of that constraint increases*, with all other data unchanged. In the NLP context this rate of change is often called the **Lagrange multiplier** as opposed to the dual variable, but the meaning is the same. There is, however, one important property of dual variables associated with LP that Lagrange multipliers in the NLP context will not generally share. Recall that in an LP the dual variable (or dual price) is constant for a range of values for the RHS of interest. It can be easily illustrated that in the NLP context this property does not generally hold true. As an illustration, consider the following simple NLP:

$$\text{Max} \quad x^2$$
$$\text{s.t.} \quad x \leq b$$
$$x \geq 0$$

In order to maximize x^2, we want to make x as large as possible. Thus, the optimal solution is $x^* = b$, and the optimal value of the objective function, which we call the OV, is $(x^*)^2 = b^2$. Thus, you can see that the OV is a function of b. That is,

$$\text{OV}(b) = b^2$$

430

CHAPTER 13
Calculus-Based
Optimization and
an Introduction
to Nonlinear
Programming

From basic calculus we know that the rate of change of this function as b increases is the derivative of $OV(b)$, namely $2b$. In other words, the Lagrange multiplier is *not* constant for a range of values of the RHS, b. It varies continuously with b.[2]

Another important difference between LP and NLP has to do with *global versus local solutions*. In an LP, it is always true that there cannot be a local solution that is not also global. This is not generally true for general nonlinear programming problems. In other words, such problems may have local as well as global solutions. This is illustrated by the hypothetical max model in Figure 13.3. In this figure, the point identified as **Local versus** "Local max" is termed a *local constrained maximizer* because the value of the objective **Global** function at this point is no smaller than at its *neighboring* feasible points. The point identified as "Global max" is termed a *global constrained maximizer* because the value of the objective function at this point is no smaller than at *all other* feasible points. As was the case with unconstrained optimization, certain convexity and concavity conditions must be satisfied to guarantee that a local constrained optimizer is also global. These properties will be defined in Section 13.6. In the absence of these properties it is generally not possible to know whether a given solution is a local or a global maximizer.

Figure 13.3
Local and Global Solutions

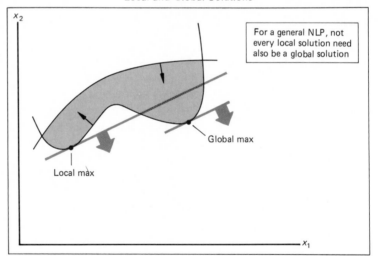

For a general NLP, not every local solution need also be a global solution

Global max

Local max

13.5

EQUALITY-CONSTRAINED MODELS AND LAGRANGE MULTIPLIERS

Many problems in business and economics are of the form

$$\text{Maximize (or Minimize)} f(x_1, \ldots, x_n) \qquad (P_1)$$

$$\text{s.t.} \quad g_i(x_1, \ldots, x_n) = b_i, \qquad i = 1, \ldots, m \quad (m < n)$$

[2]It may be briefly noted that this same example also serves to illustrate that the optimal value for an NLP *max* problem can exhibit increasing marginal returns. This can *never* happen in LP (i.e., the OV for an LP *max* models is *always* concave and hence exhibits nonincreasing marginal returns).

431

CHAPTER 13
Calculus-Based
Optimization and
an Introduction
to Nonlinear
Programming

That is, the goal is to maximize or minimize an objective function in n variables subject to a set of m ($m < n$) *equality* constraints. Here are two examples.

Example 2   A manufacturer can make a product on either of two machines. Let x_1 denote the quantity made on machine 1, and x_2 the amount on machine 2. Let

$$a_1 x_1 + b_1 x_1^2 = \text{cost of producing on machine 1}$$
$$a_2 x_2 + b_2 x_2^2 = \text{cost of producing on machine 2}$$

Determine the values of x_1 and x_2 that minimize total cost subject to the requirement that total production is some specified value, say R. The formulation of this problem is

$$\text{Min} \quad a_1 x_1 + b_1 x_1^2 + a_2 x_2 + b_2 x_2^2$$
$$\text{s.t.} \quad x_1 + x_2 = R$$

Example 3   Let p_1, p_2, and p_3 denote given prices of three goods and let B denote the available budget (i.e., B is a specified constant). Let s_1, s_2, and s_3 be given constants and let $x_1^{s_1} + x_2^{s_2} + x_3^{s_3}$ denote the "utility derived" from consuming x_1 units of good 1, x_2 units of good 2, and x_3 units of good 3. Determine the consumption mix that maximizes utility subject to the budget constraint. The formulation of this problem is

$$\text{Max} \quad x_1^{s_1} + x_2^{s_2} + x_3^{s_3}$$
$$\text{s.t.} \quad p_1 x_1 + p_2 x_2 + p_3 x_3 = B$$

In both of these examples the physical interpretations require the decision variables to be nonnegative. We shall assume that the parameters in the two models (a_i and b_i, $i = 1, 2$ in Example 2; and $p_i, s_i, i = 1, 2, 3$ and B in Example 3) are such that the optimal solutions will for sure turn out to be nonnegative and hence nonnegativity constraints need not be explicitly included. Such conditions, if appended, would convert the models to more difficult problems with both equality *and* inequality conditions.

**The Case
with Two
Variables**

Before analyzing the general problem (P_1) above, let us consider the special case of two decision variables and one equality constraint. Thus, we treat the problem

$$\text{Max} \quad f(x_1, x_2) \tag{P_2}$$
$$\text{s.t.} \quad g(x_1, x_2) = b$$

Example 4   As a particular example of (P_2), consider the problem

$$\text{Max} \quad x_1 - x_2$$
$$\text{s.t.} \quad -x_1^2 + x_2 = 1$$

The geometric analysis is shown in Figure 13.4. This analysis shows that at the optimal solution the contour of the objective function is tangent to the equality constraint. It also suggests that the optimal solution is approximately $x_1^* = 0.5$ and $x_2^* = 1.25$. We shall now show how to solve this problem analytically. To do this, we make use of the tools of differential calculus. The formal solution procedure is called the *Lagrangian technique* (also called the Lagrange multiplier method). This procedure includes four steps that are specified below for problem (P_2).

432

CHAPTER 13
Calculus-Based
Optimization and
an Introduction
to Nonlinear
Programming

Figure 13.4
Graphical Solution

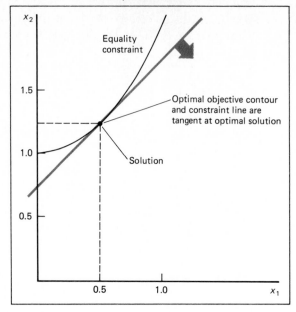

Introducing Lagrange Multipliers

■ *Step 1: Form Lagrangian:* Form a *new* function called the *Lagrangian*. This function involves a new variable, which we shall denote as λ, and which is called a *Lagrange multiplier*. The function, *for a maximization model*, is

$$L(x_1, x_2, \lambda) = f(x_1, x_2) + \lambda(b - g(x_1, x_2))$$

■ *Step 2: Take partial derivatives:* Compute the partial derivatives of the Lagrangian with respect to x_1, x_2, and λ, and set these three partial derivatives equal to zero to obtain

$$L_{x_1} = f_{x_1} - \lambda g_{x_1} = 0 \tag{13.1}$$

$$L_{x_2} = f_{x_2} - \lambda g_{x_2} = 0 \tag{13.2}$$

$$L_\lambda = b - g = 0 \tag{13.3}$$

■ *Step 3: Find all solutions:* Find the values x_1^*, x_2^*, λ^* that satisfy the equations derived in step 2. These equations are the first-order necessary optimality conditions for (P_2).

■ *Step 4: Check sufficiency conditions:* For each triple $(x_1^*, x_2^*, \lambda^*)$ determined in step 3, check whether x_1^*, x_2^* yields a constrained maximizer or constrained minimizer of f. Often this will be apparent from economic or physical considerations. Mathematically, this check can be performed as follows. Evaluate, at the point (x_1^*, x_2^*), the expression

$$D^* = -(g_{x_1})^2 L_{x_1x_1} - (g_{x_1})^2 L_{x_2x_2} + 2g_{x_1}g_{x_2}L_{x_1x_2} \tag{13.4}$$

If $D^* > 0$, then (x_1^*, x_2^*) is a local constrained maximizer. If $D^* < 0$, then (x_1^*, x_2^*) is a local constrained minimizer. If $D^* = 0$, no conclusion can be drawn.

Let us now apply the steps described above to Example 4, that is, to the problem

$$\text{Max} \quad x_1 - x_2$$
$$\text{s.t.} \quad -x_1^2 + x_2 = 1$$

■ **Step 1: Form Lagrangian:** The problem is already in the form of a *max model.* Thus, the Lagrangian is

$$L(x_1, x_2, \lambda) = f(x_1, x_2) + \lambda(b - g(x_1, x_2)) = x_1 - x_2 + \lambda(1 + x_1^2 - x_2)$$

■ **Step 2: Take partial derivatives:**

$$L_{x_1} = 1 + 2\lambda x_1 = 0$$
$$L_{x_2} = -1 - \lambda = 0$$
$$L_\lambda = 1 + x_1^2 - x_2 = 0$$

■ **Step 3: Find all solutions:** The unique solution to the above system of three equations in three unknowns x_1, x_2, λ is obtained by noting, from the second equation, that $\lambda^* = -1$. Substituting into the first equation and solving for x_1 gives $x_1^* = \frac{1}{2}$. Then the third equation gives $x_2^* = (x_1^*)^2 + 1 = 1\frac{1}{4}$. We have thus obtained

$$\lambda^* = -1, \qquad x_1^* = \tfrac{1}{2}, \qquad x_2^* = \tfrac{5}{4}$$

■ **Step 4: Check sufficiency conditions:**

$$D^* = -1(2\lambda^*) - 4(x_1^*)^2(0) + 2(-2x_1^*)(1)(0)$$
$$= 2$$

Since $D^* > 0$, the solution is a constrained maximizer.

Note that the solution in step 3 is consistent with that obtained in the geometric analysis of Figure 13.4.

Example 5 Let us use the necessary conditions given above to find the solution to the problem

$$\text{Min} \quad a_1 x_1 + a_2 x_2 + b_1 x_1^2 + b_2 x_2^2 + c_1 x_1 x_2 \qquad (13.5)$$
$$\text{s.t.} \quad x_1 + x_2 = R$$

This example will illustrate how the Lagrangian technique can be used to solve a whole class of problems. In other words, we will derive an expression for the optimal values of the decision variables (x_1^*, x_2^*) in terms of the parameters $(a_1, a_2, b_1, b_2, c_1,$ and $R)$. Having done so, we can use these general expressions to find solutions quickly and easily for any problem that is of the general form of problem (13.5). Indeed, our next example will illustrate this fact. We now turn to problem (13.5). Since the problem is in minimization form, we first convert it to max form as follows.

$$\text{Max} \quad -a_1 x_1 - a_2 x_2 - b_1 x_1^2 - b_2 x_2^2 - c_1 x_1 x_2$$
$$\text{s.t.} \quad x_1 + x_2 = R$$

■ **Step 1: Form Lagrangian:** The Lagrangian for the max problem is

433

$$L(x_1, x_2, \lambda) = -a_1 x_1 - a_2 x_2 - b_1 x_1^2 - b_2 x_2^2 - c_1 x_1 x_2 + \lambda(R - x_1 - x_2)$$

434

CHAPTER 13
Calculus-Based
Optimization and
an Introduction
to Nonlinear
Programming

■ *Step 2: Take partial derivatives:*   Taking first partial derivatives yields

$$L_{x_1} = -a_1 - 2b_1x_1 - c_1x_2 - \lambda = 0$$
$$L_{x_2} = -a_2 - 2b_2x_2 - c_1x_1 - \lambda = 0$$
$$L_{\lambda} = R - x_1 - x_2 = 0$$

■ *Step 3: Find all solutions:*   Solve for x_1^*, x_2^*, and λ^*. From the first two equations

$$a_1 + 2b_1x_1 + c_1x_2 = a_2 + 2b_2x_2 + c_1x_1$$

Thus, assuming that $2b_1 - c_1 \neq 0$,

$$x_1(2b_1 - c_1) = (a_2 - a_1) + x_2(2b_2 - c_1)$$

or

$$x_1 = \frac{(a_2 - a_1) + x_2(2b_2 - c_1)}{(2b_1 - c_1)}$$

Substituting this expression into the third equation yields

$$R - \frac{(a_2 - a_1) + x_2(2b_2 - c_1)}{(2b_1 - c_1)} - x_2 = 0$$

or

$$R(2b_1 - c_1) - (a_2 - a_1) - x_2(2b_2 - c_1) - x_2(2b_1 - c_1) = 0$$

Thus, assuming that $b_1 + b_2 - c_1 \neq 0$,

$$x_2^* = \frac{(a_1 - a_2) + R(2b_1 - c_1)}{2(b_1 + b_2 - c_1)} \tag{13.6}$$

Once a numerical value of x_2^* is determined, the third equation easily yields

$$x_1^* = R - x_2^* \tag{13.7}$$

Then the value of λ_1^* is obtained by substituting x_1^* into the first equation. This yields

$$\lambda_1^* = -a_1 - 2b_1R + x_2^*(2b_1 - c_1)$$

To determine if x_1^*, x_2^* is a local maximizer, we must check the "sufficiency conditions." The first step is to evaluate the expression for D^* given in (13.4). To perform this task we first note that $g_{x_2} = 1$, $g_{x_1} = 1$, $L_{x_2x_2} = -2b_2$, $L_{x_1x_1} = -2b_1$, and $L_{x_1x_2} = -c_1$. Substituting these values into (13.4) yields

$$D^* = -(1)^2(-2b_1) - (1)^2(-2b_2) + 2(1)(1)(-c_1)$$
$$= 2(b_1 + b_2 - c_1)$$

Thus, if $b_1 + b_2 - c_1 > 0$, we know that x_1^*, x_2^* is a local maximizer of the function

$$-a_1x_1 - a_2x_2 - b_1x_1^2 - b_2x_2^2 - c_1x_1x_2$$

which means x_1^*, x_2^* is a local minimizer of

$$a_1x_1 + a_2x_2 + b_1x_1^2 + b_2x_2^2 + c_1x_1x_2$$

We will now apply these general results to a specific problem.

A restaurant's average daily budget for advertising is $100, which is to be allocated to newspaper ads and radio commercials. Suppose that we let

$$x_1 = \text{average number of dollars per day spent on newspaper ads}$$

$$x_2 = \text{average number of dollars per day spent on radio commercials}$$

In terms of these quantities, the restaurant's total annual cost of running the advertising department has been estimated to be

$$\text{cost} = C(x_1, x_2) = 20{,}000 + 20x_1^2 + x_1x_2 + 12x_2^2 - 440x_1 - 300x_2$$

Find the budget allocation that will minimize this total annual cost.

The model to be solved is

$$\text{Min} \quad 20{,}000 + 20x_1^2 + x_1x_2 + 12x_2^2 - 440x_1 - 300x_2$$
$$\text{s.t.} \quad x_1 + x_2 = 100$$

We first note that the first term in the objective function (20,000) is a constant that does not depend on the values of the decision variables. Thus, we can ignore it in determining the optimal value of the decision variables. We thus wish to select x_1^*, x_2^* in order to

$$\text{Min} \quad -440x_1 - 300x_2 + 20x_1^2 + 12x_2^2 + x_1x_2$$
$$\text{s.t.} \quad x_1 + x_2 = 100$$

Observe that this problem is a specific case of the general class of problems given by (13.5). It follows that we can use the general equations (13.6) and (13.7) to determine x_2^* and x_1^*, respectively. To do so we first observe that $a_1 = -440$, $a_2 = -300$, $b_1 = 20$, $b_2 = 12$, $c_1 = 1$, and $R = 100$. Thus, substituting in

$$x_2^* = \frac{(a_1 - a_2) + R(2b_1 - c_1)}{2(b_1 + b_2 - c_1)} \qquad (13.6)$$

we obtain, after performing the indicated calculations, $x_2^* = 60.645$. Now turning to (13.7) we obtain $x_1^* = R - x_2^* = 100 - 60.645 = 39.355$. To consider the sufficiency conditions we simply note that $b_1 + b_2 - c_1 = 31 > 0$. Thus, $(x_1^* = 60.645, x_2^* = 39.355)$ is a local constrained minimizer of the objective function. In Problem 13–11, you are asked to argue that this is indeed a global minimizer.

***The General
Case***
We now turn to the general equality constrained problem, P_1. In this case there are m constraints, and we introduce m new variables, one for each constraint. These m new variables are called **Lagrange multipliers**. Put the problem into the maximization form. Then the Lagrangian function is

$$L(x_1, x_2, \ldots, x_n, \lambda) = f(x_1, \ldots, x_n) + \sum_{i=1}^{m} \lambda_i[b_i - g_i(x_1, \ldots, x_n)]$$

For problem P_1 we can now state a *necessary condition* for $(x_1^*, \ldots, x_n^*)$ to be optimal. In order to do this, rather technical regularity conditions must be imposed on the constraint functions $g_i(x_1, \ldots, x_n)$ at the point $(x_1^*, \ldots, x_n^*)$.[3] These conditions, called a *constraint qualification*, are usually satisfied and hence are more of theoretical than practical importance. Moreover, a precise discussion of these conditions would lead well beyond the scope of this text. Therefore, as is usually done in practice, *we shall assume that a suitable regularity condition is satisfied* at $(x_1^*, \ldots, x_n^*)$. Under this assumption:

A General Statement of the First Order Conditions

If $(x_1^*, \ldots, x_n^*)$ is a local constrained maximizer in (P_1), then there are m numbers $\lambda_1^*, \ldots, \lambda_m^*$ such that $x_1^*, \ldots, x_n^*, \lambda_1^*, \ldots, \lambda_m^*$ are a solution to the following system of $n + m$ equations in the $n + m$ unknowns $x_1, \ldots, x_n, \lambda_1, \ldots, \lambda_m$.

$$\frac{\partial f}{\partial x_1} - \sum_{i=1}^{m} \lambda_i \frac{\partial g_i}{\partial x_1} = 0 \qquad (L_{x_1} = 0)$$

$$\frac{\partial f}{\partial x_2} - \sum_{i=1}^{m} \lambda_i \frac{\partial g_i}{\partial x_2} = 0 \qquad (L_{x_2} = 0)$$

$$\vdots \qquad\qquad \vdots$$

$$\frac{\partial f}{\partial x_n} - \sum_{i=1}^{m} \lambda_i \frac{\partial g_i}{\partial x_n} = 0 \qquad (L^{x_n} = 0)$$

$$g_1(x_1, \ldots, x_n) = b_1 \qquad (L_{\lambda_1} = 0)$$

$$g_2(x_1, \ldots, x_n) = b_2 \qquad (L_{\lambda_2} = 0)$$

$$\vdots \qquad\qquad \vdots$$

$$g_m(x_1, \ldots, x_n) = b_m \qquad (L_{\lambda_m} = 0)$$

This necessary condition is a direct generalization of the two-variable case, problem (P_2), discussed above. In other words, each local constrained optimizer (maximizer or minimizer) must be a solution to the system of equations obtained by setting the $n + m$ partial derivatives of the Lagrangian equal to zero.

In theory, a global solution to problem (P_1) could be obtained by finding *all solutions* to the equations above (the necessary conditions) and then finding, among those, one that produces the largest objective value. Alternatively, one could seek a local solution to (P_1) by finding *a solution* to the equations above and then applying a complicated sufficiency test to see whether that solution is a local constrained maximizer. However, it is misleading to suggest that either of these approaches is, in general, a useful practical technique to solving problems of the form (P_1). The situation is analogous to what we encountered in the unconstrained case with n variables. There we saw that, although in special cases the necessary conditions could be explicitly solved, these conditions are more typically employed as a termination criterion in computer codes. In the current context, it is also true that special-purpose computer codes exist for solving the general problem (P_1). The Lagrangian conditions are first-order necessary conditions for a point to be optimal in (P_1). Rather than solving these conditions directly, the codes take other

---

[3] For example, it suffices to assume that the m vectors (each vector n-dimensional) $(\partial g_i/\partial x_1, \ldots, \partial g_i/\partial x_n)$, all evaluated at $(x_1^*, \ldots, x_n^*)$, are linearly independent. Although it was not explicitly mentioned, the optimality conditions for P_2 also assume that the regularity condition holds.

437

CHAPTER 13
Calculus-Based
Optimization and
an Introduction
to Nonlinear
Programming

approaches. To describe this in detail would go beyond the scope of this chapter. It suffices to say that the Lagrangian conditions provide *a termination criterion* for such codes. The point to remember is that for all NLP models it is generally true that the necessary conditions are (1) of theoretic interest (i.e., they reveal properties of the real world model being studied) and (2) used as a termination criterion in computer codes designed to solve the problem.

For (P_1), as for most NLP models, second-order sufficiency conditions also exist. However, these are entirely of theoretic interest and too complicated to discuss in the general case.

Having now discussed the general problem with equality constraints, the next level of difficult would be to add inequality constraints to the model to obtain the general constrained model (P_0). Necessary optimality conditions for this problem are the so-called Karush–Kuhn–Tucker conditions, of which the Lagrange multiplier conditions in step 2 above are a special case. Again, because of the introductory level of this chapter, a discussion of the inequality constrained model cannot be taken further. This is, more appropriately, a topic covered in a course on nonlinear programming.

Economic Interpretation of Lagrange Multipliers

Lagrange multipliers have an interesting and important economic interpretation. Indeed, as stated in Section 13.4, the Lagrange multipliers in NLP have the same interpretation as the dual variables in LP. In other words, the optimal value of the ith Lagrange multiplier λ_i^* is the instantaneous *rate of change* in the OV, the optimal value of the objective function, as the ith RHS, b_i, is increased, with all other data unchanged. Another way of saying this, in economic terminology, is that λ_i^* reflects the marginal value of the ith resource. Thus, the units of λ_i^* are

$$\frac{\text{units of objective function}}{\text{units of RHS of constraint } i}.$$

Recall Example 2, where a manufacturer wished to minimize total product cost, the objective in dollars, subject to the restriction that the total production, say in tons, of two products had to equal R. The Lagrange multiplier then has units of dollars per ton and its value is the instantaneous marginal cost of producing the Rth unit.

In order to illustrate specifically the foregoing interpretation of λ^*, for a max model, consider again the problem posed by Example 4, which was solved with geometric analysis in Figure 13.4. In this case, however, let the parameter b denote the RHS. Thus, the problem is

$$\text{Max} \quad x_1 - x_2$$
$$\text{s.t.} \quad -x_1^2 + x_2 = b$$

The Lagrangian is

$$x_1 - x_2 + \lambda(b + x_1^2 - x_2)$$

and the equations to be solved (for x_1, x_2 and λ) are

$$L_{x_1} = 1 + 2\lambda x_1 \quad = 0$$
$$L_{x_2} = -1 - \lambda \quad = 0$$
$$L_\lambda = b + x_1^2 - x_2 = 0$$

438

CHAPTER 13
Calculus-Based
Optimization and
an Introduction
to Nonlinear
Programming

The solution is

$$\lambda^* = -1, \qquad x_1^* = \tfrac{1}{2}, \qquad x_2^* = b + \tfrac{1}{4} \tag{13.8}$$

To observe the interpretation of λ^*, we will first find an expression for the optimal value of the objective as a function of b. Let $OV(b)$ be this function. By definition $OV(b) = x_1^* - x_2^*$. Thus, by substitution,

$$OV(b) = \tfrac{1}{2} - [b + \tfrac{1}{4}] = \tfrac{1}{4} - b$$

To determine the rate of change in $OV(b)$ as a function of b we take the first derivative. We see that

$$\frac{d}{db}OV(b) = -1$$

But $\lambda^* = -1$, and hence, as stated above, λ^* is the rate of change in the OV with respect to b.

In concluding this section, we mention that just as is true with LP, a dual to problem P_1 can be defined. This dual is a different optimization problem which can be expressed in only the variables $\lambda_1, \ldots, \lambda_m$, and the Lagrange multipliers will be the optimal solution to the dual problem. This topic of *nonlinear duality theory* is studied in more advanced courses in NLP.

13.6
DIFFERENT TYPES OF NLP PROBLEMS AND SOLVABILITY

The algorithms for solving general NLP problems are markedly different from the simplex approach. In LP we saw that for a problem that has an optimal solution, we could always be assured that there would in fact be at least one optimal corner solution. This is a critically important characteristic of LP models, for the corners of the feasible region can be defined by linear equations in such a way that a simple algebraic operation allows us to move from one corner to any adjacent corner at which the objective value either improves or remains at the same value. Using this technique, the simplex algorithm provides a fail-safe method for attacking LP problems. None of these comments apply to the general NLP problem (P_0), or even to the special case (P_1) involving only equality constraints.

In contrast to the LP case there is not a single preferred algorithm for solving non-linear programs. Without difficulty one can easily find 10 or 15 methods in the literature. Some of these, such as *penalty function methods* or *reduced gradient methods*, are applicable to general NLP models. But nonlinear programming is a very broad topic and many interesting special types of problems are identified in the literature. Indeed, many of the solution methods found in the literature are designed to solve special types of NLP problems. For example, some algorithms are designed exclusively for *quadratic programming problems*, others for problems with a *nonlinear objective function and linear constraints*, and so on.

Rather than confronting you with a compendium of the numerous types of algorithms for solving NLP problems, we shall give a brief description of a few major classes of nonlinear programs that one might encounter in practical applications. That is, we can "break down" this very general class of problems into more special cases, defined by the

439

CHAPTER 13
Calculus-Based
Optimization and
an Introduction
to Nonlinear
Programming

nature of the objective function and the constraint functions, and then discuss how easily solvable these special cases are. Indeed, from the managerial perspective these are important issues, to know what type of NLP one may be facing, and the prospects for finding a solution. It will be seen that these prospects are heavily dependent on the type of problem one faces.

We might begin this overview with the observation that nonlinear models are divided into two classes: (1) those that can be solved and (2) those that one can try to solve. The models that can be solved must typically conform to certain qualifications of structure and size. The hierarchy of increasing computational difficulty is shown in Figure 13.5. In this figure, the increasing Roman numerals reflect increasing computational difficulty. Let us now consider these several classes of nonlinear programs in somewhat more detail.

Figure 13.5
Increasing Computational Difficulty

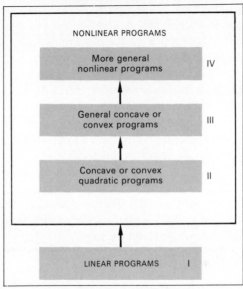

Nonlinear
Programs That
Can Be Solved:
Concave and
Convex
Programs

To define these problems it is necessary to introduce a new technical term, a **convex set of points**. Loosely speaking, this is a set of points without any "holes" or "indentations." More formally, a convex set is any set that has the following property:

Consider all possible pairs of points in the set, and consider the line segment connecting any such pair. All such line segments must lie entirely within the set.

Figure 13.6 shows two-dimensional sets of points that do not satisfy this property and hence are *not* convex sets, together with sets that are convex. The polygon in the first of these two figures may remind you of the constraint sets that occur in LP problems. This is appropriate since any constraint set for a linear program is a convex set. *The nonlinear programs that we can be reasonably sure of solving must also have convex constraint sets.*

The next question to be asked then is: What kinds of nonlinear programs have convex constraint sets? It is useful to be able to use the notion of concave and convex functions in answering this question. If the function has two independent variables,

440

CHAPTER 13
Calculus-Based
Optimization and
an Introduction
to Nonlinear
Programming

Figure 13.6
Convex and Nonconvex Sets of Points

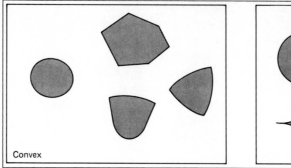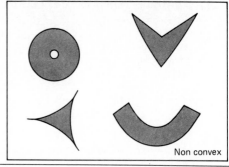

Convex

Non convex

Concave and Convex Functions

a **concave function** is shaped like an upside-down bowl. In general, a concave function, by definition, has the property that the line segment connecting any two points on the graph of the function never enters the space above the graph (if it always lies strictly under the graph then the function is *strictly concave*). Similarly, if the function has two variables, a **convex function** is shaped like a bowl. In general, a convex function, by definition, has the property that the line segment connecting any two points on the graph of the function never enters the space below the graph (if it always lies strictly above the graph then the function is *strictly convex*). The same ideas hold for functions that have a single variable, or more than two variables. It should also be remarked that a linear function is considered to be both concave and convex (the above mentioned line segments always lie in the graph).

Now suppose that we have a nonlinear program with only inequality constraints.

If the constraint function associated with each $\leq$ constraint is convex and the constraint function associated with each $\geq$ constraint is concave, the constraint set will be a convex set.

These facts are illustrated in Figure 13.7, which shows a convex function g of a single variable, given by $g(x) = x^2 + 1$. You can see that the set of x values for which $g(x) \leq 2$ is convex (i.e., this is the set $-1 \leq x \leq 1$), whereas the set of x values for which

Figure 13.7
Constraint Sets $g(x) \leq 2$ and $g(x) \geq 2$

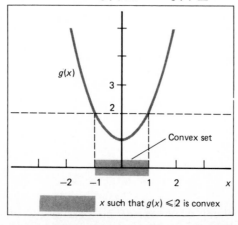

$g(x)$

3

2

Convex set

−2   −1   1   2 x

x such that $g(x) \leq 2$ is convex

441

CHAPTER 13
Calculus-Based
Optimization and
an Introduction
to Nonlinear
Programming

$g(x) \geq 2$ is not convex (i.e., this is the set $x \leq -1$, $x \geq 1$). This set is not convex because it is possible to find two points in the set (say $x = +2$ and $x = -2$) such that the straight line that connects them passes through points (e.g., the point $x = 0$) that are not in the set.

Thus, we see that in this example $g(x)$ is convex and the set defined by the inequality $g(x) \leq 2$ is convex, whereas the set defined by the inequality $g(x) \geq 2$ is not convex. A similar demonstration could be constructed to show that if $g(x)$ is concave, then the set defined by the inequality $g(x) \geq 2$ is convex, whereas the set defined by the inequality $g(x) \leq 2$ is not convex (this is related to the fact that the negative of a concave function is convex and vice-versa). We thus have a test at our disposal that will enable us to verify that certain NLPs have a convex constraint set. This test certainly will not enable us to determine if the constraint set for *any* NLP is convex or not. In particular, in the case of problems involving one or more *nonlinear equality* constraints, there is great difficulty in characterizing whether or not the constraint set is convex. Concerning the discussion in this subsection, it is worth noting that the term "concave" applies only to functions, whereas the term "convex" can apply either to a function or to a set of points, depending on the context.

Now that you understand the meaning of a convex set, it is easy, at least formally, to define a concave or convex program:

A concave program is a max model with a concave objective function and a convex constraint set.

A convex program is a min model with a convex objective function and a convex constraint set.

Convexity and Global Optima

The rationale for this characterization has to do with the fact that in the maximization context, just as in elementary calculus with one variable, concave objective functions are very convenient to work with in terms of the mathematical properties associated with the upside-down bowl shape. Convex objective functions (bowl-shaped) are convenient in the minimization context. Finally, the convexity of the constraint set endows the problem with other attractive mathematical properties that can be exploited both theoretically and computationally. A most important characteristic of concave (or convex) programming problems is that for such problems *any local constrained optimizer is a global constrained optimizer*. This fact has obvious computational implications.

Figure 13.5 indicates that the easiest type of nonlinear program is a concave or convex quadratic program. These problems, by definition, have linear (equality or inequality) constraints. The objective function must be quadratic and concave if it is a max model and quadratic and convex if it is a min model. It turns out that a variation of the simplex method can be used to solve such problems, and in practice this is reasonably efficient. It is not uncommon to solve quadratic programs with hundreds of constraints and several thousand variables. Financial models such as those used in portfolio analysis are often quadratic programs, so this class of models is of some applied importance.

In Figure 13.5 the next level of difficulty involves the general (nonquadratic) concave or convex program. There are numerous mathematical approaches and corresponding algorithms for solving such problems. For example, suppose that the problem to be solved is a max model. One typical approach proceeds as follows:

1. Find an initial feasible point "inside" the constraint set (not on the boundary).

2. Find an uphill direction and move along this straight line until either reaching a maximum along the line or until hitting some boundary of the constraint set.

3. Modify the direction of motion so as to continue uphill while remaining in the feasible region.

4. Terminate the algorithm when a point satisfying the necessary optimality conditions is found.

In this type of algorithm, as well as most others that apply to nonlinear programs that are not quadratic, there is considerable use of advanced calculus, and hence it is not possible in this development to get into much detail. Suffice it to say that *for general concave or convex programs, as opposed to linear programs, the number of nonlinear variables (i.e., those that enter into the problem nonlinearly) seems to be more significant than the number of constraints as an indicator of problem difficulty*. Without making use of additional special structure, it could well be a major task to solve a general concave or convex program with more than 100 variables.

**Nonlinear
Programs That
We Try
to Solve**

Finally, we consider problems in the next and highest level of difficulty. These problems are often called *highly nonlinear*, which usually means that the convexity and concavity properties discussed above are absent. To attack such problems, it is common practice to use the same algorithm one would use for general concave and convex programs. The results are different, however. Any NLP algorithm will generally terminate at a point at which the necessary (i.e., first-order) optimality conditions are satisfied. For a concave or convex program, such a point is guaranteed to be a global optimizer (indeed, if the objective function is *strictly* concave, or *strictly* convex, we are guaranteed that such a point is a *unique* global optimizer). But for general nonlinear programs this need not be true, as illustrated for a problem in one variable in Figure 13.8. The objective

Figure 13.8
Nonconcave Constrained Max Problem

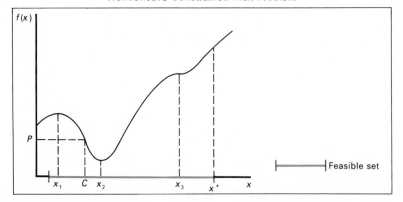

function f, which is to be maximized, is neither concave nor convex. The solution to the problem is given by x^*, but the algorithm may terminate at any of the points x_1, x_3, or x^* (for they will satisfy the necessary conditions) and, in general, the analyst has no way to determine which of these cases he or she has actually obtained. To date, no one has been smart enough to invent algorithms that overcome this possibility.

**Absence of
Convexity**

Thus, it appears that our capabilities in this realm are woefully inadequate, and you may well wonder, since we seem to have no assurance that what we are getting really

443

CHAPTER 13
Calculus-Based
Optimization and
an Introduction
to Nonlinear
Programming

provides a global constrained optimum, why do we even attempt to solve these general highly nonlinear problems? The answer and justification is surprisingly unpedantic and empirical. The firm may be currently employing the policy designated as C in Figure 13.8, with an associated profit of P. If our algorithm can produce a *better* solution, whether it be x_1, x_3, or x^*, then the use of the algorithm might well be justified. This is consistent with the overall theme that in practice there is nothing so pure as a truly optimal solution. *The goal in quantitative modeling is always to assist in the search for better decisions. The general considerations are the cost of improvement (the cost of the modeling effort and obtaining the solution) versus the benefit rendered by the solution.*

In concluding, let us address one additional practical aspect. How can we tell whether a nonlinear program in many variables is concave, convex, or neither? In other words, how do we know whether the objective function and the constraints have the right mathematical form? There are several answers to this question:

1. Sometimes, there are mathematical tests that can be applied to the problem functions to determine whether they are concave, convex, or neither.

2. Sometimes, economic intuition is used to assert that such and such a phenomenon reflects diminishing marginal returns or increasing marginal costs, and hence the associated function is concave or convex.

3. In many real problems nothing is done to address the question. One simply attempts to solve the problem and then inquires as to the practical usefulness of the terminal point (the purported "solution" produced by the algorithm). For a problem that is thought or known to be nonconvex or nonconcave, one frequently restarts the algorithm from a different initial point with the hope of producing a better terminal point.

13.7

NOTES ON IMPLEMENTATION

The practice of nonlinear programming is in some ways even more of an art than the practice of LP. Concerning LP, almost every computer library will have as part of its standard repertoire an LP software package. Also, every LP code is, in major respects, the same, since they are variants of the simplex method. Nonlinear programming codes are less easy to come by. They are generally not a standard part of computer libraries. Moreover, it would not be difficult to identify as many as 10 or 15 quite different algorithmic procedures for solving NLP problems. To find the best method for a given problem, indeed even to understand the differences between various approaches, the user, at least in this respect, must be more of an expert with mathematics. Another delicate aspect of NLP practice is the existence, from a mathematical viewpoint, of so many different types of nonlinear problems with different theoretical properties (whereas there is only one type of LP). Associated with this fact is the need to reckon with the issue of local versus global solutions to the model. The user must know enough about the mathematical structure of his or her model to have at least a feeling for the quality of the solution (e.g., local versus global) produced by the code and often he or she must experiment in order to locate improved solutions.

Although most NLP codes will print out dual prices (i.e., the optimal values of the Lagrange multipliers) along with the solution, additional sensitivity analysis is generally not available. Thus, from the manager's point of view, the NLP output contains less information than an LP output provides.

444

CHAPTER 13
Calculus-Based
Optimization and
an Introduction
to Nonlinear
Programming

Probably the most used codes in practice are GRG (a reduced gradient method) and SUMT (a penalty function method). These codes can be obtained from commercial sources for modest fees. Getting them to run on your local computer installation is, unfortunately, in some cases more a tragic comedy than a straightforward rational endeavor.

Although NLP applies to a wide spectrum of problems, the most common applications probably occur in situations where the model has special structure. For example, there may be linear constraints but a nonlinear objective function, and so on. In such cases there is hope of solving reasonably large scale models—provided that the code makes efficient use of the problem's special structure.

What do we mean by "large scale" in NLP? Again, this is much less clearly defined than it is for LP. For a concave or convex quadratic program, we can aspire to several thousand constraints and unlimited variables. This power derives from the fact that for such a model a variant of the simplex method is employed. However, for more general nonlinear problems, without special structure which is used to advantage, one would probably hesitate to attack a problem with more than 100 variables regardless of how few the constraints.

As a final note, NLP applications are probably clustered in such areas as engineering design, nonlinear estimation, electrical power transmission, physical applications such as oil drilling, and finally, optimal scheduling and equipment utilization when nonlinear costs are involved.

13.8

MAJOR CONCEPTS QUIZ

True–False

1. **T F** Economy of scale is a nonlinear relationship.
2. **T F** An applied problem involving a nonlinear relationship cannot be modeled as an LP.
3. **T F** If the necessary conditions for a local max occur, a local max occurs.
4. **T F** If a local min occurs, the necessary conditions for a local min occur.
5. **T F** If a local min is a global min, it is the only point where the sufficient conditions for a local min hold.
6. **T F** A straight line is neither a concave nor a convex function.
7. **T F** In an NLP or an LP tightening a constraint cannot help and it might hurt.
8. **T F** For a max model, a Lagrange multiplier has the same interpretation as the dual price that appears on the computer output for LP problems earlier in the text, although in general it is not constant over an RHS interval.
9. **T F** A quadratic programming problem is always a special type of concave programming problem.
10. **T F** An NLP is always either a concave or a convex programming problem.
11. **T F** The constraint set defined by the following inequalities is convex.

$$9x + 4 \le 36$$
$$4x + 12 \le 20$$

12. **T F** In practice, to find a local max of a function of several variables, one first finds all stationary points. One then applies second-order tests to these points.

13. **T F** Although nonlinear programs are more difficult than LPs, in terms of finding an optimal solution it is nevertheless true that a corner-searching technique can be applied.

14. **T F** One problem in NLP is distinguishing between local and global solutions.

_____

Multiple Choice

15. Suppose that f is a function of a single variable. The condition $f''(x^*) > 0$
    a. is a necessary condition for a local min
    b. is a sufficient condition for a local min
    c. is a sufficient condition for a local max
    d. none of the above

16. Suppose that f is a function of a single variable. The condition $f'(x^*) = 0$ is
    a. a necessary condition for x^* to be a local max
    b. a necessary condition for x^* to be a local min
    c. a necessary condition for x^* to be a global min
    d. all of the above

17. In nonlinear models differential calculus is needed
    a. to avoid multiple (local) solutions
    b. to express optimality conditions
    c. both a and b
    d. neither a nor b

18. A point x^* with the property that $f'_{(x)} = 0$ and $f''(x^*) > 0$ (where f is a function of a single variable) satisfies the sufficient conditions for x^* to be
    a. a local max
    b. a local min
    c. neither a nor b

19. Which of the following is true of a concave function?
    a. One can attempt to find a global maximizer by using a hill-climbing computer code.
    b. One can attempt to find a global maximizer by setting the first partials to zero and solving the resulting system of equations on the computer.
    c. Any local maximizer is also a global maximizer.
    d. All of the above.

20. Which of the following is true?
    a. For a general NLP, optimality conditions are directly used in solving NLP problems. That is, computer codes exist to directly solve these conditions, and this produces an NLP solution.
    b. For a general NLP, optimality conditions are indirectly used in solving NLP problems. That is, computer codes exist to directly attack the NLP, employing for example a "hill-climbing" approach. The optimality conditions provide a termination criterion for such algorithms.
    c. Optimality conditions are only of theoretic interest.

21. For concave programming problems
    a. the second-order conditions are more useful
    b. any local optimum is a global optimum as well
    c. both the constraint set and the objective function must be concave

22. Convexity
    a. is a description that applies both to sets of points and to functions
    b. is an important mathematical property used to guarantee that local solutions are also global
    c. is useful in unconstrained as well as constrained optimization
    d. all of the above

23. Which of the following is *not* generally true of a Lagrange multiplier?
    a. It has an economic interpretation similar to that of dual variable.
    b. It is the rate of change of OV as the RHS of a constraint is increased.
    c. It is valid (i.e., constant) over an RHS range.
    d. It enters into the first-order optimality conditions.

24. Which of the following is *not* true?

445

446

CHAPTER 13
Calculus-Based
Optimization and
an Introduction
to Nonlinear
Programming

a. Even when global solutions cannot be guaranteed, optimization can still be a useful tool in decision making.
b. In LP, we need never worry about local solutions (i.e., every local solution is also global).
c. Since we can only guarantee that local solutions are global when the appropriate convexity (or concavity) properties exist, these are the only types of NLP problems that yield useful information.

Answers

1. T	9. F	17. b
2. F	10. F	18. b
3. F	11. T	19. d
4. T	12. F	20. b
5. F	13. F	21. b
6. F	14. T	22. d
7. T	15. d	23. c
8. T	16. d	24. c

13.9

PROBLEMS

13-1. (a) Maximize the function $f(x) = -8x^2 - 14x - 32$.
    (b) What is the sign of the second derivative of this function at the maximizing value of x?
    (c) Maximize this function over the interval $1 \le x \le 10$.
    (d) Can you tell whether this function is concave or convex?

13-2. (a) Minimize the function $f(x) = 6x^2 - 12x + 30$.
    (b) What is the sign of the second derivative of this function at the minimizing value of x?
    (c) Minimize this function over the interval $2 \le x \le 12$.
    (d) Can you tell whether this function is concave or convex?

13-3. Lotta Crap, manager of Crap Baking Services, is considering the offer of a distributor who sells an instant croissant mix. The total cost of x pounds of the mix is given by

$$\text{total cost} = x^3 - 50x^2 + 2x$$

What quantity of this mix will minimize *total cost per pound*?

13-4. Homer Will Burst is inventory manager for the regional warehouse of a fast-food chain. The following function is used by Homer to give the monthly cost of purchasing and holding the chain's inventory of deluxe frozen dinners, where q is the size of each order:

$$\text{monthly cost} = \frac{20,000,000}{q} + 5q + 19,000 = f(q)$$

(a) Determine the order quantity q^* that minimizes the annual inventory cost.
(b) What is the minimum annual cost?
(c) Verify the nature of the stationary point i.e., is it a local or global optimizer?

13-5. Consider the function

$$f(x_1, x_2) = -2x_1^4 + 12x_1^2 - 2x_1^2 x_2 - x_2^2 + 4x_2 - 60$$

Determine whether the points below yield local minima, local maxima, or saddle points.
    (a) $(x_1 = 0, x_2 = 2)$ (b) $(x_1 = 2, x_2 = -2)$ (c) $(x_1 = -2, x_2 = -2)$

13-6. Solve the constrained optimization problem

$$\max \quad -x_1^2 - 2x_2^2 + 8x_1 + 12x_2 - 34$$
$$\text{s.t.} \quad -2x_1 - 4x_2 = -8$$

447

CHAPTER 13
Calculus-Based
Optimization and
an Introduction
to Nonlinear
Programming

13-7. *Linear Regression Analysis*   In the linear regression model, historical data points (x_i, y_i), $i = 1, \ldots, n$, are given. The linear model is an estimating equation (also called the regression line) $y = ax + b$, where a and b are chosen so as to minimize the sum of squared deviations

$$S(a, b) = \sum_{i=1}^{n} [y_i - (ax_i + b)]^2$$

(a) Use this approach to determine the estimating equation for the following data:

x	8	6	12
y	6	14	-18

(b) Use the same approach to determine the estimating equation for the following data:

x	10	12.6	14.9	17.4	20.1
y	25	20	15	10	5

13-8. (a) Solve the following problem:

$$\text{Min} \quad x_1^2 + x_2^2 - 12x_1 - 10x_2 - 61$$
$$\text{s.t.} \quad 20x_1 + 30x_2 = 60$$

(b) For this problem, what is the rate of change of OV with respect to the RHS of the constraint?

13-9. Consider the problem

$$\text{Max} \quad -3x_1^2 + 42x_1 - 3x_2^2 + 48x_2 - 339$$
$$\text{s.t.} \quad 4x_1 + 6x_2 = 24$$

(a) Solve the problem.

(b) Estimate the change in OV if the RHS of the constraint were to increase from 24 to 25.

13-10. Consider the problem

$$\text{Max} \quad -2x_1^2 + 20x_1 - 2x_1x_2 - x_2^2 + 14x_2 - 58$$
$$\text{s.t.} \quad x_1 + 4x_2 = 8$$

(a) Solve the problem.

(b) Estimate the change in OV if the RHS of the constraint were to decrease from 8 to 7.

13-11. Show that the solution found in the "optimal marketing expenditures" example (Section 13.5) is actually a global (as opposed to local) optimum.

More Challenging Problems

13-12. In Example 3, let $s_1 = s_2 = s_3 = c$, where c is a specified constant such that $0 < c < 1$. Solve Example 3 for the utility maximizing values x_1^*, x_2^*, x_3^*, and λ^*.

13-13. Solve Example 3 for the optimal x_i^*'s and λ^* with $s_i = \frac{1}{3}$, $i = 1, 2, 3$.

13-14. Assuming that all the data are positive, give the general solution to Example 2. Also state the second-order sufficiency condition in terms of the data.

13-15. Consider the function

$$f(x_1, x_2) = a_1x_1 + a_2x_2 + b_1x_1^2 + b_2x_2^2 + c_1x_1x_2 + d$$

Give a general solution to the problem of minimizing $f(x_1, x_2)$, as follows. Assume that $c_1^2 \neq 4b_1b_2$, $c_1 \neq 0$. Solve explicitly for the optimizing value of x_2^*. Solve for x_1^* in terms of x_2^*. Express the second-order sufficiency conditions in terms of the data.

CHAPTER 14

Decision Theory
and Decision Trees

1. If dual supply lines were selected, a smaller reservoir could have been chosen since the supply would have been more secure.

2. The quality of material needed in the condenser depended on the quality of water emitting from the treatment phase.

3. The residue in the water after cooling depends both on the quality of the incoming water and the number of cycles in the cooling process.

Decision trees were a particularly useful device for analyzing this problem. They allowed engineers and managers to incorporate uncertainty directly in the decision process. Perhaps more important, they provided a valuable device for visualizing and communicating the complex structure of the system.

14.1

INTRODUCTION

Decision theory provides a framework for analyzing a wide variety of management problems. The framework establishes (1) a system of classifying decision problems based on the amount of information about the problem that is available and (2) a decision criterion, that is, a measure of "the goodness" of a decision for each type of problem.

In the first part of this chapter we will present the decision theory framework and relate it to models previously discussed. The second half of the chapter is devoted to decision trees. Decision trees apply decision theory concepts to sequential decisions that include uncertain events. They are a pragmatic and practical aid to managerial decision making.

Decisions against Nature   In general terms, decision theory treats decisions against nature. This phrase refers to a situation where the result (return) from a decision depends on the action of another player (nature). For example, if the decision is to carry an umbrella or not, the return (get wet or do not) depends on what action nature takes. It is important to note that in this model the returns accrue only to the decision maker. Nature does not care what the outcome is. This condition distinguishes decision theory from game theory. In game theory both players have an interest in the outcome.

In decision theory problems, the fundamental piece of data is a payoff table like Figure 14.1. In this figure the alternative decisions are listed along the side of the table

Figure 14.1

Payoff Table

DECISION	STATE OF NATURE			
	1	2	$\cdots$	m
d_1	r_{11}	r_{12}	$\cdots$	r_{1m}
d_2	r_{21}	r_{22}	$\cdots$	r_{2m}
$\vdots$	$\vdots$	$\vdots$	$\vdots$	$\vdots$
d_n	r_{n1}	r_{n2}	$\cdots$	r_{nm}

and the possible states of nature are listed across the top. The entries in the body of the table are the payoffs for all possible combinations of decisions and states of nature.

The Decision Process

The decision process proceeds as follows:

---

1. You, the decision maker, select one of the alternative decisions $d_1, \ldots, d_n$. Suppose that you select d_1.
2. After your decision is made, a state of nature occurs. Suppose that state 2 occurs.
3. The return you receive can now be determined from the payoff table. Since you made decision 1 and state of nature 2 occurred, the return is r_{12}.

In general terms the question is: Which of the decisions should you select? You would like as large a return as possible, that is, the largest possible value of r_{ij}. It is obvious that the decision we should select will depend on our belief concerning what nature will do, that is, on which state of nature will occur. If we believe state 2 will occur, we select the decision associated with the largest number in column 2, and so on.

In the following section we will consider different assumptions about nature's behavior. Each assumption leads to a different *criterion* for selecting "the best" decision, and hence to a different procedure.

14.2

THREE CLASSES OF DECISION PROBLEMS

This section deals with three classes of decision problems against nature. Each class is defined by an assumption about nature's behavior. The three classes are: decisions under certainty, decisions under risk, and decisions under uncertainty.

Decisions under Certainty

A decision under certainty is one in which you know which state of nature will occur. Alternatively, you can think of it as a case with a single state of nature. In this case, the decision criterion is obvious. We simply select the alternative (decision) that yields the largest return for the known state of nature.

All linear programming models, integer programming models, and many other deterministic models such as the EOQ model can be thought of as decisions against nature in which there is only one state of nature. This is so because we are sure (within the context of the model) what return we will get for each decision we make. For a concrete example, consider the PROTRAC E and F model.

$$
\begin{aligned}
\max \quad & 5000E + 4000F \\
\text{s.t.} \quad & 10E + 15F \le 150 \\
& 20E + 10F \le 160 \\
& 30E + 10F \ge 135 \\
& E - 3F \le 0 \\
& E + F \ge 5 \\
& E, F \ge 0
\end{aligned}
$$

Figure 14.2 presents this problem in the form of a payoff table. In this table, a return of $-\infty$ is assigned to any infeasible decision. For example, since $E = 0$, $F = 0$ violates the third and fifth constraints, the associated return is defined to be $-\infty$. For any feasible pair (E, F) the return is defined to be the objective function value—namely, $5000E + 4000F$. For this model we know exactly what return we get for each decision (each choice of the pair E, F). We can thus list all returns in one column and think of it as representing one state of nature that we are sure will occur.

Figure 14.2

Payoff Table for the PROTRAC E and F Problem

DECISIONS	STATE OF NATURE
$E = 0, F = 0$	$-\infty$
$E = 5, F = 4$	41,000
$\vdots$	$\vdots$
$E = 6, F = 3.5$	44,000
$\vdots$	$\vdots$

Finding the Optimal Decision May be Difficult

Conceptually, you now simply select the decision that yields the highest return. In practice, as opposed to "in concept," finding such a decision may be another story. Since E and F can take on an infinite number of values, there will be an infinite number of rows for this problem (see Figure 14.2). Even in this simple problem, enumerating the alternatives and selecting the best of them is not possible. (Even enumerating all of the corners of the feasible region, though this is a finite set, is generally not possible). Additional mathematical analysis (in this case, the simplex algorithm) is needed to find the optimal decision.

Decisions Under Risk

A lack of certainty about future events is a characteristic of many if not most management decision problems. Consider how the decisions of the financial vice-president of an insurance company would change if she were to know exactly what changes were to occur in the bond market. Imagine the relief of the head buyer at Bloomingdale's if he were to know exactly how many full-length mink coats would be purchased in his store this year. This relief would be shared in part by the manufacturers of mink coats and even the operators of mink farms.

It thus seems clear that numerous decision problems are characterized by a lack of certainty. It is also clear that those who deal effectively with these problems, through either skill or luck, are often handsomely rewarded for their accomplishments. In the first book of the Old Testament, Joseph is promoted from slave to assistant Pharaoh of Egypt by accurately forecasting seven years of feast and seven years of famine.[1]

In quantitative modeling, the lack of certainty can be dealt with in various ways. For example, in a linear programming model, some of the data may be an estimate of

---

[1]As well as being an accurate forecaster, by virtue of his skill in successfully interpreting Pharaoh's dreams, Joseph has been called the first psychoanalyst. Less well known is the fact that Joseph was also the first management scientist. In anticipation of the famine, he advised Pharaoh to build storage facilities to hold inventories of grain. When it was all over and the famine had been survived, Joseph was asked how he had come to acquire such wisdom and knowledge. "Lean-year programming," was his reply.

a future value. In the PROTRAC *E* and *F* model above, next month's capacity (availability of hours) in department A (the right-hand side of the first constraint) may depend on determining factors that will occur next week, but the production plans, let us say, must be spelled out today. As described previously, management might deal with this lack of certainty by estimating the capacity as 150 and then performing sensitivity analysis.

Definition
of Risk

Decision theory provides alternative approaches to problems with less than complete certainty. One such approach is called "decisions under risk." In this context, the term "risk" has a restrictive and well-defined meaning. When we speak of "decisions under risk," we are referring to a class of decision problems for which there is more than one state of nature and for which we make the assumption that *the decision maker knows the probability with which each state of nature will occur.* Suppose, for example, that there are $m > 1$ states of nature, and let p_j be the the probability that state j will occur. We can then use equation (14.1) to calculate ER_i, the expected return if we make decision i.

$$ER_i = \sum_{j=1}^{m} r_{ij} \cdot p_j = r_{i1} p_1 + r_{i2} p_2 + \cdots r_{im} p_m \tag{14.1}$$

Optimality
Criteria

For this type of problem, *management should then make the decision i that maximizes the expected return.*[2] In other words, $i*$ is the optimal decision where

$$ER_{i*} = \text{maximum over all } i \text{ of } ER_i$$

Consider, for example, a very special version of a classic management science problem known as the newsboy problem. In this problem the newsboy buys papers from the delivery truck at the beginning of the day. During the day he sells papers. How many he will sell is unknown in advance. At the end of the day any leftover papers are worthless. Let us assume that each paper costs 10 cents and sells for 25 cents, and that the following probability distribution for demand is known:

$$P_0 = \text{Prob \{demand} = 0\} = 1/10$$
$$P_1 = \text{Prob \{demand} = 1\} = 3/10$$
$$P_2 = \text{Prob \{demand} = 2\} = 4/10$$
$$P_3 = \text{Prob \{demand} = 3\} = 2/10$$

The Payoff
Table

In this problem, each of the four different values for demand is a different state of nature and the number of papers ordered is the decision. The returns, or payoffs, are shown in Figure 14.3.

The entries in this figure represent the net cash flow associated with each combination of number ordered and number demanded. These entries are calculated with the following expression.

$$\text{payoff} = 25 \text{ (number of papers sold)} - 10 \text{ (number of papers ordered)}$$

where 25 cents is the selling price per paper and 10 cents is the cost of buying a paper.

[2]It will be shown that this is equivalent to another criterion: minimizing expected regret.

Figure 14.3

Payoff Table (Net Cash Flows) for the Newsboy Problem

DECISION	STATE OF NATURE (DEMAND)			
	0	1	2	3
0	0	0	0	0
1	−10	15	15	15
2	−20	5	30	30
3	−30	−5	20	45

It is important to note that in this model sales and demand need not be identical. Indeed, sales is the minimum of the two quantities {number demanded, number ordered}.

Once all the data are assembled for Figure 14.3, the process of finding the optimal decision is strictly mechanical. You use (14.1) to evaluate the expected return for each decision (ER_i for $i = 0, 1, 2, 3$) and pick the largest value.

Expected Returns The expected returns for all of the decisions are calculated as follows:

$$ER_0 = 0(1/10) + 0(3/10) + 0(4/10) + 0(2/10) = 0$$
$$ER_1 = -10(1/10) + 15(3/10) + 15(4/10) + 15(2/10) = 12.5$$
$$ER_2 = -20(1/10) + 5(3/10) + 30(4/10) + 30(2/10) = 17.5$$
$$ER_3 = -30(1/10) - 5(3/10) + 20(4/10) + 45(2/10) = 12.5$$

Since ER_2 is the largest of these four values, the optimal decision is to order 2 papers. With this example, we have now illustrated another class of decision problems (decisions under risk) and the associated decision criterion (maximize the expected return).

Although it was easy to find the optimal decision in the previous example, this is not necessarily always the case. For example, imagine that the demand for papers could be any integer between 1 and 1000. The tabular representation of the problem would then have 1000 columns and 1000 rows. Finding the optimal decision by calculating each of 1000 expected returns and then choosing the largest of these values is tedious at best.

Decisions under Uncertainty In this case we again have more than one possible state of nature, but now the decision maker is unwilling or unable to specify the probabilities that the various states of nature will occur. There is a long-standing debate as to whether such a situation should exist or not; that is, should the decision maker always be willing to at least subjectively specify the probabilities even when he does not "know" very much (anything) about what state of nature is apt to occur? Leaving this debate to the philosophers, we turn to the various approaches suggested for this class of problem.

Laplace Criterion The Laplace criterion interprets the condition of "uncertainty" as equivalent to assuming that all states of nature are equally likely. This is the point of view: "If I know nothing, then anything is equally likely." For example, in the newsboy problem, we had the following payoff table:

DECISION	STATE OF NATURE			
	0	1	2	3
0	0	0	0	0
1	−10	15	15	15
2	−20	5	30	30
3	−30	−5	20	45

Assuming all states of nature to be equally likely means, since there are four states, that each state occurs with probability 0.25. Using these probabilities converts the problem to a decision under risk and one could then compute the expected return. You can easily verify that, using these probabilities, expected return would again be maximized by decision 2.

Although in some situations this "equally likely" approach may produce acceptable results, in other settings it would be inappropriate. For example, consider your friend from Yugoslavia, about to watch the football game between Notre Dame and USC in a year in which one team was experiencing a bad season and the other was thus heavily favored in the betting. Although your friend knows nothing about football and has no knowledge about the probability of either team winning, these probabilities clearly exist and are *not* equal. In other words, even though one has "no knowledge," there may be underlying probabilities on the various states of nature, and these probabilities may in no way be consistent with the "equal likelihood" assumption. With this realization, there may be contexts in which you would not wish to use the criterion of expected return based on the equal likelihood assumption (i.e., the Laplace criterion). For such cases, there are three different criteria which can be used to make decisions under uncertainty: *maximin*, *maximax*, and *minimax regret*. All of these criteria can be used without specifying probabilities. The discussion will be illustrated with the newsboy problem. Look at the earlier payoff table for a moment and think what criterion you might use to make a decision. By this we mean, think of a rule that you could describe to a friend. It has to be a general rule so that your friend could apply it to any payoff table and come up with a decision. Remember, you are willing to make no assumptions about the probabilities on states of nature. Now consider the following criteria.

Does No Knowledge Mean Equally Likely?

Maximin Criterion

The maximin criterion is an extremely conservative or perhaps pessimistic approach to making decisions. It evaluates each decision by the worst thing that can happen if you make that decision. In this case, then, it evaluates each decision by the *minimum* possible return associated with the decision. In the newsboy example the minimum possible return if 3 papers are ordered is −30; thus, this value is assigned to the decision "order 3 papers." Similarly, we can associate with each other decision the minimum value in its row. Following this rule enables the decision maker to prepare a table as follows:

DECISION	MINIMUM RETURN
0	0
1	−10
2	−20
3	−30

He then selects the decision that yields the maximum value of the minimum return (hence, maximin). In this case, then, the newsboy should order 0 papers.

An Intuitive Evaluation of Maximin

This result is not intuitively appealing. The realist wonders how any activity would ever be initiated with this criterion. Those who "believe in" the maximin criterion might argue that this example is not appropriate, since the newsboy would not contemplate buying papers unless something was known about the distribution of demand. Maximin is often used in situations where the planner feels he or she cannot afford to be wrong. Defense planning might be an example. The planner chooses a decision that does as well as possible in the worst possible (most pessimistic) case.

It is, however, easy to create examples in which most people would not accept the decision selected with the maximin criterion. Consider, for example, the payoff table in Figure 14.4. Most people would prefer decision 1. It is much better than decision 2 for all states of nature except state 3, and then it is only slightly worse. Nevertheless, the maximin criterion would select decision 2. If you are among those who strongly prefer decision 1 in this example, you must then ask yourself the following question: "If the maximin criterion provides an answer that I don't like in this simple example, would I be willing to use it on more complicated and important problems? There is no correct answer to this question. The answer depends on the taste of the decision maker.

A Disturbing Example with Maximin

Figure 14.4
Payoff Table: Maximin Example

DECISION	\multicolumn{9}{c}{STATE OF NATURE}
	1	2	3	4	5	6	7	8	9
1	$\frac{100}{3}$	$\frac{100}{3}$	$\frac{2.9}{3}$	$\frac{100}{3}$	$\frac{100}{3}$	$\frac{100}{3}$	$\frac{100}{3}$	$\frac{100}{3}$	$\frac{100}{3}$
2	$\frac{3}{3}$	$\frac{3}{3}$	$\frac{3}{3}$	$\frac{3}{3}$	$\frac{3}{3}$	$\frac{3}{3}$	$\frac{3}{3}$	$\frac{3}{3}$	$\frac{3}{3}$

Maximax Criterion

The maximax criterion is as optimistic as maximin is pessimistic. It evaluates each decision by the best thing that can happen if you make that decision. In this case, then, it evaluates each decision by the maximum possible return associated with that decision. In particular, refer again to the payoff table for the newsboy problem. If the newsboy ordered 2 papers, the best possible outcome would be a return of 30. This value is thus assigned to the decision, "order 2 papers." In other words, for each decision we identify the maximum value in that row. Using this rule, the decision maker prepares a table as follows:

DECISION	MAXIMUM RETURN
0	0
1	15
2	30
3	45

He then selects the decision that yields the maximum of these maximum returns (hence, maximax). In this case, then, the newsboy should order 3 papers.

The maximax criterion is subject to the same type of criticism as maximin; that is, it is easy to create examples where using the maximax criterion leads to a decision that most people find unacceptable. Consider the payoff table presented in Figure 14.5, for example. Most people prefer decision 1 since it is much better than decision 2 for every state of nature except state 3, and then it is only slightly worse. The maximax criterion, however, selects decision 2.

Figure 14.5

Payoff Table: Maximax Example

DECISION	STATE OF NATURE								
	1	2	3	4	5	6	7	8	9
1	100	100	100	100	100	100	100	100	100
2	3	3	101.1	3	3	3	3	3	3

Regret introduces a new concept for measuring the desirability of an outcome; that is, it is a new way to create the payoff table. So far, all the decision criteria have been used on a payoff table of dollar returns as measured by net cash flows. In particular, each entry in Figure 14.3 shows the net cash flow for the newsboy for every combination of decision

Figure 14.6

Regret Table for the Newsboy Problem

DECISION	STATE OF NATURE			
	0	1	2	3
0	0	15	30	45
1	10	0	15	30
2	20	10	0	15
3	30	20	10	0

(number of papers ordered) and state of nature (number of papers demanded). Figure 14.6 shows the regret for each combination of decision and state of nature. It is derived from Figure 14.3 by

1. Finding the maximum entry in each column (e.g., 30 is the largest entry in the third column i.e., in the column under state of nature "2").
2. Calculating the new entry by subtracting the current entry from the maximum in its column. Thus, the new entry in row 2 column 3 is

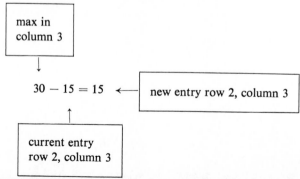

In each column, these new entries, called regret, indicate how much better we can do. In other words, "regret" is synonymous with "opportunity cost" of not making the best decision for a given state of nature. It follows that the decision maker would like to make a decision that minimizes regret, but (same old story) he does not know which state of nature will occur. If he knows a probability distribution on the state of nature, he could minimize the expected regret. (In the next section, we will see that this is equivalent to maximizing expected net cash flow.) If he does not know the probability, the typical suggestion is to use the conservative *minimax criterion*, that is, to select that decision that does the best in the worst case (the decision which has the smallest maximum regret).

For example, consider the regret table for the newsboy problem shown in Figure 14.6. If 1 paper is ordered, the maximum regret of 30 occurs if 3 papers are demanded. The value 30 is thus associated with the decision "order 1 paper." In other words, the maximum value in each row is associated with the decision in that row. Following this rule produces the following table:

DECISION	MAXIMUM REGRET
0	45
1	30
2	20
3	30

The decision maker then selects the decision that minimizes the maximum regret. In this case, the minimax regret criterion implies that the newsboy should order 2 papers. Our newsboy example illustrates that, when making decisions without using probabilities, the three criteria maximin cash flow, maximax cash flow, and minimax regret can lead to different "optimal" decisions.

14.3
THE EXPECTED VALUE OF PERFECT INFORMATION: NEWSBOY PROBLEM UNDER RISK

Let us return to the newsboy problem under risk (i.e., with a probability distribution on demand). Recall that, in this case, the optimal policy was to order 2 papers and that the expected return was 17.5. It is useful to think about this problem in a very stylized fashion in order to introduce the concept of the **expected value of perfect information**. In particular, let us assume that the sequence of events in the newsboy's day (the "current sequence of events") proceeds as follows:

1. The devil, by drawing from the demand distribution for papers, determines the number of papers that will be demanded.
2. The newsboy, not knowing what demand had been drawn, but knowing the distribution of demand, orders his papers.
3. The demand is then revealed to the newsboy and he achieves an *actual* (as opposed to expected) return determined by his order-size decision and the demand.

Now consider a new scenario. The newsboy has an opportunity to make a deal with the devil. (If you think this is silly, remember that Faust is equally improbable.) Under the new deal the sequence of events proceeds as follows:

1. The newsboy pays the devil a fee.
2. The devil determines the demand as above.
3. The devil tells the newsboy what the demand will be.
4. The newsboy orders his papers.
5. The newsboy achieves the return determined by the demand and the number of papers he ordered.

Expected Value of Perfect Information

The question is: What is the largest fee the newsboy should be willing to pay in step 1? This fee is called the *expected value of perfect information*. In general terms,

$$\text{fee} = \begin{pmatrix} \text{expected return} \\ \text{with new deal} \end{pmatrix} - \begin{pmatrix} \text{expected return with the} \\ \text{current sequence of events} \end{pmatrix}$$

With the new deal the newsboy, in step 4, will always order the number of papers that will give him the maximum return for the state of nature that will occur. However, the payment in step 1 must be made *before* he learns what the demand will be. Referring to Figure 14.3 we see that if 0 papers will be demanded, he will order 0 papers and enjoy the maximum return of 0. Since the devil is drawing from the distribution of demand, there is a probability of 1/10 that what the newsboy will learn from the devil is that demand will in fact be zero. Similarly, he will learn with a probability of 3/10 that 1 paper will be demanded. If this occurs, he will order 1 paper and enjoy the maximum return of 15. Following this reasoning, his expected return under the new deal is

$$\text{ER(new)} = 0(1/10) + 15(3/10) + 30(4/10) + 45(2/10) = 25.5$$

We have already seen that in the absence of perfect information his optimal decision (order 2 papers) gives an expected return of 17.5. Thus, if EVPI stands for the expected value of perfect information, we can calculate it as follows:

$$\text{EVPI} = 25.5 - 17.5 = 8.0$$

Practical Importance

This is the maximum amount our vendor should be willing to pay in step 1 for the deal with the devil. Although the story we have used to develop the concept is farfetched, the expected value of perfect information (EVPI) has important practical significance. It is an upper bound on the amount that you should be willing to pay to improve your knowledge about what state of nature will occur. Literally millions of dollars are spent on various market research projects and other testing devices (geological tests, quality control experiments, etc.) to determine what state of nature will occur in a wide variety of applications. The expected value of perfect information indicates the expected amount to be gained from any such endeavor and thus places an upper bound on the amount that should be spent in gathering information.

Relation between EVPI and Regret

The expected value of perfect information is always equal to the expected regret of the optimal decision under risk (the decision that maximizes expected return). We will show that this fact holds in the newsboy example.

When the probabilities on the states of nature are specified, it is a straightforward task to compute the expected regret for each decision. Using the previous probability distribution of demand and the regret table (Figure 14.6), the expected regret for the possible order quantities is computed as follows:

$$\text{expected regret (0)} = 0(1/10) + 15(3/10) + 30(4/10) + 45(2/10) = 25.5$$
$$\text{expected regret (1)} = 10(1/10) + 0(3/10) + 15(4/10) + 30(2/10) = 13.0$$
$$\text{expected regret (2)} = 20(1/10) + 10(3/10) + 0(4/10) + 15(2/10) = 8.0$$
$$\text{expected regret (3)} = 30(1/10) + 20(3/10) + 10(4/10) + 0(2/10) = 13.0$$

We see that ordering 2 papers yields the minimum expected regret. But ordering 2 papers was also the optimal decision when the criterion was to maximize the expected net dollar return.

> **It is always the case that, in decision making under risk, these two criteria (minimize expected regret, maximize expected net dollar return) will prescribe the same decision as optimal.**

Also,

> **The expected regret of the optimal decision under risk (i.e., the minimum expected regret) equals the expected value of perfect information.**

14.4
UTILITIES AND DECISIONS UNDER RISK

Utility is an alternative way of measuring the attractiveness of the result of a decision. In other words, it is an alternative way of finding the values to fill in a payoff table. Up to now we have used net dollar return (net cash flow) and regret as two measures of the goodness of a particular combination of a decision and a state of nature.

Utility suggests another type of measure. Our treatment of this topic includes three main sections:

1. A rationale for utility (i.e., why using net cash flow can lead to unacceptable decisions)
2. How to use a utility function
3. Creating a utility function

The Rationale *for Utility*   In the preceding section we saw that the maximin and maximax decision criteria could lead to unacceptable decisions in simple illustrative problems. We now point out that the criterion of maximizing expected net cash flow in a decision under risk can also produce unacceptable results. For example, consider an urn that contains 99 white balls and 1 black ball. You are offered a chance to play a game in which a ball will be drawn from this urn. Each ball is equally likely to be drawn. If a white ball is drawn, you must pay $10,000. If the black ball is drawn, you receive $1,000,000. You must decide whether to play or not. The payoff table based on net cash flow is shown in Figure 14.7.

Figure 14.7

Payoff Table (Net Cash Flows)

DECISION	STATE OF NATURE	
	White Ball	Black Ball
Play	−10,000	1,000,000
Do not play	0	0

We now use the information in this table, together with the facts that the probabilities of a white and a black ball are, respectively, 0.99 and 0.01 to calculate the expected return for each decision (play or do not play) in the usual way.

$$ER(\text{play}) = -10,000(99/100) + 1,000,000(1/100)$$
$$= -9900 + 10,000 = 100$$
$$ER(\text{do not play}) = 0(99/100) + 0(1/100) = 0$$

Since ER(play) > ER(do not play), we should play if we apply the criterion of maximizing the expected net cash flow.

Downside Risk

Now step back and ask yourself if you would decide to play this game or not. Remember that the probability is 0.99 that you will lose $10,000. Many people simply find this large "downside risk" to be unacceptable; that is, they are unwilling to accept the decision based on the criterion of maximizing the expected net cash flow. Thus, once again we see a simple example which shows a need to take care in selecting an appropriate criterion. This is all the more true in dealing with complicated, real-world problems.

Fortunately, it is not necessary to reject the concept of maximizing expected returns. To adapt the expected return criterion to general decisions under risk it is only necessary to recognize that net dollar returns do not always accurately reflect the "attractiveness" of the possible outcomes of decisions. To show what this means, ask yourself if you would be willing to win or lose 10 cents depending on the flip of a fair coin. (Most people would say yes.) How about winning or losing $10,000, depending on a flip of the same coin? (Here most people would say no.) What is the difference? A 10-cent gain seems to balance a 10-cent loss. Why does not a $10,000 gain balance a $10,000 loss? The answer is that in the latter situation most people are "risk averse," which means they would feel that the loss of $10,000 is more painful than the benefit obtained from a $10,000 gain.

Risk Averse

Decision theory deals with this problem by introducing a function that measures the "attractiveness" of money. This function is called a *utility function*, where for the sake of this discussion the word "utility" can be thought of as a measure of "satisfaction." A typical "risk-averse" utility function is shown in Figure 14.8. Two characteristics of this function are worth noting:

1. It is nondecreasing, since more money is always at least as attractive as less money.
2. It is concave. An equivalent statement is that the marginal utility of money is non-increasing. To illustrate this phenomenon, let us examine Figure 14.8.

First suppose that you have $100 and someone gives you an additional $100. Note

Figure 14.8
Typical (Risk-Averse) Utility Function

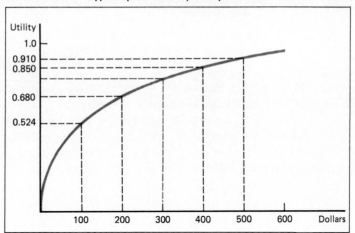

that your "utility" increases by

$$U(200) - U(100) \simeq 0.680 - 0.524 = 0.156$$

Now suppose that you start with $400 and someone gives you an additional $100. Now your utility increases by

$$U(500) - U(400) \simeq 0.910 - 0.850 = 0.060$$

In other words, 100 additional dollars is less attractive to you if you have $400 on hand than it is if you start with $100. Another way of describing this phenomenon is that the increase of a specified amount of dollars increases the utility less than the loss of the same amount of dollars decreases utility.

***Risk
Seeking*** Figure 14.9 shows two other general types of utility functions. The first is a **risk-seeking** (convex) function, where a gain of a specified amount of dollars increases the utility more

Figure 14.9
Some Utility Functions

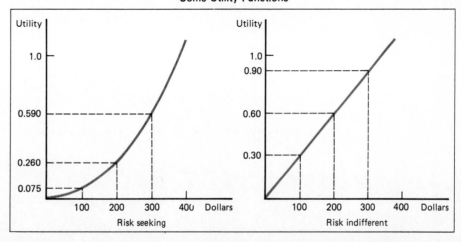

than a loss of the same amount of dollars decreases utility. As we saw, exactly the opposite statement holds for a risk-averse (concave) function like the one shown in Figure 14.8.

Risk Indifferent For the risk-indifferent function shown in Figure 14.9, a gain or a loss of a specified dollar amount produces a change of the same magnitude in your utility.

Using a Utility Function In the next section we will worry about how you go about creating a utility function. For the meantime, assume that somehow one has been created. Using this function to make decisions when the probabilities of the states of nature are known is a straightforward process. To be specific, you simply redo the payoff table, substituting the utility of the net cash flow for that cash flow, and proceed as before. Consider, for example, the newsboy problem, where we let Figure 14.10 represent the newsboy's utility

Figure 14.10
Newsboy's Utility Function

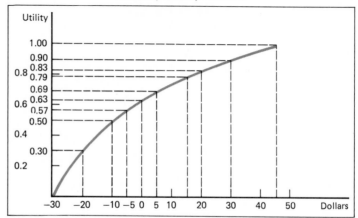

for money. The newsboy can use this figure and the payoff table of net cash flows (Figure 14.3) to create a new payoff table where the entries are the utility of the net cash flow associated each combination of a decision and a state of nature. For example, row 4, column 3 in Figure 14.3 shows a net cash flow of 20. Figure 14.10 translates this into a utility of about 0.83, which becomes the new entry in row 4, column 3. The complete table is presented in Figure 14.11. The newsboy now proceeds as before; that is, he calculates the expected utility for each decision. Using the previously employed probabilities

Figure 14.11
Newsboy Payoff Table (utilities)

DECISION	STATE OF NATURE			
	0	1	2	3
0	0.63	0.63	0.63	0.63
1	0.50	0.79	0.79	0.79
2	0.30	0.69	0.90	0.90
3	0	0.57	0.83	1.00

(1/10, 3/10, 4/10, 2/10), and letting EU$_i$ be the expected utility for decision i, the calculations are

$$EU_0 = 0.63(1/10) + 0.63(3/10) + 0.63(4/10) + 0.63(2/10) = 0.63$$

$$EU_1 = 0.50(1/10) + 0.79(3/10) + 0.79(4/10) + 0.79(2/10) = 0.761$$

$$EU_2 = 0.30(1/10) + 0.69(3/10) + 0.90(4/10) + 0.90(2/10) = 0.777$$

$$EU_3 = 0(1/10) \quad + 0.57(3/10) + 0.83(4/10) + 1(2/10) \quad = 0.703$$

Based on a criterion of maximizing the expected utility, the newsboy would order 2 papers. Referring to the discussion of decisions under risk in Section 14.2, we see that if the newsboy based his decision on maximizing the expected net cash flow, he would also order 2 papers. It is not always true that the decision which has the largest expected cash flow will also have the largest expected utility. The fact that this phenomenon occurred in this particular example does not imply that it will occur in general. A different utility function could yield a different decision.

One system of creating a utility function like the one shown in Figure 14.10 requires the decision maker, in our case the newsboy, to make a series of choices between a sure return and a lottery. In more formal language, the decision maker is called on to create an "**equivalent lottery**." This, however, is the second step. Let us start at the beginning.

The newsboy can arbitrarily select the end points of his utility function. It is a convenient convention to set the utility of the smallest net dollar return equal to 0 and the utility of the largest net return equal to 1. Since in the newsboy example the smallest return is -30, and the largest is $+45$, he sets $U(-30) = 0$ and $U(45) = 1$. Note that these values are used in Figure 14.10. These two values play a fundamental role in finding the utility of any quantity of money between -30 and 45. It is perhaps easiest to proceed by example.

Assume that the decision maker starts with $U(-30) = 0$ and $U(45) = 1$ and wants to find the utility of 10 [i.e., $U(10)$]. He proceeds by selecting a probability p such that he is indifferent between the following two alternatives:

1. Receive a payment of 10 for sure
2. Participate in a lottery in which he receives a payment of 45 with probability p or a payment of -30 with probability $1 - p$

Clearly if $p = 1$, the decision maker prefers alternative 2, since he prefers a payment of 45 to a payment of 10. Equally clear, if $p = 0$, he prefers alternative 1, since he prefers a payment of 10 to a loss of 30 (i.e., a payment of -30). It follows that somewhere between 0 and 1 there is a value for p such that the decision maker is indifferent between the two alternatives. This value will vary from person to person depending on how attractive the various alternatives are to them. We call this value of p the utility for 10. We obviously have not *proved* that using the probability p to define an equivalent lottery is a meaningful way to construct a utility function. An understandable discussion of why this approach works would carry us far beyond the scope of this text. We must be content to stop with the how and leave the why to other courses.

ANOTHER LOOK AT RISK

For many people the intuitive notion of risk is synonymous with the possibility of a meaningful or substantial loss when the results of a decision are not known with certainty. For years "widows and orphans" were advised to buy blue-chip stocks because they could count on the dividend. There was little or no risk. On the other hand, growth stocks were to be avoided since they were too risky. Although there was the opportunity for large gains, there was considerable uncertainty about the future dividends and, worse yet, the possibility of losing the original investment was significant enough to be reckoned with.

Common Conception of Risk It is evident that the amount of uncertainty and, in particular, *the probability of a "substantial" loss* is an important factor in making decisions where the results are not known in advance. In casual conversation such considerations are typically referred to as risk.

One might well wonder, at this point, whether or not the use of expected return or expected utility incorporates this intuitive notion of risk. The fundamental message is that

A decision maker's attitude toward risk is incorporated in his utility function.

In other words, by creating an appropriate utility function, the concerns of the widows and orphans (and others) about downside losses are correctly taken into account with the expected utility criterion, as illustrated in the preceding section with risk-averse, risk-seeking, and risk-indifferent utilities.

You might conclude, then, that this puts the subject of risk to rest once and for all. This is not so because in certain applications it is useful to have a measure of risk that can be calculated without having to construct a personal utility function. For this reason, ***Variance as a Measure of Risk*** in some models, especially in finance, the variability, or dispersion, or scatter of the returns associated with a decision is used as a measure of risk. The most common measure of variability is the **variance**, where the variance of the return for decision i, var(R_i), is defined as

$$\text{var}(R_i) = \sum_{j=1}^{n} (r_{ij} - \text{ER}_i)^2 p_j$$

Recall that in this expression

r_{ij} = return if the decision i is selected and state of nature j occurs.

ER_i = expected return for decision i

p_j = probability that state of nature j occurs

The square root of the variance is the **standard deviation** and the general notion is that the larger the variance (or the standard deviation) the greater the risk. To illustrate this notion consider two hypothetical investments, A and B, whose possible returns are presented in Figure 14.12. These data are grouped and plotted in Figures 14.13 and 14.14. The expected values and variances for A and B are also shown in Figures 14.13 and 14.14. Note that each decision produces the same expected return. However, it can be noted that in decision B the revenue can equal -1, whereas for decision A all revenues are at least equal to 0. Thus it could loosely be stated that B has greater downside variability,

Figure 14.12

Payoff Table for Decisions A and B

	PROBABILITY				
	0.1	0.2	0.4	0.2	0.1
	STATE OF NATURE				
DECISION	1	2	3	4	5
A	0	0	1	2	2
B	−1	0	1	2	3

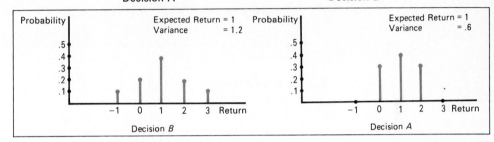

Figure 14.13

Decision A

Figure 14.14

Decision B

where *downside* means to the left of the expected return. In other words, the probability of too large a loss (too small a return) is higher with *B* than with *A*. Also note that the potential gain with investment *B* is greater than with *A*. This means that *B* has greater upside potential (or upside variability) as well as downside risk. It should be clear that as the downside risk or the upside potential becomes greater, the variance will also increase. This is reflected in the fact that, for this particular example, the variance of *A* is 0.6, and the variance of *B* is 1.2.

You can now see that variance provides a way to measure the "width" of the scatter of returns about ER_i, and in this sense variance can be considered a measure of risk. But as we mentioned at the beginning of this section, risk is commonly thought of as the probability of "too large a loss." (See Example 2 in Section 14.12 and footnote 6 for more discussion of this point.) We have seen in the above example that

---

Variance reflects upside, as well as downside, potential, and hence variance is not a measure of loss potential per se. In this sense, it may seem to be somewhat less than an ideal measure of risk.

Risk in Finance Models

In many problems it is the case that higher variance decisions have a higher expected return. In such cases the risk-averse individual will have multiple incompatible objectives. Namely, he wants a decision with low variance (because, correctly or not, he is using variance as a proxy for risk) and high expected return. A typical example occurs in portfolio models in finance, where a standard way of dealing with the problem is to enter one of the two objectives as a constraint in the model. As an example the investor may, in his model, place a lower bound on the expected returns from the portfolio. The objective would be to minimize the variance, subject to the constraint on expected return.

A MID-CHAPTER SUMMARY

The preceding four sections provide the theoretical foundation on which the rest of the chapter is based. The ensuing sections are devoted to procedures that play an important role in solving real-world problems. It is useful to summarize what we have achieved before moving ahead.

Section 14.2 provided a general framework for a class of problems identified as decisions against nature. In this framework, the problem can be described by a payoff table in which the returns to the decision maker depend on the decision he selects and the state of nature that occurs. Three specific cases were identified:

1. *Decisions under certainty:* The decision maker knows exactly what state of nature will occur. His "only" problem is to select the best decision. Deterministic problems such as linear programming, integer programming, and the EOQ model fall in this category.

2. *Decisions under risk:* A probability distribution is specified on the states of nature. The decision maker may use the following criteria to select a "best decision."
    a. Maximize expected return as measured by net dollar return
    b. Maximize expected return as measured by utility
    c. Minimize expected regret (opportunity cost)
    We saw that criteria a and c always lead to the same decision. Many inventory control and queuing problems fall into the category of decisions under risk.

3. *Decisions under uncertainty:* Here it is assumed that the decision maker has no knowledge about which state of nature will occur. The decision maker might apply the Laplace criteria, that is, assign equal probabilities to the various states of nature and then choose a decision that maximizes expected return. Alternatively, the decision maker may attack the problem without using probabilities. In this case, we discussed three different criteria for making a "best decision."
    a. Maximize minimum net dollar return
    b. Maximize maximum net dollar return
    c. Minimize maximum regret

Each of these criteria may, in general, lead to different decisions.

Section 14.3 was devoted to the concept of the expected value of perfect information (EVPI). This entity plays an important role by establishing an upper bound on the amount you should pay to gain new information about what state of nature will occur. We saw that EVPI is equal to the optimal (min) value of expected regret.

In Section 14.4 we discussed utility as an alternative measure of the attractiveness of each combination of a decision and a state of nature. The desire to use a utility function is motivated by the fact that in some cases, for example, because of the magnitudes of the potential losses, the decision that maximizes the expected net dollar return is not the decision that you would want to select. The discussion of risk is completed in Section 14.5. Here the use of the variance of returns as a measure of risk is examined.

The remaining sections in this chapter will deal with extensions of the model for decisions under risk. They consider decision trees, a technique of significant practical importance, and introduce two important concepts: the use of new information in decision making and the analysis of sequential decision problems.

DECISION TREES: MARKETING HOME
AND GARDEN TRACTORS

A *decision tree* is a graphical device for analyzing decisions under risk, that is, problems in which the probabilities on the states of nature are specified. More precisely, decision trees were created to use on problems in which there is a sequence of decisions, each of which could lead to one of several uncertain outcomes. For example, a concessionaire typically has to decide how much to bid for each of several possible locations at the state fair. The result of this decision is not certain, since it depends on what his competitors decide to bid. Once he knows his location, he must decide how much food to stock. The result of this decision in terms of profits is also not certain since it depends on customer demand.

Our discussion of decision trees is organized in the following manner. In this section we introduce the basic ideas. Section 14.8 examines the sensitivity of the optimal decision to the assessed values of the probabilities. Section 14.9 shows how Bayes Theorem is used to incorporate new information into the process, and Section 14.10 considers a sequential decision problem. The entire discussion is motivated by the following marketing problem faced by the management of PROTRAC.

The design and product testing phase has just been completed for PROTRAC's new line of home and garden tractors. Top management is attempting to decide on the appropriate marketing and production strategy to use for this product. Three major alternatives are being considered. Each alternative is identified with a single word.

Alternative Marketing and Production Strategies

1. *Aggressive (A):* This strategy represents a major commitment of the firm to this product line. A major capital expenditure would be made for a new and efficient production facility. Large inventories would be built up to guarantee prompt delivery of all models. A major marketing campaign involving nationally sponsored television commercials and dealer discounts would be initiated.

2. *Basic (B):* In this plan, E-4 (the small crawler tractor) production would be moved from Joliet to Moline. This move would phase out the trouble-plagued department for adjustable pelican and excavator production. At the same time, the E-4 line in Joliet would be modified to produce the new home and garden product. Inventories would be held for only the most popular items. Headquarters would make funds available to support local or regional advertising efforts, but no national advertising campaign would be mounted.

3. *Cautious (C):* In this plan, excess capacity on several existing E-4 lines would be used to produce the new products. A minimum of new tooling would be developed. Production would be geared to satisfy demand, and advertising would be at the discretion of the local dealer.

Management decides to categorize the condition of the market (i.e., the level of demand) as either strong (S) or weak (W). Figure 14.15 presents the payoff table and management's best estimate of the probability of a strong or a weak market. The payoffs in the body are the net profits measured in millions of dollars. They were generated by carefully calculating the sales, revenues, and costs associated with each decision–state of nature combination. It is interesting to note that a cautious (C) decision yields a higher profit with a weak market than it does with a strong market. If there is a strong market and PROTRAC is cautious, not only will the competition capture the small tractor market, but as a result of the carryover effect of these sales the competition will seriously cut into PROTRAC's current market position for accessories and other home products.

Figure 14.15

Payoffs (Millions of Dollars) and Probabilities
for the Basic Marketing Problem

	STATE OF NATURE	
	Strong, S	Weak, W
	PROBABILITY	
DECISION	0.45	0.55
Aggressive (A)	30	−8
Basic (B)	20	7
Cautious (C)	5	15

We are dealing here with what we have termed "decisions under risk" and it is, of course, possible to calculate the expected return for each decision and select the best one, just as we did in Section 14.2. The calculations follow:

$$ER(A) = 30(0.45) - 8(0.55) = 9.10$$
$$ER(B) = 20(0.45) + 7(0.55) = 12.85$$
$$ER(C) = 5(0.45) + 15(0.55) = 10.50$$

The optimal decision is to select (B), the basic production and marketing strategy.

Creating a Decision Tree

This marketing problem can also be represented by a decision tree. The first step in creating it is shown in Figure 14.16. In our exposition of decision trees, a **square node** will represent a point at which a decision must be made, and each line leading from a square will represent a possible decision. The **circular nodes** will represent situations where the outcome is not certain. Each line leading from a circle represents a possible outcome. The term **branches** will be employed for the lines emanating from the nodes, whether square or circular.

For the home and garden tractor problem, the decision tree in Figure 14.16 shows the initial node, labeled I. Since it is square, a decision must be made. Thus, management must choose one of the strategies A, B, or C. Depending on which decision is selected, a new position will be attained on the tree. For example, selecting strategy A leads us from node I to node II. Since II is a circle, the next branch that will occur is not known with certainty. If the market condition turns out to be strong, position V is attained. If, instead, the market proves to be weak, position VI is attained. Since they represent the end of the decision process, positions such as V and VI are referred to as **terminal positions**. Also, since nodes II, III, and IV are not followed by other nodes, they are called **terminal nodes**.

The decision tree presented in Figure 14.16 provides an efficient way for management to visualize the interactions between decisions and less than certain events. How-

Figure 14.16

First Step in Creating a Decision Tree for the Home
and Garden Tractor Problem

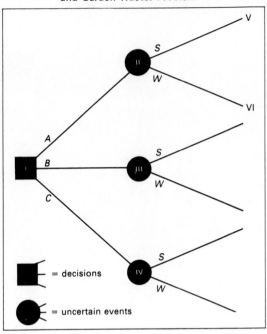

ever, if management wishes to use the decision tree to select an optimal decision, some additional information must be appended to the diagram. In particular, one must assign the return associated with each terminal position. This is called the **terminal value**. One must also assign a probability to each branch emanating from each circular node. For the basic model this is a simple task, and performing it yields the decision tree presented in Figure 14.17. You can see that the appended terminal values and branch probabilities are taken directly from Figure 14.15.

Appending Probabilities and Terminal Values

Using a decision tree to find the optimal decision is called solving the tree. To solve a decision tree one works backward or, in the jargon of the trade, by **folding back** the tree. First, the terminal branches are *folded back* by calculating an expected value for each terminal node. For example, the expected value to be obtained if one arrives at node II is 9.10. Now the branches emanating from the node are folded back (i.e., eliminated) and the expected value of 9.10 is assigned to the node, as shown in Figure 14.18.

Folding Back

Performing the same calculations for nodes III and IV yields what is termed the **reduced decision tree**, shown in Figure 14.19. Note that the expected terminal values on nodes II, III, and IV are identical to the expected returns computed earlier in this section for decisions A, B, and C, respectively. Management now faces the simple problem of choosing the alternative that yields the highest expected terminal value. In this case, as we have seen earlier, the choice is alternative B.

This completes the analysis of the basic model in terms of a decision tree. Hopefully, it is clear that for the basic model a decision tree simply provides another, more graphic, way of viewing the same problem. Exactly the same information is utilized, and the same calculations are made whether one uses the steps described in Section 14.2 or uses a decision tree to solve the problem.

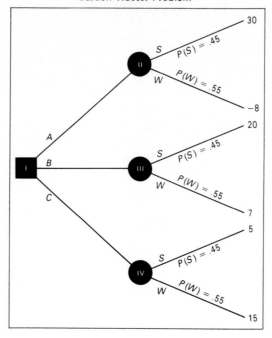

Figure 14.17
Complete Decision Tree for Home and
Garden Tractor Problem

Figure 14.19
Reduced Decision Tree of the
Home and Garden Tractor Problem

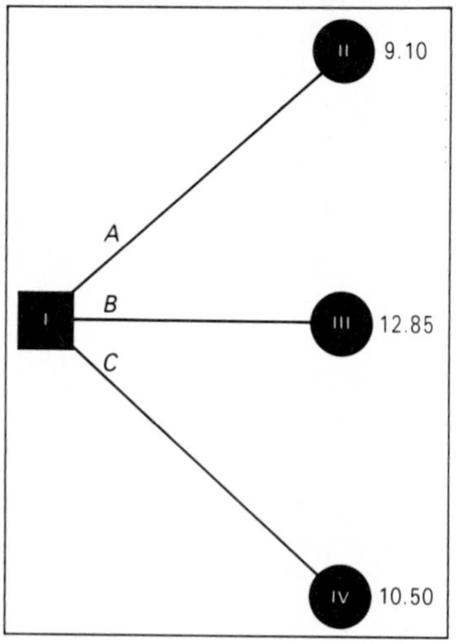

Figure 14.18
Folding Back Terminal Branches

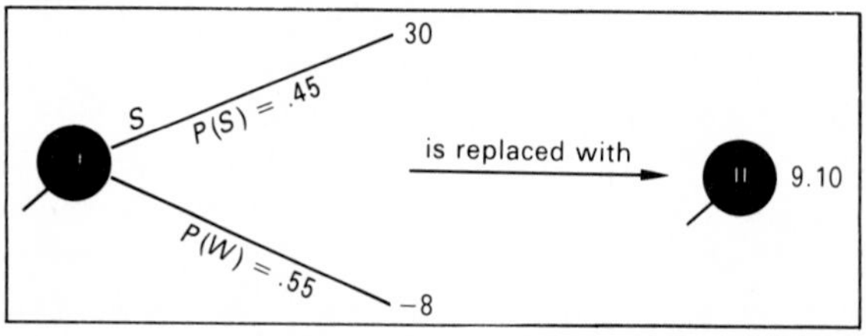

14.8

SENSITIVITY ANALYSIS

Before proceeding to the next main topic, a model in which new information becomes available concerning the likelihood of the uncertain events, it will be useful to consider again the expected return associated with each of the decisions in our previous example.

We have already noted that to calculate the expected return of strategy A, one uses the relationship

$$ER(A) = (30)P(S) + (-8)P(W)$$

where $P(S)$ is the probability of strong and $P(W)$ is the probability of weak. We also know that

$$P(S) + P(W) = 1 \quad \text{or} \quad P(W) = 1 - P(S)$$

Thus,

$$ER(A) = 30P(S) - 8[1 - P(S)] = -8 + 38P(S)$$

Expected Return as a Function of P(S) This expected return, then, is a linear function of the probability that the market response is strong.

A similar function can be found for alternatives B and C since

$$ER(B) = 20P(S) + 7[1 - P(S)] = 7 + 13P(S)$$

and

$$ER(C) = 5P(S) + 15[1 - P(S)] = 15 - 10P(S)$$

These three functions, that is, expected return as a function of the probability of "strong," are plotted on the same set of axes in Figure 14.20.

Figure 14.20
Expected Return as a Function of $P(S)$

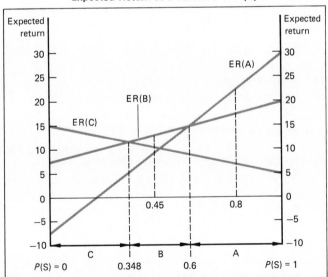

Since the criterion for making a decision when you have decisions under risk is to select the decision with the highest expected return, this figure shows which decision is optimal for any particular value of $P(S)$. For example, if as in Figure 14.15, the value of $P(S)$ is 0.45, then Figure 14.20 shows that $ER(B) > ER(C) > ER(A)$. Hence, as we have already computed, for this value of $P(S)$ the optimal decision is B. On the other hand, if $P(S) = 0.8$, we see that $ER(A) > ER(B) > ER(C)$ and thus A is the optimal decision.

In more general terms we see that if $P(S)$ is larger than the value of $P(S)$ at which the graphs of ER(A) and ER(B) cross, strategy A should be selected. The $P(S)$ value at which strategy A becomes optimal can be found by setting ER(A) equal to ER(B) and solving for $P(S)$; that is,

$$\text{ER(A)} = \text{ER(B)}$$
$$-8 + 38P(S) = 7 + 13P(S)$$
$$P(S) = 0.6$$

In a similar way, it is easily determined that the graphs of ER(C) and ER(B) cross when $P(S) = 0.348$. Thus, Figure 14.20 indicates that PROTRAC should select the basic production and marketing strategy (i.e., decision B) if $P(S)$ is larger than 0.348 and smaller than 0.6. This is consistent with what we already computed under the assumption that $P(S) = 0.45$. However, the analysis of Figure 14.20 provides considerably more

The Optimal
Policy Is
Not Very
Sensitive

information than we had previously. It is now clear, for example, that the optimal decision in this case is not very sensitive to the precision of our estimate for $P(S)$. The same strategy, B, remains optimal for an increase or decrease of more than 0.10 in the previously estimated probability of 0.45.

Although a diagram such as Figure 14.20 can only be used when there are two possible states of nature, it provides a useful pedagogical device for illustrating the sensitivity of the optimal solution to the estimate of probabilities. For higher dimensions, generalizations of this approach exist, but such a discussion would go beyond the introductory level of this chapter.

14.9

DECISION TREES: INCORPORATING NEW INFORMATION

A Market
Research
Study for
Home and
Garden
Tractors

The management of PROTRAC's domestic tractor division was just on the verge of recommending the basic marketing and production strategy (B) when the board of directors insisted that a market research study had to be performed. Only after such a study would the board be willing to approve the selection of a marketing and production strategy. As a result of the board's decision, management consulted the corporate marketing research group at PROTRAC headquarters. It was agreed that this group would perform a market research study and would report within a month on whether the study was encouraging, E, or discouraging, D. Thus, within a month the new-product planners would have this additional information. This new information should obviously be taken into account before making a decision on the marketing and production strategy.

Management could treat the new information informally; that is, once the test results are available, management's estimate of $P(S)$, the probability that the market would be strong, could be updated. If the study turns out to be encouraging, E, presumably management would want to increase the estimate of $P(S)$ from 0.45 to 0.50, 0.60, or maybe more. If the study results are discouraging, D, then $P(S)$ should be decreased.

The question is: How should the updating be accomplished? There is a formal way to do this, based on the concept of *conditional probability*. Before presenting this method we will pause to introduce the concept of conditional probability and the mechanics of working with these quantities.

Consider the following two-stage process:

1. A fair die is thrown.
2. A ball is chosen at random from one of three urns. Each urn contains 100 balls, but with a different number of white (W) and black (B) balls. The result of stage 1 determines which urn will be used. Details are presented in Figure 14.21.

Figure 14.21

Two-Stage Process

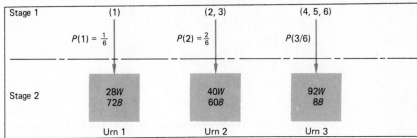

In this figure we see that if a 1 is thrown, we draw a ball from urn 1. Since we are throwing a fair die, the probability that we draw a ball from urn 1 is 1/6; that is, $P(1)$ = 1/6. Similarly, if we throw a 2 or 3, we will draw a ball from urn 2. This implies that $P(2) = 2/6$. Finally, if a 4, 5, or 6 is thrown, we draw a ball from urn 3 and thus $P(3)$ = 3/6.

The symbol $P(W|1)$ signifies a *conditional probability*. The vertical line is read as "given." Thus, $P(W|1)$ is read "the probability of W given 1." It means the probability of drawing a white ball (W) assuming that the drawing is made from urn 1. Recall that once an urn is selected, a ball is chosen at random, which means that each ball in the urn is equally likely to be drawn. Looking at Figure 14.21, we see that

$$P(W|1) = 0.28 \quad \text{and} \quad P(B|1) = 0.72$$
$$P(W|2) = 0.40 \quad \text{and} \quad P(B|2) = 0.60$$
$$P(W|3) = 0.92 \quad \text{and} \quad P(B|3) = 0.08$$

We would like to use the probabilities just presented to find $P(1|B)$. We have just seen that this means the probability that the ball was drawn from urn 1 given that we know it is black. To clarify this, assume that a friend goes through the two-stage process in the next room. He then comes in and reports that the ball is black. He then asks: "What is the probability that it came from urn 1?"

Before answering that question, suppose he had asked: "What is the probability that the ball I drew came from urn 1?" and he did *not* tell you the color of the ball. In this case all you know is that he would have drawn from urn 1 if he had thrown a 1 with his fair die. Thus, the *unconditional probability* that the ball came from urn 1 is $P(1) = 1/6$.

Now that you know the ball is black and that urn 1 has the highest percentage of black balls, your intuition may suggest that the probability of urn 1 has increased. If so, your intuition is correct. We will now use conditional probabilities to lend some precision to these remarks.

In order to calculate $P(1|B)$, we use the following relation, which is developed in courses dealing with probability and statistics. Let I denote any urn (e.g., $I = 1$). Then

$$P(I \text{ \& } B) = P(B \text{ \& } I) = P(B|I)P(I) = P(I|B)P(B) \qquad (14.2)$$

Joint
Probability where $P(B \text{ \& } I)$, which stands for $P(B \text{ and } I)$, is called the joint probability that both B and I occur. For example, if $I = 1$, then $P(B \text{ and } I)$ is the probability that the ball is black and was drawn from urn 1. We will also use the fact that

$$P(B) = P(B|1)P(1) + P(B|2)P(2) + P(B|3)P(3) \qquad (14.3)$$

We have now developed all the expressions we need to derive an expression for $P(1|B)$. From the last equality in (14.2) we obtain

$$P(I|B) = \frac{P(B|I)P(I)}{P(B)} \qquad (14.4)$$

Bayes
Theorem Then, substituting 1 for the value of I, and substituting the right-hand side of (14.3) for $P(B)$, expression (14.4) becomes

$$P(1|B) = \frac{P(B|1)P(1)}{P(B|1)P(1) + P(B|2)P(2) + P(B|3)P(3)} \qquad (14.5)$$

Equation (14.5) is called **Bayes Rule or Bayes Theorem**. Since all terms on the right-hand side of (14.5) are known, Bayes Rule provides a way to compute $P(1|B)$. Let us now apply this rule to the set of data at hand. We have previously determined that $P(B|1) = 0.72$ and $P(1) = 1/6$. Hence,

$$P(B|1)P(1) = (72/100)(1/6) = 0.12$$

This gives us the numerator. For the denominator, again using the given data:

$$P(B) = (72/100)(1/6) + (60/100)(2/6) + (8/100)(3/6) = 0.36$$

Thus, we obtain, using (14.5) and the calculations above,

$$P(1|B) = \frac{0.12}{0.36} = \frac{1}{3} \qquad (14.6)$$

Recall that the unconditional probability (i.e., with no additional information) that the ball was drawn from urn 1 is 1/6. Once we are told that the ball is black, the probability that it came from urn 1 increases. In this particular case it doubles.
The tabular display in Figure 14.22 is a convenient way to display the data required to compute all conditional probabilities.
The six entries $P(B \text{ \& } 1)$, $P(W \text{ \& } 1)$, $P(B \text{ \& } 2)$, and so on are called **joint probabilities**. They were computed using (14.2) and the already available data. For example,

$$P(B \text{ \& } 1) = P(B|1)P(1) = (72/100)(1/6) = 72/600$$
$$P(W \text{ \& } 1) = P(W|1)P(1) = (28/100)(1/6) = 28/600$$

Marginal
Probabilities and so on. The values on the lower and right rim of Figure 14.22 are called **marginal probabilities**, which is simply another term for what we have referred to as *unconditional probabilities*. You can see that each marginal probability is the sum of the joint prob-

474

Figure 14.22
Marginal and Joint Probabilities

		ROLL THE DIE			Marginal Probability
		Urn 1	Urn 2	Urn 3	
Draw a Ball	B	$P(B \& 1) = 72/600$	$P(B \& 2) = 120/600$	$P(B \& 3) = 24/600$	$P(B) = 36/100$
	W	$P(W \& 1) = 28/600$	$P(W \& 2) = 80/600$	$P(W \& 3) = 276/600$	$P(W) = 64/100$
Marginal Probability		$P(1) = 1/6$	$P(2) = 2/6$	$P(3) = 3/6$	

abilities in the corresponding row or column. For example, we see that

$$P(B) = P(B \& 1) + P(B \& 2) + P(B \& 3)$$
$$= 72/600 + 120/600 + 24/600 = 36/100$$

Now let us see how Figure 14.22 can be used to calculate conditional probabilities. To do this, we simply use expression (14.2). For example, suppose we wish to calculate $P(B|1)$. Using (14.2) we see that

$$P(B \& 1) = P(B|1)P(1)$$

which yields

$$P(B|1) = P(B \& 1)/P(1)$$

You can see that the data required to evaluate the right side of this equality is available in Figure 14.22. Thus,

$$P(B|1) = P(B \& 1)/P(1) = (72/600)/(1/6) = 0.72$$

Similarly, to calculate $P(1|B)$ we again use expression (14.2) as follows

$$P(B \& 1) = P(1|B)P(B)$$

or

$$P(1|B) = P(B \& 1)/P(B)$$

Again, the data to evaluate the right side of this equality is available in Figure 14.22. Thus,

$$P(1|B) = P(B \& 1)/P(B) = (72/600)/(36/100) = 2/6$$

Prior and Posterior Probabilities

Note that this agrees with the result shown in expression (14.6) which was obtained by applying Bayes Theorem. In summary, expression (14.2), along with a table of marginal and joint probabilities such as Figure 14.22, allows us to compute all conditional probabilities. We conclude this subsection by introducing the language that is typically used to describe the type of process just presented. The original probabilities $P(1) = 1/6$, and so on, are referred to as **prior probabilities** (i.e., before the new information that the ball

475

is black). The updated conditional probabilities [e.g., $P(1|B)$] are called **posterior probabilities** (i.e., after the new information).

The Market Research Example Continued Recall that the management of PROTRAC's domestic tractor division had all but decided to implement the basic (B) marketing and production strategy for the new line of home and garden tractors. The analysis was based on the assessment that $P(S) = 0.45$, that is, the probability of a strong market is 0.45. The board of directors has now ordered that a market research study be taken before deciding which strategy (A—aggressive, B—basic, C—cautious) to select. In this subsection we will see how to use Bayes Theorem to incorporate the results of the marketing research study into the decision process. The end result will be an updating for the values of $P(S)$ and $P(W)$.

The marketing research group has agreed to report within a month whether according to their study the test is encouraging (E) or discouraging (D). We now assume that the marketing research group is able to state the following indication of reliability: "The past results with our test have tended to be in the right direction. If a market has been strong, the test results have been encouraging 60% of the time and discouraging 40% of the time. If a market has been weak, the test results have been discouraging 70% of the time and encouraging 30% of the time." Management can use this information *Reliability of* to assess the conditional probabilities of the test results given the market conditions. *the Test* This assessment is

$$P(E|S) = 0.6 \qquad P(E|W) = 0.3$$
$$P(D|S) = 0.4 \qquad P(D|W) = 0.7$$

We now represent management's problem with the decision tree presented in Figure 14.23. The first node (I) corresponds to performing the market research. The node is circular because the outcome is not certain. There are two possible results. Either the test is encouraging (E) or discouraging (D); $P(E)$ and $P(D)$ represent the probabilities of these two outcomes.

If the test is encouraging, we proceed to node II, which is square because a decision must be made. Management must decide to select A or B or C. Suppose that management selects A. We are then led to node IV, another situation with two possible outcomes, namely whether the market is strong (S) or weak (W). If it turns out to be strong, PROTRAC will enjoy a net return of 30, which is the terminal value on the branch.

Importance of It is important to note that the tree is created in the chronological order in which infor-
Chronological mation becomes available and decisions are required: that is,
Order

1. Test result.
2. Make decision.
3. Market condition.

In order to solve this tree we must find the values for $P(S|E)$, $P(W|E)$, $P(S|D)$, $P(W|D)$, $P(E)$, and $P(D)$. This is accomplished by using Bayes Theorem with the data $P(E|S) = 0.6$, $P(D|S) = 0.4$, $P(E|W) = 0.3$, $P(D|W) = 0.7$, $P(S) = 0.45$, and $P(W) = 0.55$. Adapting (14.3) to this problem, we see that

$$P(E) = P(E|S) \cdot P(S) + P(E|W) \cdot P(W)$$
$$= (0.6)(0.45) + (0.3)(0.55) = 0.435$$

476

Figure 14.23
Decision Tree with Market Research Study

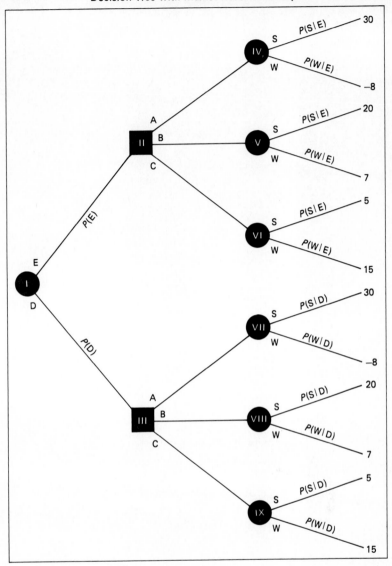

Thus, the probability that the marketing research study will be encouraging is 0.435.

Updating P(S) This implies that the probability that it is discouraging must be 0.565. Thus, $P(D) = 0.565$. In this setting, (14.4) becomes

$$P(S|E) = \frac{P(E|S)P(S)}{P(E)} = \frac{(0.6)(0.45)}{0.435} \approx 0.621$$

Thus, the event of an encouraging test result, and the use of Bayes Theorem, allows us to update the prior value of $P(S)$, namely 0.45, to a higher value, $P(S|E) = 0.621$. Similar calculations yield $P(W|E) = 0.379$, $P(S|D) = 0.318$, and $P(W|D) = 0.682$.

In Figure 14.24 the probabilities are attached to the decision tree. The first step in solving the tree is to fold it back to the terminal nodes.

Figure 14.24
Decision Tree with New Information

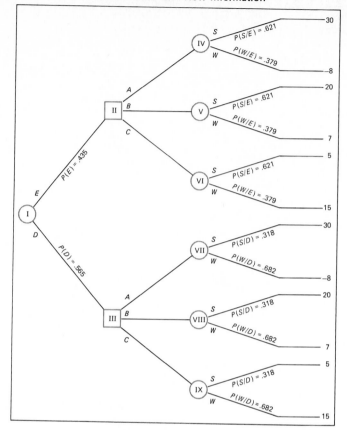

Figure 14.25 shows the tree after the first step. Figure 14.25 can be used to determine the optimal decisions. We see that if the test is encouraging (E), we arrive at node II. Then to maximize the expected return, we should take action A, that is, follow the aggressive production and marketing strategy. Similarly, if the test result is discouraging, we should take action C. Why? Because 11.81 is the largest possible expected return when the test is discouraging.

The Expected Value of Sample Information

Suppose that we use the optimal decisions determined above to fold back the decision tree shown in Figure 14.25 one more step. We obtain

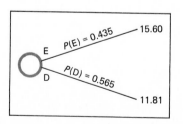

The expected return then is

$$ER = 15.60(0.435) + 11.81(0.565) \approx 13.46$$

Figure 14.25
Decision Tree after One Foldback

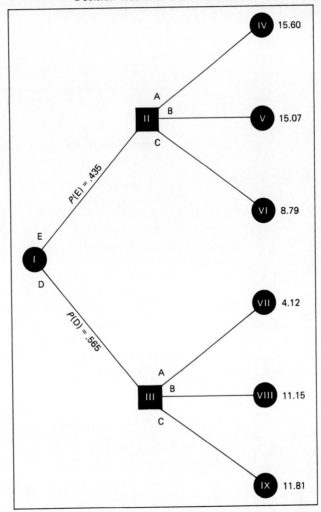

This value is the expected return of performing the market test and making optimal decisions.

In Section 14.7 we saw that if the market test is not performed, the optimal decision is to select B, the basic strategy, and that this decision has an expected return of 12.85. Clearly then, performing the market test increases PROTRAC's expected return by 13.46 − 12.85 = 0.61. Appropriately enough, this quantity is called the **expected value of sample information** (EVSI). In general terms,

$$\text{EVSI} = \begin{pmatrix} \text{maximum possible} \\ \text{expected return} \\ \text{with sample} \\ \text{information} \end{pmatrix} - \begin{pmatrix} \text{maximum possible} \\ \text{expected return} \\ \text{without sample} \\ \text{information} \end{pmatrix}$$

*Expected Value
of Sample
Information*

Let us now calculate the expected value of *perfect* information. Recall from Section 14.3 that this is the amount that management would be willing to pay for perfect information. The payoff table originally presented in Figure 14.15 is reproduced below for your convenience.

DECISION	STATE OF NATURE	
	S	W
	PROBABILITY	
	0.45	0.55
A	30	−8
B	20	7
C	5	15

*Expected
Value of
Perfect
Information*

If it were sure that the market would be strong, then management would pick decision A and enjoy a return of 30. Similarly, if it were sure that the market would be weak, management would pick decision C and enjoy a return of 15. How much would management pay for perfect information? Since perfect information will reveal a strong market with probability 0.45, and a weak market with probability 0.55, we see that

$$\text{EVPI} = (30)(0.45) + (15)(0.55) - 12.85 \approx 8.90 \qquad (14.7)$$

Equation (14.7) tells us that perfect information will bring us an expected increase over the previous expected return of 8.90. This is the maximum possible increase which can be obtained in the expected return from new information. The expected value of sample information EVSI is the increase in the expected return that was obtained with the information produced by the market test. Since EVPI = 8.9 and EVSI = 0.61, we see that the market test is not very effective. If it were, the value for EVSI would be much closer to EVPI.

14.10

SEQUENTIAL DECISIONS: TO TEST OR NOT TO TEST

In the preceding section, we assumed that the board of directors had decided to have a market research study done. We then considered the question of how the management of PROTRAC's domestic tractor division should use the information generated by the study to update the decision model. Let us step back for a moment. It seems clear that the decision to have a market study done is in essence no different from the decision to adopt one marketing and production strategy or another. Management must carefully weigh the cost of performing the study against the gain that might result from having the information that the study would produce. It is also clear that the decision on whether or not to have a market research test is not an isolated decision. If the test is given, management must still select one of the marketing and production strategies. Thus, the value of performing the test depends in part on how PROTRAC uses the information generated by the test. In other words, the value of an initial decision depends on a *sequence* of decisions and uncertain events that will follow the initial decision. This is called a *sequential decision problem*.

*Sequential
Decision
Problems*

This is an extremely common type of management problem and is actually the kind of situation that decision trees are designed to handle. It is in situations where there are a number of interrelated decisions and events with more than one possible outcome that the ability to display the problem graphically is especially useful.

Figure 14.26 shows the test or no-test tree. In terms of structure and the probabilities, you see that the upper (test) branch is the tree from Figure 14.24 and the lower (no test) branch is the tree from Figure 14.17.

Figure 14.26
Test or No-Test with Returns and Probabilities Assigned

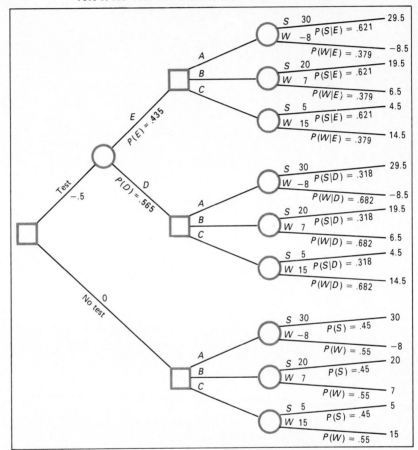

The terminal values merit some discussion. They are determined in a two-step process:

<table>
<tr><td valign="top">***Determination
of Terminal
Values***</td><td>

1. Assign the appropriate cash flow to each decision and uncertain event. In this problem we have assumed that the market test costs $500,000. Since all costs and returns are measured in millions, a figure of −0.5 is placed by the test branch and a figure of 0 is placed by the no-test branch. Similarly, a figure 30 is placed on the upper terminal branch since this is the profit if **PROTRAC** selects A and the market is strong.
2. Determine a particular terminal value by adding the costs on all branches between the first node and the terminal position. For example, the number 29.5 on the uppermost terminal position comes from adding the costs on the path Test–E–A–S (i.e., costs of −0.5 + 0 + 0 + 30 = 29.5).

</td></tr>
</table>

You solve this tree by folding it back. You fold back a circular node by calculating the expected returns. You fold back a square (decision) node by selecting the decision that yields the highest expected return. Three steps are required to solve the test or no-test tree. They are shown in Figure 14.27.

Figure 14.27
Solving the Test or No-Test Tree

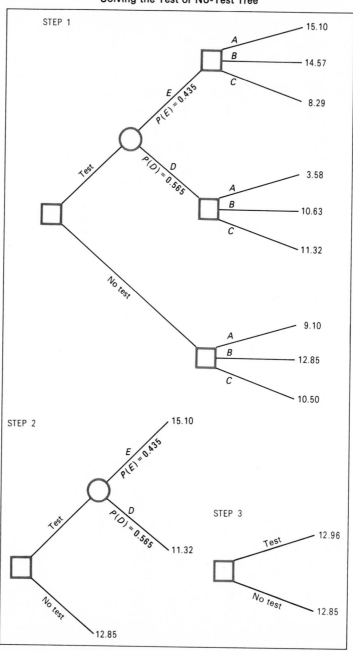

The Optimal Strategy   The *optimal strategy* is a complete plan for the entire tree. It specifies what action to take no matter which of the uncertain events occurs. To determine the optimal strategy for the test or no-test tree, we refer to Figure 14.27. From step 3 we see that since 12.96 > 12.85, PROTRAC should have the market test. From step 1 we see that if the result of the test is encouraging (E), then A is the best decision since it yields the largest expected return. Similarly, if the result of the test is discouraging (D), then C is the best decision.

14.11

EXAMPLES AND SOLUTIONS

Example 1

A firm must select between two marketing strategies, 1 and 2. The payoff table in which the entries are net returns in thousands of dollars is shown in Figure 14.28.

Figure 14.28
Payoff Table (Returns in $1000 Units)

						PROBABILITY						
	1/12	1/12	1/12	1/12	1/12	1/12	1/12	1/12	1/12	1/12	1/12	1/12
						STATE OF NATURE						
STRATEGY	1	2	3	4	5	6	7	8	9	10	11	12
1	−3	−3	−3	−1	−1	1	4	6	8	8	8	8
2	−3	0	2	2	2	3	3	3	4	4	4	6

Find the optimal decision using the criterion of maximizing expected return.

Solution to Example 1

$$ER_1 = 1/12(-3 - 3 - 3 - 1 - 1 + 1 + 4 + 6 + 8 + 8 + 8 + 8) = 32/12 = \$2667$$
$$ER_2 = 1/12(-3 + 2 + 2 + 2 + 3 + 3 + 3 + 4 + 4 + 4 + 6) = 30/12 = \$2500$$

The optimal solution is to select strategy 1.

Example 2

Refer to Example 1. Assume the firm has the utility function shown in Figure 14.29.
(a) The shape of this function describes what type of attitude toward risk?
(b) Based merely upon visual inspection of the data, which of the two strategies do you feel has more risk?
(c) Find the variance associated with the returns for each strategy. By this measure, which strategy has more risk?
(d) Calculate the expected utility associated with each strategy and select the best strategy based on the criterion of maximizing expected utility. Why is the conclusion different from that in Example 1?

Figure 14.29
Utility Function

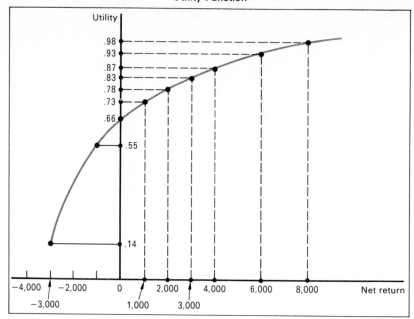

Solution to Example 2

    (a) The utility function is concave; this indicates that management is **risk averse**.

    (b) To answer this question, we create a table, shown in Figure 14.30, in which the returns and their associated probabilities are listed for each strategy. From this table, it seems reasonable to assess strategy 1 as being riskier than strategy 2 because strategy 1 has larger probabilities of losses. In particular, note that a loss of 3000 occurs with probability 3/12 in strategy 1 and only 1/12 in strategy

Figure 14.30
Strategies 1 and 2

STRATEGY 1		STRATEGY 2	
Net Return	Probability	Net Return	Probability
8000	$\frac{4}{12}$	6000	$\frac{1}{12}$
6000	$\frac{1}{12}$	4000	$\frac{3}{12}$
4000	$\frac{1}{12}$	3000	$\frac{3}{12}$
1000	$\frac{1}{12}$	2000	$\frac{3}{12}$
−1000	$\frac{2}{12}$	0	$\frac{1}{12}$
−3000	$\frac{3}{12}$	−3000	$\frac{1}{12}$

2. Moreover, there is a positive probability of losing 1000 with strategy 1, whereas this cannot happen with strategy 2.

(c) The variance of the returns from strategy i is defined by the expression

$$\text{var}(R_i) = \sum_{j=1}^{12} (r_{ij} - \text{ER}_i)^2 P_j$$

The calculations can be simplified by using the grouped data from Figure 14.30. Thus for strategy 1,

$$\text{var}(R_1) = \frac{4}{12}(8000 - 2667)^2 + \frac{1}{12}(6000 - 2667)^2 + \frac{1}{12}(4000 - 2667)^2$$

$$+ \frac{1}{12}(1000 - 2667)^2 + \frac{2}{12}(-1000 - 2667)^2 + \frac{3}{12}(-3000 - 2667)^2$$

$$= 21{,}056{,}000$$

For strategy 2,

$$\text{var}(R_2) = \frac{1}{12}(6000 - 2500)^2 + \frac{3}{12}(4000 - 2500)^2 + \frac{3}{12}(3000 - 2500)^2$$

$$+ \frac{3}{12}(2000 - 2500)^2 + \frac{1}{12}(0 - 2500)^2 + \frac{1}{12}(-3000 - 2500)^2$$

$$= 4{,}750{,}000$$

By this measure we conclude that strategy 1 has more risk.

(d) To calculate the expected utilities, one must read the utility for each return off the graph in Figure 14.29. The data and results of the calculations are shown in Figure 14.31. Strategy 2 is thus preferred to strategy 1 on the basis of the crite-

Figure 14.31
Expected Utilities

STRATEGY 1			STRATEGY 2		
Net Return	Utility	Probability	Net Return	Utility	Probability
8000	0.98	$\frac{4}{12}$	6000	0.93	$\frac{1}{12}$
6000	0.93	$\frac{1}{12}$	4000	0.87	$\frac{3}{12}$
4000	0.87	$\frac{1}{12}$	3000	0.83	$\frac{3}{12}$
1000	0.73	$\frac{1}{12}$	2000	0.78	$\frac{3}{12}$
−1000	0.55	$\frac{2}{12}$	0	0.66	$\frac{1}{12}$
−3000	0.14	$\frac{3}{12}$	−3000	0.14	$\frac{1}{12}$
Expected Utility = 0.66			Expected Utility = 0.76		

rion of maximizing expected utility. The preference has changed from 1 to 2 because 1 has more risk and the utility function is risk averse.[6]

Example 3

The customer service manager for PROTRAC is responsible for expediting late orders. To do his job effectively, when an order is late he must determine if the lateness is caused by an ordering error or a delivery error. If an order is late, one or the other of these two types of errors must have occurred. Because of the way in which this system is designed, both errors cannot occur on the same order. From past experience, he knows that an ordering error will cause 8 out of 20 deliveries to be late, whereas a delivery error will cause 8 out of 10 deliveries to be late. Historically, out of 1000 orders, 30 ordering errors and 10 delivery errors have occurred.

Assume that an order is late. If the customer service manager wishes to look first for the type of error that has the largest probability of occurring, should he look for an ordering error or a delivery error?

Solution to Example 3

Let

$$L = \text{the event that an order is late}$$
$$O = \text{the event that an ordering error is made}$$
$$D = \text{the event that a delivery error is made}$$

The problem is to find the maximum of $P(O|L)$ and $P(D|L)$. From the data in the problem it seems reasonable to assess the following probabilities:

$$P(O) = 0.03$$
$$P(D) = 0.01$$
$$P(L|O) = 0.40$$
$$P(L|D) = 0.80$$

From Bayes theorem,

$$P(O|L) = \frac{P(L|O)P(O)}{P(L|O)P(O) + P(L|D)P(D)}$$

$$P(D|L) = \frac{P(L|D)P(D)}{P(L|D)P(D) + P(L|O)P(O)}$$

---

[6]It should not be inferred that a risk-averse utility function will *always* lead to a selection of the decision with monetary returns having the smallest variance, even when expected returns are equal. In general, there will be tradeoffs between the magnitude of the various returns, the associated probabilities, and the precise shape of the utility function. A more correct inference would be the following. Given two decisions with equal expected monetary returns, a risk-averse utility function provides a way of choosing the decision with least *downside* variability. As an example, suppose $U(x) = \ln x$. Alternative 1 has returns 0.05 and 1.95, with probabilities 0.5 each. Alternative 2 has returns 0.25 and 5, with probabilities $\frac{16}{19}$ and $\frac{3}{19}$, respectively. In each case, the expected return is 1. For alternative 1, the variance is 0.90. For alternative 2, the variance is 2.58. However, the expected utility for alternative 1 is -1.164, whereas it is -0.913 for alternative 2. Hence, alternative 2, with more variance but less downside potential, is preferred. For certain special classes of utility functions, it can be shown that if two decisions have the same expected return, then utility maximization will also lead to a choice of the decision with smaller variance.

486

Thus

$$P(O|L) = \frac{(0.4)(0.03)}{(0.4)(0.03) + (0.8)(0.01)} = 0.6$$

$$P(D|L) = \frac{(0.8)(0.01)}{(0.8)(0.01) + (0.4)(0.03)} = 0.4$$

Thus the customer service manager should first check on whether an ordering error has been made.

Example 4

This example is an abstraction and simplification of a decision problem faced by a nationally known chemical company. It seems that the firm was faced with two related law suits for patent infringement. For each suit, the firm had the option of going to trial or settling out of court. The trial date for one of the suits which we will cleverly identify as suit 1 was scheduled for July 15 and the second (suit 2, of course) was scheduled for January of the following year. Preparation costs for either trial are estimated at $10,000. However, if the firm prepares for both trials, the preparation costs of the second trial will only be $6000. These costs can be avoided by settling out of court.

If the firm wins suit 1, it pays no penalty. If it loses, it pays a $200,000 penalty. Lawyers for the firm assess the probability of winning suit 1 as 0.5. The firm has the option to settle out of court for $100,000.

Suit 2 can be settled out of court for a cost of $60,000. Otherwise, a trial will result in one of three possible outcomes: (1) the suit is declared invalid and the firm pays no penalty; (2) the suit is found valid but with no infringement, and the firm pays a penalty of $50,000; (3) the suit is found valid with infringement, and the firm pays a penalty of $90,000.

The likelihood of these outcomes depends in general on the result of suit 1. The judge will certainly view suit 1 as an important precedent. The lawyers' assessment of the probability of the three possible outcomes of suit 2 under three sets of possible conditions (relating to suit 1) are presented in Figure 14.32.

Figure 14.32
Probabilities for Outcomes of Suit 2 Given the Results of Suit 1

OUTCOMES	NO INFORMATION CONCERNING SUIT 1a	FIRM WINS SUIT 1	FIRM LOSES SUIT 1
Invalid	0.3	0.7	0.1
Valid, no infringement	0.3	0.2	0.5
Valid, infringement	0.4	0.1	0.4

aThat is, suit 1 is settled out of court.

(a) Represent the firm's problem with a decision tree.
(b) Solve the decision tree and find the optimal decision rule for the firm.
(c) What is the expected loss that the firm will incur if it follows the optimal strategy?
(d) What decisions would be made if the firm treated each suit independently, ignoring any interactions between the two? What is the expected savings from the decision analysis of this scenario?

Solution to Example 4

(a) The decision tree representing the firm's problem is shown in Figure 14.33. Since all numerical entries are costs, negative values need not be used. Note that the terminal values have been determined in this figure.

Figure 14.33
Lawsuit Problem with Terminal Values

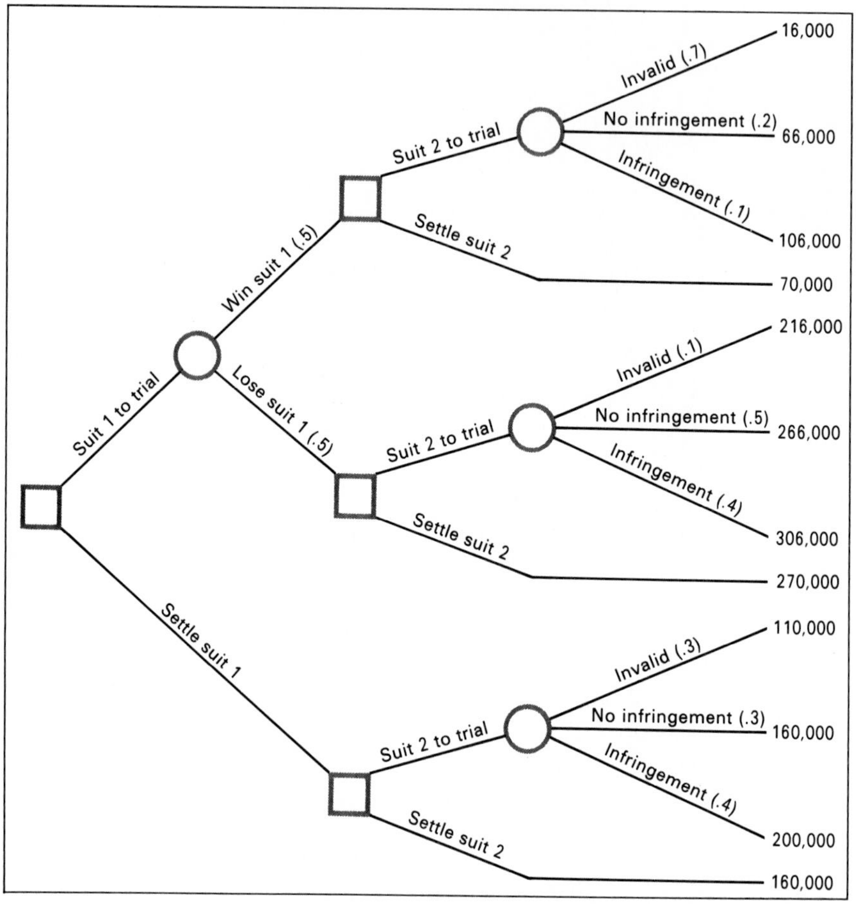

(b) Solving the decision tree requires several steps. Each circular terminal node is reduced by determining its expected cost. Figure 14.34 shows the results. The decision that minimizes the expected cost is then made for each terminal decision node. Figure 14.35 shows the results. Finally, replacing the remaining circular node by its expected cost yields the end result in Figure 14.36.

The optimal initial decision thus is to take suit 1 to trial. Figure 14.34 shows that if the firm wins suit 1, then the second decision is to take suit 2 to trial. If, on the other hand, the firm loses suit 1, then the second decision is to settle suit 2 out of court.

(c) The expected loss associated with the optimal strategy is $152,500.

(d) For suit 1, the expected cost of taking the case to trial is $(0.5)(210,000) + 0.5(10,000) = \$110,000$. The cost of settling out of court is $100,000, and thus

Figure 14.34
Lawsuit Problem after the First Reduction

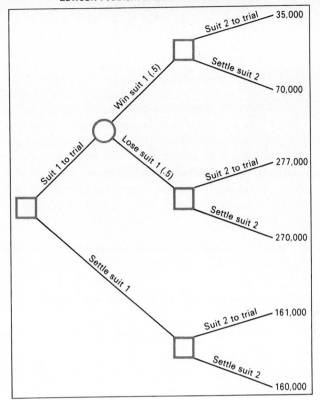

Figure 14.35
Another Reduction in the Lawsuit
Problem

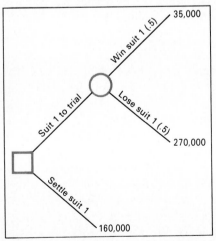

Figure 14.36
Final Tree for the Lawsuit
Problem

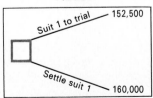

this is the optimal decision. For suit 2 by itself, the optimal decision is obtained by comparing $60,000, the cost of settling, with $61,000, the expected cost of a trial. Hence, the optimal decision is also to settle out of court. Treating cases independently, the expected total cost is thus $100,000 + 60,000 = \$160,000$, as opposed to an expected total cost of $152,500 associated with the optimal strategy. The expected savings due to the decision analysis is therefore $7500.

14.12
NOTES ON IMPLEMENTATION

In practice, the material in this chapter is included under the more general heading of "decision analysis." Ralph Keeney, a leading scholar in the field, defines decision analysis as "a formalization of common sense for decision problems which are too complex for informal use of common sense." Decision analysis, which is based on axioms originally stated by von Neumann and Morgenstern, involves assigning probabilities and utilities to possible outcomes and maximizing expected utility. This approach is applied to highly complex problems that are typically sequential in nature. It can be thought of as having four parts:

1. Structuring the problem
2. Assessing the probability of the possible outcomes
3. Determining the utility of the possible outcomes
4. Evaluating alternatives and selecting a strategy

Much of the material in this chapter concerns item 4, the technical process of evaluating alternatives and selecting a strategy. This is appropriate since this is the means of implementing decision analysis. In practice, however, this is the easy part of the problem. A significantly greater proportion of effort is frequently spent on the other three areas. Structuring the problem, which involves generating alternatives and specifying objectives in numerically measurable terms, is a particularly unstructured task. In some of the applications complex objectives have had to be quantified in the areas of environmental impact, public health and safety, and so on.

Role of Personal Judgment It is important to understand that decision analysis does *not* provide a completely objective analysis of complicated problems. Many aspects of a decision analysis require personal judgment—whether it be structuring the problem, assessing probabilities, or assigning utilities. In many important complex problems there simply are not enough empirical data to provide a basis for complete analysis. Nevertheless, experience has shown that the framework provided by decision analysis has been useful.

In the early 1960s decision analysis began to be successfully applied to a number of problems in the private sector. These include problems of gas and oil exploration as well as capital investment. Although developments have continued on private sector problems, two other general problem areas have witnessed a wide variety of applications of decision analysis. In the health care field, decision analysis has been applied to such diverse problems as the evaluation of new drugs, the analysis of treatment strategies for diseases, and the selection of medical technology for a particular facility. The second problem area concerns applications in the government. In particular, decision analysis has been applied to everything from the seeding of hurricanes, to the negotiation of international oil tanker standards, to the choice between coal and nuclear technology for large-scale power plants. A readable overview of decision analysis with an extensive bibliography is available in "Decision Analysis: An Overview," *Operations Research*, September–October 1982.

Role of Computing Computing plays a less important role in decision analysis than it does in other quantitative decision areas such as LP and IP or simulation. It is perhaps not surprising then that general-purpose decision analysis programs are not widely available from commercial software suppliers. However, at least one consulting firm has a code that it uses for analyzing its client's problems, and a major oil company has produced a package for its internal use. The increased use and importance of decision analysis, suggests that such packages may become more generally available in the future.

14.13
MAJOR CONCEPTS QUIZ

True–False

1. T F Decision trees involve sequences of decisions and random outcomes.
2. T F In decision theory, returns are dependent on the actions of an indifferent adversary termed "nature."
3. T F One underlying aspect of decision theory is that, regardless of what we assume about nature, in terms of whether or not we know probabilities of various states, we are led to the same criterion for selecting a "best decision."
4. T F Many deterministic optimization models can be thought of as decision making under certainty, where there is only one state of nature and one selects a decision that maximizes returns.
5. T F One way to deal with decision making in the "uncertainty" context is to treat all states of nature as equally likely and maximize expected return.
6. T F By paying the expected value of perfect information, the decision maker can guarantee her return.
7. T F Maximizing expected net dollar return always yields the same optimal policy as minimizing expected regret.
8. T F A risk-averse utility function is convex.
9. T F Decision trees are solved by folding forward.
10. T F Bayes Theorem provides a formula for how one can use new information to update a prior probability assessment.
11. T F Conditional probability can be defined as the ratio of a joint probability to a marginal probability.

Multiple Choice

12. Decision theory is concerned with
    a. the amount of information that is available
    b. criteria for measuring the "goodness" of a decision
    c. selecting optimal decisions in sequential problems
    d. all of the above

13. Concerning decision making under risk, which of the following is not true?
    a. We assume that the decision maker knows the probability with which each state of nature will occur.
    b. We use the criterion of maximizing return.
    c. We use the criterion of maximizing expected return.
    d. We use the criterion of minimizing expected regret.

14. Which of the following criteria does *not* apply to decision making under uncertainty?
    a. maximin return
    b. maximax return
    c. minimax regret
    d. maximize expected return

15. Maximin return, maximax return, and minimax regret are criteria that
    a. lead to the same optimal decision
    b. can be used without probabilities
    c. both a and b

16. The expected value of perfect information (EVPI)
    a. places two-sided bounds (upper and lower) on how much should be spent in gathering information
    b. can be determined without using probabilities
    c. refers to the utility of additional information
    d. equals the expected regret of the optimal decision under risk

17. The concept of utility is a way to
    a. measure the attractiveness of money
    b. take into account aversion to risk
    c. take into account inclination to take risk
    d. a and b
    e. a, b, and c

18. Which of the following does not apply to a decision tree?
    a. A square node is a point at which a decision must be made.
    b. A circular node represents an encounter with uncertainty.
    c. One chooses a sequence of decisions which have the greatest probability of success.
    d. One attempts to maximize expected return.

19. The expected value of perfect information (EVPI)
    a. shows the cost necessary to produce perfect information about the future
    b. shows the maximum possible increase in expected return with sample information
    c. shows the expected increase in information required to select the optimal decision
    d. all of the above

20. When computing the expected value of perfect information (EVPI) it is important that the payment is made
    a. in advance of receiving the information
    b. after receiving the information
    c. in an irrevocable way
    d. both a and c

21. When decisions are made sequentially in time,
    a. decision trees cannot be employed
    b. Bayes Theorem must be used
    c. the terminal value at the end of each sequence of branches is the net of the cash flows on that sequence
    d. the terminal value at the end of each sequence of branches is an expected net cash flow

Answers

1. T	8. F	15. b
2. T	9. F	16. d
3. F	10. T	17. e
4. T	11. T	18. c
5. T	12. d	19. b
6. F	13. b	20. d
7. T	14. d	21. c

14-1. Consider the following payoff table in which the entries are net dollar returns. Assume that this is a decision with no knowledge about the states of nature.

DECISION	STATE OF NATURE			
	1	2	3	4
1	35	22	25	12
2	27	25	20	18
3	22	25	25	28
4	20	25	28	33

(a) What is the optimal decision if the Laplace criterion is used?
(b) What is the optimal decision if the maximin criterion is used?
(c) What is the optimal decision if the maximax criterion is used?
(d) Create the payoff table in which the entries are regret.
(e) What is the optimal decision if the criterion of minimax regret is used?

14-2. Consider the following payoff table in which the entries are net dollars returns. Assume that this is a decision with no knowledge about the states of nature.

DECISION	STATE OF NATURE	
	1	2
1	7	1
2	5	6
3	2	8

(a) What is the optimal decision if the Laplace criterion is used?
(b) What is the optimal decision if the maximin criterion is used?
(c) What is the optimal solution if the maximax criterion is used?
(d) Create the payoff table in which the entries are regret.
(e) What is the optimal decision if the criterion of minimax regret is used?

14-3. Consider the payoff table in Problem 14-1. Assume that the following probabilities are specified for the states of nature.

$$P(1) = 0.1, \quad P(2) = 0.4, \quad P(3) = 0.3, \quad P(4) = 0.2$$

(a) Find the decision that maximizes the expected net dollar return.
(b) Find the decision that minimizes the expected regret.
(c) Comment on the relationship between the answers to parts (a) and (b).

14-4. Consider the payoff matrix in Problem 14-2. Assume that the probabilities of the states of nature are as follows:

$$P(1) = 2/3, \quad P(2) = 1/3$$

(a) Find the decision that maximizes the expected net dollar return.
(b) Find the decision that minimizes the expected regret.
(c) Plot expected net dollar return versus $P(2)$ for the three decisions in the same graph.
(d) Find the range for $P(2)$ for which each decision is optimal.

14-5. Phil Johnson of Johnson's Printing in Chicago must decide either to accept a contract for a government form printing job or fly to L.A. to bid on a brochure. Capacity constraints prohibit him from doing both jobs and he must decide on the government contract before the bidding process starts. He estimates the payoff table in terms of net dollar return as follows.

| | STATE OF NATURE | |
| | Do Not Get Brochure Job, | Get Brochure Job, |
DECISION	NJ	J
Accept government contract, G	1000	1000
Accept Brochure job, B	−1000	4000

(a) What is the optimal decision based on the maximin criterion?

(b) If the probability that he gets the brochure job is 1/3, which decision will maximize his expected net dollar return?

(c) Let $P(J)$ be the probability that he gets the brochure job. Plot the expected return for each decision as a function of $P(J)$ on the same axis.

(d) What is the smallest value of $P(J)$ for which Phil Johnson should decide to go to L.A. if he wishes to maximize his expected net dollar return?

(e) What is the optimal decision if minimax regret is the decision criterion?

(f) What is the optimal decision if minimize expected regret is the decision criterion and $P(J) = 1/3$?

(g) Assume that the purchasing agent for the brochure job has already decided who will receive the bid but Phil doesn't know the result. If Phil believes that $P(J) = 1/3$, what is the maximum amount that Phil should pay to have this information?

(h) What would you call the quantity calculated in part (g)?

14-6. A souvenir vendor discovers that his sales in July depend heavily on the weather. He must order his products in January. The wholesaler offers a small and a large variety pack at special prices, and the vendor has decided to buy one or the other. His payoff table in terms of net dollar return is shown below.

| | STATE OF NATURE | | | |
DECISION	Cold	Cool	Warm	Hot
Small	0	1000	3000	4000
Large	−3000	−1000	4000	8000

His utility function for money is presented in Figure 14.37. If the vendor believes that each state of nature is equally likely:

(a) Which decision maximizes the expected net dollar return?

(b) Which decision maximizes the expected utility?

(c) Explain the relationship between the answers to parts (a) and (b).

(d) How would you describe the vendor's risk preference?

Figure 14.37
Utility Function

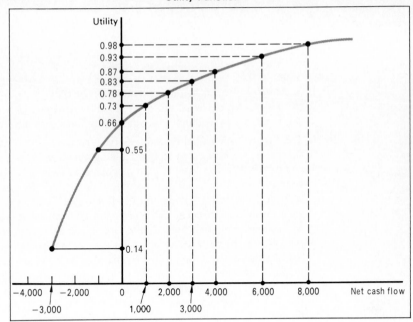

14-7. Phil Johnson of Johnson's Printing (see Problem 14-5) has decided to use the utility function shown in Figure 14.37 to determine if he should bid on the brochure job or not.
   (a) What is the optimal decision if the decision criterion is to maximize the expected net dollar return and the probability of getting the brochure job is 1/3? What is the expected net dollar return of the optimal decision?
   (b) Would you expect the decision to change if the decision criterion is to maximize the expected utility? Discuss.
   (c) What is the expected utility of the optimal decision?
   (d) What is the utility of the expected dollar return from submitting a bid for the brochure?
   (e) What is the expected utility of submitting a bid for the brochure?
   (f) Are the answers to parts (d) and (e) the same? Should they be?

14-8. Assign a utility of 0 to a net cash flow of −$20,000 and a utility of 1 to a net cah flow of $50,000. Create your own utility function by the following steps.
   (a) Find equivalent lotteries for net cash flows of $0 and $20,000.
   (b) Plot the four points on your utility function and connect them with straight lines.
   (c) Based on this utility function, are you risk averse, risk seeking, risk indifferent, or none of the above?

14-9. Assume you are risk averse and have assigned the following two end points on your utility function:

$$U(-30) = 0$$
$$U(70) = 1$$

   (a) What is a lower bound on $U(30)$?
   Suppose that you are indifferent between a sure payment of 30 and a lottery with a probability of 0.7 of winning 70 and a probability of 0.3 of losing 30.
   (b) What is a lower bound on your utility for a sure payment of 50?
   (c) What is the smallest upper bound of your utility for a sure payment of 10?
   (HINT: Recall that a utility function is nondecreasing and if the decision maker is risk averse, it is concave).

14-10. Assume that you are risk seeking and have assigned the following two end points on your utility function.

$$U(-30) = 0$$
$$U(70) = 1$$

(a) What is an upper bound on $U(30)$?

Suppose that you are indifferent between a sure payment of 30 and a lottery with a probability of 0.4 of winning 70 and a probability of 0.6 of losing 30.

(b) What is an upper bound on your utility for a sure payment of 50?

(b) What is a lower bound on your utility for a sure payment of 20?

14-11. The Scrub Professional Cleaning Service receives preliminary sales contracts from two sources: (1) its own agent and (2) building managers. Historically, $\frac{3}{8}$ of the contracts have come from Scrub agents and $\frac{5}{8}$ from building managers. Unfortunately, not all preliminary contracts result in actual sales contracts. Actually, only $\frac{1}{2}$ of those preliminary contracts received from building managers result in a sale, whereas $\frac{3}{4}$ of those received from Scrub agents result in a sale. The net return to Scrub from a sale is $3200. The cost of processing and following up on a preliminary contract that does not result in a sale is $160.

(a) What is the expected return associated with a preliminary sales contract?

Scrub keeps all of its sales filed by the source of reference; that is, it maintains one file for sales resulting from preliminary contracts submitted by Scrub agents and another for sales resulting from preliminary contracts submitted by building managers. Scrub knows that John Jones holds one of their sales contracts and they wish to have more information about him.

(b) Which file should they search first to have the higher probability of finding his name?

14-12. Clyde's Coal Company sells coal by the $\frac{1}{2}$-ton, 1-ton, or 2-ton load. The probability is 0.20 that an order is from town A; 0.30 from town B; and 0.50 from town C. The relative frequency of the number of orders of each size from each town is shown in Figure 14.38.

(a) What is the probability that an order will be for $\frac{1}{2}$ ton?

(b) If an order is for $\frac{1}{2}$ ton, what is the probability that it came from town A?

Clyde makes a different amount of profit on each type of load of coal in each city. The profit figures are shown in Figure 14.39.

(c) Find the expected profit per load for Clyde.

Figure 14.38

Relative Frequencies of Number of Orders for Each Town

TOWN	LOAD SIZE (TONS)		
	$\frac{1}{2}$	1	2
A	0.50	0.00	0.50
B	0.00	0.50	0.50
C	0.25	0.75	0.00

Figure 14.39

Profit in Dollars per Load

TOWN	LOAD SIZE (TONS)		
	$\frac{1}{2}$	1	2
A	100	190	370
B	90	200	360
C	70	130	270

14-13. Walter's Dog and Pony Show is scheduled to appear in Cedar Rapids on July 14. The profits obtained are heavily dependent on the weather. In particular, if the weather is rainy, the show loses $15,000, and if sunny the show makes a profit of $10,000. (We assume that all days are either rainy or sunny.) Walter can decide to cancel the show, but if he does he forfeits a $1000 deposit he put down when he accepted the date. The historical record shows that on July 14 it has rained $\frac{1}{4}$ of the time in the last 100 years.

(a) What decision should Walter make to maximize his expected net dollar return?

(b) What is the expected value of perfect information?

14-14. Consider the problem faced by Walter in Problem 14-13. Walter has the option to purchase a forecast from Victor's Weather Wonder. Victor's accuracy varies. On those occasions when it has rained, he has been correct (i.e., he predicted rain) 90% of the time. On the other hand, when it has been sunny, he has been right (i.e., he predicted sun) only 80% of the time.

(a) If Walter had the forecast, what strategy should he follow to maximize his expected net dollar return?

(b) How much should Walter be willing to pay to have the forecast?

14-15. A gambler has an opportunity to play the following two-stage game. At stage 1 he pays $10 and draws a ball at random from an urn containing 45 white and 55 red balls. The balls are identical except for color. The player may now quit or move on to play stage 2 at the cost of an additional $10. In stage 2, if a white ball was drawn in stage 1, the player draws a ball at random from a white urn that contains 70 blue and 30 green balls. If a red ball was drawn in stage 1, the player draws a ball at random from a red urn that contains 10 blue and 90 green balls. If in stage 2 the player draws a blue ball, the house pays him $50. If he draws a green ball, the house pays him $0. Use a decision tree to determine the optimal strategy rule for the gambler.

14-16. A certain retail firm places applicants for credit into two categories, bad risks and good risks. Statistics indicate that 10% of the population would be classified as a bad risk by the firm's standards. The firm uses a credit-scoring device to decide whether or not credit should be granted to an applicant. Experience suggests that if a good risk applies, he will get credit 90% of the time. If a bad risk applies, he will get credit 20% of the time. Management believes that it is reasonable to assume that the persons who apply for credit are selected at random from the population. What is the probability that a person granted credit will be a bad risk?

14-17. At PROTRAC's Moline plant, crankshafts are produced on each of two large automatic machines. The newer of the two machines is both faster and more reliable than the older machine. Out of a lot size of 1000 crankshafts, 600 would be produced on the new machine. The new machine produces defective crankshafts at the rate of 1 per 100, whereas the old machine produces defects at the rate of 3 per 100. What is the probability that a defective piece selected at random was produced on the new machine?

14-18. Johnson's Metal (JM), a small manufacturer of metal parts, is attempting to decide whether or not to enter the competition to be a supplier of transmission housings for PROTRAC. In order to compete, the firm must design a test fixture for the production process and produce 10 housings that PROTRAC will test. The cost of development, that is, designing and building the fixture and the test housings, is $50,000. If JM gets the order, an event estimated as occurring with probability 0.4, it will be possible to sell 10,000 items to PROTRAC for $50 each. If JM does not get the order, the development cost is essentially lost. In order to produce the housings, JM may either use its current machines or purchase a new forge. Tooling with the current machines will cost $40,000 and the per unit production cost is $20. However, if JM uses its current machines, it runs the risk of incurring overtime costs. The relationship between overtime costs and the status of JM's other business is presented in Figure 14.40. The new forge costs $260,000, including tooling costs for the transmission housing. However, with the new forge, JM would certainly not incur any overtime costs, and the production cost will be only $10 per unit. Use a decision tree to determine the optimal set of actions for JM.

Figure 14.40
Cost and Probability Data for Johnson's Metal Problem

OTHER BUSINESS	PROBABILITY	OVERTIME COST TO JM
Heavy	0.2	$200,000
Normal	0.7	100,000
Light	0.1	0

DIAGNOSTIC ASSIGNMENT

Shirley Johnson, president of Johnson's Metal (JM), is facing the decision presented in Problem 14-18, but a new element has entered the picture. Shirley has the opportunity to hire Compal, a consulting firm that does what it calls "competitive analysis." In particular, in this situation Compal offers to do a detailed study of the other firms which will compete to supply transmission housings to PROTRAC. After the analysis, Compal will report to JM that conditions for JM to get the contract are either encouraging or discouraging.

Compal states that, if conditions are encouraging, then JM will get the PROTRAC contract with probability equal to 0.5. On the other hand, if conditions are unfavorable, Compal states that the probability that JM will get the PROTRAC contract is only 0.35. At this time Compal states that the probability of encouraging and discouraging conditions are equally likely. Compal charges $1000 for its services.

Shirley asks Aline Drawer, her assistant, to determine if JM should hire Compal or not. Indeed she asks Aline to determine the optimal strategy.

Aline prepares the decision tree for the problem and by working back through it, determines that the optimal strategy is:

1. Hire Compal
2. If conditions are encouraging:
   a. Build the test fixture
   b. If JM gets the order, use current tools
3. If conditions are discouraging:
   a. Build the test fixture
   b. If JM gets the order, use current tools

He makes an appointment to discuss the results with Shirley. The meeting proceeds as follows:

SHIRLEY: "Aline! I see the decision tree and I'm duly impressed, but the result doesn't make any sense. Why should I pay Compal $1000 if we take the same action no matter what they say?"

ALINE: "Surely, Shirley, you don't mean that the analysis did not make a difference. I understand that your statement holds now that the analysis is complete, but how would you have known what strategy to follow without the decision tree?"

SHIRLEY: "Aline! You missed my point! No matter what costs or probabilities are involved, I say that we should build the test fixture, and then use the current tools if we get the order. This simply has to be a better strategy than to hire Compal and then do the same thing no matter what they say."

ALINE: "I understand, but I know I've done the decision tree right, so I don't know what to tell you."

SHIRLEY: "I don't have the time or interest to check the details of your analysis. All I know is that I want to make a decision about Compal tomorrow morning and I want to have an answer that makes sense. Your job is to provide me with that answer."

Questions

1. Is Shirley right; that is, is it impossible for Aline's strategy to be optimal?
2. Is Aline right; that is, is his analysis correct given the data at his disposal?
3. Assume Aline's role; that is, it is now your job to provide Shirley an answer that makes sense.

CASE

TO DRILL OR NOT TO DRILL

Terri Underhill has recently been assigned to the economic analysis section of Global Oil. Prescot Oil has just offered to buy the Burns Flat lease from Global for $15,000 and Terri has been assigned the task of preparing Global's response. The Burns Flat lease gives Global the right to explore for oil under 320 acres of land in western Oklahoma. Terri must recommend either to sell the lease or to drill.

If Global drills, the results are uncertain. Based on drilling records in western Oklahoma and current market prices, Terri prepares a table showing the possible outcomes, the probability of each outcome, and the net return to Global.

POSSIBLE OUTCOMES	PROBABILITY	NET RETURN
Dry well	0.2	−100,000
Gas well	0.4	40,000
Oil and gas	0.3	90,000
Oil well	0.1	200,000

1. On the basis of these data, should Global drill or sell the lease?
2. What is the most that Global should pay in advance to know what the outcome of drilling would be?

Terri, however, knows that she does not have to make the decision simply on the basis of historical records. DRI, Drilling Resource, Inc., which is Etto Oxstein's company, will perform a test for $6000 to determine the underground formation of the Burns Flat terrain. The test will indicate which of three categories (plate, varied or ridge) best describes the underground structure. The conditional probabilities of the possible outcomes vary with the underground structure. The exhibit below shows the results of the last 50 tests.

TEST RESULT/ OUTCOME	PLATE	VARIED	RIDGE	TOTAL
Dry	8	2	0	10
Gas	2	16	2	20
Gas and oil	0	14	1	15
Oil	0	0	5	5
	10	32	8	50

If the test is taken, the opportunity to sell the lease is forfeited. The market for oil leases understands that a decision to sell after the test indicates that drilling does not appear to be profitable.

3. Use a decision tree to determine the optimal strategy for Global.

4. What is the expected return associated with the optimal policy?

5. What is the maximum *additional* amount that Global should be willing to pay DRI for the test?

CHAPTER 15

Inventory Control with Known Demand

months is done on a top-down manner. In other words Kelly-Springfield sales potential is an assumed share of the projected replacement market, which in turn depends on the national economy, and so on. The inventory control section is based on the reorder point, reorder quantity model with a safety stock. The production planning system uses both linear programming and dynamic programming. The distribution system uses a heuristic based on the transportation model of linear programming to determine factory to warehouse shipments and transshipments among warehouses to eliminate critical inventory imbalances.

The total benefits from the system come from many sources. The annual savings of $2.2 million reduced inventory investment was mentioned above. Other annual returns are due to increased productivity ($4.2 million), reduced scrap ($860,000), reduced transfer tonnage ($500,000), and reduction in personnel ($175,000). Thus, the total system yields benefits totaling $8.4 million annually. As discussed above, the improved service due to the system has enabled Kelly-Springfield to expand its market share.

15.1

INTRODUCTION

STECO is the country's second largest steel wholesaler. Its main function is to supply various items to customers. In order to do this the key operations are: (1) buying items from the producer; (2) holding these items in inventory; and (3) marketing, selling, and distributing these items in response to demand.

Victor Kowalski is a success at STECO. After 18 years in marketing Victor was recently promoted to vice-president of operations. The purchasing, inventory control, and marketing functions are now his responsibility. He is confident of his ability to handle the marketing aspects of his new position, but he feels less secure in his knowledge of inventory control. Since the holding of inventory is a critical part of STECO's business, Victor's inventory-related decisions will have an important effect on his firm's performance and his own career.

From his favorite management science text, Victor learns:

Definition of Inventory

1. Inventories are defined as *idle goods in storage*, waiting to be used.
2. There are many types of inventories; for example, inventories of raw materials, inventories of in-process materials, inventories of finished goods, inventories of cash, and even inventories of individuals.
3. Inventories are held for many reasons. Some distributors hold inventory in order to fill quickly an order placed by a customer. Otherwise, in many cases, the customer would order from a competitor. This, however, is only one reason why inventories are held. They are, in fact, held for any of the following reasons.
   a. Inventories smooth out the time gap between supply and demand. The corn crop is harvested in September and October, but user demand for corn (as a raw material for animal feed, corn oil, etc.) exists throughout the year. Thus, the harvest must be stored in inventory for later use. Users are willing to pay others to worry about storing for the convenience of having the crop available when they need it.
   b. The possibility of holding inventory often contributes to lower production costs, for it is more economical to produce some items in large batches even though im-

Reasons for Holding Inventories

502

mediate orders for the items may not exist. One chooses to store the excess in inventory as opposed to producing in a more costly way—that is, a lower but more continuous rate in time.

c. Inventories provide a disguised way of storing labor. For example, in dynamic production problems the availability of labor may be a binding constraint in some later time period but slack in the earlier periods. The possibility of producing excess output in these earlier periods, and carrying the product forward in inventory, frees labor in the later periods for alternative uses.

d. Finally, as in STECO's case, inventory is a way of providing quick customer service at the time an item is needed, and customers are willing to pay for this convenience.

Inventory
Costs

4. There are generally three types of costs associated with the inventory activity: *holding costs*, *ordering costs*, and *stockout costs*.

a. *Holding costs:* One of the smaller items stocked by STECO is a piece of $\frac{3}{10}$-inch-thick high-carbon steel called an "appliance angle." Victor currently observes that there are 3000 appliance angles in stock. Each angle costs STECO $8.00. Thus, STECO currently has $24,000 tied up with the inventory of this item. Suppose that STECO were to reduce this inventory to only 1000 items. Instead of $24,000, the investment would be reduced to $8000. It would then be possible to invest some of the $16,000 which is released—in other words, by holding inventory STECO forgoes the opportunity to make other investments. This so-called **opportunity cost** is perhaps the most important contribution to inventory holding cost. The magnitude of this cost is closely tied to the interest rate. As an indication of its importance, consider that since 1970 the prime interest rate has always been above 5% and that in the early 1980s it hovered near 20%.

There are other holding costs, such as breakage, pilferage, insurance, and special handling requirements. In general, *the larger the inventories, the larger the inventory holding costs.*

b. *Ordering costs:* Each time STECO places an order to replenish its inventories an ordering cost is incurred. **This cost is independent of the quantity ordered**. It is related to the amount of time required for paperwork and accounting when an order is placed and is a direct function of the salaries of involved personnel.

c. *Stockout costs:* A stockout means that the firms runs out of inventory. In most technical uses, the term "stockout" refers to the more specific phenomenon that orders arrive after inventory has been depleted. There are, at least in the context of a model, two ways to treat such orders. One way is to save up the orders and fill them later after the inventory has been replenished. This is called *backlogging*. (Note that this is really an *assumption* in a model. In the real world, customers usually get to vote on whether they are willing to wait. The extent to which customers are willing to accept backlogging could be a major factor in determining the appropriateness of a model that makes a backlogging assumption.) Another way to deal with stockouts is simply not to accept any orders received when there is no inventory on hand. Thus, the study of inventory includes models that deal with the

Backlogging

possibility of stocking out, and in such a case some models assume backlogging—others assume no backlogging. In either case there is a cost of stocking out. This cost could include the lost profit from not making the sale (in the no-backlogging case), late delivery (the backlogging case), as well as discounts for a number of more intangible factors, such as the cost of possibly losing the customer, of losing goodwill, and of establishing a poor record of service. In the case of stockouts with no backlogging, we generally use the term **penalty** *cost*, which means the per unit cost of unsatisfied demand. In the case of stockouts with backlogging we speak of a *backlogging cost*, which means the per unit cost of backlogging demand.

It is obvious to Victor that, for a company such as STECO, with hundreds of thousands of dollars tied up in inventory, there must be a right way and a wrong way to manage the inventory function. The main trade-offs are clear: On one hand, it is good to have inventory on hand to make sure that customers' orders can be satisfied (i.e., to avoid *stockout costs*). On the other hand, carrying inventory implies a *holding cost*. This can be reduced by ordering smaller quantities more often, but this means increased *ordering costs*. These three cost factors must be balanced against each other.

*Fundamental
Questions*

Once the fundamental question of what items to order has been determined, the questions to be answered are the same for all inventory control systems. For every type of item held in inventory, someone must decide (1) *when* a replenishment order should be placed and (2) *how much* should be ordered. That much is easy. Finding good answers to these questions is not. A multitude of factors combine to make this a difficult problem. Some of the most important considerations are:

1. The extent to which future demand is known
2. The cost of stocking out and management's policy (backlogging or not)
3. The inventory holding and ordering costs
4. The possibility of long lead times—the period of time between when an order is placed and when the material actually arrives
5. The possibility of quantity discount purchasing plans

Victor realizes that he has his work cut out for him and decides to give high priority to a review of STECO's inventory system.

15.2

STECO WHOLESALING: THE CURRENT POLICY

In getting started, Victor decides to focus on a small but tractable problem, the current inventory policy for appliance angles. This is what he learns. These angles (used to construct the frames for many home appliances, such as stoves, refrigerators, freezers, etc.) are a high-volume item for STECO. Figure 15.1 shows the monthly demand for appliance angles during the preceding year.

The term **demand** means "orders received." It is not necessarily the same as **sales**. For example, in January of last year 5300 items were demanded. If *at least* 5300 items were in inventory, then sales equals demand (i.e., sales were 5300). If fewer than 5300 items were in inventory, say only 5000, then sales were 5000, which is less than the demand of 5300, and consequently a stockout occurred.

*Actual Cost
of the Current
Policy*

As a matter of fact, over a period of several years the demand for appliance angles has remained at a steady rate of about 5000 items per month. Based on this fact, management's policy last year was to add 5000 angle irons to inventory each month. Since demand is expected to hold at about the same level in the future, this is the current policy as well. Victor's question remains: "Is this a good policy?"

One way to attempt to answer this question would be to see how well the policy did last year. This turns out *not* to be an easy task. The answer depends on a considerable amount of information that Victor does not have. Consider:

1. Was there a shortage in January? Demand (5300) is larger than the amount ordered (5000). Thus there might have been. But if STECO had at least 300 angles on hand on

Figure 15.1
Monthly Appliance Angle Demand

MONTH	DEMAND (UNITS)
January	5,300
February	5,100
March	4,800
April	4,700
May	5,000
June	5,200
July	5,300
August	4,900
September	4,800
October	5,000
November	4,800
December	5,100
Total annual demand	60,000
Average monthly demand	5,000

January 1, there would not have been. Right? Not necessarily! What if the January replenishment of 5000 angles did not show up until January 10 and there was an order for 3000 angles on January 5?

2. Holding costs are equally confusing. Suppose that in March the 5000 angles from the producer arrived on March 1 and an order from one of STECO's customers, for 4800 angles, arrives on March 2. The holding cost is very small. On the other hand, if the customer order for the 4800 angles had occurred on March 31, the holding cost would be much larger.

Victor quickly gives up the task of calculating last year's actual cost. He simply does not have enough information. Instead, he decides to see what the policy of ordering 5000 angles each month *would* cost in an *abstract, idealized* world. In this world Victor assumes that

1. Orders always arrive on the first day of the month.
2. Demand is known and occurs at a constant rate of 5000 units per month.
3. All demand will be satisfied with no backlogging. In other words, stockouts are forbidden.

Victor's incentive for using this *model* is provided by his colleagues. They assure him that *on the average* these assumptions describe rather well the actual circumstances at STECO. He thus decides to use them, realizing that he may have to take the complicating factors of variability and uncertainty into account later. With these assumptions Victor can make a plot of the inventory on hand at any time. Such a plot is shown in Figure 15.2.

Notice how the inventory jumps up by 5000 units at the beginning of each month when an order arrives and decreases continuously at a constant rate of 5000 items per month (the constant monthly rate of demand). Also notice that an order from the producer arrives at the instant the inventory on hand hits zero. Thus, no stockouts occur. Given assumptions 1, 2, and 3, the cost of operating the system shown in Figure 15.2 depends only on *how much is ordered* and on the *holding and ordering costs*. Since in this

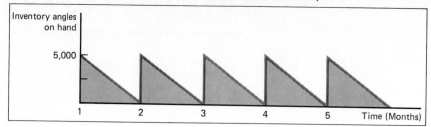

Figure 15.2

Inventory on Hand, 5000 Order Quantity

ideal world there are no stockouts, Victor need not worry about stockout costs. Let us see how the operating cost arises.

In cooperation with his accountants Victor learns that (1) it costs $25.00 to place an order and (2) it costs $1.92 to hold an angle in inventory for a year. Given his assumptions, Victor is now in a good position to compute, within his model, the annual cost of *ordering 5000* items per month. Since orders are placed once a month

Annual Ordering Cost

$$\text{annual ordering cost} = 12(25) = \$300$$

To calculate the annual holding cost, Victor uses the following logic:

$$\text{average time each item remains in inventory} = \tfrac{1}{2} \text{ month}$$

Expressed in terms of years, then, for each batch

$$\text{average time each item remains in inventory} = \tfrac{1}{24} \text{ year}$$

Since the cost to hold 1 item for 1 year is $1.92, it must follow that for each batch

$$\text{cost to hold 1 item for } \tfrac{1}{24} \text{ year} = (1.92)(\tfrac{1}{24})$$

Thus, for each batch of 5000 items,

$$\text{holding cost per batch} = 5000(1.92)(\tfrac{1}{24})$$

Since 12 of these batches are ordered each year,

Annual Holding Cost

$$\text{annual holding cost} = (12)(5000)(1.92)(\tfrac{1}{24}) = \$4800$$

Victor's simplifying assumptions and calculations in the idealized world have produced an annual holding cost of $4800. Another derivation may be more intuitive. First note that the average inventory level is one-half of the maximum inventory level when demand is constant (see Figure 15.3). Thus, over the year the average inventory level is 2500 units, and we have

$$\text{annual holding cost} = (\text{average inventory level}) \cdot (\text{holding cost per item per year})$$
$$= (2500) \cdot (1.92) = \$4800$$

Now combining the yearly holding and ordering costs, Victor computes that, in terms of his model, the annual inventory costs for appliance angles are

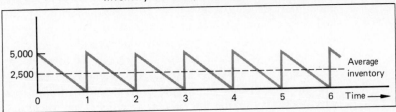

Figure 15.3
Inventory on Hand, 5000 Order Quantity

annual holding and ordering cost = annual holding cost + annual ordering cost

$$= 4800 + 300 = \$5100$$

As we have pointed out, this figure is based on the policy of ordering 5000 items each month. Suppose that we had placed larger orders, say for 10,000 items each time an order was placed. In this case an order would now be placed every 2 months (i.e., six per year) and the average inventory is 5000 items. The annual holding and ordering cost would then be computed as follows:

Comparing
Annual
Holding
and Ordering
Costs

annual holding and ordering cost = annual holding cost + annual ordering cost

$$= (5000)(1.92) + 6(25) = \$9750$$

Note that *increasing* the order quantity *increased* the annual holding cost and *decreased* the annual ordering cost.

In contrast, suppose that a policy of ordering 2500 items twice a month were followed. Then the average inventory is 1250 items and 24 orders would be placed each year. In this case

annual holding and ordering cost = annual holding cost + annual ordering cost

$$= (1250)(1.92) + (24)(25) = \$3000$$

Note that *decreasing* the order quantity *decreased* the annual holding cost and *increased* the annual ordering cost.

Victor now clearly understands the general effect of changing the amount that is ordered each time an order is placed. What he wonders is whether or not the policy followed last year by STECO, and currently being followed, is optimal in the *idealized model*. This policy is to order 5000 units per month. It would appear from the last calculation above that a policy of ordering 2500 items twice a month would be superior. Is there even a better policy?

In his search for the answer to this question, Victor comes across a computer-based inventory control system called ICON.[1] This system is designed to answer two key questions: (1) when to order[2] and (2) how much to order. With reference to the appliance angle policy, this is just what Victor wants to know. When should orders be placed? How much should be ordered?

[1]This is a hypothetical system in our scenario that resembles several currently available commercial systems.

[2]We have already seen that, assuming a known rate of demand (5000 items per month), as soon as we choose an order quantity we also implicitly determine "how often" we order (e.g., once a month, once every 2 months, etc). The "when to order" question has not yet been addressed. It asks, *when* we should order, in terms of the level of the current inventory on hand. This will be seen to depend on lead time to delivery.

He decides to explore further this ICON system. He is amazed to discover that this system is based in part on an adaptation of a simple model that he recalls having studied as an undergraduate almost 20 years ago, the **economic order quantity (EOQ) model**. Victor had always thought of it as a textbook model with unrealistic assumptions, a model selected to give a simple and easily taught result. In part, Victor was correct. The EOQ model does ignore a number of important factors. He was, however, wrong in his estimate of its usefulness. This model attempts to balance the cost of placing orders with the cost of holding inventory. In the present appliance angle context, that is just what Victor is looking for. In a larger context, the EOQ model forms the backbone for most of the commercially available computer-based inventory control systems.

As Victor is soon to learn, the ICON system is able to use the EOQ model because it is a two-step process. First, it uses the EOQ model to answer the "when" and "how much" questions with or without quantity discounts, and then it modifies these answers to allow for variabilities in demand. The latter topic will be discussed in Chapter 16.

Victor decides to see how this system works by first applying the EOQ model to the trial problem posed above. Would any improvements have been obtained?

15.3

THE ECONOMIC ORDER QUANTITY MODEL

Developing
the Model
The EOQ model in its simplest form assumes that

1. No stockouts are allowed. That is, each new order arrives (in totality) as soon as the inventory level hits zero.
2. There is a constant rate of demand.
3. The relevant costs are ordering and holding costs.

Victor notes that these three assumptions are precisely the assumptions he has already made in his calculation (i.e., using his model) that STECO's annual inventory cost is $5100. Recall that this cost is based on a policy of adding to the stock 5000 angles each month. The EOQ model will give Victor some feeling for the "goodness" of that policy, for it will calculate the *optimal order quantity*, which is defined to be the quantity that under the three assumptions above *minimizes the total cost per year of ordering appliance angles and holding them in inventory*. It is based on:

Costs in
the EOQ
Model
1. *Ordering cost = C_0:* Every time an order is placed, the purchasing department must contact the supplier to determine the current price and delivery time, complete and mail the order form, enter the order into the inventory control system, and initiate the receiving and stock-keeping records. When the order arrives, receiving must complete the receiving and stock-keeping records and update the order status in ICON. All of this costs money. As we have already seen, STECO estimates the cost of placing an order for appliance angles, *regardless of the number of units ordered*, to be $25.00. This includes two-thirds of an hour of clerk-category labor at $18.00 per hour for wages and fringe benefits, one-third of an hour of an assistant purchasing agent's time at $24.00 per hour, plus $5.00 in material, phone, and mailing costs. Thus,

$$C_0 = \tfrac{2}{3}(18) + \tfrac{1}{3}(24) + 5 = \$25.00$$

2. *Inventory carrying cost = C_h:* Every dollar invested in inventory could be put to use elsewhere by STECO. For example, it could be put in a bank or invested in Treasury

bills and earn interest for STECO. When a dollar is tied up in inventory, STECO loses the opportunity to invest it elsewhere. This lost opportunity is called the "opportunity cost." Typically, the opportunity cost accounts for a large part of the cost of holding inventory. In addition, there are overhead costs such as rent, light, and insurance that must be allocated to the items in inventory.

The cost of holding inventory is typically expressed as the cost of holding 1 unit for 1 year and is calculated as a percentage of the cost of the item. STECO estimates that the cost of holding an appliance angle in inventory for 1 year is 24% of its purchase price. The 24% figure can be subdivided into an opportunity cost of 20% plus an overhead allocation per item of 4%. Since each angle costs $8.00, the cost of holding each item in inventory for 1 year is

$$C_h = 0.24 \times \$8.00 = \$1.92$$

which is the figure Victor used in his calculations.

The Annual Holding and Ordering Cost

The first step in calculating the optimal (i.e., cost minimizing) order quantity is to derive an expression for the annual holding and ordering cost (AHO) as a function of the order quantity. It consists of two parts, annual ordering cost and annual holding cost.

$$\text{annual ordering cost} = C_0 \cdot (\text{number of orders per year}) \tag{15.1}$$

If

$$N = \text{number of orders per year}$$
$$D = \text{annual demand}$$
$$Q = \text{order quantity}$$

then, in general,

$$\text{annual ordering cost} = C_0 N = C_0 D/Q \tag{15.2}$$

To compute the annual holding cost Victor makes use of two facts: (1) the annual holding cost is equal to C_h times the average inventory and (2) the average inventory is equal to one-half of the maximum inventory when demand occurs at a constant rate. Since the order quantity is also the maximum amount of inventory on hand (see Figure 15.3), it follows that

$$\text{annual holding cost} = C_h Q/2 \tag{15.3}$$

If we add together expressions (15.2) and (15.3), we see that the assumptions of the EOQ model have enabled Victor to obtain the following expression for the annual holding and ordering cost as a function of the order quantity Q:

$$\text{AHO}(Q) = C_0 D/Q + C_h Q/2 \tag{15.4}$$

For appliance angles, the relevant values of C_0, D, and C_h can be plugged into expression (15.4) to give

$$\text{AHO}(Q) = \$25(60,000/Q) + \$1.92(Q/2) = (1,500,000/Q) + 0.96Q \tag{15.5}$$

Using (15.5), Victor can represent the annual holding and ordering cost for angles as a function of the order quantity Q in graphical form. The result is shown in Figure 15.4.

Figure 15.4
Graph of Annual Holding and Ordering Costs as a Function of Order Quantity

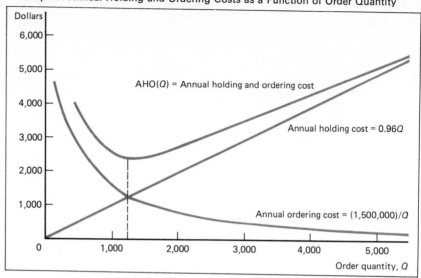

From this graph it is clear that the optimal order quantity [the one that minimizes AHO(Q)] is somewhat larger than 1000 items. Victor is amazed at how much this differs from the current policy of 5000 items per month.

**The EOQ
Formula**

It would obviously be useful to have an expression for Q^*, the optimal order quantity. (The asterisk indicates the value of Q that is the optimal solution to the model.) A formula can be derived to calculate its value as a function of the parameters in the problem. One way to derive this equation is to note that the optimal value of Q occurs where the annual ordering cost equals the annual holding cost (see Figure 15.4). Note that both are around $1200. Following this approach yields

$$\text{annual holding cost} = \text{annual ordering cost}$$
$$C_h \cdot Q^*/2 = C_0 D/Q^* \tag{15.6}$$

or

$$Q^* = \sqrt{\frac{2DC_0}{C_h}} \tag{15.7}$$

**Alternative
Form**

Alternatively, this formula can be derived by using differential calculus to minimize the function AHO(Q) presented in (15.4) (see Appendix 15.1). An alternative form of (15.7) that is sometimes used is

$$Q^* = \sqrt{\frac{2DC_0}{iP}} \tag{15.8}$$

where P = purchase price ($8.00 for angles)
i = fraction of P that is used to calculate C_h (0.24 for angles)

This quantity Q^* is often termed the *economic order quantity*, and it should be noted that it is expressed in terms of the input parameters C_0, C_h, and D. By substituting the appliance angle values for D, C_0, and C_h into (15.7), Victor can find the optimal order quantity for his problem:

$$Q^* = \sqrt{\frac{2 \times 60,000 \times 25}{1.92}} = 1250$$

Plugging this value into the expression for the annual holding and ordering cost for angles [equation (15.5)] yields

$$\text{AHO}(Q^*) = \text{AHO}(1250) = (1,500,000)/1250 + (0.96)(1250)$$
$$= \$1200 + \$1200 = \$2400$$

The calculation above illustrates the fact that when Q equals Q^*, the associated annual holding cost $(C_h Q^*/2)$ and the annual ordering cost $(C_0 D/Q^*)$ are equal. This fact is rigorously proved in Appendix 15.1.

Victor has already observed that the policy of ordering 5000 units at a time produces in the model a total annual cost of \$5100. If the quantity 1250 were to be used instead, the cost in the model would be \$2400, resulting in over a 50% savings. Victor is convinced that the idealized economic order quantity model is a good enough representation of STECO to make these results quite interesting.

Related Expressions Although Victor is happy to learn of the optimal order quantity and the savings that come with it, he is not satisfied. He realizes there are other questions yet to be resolved. For example, he is curious to know the optimum number of times appliance angles should be ordered each year and the **cycle time,** which is defined as the interval between the arrival of two consecutive orders.

Optimal Number of Orders He has already used the fact that $N = D/Q$ to calculate the annual ordering cost. Thus, N^*, the optimal number of times to order each year, is given by the expression

$$N^* = D/Q^* \qquad (15.9)$$

For angles, this yields a result of $N^* = 60,000/1250 = 48$. Recall that with the current policy STECO places only 12 orders per year. The new result is quite different.

Optimal Cycle Time Victor has also noted that the cycle time, the time required to use up an order, is Q/D years. Letting T^* denote the optimal cycle time, we see that

$$T^* = Q^*/D = 1250/60,000 = 0.020833 \qquad (15.10)$$

which implies that STECO should order angles every 0.25 month since $(0.020833)(12) = 0.25$. Note that when the cycle time is 0.25 month we must order four times per month and thus 48 times per year. This is the same as the value for N^* above. Note that expression (15.4) for $\text{AHO}(Q)$ depends on the given parameters C_0, C_h, and D, as well as the variable Q. It is possible to obtain an expression for the *optimal value* of AHO, in terms of only the input parameters C_0, C_h, and D (i.e., eliminating Q) as follows. Substitute the expression for Q^* [expression (15.7)] into (15.4) to obtain

$$AHO^* = AHO(Q^*) = C_0(D/Q^*) + C_h(Q^*/2)$$

Minimum
Annual
Holding
and Ordering
Cost

$$= C_0\left(D\Big/\sqrt{\frac{2DC_0}{C_h}}\right) + C_h\left(\sqrt{\frac{DC_0}{2C_h}}\right)$$

$$= C_0 D\sqrt{\frac{C_h}{2DC_0}} + C_h\sqrt{\frac{DC_0}{2C_h}}$$

$$= \sqrt{\frac{C_0 DC_h}{2}} + \sqrt{\frac{C_0 DC_h}{2}} = \sqrt{2C_0 DC_h} \tag{15.11}$$

For angles this becomes $AHO^* = \sqrt{2 \times \$25 \times 60{,}000 \times \$1.92} = \$2400$, a value that Victor has previously calculated.

Lead Times and When-to-Order Under the assumptions of the EOQ model, the "how-much-to-order" decision is provided by the derived quantity Q^*. The number of orders per year is given by $N^* = D/Q^*$. The remaining basic question is "when-to-order." The answer to this question is straightforward, but it depends on the *lead time to delivery*. Under the assumptions of the EOQ model, the entire order quantity Q^* arrives in a single batch precisely when the inventory level hits zero. Thus, if it takes ℓ days for an order to arrive, the order should be placed ℓ days before the end of each cycle. This is illustrated for two different values of ℓ in Figure 15.5. Here T^* is the optimal cycle length, i.e., the cycle length that arises from ordering

Figure 15.5

When-to-Order Decision

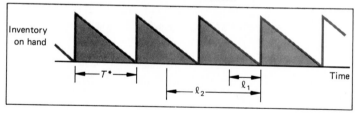

Q^* items, and ℓ_1 and ℓ_2 are two examples of lead times. If the order is to arrive at time A and the lead time is ℓ_1, the order should be placed at time $A - \ell_1$. If the order is to arrive at time A and the lead time is ℓ_2, the order should be placed at time $A - \ell_2$. In practice, the actual demand will not strictly obey the constant rate assumption shown in Figure 15.5. For this reason, in reality, point A may not be well defined, and hence "order at time $A - \ell_1$" is not a suitable rule. Rather, in practice, the when-to-order rule is typically stated as follows.

WHEN-TO-ORDER RULE: An order should be placed when the *inventory position* equals the demand during the lead time.

---

where by definition

Inventory Position

$$\text{inventory position} = \text{inventory on hand} + \text{inventory on order}$$

In the case when demand is at a constant rate, this rule is equivalent to the more intuitive timing rule; that is, order ℓ days before you want the order to arrive.

We first note that there are 240 working days in a year at STECO. Since yearly demand, D, for angles is 60,000 items, assumed to occur at a constant rate, this implies that d, the daily demand, is

$$d = D/240 = 60{,}000/240 = 250 \text{ per day}$$

We have seen in (15.10) that the optimal cycle time T^* is $1250/60{,}000$ years. Since there are 240 days per year, this becomes

$$T^* = \frac{1250}{60{,}000} \times 240 = 5 \text{ days}$$

**Lead Time
Less Than
Cycle Time**

We first consider a case in which the lead time (ℓ) is less than the optimal cycle time T^*. In particular, let $\ell = 3$. The timing rule says to order 3 days before you want an order to arrive. Thus 2 days after an order of 1250 angles arrives (3 days before the next order) an order for 1250 angles is placed. The situation is illustrated in Figure 15.6. Note that

**Figure 15.6
When-to-Order If $\ell < T^*$**

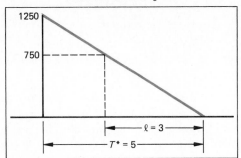

when the order is placed there are no other orders outstanding (no items on order) and since daily demand is $1250/5 = 250$, the order is placed when there are 750 items on hand. Since

$$\text{inventory position} = \text{inventory on hand} + \text{inventory on order}$$
$$= 750 + 0 = 750$$

and

$$\text{demand over the lead time} = 3 \text{ days} \times 250 \text{ items/day} = 750 \text{ items}$$

this example illustrates that the reorder point is when

$$\text{inventory position} = \text{demand over the lead time}$$

**Lead Time
Greater Than
Cycle Time**

Now consider a case where ℓ is greater than T^*. In particular, suppose that $\ell = 8$, $T^* = 5$ and you want the order to arrive on day 30. Then as shown in Figure 15.7, the order must be placed 8 days (on day 22) before you want it to arrive. Note in Figure 15.7 that at time 22 inventory on hand $= 750$. Further, the order that will arrive at time 25 was placed at time 17 because the lead time is 8. This order is still outstanding. It is the only order outstanding. Thus, inventory on order $= 1250$. Again by definition,

$$\text{inventory position} = \text{inventory on hand} + \text{inventory on order}$$
$$= 750 + 1250 = 2000$$

Figure 15.7
When-to-Order If $\ell > T^*$

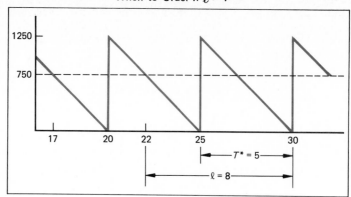

The demand during the lead time is given by the calculation

$$8 \text{ days} \times 250 \text{ items/day} = 2000$$

Once again we see that the rule "*order when the inventory position equals the demand during the lead time*" yields the same result as the timing rule.

Inventory Position in Practice

The when-to-order rule based on inventory position may seem needlessly complicated. In practice, however, it is easy to implement. The inventory clerk simply keeps a running total of the inventory position for each item. *When an order is placed* (not when an order arrives), *he adds the order quantity to the inventory position.* When an order arrives there is no change in inventory position for this is merely a transfer of Q^* items from inventory on order to Q^* items on hand. *When an order is sent to a customer, the clerk must subtract the amount from the inventory position.* When the inventory position reaches a specified precomputed number, the demand during the lead time, he places an order.

In a system where there is uncertainty in demand, we shall see that the concept of safety stock can be easily incorporated within the inventory position rule. This provides a simple and effective inventory control procedure.

Sensitivity

Victor now feels that he understands the application of the EOQ model to angles quite well. But let us at this point very carefully and clearly summarize exactly what he has shown:

1. Using the company's current policy of ordering 5000 items each time an order is placed, the inventory costs in the model are $5100.
2. If the company would use the optimal EOQ policy of ordering 1250 items each time an order is placed, the inventory costs from the model would be $2400.

Whether or not the optimal EOQ policy should be used in the future depends on the realism of the assumptions. After all, the EOQ model, like any other model, is idealized. It is no more than a selective representation of reality: an abstraction and an approximation. In this case, as with all models, the main question is: "How sensitive are the results of the model to the assumptions and the data?"

Victor has already determined that the assumptions (no stockouts are allowed, all goods arrive in a batch, the only relevant costs are ordering and holding costs, demand is on average 5000 items per month) are realistic in terms of STECO's policies and operations. Since the model is fairly realistic, it seems reasonable that the inventory costs obtained within the model are fairly good estimates of the costs that STECO is actually incurring. Therefore, using a policy that is optimal in the model (order quantity of 1250) seems preferable to the traditional policy of ordering 5000. However, Victor must still be concerned about how sensitive the optimal order quantity and, more impor-

Errors in the Cost Estimates

tant, the optimal annual cost are to the data. After all, each of the parameters C_0 and C_h is in itself an estimate. He is worried about how sensitive the EOQ results might be to the estimates for these parameters. If he errs in estimating these parameters, how much effect would that have on the difference between the calculated Q^* and AHO*, and the true Q^* and AHO*? If the results are highly sensitive to the values of the estimates, it is not clear whether the optimal policy for the model should actually be implemented by STECO. Moreover, Victor's overall task is to deal with the inventory control on all of STECO's thousands of products. Substantial resources would be needed to estimate the parameters for all the products with great accuracy, if that is required.

Let us therefore consider how the EOQ results might vary with changes in our estimated holding and ordering costs. Recall that Victor assumed that $C_h = 1.92$ and $C_0 = \$25$. We will consider four cases in which the true parameters are different from the values selected by Victor. These "true values" are shown in the first two columns of Figure 15.8. In case (i) Victor has overestimated both cost parameters by about 10%

Figure 15.8

Sensitivity to C_h and C_0

(1) TRUE PARAMETERS C_h	C_0	(2) OPTIMAL Q	(3) MINIMUM COST	(4) VICTOR'S DECISION[a]	(5) VICTOR'S COST	(6) LOSS (%)
(i) 1.72	23	1267	2179	$Q = 1250$	2179	0
(ii) 1.72	27	1372	2361	$Q = 1250$	2371	0.42
(iii) 2.12	23	1141	2419	$Q = 1250$	2429	0.41
(iv) 2.12	27	1236	2621	$Q = 1250$	2621	0

[a]Based on $C_h = 1.92$, $C_0 = 25$.

each. Had he estimated the parameters correctly he would have ordered 1267 items and incurred an annual holding and ordering cost of 2179. Because of his estimation errors he orders 1250. In order to find out what costs he will actually incur, Victor must evaluate the AHO equation with its true parameter values [$C_h = 1.72$ and $C_0 = 23$ in case (i)] and the value of Q determined by his estimates (1250). This calculation follows:

$$\text{AHO}(Q) = C_0 D/Q + C_h Q/2$$
$$= 23(60,000/1250) + 1.72(1250/2) = 2179.$$

The Effect Is Negligible

This number is shown as Victor's Cost in column (5). We thus see that if Victor over-estimates the two cost parameters as shown, it has no effect on the annual holding and ordering cost (to the nearest dollar). The other three cases show that the effect on the annual holding and ordering cost of any combination of 10% errors in the estimates of C_0 and C_h is negligible.

Our analysis suggests that in Victor's case the EOQ model is insensitive even to approximately 10% variations or errors in the cost estimates. It turns out that this is a property enjoyed by EOQ models in general. Thus, Victor concludes that if he can obtain at least reasonable estimates of ordering and holding costs, the value of Q thereby obtained will yield an AHO very close to the true minimum.

If future demand were known with complete certainty and were truly at a constant monthly rate, then under the other assumptions that ordering and holding costs are the only relevant costs, and no stockouts are allowed, it is true that the values Q^* and $\text{AHO}(Q^*)$ as produced by the idealized EOQ model would indeed be optimal, not just in the model but in the real problem as well. However, in practice, as we repeatedly emphasize, the real-world problem rarely satisfies the assumptions of the model exactly. In Chapter 16 Victor will enlarge his perspective to see how the ICON system deals with uncertainty in future demand in formal ways. As a first step, however, he must recognize that using the previously derived reorder point of 750 items (for 3-day lead times) will almost surely lead to some stockouts. A stockout will occur whenever the demand during the 3-day lead time exceeds 750 items. Another possible cause for a stockout could be the occurrence of a longer lead time for unforeseen reasons. The job of the manager is to deal successfully with uncertainty. In the STECO context, if stockouts are truly to be avoided, then Victor as manager may choose to increase the reorder point (leaving the reorder quantity unchanged). He may, for example, choose to reorder when 1000 items are on hand. What would he achieve with such a change?

Since, during the expected 3-day lead time, 750 items are estimated to be demanded (assuming that the constant demand rate holds), we see that 250 items will still remain in inventory when the order arrives. This extra 250 units serves as a precaution against larger than expected demand or a delay in the scheduled delivery. It is called a safety or buffer stock.

Using a Safety Stock

> **A safety stock is the difference between the reorder point and the expected leadtime demand.**

In the appliance angle example, carrying a safety stock of 250 items would raise the average inventory level by 250 items. This will affect only the yearly carrying charge, which will increase by

$$C_h(250) = (1.92)(250) = \$480$$

and hence the only effect of the 250-item buffer stock is to raise the annual cost estimate from \$2400 to \$2880, still a considerable savings over the current policy. (This statement ignores any changes in costs due to stockouts.)

Thus, as a first-order consideration, possible uncertainties in demand, or in lead time, can be treated with a managerial judgment on a suitable safety stock level. This is handled by simple modification of the reorder point rule. Whether or not a simple modification should be made is in itself a matter of managerial judgment. It is a question of the extent to which stockouts are to be avoided, and a question of whether or not a deeper treatment should be undertaken. After all, the question of "what a suitable safety stock level is" remains unanswered. In Chapter 16 this question will be analyzed in greater depth.

Other variations in the basic model might be called for to capitalize on the opportunity to get quantity discounts. This is treated in the following section.

15.4

QUANTITY DISCOUNTS AND STECO'S OVERALL OPTIMUM

The EOQ model that Victor has been working with minimizes the annual holding and ordering cost. There was previously no need to take into account the cost of purchasing the product, for the per item cost to STECO was assumed to be a constant independent of Q. Victor now learns that STECO's supplier will make a special offer as an incentive for more business. The supplier has agreed to offer a $0.10 discount on every angle purchased if STECO orders in lots of at least 5000 items. Of course, higher order quantities will also reduce the number of orders placed, and hence the annual ordering cost. However, as already discussed a high order quantity leads to a higher average inventory level and hence higher holding costs. Whether or not the discount will, on balance, be advantageous to STECO is not obvious.

An All Units Discount

Victor decides to proceed as before, that is, to develop an annual cost curve and then find the order quantity that minimizes it. His annual total cost [ATC(Q)] is the sum of the annual holding and ordering cost [AHO(Q)] and the annual purchase cost [APC]: that is,

$$\text{ATC}(Q) = \text{AHO}(Q) + \text{APC}.$$

From equation (15.4) and the fact that

$$\text{APC} = PD$$

it follows that

Annual Total Cost

$$\text{ATC}(Q) = C_0 D/Q + iPQ/2 + PD.$$

Victor wishes to evaluate this function for two different prices, the regular price of $8.00 per unit and the potential discounted price of $7.90 per unit. He obtains the following two functions:

Regular price equation:

$$\text{ATC}(Q) = \frac{25 \times 60{,}000}{Q} + (0.24)(8.00)(Q/2) + (8.00)(60{,}000).$$

Discount price equation:

$$\text{ATC}(Q) = \frac{25 \times 60{,}000}{Q} + (0.24)(7.90)(Q/2) + (7.90)(60{,}000).$$

The general shape of these curves is shown in Figure 15.9. There are two facts to notice.

1. The discount curve lies below the regular cost curve. This is so since each term in the regular price ATC(Q) is greater than or equal to the corresponding term in the discount price ATC(Q).
2. The value of Q, say Q_D^*, that minimizes the discount price ATC(Q) is larger than the value of Q, say Q_R^*, that minimizes the regular price ATC(Q). This is true because, using (15.8),

$$Q_D^* = \sqrt{\frac{2 \times 25 \times 60{,}000}{(0.24) \times (7.90)}} > \sqrt{\frac{2 \times 25 \times 60{,}000}{(0.24) \times (8.00)}} = Q_R^*$$

Figure 15.9

Annual Total Cost for Regular and Discount Prices

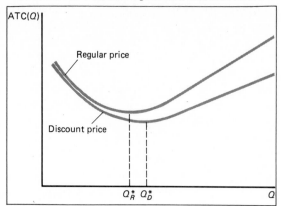

Obviously, Victor would like to minimize his annual total cost, ATC(Q). If he could get the discount price, regardless of the order quantity, he would of course order Q_D^*. However, assume that the discount price holds only if he orders at least B items at a time. Two situations could arise. These are illustrated in Figure 15.10.

Figure 15.10

Effect of B

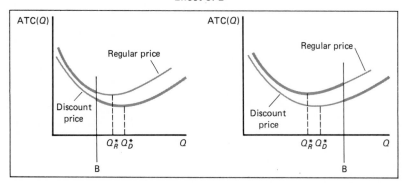

The Importance of the Price Break

The heavily shaded curves in these figures indicate the actual cost function that Victor faces. It illustrates that the regular price curve must be used for order quantities of less than B and that the discount price curve is used for order quantities of B or more.

We see that if $B \leq Q_D^*$, Victor will achieve the minimum cost by ordering Q_D^*. If, however, $B > Q_D^*$, the optimal decision, in general, is not immediately obvious. The best Victor can do on the regular price curve is to order Q_R^*. The best he can do on the discount price curve is to order B. (He cannot order less than B and get the discount price, and ordering more than B increases ATC.) In Figure 15.10 you can see that the quantity B is preferred to Q_R^*. In general, to determine whether B or Q_R^* is optimal Victor must calculate the ATC(Q) at these two points and compare them. The general rule then is

If $B \leq Q_D^*$, order Q_D^*.		

If $B > Q_D^*$, order $\begin{cases} Q_R^* \\ B \end{cases}$ $\begin{array}{l} \text{if regular price} \\ \text{ATC}(Q_R^*) \\ \text{if not} \end{array}$ $\leq$ $\begin{bmatrix} \text{discount price} \\ \text{ATC}(B) \end{bmatrix}$

To apply this rule, Victor notes that he must order at least 5000 items to get the discount. Thus $B = 5000$. To calculate Q_D^* he uses the EOQ formula as follows:

$$Q_D^* = \sqrt{\frac{2 \times 25 \times 60,000}{(0.24)(7.90)}} = 1257.9 \sim 1258. \qquad (15.12)$$

Since $Q_D^* = 1258 < 5000 = B$, he must compare two alternatives to determine the optimal order quantity. From his previous calculations [those following (15.8)] he knows that Q_R^* equals 1250. Thus, the value $\text{ATC}(Q_R^*)$ is calculated by the regular price equation above.

$$\text{ATC}(Q_R^*) = \frac{25 \times 60,000}{1250} + (0.24)(8.00)\frac{1250}{2} + (8.00)(60,000) = 482,400.$$

Similarly, the value $\text{ATC}(B)$ is calculated by the discount price equation.

$$\text{ATC}(B) = \frac{25 \times 60,000}{5,000} + (0.24)(7.90)\frac{5000}{2} + (7.90)(60,000) = 479,040.$$

These calculations show that Victor should order 5000 items to take advantage of the quantity discount. This decision saves

$$\$482,400 - \$479,040 = \$3360$$

per year over the next best decision (ordering Q_R^*). What this discussion suggests is that quantity discounts can play an important role in determining the optimal inventory policy. Indeed, it is so important that STECO's ICON system has been designed to deal with this problem. ICON first solves the basic EOQ model, and then in a second stage, when quantity discounts are available, the system runs through the calculations that Victor has just made.

15.5

THE EOQ MODEL WITH BACKLOGGING

One of the important functions of inventory is to protect against stockouts. We have already seen earlier in this chapter how a manager can add a safety stock to the reorder point to decrease the likelihood of stockouts with an EOQ model. However, in some cases it may be advantageous to both the buyer and the seller if not all orders are satisfied out of inventory immediately on hand. Indeed, the seller sometimes plans on running out and knows that there will be some demand when there is no inventory on hand. Holding this demand in abeyance and then satisfying it out of later inventory is called *backlogging demand*.

We thus wish to drop the no-stockout assumption in the basic model and examine the implications of doing so. The essence of backlogging in the EOQ context is illustrated in Figure 15.11.

Figure 15.11
EOQ Model with Planned Backorders

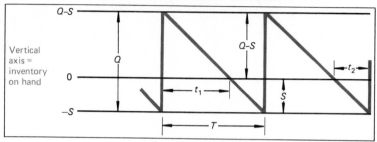

Much of Figure 15.11 is familiar. An order for Q items arrives every T days. The order arrives all at once (in a batch) at which time the inventory on hand jumps up by Q items. Between the arrival of orders inventory depletes at a constant rate, reflecting the fact that demand is occurring at a constant rate. The new wrinkle is the fact that not all demand is immediately satisfied out of inventory on hand. Certain customers are asked to wait and their demand is satisfied when the next order arrives. In a strict sense those customers whose orders arrive during the first t_1 days of an inventory cycle have their demand satisfied out of inventory immediately on hand. Those whose orders arrive during the rest of the cycle (t_2 days) wait until the next replenishment to receive their goods. The process of asking customers to wait (called backlogging) is indicated in Figure 15.11 with the introduction of negative values for inventory on hand.

Cost of Backlogging Typically, the supplier must offer some sort of financial incentive to his customers to accept a waiting period. This incentive might take the form of financial considerations; that is, the supplier might accept payment up to 90 days after delivery at no extra charge, whereas immediate delivery implies immediate payment or the addition of finance charges. Another approach is simply to offer a price reduction for backlogged orders. The point is that the supplier typically incurs a cost for these items, but sometimes it is sensible to incur these costs intentionally.

Returning to Figure 15.11, note that during the cycle time (T) the firm holds inventory during t_1 and accepts backorders (i.e., backlogged demand) during t_2 when the inventory has been depleted. Clearly, $t_1 + t_2 = T$. The symbol S indicates the total number of units backlogged during a cycle, that is, the total number of units of unsatisfied demand accumulated during t_2. We see then that, with an order size of Q, the maximum level of inventory on hand is $Q - S$, since S items from each new order must be used to fill previously backlogged orders and the remaining $Q - S$ are placed in inventory.

In the basic EOQ model management has to make one decision, the value of Q, since this determines the cycle time and the entire policy. When backorders are permitted, management must select both Q and S. As before, Q, together with the constant rate of demand D, determines T, the cycle length, but S must be specified before it is clear how many units will be backlogged on each cycle and how much inventory will be **Two Decisions** held. The values of the decision variables Q and S are selected to minimize the sum of the annual ordering, holding, and backlogging costs. Backlogging costs are assessed in **520** exactly the same manner as holding costs; that is, the cost to backlog an item for a year must be specified, and the cost per cycle is built up from this quantity. The cost per cycle is used in turn to calculate the annual cost. A detailed development follows.

The Annual Cost Expression
Let AHOB(Q, S) be the annual holding, ordering, and backlogging cost as a function of Q and S. Also, let C_b be the cost of backlogging an item for a year. We now proceed to develop the cost of a cycle.

1. **Ordering cost:** Since one order is placed each cycle, this is simple. The ordering cost equals C_0.

2. **Holding cost:** The maximum inventory level is $Q - S$. Demand occurs at the constant rate of D items per year. It follows that the quantity $(Q - S)$ will last for a time (in years) given by

$$t_1 = \frac{Q - S}{D}$$

if it is consumed at the *rate* D. The average time (in years) that a unit is held in inventory is $t_1/2$ and $(Q - S)$ items are held. Thus, the holding cost per cycle is

$$C_h(Q - S)t_1/2 = C_h(Q - S)(1/2)[(Q - S)/D]$$
$$= \frac{C_h}{2} \frac{(Q - S)^2}{D}.$$

3. **Backlogging cost:** A maximum of S units are backlogged. Since backlogging occurs at the rate of demand D, the time for backlogging must be

$$t_2 = S/D$$

A total of S items are backlogged for an average of $t_2/2$ years; thus, the backlogging cost per cycle is

$$C_b S t_2/2 = C_b S(1/2)(S/D)$$
$$= \frac{C_b}{2} \frac{S^2}{D}.$$

Annual Holding, Ordering, and Backlogging Cost
The annual holding, ordering, and backlogging cost, AHOB(Q, S), can now be obtained by adding the costs from 1, 2, and 3 above to obtain the cost per cycle and then multiplying by the number of cycles per year. As in the basic EOQ model there are D/Q cycles per year. Thus,

$$\text{AHOB}(Q, S) = D/Q \left[C_0 + \frac{C_h}{2} \frac{(Q - S)^2}{D} + \frac{C_b}{2} \frac{S^2}{D} \right]. \tag{15.13}$$

Management can now use (15.13) to calculate the annual holding, ordering, and backlogging cost for any choice of the decision variables Q and S. With differential calculus one can also use the same equation to derive the expressions for Q^* and S^*, the optimal values of Q and S. The results of this derivation are presented in (15.14) and (15.15).

Optimal Decisions

$$Q^* = \sqrt{\frac{2C_0 D}{C_h} \left(\frac{C_h + C_b}{C_b} \right)} \tag{15.14}$$

$$S^* = Q^* \left(\frac{C_h}{C_h + C_b} \right). \tag{15.15}$$

Plugging the expressions for Q^* and S^* into (15.13) yields AHOB(Q^*, S^*), the minimum annual holding, ordering, and backlogging cost. The result is shown in (15.16).

$$\text{AHOB}(Q^*, S^*) = \left[2C_0DC_h\left(\frac{C_b}{C_h + C_b}\right)\right]^{1/2}. \tag{15.16}$$

It is interesting to compare these expressions to those for Q^* and $\text{AHO}(Q^*)$ in the basic EOQ model. Recall that in the basic model

$$Q^* = \sqrt{\frac{2C_0D}{C_h}} \quad \text{and} \quad \text{AHO}(Q^*) = (2C_0DC_h)^{1/2}$$

We first note that since $(C_h + C_b)/C_b \geq 1$, the optimal order quantity in the backlogged case is at least as large as the optimal order quantity in the basic model. Similarly, since $C_b/(C_b + C_h) \leq 1$, the annual cost for the backlogged model is at most as large as the annual cost in the basic model.

Suppose that the cost of backlogging an item for a year is twice as large as the cost of holding the same item for a year; that is, assume that $C_b = 2C_h$. Does your intuition tell you that you would never choose to backlog in this case? If it did you have learned again how easily we are misled by our intuition. From (15.15) we see that since $C_h/(C_h + C_b) = \frac{1}{3}$, $S^* = Q^*(\frac{1}{3})$ which implies that one-third of the orders will be backlogged. Now from (15.16) and the facts that

$$\frac{C_b}{C_h + C_b} = \frac{2}{3} \quad \text{and} \quad \left(\frac{C_b}{C_h + C_b}\right)^{1/2} = 0.816$$

we conclude that the annual cost in the backlogged model is only 0.816 times as much as the annual cost in the basic model. In other words, what to many people seems like an unattractive alternative (backlogging when it is twice as expensive as holding inventory) turns out to play an important role in the optimal inventory policy. One-third of the orders are backlogged. This policy has an important effect on the costs (approximately a 20% reduction).

One way to think about the basic model is to assume that backlogging is allowed, but that since C_b is extremely large (infinite) no orders are ever backlogged. It is reassuring to note that if C_b is set equal to infinity in (15.14), (15.15), and (15.16), then $S^* = 0$, and Q^* and $\text{AHOB}(Q^*, S^*)$ reduce to the appropriate expressions for the no-backlog case.

15.6

THE PRODUCTION LOT SIZE MODEL:
VICTOR'S HEAT TREATMENT PROBLEM

Although STECO is primarily a steel wholesaler, it does have some productive capacity. In particular, it has an extensive and modern heat-treatment facility which it uses to produce a number of items that it then holds in inventory. The heat treatment facility has two important characteristics: There is a large setup cost associated with producing each product, and once the setup is complete, production is at a steady and known rate.

The setup cost, which is analogous to the ordering cost in the EOQ model, is incurred because it is necessary to change the chemicals and the operating temperature in the heat-treatment facility to meet the specifications set forth by the metallurgical laboratory. Also, each item must spend a specified time at a specific temperature in each of several chemical baths. Thus, an order quantity of heat-treated steel does not arrive in inventory all at once. Rather, it arrives steadily over a period of several days. This change requires a modification in the EOQ formula, even if the assumptions of a constant rate of demand and the inventory carrying cost being equal to C_h times the average inventory are maintained.

It is usually more convenient to work with this model in terms of daily production and demand rates. Thus, consider a product in which

d = number of units demanded each day

p = number of units produced each day during a production run

C_0 = setup cost that is independent of the quantity produced

C_h = cost per *day* of holding inventory

It is obvious that p must be greater than d for the problem to be interesting. If $p < d$, demand is greater than STECO's ability to produce and holding inventory is the least of their problems.

Figure 15.12 presents a plot of what the inventory on hand would look like if STECO decides to produce in lots of Q items each.

Figure 15.12
Inventory on Hand for the Production Lot Size Model

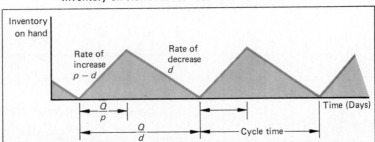

There are several aspects of this graph that must be noted in order to calculate the average holding and setup cost per day.

1. During a production run items are added to inventory at a rate of p units per day and removed at the rate of d per day. The net effect is an increase at the rate of $p - d$ units per day.
2. At other times, items are removed from inventory at a rate of d items per day.
3. Since Q items are produced in a run, at the rate of p items per day, each production run is Q/p days long.
4. Since Q items are produced in a run, and d is the daily demand rate, each cycle time is Q/d days long.

Facts 1 and 3 can be used to find the maximum amount of inventory on hand (see Figure 15.12).

$$\text{maximum inventory} = (p - d)Q/p.$$

Since the average inventory equals one-half of the maximum inventory, it follows that

$$\text{average inventory} = 1/2(p - d)Q/p.$$

Rearranging the terms in the expression above, we obtain

$$\text{holding cost per day} = C_h Q/2(1 - d/p).$$

Similarly, since there is one setup every cycle and a cycle lasts Q/d days,

$$\text{setup cost per day} = \frac{C_0}{Q/d} = C_0 \frac{d}{Q}.$$

Thus, the daily holding and setup cost, denoted DHS(Q), is given by the expression

$$\text{DHS}(Q) = C_0 \frac{d}{Q} + C_h \frac{Q}{2}\left(1 - \frac{d}{p}\right).$$

If you think of $C_h(1 - d/p)$ as a constant, this expression takes the same form as given by (15.4), the expression for the annual holding and operating cost in the EOQ model.

It follows, then, that the value of Q that minimizes DHS(Q) will be given by the EOQ equation (15.8) with C_h appropriately modified. Thus, for the production lot size model,

$$Q^* = \sqrt{\frac{2dC_0}{C_h(1 - d/p)}}. \tag{15.17}$$

***Optimal
Production
Lot Size***
The result could also be derived with differential calculus, analogous to the derivation in Appendix 15.1.

To apply this analysis to any particular product, Victor must estimate the various parameters for that product and then evaluate (15.17) to obtain Q^*. Thus, once the parameters are estimated, finding Q^* is reduced to a matter of "plug and chug."

Just to confirm his understanding of the production lot size model, Victor decides to work his way through the calculations for a $\frac{3}{8}$-inch hardened reinforcing rod, a product used in reinforced concrete construction.

The demand for this product averages 200 rods per day. It costs $100 to setup to heat treat the rods and they can be produced at a rate of 400 rods per day. Victor estimates the holding cost per day as ($1.00)(0.24)/240 = 0.001, where $1.00 is the cost of the rod and 0.24 is the annual interest rate used by STECO for all products. The figure 240 is the assumed number of working days per year.

The optimal production lot size for this product, then, is

$$Q^* = \sqrt{\frac{2 \times 200 \times 100}{0.001(1 - 200/400)}} = 8944$$

A production run of this size yields a supply of rods large enough to satisfy demand for

$$\frac{8944}{200} = 44.72 \text{ days}$$

Other Considerations

In practice, Victor might adjust this quantity to take into account the fact that a number of other products also have to make use of the heat-treatment facility. He would perhaps add a safety stock to allow for the possibility that demand might run ahead of production at the beginning of a production run. Quantity discounts would probably not play a role in his decision since the rods that are heat treated are drawn from STECO's general inventory of $\frac{3}{8}$-inch-high carbon steel rods. These rods are used for a number of purposes and their purchase must be determined by total demand.

15.7
MATERIAL REQUIREMENTS PLANNING: FARMCRAFT MANUFACTURING CO.

The directors of STECO have recently approved the purchase of Farmcraft Manufacturing Co., a major producer of planting equipment. As a manufacturer, Farmcraft maintains inventories of intermediate goods which are to be used in producing finished products. During a major restudy of Farmcraft's inventory management, Victor is called in as a consultant. He quickly learns that his experience at STECO has little direct application. STECO maintains finished product inventories to satisfy consumer demand. There is a big difference between this activity and that which occurs at Farmcraft.

Intermediate Goods

In a typical manufacturing process certain parts and subassemblies are used in a number of finished products. For a firm like Farmcraft you would expect to see basic parts like bolts and nuts, custom parts like wheels and treads, and subassemblies like transmissions and engines used in a number of finished products. We shall use the term **intermediate goods** to refer to all parts and subassemblies.

It is, of course, clear that the demand for intermediate goods is generated by the demand for the finished product. The question to be asked is: "What levels of intermediate good inventories are required to assure that finished product demand will be satisfied?" We shall see that the relationships between intermediate goods and final product, if properly taken into account, can lead to important efficiencies in establishing appropriate inventory levels. **Material requirements planning**, abbreviated MRP, is an important technique to deal with dependencies in demand. Let us use a simple example to explain the approach.

In Figure 15.13 we see a display of some of the requirements for a 12-row beet and bean planter. The flow in this figure illustrates that the gearbox must be available in order to produce the transmission, for indeed the gearbox is part of the transmission. Moreover, the transmission must be available in order to produce the power train, for it is part of the power train, and this power train in turn goes into the final product. Thus, Figure 15.13 gives you an indication of some of the dependencies among intermediate goods. It is this type of dependency that will be used in the MRP analysis of required inventory levels.

Proceeding, suppose that Farmcraft's production schedule calls for 1000 units of finished product (12-row planters) to be assembled by April 1 of next year. In order to meet this schedule the power train, wheel assembly, and earth turning units must be

Figure 15.13

Material Input List

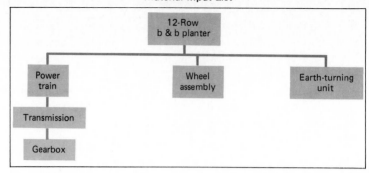

Bill of
Materials

completed by March 15, allowing 2 weeks for the final assembly. Let us now focus on the inventory control aspects of the power train. The number of units currently in inventory are shown in Figure 15.14. The first question to be asked is: "How many units of each component will ultimately be required in inventory to fulfill the requirement that 1000 units of finished product are assembled by April 1?"

Figure 15.14

Current Inventory for Farmcraft

COMPONENT	UNITS CURRENTLY IN INVENTORY
Power train	360
Transmission	250
Gearbox	400

Computing
Additional
Requirements

You may believe that the answer is obvious: namely, 1000 units of each component are required. Therefore, you may say that the *additional requirements*, above and beyond current inventory levels, are obtained by subtracting current levels from 1000, as shown in Figure 15.15. The problem with this answer is that it does not take into account the dependencies revealed in Figure 15.13. It ignores the facts that gearboxes are already

Figure 15.15

Additional Requirements: A Wrong Answer

COMPONENT	NUMBER REQUIRED TO MEET DEMAND FOR 1000 PLANTERS	NUMBER IN INVENTORY	ADDITIONAL REQUIREMENT
Power train	1000	360	640
Transmission	1000	250	750
Gearbox	1000	400	600

installed in the 250 transmissions on hand, and transmissions are already installed in the 360 power trains on hand. Taking these facts into account, the MRP analysis of additional requirements would proceed as follows:

units of finished product to be assembled	1000
total requirement for power trains	1000

power trains in current inventory	360
additional power trains required	640

Now since each additional power train will require a transmission, we have

total requirement for transmissions	640
transmissions in current inventory	250
additional transmissions required	390

Similarly, since each of the additional transmissions will require a gearbox, one obtains

total requirement for gearboxes	390
gearboxes in current inventory	400
additional gearboxes required	0

You can now see how MRP was used to take the dependency of intermediate goods into account and to produce an improved list of additional requirements as given in Figure 15.16. The analysis using MRP clearly leads to lower inventory levels and hence lower inventory charges.

Figure 15.16

Comparison of Results

COMPONENT	ADDITIONAL REQUIREMENTS WITHOUT DEPENDENCY (FIGURE 15.15)	ADDITIONAL REQUIREMENTS TAKING DEPENDENCY INTO ACCOUNT
Power train	640	640
Transmission	750	390
Gearbox	600	0

Since each component of the power train requires production and assembly time, some planning must be done in order to deliver the 640 additional power trains on schedule. The necessary information is given in Figure 15.17. The lead time in this context is the amount of time it will take to produce the additional requirements given that all components are available at the start of the process. For example, it requires 20 working days to produce 640 power trains once the 640 transmissions (250 from inventory and 390 newly produced) as well as all of the other materials in the power train are available.

Figure 15.17

Additional Requirements and Lead Times for the Power Train Assembly

COMPONENT	ADDITIONAL REQUIREMENTS	LEAD TIME (WORKING DAYS)
Power train	640	20
Transmission	390	5
Gearbox	0	0

With the information in Figure 15.17 we can construct the time line shown in Figure 15.18. As previously stated, the 1000 complete planters are due on April 1, the sixtieth working day of the year. This date marks the end of the production and assembly

Figure 15.18
Time Phasing Planter Production

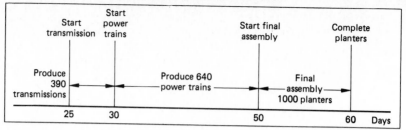

process and the start of our calculation. It was also previously stated that the power trains must be available on March 15, to allow the 10 working days required to assemble final components into the planters. Figure 15.18 was constructed by starting at the desired completion time and working backward. This process is often called *time phasing* or *lead-time offsetting*. We see from this construction that the process of producing the 390 additional transmissions must be started on the twenty-fifth working day (roughly February 5; the exact date, of course, depends on the year). If Farmcraft did not already have at least 390 gear boxes in inventory, the date at which the entire process of producing power trains started would have been even earlier.

Time Phasing

The popularity of MRP in real applications is partly due to its conceptual simplicity.

> **To apply MRP, start backward from the finished product and successively compute net additional requirements for the dependent intermediate goods.**

However, in spite of its simplicity an enormous volume of calculations must be performed to apply MRP in most real manufacturing environments. Consequently, the success of MRP is to a large extent due to the capabilities of large-scale computers.

15.8
MAJOR CONCEPTS QUIZ

True–False

1. **T F** The opportunity cost segment of the holding cost is determined by factors such as breakage, pilferage, and insurance.
2. **T F** Demand is always greater than or equal to sales.
3. **T F** In the EOQ model the annual ordering cost is directly proportional to the order quantity.
4. **T F** If the lead time is smaller than the cycle time, an order should be placed when the inventory on hand equals the demand during the lead time (assuming zero safety stock).
5. **T F** In the EOQ model the annual holding and ordering cost is reasonably insensitive to errors in estimating the cost parameters.
6. **T F** The safety stock is the difference between the reorder point and the actual demand over the lead time.
7. **T F** For any set of demand and cost parameters, the minimum annual holding and ordering cost (backlogging not permitted) is never less than the minimum annual holding, ordering, and backlogging cost (backlogging permitted).

8. T F In the production lot size model, since production is at a steady rate, no setup cost is included in the model.

9. T F Material requirements planning takes the dependency of intermediate goods into account to determine the additional requirements of component parts.

Multiple Choice

10. The following are some of the reasons inventory is held:
   a. protect against uncertainty in demand
   b. lower production costs
   c. store labor
   d. all of the above

11. Important considerations in deciding *when* and *how much* to order include all factors except:
   a. the lead time
   b. the proportion of the holding cost that is due to the opportunity cost
   c. the possibility of quantity discounts
   d. the extent to which future demand is known

12. In the EOQ model
   a. orders arrive in a batch
   b. demand is known and occurs at a constant rate
   c. all demand must be satisfied
   d. all of the above

13. In the EOQ model if the price of the item increases and all other parameters remain the same, the optimal order quantity will typically
   a. increase
   b. decrease
   c. stay the same

14. In the EOQ model the optimal number of orders per year
   a. increases directly with
   b. increases as the square root of
   c. decreases directly with
   d. does not change with
   the annual rate of demand.

15. Consider an EOQ model with a quantity discount where a smaller per unit price applies to all units if B or more units are purchased. If Q_D^* minimizes AHO assuming the smaller price, and Q_R^* minimizes AHO assuming the regular price, and $Q_D^* > B$, the optimal order quantity is always
   a. Q_D^*
   b. either Q_R^* or B, depending on which yields the smaller annual total cost
   c. Q_R^*
   d. B

16. In the EOQ model with backlogging the optimal number of orders to backlog is
   a. directly proportional to
   b. directly proportional to the square root of
   c. not dependent on
   d. directly proportional to the reciprocal of
   the annual rate of demand.

17. In the production lot size model, increasing the rate of production
   a. increases
   b. does not influence
   c. decreases the optimal number of orders to place each year.

Answers

1. F	7. T	13. b
2. T	8. F	14. b
3. F	9. T	15. a
4. T	10. d	16. b
5. T	11. b	17. a
6. F	12. d	

529

15-1. A local hardware store sells 364,000 pounds of nails a year. It currently orders 14,000 pounds of nails every 2 weeks at a price of $0.50 per pound. Assume that

1. Demand occurs at a constant rate.
2. The cost of placing an order is $50.00 regardless of the size of the order.
3. The annual cost of holding inventory is 12% of the value of the average inventory level.
4. These factors do not change over time.

(a) What is the average inventory level?
(b) What is the annual holding cost?
(c) What is the annual ordering cost?
(d) What is the annual holding and ordering cost?
(e) What is the annual total cost?
(f) Would it be cheaper for the owner to order in larger lots (and less frequently) or smaller lots (and more frequently)?

15-2. The campus ice cream store sells 200 quarts of vanilla ice cream each month. The store currently restocks its inventory at the beginning of each month. The wholesale price of ice cream is $1 per quart. Assume that

1. Demand occurs at a constant rate.
2. The annual cost of holding inventory is 18% of the value of the average inventory level.
3. Last year the annual total cost was $2604.00.
4. These factors do not change over time.

(a) Compute average inventory level.
(b) Compute annual holding cost.
(c) Compute annual ordering cost and cost/order.
(d) Compute annual holding and ordering cost.
(e) Should the store order in larger lots (and less frequently) or smaller lots (and more frequently)?

15-3. A local entrepreneur and renowned visionary, sells pencils at a constant rate of 25 per day. Each pencil costs 5 cents. If ordering costs are $5 and inventory holding costs are 20% of the cost of the average inventory, what is the optimal order quantity and the optimal number of orders that should be placed each year?

15-4. Hong Kong's leading optical products center, I. Kant C. U., experiences demand for its eyeglasses at a constant annual rate of 5000 pairs. The store sells the glasses for $9 a pair, which is 150% of their cost. If ordering costs are $20 and annual inventory holding costs are 10% of the cost of average inventory, what is the economic order quantity and cycle time for I. Kant C. U. purchases of eyeglasses?

15-5. Specific Electric is a giant manufacturer of electrical appliances in the United States. It uses electric motors that it purchases from another firm at a constant rate. Total purchase costs during the year are $2,400,000. Ordering costs are $100 and annual inventory holding costs are 20% of the cost of the average inventory.
(a) What is the dollar value of the optimal order quantity?
(b) How many times a year should SE order?
(c) What is the optimal cycle time in years and in days if there are 250 working days per year?
(HINT: If P is the cost per unit to Specific Electric and Q^* is the optimal order quantity, PQ^* is the dollar value of the optimal order quantity).

15-6. Suppose that the actual holding cost in Problem 15-5 is 30% of the cost of average inventory. Assume that Specific Electric uses the optimal policy derived in Problem 15-5.
(a) Calculate the ratio

$$\frac{\text{actual annual holding cost}}{\text{annual holding cost of optimal policy}}$$

(b) Calculate the ratio

$$\frac{\text{actual annual holding and ordering cost}}{\text{annual holding and ordering cost of optimal policy}}$$

(c) Comment on the implications of parts (a) and (b).

15-7. Strumm and Howell is a local record store that specializes in country music. The store has been quite successful in recent years, with retail sales of $400,000 per year. Sales occur at a constant rate during the year. S and H buys its records from a major recording company. The retail sales price equals $\frac{5}{3}$ times the cost to S and H. The ordering cost for each shipment of orders is $75, independent of the size of the order. Annual inventory holding costs are 10% of the cost of the average inventory level.
(a) What is the dollar value of the optimal order quantity?
(b) How often should S and H order each year?
(c) What is the optimal cycle time in years?
(HINT: If P is the cost per unit to S and H and Q^* is the optimal order quantity, PQ^* is the dollar value of the optimal order quantity).

15-8. In reevaluating its cost estimates, the cost accountants for Strumm and Howell (see Problem 15-7) conclude that the ordering cost is $100 and the cost of holding inventory is 8. Assume that S and H uses the policy derived in Problem 15-7. Consider the ratio

$$R = \frac{\text{actual AHO}(Q_7)}{\text{AHO}(Q^*)}$$

where AHO(Q) = annual holding and ordering cost as a function of Q
$\qquad Q_7$ = optimal value of Q for the parameter values in Problem 15-7
$\qquad Q^*$ = optimal value of Q for parameter values described above

(a) Find R.
(b) Comment on the magnitude of R.

15-9. The Waukon, Iowa, outlet of Cheap Cheep Chicks orders baby chickens from the firm's central incubator in Des Moines. Ten dozen chicks are demanded each day of the 250-workday year. It costs $40 to process an order independent of the number of chicks ordered and $80 to hold a dozen chicks in inventory for a year. Assume that Cheap Cheep calculates inventory holding costs based on the average inventory level. The incubation period for eggs is 20 days, and thus it takes 20 days between the time an order is placed and the chicks are delivered.
(a) What is the optimal order quantity?
(b) How many orders should be placed each year?
(c) What is the optimal cycle time in years? In working days?
(d) What is the lead time?
(e) What is the inventory position at each order point?
(f) What is the demand during the lead time?

15-10. Suppose that the Waukon, Iowa, outlet of Cheap Cheep Chicks (see Problem 15-9) had its own incubator and could get same-day delivery of fresh eggs. These eggs must be placed in the incubator the day they arrive, and they are guaranteed to hatch in 20 days. It costs $40 to process an order for eggs independent of the number of eggs ordered. All other facts about the operation are the same as in Problem 15-9.
(a) What is the optimal order quantity for eggs?
(b) How many orders should be placed each year?
(c) What is the optimal cycle time in years? In working days?

(d) What is the lead time?

(e) What is the inventory position at each order point?

(f) What is the demand during the lead time?

15-11. Bed Bug, a local manufacturer of orthopedic mattresses, currently satisfies its constant production requirements of 500 coiled springs per day by using an EOQ model based on an ordering cost of $90, a product cost of $1 per spring, and an inventory holding cost of 15% of the cost of average inventory. Springy Steel, its supplier, has recently offered a 0.5% discount if Bed Bug orders in quantities of at least 20,000 springs, or a 0.7% discount if it orders quarterly. Assume 240 workdays per year.

(a) Find Q^*, T^*, N^*, and the annual total cost under the current cost assumptions.

(b) Calculate annual total cost for each of the discount alternatives.

(c) What should Bed Bug do?

15-12. Threadbare Haberdashery sells suits at a constant rate of 20 per day. Assume 300 days in a year. Suits cost $100 each and the annual inventory carrying costs are 20% of the cost of average inventory. It costs $54 to place an order. Currently, Threadbare orders four times per year.

(a) How much more per suit would they be willing to pay if they could order optimally? Find an *approximate* solution by ignoring the effect of the new price on AHO.

(b) Show the equaion you would have to solve to find an exact value, that is, one that takes the effect of the new purchase price on AHO into account.

15-13. The Reefer Tobacco Company, the nation's largest distributor of California-grown smoking products, has a constant demand of 192 packs per month for its most popular product, Wachy Tabachy. Its ordering cost is $100, annual holding costs are 25% of the average inventory (due to the high risk of seizure), and the product costs $200 per pack. Currently, it does not backlog demand and follows the optimal ordering policy. Recently, a local consultant recommended that the company backlog demand. This requires a price discount. Reefer feels that it must offer a discount of $0.20 per day. Allowing for vacations and religious holidays, there are 200 days per year.

(a) Under the current policy (no backlogging), find Q^*, N^*, T^*, and AHO(Q^*).

(b) What is the value for C_b, the cost of backlogging a unit for a year?

(c) For the suggested backlogging policy, find Q^*, S^*, N^*, T^*, and AHOB(Q^*).

(d) Which policy should Reefer implement?

15-14. The demand for general books at the University Bookstore occurs at a constant rate of 25,000 books per year. The manager satisfies this demand without backlogging. He calculates the optimal order quantity based on ordering costs of $25, and an annual holding cost of $5 per book. Orders are delivered 7 days after they are received by telephone. Assume 250 days per year.

(a) What are the values for Q^*, N^*, T^*, and AHO*?

(b) When an order is placed, what is the level of

    (i) Inventory on hand?

    (ii) Inventory on order?

    (iii) Inventory position?

(c) What is the demand during the lead time?

15-15. Suppose that in Problem 15-14 the bookstore has the option of backlogging orders and that it costs $1.667 to backlog a unit of demand for a year. (When backlogging is permitted inventory position is defined as inventory on hand plus inventory on order plus S^*.)

(a) What are the values for Q^*, N^*, T^*, S^*, and AHOB*?

(b) When an order is placed, what is the level of

    (i) Inventory on hand?

    (ii) Inventory on order?

    (iii) Inventory position?

(c) What is the demand during the lead time?

(d) Should the bookstore backlog orders?

15-16. XXX Distillery, a major producer of arthritis and nerve medicine in the Southeast, produces its stock in batches. In order to begin each run, the company owners must select a suitable location and assemble the equipment. The cost of this operation is $750. Production yields 48 gallons of product each day, each of which costs $0.05 per day to hold in inventory. Demand is constant at 600 gallons per month. Assume 12 months, 300 days per year, and 25 days per month.

(a) Find Q^*, N^*, and T^* for the optimal production lot size.

(b) Find the maximum inventory and the length (in days) of each production run for the optimal production lot size.

(c) Find AHO(Q^*).

15-17. Because of the importance of business confidentiality, XXX Distillery in Problem 15-16 decides to make four production runs per year.

(a) Find the production order quantity, Q^*, cycle time (in days), length of production run, and maximum inventory level.

(b) Find AHO for the policy in part (a).

15-18. Consider Problem 15-16.

(a) Suppose that XXX Distillery purchased rather than produced its product and that the cost of placing an order is $750. Find Q^* and AHO(Q^*).

(b) How does AHO(Q^*) in part (a) compare with AHO(Q^*) when there is a production rate of 48 gallons per day? Explain this relationship.

(c) Assume that the production rate is 96 gallons per day. Use the results of Problem 15-16 and part (a) to give upper and lower bounds for the optimal lot size and AHO.

15-19. Due to technical obsolescence of its equipment, XXX Distillery (Problem 15-16) stops producing and functions only as a marketing organization. It now purchases its product from another producer. XXX must buy at least 1200 gallons per order to qualify for a quantity discount. What is the smallest discount per gallon that would persuade XXX to order 1200 gallons?

15-20. The Clunker Car Company (CCC) produces automobiles based on the latest Model T technology. Part of the materials used in its newest line of import-competing automobiles, the C-Cars, are shown in Figure 15.19. CCC's current inventory levels include 300 throats, 200 butterfly valves, 250 spark plug sets (1 set per engine), 50 carburetors, and 75 engines.

Figure 15.19

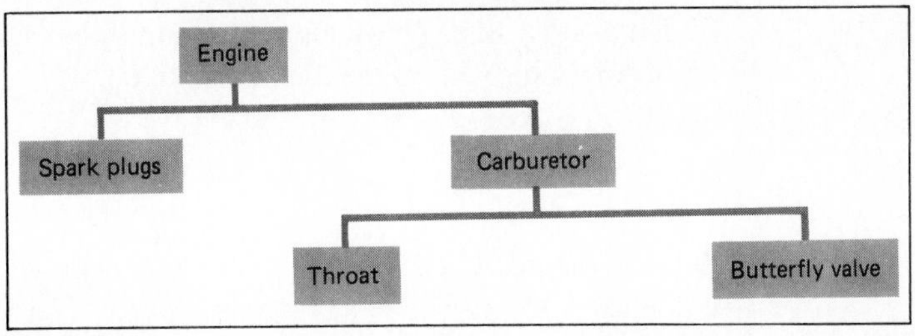

(a) What additional amounts of each part will be needed to satisfy an order for 375 engines?

(b) Assume that the lead time for assembly is 10 days for engines and 5 days for carburetors. Assume further that the lead time for ordering throats is 3 days, butterfly valves is 2 days, and spark plugs is 6 days. Find the ordering and assembly schedule for an order due in 30 days.

15-21. Solve Problem 15-20 with the following data:

    Current inventory
      150 throats
      100 butterfly valves
      125 spark plug sets
      90 carburetors
      130 engines
    Assembly time
      Engines, 8 days
      Carburetors, 6 days
    Ordering time
      Throats, 5 days
      Butterfly valves, 3 days
      Spark plugs, 5 days

What is the date that the first action must be taken? Which action is it?

APPENDIX 15.1

The EOQ Model

To derive expression (15.7), the optimal value of Q in the EOQ model, you must find the value of Q that minimizes expression (15.4), the annual holding and ordering cost.

$$\text{AHO} = C_0\left(\frac{D}{Q}\right) + C_h\left(\frac{Q}{2}\right)$$

Taking the first derivative with respect to Q yields

$$\frac{d}{dQ}\text{AHO} = \frac{-C_0 D}{Q^2} + \frac{C_h}{2}$$

Setting this result equal to zero and solving for Q gives

$$Q^* = \sqrt{\frac{2C_0 D}{C_h}}$$

which is (15.7).

    To demonstrate that Q^* yields a minimum, you take the second derivative of AHO with respect to Q and determine if it is positive:

$$\frac{d^2}{dQ^2}\text{AHO} = \frac{2C_0 D}{Q^3}$$

Since the result is positive for all $Q > 0$, you can conclude that Q^* yields a minimum.

Equality of the Annual Holding and Ordering Cost

It is useful to show that

$$C_0\left(\frac{D}{Q^*}\right) = C_h\left(\frac{Q^*}{2}\right)$$

that is, that the optimal order quantity yields equal values for the annual holding and annual ordering costs.

The demonstration is achieved by substituting the expression for Q^* into the left-hand side of the inequality and obtaining the right-hand side.

$$C_0\left(\frac{D}{Q^*}\right) = C_0 \frac{D}{(2C_0D/C_h)^{1/2}}$$

$$= C_0\left(\frac{2}{2}\right)\frac{DC_h^{1/2}}{(2C_0D)^{1/2}}\left(\frac{C_h}{C_h}\right)^{1/2}$$

$$= C_h\frac{1}{2}\left(\frac{2C_0D}{C_h}\right)^{1/2}$$

$$= C_h\left(\frac{Q^*}{2}\right)$$

Q. E. D.

CHAPTER 16

Inventory Models with Probabilistic Demand

16.1

INTRODUCTION

There are many sources of uncertainty in a typical production and distribution system. There is uncertainty as to how many items customers will demand during the next week, month, or year. There is uncertainty about delivery times. If one of your suppliers says that you will receive your order before January 5, can you rely on it or will your order arrive weeks or months later? There is uncertainty in the production processes. What happens to your production and delivery plans if a worker is sick or if a critical machine breaks down? Uncertainty exacts a toll from management in a variety of ways. A spurt in demand or a delay in production may lead to stockouts with the potential for lost revenue and customer dissatisfaction. Alternatively, a firm might react to a current or anticipated stockout by expediting orders, placing special orders with a supplier, or working overtime. All of these activities can be costly.

Firms typically hold inventory to provide protection against uncertainty. Clearly, a cushion of inventory on hand allows management to face unexpected demands or delays in delivery with a reduced chance of incurring a stockout. We have, however, already observed that holding inventory is not free. The question, then, is: How much inventory should a firm hold to provide reasonable protection against uncertainty?

In previous chapters we have seen that management attempts to deal with such questions about uncertainty in a variety of ways. For example, in LP models, sensitivity analysis is typically used to assure management that its decisions are not vulnerable to changes in the parameters of the model. This chapter considers uncertainty in a more formal fashion. It looks at models in which uncertainty is dealt with explicitly by incorporating a *probability distribution of demand* into the evaluation of the various alternative inventory control schemes.

The chapter has two main divisions. The first deals with the *reorder point–reorder quantity* models that were introduced in the preceding chapter. The new twist is that a distribution for lead-time demand will be introduced. Also, no backlogging will be allowed. The second division introduces *one-period inventory models*. These models are appropriate for situations in which only one ordering decision is to be made in anticipa-

536

tion of future demand. Such models are directly applicable to purchase decisions involving, for example, style goods or perishable products. The rationale for these models also provides the basis for more complex models involving a sequence of ordering decisions.

16.2

THE REORDER POINT-REORDER QUANTITY MODEL

In the preceding chapter we have seen Victor Kowalski develop a reorder point–reorder quantity model to control the inventory of appliance angles. There are three main points to review:

1. *The rule itself:* The operating rule in a reorder point–reorder quantity model is specified by two parameters: the reorder point (r) and the reorder quantity (Q). The operating rule states that when the inventory position[1] equals r, an order for Q items should be placed. Because this model is defined by its two parameters, it is commonly referred to as an (r, Q) model. We will adopt this notation.
2. *Determining Q:* The reorder quantity, Q, is determined using the EOQ (economic order quantity) model. This model must be modified to take quantity discounts and backlogging into account when such factors are appropriate.
3. *Determining r:* The reorder point, r, is chosen to protect the firm from running out of stock during the lead time. If demand is known with certainty, then r is set equal to the demand during the lead time.

16.3

THE APPLIANCE ANGLE PROBLEM

A Review　　Let us review some of the details of Victor's problem and the EOQ model that he used to solve it. The model assumed that demand occurred at a constant and known rate of 5000 items per month. The cost of placing an order and the annual holding cost per item were specified as $25.00 and $1.92, respectively. STECO purchased items from the mill at $8.00 each unless orders were placed in lots of at least 5000 items, in which case the price was $7.90 per unit. Under these conditions Victor discovered, using the EOQ formulas, that an order quantity of 5000 items minimized the annual total cost (ATC), defined as the sum of the purchase, ordering, and inventory costs during the year.

Model with　　Under the assumption that demand is known and occurs at a constant rate, we saw
Known　　that the reorder point r, as noted in point 3, should be set equal to the demand during
Demand　　the lead time. Since demand was assumed to be 5000 items per month, if the lead time was one-half a month, Victor would select the reorder point of 2500 angles (i.e., $r = 2500$). With these assumptions, inventory would run out at just the instant the order arrived (see Figure 16.1).

　　We also noted in Chapter 15 that in reality demand is almost never known with certainty and thus that selecting the reorder point r, as described above, may well result in a stockout. In the previous example anytime demand during the 2-week lead time exceeds 2500, there will be a stockout. Each unfilled order could represent a serious loss to

537　　[1]Inventory position is defined as inventory on hand plus that already on order.

Figure 16.1
(r, Q) Model with Known Demand

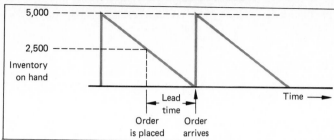

STECO. If the customer were not willing to wait for a late delivery (i.e., demand cannot be backlogged), STECO would lose the profit from this potential sale. In addition, the customer might choose to do business in the future with a firm that can provide better service.

One obvious way to reduce the chance of running out of stock is to increase the value of r. There is another side to this story, however. Increasing r increases on the average the amount of inventory that Steco will hold. If Victor increases r to 2750 and the average demand is 2500, then clearly, on the average, he will have 250 items on hand when the next order arrives. Holding inventory is not free. Indeed, one of the two cost components considered in the EOQ model is the cost of holding inventory. Victor is thus faced with a classical management problem. If he increases r, the reorder point, he decreases the chance that he will run out of stock, but he increases his average inventory

**The
Trade-Offs** holding cost. If he decreases r, he increases the chance of running out, but decreases the average inventory holding cost. The question is: "How large should r be to achieve the proper balance between these two factors?" In the preceding chapter it was suggested that a manager might *intuitively* add an appropriate safety stock to the average lead-time demand to solve this problem. In this chapter we give a formal framework for thinking about the choice of r. It will be seen that this framework can assist management in making a more informed decision.

16.4

VICTOR'S CHOICE OF r: UNIFORM LEAD-TIME DEMAND

The analytic approach that is commonly used to determine the reorder point is to assume that the probability distribution of demand during the lead time is known. In other words, it is not assumed that demand is exactly known but, rather, the probabilities with which it might assume various values are assumed to be known. For example, rather than assuming that demand during the lead time is 2500 units, it might be assumed that demand would equal 2475 with probability one-half and 2525 with probability one-half. Indeed, the term "decisions under risk" is used by many authors to indicate a situation in which the probabilities of the uncertain events are known.

Victor knows something about the demand for angles from his experience in sales. It seems to him that the demand during the $\frac{1}{2}$-month lead time is never more than 3000 items or less than 2001. Between these two extremes one level of demand seems about as likely as the next. Since there are 1000 numbers in this interval, this implies that the probability that demand equals 2482 or 2535 or any other number in the interval is 1/1000. In other words, Victor initially approaches the problem of choosing r by assuming that lead-time demand is uniformly distributed over the interval from 2001 to 3000. With this assumption, Victor can easily control the probability of a stockout. Consider the following examples:

1. If Victor sets r equal to any value larger than 3000, he will never run out during the lead time. For example, if he sets r equal to 3010, he will always have at least 10 angles on hand when the next order arrives. Since demand during the lead time is ≤ 3000 and he starts with 3010 on hand, he must have at least 10 on hand at the end of the lead time.

2. If an r of 2995 is selected, a stockout will occur if demand is 2996, 2997, 2998, 2999, or 3000. Since the probability of each of these quantities is 1/1000, the probability of a stockout is $5/1000 = 0.005$.

These examples indicate how the probability of a stockout can be controlled by the choice of r. Generalizing this discussion, we see that if the reorder point is r, with $r < 3000$, then a stockout will occur if demand is $r + 1, r + 2, \ldots, 3000$. If we let $p(s)$ be the probability of a stockout, then if $r \geq 3000$, $p(s)$ is zero. If $r < 3000$, then

$$- \qquad p(s) = \frac{3000 - r}{1000}$$

Some values of $p(s)$ and r are shown in Figure 16.2.

Selecting r
Determines the
Probability of
a Stockout

Figure 16.2 illustrates the intuitively appealing fact that as r increases, $p(s)$ decreases. It also establishes the idea that specifying $p(s)$ dictates a value for r. To see this you must simply read Figure 16.2 from right to left. If Victor wants the probability of stocking out to equal 0.05, then he must choose $r = 2950$. Similarly, a $p(s)$ of 0.13 implies an r of 2870.

Victor now understands that choosing $p(s)$ implies a value for r, and vice versa. He still does not know how to choose a "good" value for r, or $p(s)$. One approach would be to assign a "penalty cost" per unit stockout. Victor would then choose r to minimize the expected holding and penalty cost during the lead time. One problem with this would be that penalty costs can be difficult to assess. In any case, an example of this

Figure 16.2
r, the Reorder Point versus $p(s)$,
the Probability of a Stockout,
Assuming Uniform Lead-Time
Demand

r	$p(s)$
3010	0
3000	0
2950	0.05
2920	0.08
2870	0.13
2750	0.25
2500	0.50

type of approach is presented in the second half of this chapter in connection with the discussion of one-period inventory models.

Another way to determine r, or $p(s)$, is to intuitively balance several implications. This is discussed in the next three sections.

SELECTING A PROBABILITY OF STOCKING OUT

We have just illustrated the fact that choosing the reorder point r is equivalent to choosing $p(s)$, the probability of stocking out during the lead time to delivery. In thinking about the appropriate value for $p(s)$ in the case of appliance angles Victor considers the following facts:

1. Appliance angles are carried by all steel wholesalers.
2. The lead time for delivery from the steel mill is 2 weeks. Thus, STECO cannot quickly replenish its supply.

The result of these two facts is that if STECO is unable to fill an order when it is placed, the customer will almost always go to another supplier. Victor thus wants to make sure that STECO does not run out very often. Consequently, he wants to select a small value for $p(s)$.

Number of Stockouts per Year
To get a feeling for the effects of a particular choice of $p(s)$, he might ask: "Suppose I choose $p(s) = 0.05$. How often will I stockout *during a year*?" There is no certain numerical answer to Victor's question. We can, however, make the following observations:

1. Since the order quantity Q is 5000, and since annual demand is 60,000, there are 12 orders placed per year. Thus, during each year there are 12 lead times, which means 12 opportunities to stockout. This is the maximum number of stockouts that can occur.
2. During *each* lead time STECO will stockout with a probability of $p(s)$. This is independent of whether a stockout occurred during any previous lead time or not.

Thus, if $p(s) = 0.05$ for *each* lead time, and we have 12 lead times a year, there will be, on the average, $(0.05)(12) = 0.6$ stockout per year, which means an average of 6 stockouts every 10 years. Victor may well be willing to select a value for $p(s)$ on the basis, as above, of *average stockouts per year*. But he can also obtain more specific information.

The two observations above imply that the **binomial distribution** can be used to calculate the probability of incurring any specific number of stockouts during a year. In general terms, the binomial distribution assumes two inputs: (1) an event that has a probability, say α, of occurring at a given trial and (2) a sequence of n independent trials. Then[2]

Binomial Distribution

The probability of having the event occur exactly x times in n trials

$$= \frac{n!}{x!\,(n-x)!}\alpha^x(1-\alpha)^{n-x} \qquad \text{for } x = 0, 1, 2, \ldots, n \qquad (16.1)$$

In the angles example the interpretation of a "trial" would be "lead time," and the "event" under consideration would be "a stockout during a lead time." Thus, $\alpha = p(s)$. Since there are 12 lead times per year, we would have $n = 12$. Choosing, as above, $p(s) = 0.05$, we can compute the probability of exactly x stockouts from the expression

[2]The term $n! = n(n-1)(n-2) \cdots 1$. For example, $4! = 4 \cdot 3 \cdot 2 \cdot 1 = 24$. By convention, $0!$ is assigned the value 1.

$$\frac{12!}{x!(12-x)!}(0.05)^x(0.95)^{n-x}$$

Victor can use this expression to calculate probability of any specific number of stockouts in a year. For example, he computes that the probability of zero stockouts is 0.54, and there will be exactly 1 stockout (in a year) with probability 0.34. Although he now has the possibility of deriving considerable specific information, he would like a simple statistic to use in comparing the effects of alternative values of $p(s)$. Since he does not want to stockout "very often," he decides to compute the probability that he will stockout more than once during a year.

He makes use of the following relationship:

Prob {more than one stockout}
$$= 1 - \{\text{Prob [zero stockouts]} + \text{Prob [one stockout]}\} \qquad (16.2)$$

In particular, when $p(s) = 0.05$,

$$P\{\text{more than one stockout}\} = 1 - \{0.54 + 0.34\} = 0.12$$

Probability of More Than One Stockout where, as given above, Prob {0 stockouts} = 0.54, and Prob {1 stockout} = 0.34. Similar analysis can be used to construct a table such as the one shown in Figure 16.3. This table incorporates two implications which follow from a choice of $p(s)$ or r: (1) probability of more than one stockout in a year and (2) average number of stockouts per year.

In concluding this section, two points should be emphasized:

1. The first two columns of Figure 16.3 [i.e., the relation between r and $p(s)$] depend on the probability distribution of demand during the lead time. Recall in the discussion above that Victor assumed a probability of 1/1000 for all integer demands from 2001 to (and including) 3000.

2. The last two columns of Figure 16.3 have nothing to do with the probability distribution of lead time demand. They are based on
   a. The probability of a stockout during *each* lead time [the value of $p(s)$]
   b. The number of orders placed each year (the value of n, which is determined by Q)

Effect of Changing Q To emphasize the last point, recall that Victor selected an order quantity Q of 5000 items. Since his model anticipates an annual demand of 60,000 items, $n = 12$ (i.e., 60,000/5000) orders are planned for each year. Suppose that, instead of 5000, an order quantity of $Q = 10,000$ items had been selected. In this case only six orders would be planned each

Figure 16.3
Data When Demand Is Uniform

$p(s)$	r	PROBABILITY OF MORE THAN ONE STOCKOUT PER YEAR	AVERAGE NUMBER OF STOCKOUTS PER YEAR
0	3000	0	0
0.02	2980	0.03	0.24
0.05	2950	0.12	0.6
0.10	2900	0.34	1.2
0.25	2750	0.84	3
0.50	2500	0.997	6

year; that is, there would be six times throughout the year during which a stockout could occur. Then, with $p(s) = 0.05$ and $n = 6$, expression (16.1) produces

$$\text{probability of no stockouts} = \frac{6!}{0!\,6!}(0.05)^0(0.95)^6 = 0.735$$

$$\text{probability of one stockout} = \frac{6!}{1!\,5!}(0.05)^1(0.95)^5 = 0.232$$

Thus, the probability of more than one stockout during the year becomes $1 - (0.735 + 0.232) = 0.033$. This compares with 0.12 for the case of 12 orders per year. Also note that, with six orders per year there are, on the average, 0.3 stockouts per year, as opposed to 0.6 in the previous case. We see, then, that only Q and $p(s)$ play a role in determining the last two columns of Figure 16.3.

16.6

VICTOR'S CHOICE OF r: NORMAL LEAD-TIME DEMAND

Practical Victor assumed that demand during lead time was uniformly distributed between 2001
Motivation and 3000. Many of the commercial inventory control systems find it useful to assume
for Using the that the demand during the lead time has a normal probability distribution. This assump-
Normal tion is popular for two main reasons:

1. It is a good enough approximation to reality to yield useful results.
2. The normal probability distribution is completely characterized by two parameters: the mean, μ, and the standard deviation, σ. Since only two numbers are required to specify the demand for each product, it is easy to store in a computer the probability distribution for many (in some cases, thousands) products. Think how much space would be required if you had to specify, for each product, a different probability distribution with 1000 possible outcomes.

Victor has just learned that ICON, the inventory control system used at STECO, assumes that demand during the lead time has a normal distribution. Since the inventory of angles will actually be controlled by this system, Victor decides to find out how this system would select r. He learns that by using past demands, the system has estimated that the demand during the lead time has a mean, μ, of 2500 and standard deviation, σ, of 250. A diagram of this distribution is shown in Figure 16.4.

Determination The assumption that demand during the lead time has a normal distribution with $\mu = $
of r 2500 and $\sigma = 250$ makes it possible for Victor to find the appropriate r for any value of
$p(s)$, the probability of a stockout during a lead time, that he chooses. For example, suppose that he wants to have, as previously, $p(s) = 0.05$. Refer to Table T.1 in Appendix B, and you will see that an r value that is 1.645 standard deviations above the mean corresponds to a $p(s)$ of 0.05. It follows that for the assumed normal distribution with $\mu = 2500$ and $\sigma = 250$, as shown in Figure 16.4, the reorder point r is given by $r = 2500 + 1.645(250) = 2911.25$. Similar calculations, using different values for $p(s)$, yield the data shown in Figure 16.5.

These data should be compared with Figure 16.3. You can see that for the same

Figure 16.4

Normal Demand for Angles with $\mu = 2500$, $\sigma = 250$

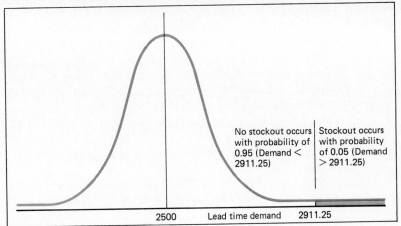

No stockout occurs with probability of 0.95 (Demand < 2911.25)

Stockout occurs with probability of 0.05 (Demand > 2911.25)

2500   Lead time demand   2911.25

values of $p(s)$ the two figures give different values for r. This shows how changing the distribution of lead-time demand changes the relation between r and $p(s)$. However, since the order quantity Q is 5000 and thus there are 12 orders per year, the last two columns of Figure 16.5 remain the same as in Figure 16.3.

Figure 16.5

Data When Demand Is Normal with $\mu = 2500$, $\sigma = 250$

$p(s)$	r	PROBABILITY OF MORE THAN ONE STOCKOUT PER YEAR	AVERAGE NUMBER OF STOCKOUTS PER YEAR
0.02	3013.5	0.03	0.24
0.05	2911.2	0.12	0.6
0.10	2820.2	0.34	1.2
0.25	2668.5	0.84	3
0.50	2500.0	0.997	6

16.7

EXPECTED ANNUAL COST OF SAFETY STOCK

We have discussed several implications of selecting a particular value for the reorder point, r. One is the average number of stockouts per year. Another is the probability of stocking out more than once during a year. Associated with various choices for r will be a safety stock, and a consideration of importance is the expected annual holding cost that is associated with keeping this safety stock. Recall that the **safety stock** has been defined as the quantity that is added to the expected demand during the lead time to protect against uncertainty. Thus,

safety stock $= r -$ expected demand during the lead time[3]

[3]Expected demand during the lead time is the mean of the lead-time demand distribution.

It is a fact that the average inventory on hand during a year is increased by an amount equal to the safety stock. To understand this, recall if Victor selected a $p(s) = 0.05$, the appropriate value of r using the normal distribution for lead-time demand is 2911.2 (see Figure 16.5). Since the expected demand during the lead time is the mean of our normal distribution, namely 2500, we see that the safety stock, in this instance is 411.2 units. This situation is shown in Figure 16.6. Here we see that sometimes demand is less than and sometimes greater than the mean demand (2500). On the average, however, demand will equal 2500 units and thus STECO will have increased the average amount of inventory on hand by the safety stock. Recall from Chapter 15 that C_h, STECO's cost of holding an angle in inventory for a year, is $1.92. Then,

$$\text{expected annual cost of safety stock} = C_h \cdot (\text{safety stock}) = 1.92(411.2) = 789.50$$

Other costs could be calculated for other values of r. These calculations are combined with previous calculations in Figure 16.5 to yield Figure 16.7.

Figure 16.6
Random Demand during the Lead Time

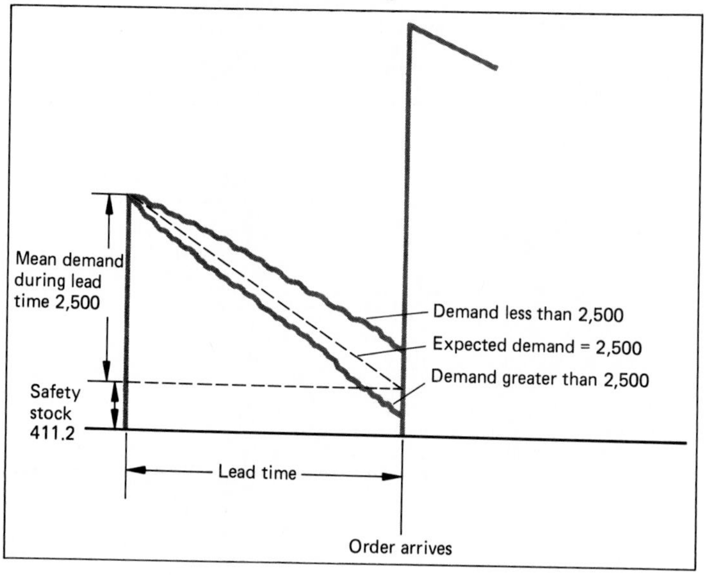

Figure 16.7
Characteristics When Demand Is Normal with $\mu = 2500$, $\sigma = 250$

$p(s)$	r	SAFETY STOCK	PROBABILITY OF MORE THAN ONE STOCKOUT PER YEAR	AVERAGE NUMBER OF STOCKOUTS PER YEAR	EXPECTED ANNUAL COST OF SAFETY STOCK
0.02	3013.5	513.5	0.03	0.24	$985.92
0.05	2911.2	411.2	0.12	0.6	789.50
0.10	2820.2	320.2	0.34	1.2	614.78
0.25	2668.5	168.5	0.84	3	323.52
0.50	2500	0	0.997	6	0

This table makes it easier for management to understand the trade-off between holding inventory and stocking out, and provides the basis for at least a partially enlightened choice for the reorder point, r. Management can compare, for example, the case when $p(s) = 0.05$ and $r = 2911$ with the no-safety-stock situation, $p(s) = 0.5$ and $r = 2500$. Here it costs \$789.50 to decrease the probability of more than one stockout per year from 0.997 to 0.12 (also, to decrease the average number of stockouts per year from 6 to less than 1). Rather than asking himself, "Do I prefer a $p(s)$ of 0.50 to one of 0.05?" a manager can ask, "Is it worth about \$789.50 to decrease the probability of more than one stockout per year from 0.997 to 0.12?" With $p(s) = 0.50$ he would expect to stockout more than once essentially every year, whereas with $p(s) = 0.05$ he would expect to stockout more than once (during the year) only about once in every 8 years ($\frac{1}{8} = 0.125$).

*Role of
Management
Judgment*

A table like Figure 16.7 provides an excellent example of how management could typically make use of formal models. The models are used to generate data, such as those shown in the table. Based on these data, and his own experience, the manager uses his judgment in making his decision.

16.8

ONE-PERIOD MODELS WITH PROBABILISTIC DEMAND (WILES' HOUSEWARES PROBLEM)

Peggy McConnel is the chief buyer for housewares at Wiles, Chicago's leading retailer. The chief buyer's role is important in a retail organization like Wiles. Peggy is responsible for designing the overall retailing strategy and operating procedures for her area. She also supervises a group of buyers who make specific purchase decisions.

Certain sections of the housewares department have just suffered their second consecutive bad year. Competing shops, such as Box and Barrel, which specialize in imported cooking and dining articles, have made serious inroads into Wiles' once secure position. The gourmet cooking, glassware, stainless flatware, and contemporary dishes sections of Wiles are not generating enough revenue to justify the amount of floor space currently committed to them.

Peggy plans to meet this challenge head-on. She has reorganized the sections that are in trouble to create a store within a store. To achieve the same ambience as her competitors, she has adopted display techniques that feature natural wood and modern lighting. She has essentially created a specialty shop, like her competitors, within the housewares department. With these changes, plus Wiles' reputation for quality and service, she feels that they can effectively compete.

*Special
Sale*

To introduce the new facility at Wiles, Peggy decides to make the month of October "International Dining Month." This promotion will feature a sale on five special articles, each from a different country. These articles will be especially made for Wiles and include a copper omelet pan from France, a set of 12 long-stem wine glasses from Spain, and so on. Each of the items has been selected by a buyer on Peggy's staff. The design and price are agreed on. The items have to be ordered at least 6 months in advance and they will not become part of Wiles' regular product line. Any items left at the end of October will be sold to a discount chain at a reduced price. In addition, Wiles has adopted the policy that if they run out of the special sale items, a more expensive item from their regular line of merchandise will be substituted at the sale price. It is all part of the "once in a lifetime" promotion.

Peggy and her buyers must decide how many of these items to order now, 6 long months before the sale takes place in October. If demand were known, the decision would be easy. Order the quantity demanded. But demand is uncertain. *If they order too many, excess items will be sold at a loss. If they order too few, substitute items must be sold at a loss.* Unfortunately, they cannot find help by examining the (r, Q) inventory system that Wiles uses for stock items in housewares. This problem does not fit that mold. The (r, Q) model balances reorder costs and inventory holding costs. Here the ordering cost is not in question. Each item will be ordered once. Peggy needs to balance the cost of ordering too much against the cost of ordering too little. A new approach is required.

16.9
THE NEWSBOY PROBLEM

The problem faced by Peggy and her staff is a classic management science problem known as the newsboy problem, first seen in Section 14.2. In this problem the newsboy buys Q papers from the delivery truck driver at the beginning of the day. During the day he sells papers. How many he will sell is unknown in advance. At the end of the day any leftover papers are worthless. If he buys more than he sells, he loses the money associated with the leftover papers. If he does not buy enough, he loses the potential profits from additional sales.

Suppose that he pays C dollars for each paper and sells them for S dollars each. Let $C = \$0.10$ and $S = \$0.25$. The model is built on three components.

Components
of the
Newsboy
Problem

1. The holding cost, h, is the cost per unit to the newsboy of each leftover paper. In this example
$$h = C = \$0.10$$

2. The penalty cost, p, is the potential profit that the newsboy "loses" with each paper that could have been sold but was not because he had run out. In this example,
$$P = S - C$$
$$= \$0.25 - \$0.10$$
$$= \$0.15$$

3. The probability distribution of demand.

Probability
Distribution
of Demand

The information about the probability that demand takes on particular values is contained in the probability distribution of demand. One would expect this distribution to be different for different products, times, and so on. Indeed, the form of the distribution can change. In some cases a normal distribution is appropriate. Other distributions may be more realistic in other cases. In this example, suppose, for simplicity, that the newsboy employs a *uniform* distribution. In particular, suppose he believes that any demand between 1 and 100 is equally likely. Thus,

$$\text{Prob \{demand} = \text{any integer from 1 through 100\}} = 1/100$$

It thus follows that

$$\text{Prob \{demand} \le x\} \begin{cases} = 0 & \text{where } x \le 0 \\ = x/100 & \text{where } x = 1, 2, \ldots, 100 \\ = 1 & \text{where } x \ge 100 \end{cases}$$

The three components (p, h, and the probability distribution of demand) come together in the following rule to determine Q^*, the optimal (i.e., *cost minimizing*) order quantity.[4]

Optimal Order Quantity

Q^* is the smallest integer such that $P\{\text{demand} \leq Q^*\} \geq \dfrac{p}{p+h}$ (16.3)

In our example, $p = \$0.15$, $h = \$0.10$, and

$$P\{\text{demand} \leq x\} = \frac{x}{100} \quad \text{for } x = 1, 2, \ldots, 100$$

Substituting these values into (16.3) tells us to find the smallest integer Q^* such that $P\{\text{demand} \leq Q^*\} \geq P/p + h$, which means Q^* is the smallest integer satisfying $Q^*/100 \geq 0.15/(0.15 + 0.10) = 0.60$, which means $Q^* = 60$.

If Peggy is to fit her problem into the newsboy model, she must specify each of the three components. Consider the copper omelet pan. Wiles will buy these pans for $22.00 each and will sell them for $35.00. Any pans left at the end of the sale will be sold to Clampton's Discount Chain for $15.00 each. If Wiles runs out of these pans, they will substitute one of their regular copper omelet pans and sell it for the sale price of $35.00. These regular pans cost $32.00 each and normally sell for $65.00. These data provide the basis for calculating the cost parameters in the newsboy problem.

Determining the Cost Parameters

1. Let us first determine the holding cost, h. Since Wiles pays $22.00 for each pan and sells each leftover pan for $15.00, the store loses $7.00 on each pan not sold during the sale. Thus, $h = \$7.00$.
2. Next, let us look at the penalty cost, p. Each time a regular pan is substituted for a sale pan to satisfy excess demand, Wiles gains $3.00 ($35.00 $-$ $32.00). If a sale pan had been available, Wiles would have gained $13.00 ($35.00 $-$ $22.00). Taking into account this "foregone gain," and treating it as an "opportunity cost," we see that the cost per unit of running out of sale omelet pans is $10.00 ($13.00 $-$ $3.00).

Specifying the Probability Distribution of Demand

3. Peggy must also specify the probability distribution of demand. This is not easy. There are no directly applicable historical data. Wiles has not tried exactly this promotion before. There is, however, information about the results of other sales. In addition, Peggy has opinions and information about the state of the economy, the desirability of this particular item, and so on.

Faced with the fact that she must specify a probability distribution, she uses the following approach.
   a. Her best guess for demand during the sale is 1000 pans. She feels it is equally likely that actual demand may exceed or fall short of this best guess.
   b. She feels confident that demand will not be less than 700 pans or more than 1300.
   c. A demand near 1000 seems much more likely than one near 700 or 1300.

Based on these three observations, Peggy decides on the following model:

1. Demand is normal.
2. The mean, μ, equals her best estimate of demand, $\mu = 1000$.

[4]The derivation of this result would require a technical discussion which we have chosen to omit because of constraints on space. Although this formulation of the Newsboy problem may appear to differ from the formulation in Section 14.2, it can be shown that either formulation leads to the same optimal order quantity. These are two equivalent ways of viewing the same problem.

3. The standard deviation, σ, is given by the calculation

$$\sigma = \frac{1300 - 700}{6} = 100$$

This calculation is based on the observation that an interval 3 standard deviations above and 3 standard deviations below the mean includes almost all possible outcomes. In other words, the distance between the largest and the smallest potential outcomes is $3 + 3 = 6$ standard deviations. This distribution is shown in Figure 16.8.

With the assumption that demand is normal with $\mu = 1000$ and $\sigma = 100$, and using the values determined above for h and p, the optimal order quantity Q^* is found by solving equation (16.3). Peggy must select Q^* to be the smallest integer such that

$$P\{\text{demand} \leq Q^*\} \geq \frac{p}{p + h} = 0.588$$

Figure 16.8
Normal Distribution with $\mu = 1000$ and $\sigma = 100$

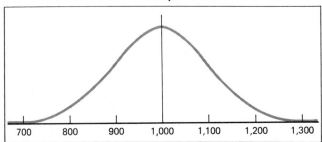

| 700 | 800 | 900 | 1,000 | 1,100 | 1,200 | 1,300 |

Optimal We see from Table T.1 in Appendix B that 0.588 of the area under the curve for a normal
Number of distribution lies to the left of a point that is about 0.22 standard deviation above the
Pans mean. Since Peggy has assumed a mean of 1000 and a standard deviation of 100,

$$Q^* = 1000 + 0.22(100) = 1022$$

In other words, given her specification of of h, p, and the probability distribution of demand, the newsboy model indicates that Peggy should order 1022 omelet pans.

Let us now suppose that Peggy changes her distribution. Instead of using the normal, suppose that she were to assume a uniform distribution on the interval from 700 to 1300. In this case,

$$P\{\text{demand} \leq x\} = \frac{x - 700}{600} \qquad \text{for } x = 701, 702, \ldots, 1300$$

and solving (16.3) for Q^* gives

$$P\{\text{demand} \leq Q^*\} = \frac{Q^* - 700}{600} \geq 0.588$$

$$Q^* = 600(0.588) + 700 = 1052.8$$

and hence $Q^* = 1053$. With the normal assumption she orders 1022. Had she used the uniform distribution, she would order 1053. You can see that the assumption about the distribution of demand can be of considerable importance. It is typical of probabilistic inventory models that assumptions about the distribution of demand can greatly affect the recommended decision. That is why care must be exercised to find a distribution that best approximates reality. You can think of the distribution itself as a model of reality—a model that we then use in another model to recommend a decision.

16.10

NOTES ON IMPLEMENTATION

Two-Bin System
Inventory control is one of the oldest and most common applications of quantitative models. In manufacturing companies, the most popular implementation of inventory control models has been historically the "two-bin" inventory system. In this system a certain number of items are set aside, in bin 1, so to speak. All other items are held in another location, bin 2. Items are removed from bin 2 in order to satisfy demand. When bin 2 is empty and the stock clerk starts to use items from bin 1, this is the signal to place an order for a predetermined quantity of items. In the 1950s a computer card would be attached to bin 1. When the clerk removed the first item from bin 1 he also removed the computer card and sent it to inventory control. This card initiated the order for the item.

The two-bin system is a method of implementing the reorder point–reorder quantity model. The age of cheap computing and remote terminal entry has made this system less important. In more current versions, the process of billing a customer will often automatically adjust the inventory level. For example, the cash register in a department store, as well as itemizing your bill, will often make a record of the item you purchased. This information is fed to a computer, which adjusts the inventory level and triggers a reorder when appropriate. The data accumulated with such devices can also be used in evaluating the success of a product line and forecasting future demand.

Commercial Inventory Software Packages
A number of computer manufacturers offer an inventory control package as a standard part of their software package. Packages of some long standing include IBM's IMPACT, Honeywell's PROFIT, and RCA's WISDOM. IBM also has a more recent entry in the field entitled INFOREM, *In*ventory *Fo*recasting and *Re*plenishment *M*odels.

To the extent that one can generalize, these packages are based on the use of exponential smoothing (see Chapter 17) for forecasting and a reorder point–reorder quantity model as the inventory control mechanism. Each package has its own features, and we do not intend to go into detail here. It is, however, interesting to note that simulation (see Chapter 18) is an option in certain cases. This makes it possible to evaluate the operation of the system under various sets of parameters (e.g., reorder point, reorder quantity, or demand distribution) or to compare the operations of different types of systems. The very existence of these different packages indicates the importance of the inventory management function.

In some industries (or activities) inventory control has a special significance and the assumptions underlying the standard packages (IMPACT, etc.) do not fit very well. In such cases it pays for the organization to develop its own inventory control system. One example is provided by the steel wholesaling business (like STECO). Here, for certain products, the idiosyncrasies of the supplier, the steel manufacturers, make it difficult to use a standard approach. Certain types of steel are produced in large batches (heats) on a schedule that is known a year or so in advance. The wholesaler must determine if he wishes to buy part of a particular heat or not. Once a heat is sold out, prospective buyers must wait for the next heat. This uncertainty in supply must be reflected in the inventory control system for these items.

Replacement Parts Another example, where organizations may need to develop their own self-tailored systems, is provided by the inventory of replacement parts for complicated systems. The military services have an enormous number of items of this sort. Consider an electric generator that is an important part of a nuclear sub. The number of such items in service is small and they fail infrequently. Since they are expensive, the inventory carrying cost is high. One thus would like to hold a minimal inventory. On the other hand, the penalty cost of running out is also high. Losing the service of a multimillion dollar sub for several weeks while a new generator is built has high opportunity costs. In many such cases, the following type of rule is employed. "Order an item for inventory each time an item is withdrawn."

The bottom line is that inventory control is an important management function and that quantitative models have made and are making an important contribution in this area. Although the mathematics may vary from one specific model to another, the concept of balancing ordering, holding, and stockout costs remains valid across many applications. General managers should understand the assumptions and operating implications of their own system. The blind assumption that because an inventory control system is large, complex, and computerized, it therefore cannot be understood, and/or must be all right, is a large first step in the wrong direction.

16.11
MAJOR CONCEPTS QUIZ

True–False

1. **T F** In probabilistic inventory models, penalty costs are typically used to prevent ordering too frequently.

2. **T F** The reorder point must be chosen to balance the number of stockouts versus holding cost.

3. **T F** The expected annual cost of a safety stock depends on only three quantities: r, the mean of the lead-time demand distribution, and the holding cost C_h.

4. **T F** For different lead-time demand distributions, as long as $p(s)$ is the same, the safety stock level will also be the same.

5. **T F** Q plays an important role in determining the average number of stockouts per year.

6. **T F** The tools developed in this chapter serve to automate the choice of r.

7. **T F** In the newsboy model, the proper definition of penalty cost involves the concept of foregone profit, or so-called "opportunity" cost.

8. **T F** Suppose that known annual demand is 60,000, and each order is for 15,000 items. Then a maximum of 4 stockouts per year can occur.

Multiple Choice

9. The probability of incurring exactly 2 stockouts in a given year can be determined by using
   a. the uniform distribution
   b. the normal distribution
   c. the binomial distribution
   d. all of the above

10. The correspondence between $p(s)$ and r depends on
   a. the average number of stockouts in a year
   b. the lead time demand distribution
   c. the safety stock level

11. The choice of $p(s)$, as well as the number of orders placed per year, determine
   a. average number of stockouts per year
   b. the probability of more than 1 stockout in a year
   c. parameters for the binomial distribution
   d. all of the above
   e. none of the above

12. The normal distribution is convenient to work with because
   a. it is specified by only two parameters, μ and σ
   b. the same table is used no matter how one chooses μ and σ (i.e., for *any normal distribution*)
   c. it is often a good approximation to reality
   d. all of the above
   e. none of the above

13. The newsboy model
   a. balances holding and penalty cost for a one-period problem
   b. minimizes ordering, holding, and penalty cost for a one-period problem
   c. applies only to problems for which there is a uniform or normal distribution of demand
   d. all of the above

14. Consider the smallest integer Q^* that satisfies

$$P\{\text{demand} \leq Q^*\} \geq \frac{p}{p + h}$$

   a. The value of Q^* will depend on the assumed distribution of demand.
   b. The value of Q^* provides the optimal order quantity for the newsboy model.
   c. The value of Q^* minimizes the sum of expected holding and penalty costs in the newsboy model.
   d. All of the above.

15. The assumption about the lead-time demand distribution
   a. can affect the cost of keeping a given safety stock level
   b. will typically affect the choice of a safety stock level
   c. will affect the average number of stockouts per year
   d. both a and b

Answers

1. F	6. F	11. d
2. T	7. T	12. d
3. T	8. T	13. a
4. F	9. c	14. d
5. T	10. b	15. b

16.12

PROBLEMS

16-1. At PROTRAC's Seattle outlet the demand during a week for the overhaul kit for small marine engines is a random variable with the following distribution:

$$p(0) = 0.01 \qquad p(7) = 0.13$$
$$p(1) = 0.03 \qquad p(8) = 0.11$$
$$p(2) = 0.06 \qquad p(9) = 0.09$$
$$p(3) = 0.09 \qquad p(10) = 0.06$$
$$p(4) = 0.11 \qquad p(11) = 0.03$$
$$p(5) = 0.13 \qquad p(12) = 0.01$$
$$p(6) = 0.14$$

The kits cost $166.67 each, the cost of placing an order is $50, the cost of holding a kit in inventory for a year is 20% of the purchase price, and delivery lead time is 1 week. Assume 50 weeks per year and derive an (r, Q) model with a probability of 0.04 of stocking out during a cycle.

16-2. Pierce Dears, the lead salesman for PROTRAC's Seattle outlet, has just negotiated a contract to sell 18 overhaul kits per week to Goal, the discount chain store, for the foreseeable future. Since this demand is deterministic Pierce decides to adjust the inventory control policy as shown in Figure 16.9.

Figure 16.9

CHARACTERISTIC	PARAMETERS FOR THE INVENTORY POLICY IN PROBLEM 16-1	PARAMETER FOR THE INVENTORY POLICY IN PROBLEM 16-2
Order quantity	Q^*	$Q^* + 18T^*$
Cycle time (weeks)	T^*	T^*
Reorder point	r^*	r^*

In words, he has simply increased the order quantity to cover the demand during the cycle time. Since the additional demand is deterministic he says there is no need to change r.

(a) Is this a good policy? Explain your answer.

(b) What policy would you recommend if Pierce wanted to maintain a 0.04 probability of stocking out during an inventory cycle?

16-3. Assume that PROTRAC's Seattle outlet uses the optimal policy in Problem 16-1.

(a) What is the probability of exactly 2 stockouts during the year?

(b) What is the probability of more than 1 stockout during the year?

16-4. After receiving Goal's order in Problem 16-2, management at PROTRAC's Seattle outlet decided that a 0.10 probability of a stockout per cycle would be best for them.

(a) Find Q^* and r^*.

(b) What is the probability of exactly 2 stockouts during a year?

(c) What is the probability of more than 1 stockout during a year?

16-5. Increasing Q, the order quantity, will have what effect on:

(a) The probability of a stockout *during an inventory cycle*?

   (i) Increase it?

   (ii) Decrease it?

   (iii) Leave it unchanged?

Explain your choice.

(b) The probability of more than 1 stockout per year?

   (i) Increase it?

   (ii) Decrease it?

   (iii) Leave it unchanged?

Explain your choice.

16-6. Increasing r, the reorder point, will have what effect on:

(a) The probability of a stockout *during an inventory cycle*?

   (i) Increase it?

   (ii) Decrease it?

   (iii) Leave it unchanged?

Explain your choice.

(b) The probability of more than 1 stockout per year?

   (i) Increase it?

   (ii) Decrease it?

   (iii) Leave it unchanged?

Explain your choice.

16-7. At Steco the weekly demand for high-titanium rods is normally distributed with mean 100 and standard deviation 5. These rods cost $5 each and the cost of holding a rod in inventory for a year is equal to 20% of its cost. The cost of placing an order is $25 independent of the quantity ordered. Delivery lead time is 1 week. Management wants a 0.06 probability of stocking out during an inventory cycle. Assume 50 weeks per year. What (r, Q) system would you recommend?

16-8. Consider the data presented in Problem 16-7. Now assume that increased demand has forced Steco's supplier to increase the delivery lead time for high-titanium rods from 1 week to 4 weeks. (*Hint:* Demand during the lead time is the sum of the demands during each of the four weeks. The demand each week has a normal distribution and it is reasonable to assume that demands are independent from week to week.)

    The following information is useful in solving Problem 16-8. Assume that X is normally distributed with mean μ_X and standard deviation σ_X and Y is also normally distributed with mean μ_Y and standard deviation σ_Y. Let $Z = X + Y$ and assume X and Y are independent. Then Z is normally distributed with mean $\mu_Z = \mu_X + \mu_Y$ and standard deviation $\sigma_Z = \sqrt{\sigma_X^2 + \sigma_Y^2}$

(a) What (r, Q) policy would you recommend in view of this change?

(b) What effect has the change in delivery lead time had on the value for Q? Explain why.

(c) Does r increase:
    (i) Less rapidly than
    (ii) The same rate as
    (iii) More rapidly than
    the lead time? Explain why.

16-9. What is the expected annual cost of the safety stock associated with the (r, Q) policy you recommended in Problem 16-7?

16-10. What is the expected annual cost of the safety stock associated with the (r, Q) policy you recommended in Problem 16-8?

16-11. The regional distribution center for Deuce Hardware sells small window air conditioners for $250 each. These units cost $200. All units not sold by September 1 are sold for one-half of the retail price in an end-of-the-season sale. Assume that demand for this air conditioner during the season is normally distributed with a mean of 600 and a standard deviation of 100.

(a) How many air conditioners should Deuce order at the beginning of the season?

(b) What is the probability that Deuce will not satisfy all demand during the season? The management of Deuce decides to select the order quantity so that the probability of a stock out is 0.10.

(c) How many air conditioners should be ordered at the beginning of the season?

(d) What "cost of goodwill" has to be added implicitly to the financial penalty cost to justify this decision?

16-12. The question the concessionaire must answer is how many soft pretzels to buy for the Great Fond du Lac Boat Race. The pretzels cost 15 cents and sell for 25 cents. Unsold pretzels can be returned to the supplier for an 8-cent refund. (The supplier then sells them in its Day Old Shoppe for 15 cents.) Demand is normal with a mean of 2000 and a standard deviation of 250.

(a) How many pretzels should be ordered?

(b) What is the probability that not all demand will be satisfied? Since the purchase of a pretzel typically leads to other purchases—beer, soft drinks, etc.—the concessionaire decides to set the probability of a stockout at 0.07.

(c) How many pretzels should be ordered?

(d) What additional cost of a lost sale must implicitly be added to the financial loss to justify this decision?

INVENTORY TURNS

INTRODUCTION

Contributing to the operation of an enterprise through its various committees is an important part of the managerial function. This vignette attempts to capture some of that experience. Assume the role of Larry Luchek. You will attend the next meeting of the management committee as a replacement for Victor Kowalski. Be prepared to make a presentation to the group on the topic of inventory turns if you feel there is more to be said. Remember that the other members of the committee are not necessarily experts in up-to-date inventory control technology, so if you have a point to make you should be prepared to illustrate it with numerical examples. As you will see, such arguments are the medium of exchange in the committee under consideration.

A Management Committee Meeting
STECO's management committee is having its biweekly meeting. Frank Watson, the president; Jayne Frazier, the treasurer, and Tom Galanti, vice-president of marketing, are all assembled in the conference room. Victor Kowalski, vice-president of operations, is on a tour of west coast facilities and cannot attend the meeting. He is represented by his assistant, Larry Luchek. The discussion proceeds as follows:

FRANK: This probably isn't the best time to raise the topic since Vic isn't here, but I want to mention it anyway so that it will be on the agenda for the next meeting. I was just reading in *Business Week* that the Japanese are beating our pants off in inventory control methods. Since inventory is our main business we have to be sure that we are doing as well as possible.

JAYNE: I read the same article and frankly it wasn't very clear to me. The entire discussion was in terms of "turns." I'm quite familiar with our system and that isn't a term we use. At any rate the bottom line of the article is that the Japanese are doing so much better because they have many more inventory turns than the typical U.S. firm, and I inferred that more turns means you pay less inventory charges. As I recall, the typical Japanese firm averaged about 20 turns whereas the U.S. average was about six. The article also mentioned that European firms on the average have even a smaller number of turns; I think the average was about two turns. Whatever all of that proves.

LARRY: I'm sure that Vic could give you a more complete analysis of the situation than I can because I'm rather new to this assignment. However, I may be able to shed some light on the subject. Turns are defined as

$$\text{turns} = \text{annual demand/average inventory}$$

Jayne, your remarks are right on target. For a given annual demand, more turns means lower average inventory and, hence, lower holding costs. However, since average inventory is a function of the order quantity and our order quantities are determined by the EOQ formula, the number of turns that we have for our products must be optimal. Let's look at a specific example. We assume that demand in each month for reinforced appliance angles is a normal random variable with a mean of 50 and a standard deviation of 15. Note that this assumption yields an annual demand of 12(50) equals 600. The typical lead time is one month and, as you know, Steco's standard practice is to have a stockout probability of 0.05. We have estimated an ordering cost of $25.00 and a holding cost of $1.92 per unit per year. By using the EOQ formula we can verify that Q^*, the optimal order quantity, is 125. The average inventory is one-half of the order quantity, or 62.5 angles. This yields 9.6 turns per year. Here, I'll put the calculations on the board.

$$\text{Annual demand} = D = 600 \text{ angles}$$
$$\text{Ordering cost} = C_o = \$25.00$$
$$\text{Holding cost} = C_h = \$1.92 \text{ per angle per year}$$
$$\text{Optimal order quantity} = Q^* = \sqrt{2C_oD/C_h} = 125$$
$$\text{Average inventory} = Q^*/2 = 62.5$$
$$\text{Turns} = D/(Q^*/2) = 9.6$$
$$\text{Orders per year} = N^* = D/Q^*$$
$$\text{therefore}$$
$$\text{Turns} = 2N^*$$

JAYNE: Are you sure about that, Larry? I understand your calculations, but, as I recall, our inventory audit shows a larger average inventory.

LARRY: There may be some random fluctuations, but we use an (r, Q) model and on the average it will indicate how the system works. In particular, these calculations form the basis for two observations. First we see that the number of turns (9.6) that results from our calculations is indeed smaller than the figure of 20 that you cite for Japanese firms. However, the number of turns is optimal given our current costs. In order to change the number of turns we must change the costs. Next we see that the number of turns is simply two times the number of orders we place during a year. Thus, to increase the optimal number of orders without increasing the annual cost, we would have to lower the cost of placing an order. Since our system is already computerized, this doesn't sound very promising to me. Frankly, I don't see that there is a lot of room for improvement.

TOM: Larry, this situation reminds me of the nonreinforced appliance angle problem. I remember discussing that order with Vic because it was the case he used to learn about ICON, our inventory control system. It seems to me that because of quantity discounts we increased our order quantity from 1250 to 5000. Obviously this large increase in the order quantity would cause a large decrease in the number of turns. If I understood your formulae correctly, increasing the order quantity by a factor of four would reduce the number of turns by the same factor, four. So it is obvious that quantity discounts can play an important role in determining the number of turns. I suppose that it is possible that suppliers in the United States are more able than their Japanese competitors to demand larger order quantities in order to obtain quantity discounts, and thus the number of turns on the average is smaller here. I must say that does not sound like a reasonable hypothesis to me. There must be another explanation.

FRANK: I think that we have devoted as much time to this topic as we should in Vic's absence. We'll put it on the agenda for the next meeting. I now want to bring your attention to our current cash flow problems. The combination of slow payment by our customers and the high interest costs are causing serious problems . . . .

Questions

1. What main point has Larry omitted from his analysis and how (if at all) would this affect his calculation for the number of turns?
2. Larry has correctly pointed out that ordering cost will affect the number of turns. Tom has correctly pointed out that quantity discounts play a role. As a result of your analysis, what other features might management consider?

CHAPTER 17

Forecasting

17.1
INTRODUCTION

The date is June 15, 1941. Joachim von Ribbentrop, Hitler's special envoy, was meeting in Venice with Count Ciano, the Italian foreign minister, whereupon von Ribbentrop says: "My dear Ciano, I cannot tell you anything as yet because every decision is locked in the impenetrable bosom of the Führer. However, one thing is certain: If we attack, the Russia of Stalin will be erased from the map within eight weeks."[1] Nine days later, on June 24, Nazi Germany launched operation Barbarossa and declared war on Russia. With this decision a chain of events that led to the end of the Third Reich had been set in motion and the course of history was dramatically changed.

The Role of Forecasting Although few decisions are this significant, it is clearly true that many of the most important decisions made by individuals and organizations crucially depend on an assessment of the future. Predictions or forecasts with greater accuracy than that achieved by the German General Staff are thus fervidly hoped for and in some cases diligently worked for.

Economic forecasting considered by itself is an important activity. Government policies and business decisions are based on forecasts of the GNP, the level of unemployment, the demand for refrigerators, and so on. Among the major insurance companies, one is hard-pressed to find an investment department that does not have a contract with some expert or firm to obtain economic forecasts on a regular basis. Billions of dollars of investments in mortgages and bonds are influenced by these forecasts. Over 2000 people show up each year at the Annual Forecast Luncheon sponsored by the University of Chicago to hear the views of three economists on the economic outlook. The data are overwhelming. Forecasting is playing an increasingly important role in the modern firm.

[1] A. L. C. Bullock, *Hitler: A Study in Tyranny* (New York: Harper & Row, Publishers, 1962).

The Increasing Importance of Quantitative Models

Not only is forecasting increasingly important, quantitative models are playing an increasingly important role in the forecasting function. There is clearly a steady increase in the use of quantitative forecasting models at many levels in industry and government. A conspicuous example is the widespread use of inventory control programs which include a forecasting subroutine. For economic entities such as the GNP or exchange rates many firms now rely on econometric models for their forecasts. These models, which consist of a system of statistically estimated equations, have had a significant impact on the decision processes both in industry and government.

There are numerous ways to classify forecasting models and the terminology varies with the classification. For example, one can refer to "long-range," "medium-range," and "short-range" models. There are "regression" models, "extrapolation" models, and "conditional" or "precedent-based" forecasting models, as well as "nearest-neighbor" models. The major distinction we employ will be between *quantitative* and *qualitative* *forecasting techniques*.

17.2
QUANTITATIVE FORECASTING

Quantitative forecasting models possess two important and attractive features:

Quantitative Models Are Unambiguous

1. They are expressed in mathematical notation. Thus, they establish an unambiguous record of how the forecast is made. This provides an excellent vehicle for clear communication about the forecast among those who are concerned. Furthermore, it provides an opportunity for systematic modification and improvement of the forecasting technique. In a quantitative model coefficients can be modified and/or terms added until the model yields good results. (This assumes that the relationship expressed in the model is basically sound.)

2. With the use of computers, quantitative models can be based on an amazing quantity of data. For example, a major oil company was considering a reorganization and expansion of its domestic marketing facilities (gasoline stations). Everyone understood that this was a pivotal decision for the firm. The size of the proposed capital investment alone, not to mention the possible influences on the revenue from gasoline sales, dictated that this decision be made by the board of directors. In order to evaluate the alternative expansion strategies, the board needed forecasts of the demand for gasoline in each of the marketing regions (more than 100 regions were involved) for each of the next 15 years. Each of these 1500 estimates was based on a combination of several factors, including the population and the level of new construction in each region. Without the use of computers and quantitative models a study involving this level of detail would generally be impossible. In a similar way, inventory control systems which require forecasts that are updated on a monthly basis for literally thousands of items could not be constructed without quantitative models and computers.

Large Data Bases

The technical literature related to quantitative forecasting models is enormous and a high level of technical, mainly statistical, sophistication is required to understand the intricacies of the models in certain areas. In the following two sections we summarize some of the important characteristics and the applicability of such models. We shall

557

distinguish two categories based on the underlying approach. These are **causal models** and **time-series models**.

17.3
CAUSAL FORECASTING MODELS

In a causal model, the forecast for the quantity of interest "rides piggyback" on another quantity or set of quantities. In other words, our knowledge of the value of one variable (or perhaps several variables) enables us to forecast the value of another variable. In more precise terms, let y denote the true value for some variable of interest, and let $\hat{y}$ denote a predicted or forecast value for the variable. Then, in a causal model,

$$\hat{y} = f(x_1, x_2, \ldots, x_n)$$

Independent and Dependent Variable   where f is a forecasting rule, or function, and $x_1, x_2, \ldots, x_n$ is a set of variables. In this representation the x variables are often called **independent variables**, whereas $\hat{y}$ is the **dependent** *or* **response variable**. The notion is that we know the independent variables and use them in the forecasting model to forecast the dependent variable.

Consider the following examples:

1. If y is the demand for baby food, then x might be the number of children between 7 and 24 months old.
2. If y is the demand for plumbing fixtures, then x_1 and x_2 might be the number of housing starts and the number of existing houses, respectively.
3. If y is the traffic volume on a proposed expressway, then x_1 and x_2 might be the traffic volume on each of two nearby existing highways.
4. If y is the yield of usable material per pound of ingredients from a proposed chemical plant, then x might be the same quantity produced by a small-scale experimental plant.

For a causal model to be useful, the independent variables must either be known in advance or it must be possible to forecast them more easily than $\hat{y}$, the dependent variable. For example, knowing a functional relationship between the pounds of sauerkraut and the number of bratwurst sold in Milwaukee in the same year may be interesting to sociologists, but unless sauerkraut usage can be easily predicted, the relationship is of little value for anyone in the bratwurst forecasting business.

To use a causal forecasting model, then, requires two conditions:

1. A relationship between values of the independent and dependent variables such that the former provides information about the latter.
2. The values for the independent variables must be known and available to the forecaster at the time the forecast must be made.

One commonly used approach in creating a causal forecasting model is called *curve fitting*.

Curve Fitting: An Oil Company Expansion

The fundamental ideas of curve fitting are easily illustrated by a problem in which one independent variable is used to predict the value of the dependent variable. As a specific example, consider an oil company that is planning to expand its network of modern self-service gasoline stations. They plan to use traffic flow (measured in the average number of cars per hour) to forecast sales (measured in average dollar sales per hour).

The firm has had five stations in operation for more than a year and has used historical data to calculate the averages shown in Figure 17.1.

Figure 17.1
Sales and Traffic Data

STATION	CARS PER HOUR	SALES PER HOUR
1	150	$220
2	55	75
3	220	250
4	130	145
5	95	200

These data are plotted in Figure 17.2. Such a plot is often called a **scatter diagram**. We now wish to use these data to construct a function that will enable us to forecast the sales at any proposed location by measuring the traffic flow at that location and plugging its value into the function we construct. In particular, suppose that the traffic flow at a proposed location in Buffalo Grove is 183 cars per hour. How might we use the data in Figure 17.2 to forecast the sales at this location?

Figure 17.2
Sales versus Traffic

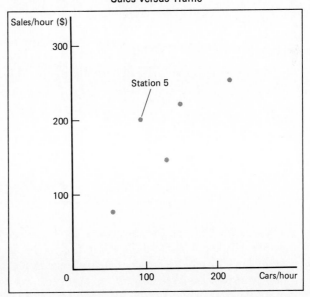

Quick and Dirty Fits A method that is commonly used when there is a single independent variable and a need to produce a forecast quickly is to fit a particular type of curve to the data "by eye." The goal is to find a "curve" that comes close enough to the points in the scatter diagram to satisfy the person who needs the forecast. We note that in this process it is not necessary to "touch" any data point, but the line could pass through a point if it yields a good fit.

A straight line is the type of curve most commonly selected. This process is illustrated in Figure 17.3. The line shown has no special properties except that it appears (at least to the authors) to lie close to the data. Once the line is drawn, one can read from the graph a forecast of sales for any particular traffic flow. The figure shows that this particular line yields a forecast of $202.50 for a traffic flow of 183.

The better equipped office is not limited to fitting a straight line by eye. A French curve enables the decision maker to select a function that lies closer to the data. Figure 17.4 illustrates this point. Again, a forecast for a traffic flow of 183 is shown.

The straight line and the curve selected in Figures 17.3 and 17.4 yield approximately the same forecast for demand (sales/hr) when the traffic flow is 183. A larger difference, both in absolute and relative terms, would occur if these figures were used to forecast demand at a location with a traffic flow of 60. The straight line yields a forecast of 133, whereas the curve yields a forecast of 117. So which model is right?

Figure 17.3
Fitting a Line by Eye

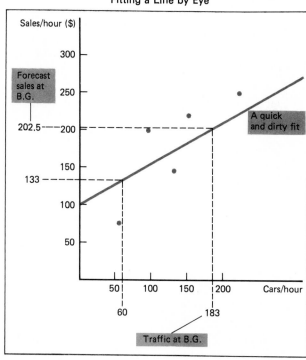

The Manager Still Must Decide There is no black-and-white answer to that question at the time the company must decide whether or not to build the station in Buffalo Grove. Forecasting models, like all other models, require the final step of managerial approval. *Based on judgment, which may be strongly influenced by direct experience with a forecasting model, the manager must decide whether to accept a particular forecast or to devote more resources to obtaining a* **560** *better forecast (i.e., one in which he has more confidence).*

Figure 17.4

Fitting a Curve by Eye

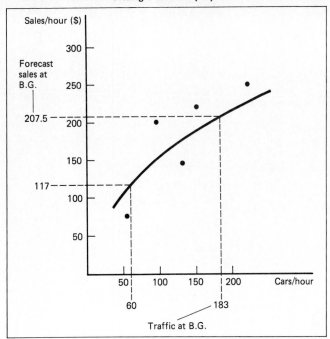

The quick and dirty method just described has two major deficiencies:

1. It is impossible to extend to problems with more than one independent variable. Think of trying to use this approach if you were given historical values of sales, traffic flow, *and* the number of competing stations in a 3-mile radius. It quickly becomes clear that a ruler and/or a French curve will not provide enough help.

2. There is no measure of what a "good fit" means. Once a manager has chosen a specific functional form (say a straight line), there is no automatic way to select one line that is better than other possible lines. Sure, the manager can look at them and pick the one he likes. However, if he can specify a measure of goodness, the process of curve fitting can be reduced to a standard and more objective technical operation.

Least-Squares The method of least squares is a formal procedure for curve fitting that overcomes the
Fits two deficiencies just discussed. It is a two-step process:

1. Select a specific functional form (e.g., a straight line).
2. Within the set of all possible functions specified in step 1, choose the specific function that minimizes the sum of the squared deviations between the data points and the function values. (We hasten to illustrate this idea.)

Consider the sales–traffic flow example. In step 1, assume that we select a straight line; that is, we restrict our attention to functions of the form $y = a + bx$. Step 2 involves the problem of how to select a and b. In Figure 17.5, specific values for a and b were chosen, the appropriate line $y = a + bx$ was drawn, and the deviations between observed points and the function are indicated. For example,

Figure 17.5
Method of Least Squares

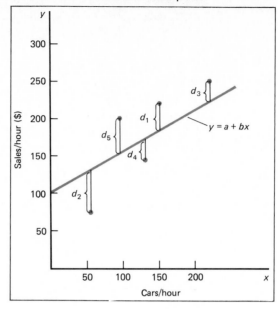

$$d_1 = y_1 - [a + bx_1] = 220 - [a + 150b]$$

where y_1 = actual (observed) sales/hr at location 1 (i.e., 220)
   x_1 = actual (observed) traffic flow at location 1 (i.e., 150)
   a = intercept (on the vertical axis) for function in Figure 17.5
   b = slope for the function in Figure 17.5

The value d_1^2 is a measure of how close the value of the function $[a + bx_1]$ is to the observed value, y_1; that is, it indicates how well the function fits at this one point.

***Sum of
Squared
Deviations***

We want the function to fit well at all points. One measure of how well it fits overall is the sum of the squared deviations, which is $\sum_{i=1}^{5} d_i^2$. Let us now consider a general problem with n as opposed to 5 observations. Then, since each $d_i = y_i - (a + bx_i)$ the sum of the squared deviations can be written as

$$\sum_{i=1}^{n} (y_i - [a + bx_i])^2 \tag{17.1}$$

The method of least squares tells us to select a and b so as to minimize the sum shown in expression (17.1). The rules of calculus can be used to determine the values of a and b that minimize this sum. The procedure is to take the partial derivative of the sum in expression (17.1) with respect to a and set the resulting expression equal to zero. This yields one equation. A second equation is derived by following the same procedure with b. The equations that result from this procedure are

$$\sum_{i=1}^{n} -2(y_i - [a + bx_i]) = 0 \quad \text{and} \quad \sum_{i=1}^{n} -2x_i(y_i - [a + bx_i]) = 0$$

Recall that the values for x_i and y_i are the observations and our goal is to find the values of a and b that satisfy these two equations. The solution can be shown to be

Slope and Intercept

$$b = \frac{\sum_{i=1}^{n} x_i y_i - \frac{1}{n}\sum_{i=1}^{n} x_i \sum_{i=1}^{n} y_i}{\sum_{i=1}^{n} x_i^2 - \frac{1}{n}\left(\sum_{i=1}^{n} x_i\right)^2} \tag{17.2}$$

$$a = \frac{1}{n}\sum_{i=1}^{n} y_i - b\sum_{i=1}^{n} x_i$$

The next step is to determine the values for $\sum x_i$, $\sum x_i^2$, $\sum y_i$, $\sum x_i y_i$. Note that these quantities depend only on the data we have observed and that we can find them with simple arithmetic operations. The table in Figure 17.6 is devoted to this purpose.

Figure 17.6

Least-Squares Calculations: The Linear Case

i	x_i(CARS/HR)	y_i(SALES/HR)	$x_i y_i$	x_i^2
1	150	220	33,000	22,500
2	55	75	4,125	3,025
3	220	250	55,000	48,400
4	130	145	18,850	16,900
5	95	200	19,000	9,025
Σ	650	890	129,975	99,850

Plugging the numerical values into the equations shown in expression (17.2) and setting $n = 5$, yields

$$b = 0.93 \qquad a = 57.1$$

Least Squares versus Quick and Dirty

The resulting least-squares line is shown in Figure 17.7 as a solid line. The quick and dirty line from Figure 17.3 is shown as a dashed line. This figure suggests that at least some individuals (e.g., the authors) are not too good at selecting by eye a line that well fits the data (by the least squares criterion).

The example above has shown how to make *linear fits* for the case of 1 independent variable. But the method of least squares can be used with any number of independent variables and with any functional form. As an illustration, suppose that we wish to fit a quadratic function of the form

$$y = a_0 + a_1 x + a_2 x^2$$

Fitting a Quadratic

to our previous data with the method of least squares. Our goal, then, is to select a_0, a_1, and a_2 in order to minimze the sum of squared deviations, which is now

$$\sum_{i=1}^{5} (y_i - [(a_0 + a_1 x_i + a_2 x_i^2])^2 \tag{17.3}$$

We proceed by setting the partial derivatives with respect to a_0, a_1, and a_2 equal to zero. This gives the equations

$$\begin{aligned} 5a_0 + (\textstyle\sum x_i)a_1 + (\sum x_i^2)a_2 &= \textstyle\sum y_i \\ (\textstyle\sum x_i)a_0 + (\sum x_i^2)a_1 + (\sum x_i^3)a_2 &= \textstyle\sum x_i y_i \\ (\textstyle\sum x_i^2)a_0 + (\sum x_i^3)a_1 + (\sum x_i^4)a_2 &= \textstyle\sum x_2^i y_i \end{aligned} \tag{17.4}$$

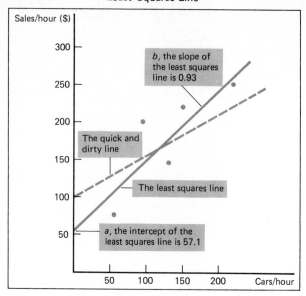

Figure 17.7
Least-Squares Line

Finding the numerical values of the coefficients is a straightforward task. We proceed in the same tabular manner as in Figure 17.6. Indeed, we need all of the values calculated there. To conserve space, we use scientific notation and express numbers in powers of 10. For example, we will write 22,500 as 2.25×10^4. The calculations, to two decimals of accuracy, are shown in Figure 17.8.

Figure 17.8
Least-Squares Calculations: The Quadratic Case

i	$x_i \times 10^2$	$y_i \times 10^2$	$x_i y_i \times 10^4$	$x_i^2 \times 10^4$	$x_i^3 \times 10^6$	$x_i^4 \times 10^8$	$x_i^2 y_i \times 10^6$
1	1.50	2.20	3.30	2.25	3.38	5.06	4.95
2	0.55	0.75	0.41	0.30	0.17	0.09	0.23
3	2.20	2.50	5.50	4.84	10.65	23.43	12.10
4	1.30	1.45	1.89	1.69	2.20	2.86	2.45
5	0.95	2.00	1.90	0.90	0.86	0.81	1.80
Σ	6.50	8.90	13.00	9.98	17.26	32.25	21.53

The numerical values from Figure 17.8 can now be plugged into the equations presented in (17.4) to yield

$$5a_0 + 650a_1 + 99{,}800a_2 = 890 \tag{17.5}$$

$$6.50a_0 + 998a_1 + 172{,}600a_2 = 1300 \tag{17.6}$$

$$9.98a_0 + 1726a_1 + 322{,}500a_2 = 2153 \tag{17.7}$$

Both sides of (17.6) have been divided by 10^2 and both sides of equation (17.7) have been divided by 10^4 to obtain the form shown.

We are now left with the straightforward but tedious task of solving three linear equations in three unknowns. Completing this exercise yields

$$a_0 \approx -65.726$$

$$a_1 \approx 3.015$$

$$a_2 \approx -0.0074$$

Figure 17.9
Evaluating the Quadratic Function

x	$-65.726 + 3.015x - 0.0074x^2$
0	-65.726
50	66.46
100	161.52
200	240.22

To plot this function, we first evaluate it for four values of x as shown in Figure 17.9.[2]

These points are plotted in Figure 17.10 and a curve is drawn through them. The linear least-squares fit is also shown. The quadratic function appears to fit the data better, but beware. As we have seen in the use of quick and dirty methods, the eye is not always a reliable guide to what is happening.

Figure 17.10
Quadratic Least-Squares Function

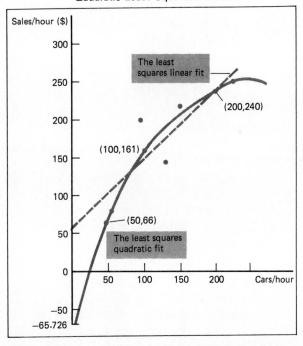

Goodness of Fit   In the method of least squares, we have selected the sum of the squared deviations as our measure of "goodness of fit." We can thus compare the linear and the quadratic fit with

[2]One can use differential calculus to show that the function has a maximum value at

$$x = -a_1/2a_2 \approx 241.3$$

this criterion. The calculations are shown in Figure 17.11, where columns (1) and (2) are the actual historical data from Figure 17.1, column (3) is the least-squares linear fit, and the column identified as (4) is the least-squares quadratic fit.

We see that the sum of the squared deviations for the quadratic function is indeed smaller than that for the linear function (i.e., 5398 < 5923). Indeed, the quadratic gives us roughly a 10% decrease in the sum of squares. The general result has to hold in this direction; that is, the quadratic function must always fit better than the linear function. A linear function is, after all, a special type of a quadratic function (one in which $a_2 = 0$). It follows then that the best quadratic function must be at least as good as the best linear function. This concept seems to have some general merit. Why not choose even a more

The Quadratic Function Gives a Better Fit

Figure 17.11
Sum of the Squared Deviations

i	(1) x_i	(2) y_i	(3) $a + bx_i$	$[(2) - (3)]^2$ d_i^2	(4) $a_0 + a_1x_i + a_2x_i^2$	$[(2) - (4)]^2$ d_i^2
1	150	220	196	576	220.57	0.32
2	55	75	108	1089	77.64	6.96
3	220	250	262	144	261.87	140.85
4	130	145	178	1089	200.71	3104
5	95	200	145	3025	246.31	2145
Σ				5923		5398

general form, such as a cubic or a quartic, thereby getting even a better fit? In principle the method can be applied to any specified functional form. In practice, functions of the form (again using only a single independent variable for illustrative purposes)

$$y = a_0 + a_1x + a_2x^2 + \cdots + a_nx^n$$

are often suggested. Such a function is called a polynomial of degree n and it represents a broad and flexible class of functions (for $n = 2$ we have a quadratic, $x = 3$ a cubic, $n = 4$ a quartic, etc.). One can obtain an amazing variety of curves with polynomials, and thus they are popular among curve fitters. One must, however, proceed with caution when fitting data with a polynomial function. Under quite general conditions it is possible, for example, to find a $(k - 1)$-degree polynomial that will perfectly fit k data points. To be more specific, suppose that we have on hand seven historical observations, denoted (x_i, y_i), $i = 1, 2, \ldots, 7$. It is possible to find a sixth-degree polynomial

Polynomial Fits

$$y = a_0 + a_1x + a_2x^2 + \cdots + a_6x^6$$

that exactly passes through each of these seven data points (see Figure 17.12).

This perfect fit (giving zero for the sum of squared deviations), however, is deceptive, for it does not imply as much as you may think about the predictive value of the model. For example, refer again to Figure 17.12. When the independent variable (at some future time) assumes the value x_8, the true value of y might be given by y_8, whereas the predicted value is $\hat{y}_8$. Despite the previous perfect fit, the forecast is very inaccurate. In this situation a linear fit (i.e., a first-degree polynomial) such as the one indicated in Figure 17.12 might well provide more realistic forecasts for the future, although by the criterion of least squares it does not "fit" the historical data nearly as well as the sixth-degree polynomial. Also, note that the polynomial fit has hazardous extrapolation prop-

Figure 17.12
A Sixth-Degree Polynomial Produces a Perfect Fit

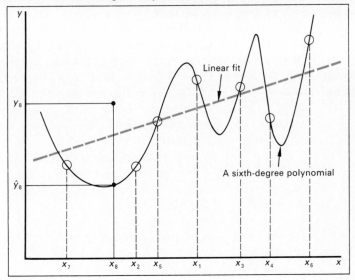

erties. That is, the polynomial "blows up" at its extremes; x values only slightly larger than x_6 produce very large predicted y's. Looking at Figure 17.12, you can understand why high-order polynomial fits are referred to as "wild."

    The intent of the paragraph above is to suggest that a model which has given a good fit to historical data may provide a terrible fit to future data. That is, a good historical fit may have poor predictive power. So what is a good predictive model?

Regression Analysis
The answer to this question involves considerations both philosophic and technical. The answer to the question depends, first, on whether or not one has some idea about the underlying real-world process which relates the y's and the x's. To be an effective forecasting device, the forecasting function must to some extent capture important features of that process. The more one knows, the better one can do. To go very far into this topic, one must employ a level of statistics that would extend well beyond this introductory coverage. For our purposes it suffices to state that knowledge of the underlying process is typically phrased in statistical language. For example, linear curve fitting, in the statistical context, is called *linear regression analysis*. If the statistical assumptions about the linear regression model are precisely satisfied, then in a precise and well-defined sense statisticians can prove that the linear fit is the "best possible fit." But in a real sense, this begs the question. In the real world one can never be completely certain about the underlying process. It is never "served to us on a platter." One only has some (and often not enough) historical data to observe. The question then becomes: How much confidence can we have that the underlying process is one that satisfies a particular set of statistical assumptions? Fortunately, quantitative measures do exist. Statistical analysis, at least for simple classes of models like linear regression, can reveal how well the historical data do indeed satisfy those assumptions.

    And what if they do not? One tries a different model. Let us regress (digress) for a moment to recall some of the philosophy involved with the use of optimization models. There is an underlying real-world problem. The model is a selective representation of that problem. How good is that model, or representation? One usually does not have precise measures, and many paragraphs in this text have been devoted to the role of managerial judgment and sensitivity analysis in establishing a model's credibility. Ideally, to test the goodness of a model, one would like to have considerable experience with its use. If, in repeated use, we observe that the model performs well, then our confidence is high.[3] However, what confidence can we have at the outset, without experience? One benchmark, which brings us close to the current context, is to ask the question: Suppose the model were used to make past decisions. How well would the firm have fared? This approach "creates" experience by **simulating the past**. This is often referred to as **validating** the model. One way to use this approach, in the forecasting context, is called "divide and conquer" and is discussed at some length in Section 17.5. Typically, one uses only a portion of the historical data to create the model—for example, to fit a polynomial of a specified degree. One can then use the remaining data to see how well the model would have performed. This procedure is specified in some detail in Section 17.5. At present, it suffices to conclude by stressing that in curve fitting the question of "goodness of fit" is both philosophic and technical, and you do not want to lose sight of either issue.

*Validating
the Model*

*The Role of
the Computer*

These few examples of causal forecasting models demonstrate that even in simple problems the required calculations are tedious. In most problems of an interesting size, it is impractical to perform the calculations by hand. This is especially true in problems where there are several independent variables. Fortunately, this is not a serious problem. The wide availability of computers and the steadily decreasing cost of computing have reduced the problem of performing the necessary calculations so that, at least in many applications, it is insignificant. The important questions are: What model, if any, can do a reliable job of forecasting, and are the data required for such a model available and reliable?

*Summary
Comments*

A causal forecasting model uses one or more independent variables to forecast the value of a dependent or response variable. The model is often created by fitting a curve to an existing set of data and then using this curve to determine the response associated with new values of the independent variable(s). The method of least squares is a particularly useful method of fitting a curve. We have illustrated the general concept of this method and considered the specific problems of fitting a straight line, a quadratic function, and higher-order polynomials to a set of data. For simplicity, all of our illustrations have involved a single independent variable but the same techniques, except for "quick and dirty," apply to problems with many variables.

In concluding, we have discussed both philosophic and technical issues which the "curve fitter" must address. Comments on the role of causal models in managerial decision making are reserved to Section 17.7. We now turn our attention to time-series analysis.

17.4

TIME-SERIES FORECASTING MODELS

*Extrapolating
the Past*

Another class of quantitative forecasting techniques comprises the so-called **time-series models**. These models produce forecasts by *extrapolating* the *historical behavior of the values of a particular single variable of interest*. For example, one may be interested in

[3]No matter how much observation seems to substantiate the model, we can never conclude that the model is "true." Recall the high degree of "substantiation" of the flat earth model: "If you leave port and sail westward you will eventually fall off the earth and never be seen again."

the sales for a particular item, or a fluctuation of a particular market price with time. Time-series models use some technique to *extrapolate* the historical behavior into the future. Figuratively, the series is being lifted into the future "by its own bootstraps."

In order to provide several examples of bootstrap methods, let us suppose that we have on hand the daily closing prices of a January soybeans futures contract for the past 12 days, including today, and that from this past stream of data we wish to predict tomorrow's closing price. Several possibilities come to mind.

1. If it is felt that all historical values are important, and that all have equal predictive power, we might take the *average* of the past 12 values as our best forecast for tomorrow.

2. If it is felt that today's value (the twelfth) is far and away the most important, this value might be our best prediction for tomorrow.

3. It may be felt that in the current "fast-trending market" the first six values are too antiquated, but the most recent six are important and each has equal predictive power. We might then take the average of the most recent six values as our best estimate for tomorrow.

4. It may be felt that *all* past values contain useful information, but today's (the 12th observation) is the most important of all, and, in succession, the 11th, 10th, 9th, and so on, observations have decreasing importance. In this case we might take a *weighted average* of all 12 observations, with increasing weights assigned to each value in the order 1 through 12 and with the 12 weights summing to 1.

5. We might actually plot the 12 values as a function of time and then draw a linear "trend line" which lies close to these values. This line might then be used to predict tomorrow's value.

A Preview Let us now suppose that tomorrow's actual closing price is observed and consider our forecast for the day after tomorrow, using the 13 available historical values. Methods 1 and 2 can be applied in a straightforward manner. Now consider method 3. In this case we might take tomorrow's actual observed price, together with today's and the previous four prices, to obtain a new 6-day average. This technique is called *a simple six-period moving average*, and it will be discussed in more detail in the following sections.

Let us now refer to method 4. In this instance, since we employ all past values, we would be using 13 rather than 12 values, with new weights assigned to these values. An important class of techniques called *exponential smoothing models* operate in this fashion. These models will also be explored in the ensuing discussion.

Finally, we shall explore in more detail the technique mentioned in item 5. This provides another illustration of forecasting by a *curve-fitting method*.

We mention at this point that whenever we have values for a particular (single) variable of interest, which can be plotted against time, these values are often termed a *time series*, and any method used to analyze and extrapolate such a series into the future falls within the general category of *time-series analysis*. This is currently a very active area of research in statistics and management science. We will be able to barely scratch the surface in terms of formal development. Nevertheless, some of the important concepts, from the manager's viewpoint, will be developed.

Curve Fitting We have already considered this topic in the discussion of causal models. In using curve fitting in the time-series context the main difference is that in this situation the independent variable is time. The historical observations of the dependent variable are plotted against time and a curve is then fit to these data. The curve is then extended into the future to yield a forecast. In this context, extending the curve simply means evaluating the derived function for larger values of t, the time. This procedure is illustrated for a straight line in Figure 17.13.

Figure 17.13
Fitting a Straight Line

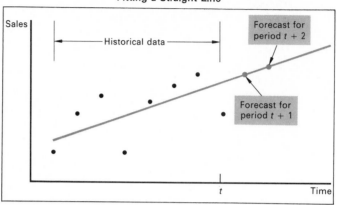

The use of time as an independent variable has more serious implications than altering a few formulas, and a manager should understand the important difference between a causal model using curve fitting and a time-series model using curve fitting. The mathematical techniques for fitting the curves are identical, but the rationale, or philosophy, behind the two models is basically quite different. To understand this difference, think of the values of y, the variable of interest, as being produced by a particular underlying process or system. The causal model assumes that as the under-lying system changes to produce different values of y, it will also produce corresponding differences in the independent variables and thus, by knowing the independent variables, a good forecast of y can be deduced. The time-series model assumes that the system that produces y is essentially *stationary* (or *stable*) and will continue to act in the future as it has in the past. Future patterns in the movement of y will closely resemble past patterns. This means that time is a surrogate for many factors which may be difficult to measure but which seem to vary in a consistent and systematic manner with time. If the system that produces y significantly changes (e.g., because of changes in environment, tech-nology, or government policy) then the assumption of a *stationary process* is invalid and consequently a forecast based on time as an independent variable is apt to be badly in error.

Time as the Independent Variable

Just as for causal models, it is, of course, possible to use other than linear functions to extrapolate a series of observations (i.e., to forecast the future). As you might imagine, one alternative that is often suggested in practice is to assume that y_t is a higher-order polynomial in t, that is,

$$y_t = b_0 + b_1 t + b_2 t^2 + \cdots + b_k t^k$$

As before, appropriate values for the parameters $b_0, b_1, \ldots, b_k$ must be mathematically derived from the values of previous observations. The high-order polynomial, however, suffers from the pitfalls described earlier. That is, perfect (or at least extremely good) historical fits with little or no predictive power may be obtained.

The assumption behind models of this type is that the average performance over the recent past is a good forecast of the future. It is perhaps surprising that these "naive" models are extremely important in applications. Almost all of the inventory control packages include a forecasting subroutine based on a particular type of moving average called exponentially weighted moving averages. On the basis of a criterion such as "frequency of use," the method of moving averages is surely an important forecasting procedure.

One person who is deeply concerned about the use of simple forecasting models is Victor Kowalski, the new vice-president of operations at STECO. His introduction to inventory control models is discussed in Chapter 15. Since he is responsible for the inventory of thousands of items, simple (i.e., inexpensive) forecasting models are important to him. In order to become familiar with the various models he decides to "try out" different models on some historical data. In particular he decides to use last year's monthly sales data for stainless steel struts to learn about the different models and to see how well they would have worked if STECO had been using the models last year. He is performing what is called a *validation* study.

The forecasting models are presented, of course, in symbols. Victor feels that it would be useful to use a common notation throughout his investigation. He thus decides to let:

$$y_{t-1} = observed\ sales\ \text{of struts in month } t-1$$
$$\hat{y}_t = forecast\ \text{of sales for struts in period } t$$

He is interested in forecasting the sales one month ahead; that is, he will take the known historical values $y_1, \ldots, y_{t-1}$ (demand in months 1 through $t-1$) and use this information to produce $\hat{y}_t$, the forecast for y_t. In other words, he will use the actual past sales, through May, for example, and use them to forecast the sales in June, then he will use the sales through June to forecast sales in July, and so on. This process produces a sequence of $\hat{y}_t$ values. By comparing these values with the observed y_t values, one obtains an indication of how the forecasting model would have worked, had it actually been in use last year.

The simplest model in the moving-average category is the *simple n-period moving average.* In this model the average of a fixed number (say n) of the most recent observations is used as an estimate of the next value of y. For example, if n equals 4, then after we have observed the value of y in period 15, our estimate for period 16 would be

$$\hat{y}_{16} = \frac{y_{15} + y_{14} + y_{13} + y_{12}}{4}$$

In general,

$$\hat{y}_{t+1} = \frac{1}{n}(y_t + y_{t-1} + \cdots + y_{t-n+1})$$

The application of a three-period and a four-period moving average to STECO's strut sales data is shown in Figure 17.14.

We see that the three-month moving average forecast for sales in April is the average of January, February, and March sales, $(20 + 24 + 27)/3$ or 23.67. *Ex post*

Figure 17.14
Three- and Four-Month Simple Moving Averages

MONTH	ACTUAL SALES (THOUSANDS)	THREE-MONTH SIMPLE MOVING AVERAGE FORECAST	FOUR-MONTH SIMPLE MOVING AVERAGE FORECAST
Jan.	$20		
Feb.	24		
Mar.	27		
Apr.	31	(20 + 24 + 27)/3 = 23.67	
May	37	(24 + 27 + 31)/3 = 27.33	(20 + 24 + 27 + 31)/4 = 25.50
June	47	(27 + 31 + 37)/3 = 31.67	(24 + 27 + 31 + 37)/4 = 29.75
July	53	(31 + 37 + 47)/3 = 38.33	(27 + 31 + 37 + 47)/4 = 35.50
Aug.	62	(37 + 47 + 53)/3 = 45.67	(31 + 37 + 47 + 53)/4 = 42.00
Sept.	54	(47 + 53 + 62)/3 = 54.00	(37 + 47 + 53 + 62)/4 = 49.75
Oct.	36	(53 + 62 + 54)/3 = 56.33	(47 + 53 + 62 + 54)/4 = 54.00
Nov.	32	(62 + 54 + 36)/3 = 50.67	(53 + 62 + 54 + 36)/4 = 51.25
Dec.	29	(54 + 36 + 32)/3 = 40.67	(62 + 54 + 36 + 32)/4 = 46.00

(that is, after the forecast) actual sales in April were 31. Thus, in this case the sales forecast differed from the actual sales by $31 - 23.67$ or 7.33.

Inspection of the data in Figure 17.14 suggests that neither forecasting method seems particularly accurate. It is, however, useful to replace this *qualitative impression* with some *quantitative measure* of how well the two methods performed. A commonly used measure of comparison is the average of the squared errors, where

Average Squared Error

$$\text{average squared error} = \frac{\displaystyle\sum_{\text{all forecasts}} (\text{forecast sales} - \text{actual sales})^2}{\text{number of forecasts}}$$

The average squared error is calculated for the three-month (beginning with April) and four-month (beginning with May) moving average forecast in Figure 17.15. Since the three-month moving average yields an average squared error of 195.78, whereas the four-month moving average yields an average squared error of 267.21, it seems (at least historically) that including more historical data harms rather than helps the forecasting accuracy.

Shortcomings of the Simple Moving Average

The simple moving average has two shortcomings, one philosophical and the other operational. The *philosophical* problem centers on the fact that in calculating a forecast (say $\hat{y}_8$), the most recent observation (y_7) receives no more weight or importance than an older observation such as y_5. This is because each of the last n observations is assigned the weight $1/n$. This procedure of assigning equal weights stands in opposition to one's intuition that in many instances the more recent data should tell us more than the older data about the future. Indeed, the analysis in Figure 17.15 suggests that better predictions for strut sales are based on the most recent data.

The second shortcoming, which is *operational*, is that if n observations are to be included in the moving average, then $(n - 1)$ pieces of past data must be brought forward to be combined with the current (the nth) observation. These past data must be stored in some way, in order to calculate the forecast. This is not a serious problem when a small number of forecasts are involved. The situation is quite different for the firm that needs to forecast the demand for thousands of individual products on an item-by-

Figure 17.15

Average Squared Error

MONTH	ACTUAL SALES (THOUSANDS)	THREE-MONTH SIMPLE MOVING AVERAGE FORECAST	SQUARED ERROR	FOUR-MONTH SIMPLE MOVING AVERAGE FORECAST	SQUARED ERROR
Apr.	$31	23.67	53.73		
May	37	27.33	93.51	25.50	132.25
June	47	31.67	235.01	29.75	297.55
July	53	38.33	215.21	35.50	306.25
Aug.	62	45.67	266.67	42.00	400.00
Sept.	54	54.00	0	49.75	18.06
Oct.	36	56.33	413.31	54.00	324.00
Nov.	32	50.67	348.57	51.25	370.56
Dec.	29	40.67	136.19	46.00	289.00
Total			1762.20		2137.67
Average			195.78		267.21

item basis. If, for example, STECO is using eight-period moving averages to forecast demand for 5000 small parts, then for each item 7 pieces of data must be stored for each forecast. This implies that a total of 35,000 pieces of data must be stored. In such a case storage requirements, as well as computing time, may become important factors in designing a forecasting and inventory control system.

Weighted n-Period Moving Average The notion that recent data are more important than old data can be implemented with a **weighted n-period moving average**. This generalizes the notion of a simple n-period moving average, where, as we have seen, each weight is $1/n$. In this more general form, taking $n = 3$ as a specific example, we would set

$$\hat{y}_7 = \alpha_0 y_6 + \alpha_1 y_5 + \alpha_2 y_4$$

where the α's (which are called weights) are nonnegative numbers which are chosen so that smaller weights are assigned to more ancient data and all the weights sum to 1. There are, of course, innumerable ways for selecting a set of α's to satisfy these criteria. For example, if as above the weighted average is to include the last three observations (a weighted three-period moving average) one might set

$$\hat{y}_7 = \tfrac{3}{6} y_6 + \tfrac{2}{6} y_5 + \tfrac{1}{6} y_4$$

Alternatively, one could define

$$\hat{y}_7 = \tfrac{5}{10} y_6 + \tfrac{3}{10} y_5 + \tfrac{2}{10} y_4$$

In either of these expressions we have decreasing weights that sum to 1. In practice, the proper choice of weights could well be a study in itself. Rather than discussing the rationale for various choices of weights, our desire is to illustrate the use of the model.

To get some idea about its performance, Victor applies the three-month weighted moving average with weights 3/6, 2/6, 1/6 to the historical stainless strut data. The forecasts and the average squared error are shown in Figure 17.16.

Figure 17.16

Three-Month Weighted Moving Average

MONTH	ACTUAL SALES (THOUSANDS)	THREE-MONTH WEIGHTED MOVING AVERAGE FORECAST	SQUARED ERROR
Jan.	$20		
Feb.	24		
Mar.	27		
Apr.	31	$[(3 \times 27) + (2 \times 24) + (1 \times 20)]/6 = 24.83$	
May	37	$[(3 \times 31) + (2 \times 27) + (1 \times 24)]/6 = 28.50$	38.07
June	47	$[(3 \times 37) + (2 \times 31) + (1 \times 27)]/6 = 33.33$	72.25
July	53	$[(3 \times 47) + (2 \times 37) + (1 \times 31)]/6 = 41.00$	186.87
Aug.	62	$[(3 \times 53) + (2 \times 47) + (1 \times 37)]/6 = 48.33$	144.00
Sept.	54	$[(3 \times 62) + (2 \times 53) + (1 \times 47)]/6 = 56.50$	186.87
Oct.	36	$[(3 \times 54) + (2 \times 62) + (1 \times 53)]/6 = 56.50$	6.25
Nov.	32	$[(3 \times 36) + (2 \times 54) + (1 \times 62)]/6 = 46.33$	420.25
Dec.	29	$[(3 \times 32) + (2 \times 36) + (1 \times 54)]/6 = 37.00$	205.35
			64.00
Total			1323.91
Average			147.10

Comparing the Results   Comparing the average squared errors of the three-month simple moving average (195.78), the four-month simple moving average (267.21), and the three-month weighted moving average (147.10) confirms the suggestion, based on Figure 17.15, that recent sales results are a better indicator of future sales than are older data. Although the weighted moving average places more weight on more recent data, it does not solve the operational problems of data storage since $n - 1$ pieces of historical sales data must still be stored. We now turn to a weighting scheme that cleverly addresses this problem.

Exponential Smoothing: The Basic Model   We saw that, in using a weighted moving average, there are many different ways to assign decreasing weights that sum to 1. One way is called exponential smoothing, which is a shortened name for an **exponentially weighted moving average**. This is a scheme that weights recent data more heavily than past data, with weights summing to 1, but it avoids the operational problem just discussed. In this model, for any $t \geq 1$ the forecast for period $t + 1$, denoted $\hat{y}_{t+1}$, is a weighted sum (with weights summing to 1) of the actual *observed sales in period t* (i.e., y_t) and *the forecast for period t* (which was $\hat{y}_t$). In other words,

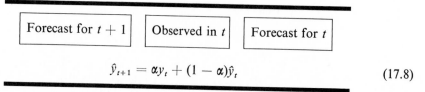

$$\hat{y}_{t+1} = \alpha y_t + (1 - \alpha)\hat{y}_t \qquad (17.8)$$

where α is a user-specified constant such that $0 < \alpha < 1$. Thus, to compute $\hat{y}_{t+1}$, only $\hat{y}_t$ need be stored (together with the value of α). As soon as the actual y_t is observed, we compute $\hat{y}_{t+1} = \alpha y_t + (1 - \alpha)\hat{y}_t$. If STECO wanted to forecast demand for 5000 small parts, in each period, then 5001 items would have to be stored (the 5000 $\hat{y}_t$ values, and the value of α), as opposed to the previously computed 35,000 items needed to implement an eight-period moving average.

In order to obtain more insight into the exponential smoothing model, let us note that when $t = 1$ the expression used to define $\hat{y}_2$ is

$$\hat{y}_2 = \alpha y_1 + (1 - \alpha)\hat{y}_1$$

In this expression $\hat{y}_1$ is an "initial guess" at the value for y in period 1, and y_1 is the observed value in period 1. At this point Victor decides to select an α of 0.6 and a $\hat{y}_1$ of 40 and to apply the model to the stainless steel strut data. His efforts are shown in Figure 17.17. As this figure shows, Victor has actual and estimated sales for 12 months. However, before beginning his computations he decides that he will calculate the average squared error only for the last nine months (April through December). This, he believes, will give a better comparison with the results obtained from the other models (see Figures 17.15 and 17.16).

Figure 17.17
Exponential Smoothing (α = 0.6)

MONTH	ACTUAL SALES (THOUSANDS)	$\hat{y}_t$	$\alpha \hat{y}_t + (1 - \alpha)\hat{y}_t$	SQUARED ERROR
Jan.	$20	40	0.6 × 20 + 0.4 × 40 = 28.00	
Feb.	24	28	0.6 × 24 + 0.4 × 28 = 25.60	
Mar.	27	25.60	0.6 × 27 + 0.4 × 25.60 = 26.44	
Apr.	31	26.44	0.6 × 31 + 0.4 × 26.44 = 29.18	20.79
May	37	29.18	0.6 × 37 + 0.4 × 29.18 = 33.87	61.15
June	47	33.87	0.6 × 47 + 0.4 × 33.87 = 45.35	172.40
July	53	45.35	0.6 × 53 + 0.4 × 45.35 = 49.94	58.52
Aug.	62	49.94	0.6 × 62 + 0.4 × 49.94 = 57.18	145.44
Sept.	54	57.18	0.6 × 54 + 0.4 × 57.18 = 55.27	10.11
Oct.	36	55.27	0.6 × 36 + 0.4 × 55.27 = 43.71	371.33
Nov.	32	43.71	0.6 × 32 + 0.4 × 43.71 = 36.68	137.12
Dec.	29	36.68		58.98
Total				1035.84
Average				115.09

Victor is delighted with the results. The average squared error is smaller than what he obtained with the previous three models and the calculations are simple. From a computational view it is reasonable to consider exponential smoothing as an affordable way to forecast the sales of the thousands of products that STECO holds in inventory.

Although the results obtained from the exponential smoothing model are impressive, it is clear that the particular numerical values that appear in Figure 17.17 depend on the values selected for the smoothing constant α, and the "initial guess" $\hat{y}_1$.

Because of the importance of the basic exponential smoothing model, it is worth exploring in more detail how it works and when it can be successfully applied to real problems. We will now examine some of its properties. To begin, note that if $t \geq 2$ it is possible to substitute $t - 1$ for t in (17.8) to obtain

$$\hat{y}_t = \alpha y_{t-1} + (1 - \alpha)\hat{y}_{t-1}$$

Substituting this relationship back into the original expression for $\hat{y}_{t+1}$ [i.e., into (17.8)] yields for $t \geq 2$,

$$\hat{y}_{t+1} = \alpha y_t + \alpha(1 - \alpha)y_{t-1} + (1 - \alpha)^2 \hat{y}_{t-1}$$

By successively performing similar substitutions one is led to the following general expression for $\hat{y}_{t+1}$:

$$\hat{y}_{t+1} = \alpha y_t + \alpha(1 - \alpha)y_{t-1} + \alpha(1 - \alpha)^2 y_{t-2} + \cdots + \alpha(1 - \alpha)^{t-1}y_1 + (1 - \alpha)^t\hat{y}_1$$

(17.9)

For example,

$$\hat{y}_4 = \alpha y_3 + \alpha(1 - \alpha)y_2 + \alpha(1 - \alpha)^2 y_1 + (1 - \alpha)^3\hat{y}_1$$

Since $0 < \alpha < 1$, it follows that $0 < 1 - \alpha < 1$. Thus,

$$\alpha > \alpha(1 - \alpha) > \alpha(1 - \alpha)^2$$

In other words, in the previous example y_3, the most recent observation, receives more weight than y_2, which receives more weight than y_1. This illustrates the general property of an exponential smoothing model—that *the coefficients of the y's decrease as the data become older*. It can also be shown that *the sum of all of the coefficients (including the coefficient of $\hat{y}_1$) is 1*; that is in the case of $\hat{y}_4$, for example,

$$\alpha + \alpha(1 - \alpha) + \alpha(1 - \alpha)^2 + (1 - \alpha)^3 = 1$$

Initial Guess   We have thus seen in expression (17.9) that the general value $\hat{y}_{t+1}$ is a weighted sum of *all previous observations* (including the last observed value, y_t). Moreover, the weights sum to 1 and are decreasing as historical observations get older. The last term in the sum, namely $\hat{y}_1$, is not a historical observation. Recall that it was a "guess" at y_1. We can now observe that as t increases, the influence of $\hat{y}_1$ on $\hat{y}_{t+1}$ decreases and in time becomes negligible. To see this, note that the coefficient of $\hat{y}_1$ in (17.9) is $(1 - \alpha)^t$. Thus, the weight assigned to $\hat{y}_1$ decreases exponentially with t. Even if α is small [which makes $(1 - \alpha)$ nearly 1] the value of $(1 - \alpha)^t$ decreases rapidly. For example, if $\alpha = 0.1$ and $t = 20$, then $(1 - \alpha)^t = 0.12$. If $\alpha = 0.1$ and $t = 40$, then $(1 - \alpha)^t = 0.015$. Thus, as soon as enough data have been observed, the value of $\hat{y}_{t+1}$ will be quite insensitive to the choice for $\hat{y}_1$.

Choosing α   Obviously, the value of α, which is a parameter input by the analyst, affects the performance of the model. As you can see explicitly in (17.8), it is the weight given to the data value (y_t) most recently observed. This implies that, the larger value of α, the more strongly the model will react to the last observation, which, as we will see, may or may not be desirable. Figure 17.18 shows values for the weights [in expression (17.9)] when $\alpha = 0.1$, 0.3, and 0.5. You can see that for the larger values of α (e.g., $\alpha = 0.5$) more relative weight is assigned to the more recent observations and the influence of older data is more rapidly diminished.

To illustrate further the effect of choosing various values for α (i.e., putting more or less weight on recent observations), we consider three specific cases.

Figure 17.18
Weights for Different Values of α

VARIABLE	COEFFICIENT	$\alpha = 0.1$	$\alpha = 0.3$	$\alpha = 0.5$
y_t	α	0.1	0.3	0.5
y_{t-1}	$\alpha(1 - \alpha)$	0.09	0.21	0.25
y_{t-2}	$\alpha(1 - \alpha)^2$	0.081	0.147	0.125
y_{t-3}	$\alpha(1 - \alpha)^3$	0.07290	0.10290	0.0625
y_{t-4}	$\alpha(1 - \alpha)^4$	0.06561	0.07203	0.03125
y_{t-5}	$\alpha(1 - \alpha)^5$	0.05905	0.05042	0.01563
y_{t-6}	$\alpha(1 - \alpha)^6$	0.05314	0.03530	0.00781
y_{t-7}	$\alpha(1 - \alpha)^7$	0.04783	0.02471	0.00391
y_{t-8}	$\alpha(1 - \alpha)^8$	0.04305	0.01729	
y_{t-9}	$\alpha(1 - \alpha)^9$	0.03874	0.01211	
y_{t-10}	$\alpha(1 - \alpha)^{10}$	0.03487	0.00847	
Sum of the weights		0.68619	0.98023	0.99610

Step Change ■ *Case 1:* Suppose that at a certain point in time the underlying system experiences a rapid and radical change. How does the choice of α influence the way in which the exponential smoothing model will react? As an illustrative example consider an extreme case in which

$$y_t = 0 \quad \text{for } t = 1, 2, .., 99$$
$$y_t = 1 \quad \text{for } t = 100, 101, \ldots$$

This situation is illustrated in Figure 17.19. Note that in this case if $\hat{y}_1 = 0$, then $\hat{y}_{100} = 0$ for any value of α, since we are taking the weighted sum of a series of zeros.

Figure 17.19
System Change When $t = 100$

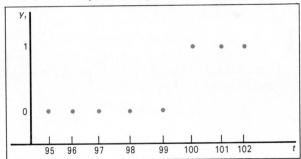

Thus, at time 99 our best estimate of y_{100} is 0, whereas the actual value will be 1. At time 100 we will first see that the system has changed. The question is: How quickly will the forecasting system respond as time passes and the information that the system has changed becomes available?

To answer this question, we plot $\hat{y}_{t+1}$ for $\alpha = 0.5$ and $\alpha = 0.1$ in Figure 17.20. Note that when $\alpha = 0.5$, $\hat{y}_{106} = 0.984$; thus at time 105 our estimate of y_{106} would be 0.984, whereas the true value will turn out to be 1. When $\alpha = 0.1$ our estimate of y_{106} is only 0.468.

Figure 17.20

Response to a Unit Change in y_t

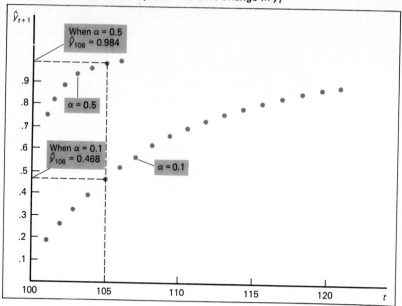

We see then that a forecasting system with $\alpha = 0.5$ responds much more quickly to changes in the data than does a forecasting system with $\alpha = 0.1$. The manager would thus prefer a relatively large α if the system is characterized by a low level of random behavior, but is subject to occasional enduring shocks. (Case 1 is an extreme example of this situation.) However, suppose that the data are characterized by large random errors but a stable mean. Then if α is large, a large random error in y_t will throw the forecast value, $\hat{y}_{t+1}$, way off. Hence, for this type of process a smaller value of α would be preferred.

Linear Ramp

■ *Case 2:* As opposed to the rapid and radical change investigated in Case 1, suppose now that a system experiences a *steady* change in the value of y. An example of a steady growth pattern is illustrated in Figure 17.21. This example is called a *linear ramp*. Again the question is: How will the exponential smoothing model respond and how will this response be affected by the choice of α?

Figure 17.21

Steadily Increasing Values of y_t (a Linear Ramp)

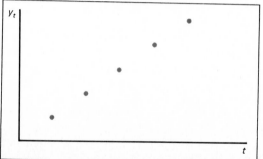

In this case, recall that

$$\hat{y}_{t+1} = \alpha y_t + \alpha(1 - \alpha)y_{t-1} + \cdots$$

Since all previous y's ($y_1, \ldots, y_{t-1}$) are smaller than y_t and since the weights sum to 1, it can be shown that, for any α between 0 and 1, $y_{t+1} < y_t$. Also, since y_{t+1} is greater than y_t, we see that $\hat{y}_{t+1} < y_t < y_{t+1}$. Thus our forecast will always be too small. Finally, since smaller values of α put more weight on older data, the smaller the value of α, the worse the forecast becomes. But even with α very close to 1 the forecast is not very good if the ramp is steep. The moral for managers is that exponential smoothing (or indeed any weighted moving average), without an appropriate modification, is not a good forecasting tool in a rapidly growing market. The model could be adjusted to include a trend, but this topic lies beyond the introductory scope of this chapter.

Seasonal Demand

■ *Case 3:* Suppose that a system experiences a regular *seasonal pattern* in y (such as would be the case if y represents, for example, the demand in the city of Chicago for swimming suits). How then will the exponential smoothing model respond, and how will this response be affected by the choice of α? Consider, for example, the seasonal pattern illustrated in Figure 17.22, and suppose it is desired to extrapolate *several periods forward*. For example, suppose we wish to forecast demand in periods 8 through 11 based only on data through period 7. Then

$$\hat{y}_8 = \alpha y_7 + (1 - \alpha)\hat{y}_7$$

Figure 17.22
Seasonal Pattern in y_t

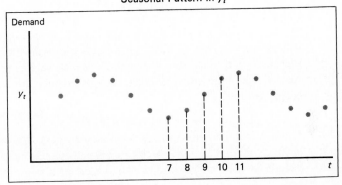

Now to obtain $\hat{y}_9$, since we have data only through period 7, we assume that $y_8 = \hat{y}_8$. Then

$$\hat{y}_9 = \alpha y_8 + (1 - \alpha)\hat{y}_8 = \alpha\hat{y}_8 + (1 - \alpha)\hat{y}_8 = \hat{y}_8$$

Similarly, it can be shown that $\hat{y}_{11} = \hat{y}_{10} = \hat{y}_9 = \hat{y}_8$. In other words, $\hat{y}_8$ is the best estimate of all future demands. Now let us see how good these predictions are. We know that

$$\hat{y}_{t+1} = \alpha y_t + \alpha(1 - \alpha)y_{t-1} + \alpha(1 - \alpha)^2 y_{-2} + \cdots$$

Suppose that a small value of α is chosen. By referring to Figure 17.18 we see that when α is small (say 0.1) the coefficients for the most recent terms change relatively slowly (i.e., they are nearly equal to each other). Thus, $\hat{y}_{t+1}$ will resemble a simple moving average of a number of terms. In this case the future predictions (e.g., $\hat{y}_{11}$) will all be somewhere near the average of the past observations. The forecast thus essentially ignores the seasonal pattern. If a large value of α is chosen, $\hat{y}_{11}$, which equals $\hat{y}_8$, will be close in value to y_7, which is obviously not good. In other words, the model fares poorly in this case regardless of the choice of α.

Using Exponential Smoothing

The exponential smoothing model $\hat{y}_{t+1} = \alpha y_t + (1 - \alpha)\hat{y}_t$, is intended for situations in which the behavior of the variable of interest is essentially stable, in the sense that deviations over time have nothing to do with *time*, per se, but are caused by *random effects* which do not follow a regular pattern. This is what we have termed the *stationarity* assumption. Not surprisingly, then, the model has various shortcomings when it is used in situations (such as swimming suit demand) that do not fit this prescription. Although this statement may be true, it is not very constructive. What approach should a manager take when the exponential smoothing model as described above is not appropriate? In the case of a seasonal pattern a naive approach would be to use the exponential smoothing model on "appropriate" past data. For example, to forecast sales in June one might take a smoothed average of sales in previous Junes. This approach has two problems. First, it ignores a great deal of useful information. Certainly sales from last July through this May should provide at least a limited amount of information about the likely level of sales this June. Second, if the cycle is very long, say a year, this approach means that very old data must be used to get a reasonable sample size. The above assumption, that the system or process producing the variable of interest is essentially *stationary* over time, becomes more tenuous when the span of time covered by the data becomes quite large.

If the manager is convinced that there is either a trend (Case 2) or a seasonal effect (Case 3) in the variable being predicted, a better approach is to develop modified exponential smoothing models that incorporate these features. References to models of this sort exist in the technical literature and the models are not exceptionally complicated. Presentation of these developments, however, carries us too far into the realm of a quite special technique and too far from our goal in this chapter of presenting mainly the basic concepts.

The Random Walk

The moving-average techniques discussed above are examples of what are called time-series models. Recently, much more sophisticated methods for time-series analysis have become available. These methods, based primarily on developments by G. E. P. Box and G. M. Jenkins[4] in the late 1960s, have already had an important impact on the practice of forecasting, and indeed the Box–Jenkins approach is incorporated in certain computer packages.

These time-series forecasting techniques are based on the assumption that the true values of the variable of interest, y_t, are generated by a stochastic (i.e., probabilistic) model. Introducing enough of the theory of probability to enable us to discuss these models in any generality seems inappropriate, but one special and very important (and very simple) process, called a *random walk*, serves as a nice illustration of a stochastic model. Here the variable y_t is assumed to be produced by the relationship

$$y_t = y_{t-1} + \epsilon$$

[4]G. E. P. Box and G. M. Jenkins, *Time Series Analysis, Forecasting and Control* (San Francisco: Holden-Day, Inc., 1970).

where the value of ϵ is determined by a random event. To illustrate this process even more explicitly, let us consider a man standing at a street corner on a north-south street. He flips a fair coin. If it lands with a head showing, he walks one block north. If it lands with a tail showing, he walks one block south. When he arrives at the next corner (whichever one it turns out to be) he repeats the process. This is the classic example of a random walk. To put this example in the form of the model, label the original corner zero. We shall call this the value of the first observation, y_1. Starting at this point, label successive corners going north $+1, +2, \ldots$. Also starting at the original corner label successive corners going south $-1, -2, \ldots$ (see Figure 17.23). These labels that describe the location of our random walker are the y_t's.

Figure 17.23
Classic Random Walk

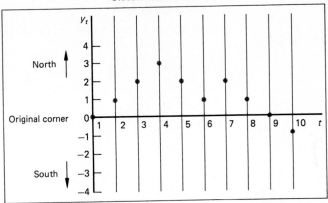

In the model, $y_t = y_{t-1} + \epsilon$, where (assuming a fair coin) $\epsilon = 1$ with probability $1/2$ and $\epsilon = -1$ with probability $1/2$. If our walker observes the sequence, H, H, H, T, T, H, T, T, T, he will follow the path shown in Figure 17.23.

Using the Conditional Expected Value as a Forecast

Suppose that after our special agent has flipped the coin nine times (i.e., he has moved nine times, and we have, starting with corner 0, 10 observations of corners) we would like to forecast where he will be after another move. This is the typical forecasting problem in the time-series context. That is, we have observed $y_1, y_2, \ldots, y_{10}$ and we need a good forecast $\hat{y}_{11}$ of the forthcoming value y_{11}. In this case, according to a reasonable criterion, the best value for $\hat{y}_{11}$ is the *conditional expected value* of the random quantity y_{11}. In other words, the best forecast is the expected value of y_{11} given that we know $y_1, y_2, \ldots, y_{10}$. From the model we know that y_{11} will equal $y_{10} + 1$ with a probability equal to $1/2$ and y_{11} will equal $y_{10} - 1$ with a probability equal to $1/2$. Thus, $E(y_{11}|y_1, \ldots, y_{10})$, the conditional expected value of y_{11} given $y_1, y_2, \ldots, y_{10}$, is calculated as follows:

$$E(y_{11}|y_1, \ldots, y_{10}) = (y_{10} + 1)\tfrac{1}{2} + (y_{10} - 1)\tfrac{1}{2} = y_{10}$$

Thus we see that for this model the data $y_1, \ldots, y_9$ are irrelevant and *the best forecast of the random walker's position one move from now is his current position.* We note that in fact y_{11} can never equal y_{10}. Thus if we were actually betting on the value for y_{11} this forecast would not be useful. If, however, you were betting on the *average value* of y_{11}, for many walkers leaving y_{10}, then y_{10} is the best bet.

A further fact of interest is that the best forecast of y_{12} given $y_1, \ldots, y_{10}$ is also

y_{10}. Indeed, the best forecast for any future value of y, given this particular model, is its current value.

Application to Stock Prices This example is not as silly as it may seem at first glance. Indeed, there is a great deal of evidence that supports the idea that stock prices behave like a random walk and that the best forecast of a future stock price is its current value. Not surprisingly, this conclusion is not warmly accepted by research directors and technical chartists who make their living forecasting stock prices. One reason for the resistance to the random walk hypothesis is the almost universal human tendency when looking at a set of data to observe certain patterns or regularities no matter how the data are produced. Consider the time-series data plotted in Figure 17.24. It does not seem unreasonable to believe

Figure 17.24

Time-Series Data

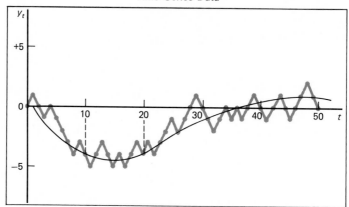

that the data are following a sinusoidal pattern as suggested by the smooth curve in the figure. In spite of this impression, the data was in fact generated by the random walk model presented earlier in this section. This illustrates the tendency to see patterns where there are none. In Figure 17.24, any attempt to predict future values by extrapolating the sinusoidal pattern would have no more validity than flipping a coin.

In concluding this section we should stress that it is *not* a general conclusion of time-series analysis that the best estimate of the future is the present [i.e., that $\hat{y}(t + l) = y_t$]. This result holds for the particular random walk model presented above. The result depends crucially on the assumption that the expected or mean value of ϵ, the random component, is zero. If the probability that ϵ equals 1 had been 0.6 and the probability that ϵ equals -1 had been 0.4, the best forecast of y_{t+1} would not have been y_t. To find this forecast one would have had to find $E(y_{t+1} \mid y_1, \ldots, y_t)$. Such a model is called *a random walk with a drift*.

17.5

THE ROLE OF HISTORICAL DATA: DIVIDE AND CONQUER

Historical data play a critical role in the construction and testing of forecasting models. Hopefully, a rationale precedes the construction of a quantitative forecasting model. There may be theoretical reasons for believing that a relationship exists between some independent variables and the dependent variable to be forecast and thus that a causal model is appropriate. Alternatively, one may take the time-series view that the "behavior of the past" is a good indication of the future. In either case, however, if a quantitative model is to be used, the parameters of the model must be selected. For example:

1. In a causal model using a linear forecasting function, $y = a + bx$, the values of a and b must be specified.

2. In a time-series model using a weighted n-period moving average, $\hat{y}_{t+1} = \alpha_0 y_t + \alpha_1 y_{t-1} + \cdots + \alpha_{n-1} y_{t-n+1}$, the number of terms, n, and the values for the weights, $\alpha_0, \alpha_1, \ldots, \alpha_{n-1}$, must be specified.

3. In a time-series model using exponential smoothing, $\hat{y}_{t+1} = \alpha y_t + (1 - \alpha)\hat{y}_t$, the value of α must be specified.

In any of these models, in order to specify the parameter values, one typically must make use of historical data. A useful guide in seeking to use such data effectively is to "divide and conquer." More directly, this means that it is often a useful practice to use part of the data to estimate the parameters and the rest of the data to test the model.

For example, suppose that a firm has weekly sales data on a particular product for the last two years and plans to use an exponential smoothing model to forecast sales for this product. The firm might use the following procedure.

---

1. Pick a particular value of α and compare the values of $\hat{y}_{t+1}$ to y_{t+1} for $t = 25$ to 75. The first 24 values are not compared so as to negate any initial or "startup" effect, that is, to nullify the influence of the initial guess, $\hat{y}_1$. The analyst would continue to select different values of α until the model produces a satisfactory fit during the period $t = 25$ to 75.

2. Test the model derived in step 1 on the remaining 29 pieces of data. That is, using the best value of α from step 1, compare the values of $\hat{y}_{t+1}$ and y_{t+1} for $t = 76$ to 104.

If the model does a good job of forecasting values for the last part of the historical data, there is some reason to believe that it will also do a good job with the future. On the other hand, if by using the data from weeks 1 through 75, the model cannot perform well in predicting the demand in weeks 76 through 104, the prospects for predicting the future with the same model seem dubious. In this case, another forecasting technique might be applied.

*Simulating
the Past*

The same type of divide-and-conquer strategy can be used with any of the forecasting techniques we have presented. This approach amounts to *simulating* the model's performance on past data. It is a popular method of testing models. It should be stressed, however, that this procedure represents what is termed a "null test." If the model fails on historical data, the model probably is not appropriate. If the model succeeds on historical data, *one cannot be sure that it will work in the future.* Who knows, the underlying system that is producing the observations may change. It is this type of sober experience that causes certain forecasters to be less so.

QUALITATIVE FORECASTING

Expert Judgment

A considerable amount of current research is aimed at comparing expert judgment with the use of formal quantitative models, and an increasing body of evidence casts doubt on whether, at least in many contexts, expert judgment can outperform even the simplest formal models.

Nevertheless, in current practice, many important forecasts are not based on formal models. This point seems obvious in the realm of world affairs—matters of war and peace, so to speak. Perhaps more surprisingly it is also often true in economic matters. For example, during the high interest-rate period of 1980 and 1981, the most influential forecasters of interest rates were not two competing econometric models run by teams of econometricians. Rather, they were Henry Kaufman of Salomon Brothers and Albert Wojnilower of First Boston, the so-called Doctors Doom and Gloom of the interest-rate world. These gentlemen combined relevant factors such as the money supply and unemployment, as well as results from quantitative models, in their own intuitive way (their own "internal" models) and produced forecasts that had widespread credibility and impact on the financial community.

The moral for managers is that qualitative forecasts can well be an important source of information. Managers must consider a wide variety of sources of data before coming to a decision. Even when formal models are being used, expert opinion is often relied on to qualitatively assess attributes which feed into the formal model. A sobering and useful measure of all forecasts—quantitative and qualitative—is a record of past performance. Good performance in the past is a sensible type of null test. An excellent track record does not promise good results in the future. A poor record, however, hardly creates enthusiasm for high achievement in the future. Managers should. thus, listen to experts cautiously and hold them to a standard of performance.

There is, however, more to qualitative forecasting than selecting "the right" expert. Techniques exist to elicit and combine forecasts from various groups of experts and we now turn our attention to these techniques.

The Delphi Method and Consensus Panel

The Delphi Method confronts the problem of obtaining a combined forecast from a group of experts. One approach is to bring the experts together in a room and let them discuss the event until a consensus emerges. Not surprisingly, this is called a **consensus panel**. This approach suffers because of the group dynamics of such an exercise. One strong individual can have an enormous effect on the forecast because of his or her personality, reputation, or debating skills. Accurate analysis may be pushed into a secondary position.

The Delphi Method was developed by the Rand Corporation to retain the strength of a joint forecast, while removing the effects of group dynamics. The method uses a coordinator and a set of experts. Each expert does not know who else is in the group. All communication is through the coordinator. The process is illustrated in Figure 17.25.

After three or four passes through this process, a consensus forecast typically emerges. The forecast may be near the original median, but if a forecast that is an outlier in round 1 is supported by strong analysis, the extreme forecast in round 1 may be the group forecast after three or four rounds.

Figure 17.25
Delphi Method

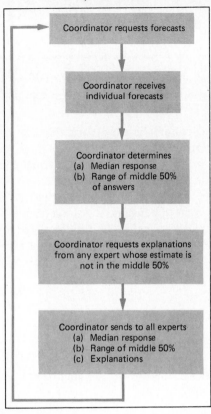

Coordinator requests forecasts

Coordinator receives
individual forecasts

Coordinator determines
(a) Median response
(b) Range of middle 50%
of answers

Coordinator requests explanations
from any expert whose estimate is
not in the middle 50%

Coordinator sends to all experts
(a) Median response
(b) Range of middle 50%
(c) Explanations

Grass-Roots
Forecasting
and Market
Research

Other qualitative techniques focus primarily on forecasting demand for a product or group of products. They are based on the concept of asking either those who are close to the eventual consumer, such as salesmen, or the consumer himself about a product or his purchasing plans.

Consulting
Salesman

In grass-roots forecasting, salesmen are asked to forecast demand in their district. In the simplest situations, these forecasts are added together to get a total demand forecast. In more sophisticated systems individual forecasts or the total may be adjusted on the basis of the historical correlation between the salesman's forecasts and the actual sales. Such a procedure makes it possible to adjust for an actual occurrence of the stereotyped salesman's optimism.

Grass-roots forecasts have the advantage of bringing a great deal of detailed knowledge to bear on the forecasting problem. The individual salesman who is keenly aware of the situation in his district should be able to provide better forecasts than more aggregate models. There are, however, several problems:

1. *High cost:* The time salesmen spend forecasting is not spent selling. Some view this opportunity cost of grass roots forecasting as its major disadvantage.
2. *Potential conflict of interest:* Sales forecasts may well turn into marketing goals

that can affect a salesman's compensation in an important way. Such considerations exert a downward bias in individual forecasts.

3. *Product schizophrenia (i.e., stereotyped salesman's optimism):* It is important for salesmen to be enthusiastic about their product and its potential uses. It is not clear that this enthusiasm is consistent with a cold-eyed appraisal of its market potential.

In summary, grass-roots forecasting may not fit well with other organization objectives and thus may be of limited value in an overall sense.

Consulting Consumers

Market research is a large and important topic in its own right. It includes a variety of techniques, from consumer panels through consumer surveys and on to test marketing. The goal is to make predictions about the size and structure of the market for specific goods and/or services. These predictions (forecasts) are usually based on small samples and are qualitative in the sense that the original data typically consists of subjective evaluations of consumers. A large menu of quantitative techniques exist to aid in determining how to gather the data and how to analyze it.

Market research is an important activity in most consumer products firms. It also plays an important role in the political and electoral process.

17.7
NOTES ON IMPLEMENTATION

Whether in the private or public sector, the need to deal with the future is an implicit or explicit part of every management action and decision. As such, managing the forecasting activity is a critical part of a manager's responsibility. A manager must decide what resources to devote to a particular forecast and what approach to use to obtain it.

The question of "what resources" hinges on two issues.

1. The importance of the forecast, or more precisely, the importance of the decision awaiting the forecast and its sensitivity to the forecast

2. The quality of the forecast as a function of the resources devoted to it

In other words, how much does it matter and how much does it cost; these are the same questions that management must ask and answer about many of the services it purchases.

In actual applications, the selection of the appropriate forecasting method for a particular situation depends on a variety of factors. Some of the features that distinguish one situation from the next are:

1. The importance of the decision
2. The availability of relevant data
3. The time horizon for the forecast
4. The cost of preparing the forecast
5. The time until the forecast is needed
6. The number of times such a forecast will be needed
7. Stability of the environment

The importance of the decision probably plays the strongest role in determining what forecasting method to use. Curiously, *qualitative approaches* (as opposed to *quantitative*) dominate the stage at the extremes of important and not very important forecasts.

On the low end of the importance scale, think of the many decisions a supermarket manager makes on what are typically implicit forecasts: What specials to offer, what to display at the ends of the aisles, how many baggers to employ. In such cases, forecasts are simply business judgment. The potential return is not high enough to justify the expenditure of resources required for formal and extensive model development.

On the high end, the decisions are *too important* (and perhaps too complex) to be left entirely to formal quantitative models. The future of the company, to say nothing of the executive, may hinge on a good forecast and the ensuing decision. *Quantitative models may certainly provide important input. In fact, the higher the planning level, the more you can be sure that forecasting models will at least to some extent be employed.* But for very important decisions, the final forecast will be based on the judgment of the executive and his colleagues. The extent to which a quantitative model is employed as an input to this judgment will depend, in the final analysis, on management's assessment of the model's validity. A consensus panel (a management committee) is often the chosen vehicle for achieving the final forecast. For example, what forecasts do you think persuaded Henry Ford IV to reject Lee Iacocca's plan to move Ford into small energy-efficient cars in the late 1970s? Also, what forecasts led Panasonic to introduce a tape-based system while RCA introduced a disk-based system for the TV player market? And what about the Cuban missile crisis? The Bay of Pigs? Clearly, management's personal view of the future played an important role.

Quantitative models play a major role in producing directly usable forecasts in situations that are deemed to be of "midlevel importance." This is especially true in short-range (up to 1 month) and medium-range (1 month to 2 years) scenarios. Time-series analyses are especially popular for repetitive forecasts of midlevel importance in a relatively stable environment. The use of exponential smoothing to forecast the demand for mature products is a prototype of this type of application.

Causal models actively compete with various experts for forecasting various economic phenomena in the midlevel medium range. Situations in which a forecast will be repeated quite often and where much relevant data are available are prime targets for quantitative models, and in such cases many successful models have been constructed. As our earlier discussion of interest rates forecasts indicated, there is ample room in this market for the "expert" with a good record of performance. In commercial practice one finds that many management consulting groups, as well as specialized firms such as DRI, provide forecasting "packages" for use in a variety of midlevel scenarios.

As a final comment, we can make the following observation about the use of forecasting in decision making within the public sector. Just as in private industry, it is often the case that the higher the level of the planning function, the more one sees the use of forecasting models employed as inputs. In such high-level situations there is a high premium on expertise and forecasting is, in one sense, a formal extension of expert judgment. Think of the Council of Economic Advisors, the Chairman of the Federal Reserve Board, or the Director of the Central Intelligence Agency. You can be sure that forecasts are of importance in these contexts and you can be sure that there is within these environments a continuing updating and, one hopes, improvement of forecasting techniques. As always, the extent to which the results of existing models are employed is a function of the executive's overall assessment of the model itself.

17.8

MAJOR CONCEPTS QUIZ

True–False

1. T F Quick-and-dirty forecasting methods are typically based on the method of least squares.
2. T F Minimizing total deviations (i.e., $\sum_{i=1}^{n} d_i$) is a reasonable way to define a "good fit."
3. T F Least-squares fits can be used for a variety of curves in addition to straight lines.
4. T F Regression analysis can be used to prove that the method of least squares produces the best possible fit for any specific real problem.
5. T F The method of least squares is used in causal models as well as in time-series models.
6. T F In a weighted three period moving-average forecast the weights can be assigned in many different ways.
7. T F Exponential smoothing automatically assigns weights that decrease in value as the data gets older.
8. T F Average squared error is one way to compare various forecasting techniques.
9. T F "Validation" refers to the process of determining a model's credibility by simulating its performance on past data.
10. T F A "random walk" is a stochastic model.
11. T F At higher levels of management, qualitative forecasting models are important in terms of current practice.

Multiple Choice

12. Quick-and-dirty forecasting methods
    a. consider only the last k data points
    b. primarily apply to problems with one independent variable
    c. use an intuitive measure of good fit
    d. both b and c

13. Linear regression (with 1 independent variable)
    a. requires the estimation of three parameters
    b. is a special case of polynomial least squares
    c. is a quick and dirty method
    d. uses total deviation as a measure of good fit

14. An operational problem with a simple k-period moving average is that
    a. it assigns equal weight to each piece of past data
    b. it assigns equal weight to each of the last k observations
    c. it requires storage of $k - 1$ pieces of data
    d. none of the above

15. A large value of α puts more weight on
    a. recent
    b. older
    data in an exponential smoothing model.

16. If the data being observed can be best thought of as being generated by random deviations about a stationary mean, a
    a. large
    b. small
    value of α is preferable in an exponential smoothing model.

17. A divide-and-conquer strategy means:
    a. Divide the modeling procedure into two parts: (1) use all the data to estimate parameter values and (2) use the parameter values from part (1) to see how well the model works.

    b. Divide the data into two parts. Estimate the parameters of the model on the first part. See how well the model works on the second part.
    c. Compare two models on the same data base.
    d. None of the above.

18. The Delphi Method
    a. relies on the power of written arguments
    b. requires resolution of differences via face-to-face debate
    c. is mainly used as an alternative to exponential smoothing
    d. none of the above

19. Conflict of interest can be significant problem in
    a. the Delphi Method
    b. asking salesmen
    c. marketing research based on consumer data
    d. none of the above

20. Quick-and-dirty forecasting methods are deficient in that
    a. they require the evaluation of squares and square roots
    b. they cannot be extended to more than one independent variable
    c. they have no objective measure for obtaining a good fit
    d. both b and c

Answers

1. F	**8.** T	**15.** a
2. F	**9.** T	**16.** b
3. T	**10.** T	**17.** b
4. F	**11.** T	**18.** a
5. T	**12.** d	**19.** b
6. T	**13.** b	**20.** d
7. T	**14.** c	

17.9

PROBLEMS

17-1. Consider the following set of data:

x	y	x	y
100	57	60	46
70	40	50	45
30	35	20	26
40	33	10	26
80	56	90	53

    (a) Plot a scatter diagram of these data.
    (b) Fit a straight line to the data using the method of least squares.
    (c) Use the function derived in part (b) to forecast a value for y when $x = 120$.

17-2. Consider the following set of data, where x is the independent and y the dependent variable.
    (a) Plot the scatter diagram for these data.
    (b) Fit a straight line to the data by the method of least squares.

x_i	y_i
30	35
25	26
20	25
15	5
10	9
5	1

17-3. Consider the following set of data:

x	y
1	2.00
2	1.50
3	4.50
4	4.00
5	5.50
6	4.50
7	6.00

(a) Plot a scatter diagram of the data.

(b) Fit a straight line to the data by the method of least squares. Plot the line on the scatter diagram.

(c) Fit a quadratic function to the data by the method of least squares. Plot the curve on the scatter diagram.

17-4. Fit a quadratic function to the data in Problem 17-2 by the method of least squares.

17-5. Compare the goodness of fit on the data in Problem 17-2 for the least-squares linear function and the least-squares quadratic function (derived in Problem 17-4) by calculating the sum of the squared deviations.

17-6. Compare the goodness of fit on the data in Problem 17-3 for the least-squares linear function and the least-squares quadratic function by calculating the sum of the squared deviations.

17-7. Further investigation reveals that the x variable in Problem 17-1 is simply 10 times the time at which an observation was recorded and the y variable is demand. For example, a demand of 57 occurred at time 10; a demand of 26 occurred at times 1 and 2.

(a) Plot actual demand against time.

(b) Use a simple four-period moving average to forecast demand at time 11.

(c) By inspecting the data, would you expect this to be a good model or not? Why?

17-8. Consider the following data set:

TIME	1	2	3	4	5	6	7	8	9	10	11	12
DEMAND	20	34	14	7	18	30	22	9	20	35	25	13

(a) Plot this time series. Connect the points with a straight line.

(b) Use a simple four-period moving average to forecast the demand for period 13.

(c) Does this seem like a reasonable forecasting device in view of the data?

17-9. Consider the data in Problem 17-7.

(a) Use a four-period weighted moving average with the weights 4/10, 3/10, 2/10, and

1/10 to forecast demand for time 11. Heavier weights should apply to more recent observations.

(b) Do you prefer this approach to the simple four-period model suggested in Problem 17-7? Why?

17-10. Consider the data in Problem 17-8.

(a) Use a six-period weighted moving average with the weights 10/30, 8/30, 6/30, 3/30, 2/30, and 1/30 to forecast demand for time period 13.

(b) Do you prefer this approach to the simple four-period model suggested in Problem 17-8? Why?

17-11. Consider the data in Problem 17-7.

(a) Let $\hat{y}_1 = 22$ and $\alpha = 0.4$. Use an exponential smoothing model to forecast demand in period 11.

(b) If you were to use an exponential smoothing model to forecast this time series, would you prefer a larger (than 0.4) or smaller value for α? Why?

17-12. Consider the data in Problem 17-8.

(a) Assume that $\hat{y}_1 = 18.35$ and $\alpha = 0.3$. Use an exponential smoothing model to forecast demand in period 13.

(b) If you were to use an exponential smoothing model to forecast this time series, would you prefer $\alpha = 0.3$, a larger (than 0.3), or smaller, value of α? Why?

17-13. The president of Quacker Mills wants a subjective evaluation of the market potential of a new nacho-flavored breakfast cereal from a group consisting of (1) the vice-president of marketing, (2) the marketing manager of the western region, (3) 10 district sales managers from the western region. Discuss the advantages and disadvantages of a consensus panel and the Delphi Method for obtaining this evaluation.

17-14. The president of a midwestern university is considering a new budgeting system in which the large professional schools (business, law, and medicine) will become "profit" centers. She would like to get an evaluation of this plan from the deans of these schools. Would you recommend a consensus panel or the Delphi approach?

17-15. Given your current knowledge of the situation, would you recommend a causal or a time-series model to forecast next month's demand for Kellogg's Rice Crispies? Why?

17-16. Given your current knowledge of the situation, would you recommend a causal or a time-series model to forecast the number of new housing starts one year from now? Why?

More Challenging Problems

17-17. In some cases it is possible to obtain better forecasts by using a trend adjusted forecast. For example, consider the following two-step procedure:

1. Calculate $\hat{y}_t$ as before
2. Let $\hat{w}_t$ be the forecast of demand in period $t + 1$ based on data through period t, given as

$$\hat{w}_t = \hat{y}_t + \alpha[\hat{y}_t - \hat{y}_{t-1}] + (1 - \alpha)[\hat{y}_{t-1} - \hat{y}_{t-2}]$$

(a) Use the above trend-adjusted model with $\alpha = 0.4$ to forecast the sequence of demands in Problem 17-11.

(b) Use the average squared error measure to compare the simple exponential smoothing model (Problem 17-11) with the trend-adjusted model from part (a) on forecasting demand for periods 4 through 10, i.e. compare $1/7 \sum_{t=4}^{10} (y_t - \hat{y}_{t-1})^2$ with $1/7 \sum_{t=4}^{10} (y_t - \hat{w}_{t-1})^2$.

17-18. (a) Use the trend-adjusted model with $\alpha = 0.3$ to forecast the sequence of demands in Problem 17-12.

(b) As in Problem 17-17, compare the above result with the result from Problem 17-12. That is, compare $1/9 \sum_{t=4}^{12} (y_t - \hat{y}_{t-1})^2$ with $1/9 \sum_{t=4}^{12} (y_t - \hat{w}_{t-1})^2$.

17-19. Discuss the merit of the measure "average squared error." In comparing two methods, is the one with a smaller average squared error *always* superior?

17-20. With reference to Problem 17-19, what other quantitative measures can you think of for comparing different forecasting methods?

CHAPTER 18

Simulation Models

NAVAL SHIP PRODUCTION*

Ingalls Shipbuilding, a division of Litton Industries, Inc., is one of the largest shipyards in the world. From 1974 through 1977 the division's sales ranged from $500 million to $800 million with employment of approximately 20,000.

In 1969 and 1970 Ingalls was awarded Total Package Procurement contracts for five amphibious assault ships (LHAs) and 30 DD963 destroyers. These were firm-fixed-price contracts in which Ingalls received performance specifications and assumed sole responsibility for system design, detailed design, material procurement, planning, testing, and construction.

These contracts led to unanticipated cost overruns of $500 million dollars and a claim for this amount against the Navy. The basis for this claim rested on Ingalls' contention that Navy-responsible delays and design changes had created disruptions which had spread difficulties throughout the system and eventually produced the cost overruns. Although detailed data were submitted with the claim the difficulty of estimating the costs of second- and third-order "ripple effects" led to an adversary relationship between Ingalls and the Navy. This relationship endangered not only Ingalls' current profit position but the potential for future business.

To clarify its claim, Litton had a simulation program constructed to correctly quantify Navy-responsible delay and disruption costs and to demonstrate the ripple effects. Simulation was selected because it permitted:

1. Direct answering of "what if" questions. In particular, what if the Navy-initiated delays had not occurred?

*Kenneth G. Cooper, "Naval Ship Production: A Claim Settled and a Framework Built," *Interfaces*, Vol. 10, No. 6, December 1980, pp. 20–30.

2. A more complete and realistic representation of the system.

3. Clear and defensible attribution of impacts to specific sources.

The short-run impact of the model was to obtain a $447 million settlement for Ingalls from the Navy. Since the claim was settled out of court both the direct cost of further litigation (perhaps from $170 to $350 million) as well as a vast amount of managerial and professional time and talent were saved.

Perhaps the long-run effects are more important. Since its original application eight different shipbuilding programs totaling 55 ships and approximately $7 billion of business have been modeled. In these applications the model is used to estimate the effect of various actions in scheduling or managing resources as well as the impact of a multitude of exogenous factors.

APPLICATION CAPSULE •

PLANNING TO GET THE LEAD OUT*

In the mid-1970s concern over the use of tetraethyl lead (TEL) and the amount of sulfur in automobile gasoline became a topic of national concern. One result was that the California legislature passed a law requiring a scheduled lead and sulfur phase down. Under this law the maximum TEL content had to be decreased in phased steps from 1.4 to 0.4 grams per gallon over a 3-year horizon.

This law presented a major challenge to Exxon's Benicia Refinery since it fundamentally changed the way in which gasoline was produced. Gasoline production is performed in two steps: refining in which crude oil is separated into various components that are stored in large (component) tanks, and blending in which the components are mixed together to produce finished products which are stored in (finished product) tanks. TEL was an important part of this process because of the flexibility it provided. If a batch of gasoline did not meet the octane specification a little more TEL could be added to bring it up to standard.

Reducing the use of TEL had a particularly dramatic influence on the storage of components and finished products. Without the ability to enhance octane ratings with TEL it was necessary to expand the inventory of higher-octane components or blended products or perhaps both to ensure an adequate supply of the full range of finished products. Preliminary calculations indicated at least two new component tanks and one or two new finished product tanks would be needed. At a cost of over $1 million per tank this was clearly a problem that deserved careful attention.

Exxon constructed a discrete time simulator to analyze this problem. The program simulates the operation of the gasoline production facilities on an hour-to-hour basis. The simulator had several advantages: gathering of input data was easy and

*Lewis Golovin, "Product Blending: A Simulation Case Study in Double-Time," *Interfaces*, Vol. 9, No. 5, pp. 64–76.

594

straightforward, management became involved in determining the blending strategy used in the simulation, and results were produced on operations reports very similar to those in actual use. Each of these factors make the results more "believable" to management and thus made the recommendations more acceptable.

As a result of the analysis, Exxon management decided to change the way in which components and final products were stored and to authorize the construction of one additional component tank and one additional finished product tank. Thus the company was able to reduce its planned capital expenditure by at least one tank—an estimated savings of at least $1.4 million.

APPLICATION CAPSULE •

THE CAMPAIGN AGAINST BRUCELLOSIS*

In the late 1970s Australia (as well as the United States, United Kingdom, Canada, New Zealand, and Japan) was engaged in a nationwide campaign to eradicate the disease bovine brucellosis from its cattle. This disease is highly contagious and reduces productivity in the beef and dairy industry by causing fertility problems in cattle.

The approach used in Australia for eradicating brucellosis involved testing of all herds and slaughter of infected cattle. In particular, the procedure set down by the Australian Bureau of Animal Health required: (1) all breeding animals in all herds had to be tested and all infected animals slaughtered within 21 days of detection; (2) herds had to be retested within 30 to 60 days (and diseased cattle slaughtered) until no disease was uncovered in two consecutive tests. This program was the responsibility of each of the six Australian state governments. The enormity of the task is evident from the fact that in just one state, New South Wales, there are approximately 5.2 million breeding cattle in about 17,000 herds.

Those responsible for the campaign had to decide how many test teams to put into the field and how many herds to test at any particular time. These decisions are restricted by three sets of constraints: the capacity of the laboratories that analyze the samples collected by the test teams, the capacity of the slaughter houses in the particular region to process infected cattle, and the requirements for retesting set by the Bureau of Animal Health. In addition, in order for Australian beef to remain competitive on the world market brucellosis had to be effectively eliminated by the mid-1980s. Planning for the campaign was difficult because of uncertainty over the original incidence of the disease and the rate of reinfection during the interval between tests.

A simulator based on a Markov chain model was constructed to aid in the planning process. Inputs included estimates of retest and slaughter rates and initial disease status. The output included an estimate of the number of herds tested and the number

*A. C. Beck, and L. W. Valentine, "A Simulation Model to Aid Decision Making in a Campaign to Eradicate Brucellosis from Cattle," *Interfaces*, Vol. 10, No. 1, February 1980, pp. 28–38.

of cattle slaughtered for each time period during the campaign. Estimates of the various probabilities were updated and the model run again as new data became available. The model allowed the planners to focus on the number of teams and the testing intensity required to organize a feasible and cost-effective program. It was estimated that the model produced a savings of approximately 1 million Australian dollars during the campaign and helped guarantee the status of the annual 160 million Australian dollar New South Wales beef export market.

18.1
INTRODUCTION

Any discussion of models in managerial decision making, no matter how broad, is pointedly incomplete without some reasonable amount of attention to the topic of simulation. If you would select at random a practitioner of management science or an analyst from a corporate planning department, the chances are high that he would be working with a simulation model. Our goal in this chapter is to develop a reasonable understanding of how such models work and where they fit into the spectrum of applications.

Uses of Simulation
At the outset, it is important to recognize that simulation is one of those words that means different things to different people. The president of PROTRAC uses a simulation model to assist in long-range corporate planning. This is a strategic planning model. A project director at NASA uses a simulation model to assist in planning the next trip to Mars. Simulation models are used by the Federal Reserve Board in economic planning and by the Department of Defense in military planning. A simulation model is used by a commodities speculator to test her latest theory on how to profit in futures trading in the soybean market. A job-shop scheduler uses a simulation model to help plan the acquisition of new machinery.

All of these models have little in common, and yet they are all referred to as "simulation." The concept of simulation applies to any situation in which someone is interested in the behavior of a particular system.

> **The basic idea of a simulation is to build an experimental device that will "act like" (simulate) the system of interest in certain important respects.**

This approach has a long history in the applied physical and engineering sciences. Consider the following examples:

1. Models of yachts to be built for the America's Cup race are tested in a tow tank at MIT. Towing the model through the tank *simulates* the flow of the water over the hull of the actual ship.
2. Models of planes are tested in wind tunnels to test the aerodynamic properties of the plane. The wind tunnel experience *simulates* actual flight.
3. Pilots train in models of actual airplane cabins under *simulated* conditions.
4. Pilot plants are used to *simulate* the behavior of chemical processes in order to reduce the risk associated with the construction of the actual processor.

596

5. New products are subjected to tests that *simulate* the conditions they will later encounter.

In spite of its popularity in other fields, simulation is a relatively new technique for studying management systems. Its popularity and growth have coincided with the availability and the computational power of digital computers. Computers provide the student of management with a device that can work through amazingly complicated logical structures unerringly, rapidly, and at a reasonable cost. Thus, with the aid of a computer it is possible to describe the logical operation of a management system and to experiment with it.

In the following sections, several examples will be presented to illustrate the different meanings of simulation. These examples will give some understanding of how simulation models are constructed and how they can be properly and improperly used.

18.2
SIMULATION AND RANDOM NUMBERS

Dealing with Uncertainty

Simulation is an important tool for analyzing problems in which there are elements of uncertainty. In particular, in many simulation models it is assumed that the behavior of one or more factors can be represented by a probability distribution. This is what we have previously called (see Chapter 14) decision making under risk. Using simulation to deal with this type of problem is sometimes called a *Monte Carlo* approach. The importance of simulation in this context stems from the fact that in such cases it is often difficult to get analytic results for many interesting and important problems. This is, for example, often true of the so-called queuing or waiting-line models. In fact, apparently enough people are interested in simulating queuing situations that more than one supplier of computer software has found it to be an advantage to introduce general-purpose simulation packages for queuing systems. In the following pages, we consider several applications of simulation to problems in which uncertainty is captured in terms of probability distributions. To deal with this phenomenon, simulation models use **random numbers**. That is,

> **Random numbers are used, in the simulation context, to generate uncertain events. In particular, they are used to make random draws from a probability distribution.**

To focus more clearly on what is meant by a random number, let us consider an experiment in which a set of identical balls is numbered from 0 through 99 and placed in an urn. A ball is then drawn from the urn *at random*; that is, each ball is *equally likely* to be drawn. The number on the ball is recorded, the ball is returned to the urn, and the experiment is repeated. Suppose that this experiment is repeated 400 times and the results are recorded in a table.

The sequence of 400 numbers shown in Figure 18.1, called a *table of random digits*, was created by a computer using a device conceptually equivalent to the procedure just described.

As a first glimpse at how such a table can be used in a simulation, consider simulating a coin-flipping game in which the house pays $2 if a head occurs and nothing if a tail occurs. Suppose that you wanted to obtain a better feeling for the potential sequence

Figure 18.1

Table of Random Digits

	1	2	3	4	5	6	7	8	9	10
1	97	95	12	11	90	49	57	13	86	81
2	02	92	75	91	24	58	39	22	13	02
3	80	67	14	99	16	89	96	63	67	60
4	66	24	72	57	32	15	49	63	00	04
5	96	76	20	28	72	12	77	23	79	46
6	55	64	82	61	73	94	26	18	37	31
7	50	02	74	70	16	85	95	32	85	67
8	29	53	08	33	81	34	30	21	24	25
9	58	16	01	91	70	07	50	13	18	24
10	51	16	69	67	16	53	11	06	36	10
11	04	55	36	97	30	99	80	10	52	40
12	86	54	35	61	59	89	64	97	16	02
13	24	23	52	11	59	10	88	68	17	39
14	39	36	99	50	74	27	69	48	32	68
15	47	44	41	86	83	50	24	51	02	08
16	60	71	41	25	90	93	07	24	29	59
17	65	88	48	06	68	92	70	97	02	66
18	44	74	11	60	14	57	08	54	12	90
19	93	10	95	80	32	50	40	44	08	12
20	20	46	36	19	47	78	16	90	59	64
21	86	54	24	88	94	14	58	49	80	79
22	12	88	12	25	19	70	40	06	40	31
23	42	00	50	24	60	90	69	60	07	86
24	29	98	81	68	61	24	90	92	32	68
25	36	63	02	37	89	40	81	77	74	82
26	01	77	82	78	20	72	35	38	56	89
27	41	69	43	37	41	21	36	39	57	80
28	54	40	76	04	05	01	45	84	55	11
29	68	03	82	32	22	80	92	47	77	62
30	21	31	77	75	43	13	83	43	70	16
31	53	64	54	21	04	23	85	44	81	36
32	91	66	21	47	95	69	58	91	47	59
33	48	72	74	40	97	92	05	01	61	18
34	36	21	47	71	84	46	09	85	32	82
35	55	95	24	85	84	51	61	60	62	13
36	70	27	01	88	84	85	77	94	67	35
37	38	13	66	15	38	54	43	64	25	43
38	36	80	25	24	92	98	35	12	17	62
39	98	10	91	61	04	90	05	22	75	20
40	50	54	29	19	26	26	87	94	27	73

of outcomes of this game. This can be done by simulation as follows. Adopt the convention that if the random number that is chosen is any integer from 00 through 49, we will say that a head has occurred, and if the random number is any integer from 50 through 99, a tail occurs. Note that since there are 100 numbers in total (the integers from 00 through 99), and since each number is equally likely, the probability of each number is 1/100. The probability that a head occurs is the probability that an integer from 00 through 49 will be drawn, which is clearly 50/100 = 1/2. Similarly, the probability of a tail will be 1/2.

Now one simply starts at a random (i.e., an arbitrary) position in the table of random numbers and reads them consecutively (down columns) in order to simulate the game.[1] Suppose that the simulation starts with the integer in column 3, row 16. For 10 trials, the results are recorded in Figure 18.2.

Figure 18.2
Simulating a Coin Flip

TRIAL	RANDOM NUMBER	EVENT	RETURN
1	41	H	$2
2	48	H	2
3	11	H	2
4	95	T	0
5	36	H	2
6	24	H	2
7	12	H	2
8	50	T	0
9	81	T	0
10	02	H	2
Total return			$14.00
Average return			$ 1.40

Based on these results, our estimate of *average return* is $1.40. It can also be noted that after 20 trials the total return is $22.00, which gives an average return of $1.10 per trial. Actually, in this example it is a trivial analytic matter to calculate that the *expected return* of the game is $1.00, and hence you should be willing to pay the house a fee of up to $1.00 per flip of the coin in order to play the game. As the simulation above becomes longer and longer you would expect the average return to come closer and closer to $100. In later sections we will expand upon this relation between an *average value* (an empirical concept) as determined by simulation, and an *expected value* which is an *analytic concept* (i.e., a theoretic property of a model). For the moment, let us simply observe that in many real-world problems, it is difficult if not impossible to calculate the expected return associated with the various alternatives. Often the mathematics is simply too complicated. In such cases the hope is that, just as in the coin-flipping example, a simulation will provide an empirical way to obtain a decent estimate of the expected return.

The example above provides an oversimplified springboard of just how a simulation might work. Let us now proceed to deepen our understanding.

18.3
A SIMPLE HAND SIMULATION:
THE FRAME-PROCESSING MACHINE

The following problem is faced by the manufacturing superintendent at PROTRAC's Moline plant. One of his most expensive pieces of capital equipment is called a *frame-processing machine*. This machine performs a number of machining operations on the

---

[1] It is a property of a table of random numbers that we could choose to read down columns, or across rows, or any other rule to generate our sequence. Any such rule will produce a random sequence.

frame for the E-9. After this machining is completed, the frame is transported to inventory at the head of the assembly line. Plant engineering is proposing to install an overhead monorail crane system that would remove the frame from the machining operation and transport it to the assembly line. This monorail crane, however, would also serve other functions in the plant. The crane would move along its track visiting each of a number of different locations in the plant where it has specific tasks to perform. The frame-processing machine would represent only one such location. Should there be a completed frame waiting at this location when the crane arrives, the frame would be picked up by the crane. If no frame is ready, however, the crane operator would not wait. The situation is represented in Figure 18.3.

Figure 18.3

Transportation System for Frames

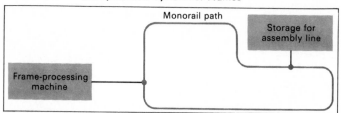

The time required to process the frames varies greatly, depending on the amount of straightening required and on the surface condition of the frame. The time between visits of the crane at the frame-processing machine also varies, depending on what other tasks it encounters as it makes its rounds. Any idle time on the frame-processing machine has a significant opportunity cost to PROTRAC since this machine is a major bottleneck in the overall processing operation.

After a group of four frames has been completed, the frame-processing machine is shut down in order to readjust the tools. Since the crane is used in the final part of this readjustment operation, it turns out that as part of its regular routine the crane begins its rounds from the frame-processing machine as soon as that machine is ready to begin operating again. In other words, both the processing machine and the crane begin at the same time. The industrial engineering department has provided the estimates of operating data shown in Figure 18.4. This table portrays what is called *a discrete probability distribution*.

The production superintendent would like to know how much idle time he will have on the average during a production run of four frames. With the data in Figure 18.4

Figure 18.4

Data for E-9 Frame Production

PROCESSING TIME [TIME ON THE FRAME-PROCESSING MACHINE (MIN)]	PROBABILITY	ROUTE TIME [TIME BETWEEN ARRIVALS FOR THE CRANE (MIN)]	PROBABILITY
45	$\frac{1}{5}$	10	$\frac{1}{4}$
60	$\frac{3}{5}$	15	$\frac{2}{4}$
75	$\frac{1}{5}$	20	$\frac{1}{4}$

and the table of random numbers provided in Figure 18.1, he decides to simulate the behavior of the E-9 frame-processing machine. He first defines the following variables:

$P(N)$ = processing time of frame N

$R(M)$ = time required for round M by the crane

$T(N)$ = time at which the processing of frame N will be complete

$S(M)$ = time at which the crane will complete its Mth round and arrive at the frame-processing machine

Flow Charting the Simulation

With the aid of this notation, he develops the flowchart shown in Figure 18.5. Before the superintendent can use this flowchart, the boxes labeled *Determine P(N)* and *Determine R(M)* must be specified. The idea, of course, is to select *processing times* and *route times* according to the probabilities shown in Figure 18.4. This idea is implemented by using the table of random numbers provided in Figure 18.1. For example, since the probability is 1/5 that the processing time is 45 minutes, we assign the 20 random digits 00 through 19 to this event. In other words, if a 16 is selected, we will say that the processing time is 45

Figure 18.5

Flow Diagram for E-9 Frame-Processing Simulation

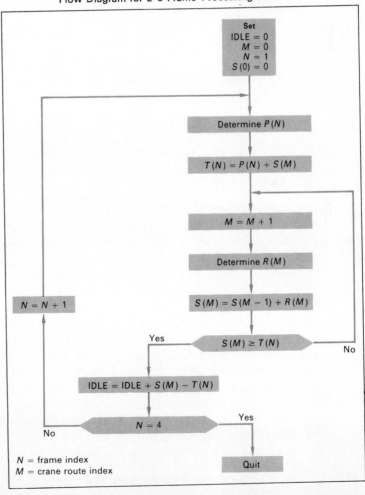

minutes. The relationship between the random digits and the processing times is shown in Figure 18.6. The relationship between the random digits and the route times is also presented in this figure. There is nothing particularly sacred about the correspondence between events and random numbers shown in Figure 18.6. Many assignments of random digits to processing times would be correct. The essential condition is that 1/5 of the digits be assigned to a processing time of 45 minutes, 3/5 of the digits to 60 minutes, and so on. Thus, *any* 20 digits could have been substituted for 00–19, and so on. The assignment in Figure 18.6 is, in theory, no better or worse than any other correct assignment, but the one we have chosen was particularly simple to construct, and is also simple to work with. In other words, having drawn a number, you determine what event has occurred by locating that number in its appropriate interval, a particularly simple task. That is why *intervals of random numbers*, as in Figure 18.6, are the preferred usage.

Figure 18.6

Using Random Digits

PROCESSING TIME (MIN)		PROBABILITY	RANDOM DIGITS
	45	$\frac{1}{5}$	00–19
Events	60	$\frac{3}{5}$	20–79
	75	$\frac{1}{5}$	80–99

ROUTE TIME (MIN)		PROBABILITY	RANDOM DIGITS
	10	$\frac{1}{4}$	00–24
Events	15	$\frac{2}{4}$	25–74
	20	$\frac{1}{4}$	75–99

Beginning the Simulation The superintendent can now start his simulation. Suppose that he starts arbitrarily with the digit from column 9, row 33 in Figure 18.1. Since this number is 61, the value of $P(1)$, the time required to process the first frame, is 60 minutes. Since the next number (column 9, row 34) is 32, he knows that $R(1)$, the time required for the crane to complete its first route, is 15 minutes. Thus, the crane will arrive back at the frame-processing machine (where it initially started) at time 15. Since the first frame is still being processed, the crane moves on. More route times will be generated until the first frame can be picked up. The entire simulation for four frames is shown in Figure 18.7. The notation used corresponds to the notation in the flow chart (Figure 18.5). Each processing time and route time is recorded in the appropriate box. The other two numbers in parentheses in each box are the random number that was drawn to generate value for the processing time or route time and which random number it is in the overall sequence of draws. The latter figure is included to allow you to follow the development of the simulation in the order in which it occurred. We recommend that you follow this development closely in order to understand better how a simulator works.

This particular run proceeded as follows:

1. Random number 61 was chosen. This implied that $P(1) = 60 = T(1)$.

Figure 18.7
Simulation of Processing Four Frames

PROCESSING MACHINE

P(1) = 60   P(2) = 45   Idle = 10

CRANE

R(1) = 15 (32, 2)   S(1) = 15
R(2) = 15 (62, 3)   S(2) = 30
R(3) = 15 (67, 4)   S(3) = 45
T(1) = 60 (61, 1)
R(4) = 15 (25, 5)   S(4) = 60
R(5) = 20 (75, 7)   S(5) = 80
R(6) = 15 (27, 8)   S(6) = 95
R(7) = 20 (81, 9)   S(7) = 115
T(2) = 105 (17, 6)

PROCESSING MACHINE

P(3) = 45   T(3) = 160 (02, 10)   Idle = 10   P(4) = 60

CRANE

R(8) = 15 (60, 11)   S(8) = 130
R(9) = 10 (04, 12)   S(9) = 140
R(10) = 15 (46, 13)   S(10) = 155
R(11) = 15 (31, 14)   S(11) = 170
R(12) = 15 (25, 16)   S(12) = 185
R(13) = 10 (24, 17)   S(13) = 195
R(14) = 10 (10, 18)   S(14) = 205
R(15) = 15 (40, 19)   S(15) = 220
R(16) = 10 (02, 20)   S(16) = 230
T(4) = 230 (67, 15)

2. Random number 32 was chosen, so $R(1) = 15$. Now $S(1) = 15 + 0 = 15$. Thus $S(1) < T(1)$.

3. With $S(1) < T(1)$, the next random number, 62, was chosen. This implied that $R(2) = 15$. Then, since $S(2) = R(2) + S(1)$, it follows that $S(2) = 30$.

4. Since $S(2) < T(1)$, the next random number, 67, was drawn. Thus $R(3) = 15$. Now $S(3) = R(3) + S(2) = 45$.

5. Since $S(3) < T(1)$, the next random number, 25, was drawn. Now $S(4) = 60$, which equals $T(1)$. Thus, the first frame was completed with no idle time.

6. To start the next frame, the next random number, 17, was drawn, so $P(2) = 45$.

By following the complete development, it should be clear that a total of 20 minutes of idle time and 16 rounds of the crane occurred during this particular processing of four frames. The idle time, in general, is a chance phenomenon, and in another run it could turn out to be some other number. Suppose, for example, that the last random number (the twentieth) chosen in this run was 84 (rather than 02). In this case, the final route time would have been 20 minutes and the fourth frame would have had to wait 10 minutes to be picked up. Under this set of circumstances, the total idle time would have been 30 rather than 20 minutes.

It is easy to see that the logical operations and the bookkeeping associated with a simulation can become complicated and burdensome as the complexity of the system under consideration increases. Even for the extremely simple system presented here, the prospect of accurately completing many runs by hand is hardly encouraging. Unfortunately, for most simulations large samples are required to produce good estimates of the quantities of interest. Thus, except for very simple systems, hand simulation is not really a viable tool for analysis. The frame-processing example has been presented for its pedagogical value. To understand and interpret the results of a simulation accurately, one must understand the concept of using random numbers to generate uncertain events. The frame-processing example clearly illustrates this concept and, accordingly, the 'role of random numbers in creating a simulation model. This example provides a good idea of how many simulation models actually work.

Two Inventory Models We shall now use simulation to tackle two problems encountered previously in Chapter 16, the omelet pan problem featuring Peggy McConnel from Wiles Department Store, and the (r, Q) inventory model starring Victor Kowalski. As discussed in Chapter 16, both of these problems can be attacked with analytic methods. As a matter of fact, this would be the preferred approach for those specific examples. However, the pedagogical advantages of being able to compare the analytic and simulation approaches on the same problem motivate us to base our presentations on these models. As we shall see later, in the real world, simulation is typically used when it is impossible or too expensive to obtain analytic results.

18.4

THE ANALYTIC APPROACH VERSUS SIMULATION: INVENTORY AT WILES' HOUSEWARES

The Omelet Pan Problem Consider the omelet pan problem described in Chapter 16. In this problem Peggy McConnel, the chief buyer for housewares at Wiles Department Store, is trying to decide how many special omelet pans to order for a promotion. Wiles will buy the special pans for $22 and will sell them for $35. Any pans left at the end of the sale will be sold to Clampton's Discount Chain for $15 each. We thus see that Wiles will lose $7 for each special pan left unsold at the end of the promotion. This per unit amount, for each unsold special pan, is called *the per unit holding cost, h*. Thus, $h = \$7$.

As part of the promotion, Peggy has decided to use regular omelet pans to satisfy demand if she runs out of the special pans. Regular pans cost $32 each. In this case, then, the per unit cost of running out of special pans, called the *per unit penalty cost*, consists entirely of foregone revenue. This forgone revenue is termed "opportunity cost." If Peggy is out of special pans and a customer orders one, she will sell for $35 a regular pan that cost $32, and enjoy a contribution margin of only $3 ($35 − $32). However, if a special pan had been available, she would have sold this pan that cost $22 for $35, and thereby enjoyed a contribution margin of $13. She thus incurs a $10 ($13 − $3) "opportunity loss" (decline in contribution margin) for stockouts of special pans. This foregone revenue is *the per unit penalty cost, p*. Note that Peggy's calculations assume that using regular pans to satisfy the promotional demand will *not* create any unsatisfied regular demand. Because of the location of her regular pan supplier, the supply is large enough that this complication need not be considered.

The problem facing Peggy is how many special pans to order in view of an uncertain demand. We will see how to attack this question with simulation, beginning with an illustrative simple example. Later, we will invoke the assumption of a normal demand distribution ($\mu = 1000$, $\sigma = 100$) which is the situation treated in Chapter 16. But for the present discussion let us simplify the presentation by assuming that demand has the following discrete probability distribution.

$$\text{Prob \{demand} = 8\} = 0.1$$
$$\text{Prob \{demand} = 9\} = 0.2$$
$$\text{Prob \{demand} = 10\} = 0.3$$
$$\text{Prob \{demand} = 11\} = 0.2$$
$$\text{Prob \{demand} = 12\} = 0.1$$
$$\text{Prob \{demand} = 13\} = 0.1$$

Figure 18.8

Associating Random Numbers with Demands

RANDOM NUMBERS	PROPORTION OF TOTAL NUMBERS ASSIGNED	DEMAND FOR OMELET PANS	PROBABILITY
00–09	0.10	8	0.1
10–29	0.20	9	0.2
30–59	0.30	10	0.3
60–79	0.20	11	0.2
80–89	0.10	12	0.1
90–99	0.10	13	0.1

The relationship between random digits and events is shown in Figure 18.8. Again note that an interval of digits has been assigned to each uncertain event. The general rule for such an assignment is

$$\frac{\text{number of digits in interval } i}{100} = \text{probability of event } i$$

With this demand information Peggy could construct the simulator shown in Figure 18.9. To see how the simulator works, assume that Peggy decides to order 11 omelet pans. Then $y = 11$. Let us arbitrarily begin with the random digit 26 in row 6, column 7 of Figure 18.1. Then, according to Figure 18.8, the corresponding randomly generated demand is $D = 9$ pans. This means $y > D$ and the simulator takes the "yes" branch in the flowchart. The cost of this *simulated* promotion is $7(11 - 9) = \$14$. This, of course, is the appropriate cost since, if Peggy ordered 11 pans and only 9 were sold, Wiles would have 2 left over. Since the per unit holding cost is $7, this implies a cost of $14.

Figure 18.9

Simulating the Cost of Ordering y Pans

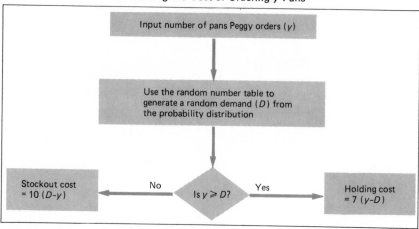

In problems such as this, the theoretic statistical concept of *expected cost* is of interest. In this simple example Peggy could calculate the *expected cost* of ordering 11 pans. Before doing so, let us use the simulator to *estimate* this value. We must make a number of trials, setting $y = 11$ and generating a new random demand on each trial. The cost that results on any given trial depends, of course, on the value of demand that was generated on that particular trial. The *average cost* over all trials, then, is an empirically obtained estimate of the expected cost. This process, for 10 trials, is illustrated in Figure 18.10, where we have proceeded to generate subsequent random demands by reading down column 7 in Figure 18.1, beginning from our initially selected entry in row 6. The results show that the total cost for the 10 trials is $96, and the average cost is $96/10 = \$9.60$. Thus based on these trials, Peggy's best estimate of the expected cost of ordering 11 pans is $9.60.

Obtaining an Average Cost for Each Order Quantity

If Peggy wanted to use simulation to determine how many pans to order, she would:

1. Select an order size (in the example above, the order size is 11).
2. Run a number of trials (say 10), *beginning from the same random number* (row 6, column 7).
3. Calculate the average cost.
4. Repeat steps 2 and 3 for a different order size.
5. Select the order size with the smallest cost.

Figure 18.10

Ten Simulated Trials

TRIAL NUMBER	QUANTITY ORDERED	RANDOM DEMAND	PANS LEFT OVER	PANS SHORT	COST
1	11	9	2		7 × 2 = 14
2	11	13		2	10 × 2 = 20
3	11	10	1		7 × 1 = 7
4	11	10	1		7 × 1 = 7
5	11	9	2		7 × 2 = 14
6	11	12		1	10 × 1 = 10
7	11	11	0		7 × 0 = 0
8	11	12		1	10 × 1 = 10
9	11	11	0		7 × 0 = 0
10	11	9	2		7 × 2 = 14
Total cost					$96

The results of such a study, for order sizes 9, 10, 11, and 12, are shown in the third column of Figure 18.11. It is seen that an order size of 11 pans gives the smallest average cost, *based on 10 trials*.

Figure 18.11

Expected Costs and Simulated Average Costs

NUMBER ORDERED	EXPECTED COST	SIMULATED AVERAGE COST BASED ON 10 TRIALS
9	$14.70	$16.00
10	9.80	11.10
11	10.00	9.60
12	13.60	11.50

It is worth noting that in order to compare each order size for the same demand pattern, each set of 10 trials must use the some sequence of random numbers, as stipulated in step 2 above. If Peggy were to run the same study, beginning with a different random number, the simulator would generate a different series of demands and thus would most likely obtain a different set of average costs.[2] This fact leads to the following important observation.

[2]The important point here is that a simulation study is like a laboratory test. In performing such a study one wants to be as scientific as possible, which implies that one wants to eliminate as much extraneous variability as possible. As an analogy, suppose that you are comparing the taste of two different species of corn. The analogy goes as follows. "Corn type A tastes better than type B" is analogous to "An order size of A pans gives lower cost than an order size of B pans." So now you design a study. If corn type A is grown in Connecticut and type B in Iowa, you might worry that the soil composition is partly responsible for the different results. This would correspond to comparing the results of two different order sizes in simulation experiments using different random numbers. Consequently, you would want to grow both corn types side by side in the same soil (i.e., use the same random number to generate a demand). However, having grown both corn types in Iowa, you now wonder whether the results would be the same (e.g., type A tastes better than type B) if the corn had been grown in Connecticut. Thus, if you want to have high confidence in your conclusions, more work must be done. You would grow both corn types in numerous different types of soil and then study the overall results. But what is important is that you would not grow type A in 10 types of soil and then type B in 10 *different* types of soil. You would grow them side by side in the same 10 types of soil. This corresponds to performing the simulations with the same sequence of random numbers.

Suppose that, in a decision under uncertainty, management would like to make that decision that minimizes expected cost or maximizes expected profit. With simulation, it is impossible to guarantee that this decision can be identified. In other words, the decision that leads to the minimum average cost, as computed by simulation, may not be the same as the decision that produces, in a mathematical sense, the minimum expected cost.

In order to see this, suppose that Peggy now uses algebra to calculate the expected cost of ordering 11 pans. The calculation is shown below.

$$\text{expected cost} = \quad 10(13-11)\,\text{Prob}\,\{D=13\} + 10(12-11)\,\text{Prob}\,\{D=12\}$$
$$+ \;\; 7(11-11)\,\text{Prob}\,\{D=11\} + \;\; 7(11-10)\,\text{Prob}\,\{D=10\}$$
$$+ \;\; 7(11-\;\;9)\,\text{Prob}\,\{D=\;\;9\} + \;\; 7(11-\;\;8)\,\text{Prob}\,\{D=\;\;8\}$$

or

$$\text{expected cost} = 20(0.1) + 10(0.1) + 0(0.2) + 7(0.3) + 14(0.2) + 21(0.1) = 10$$

Simulated
Average
versus
True Expected
Value

It is no surprise that the average cost generated by 10 simulated trials ($9.60) does not exactly equal the expected cost ($10) since, according to the remarks above, different sets of 10 runs, beginning each set with a different random number, will typically produce different values for the average. The implication of this fact on the process of making a decision is interesting. Figure 18.11 compares the algebraically computed expected cost and a simulated average cost, based on order sizes of 9, 10, 11, and 12 pans.

Here we see that if Peggy were to base her decision on the simulated average costs the cost-minimizing decision would be to order 11 pans, whereas to minimize the expected cost she should order 10 pans. This is, of course, a deliberately oversimplified example, but it is an excellent illustration of the fact that

Simulation, in general, does not achieve optimality.

We should at this point reemphasize that in a real problem you would not both calculate the expected cost and use simulation to calculate an average cost. As we have mentioned, simulation is used when it is computationally impractical or even not possible to calculate the expected cost associated with the alternative decisions. This simple example serves to illustrate important relationships between simulation and analytic models.

Up until this point we have used *discrete* probability distributions in all of our examples. The next section broadens our coverage by showing how random events characterized by continuous distributions can also be simulated with random numbers. First, let us summarize and comment on several aspects of what we have seen to date.

Recapitulation

1. A simulator takes parameters and decisions as inputs and yields a measure (or measures) of effectiveness as output. In Peggy's problem the parameters were holding cost, h, and penalty cost, p. Peggy input the values $h = 7$ and $p = 10$. The decisions were "number of pans to order." The measure of effectiveness was cost.

2. If the simulator contains random events, each pass through the simulator (i.e., each choice of a random number) for the same parameters and decisions will generally yield a different value for the measure of effectiveness.

3. In Peggy's problem the measure of effectiveness for an order of size 11, in each trial, was taken to be cost (each row of Figure 18.10). The 10 trials taken together combine to produce another measure of the goodness of order size—namely, average cost. It is to be noted that even more information is available. Figure 18.10 shows a 30% probability of obtaining a shortage (this occurred in 3 of the 10 trials). This is additional data with which to assess the "goodness" of ordering 11 pans, and it shows how, with simulation, numerous "measures of effectiveness" can be produced. There is another important property of simulation that is illustrated by Figure 18.10. The 10 trials have actually produced a distribution of costs. They vary from 7 to 20 and the mean is 9.6. This provides some indication as to the **variability** associated with the policy being measured (order 11 pans).

Indicators of variability are important products of simulation studies. Management usually seeks policies for which the potential outcome is highly predictable, which means low variability.

---

4. If the simulator contains random events, then increasing the number of passes through the simulator (for the same parameters and decisions) will, "on the average," improve the accuracy of the estimate of the expected value of the measure of effectiveness (see Figure 18.14 and the subsequent discussion). In other words, if Peggy had used 100 or 1000 trials in Figure 18.11, the average cost for each order quantity would "on the average" be closer to the corresponding expected cost.

5. In a simulator we can never be sure that we have found the optimal decision. We can simply identify the best decision among those evaluated. Management should ask the following questions:

   a. Have enough trials been performed for each decision so that the average value of the measure (or measures) of performance is a good indication of the expected value?

   b. Have enough decisions and the right decisions been evaluated so that we can believe that the best answer found is "close enough" to the optimum?

18.5

USING CONTINUOUS DISTRIBUTIONS TO GENERATE RANDOM EVENTS

The Normal Distribution

The normal distribution plays an important role in many analytic and simulation models. In simulation, we often assume that random quantities are normally distributed. To illustrate, we return to Peggy McConnell and Wiles' omelet pan problem. The above discussion presented, for pedagogical reasons, a simplified discrete distribution of demand for the problem. In the problem she actually faced (Chapter 16) Peggy assumed that a normal distribution with a mean of 1000 and a standard deviation of 100 reasonably approximated the demand that would occur. She then used this distribution to determine the optimal number of pans to order, which turned out to be 1022.

Suppose that she had chosen to use simulation to estimate the expected cost associated with any particular order quantity (the approach described in Section 18.4). In order to accomplish this, on each simulation trial she would have to draw a random demand from a normal distribution with a mean μ of 1000 and a standard deviation σ of 100. This is a two-step process:

1. Take a number from the random number table and divide by 100. For example, suppose that we arbitrarily start in row 28, column 3, of Figure 18.1 and obtain the number 0.76.

2. Use Table T.1 in Appendix B to find the number (say v) such that the area under the normal curve to the left of v equals the number selected in 1. In this example we must find v such that the area under the normal curve to the left of v equals 0.76. From Table T.1 we see that v must be 0.706 standard deviation to the right of the mean. Thus, $v = \mu + 0.706\sigma = 1000 + 0.706(100) = 1070.6$. This is the first randomly generated demand.

To generate another demand, we would take the next random number (82) from Figure 18.1 and start the process over again.

Other Distributions

The general concept of the two-step process used to generate normally distributed random quantities can be used for any other distribution. The process is illustrated in Figure 18.12, where W denotes a random quantity such as demand. The crucial element is a plot of the Prob $\{W \le w\}$. The figure shows a typical function of this type, namely, one that goes from 0 to 1 and is nondecreasing. We should stress that Figure 18.12 motivates the *concept* underlying the technique of generating an arbitrary random quantity. In practice, the process is typically performed in the computer with either a tabular or analytic representation of a graph like Figure 18.12. The process starts as before, by selecting a number, say, 80, from the random number table. The value of this random number (divided by 100) is then located on the vertical axis (or, in the computer, in an appropriate table). You then read from the graph (or the computer does a "table

Figure 18.12
Generating Random Quantities

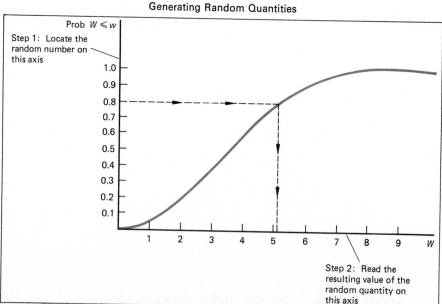

lookup") to obtain on the horizontal axis the value of the random quantity (approximately 5.1 in Figure 18.12). This is exactly how we used Table T.1 to generate normally distributed random quantities.

18.6
COMPUTER SIMULATION OF WILES' PROBLEM

By now you should already have the feeling that simulation by hand is time consuming and tedious (to put it kindly) even for simple models like the omelet pan problem. For more complicated models, these characteristics are exacerbated and, in addition, it becomes increasingly difficult to avoid making logical and/or computational errors. On the other hand, computers are specifically designed to perform a large number of logical and numerical operations rapidly and accurately. In addition, computers can be easily programmed to generate random quantities from any specific distribution. The process is essentially the one described in the preceding section. The random numbers are produced internally by the computer and used to obtain the appropriate random quantity. In most computer simulation packages it is possible to request observations from one of a number of standard probability distributions simply by stating what distribution you want and providing the parameters for that distribution. For all of these reasons, almost all simulations are performed on computers. Indeed, a number of general-purpose simulation packages are used to investigate inventory and queuing problems. Some of these packages are commercially available and others exist in specific firms or universities.

One such package is used for research on multiechelon inventory systems at the University of Chicago. It is an on-line system that can be used to study a great variety of inventory systems. Indeed, the following discussion shows how it could be used to study Peggy McConnel's omelet pan problem. In particular, the system is used to *estimate* the expected holding and penalty cost if 1022 pans are ordered. The mathematical analysis in Chapter 16 revealed that, assuming a normal distribution of demand (with $\mu = 1000, \sigma = 100$), 1022 is the optimal number of pans, that is, the number that minimizes expected cost.

Figure 18.13 shows the input and the output for a set of 1000 trials on this problem. To use this system the user must input various parameters. In this particular set of experiments we used the same parameters that were used in the analytic solution in Chapter 16. Note, for example, that the per unit holding cost is $7.00 and the per unit penalty cost is $10.00. Also note that many features of the program, such as multiple stocking points, order setup costs, safety stocks, and lead times, are not part of Peggy's problem.

Computer
Model

Our goal is to simulate 1000 trials. Of course, Peggy's problem is a one-period model (formally, in Chapter 16, called the newsboy model). Our simulator is for a multiperiod inventory system. How can we adapt this to Peggy's problem? In Figure 18.13 we see that the value 1022 is entered for the *initial inventory* (initial stock OH) and for both the *order-up-to-level* and the *reorder point*. Consider for a moment what happens in the simulation. The inventory model will consider 1000 periods. In each period the computer will simulate a random demand of Peggy's problem, i.e., it will draw a random sample from a normal distribution with mean 1000 and standard deviation of 100. The initial inventory (inventory on hand at the beginning of period 1) is 1022. During the first

Figure 18.13
Computer Simulation of Wiles' Problem

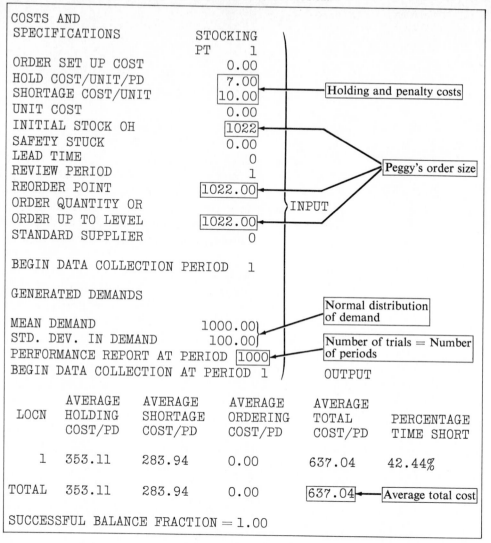

```
COSTS AND
SPECIFICATIONS              STOCKING
                           PT      1
ORDER SET UP COST                0.00
HOLD COST/UNIT/PD                7.00     ◄── Holding and penalty costs
SHORTAGE COST/UNIT             10.00
UNIT COST                        0.00
INITIAL STOCK OH                1022   ◄──┐
SAFETY STUCK                     0.00     │
LEAD TIME                           0     │
REVIEW PERIOD                       1     ├── Peggy's order size
REORDER POINT                1022.00   ◄──┤
ORDER QUANTITY OR                         │  INPUT
ORDER UP TO LEVEL            1022.00   ◄──┘
STANDARD SUPPLIER                   0

BEGIN DATA COLLECTION PERIOD     1

GENERATED DEMANDS
                                          ┌── Normal distribution
MEAN DEMAND                  1000.00      │   of demand
STD. DEV. IN DEMAND           100.00      └──
PERFORMANCE REPORT AT PERIOD  1000   ◄── Number of trials = Number
BEGIN DATA COLLECTION AT PERIOD 1            of periods
                                          OUTPUT

       AVERAGE   AVERAGE   AVERAGE   AVERAGE
 LOCN  HOLDING   SHORTAGE  ORDERING  TOTAL     PERCENTAGE
       COST/PD   COST/PD   COST/PD   COST/PD   TIME SHORT

   1   353.11    283.94    0.00      637.04    42.44%

TOTAL  353.11    283.94    0.00      637.04  ◄── Average total cost

SUCCESSFUL BALANCE FRACTION = 1.00
```

period our normal distribution is used to generate a random demand that must be satisfied out of initial inventory. Thus, inventory on hand at the end of the first period (the beginning of period 2) is less than 1022, which is the *reorder point*. Therefore, an order is placed to bring the inventory up to the *order-up-to-level*, 1022. Since the lead time is input as zero, the order arrives instantaneously, and thus the inventory on hand at the beginning of period 2 is 1022. This process is repeated 1000 times in the simulation. We thus have a sample of 1000 periods in which the inventory on hand at the beginning of each period is 1022. This can be interpreted as simulating 1000 trials in Peggy's scenario.

The output shows that the average total cost per period is $637.04, with stockouts occurring in 42.44% of the trials. The output also shows average holding cost per period and average shortage (penalty) cost per period. Similar experiments were performed with 500 and 10,000 trials. The average costs are shown in Figure 18.14. The expected cost that was calculated using analytic techniques not covered in this text is also shown.

Figure 18.14

Costs for the Omelet Pan Problem If 1022 Pans Are Ordered

AVERAGE COST NUMBER OF TRIALS			
500	**1000**	**10,000**	**EXPECTED COST**
$648.46	$637.04	$661.09	$662.00

Interpreting the Results
It is interesting to note that a sample of 500 trials yielded a "better" estimate of the expected cost than the sample of 1000 trials. Although one expects to get "better" results with larger samples, this example drives home the fact that results from a simulation of this sort are indeed random, and thus

We cannot be assured that with any particular sample the average cost will be closer to expected cost just because we take a larger sample.

All we can say is that "on the average," larger samples will get us closer (see the concluding comments in Section 18.4). Thus, when 10,000 trials were taken, the average cost is, as we would expect, closer to the true expected cost. In some sense, then, the result with 1000 trials is a fluke. But that is the point. When a simulator contains random events, the output is random and your results must be interpreted accordingly.

18.7

SIMULATING THE PAST

You may wonder why anyone would wish to simulate the past, since it is already known with complete certainty. *Simulating the past is a device commonly used by modelers to gain some measure for the credibility of a model.* The general notion of simulating the past applies to models that attempt to predict real-world phenomena or prescribe decisions to be made in some particular context. Such a model may be tested on historical data in two steps:

1. First, decisions (in the past) are made by the model as they would have been made if the model had been available at that time.
2. Then the model is evaluated on the basis of its performance on past data. For example, a forecasting model would be evaluated by comparing its predictions with the actual historical outcomes. One can thereby determine the costs (or savings) that would have been incurred if the model actually had been used.

This provides a type of null test. If the model did not perform well on historical data, it is probably difficult to believe that it will perform well in the future. Unfortunately, the fact that it *did* work well on historical data does not prove that it will work well in the future. Assessing how well it will work in the future involves a great deal of judgment. This judgment should rest on an understanding of why the model worked in the past and how stable the system is. In other words, the model captures a particular logical structure or collection of relationships that appear to explain the reality of the past. How likely is it that the reality of the future will be explained by the same collection of relationships? That is what we mean by judging the stability of the system. The following specific example is intended to illustrate and clarify the general statements made in this paragraph.

Market Simulations   A commodities speculator has developed a set of quantitative rules for buying and selling futures contracts on frozen pork bellies. These rules are based on historical price relationships that existed during the past 15 years between the various contract months. Historical storage charges and interest rates also entered into the development of his rules. In this case, then, the speculator's mathematical theory, along with an analysis of historical data, has led to his trading model. In order to use his model on any given day, he must input the closing prices for each contract on the previous day. He also inputs the 30-day interest rate and the current storage charges. The model then tells him which contracts to buy or sell, and respective quantities thereof.

In order to evaluate his model with a simulation, the trader might typically employ the past data as follows. Beginning, for example, in 1965, he acts as though he were actually trading with his model. He takes the actual daily closing prices from then to the present, along with the then-current interest rates and storage charges, inputs this data to the computer, and has the computer execute his trading rules and compute yearly profits, losses, margin requirements, and so on. If he is disappointed in the results, he may modify some of the rules and then repeat the simulation in the hope of achieving a better past performance. Thus, he simulates the past to develop more confidence in the way his model might perform if he uses it today, in the present, with real dollars.

The idea of simulating the past is important in numerous and diverse applications. For example, a large government agency was recently concerned about the effect of money supply on the rate of inflation. Some of the analysts in the agency were working with a *conditional forecasting model* that would predict the national inflation rate five quarters into the future as a function of the global and domestic money supplies. The model was based on two factors:

1. The strongly held belief on the part of the economists for the agency that the global and domestic money supplies are primary determinants of the rate of inflation.
2. A very successful one-period forecasting model.

Econometric Forecasting   This model used data in the current quarter to predict the rate of inflation in the next quarter. Inputs were the rate of inflation, the global money supply, and the domestic money supply in the current quarter, and the output was the rate of inflation in the next quarter. In particular, the model was a system of equations, and the parameters in the equations were estimated by using standard statistical techniques on past data, starting with the first quarter of 1965 through the present. Such models are often called *econometric models*, and many such models have been developed for macroeconomic forecasting. This model was a "good fit" in the sense that, in terms of past data, there was close correspondence between each quarter's actual inflation rate and that quarter's predicted inflation rate (based upon the previous quarter's actual inflation rate and the previous quarter's actual money supplies).

The analysts hoped to transform this one-quarter forecasting model into the desired *conditional* forecasting model. As different values for the money supply were input into this proposed model, different rates of inflation would be produced, and hence the effect of such policy changes (i.e., changes in the money supply) could be studied. In essence, the analyst's model was a function machine like the one shown in Figure 18.15.

Since this agency could influence the domestic money supply, this model could be tremendously useful in determining the policies to be supported.

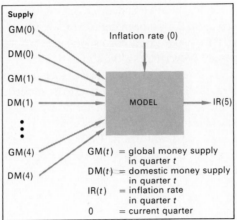

Figure 18.15

Model for Predicting Inflation

Conditional Forecasting Model

This particular model was designed to operate as follows. The model accepts the actual global and domestic money supplies and the actual rate of inflation during the current quarter (say $t = 0$) as *inputs* and yields a predicted rate of inflation for next quarter as intermediate output. This *predicted* value of the rate of inflation for next quarter along with an *assigned* level for the money supplies during the next quarter would then lead to a *prediction* of the inflation rate two quarters into the future. Continuing to iterate in this way, the model could presumably predict the inflation rate five quarters into the future ($t = 5$), *conditional* upon the assigned intermediate money supply values. Of course, there is no particular importance to the symbols $t = 0$ and $t = 5$. The important point is that, given data on money supply for any particular quarter and rate of inflation for that quarter, and given hypothetical money supply values for four succeeding quarters, then the inflation rate in the fifth succeeding quarter is estimated. Thus, for example, one could take the data in quarter 3 as given, and predict the inflation rate in quarter 8, and so on.

The analysts and the economists for the agency were convinced that the proposed model would yield accurate results. After all, they had a well-developed theory and the impressive statistics on the one-period forecasting model to support their position. Nevertheless, the client, being rather cautious, wanted to test this model somehow. The model purports to estimate reasonably well the inflation rate that will be produced by various money supply levels in the five preceding periods. One obvious test would be to look at past money supply levels and see if the model's prediction was close to the actual past rates of inflation. This procedure is an example of *simulating the model's performance with past data.*

The client began with the first quarter of 1965 ($t = 0$), inputting the then-current actual money supplies and the actual rate of inflation at that time and allowing the model to predict the rate of inflation during the second quarter ($t = 1$). He then took the *actual* money supply during the second quarter and the *predicted* (rather than actual) rate of inflation to predict the rate of inflation in the third quarter. This process is continued on into quarter 5, where the predicted inflation rate and actual inflation rate are then compared. Next, the client began with the second quarter of 1965 ($t = 1$), inputting the then-current actual money supplies and the actual rate of inflation at that time. The actual money supplies for the next five quarters were then used to obtain an estimated inflation rate for quarter 6, and this was compared with the actual value in quarter 6. Continuing the simulation in this way, it soon became apparent that the model's predictions were enormously different from the rates of inflation that actually existed. This caused the client considerable discomfort. Had the correspondence between actual and predicted inflation been good, nothing would have been proved, for this would not imply that an equally good correspondence would have been obtained if the data had been different. Nevertheless, the simulation run by the client was really the only test available, and good results would at least have given a sort of null test for the model. As it was, the results of this simulation left the model on very shaky ground. The client's attitude was the following: "I don't care how good the statistics are. I don't even want to look at them. Our job is to predict the future. Give me a model that is not ridiculous at predicting the past and I will use it. I don't care what the theoretic justification is." This type of pragmatic response is not unusual among those who must live with a decision to be made on the basis of a model.

18.8
NOTES ON IMPLEMENTATION

Simulation is a powerful and flexible analytic tool that can be used to study a wide variety of management problems. It is generally used in cases where a good analytic model either does not exist or is too complicated to solve. This description encompasses a large segment of real-world problems and, as a result, surveys of the use of management science techniques typically put simulation at or near the top. However, there are a number of important factors for management to consider before making a commitment to a simulation study.

A Last-Resort Technique

Although the language varies from source to source, there is an often expressed sentiment that simulation is a last-resort technique. In other words, as stated above, simulation is frequently used when no convenient analytic model is available. With an analytic model the laws of mathematics can be used, often to obtain optimal decisions and sometimes sensitivity data, provided, of course, that the analysis is not so complex as to be prohibitive. In a simulation with random events, optimality is out of the question. Often a number of runs are required just to get a good estimate of the "goodness" of a particular decision.

In a simulation study, it is often necessary to use some sort of search procedure to find a good decision. This can be a formidable task. Suppose, for example, that there are 10 decision variables, each of which can assume 10 different values. There are then 10^{10} (10 billion) possible decisions to consider. For the sake of calculation, assume that it is necessary to evaluate only 1% of the possible decisions in order to be confident that a good decision has been reached and that 20 trials are required to get a good estimate of an expected value of the measure of effectiveness for each particular decision. In this case, $(0.01)(10^{10})(20) = 2 \times 10^9$ (2 billion) passes through the simulator would be required.

In such a case, the moral is clear. Do not simulate unless you have to.

The acronym KISS for "Keep It Simple, Stupid" is popular among professionals in the quantitative analysis business. The idea applies with special force to simulation. A common and often fatal error of simulation studies is that they are too complicated. This may be an overreaction to the freedom gained by moving from analytic models to simulation models. Analytic models are often quite restrictive in their assumptions. Once we depart from linear functions or very simplistic assumptions, the mathematics gets harder by an order of magnitude.

Simulation can be much more permissive about functional forms. Since we are typically just generating an observation from a function (not solving a set of equations), linear functions do not command the same premium in simulation as they do in analytic models.

Whatever the motivation, there is typically a strong urge to include many factors in a simulation model. For example, it may not seem difficult to add a customer return feature to an inventory control model. In essence, all that is required is some additional computer code to generate this feature and incorporate it into the model. "There is no theoretic barrier, so why not do it." This impression can be seriously wrong.

Large complicated simulations incorporating a large number of "lifelike" features are at first blush appealing to management. However, they suffer from at least three serious problems:

1. They are often expensive to write and document.
2. They are an expensive experimental device. In the first place, the computer code may become so complex that each run is time consuming and therefore expensive. Moreover, the more complex the simulation, the more runs one generally wants to make. Consider a very simple model with two parameters and one decision (e.g., Peggy McConnel's problem). Suppose that we wish to simulate the effect of five different decisions (e.g., five order sizes). For each decision we run 10 trials. Thus, for each set of specified values for the parameters, we make $5(10) = 50$ runs. If we want to explore this system with three different sets of values for each parameter ($3^2 = 9$ combinations), we must make $9(50) = 450$ runs. Suppose that in a more complex model there are 10 instead of two parameters, and again each parameter may assume (because, say, of uncertainty) three different values ($3^{10} = 59,049$ combinations). In this case we must make $(59,049)50 = 2,952,450$ runs! In multiplying the number of parameters by 5 we multiplied the number of runs by 6561. Since increasing complexity invariably leads to increasing the number of parameters, you can see how troublesome this can become. The amount of freedom one has in constructing a simulation model, if abused, can be the very downfall of the model.
3. Complex simulations often produce so much data that the results are difficult to interpret.

Lean abstract models that capture the essence of the real problem and set encumbering details aside are as important to successful simulation studies as they are to good analytic models. Casual observation suggests that more simulation projects have died from too grand an original conception than from any other disease.

It seems almost innocuous to say that simulation studies should be carefully planned before they are run. But this planning can be intricate and may well require statistical expertise. Should we do one trial of 1000 periods or 10 trials of 100 periods each? In other words, the analyst must decide how much and what kind of sampling to do with each decision and how many different decisions to try. Management's problem can be conceptually illustrated in Figure 18.16, where we imagine that simulation is being used to find a low-cost decision for a particular problem. The notion is that by increasing the cost of experimentation (i.e., the amount of computer time), a better simulated solution can be found.

Figure 18.16
When Is Enough Enough?

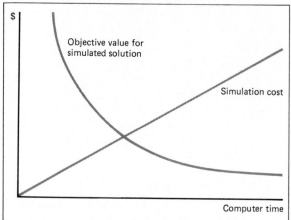

Although this concept has merit, the application is not easy. The shape of the "objective value for simulated solution" function is not well known. It is just not clear how much the solution can be expected to improve with increased experimentation. In view of this fact, two general strategies are useful:

1. Search in a sequential manner: that is, use the results of earlier simulations to suggest the next decision to try.
2. Use a relatively small number of trials for each decision in an attempt to locate the general area in which the decisions are good. Then increase the number of trials to obtain more precision within this area.

Simulation
Languages

The importance and widespread use of simulation has lead to the creation of special simulation languages. In general, these languages are intended to

1. Facilitate model formulation
2. Be easy to learn
3. Provide good debugging and error diagnostics
4. Be flexible enough to use on a wide range of problems

Different languages have different strengths and are intended for different types of simulation studies. A detailed examination of these languages is beyond the scope of this book. It is useful, however, to know of some of the more popular entries in this field.

GPSS (General-Purpose Systems Simulator) was developed in the early 1960s. Flowchart concepts provide the underlying rationale for this language. SIMSCRIPT 2.5 and GASP II are both based on the FORTRAN IV computer language. Both were developed in the early to mid-1960s. The former was developed by H. M. Markowitz at the Rand Corporation and the latter by A. Alan B. Pritsher.

Pritsher and N. Hurst produced GASP IV in 1973. It incorporates the features of GASP II, and provides a number of new and attractive features as well.

Even this brief comment on programming languages suggests that programming computer simulators is an arcane subject and managers should rely on expert guidance both in the formulation and experimentation phases. All managerial concerns about the use of experts apply *a fortiori* to simulation projects.

Two guidelines that are useful in all quantitative studies are especially important in simulation studies.

Documenta-
tion

Insist on good documentation. A new manager (in contrast to an analyst) should be able to understand the input required, the assumptions of the model, and the meaning of the output with a reasonable amount of effort. This requires clear documentation. Too often the usefulness of a simulation program effectively ends with the tenure of the originator. The only reasonable cure for this problem is good documentation. It is difficult to overemphasize the importance of this guideline.

Group
Dynamics

Most quantitative modeling efforts require interaction and communication between the modeler and the user. This is particularly true of simulation projects. The users must understand how to enter decisions and parameters and how to analyze the output. The firsthand knowledge of the users is essential in making sure that the simulation captures the essence of the real problem. Also, the fact that the user possesses an intimate knowledge of the real problem can be an important part of the search for good solutions.

Good documentation and group dynamics are closely interrelated and are an important part of managing any project based on quantitative modeling and analysis.

18.9

SIMULATION VERSUS OPTIMIZATION

Now that a variety of examples have been studied, you should have a fairly accurate picture of what simulation does and how it works. It may be useful at this juncture, as a sort of concluding overview, to compare simulation with optimization. The two types of models are compared in Figures 18.17 and 18.18.

These two figures indicate that in each type of model the user inputs parameters as data. In each case, a certain amount of useful information is created by the model and printed as output. In the optimization model, the output includes decisions (optimal

Figure 18.17
Typical Simulator

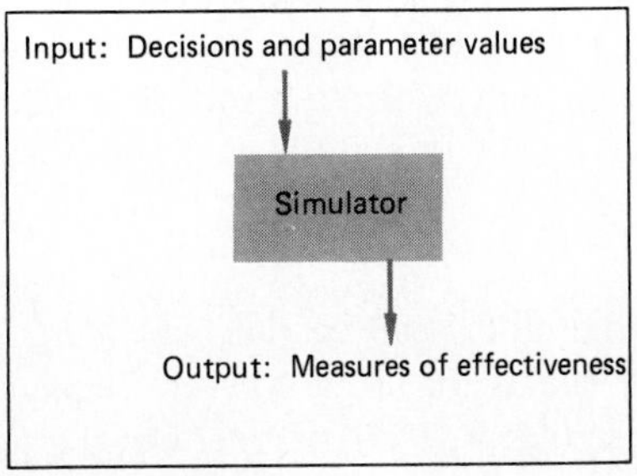

Input: Decisions and parameter values

Simulator

Output: Measures of effectiveness

Figure 18.18
Optimization Model

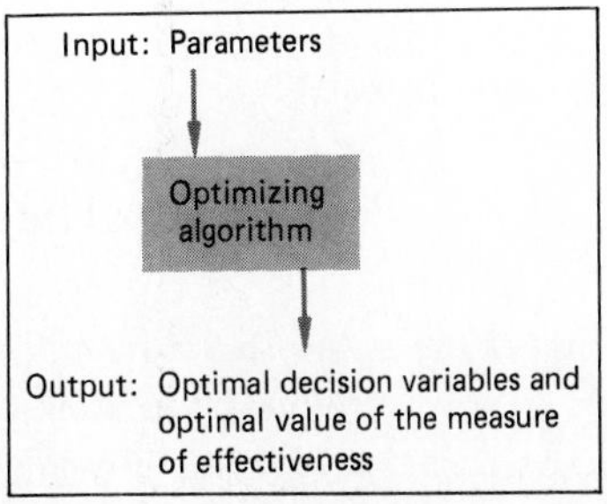

Input: Parameters

Optimizing
algorithm

Output: Optimal decision variables and
optimal value of the measure
of effectiveness

values of the decision variables) and the OV (the optimal value of the objective function). Also, the optimal values of the decision variables can be used to compute the values of the constraint functions at the optimal solution. A simulation model does not have the formal structure of an objective function and constraints. The output may include the values of numerous functions of interest. A strategic planning simulation model may have as outputs yearly profits, total 15-year discounted profits, yearly sales, final market share, and so on. A major difference between the two types of models is this:

In a simulation model, the decisions of primary interest are input by the user.
In an optimization model, the decisions of interest are produced by the model.

This assertion must be taken in the proper context, for in earlier discussions in the text we saw applications in which, in some sense, one could input a decision to an optimization model, but that is not an accurate description of what was going on. For example, in Chapter 9 we saw a study in which a capacity decision could be input as a value for an RHS parameter. By assigning a sequence of possible RHS values, we generated the optimal value function, and this function became the tool for determining the optimal capacity level. This process of running the optimization model many times, with a sequence of differing capacity levels, casts the model into a "what if" type of scenario. Explicitly, we were saying, "If the capacity is b_1 then what is the OV, and if the capacity is b_2 then what is the OV?" In this instance, the decision of *primary interest* was the capacity. Possible values of the capacity were being input to a simulation. The simulation consisted of running a linear program. Thus, it is reasonable to assert that the key concept above provides a main distinction between simulation and optimization. That is, in a simulation model the decision variables of interest are input by the user. The model then *describes* what happens under the assumption that those decisions are made. The simulator may "make" endogenous decisions in order to describe what happens, but these are not the decisions being studied. The optimization model may take as an input a value for a decision of interest (such as capacity), but then the decisions produced by the optimization model are not the ones of major interest, and the optimization model is really a component of a simulation.

18.10
ADVANTAGES AND LIMITATIONS OF SIMULATION

Uncertainty   A major advantage of simulation models is that they provide a means of dealing with uncertainty, whether it be uncertainty in tomorrow's demand, tomorrow's interest rates, or tomorrow's militaristic behavior of a hostile power. These models typically deal with a multitude of uncertainties, as opposed to the expository examples in the text where only a single uncertain event (e.g., product demand) was involved. A typical complex simulation may deal with the unfolding of thousands of random events before the outputs are finally determined.

Versatility   Another advantage is that the model can be run many times, either varying parameter values to explore sensitivity effects, or using different sequences of random numbers in order to study the magnitude of possible statistical variations.

Variability   It should be emphasized that variability in the results of different trials is intrinsically neither good nor bad. The important fact is that the simulation should do a reasonable job of reproducing the amount of variability that actually occurs in the system being simulated. For example, if in the real world there is a large degree of variability between forecast demand and actual demand, then the same condition should exist in the simulation model. If in the real world there is a high degree of correspondence between the forecast for an event and the realization of that event, then this high degree of correspondence should also hold true in the simulation model.

Multiple Outputs   A third advantage of simulation is that many different measures of effectiveness can be observed, whereas optimization models are generally limited to a single objective function (although goal programming, discussed in Chapter 10, provides an alternative means of dealing with multiple objectives).

Rational Tool   As is the case with all types of quantitative models, simulation models handle a large number of interactions in a consistent but adjustable manner. In this way they provide a means for the consistent evaluation of alternative policies. As with models in general, another advantage is the explicit identification and specification of the relations of interest. Human beings are not particularly good at consistently tracing through the implications of a decision that must interact with numerous other decisions or exogenous variables before its impact is realized.

At least two limitations should be mentioned. The first might be identified as the size of the model. Big models are expensive to built and operate. A common error when people first begin to build models is to make them too realistic and too comprehensive. The number of interactions that must be specified is large, and the data required to make these specifications in a reasonable manner are both expensive and time-consuming to obtain. Often, attempts to model a complicated situation are stillborn because the projects are simply too ambitious. In addition, a large simulation model with many parameters will require many, many executions in order to study variability and to test the sensitivity of the output to parameter values. This can be prohibitively expensive.

A second limitation, beyond sheer size, is that in a highly complex scenario it may well be the case that no one understands the interactions and the relationships well enough to build even a simulation model that works effectively. Simple extrapolations of policies that have worked well in the past for reasons not well understood may be more useful than recommendations from elaborate models based on dubious relationships. For example, there are many people who have more confidence in the economic forecasts made by "experts" combining facts in a heuristic manner than in the forecasts emanating from large simulation models.

In concluding this section, a word of warning is probably appropriate. Simulation is an appealing concept that is deceptively simple in appearance. The idea of having a device that can be used to evaluate alternative decisions without employing higher mathematics is typically appealing to a manager. The fact of the matter, however, is that using a simulator as an aid to decision making in any reasonably complicated environment is anything but a trivial task. The modeling problem remains as formidable as ever. That is, one must still find a selective representation of reality that captures the essence of the real problem. Furthermore, in order to arrive at valid conclusions one must design appropriate experiments and analyze the resulting data. This often involves formal statistical methods and a high degree of technical expertise.

MAJOR CONCEPTS QUIZ

True–False

1. **T F** The basic concept of simulation is to build an experimental device that will "act like" the system of interest in important respects.

2. **T F** A deterministic model (one with no random elements) can be used as a simulation model.

3. **T F** If a simulator includes random elements, two successive trials with the same parameter values will produce the same value for the measure of effectiveness.

4. **T F** In a simulation with random elements it is impossible to guarantee that the decision that maximizes expected profit can be determined.

5. **T F** In real-world problems it is common practice to compare the expected cost associated with a decision with the average cost for that decision produced by a simulator.

6. **T F** In a simulation involving several distinct random outcomes a correct association of random numbers and events implies that each random number must represent a different outcome.

7. **T F** Simulation is sometimes described as a last-resort technique since it is generally not employed until analytic approaches have been examined and rejected.

8. **T F** A common error in designing a simulator is to use such restrictive assumptions that the model fails to capture the essence of the problem.

9. **T F** Additional experimentation with a simulator is sure to increase the simulation cost but may also improve the quality of the solution.

Multiple Choice

10. In a typical simulation model input provided by the analyst includes
    a. values for the parameters
    b. values for the decision variables
    c. a value for the measure of effectiveness
    d. all of the above
    e. both a and b

11. An advantage of simulation, as opposed to optimization, is that
    a. often multiple measures of goodness can be examined
    b. some appreciation for the variability of outcomes of interest can be obtained
    c. more complex scenarios can be studied
    d. all of the above

12. Consider a simulator with random elements which uses profit as a measure of effectiveness. For a specified assignment of parameter values
    a. the average profit over a number of trials is used as an estimate of the expected profit associated with a decision
    b. the average profit is always closer to the expected profit as the number of trials increases
    c. the average profit over 10 trials is always the same
    d. none of the above

13. A random number refers to
    a. an observation from a set of numbers (say the integers 0–99) each of which is equally likely
    b. an observation selected at random from a normal distribution
    c. an observation selected at random from any distribution provided by the analyst
    d. none of the above

14. The random number 0.63 has been selected. The corresponding observation, say v, from a *normal* distribution is determined by the relationship:
    a. v is "the probability that the normally distributed quantity is ≤ 0.63"
    b. v is the number such that "the probability that the normally distributed quantity is $\leq v$" equals 0.63

c. v is the number such that "the probability that the normally distributed quantity equals v" is 0.63

d. none of the above

15. To reduce the effect of initial conditions in a simulation study one can
   a. vary the values of the system parameters
   b. increase the number of alternative decisions studied
   c. increase the sample size and ignore data from a number of the first runs for each set of parameters and decisions
   d. all of the above

16. If both an analytic model and a simulation model could be used to study a problem including random events, the analytic model is often preferred because
   a. the simulator generally requires a number of runs just to get a good estimate of the objective value (such as expected cost) for a particular decision
   b. the analytic model may produce an optimal decision
   c. the simulation study may require evaluating a large number of possible decisions
   d. all of the above

17. Large complicated simulation models suffer from the following:
   a. average costs are not well defined
   b. it is difficult to create the appropriate random events
   c. they may be expensive to write and to use as an experimental device
   d. all of the above

18. In performing a simulation it is advisable to
   a. use the results of earlier decisions to suggest the next decision to try
   b. use the same number of trials for each decision
   c. simulate all possible decisions
   d. none of the above

Answers

1. T	7. T	13. a
2. T	8. F	14. b
3. F	9. T	15. c
4. T	10. e	16. d
5. F	11. d	17. c
6. F	12. a	18. a

18.12
PROBLEMS

In the following problems you will be asked to perform a number of simulations. In all cases, assign consecutive random numbers to each event and assign smaller values of random numbers to smaller numerical values of the event. For example:

EVENT (DEMAND)	PROBABILITY	PROPER ASSIGNMENT	IMPROPER ASSIGNMENT
3	0.2	00–19	30–49
4	0.7	20–89	00–29 and 60–99
5	0.1	90–99	50–59

In each simulation problem a row and column will be indicated. Select the first random number at this position in Figure 18.1 and read as instructed in the problem statement.

18-1. Cite examples of the use of simulation (in the broad sense) by the military.

18-2. Cite examples of the use of simulation (in the broad sense) in professional sports.

18-3. Use the flowchart in Figure 18.5 to simulate the processing of four E-9 frames. Determine the idle time. Start where the example in the text ended, namely, with the number in row 13, column 10, of Figure 18.1. (This number is 39.)

18-4. Comment on the following statement: In order for a mathematical model to be a simulation, the model must include random elements and thus employ random numbers in its operation.

18-5. A major oil company has a complicated nonlinear programming model that finds an optimal production schedule, including optimal quantities of each of several crude oils to use in the refining process, as a function of both the sales price and demand for the firm's retail products. The objective of this model is to maximize profits. The marketing department is attempting to develop a solid program for next year. The department manager must select a strategy in which both the promotional effort and product prices are specified. Given any strategy, the manager believes that he can accurately forecast the demand for retail products (perhaps using another model). There are currently three strategies he is thinking of using, and he plans to use the model to select the best of these.

Describe the sense in which the marketing department manager, although using an optimization model, is actually employing a simulation approach.

18-6. In a simulation model containing random elements, it is typically necessary to run a simulator a number of times for the same decision in order to get a good estimate of the true cost (or benefit) of the decision under consideration. Can you think of another reason for running a number of trials for the same decision?

18-7. Comment on the following statement: Variability is a natural enemy of simulation. Simulations should be designed to keep variability to a reasonably low level so that accurate estimates of the effectiveness of alternative policies can be arrived at with a reasonable number of simulation trials.

18-8. Consider the inflation model discussed in Section 18.7. The analyst defends his rejected model as follows:

The test you have applied is unfair. You assume that the actual values for $GM(t)$ and $DM(t)$ $t = 0, \ldots, 4$ are available but that $IR(t)$ is not. That is nonsense. Either you know the values from period t or you don't. Why assume that you only know some of them? The model will yield excellent results if we put the true values for $GM(t)$, $DM(t)$ and $IR(t)$ into the model, rather than using the predicted values for the inflation rate, say $\widehat{IR}(t)$, as you've done in your test. You should change your mind and adopt the model.

Discuss the difference between this point of view and the one taken in the text.

18-9. In Chapter 17 the role of historical data in constructing forecasting models was considered. A "divide-and-conquer" approach was suggested. In this approach, one used the first half of the data to select parameter values so that the model fit the data. The ability of the model to forecast was then tested on the second half of the data. In Section 18.7, a commodity-pricing example was given in which a model was both derived and tested on the same set of historical data.

Is the advice given in these two sections contradictory? Try to specify some general guidelines to use in deciding when one should "divide and conquer" and when one can both derive and test a model on the same set of data. Is the "divide-and-conquer" rule applicable to the model described by the analyst in Problem 18-8?

18-10. Consider PROTRAC's cash balance problem. The change in the cash balance from one morning to the next is a random variable. In particular, it increases by $10,000 with probability 0.3, decreases by $10,000 with probability 0.2, and remains the same with probability 0.5. Associate random numbers with these events so as to accurately reflect the correct probabilities in a simulation study.

18-11. Consider the following brand-switching problem. In this problem probabilities are used to describe the behavior of a customer buying beer. Three particular beers (B, M, and S) are incorporated in the model. Customer behavior is summarized in Figure 18.19. Thus, we see in the first row that a customer who buys beer B in week 1 will buy the same beer in week 2 with probability 0.85, will buy beer M with probability 0.10, and will buy beer S with probability 0.05. A similar interpretation holds for the other rows. Consider a customer who buys beer B in week 1. Assume that you wish to simulate his behavior for the next 10 weeks. We know that in week 2 he would buy beers B, M, and S with probabilities 0.85, 0.10, and 0.05. If in week 2 he bought beer M, he would buy beers B, M, and S with probability 0.08, 0.85, and 0.07, respectively. Define the events you would need and associate random numbers with these events so as to accurately reflect the correct probabilities.

Figure 18.19

	PROBABILITY OF PURCHASE IN WEEK $i + 1$		
BEER PURCHASED IN WEEK i	B	M	S
B	0.85	0.10	0.05
M	0.08	0.85	0.07
S	0.13	0.17	0.70

18-12. Assume that you want to generate a sample from a normal distribution that has a mean of 100 and a standard deviation of 10. If the number you obtain from the table of random numbers is 94, what is the value of the normal random variable?

18-13. Assume that you want to generate a sample from a normal distribution that has a mean of 600 and a standard deviation of 50. If the number you obtain from the table of random numbers is 37, what is the value of the normal random variable?

18-14. The probability that $W \leq x$ is plotted in Figure 18.20. Use this function to generate three sequential observations of the random variable W. Start in row 17, column 4 of Figure 18.1 and read down.

Figure 18.20

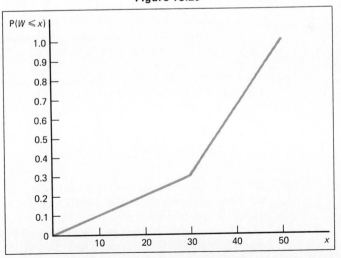

18-15. The probability that the random variable Z is less than or equal to x is specified below:

$$P(Z \leq x) = 0 \qquad\qquad x \leq 0$$
$$= 0.25x \qquad\qquad 0 \leq x \leq 2$$
$$= 0.25 + 0.125x \qquad 2 \leq x \leq 4$$
$$= -0.25 + 0.25x \qquad 4 \leq x \leq 5$$
$$= 1 \qquad\qquad\qquad x \geq 5$$

Plot this function and use it to generate three observations of the random variable Z. Use the random numbers 40, 60, and 90.

18-16. Simulate a sample of 10 periods for the omelet pan problem described in this chapter. Assume that you have 10 pans on hand at the beginning of each period. Use the random numbers starting in row 20, column 8, reading down Figure 18.1. Use the association of random numbers with demand given in Figure 18.8.
(a) Calculate the average cost per period.
(b) Record the number of stockouts (count a stockout as occurring when demand > 10).

18-17. The weekly demand for milk for the last 50 weeks at the All-Ways-Open convenience market is shown in Figure 18.21.
(a) Assign random numbers to demands so that the probability of a particular demand in the simulation is equal to the relative frequency of that demand over the last 50 weeks.
(b) Simulate 10 weeks of demand. Begin in row 11, column 4 of Figure 18.1 and read down.

Figure 18.21

SALES (CASES)	NUMBER OF WEEKS
20	2
21	4
22	8
23	10
24	8
25	10
26	5
27	3
Total	50

Figure 18.22

NUMBER OF BRAKE JOBS	NUMBER OF WEEKS
5	3
6	8
7	9
8	6
9	4
Total	30

18-18. The number of disk-brake jobs performed by the service department of the Green Cab Company during each of the last 30 weeks is shown in Figure 18.22.
(a) Assign random numbers to the number of brake jobs performed so that the probability of a particular number of jobs in the simulation is equal to the relative frequency of that number of jobs over the last 30 weeks.
(b) Simulate 10 weeks of demand. Begin in row 5, column 3 of Figure 18.1 and read down.

18-19. STECO currently carries inventory for stainless steel sheets in two nearby cities, L and A. Weekly demands (in trucks) and the probabilities for each city are shown in Figure 18.23. Assume that the demands are independent. L starts each week with 8 trucks of inventory on hand. A starts each week with 10 trucks of inventory on hand.
(a) Simulate 20 weeks of demand at L and record the number of stockouts. Begin in row 21, column 6 of Figure 18.1 and read down.

(b) Start in row 1, column 7 and read down to simulate 20 weeks of demand at A and record the number of stockouts.

Suppose that STECO centralized its stainless steel sheet inventory and satisfied all demand from L and A out of one new warehouse (call it LA).

(c) If LA started each week with 18 trucks of inventory on hand, would you expect the number of stockouts to increase, decrease, or remain the same as compared to when L and A operated independently? Why?

(d) Use the same sequence of demands you used in parts (a) and (b) to simulate 20 weeks of operation for the new warehouse, LA. Record the number of stockouts. Does this result agree with your answer to part (c)?

Figure 18.23

	PROBABILITY	
DEMAND	L	A
5	0.10	
6	0.10	
7	0.60	0.10
8	0.10	0.10
9	0.10	0.40
10		0.20
11		0.20

Figure 18.24

TIME BETWEEN ARRIVALS (MIN)	PROBABILITY
5	0.25
10	0.50
15	0.25

18-20. The time between arrivals at the drive-up window of the Slippery Savings and Loan is shown in Figure 18.24.

All customers form a single line and are served in the order of arrival. Assume that it takes 8 minutes to serve each customer. Also assume that no one is being served or waiting to be served when the first customer arrives. Simulate the arrival of 16 customers and record the number of customers who have to wait. Begin in row 1, column 1 of Figure 18.1 and read down.

18-21. The Homeburg Volunteer Fire Department makes an annual door-to-door solicitation for funds. They ask each household to be supporters (a $5 donation) or patrons (a $10 donation). An analysis of data from previous years indicates:

1. No one is home at 35% of the homes visited. If no one is home, the home is *not* revisited, and thus no donation is obtained. When someone is home, 70% of the time a woman answers the door and 30% of the time a man answers the door.

2. 20% of the women make a contribution. 40% of them are supporters and 60% are patrons.

3. 25% of the men make a contribution. 55% of them are supporters and 45% are patrons.

(a) Make a flowchart for this process. The output should be the contribution that occurs from calling on a house.

(b) Use the flowchart in part (a) to simulate 15 visits and record the total contribution from these 15 visits. Begin in row 11, column 8 of Figure 18.1 and read down.

(c) If there are 20,000 households to solicit in Homeburg, what is your estimate of the return from the annual solicitation?

SCHEDULING TANKER ARRIVALS

Simulation is a popular method for studying systems with random components. It follows that managers are often placed in the position of accepting or rejecting recommendations based on simulation studies, or perhaps recommending additional analysis. This vignette illustrates such a situation.

David O'Brien is the manager of Global Oil's St. Croix refinery. This refinery was built in 1954 and is served by a dock facility designed to handle 250,000-barrel tankers. Tankers arrive at the dock and unload into a 700,000-barrel storage tank at the rate of 400,000 barrels per day. The refinery itself accepts oil from the storage tank at the rate of 250,000 barrels per day. This is called the input pipeline capacity. The storage tank thus serves as a buffer storage facility, allowing the tankers to unload more rapidly. If the storage tank is full, however, the rate at which a tanker can unload decreases to 250,000 barrels per day.

Global installed the storage tank because the firm must pay a penalty cost, a so-called demurrage fee, if a tanker has to wait too long before it is able to start unloading its oil. In particular, a demurrage fee of $1400 per day is charged if a 250,000-barrel tanker must wait more than two days to start unloading. The charge is a pro-rata charge so that, for example, if a tanker waits 3.5 days before the start of unloading, then its total fee is $(3.5 - 2.0) \times \$1400$ or $2100.

Global is considering servicing the St. Croix refinery with its fleet of new 500,000-barrel supertankers. The harbor is deep and can easily accommodate the new tankers, but because of the limited unloading capacity, demurrage charges are a concern. A 500,000-barrel tanker incurs demurrage fees at the rate of $3000 per day if it must wait more than 2 days to start unloading.

Currently, one 250,000-barrel tanker arrives every 1.5 days on the average, that is, at a rate of 2/3 tanker per day, or 166,667 barrels of oil per day. Dave has proposed that if Global moves to the 500,000-barrel tankers, demurrage charges should remain about the same as long as the average daily arrival of oil is held constant. He therefore decides that the supertankers should arrive at the rate of 1/3 tanker per day or one every three days, since 500,000-barrels/tanker $\times$ 1/3 tanker/day or 166,667 barrels/day.

Dave learns that if the 500,000-barrel tankers are used, Global in fact is willing to incur a small increase in the total annual demurrage charges. This is because one supertanker requires less crew than two of the current tankers. However, the firm would not like to see a large increase in these charges.

To check his intuitive notion that the effects of doubling the tanker size and cutting the arrival rate in half should cancel each other, Dave decides to use Tanker, Global's on-line simulator, which was written to aid him in operating the dock. This simulator assumes that the arrivals are drawn from an exponential distribution with a user-specified mean. The item of interest is the total annual demurrage charges. The simulation will provide two ways to estimate this quantity:

1. *Average cost per tanker method:* Use the simulated results to compute the average cost per tanker as

$$\frac{\text{total demurrage fees}}{\text{number of tankers}}$$

and multiply this figure by the average number of tankers per year. Since super-tankers arrive at the rate of one every three days, this implies 120 per year (assuming a 360-day year). Thus, for supertankers we obtain the estimate

$$\text{total annual cost} = (\text{average cost per tanker}) \times (120)$$

2. *Average cost per day method:* Use the simulated results to compute the average cost per day as

$$\frac{\text{total demurrage fees}}{\text{number of days}}$$

and multiply this figure by 360, the number of days in a year. Using this method, we obtain the estimate (for either type of tanker)

$$\text{total annual cost} = (\text{average cost per day}) \times (360)$$

Actually Dave decides to run two simulations: one with parameters describing the current situation and the other with parameters describing the proposed situation. In each case he decides to sample roughly 2 months of data. He thus plans to simulate the arrival and unloading of 44 of the 250,000-barrel tankers (an expected duration of 44 × 1.5 or 66 days) and 22 of the 500,000-barrel tankers (an expected duration of 22 × 3.0 or 66 days). The simulation with current parameters is used as a test to see if the results are a reasonable approximation of the current situation.

The results of the simulations are shown in Figures 18.25 and 18.26.

Figure 18.25
250,000-Barrel Tankers

```
$PARAMS
PIPCAP = 250000.0,   TNKCAP = 700000.0,   UNLOAD = 400000.0,
SHPSIZ = 250000.0,   ARRIVAL = 0.6670000, DEMLMT = 2.000000,
CHARGE = 1400.000,   NUMBAT = 1,          NUMSHP = 44
SEED   = 345671
WANT MORE CHANGES? N      Initial random      Number of batches (trials)
                          number              of 44 ships


END OF SIMULATION AT TIME      50.399    Simulated time required for
                                         arrival of 44 ships

A TOTAL OF        44 TANKERS WERE UNLOADED
AVERAGE TIME IN PORT WAS       1.718
A TOTAL OF        1 TANKERS WERE WAITING AT END
A TOTAL OF    41.142 DAYS WERE SPENT WAITING        Total demur-
A TOTAL OF   7388.640  DOLLARS IN FEES CHARGED      rage cost dur-
                                                    ing simulated
TANK WAS EMPTY 6.774                                period of
TANK WAS FULL 18.533                                50.399 days
```

Figure 18.26
500,000-Barrel Tankers

```
$PARAMS
PIPCAP = 250000.0,    TNKCAP = 700000.0,    UNLOAD = 400000.0,
SHPSIZ = 500000.0,    ARIVAL = 0.3330000,   DEMLMT = 2.000000,
CHARGE = 3000.000,    NUMBAT = 1,           NUMSHP = 22,
SEED   = 345671
WANT MORE CHANGES? N



END OF SIMULATION AT TIME        52.192

A TOTAL OF       22   TANKERS WERE UNLOADED
AVERAGE TIME IN PORT WAS        1.915
A TOTAL OF        3   TANKERS WERE WAITING AT END
A TOTAL OF      12.364   DAYS WERE SPENT WAITING
A TOTAL OF      3982.455   DOLLARS IN FEES CHARGED
TANK WAS EMPTY      10.992
TANK WAS FULL       6.035
```

The relevant data are summarized in Figure 18.27.

Dave finds the data in Figure 18.27 to be interesting from several points of view. First, concerning the results from the 250,000-barrel tankers (i.e., the current situation), experience has shown that, over the last several years of operation, more than half of the time no demurrage charge has been incurred during a 2-month interval. However, a $7000 charge for a 2-month period in which a charge is incurred is not rare. Dave thus feels that the simulator is by chance giving a conservative

Figure 18.27
Summary Data

TANKER SIZE:	250,000	500,000	TANKER SIZE:	250,000	500,000
(a) Total demurrage charges	$7388.640	$3982.445	(e) = (a)/(c) Average cost per day	$146.60	$76.304
(b) Number of tankers unloaded	44	22	(f) Expected tankers per year	240	120
(c) Number of days	50.399	52.192	(g) = (d) × (f) Tanker-based cost per year	$40,301.52	$21,722.40
(d) = (a)/(b) Average cost per tanker	$167.923	$181.020	(h) = (e) × 360 Day-based cost per year	$52,776.00	$27,469.44

estimate (in the sense of an overestimate) of the average demurrage charges and it should thus be a good test of the proposed system.

Second, he is surprised that 500,000-barrel tankers yield a considerably lower annual cost with both estimation techniques. His intuition had suggested that the costs for the two systems would be about equal. However, he knows that the difference could easily be a random event, because this particular result is, of course, based on a sample. The good news, however, is that there is nothing in the data to suggest that the demurrage charges would be significantly larger with the 500,000-barrel tankers.

The mark of a good manager is to know when to decide as well as what to decide. With the simulation analysis for back-up, Dave confidently recommends that Global switch to the 500,000-barrel tankers with a 0.333 rate of arrival.

Questions

1. Explain the cause of the difference Dave encountered with the two methods of estimating total annual demurrage fees in the simulation with 500,000-barrel tankers.

2. Do you believe the results of the study? Comment on Dave's recommendation and study.

CHAPTER 19

Queuing Models

19.1
INTRODUCTION

Monte Jackson might not subscribe to the notion that all of life is a queue, but as administrative director of St. Luke's Hospital in Philadelphia, he must deal with a number of situations that can be described as queuing problems. Briefly, a queuing problem is one in which you have a sequence of items (such as people) arriving at a facility for service, as shown in Figure 19.1. At this moment, Monte is concerned about three particular "queuing problems."

Figure 19.1

General Queuing Problems

Arrivals

00000 $\longrightarrow$ Service facility $\longrightarrow$

Problem 1:
St. Luke's
Hematology
Lab

St. Luke's treats a large number of patients on an outpatient basis; that is, there are many patients who come to the hospital to see the staff doctors for diagnosis and treatment who are not admitted to the hospital. Outpatients plus those admitted to the 600-bed hospital produce a large flow of new patients each day. Most new patients must visit the hematology laboratory as part of the diagnostic process. Each such patient has to be seen by a technician. The system works like this. After seeing a doctor, the patient arrives at the laboratory and checks in with a clerk. Patients are assigned on a first-come, first-served basis to test rooms as they become available. The technician assigned to that room performs the tests ordered by the doctor. When the testing is complete, the patient goes on to the next step in the process (perhaps X-ray) and the technician sees a new patient.

Monte must decide how many technicians to hire. Superficially, at least, the trade-off is obvious. More technicians mean more expense for the hospital and quicker service for the patients.

As part of its remodeling process, St. Luke's is designing a new communications system. Monte must decide how many WATS lines the hospital should buy. He knows that when people pick up the phone, they want to get through without having to try several times. How many lines he needs to achieve that result at a reasonable cost is not so clear.

Problem 3:
Hiring
Repairmen

St. Luke's hires repairmen to maintain 20 individual pieces of electronic equipment. The equipment includes measuring devices like the electrocardiogram machine, small dedicated computers like the one used for lung analysis, and equipment like the CAT scanner. If a piece of equipment fails and all the repairmen are occupied, it must wait to be repaired. Monte must decide how many repairmen to hire. He must balance the cost of the repairmen against the cost of having broken equipment.

As Figure 19.2 indicates, all three of these problems fit the general description of a queuing model. Monte will resolve these problems by using a combination of analytic and simulation models. However, before we reach the level of sophistication required to deal with Monte's specific problems, it is necessary for us to spend some time with the basic queuing model. In the process we will learn some terminology and we will see the type of analytic results that are available.

Figure 19.2
Some Queuing Problems

PROBLEM	ARRIVALS	SERVICE FACILITY
1	Patients	Technicians
2	Telephone Calls	Switchboard
3	Broken Equipment	Repairmen

19.2

THE BASIC MODEL

Consider the Xerox machine located in the fourth-floor secretarial service suite. Assume that users arrive at the machine and form a single line. Each arrival in turn uses the machine to perform a specific task. These tasks vary from obtaining a copy of a 1-page letter to reproducing 100 copies of a 25-page report. This system is called a single-channel queue. Questions about this or any other queuing system center around four quantities:

1. The number of people in the system: the number of people currently being served, as well as those waiting for service.
2. The number of people in the queue: the number of people waiting for service.
3. The waiting time: the interval between when an individual enters the system and when he leaves the system. Note that this interval includes the service time.
4. The waiting time in the queue: the time between entering the system and the beginning of service.

To answer questions about these quantities, it is necessary to make some basic assumptions about particular aspects of the system. In the basic model the following assumptions are made.

Arrival Process Each arrival will be called "a job." Since the time between arrivals is not known with certainty, we will need to specify a probability distribution for it. In the basic model a particular distribution called the **exponential distribution** (sometimes called the *negative exponential distribution*) is used. This distribution plays a central role in many queuing models. It provides a reasonable representation of the arrival process in a number of situations and its so-called lack of memory property makes it possible to obtain analytic results. The words "Poisson input" are also used to describe the arrival process when the time between arrivals has an exponential distribution. This is because of the relationship between the exponential distribution and the Poisson distribution. In particular, if the interarrival time has an exponential distribution, the number of arrivals in a specified length of time (say, three hours) has a Poisson distribution. But we digress. The exponential distribution and its relationship to the Poisson is discussed in some detail in Section 19.9. At this point, it is only necessary to understand that the exponential distribution is completely specified by one parameter. This parameter, called λ, is the **mean arrival rate**, i.e., how many jobs arrive (on the average) during a specific period of time. In a moment we will consider an example where

$$\lambda = 0.05 \text{ jobs per minute}$$

This implies that *on the average* five hundredths of a job arrives every minute. It is probably more natural to think in terms of a longer time interval. An equivalent statement is that *on the average* one job arrives every 20 minutes. Using more technical terms, we say that *the mean interarrival time* is 20 minutes. Mean interarrival time is the average time between two arrivals.

Thus, for the exponential distribution
$$\text{average time between jobs} = \text{mean interarrival time} = 1/\lambda \qquad \textbf{(21.1)}$$

Thus, if $\lambda = 0.05$,

$$\text{mean interarrival time} = 1/\lambda = 1/0.05 = 20$$

Service Process In the basic model, the time that it takes to complete a job (the service time) is also treated with the exponential distribution. The parameter for this exponential distribution is called μ. It represents **the mean service rate** in jobs per minute. In other words, μT is the number of jobs that would be served (on the average) during a period of T minutes if the machine were busy during that time. In the upcoming example we will assume that $\mu = 0.10$. This implies that on the average 0.10 of a job is completed each minute. An equivalent statement is that on the average one job is completed every 10 minutes.

The mean, or average, service time (the average time to complete a job) is $1/\mu$. When μ, the mean service rate, is 0.10, the average service time is 10 since $1/\mu = 1/0.10 = 10$.

Queue Size There is no limit on the number of jobs that can wait in the queue. The queue is said to be infinite.

Jobs are served on a first-come, first-served basis, that is, in the same order as they arrive at the queue.

The system operates as described continuously over an infinite horizon.

Consider these assumptions in the context of the Xerox problem. Suppose that the average arrival time between jobs is 20 minutes. As we have seen, the fact that the inter-arrival time has an exponential distribution [see (19.1)] means that $1/\lambda = 20$, and thus $\lambda = 0.05$, or that the jobs arrive at the rate of 0.05 job per minute. Similarly, if the average time to complete a job is 10 minutes, we know that $1/\mu = 10$, $\mu = 0.10$, and that jobs are completed at the rate of 0.10 job per minute when the machine is operating.

The values of these two parameters (together with the assumptions) are all that is needed to calculate several important characteristics of the basic model. The necessary formulas are presented in Figure 19.3. **WARNING!** The formulas in Figure 19.3 hold only if $\lambda < \mu$. If this condition does not hold (i.e., if $\lambda > \mu$), the number of people in the queue will grow without limit. Consider, for example, a specific case where $\lambda = 0.25$ and $\mu = 0.10$. Remember that $1/\lambda$ is the average interarrival time. Thus, since $1/\lambda = 1/0.25 = 4$, on the average a job arrives every 4 minutes. Similarly, $1/\mu$ is the average time it takes to complete a job. Since $1/\mu = 1/0.10 = 10$, on the average it takes 10 minutes to complete a job. It seems clear that in this case the service operation will get further behind (the queue will grow longer) as time goes by.

Figure 19.3

Operating Characteristics for the Basic Model

CHARACTERISTIC	SYMBOL	FORMULA
Expected number in system	L	$\dfrac{\lambda}{\mu - \lambda}$
Expected number in queue	L_q	$\dfrac{\lambda^2}{\mu(\mu - \lambda)}$
Expected waiting time (includes service time)	W	$\dfrac{1}{\mu - \lambda}$
Expected time in queue	W_q	$\dfrac{\lambda}{\mu(\mu - \lambda)}$
Probability that the system is empty	P_0	$1 - \lambda/\mu$

Now return to the Xerox problem, in which $\lambda < \mu$ and the formulas in Figure 19.3 hold. Plugging the numerical values from the Xerox problem, $\lambda = 0.05$ and $\mu = 0.10$, into the formulas yields the results presented in Figure 19.4.

These numbers require some interpretation. L, for example, is the expected number of people in the system (those being served plus those waiting) after the queue has reached **steady state**. In this sentence, the phrase "steady state" means that the probability that you will observe a certain number of people (say 2) in the system does not depend on the time at which you count them. If a steady state has been achieved, the probability that there are two people using and/or waiting for the Xerox machine should be the same at 2:30 P.M. and at 4:00 P.M.

Figure 19.4
Evaluating the Operating Characteristics of the Basic Model
when $\lambda = 0.05$, $\mu = 0.10$

expected number in system	$L = \dfrac{\lambda}{\mu - \lambda} = \dfrac{0.05}{0.10 - 0.05} = 1$
expected number in queue	$L_q = \dfrac{\lambda^2}{\mu(\mu - \lambda)} = \dfrac{0.0025}{0.10(0.10 - 0.05)} = 0.5$
expected waiting time	$W = \dfrac{1}{\lambda - \mu} = \dfrac{1}{0.10 - 0.05} = 20$
expected time in queue	$W_q = \dfrac{\lambda}{\mu(\mu - \lambda)} = \dfrac{0.05}{0.10(0.10 - 0.05)} = 10$
probability that the system is empty	$P_0 = 1 - \dfrac{\lambda}{\mu} = 1 - \dfrac{0.05}{0.10} = 0.5$

The other characteristics presented in Figures 19.3 and 19.4 have a similar interpretation. Thus, in a steady state, (1) the system is empty with a probability of one-half ($P_0 = 0.5$); (2) on the average there is 0.5 person in the queue ($L_q = 0.5$), (3) on the average an arrival must wait 10 minutes before starting to use the machine ($W_q = 10$); and (4) on the average an arrival will spend 20 minutes in the system ($W = 20$).

Implications for Management These results hold for the basic model and the particular values for the parameters ($\lambda = 0.05$ and $\mu = 0.10$). They provide information that is useful to management in analyzing this service facility. Suppose, for example, that management makes the following calculations. Since $\lambda = 0.05$, on the average five hundredths of a job arrives each minute. During each 8-hour day there are $8 \times 60 = 480$ minutes. Thus during each day there is on the average a total of $(0.05)(480) = 24$ arrivals. From the calculations in Figure 19.4 we know that on the average each person spends 20 minutes in the system ($W = 20$). Thus, a total of (24 arrivals per day)(20 minutes per arrival) = 480 minutes or 8 hours is spent at this facility. Management might well feel that this is too long. A variety of steps might be taken.

1. A new machine might be purchased with a smaller mean service time.
2. Another machine might be purchased and both machines used to satisfy the demand.
3. Some personnel might be sent to a different and less busy copying facility. This would change the arrival process.

Management might select one of these alternatives, or perhaps some other option. But in any case, management must balance the cost of providing service against the cost of waiting. The results in Figure 19.4 and similar results for other systems would be a central part of the analysis. These ideas will be developed in more detail in the context of Monte Jackson's problems.

19.3

LITTLE'S FLOW EQUATION AND OTHER GENERALITIES

It has been proven that in a steady state queuing process

$$L = \lambda W \tag{19.2}$$

This result states that L, the expected number of people in the system equals λ, the arrival rate, times W, the expected waiting time. To perform a quick numerical check, see if the numbers derived for the Xerox problem (Figure 19.4) satisfy (19.2). The calculation is shown in (19.3).

$$L = 1.0 = 0.05 \times 20 = \lambda W \tag{19.3}$$

An Intuitive Development

To understand the intuitive foundation for this result, consider the diagram in Figure 19.5. In Scene 1 our hero arrives and joins the queue. In Scene 2 he has just completed service. Assume the system is in steady state. Since in this case the average number of people in the system is independent of time, let us measure this quantity when our hero completes being served. At this time, the number of people in the system is precisely the total number who arrived after he did (i.e., the individuals who arrived during his waiting time). Therefore, if W is his waiting time and people arrive at a rate of λ, we would expect L, the average number in the system, to equal λW.

Figure 19.5
Little's Flow Equation

Equation (19.2) is often called Little's flow equation. Note that it applies to any steady state queuing process and is thus applicable to a wide variety of problems. The proof used to establish (19.2) also shows that

$$L_q = \lambda W_q \tag{19.4}$$

A numerical check for the Xerox problem shows that

$$L_q = 0.5 = 0.05 \times 10 = \lambda W_q$$

Do All Arrivals Join the Queue?

which again agrees with the result in Figure 19.4. One must take some care in applying this result in more complicated cases. It is essential that λ represents the rate at which arrivals **join** the queue. This may be different from the rate at which people "arrive." Consider, for example, a queue with an upper limit on the number of items that can wait in the queue. A modern phone system that will hold a certain number of calls (say 10) in a queue until a service representative becomes available provides a good example. In such a system a person who calls and finds the system full simply receives a busy signal. In other words, he is sent away. He does not join the queue. Thus, if $\lambda = 0.25$ (the arrival rate) and the mean time between calls is 4 minutes, this is *not* the rate that people *join*. Thus, the relationship $L = 0.25W$ will not hold for this system.

Another important general result depends on the observation that

---

expected waiting time = expected waiting time in queue + expected service time

---

For the basic model we have already made use of the fact that

$$\text{expected service time} = 1/\mu$$

Putting the general result in symbols yields

$$W = W_q + 1/\mu \tag{19.5}$$

AnAlternative Approach to Finding L, L_q, W, and W_q

For the Xerox problem we have

$$W = 20 = 10 + 1/0.10 = W_q + 1/\mu$$

Not only does this hold for the basic model, but the general result [equation (19.5)] holds for any queuing model in which a steady state occurs.

Equations (19.2), (19.4), and (19.5) make it possible to compute the four operating characteristics L, L_q, W, and W_q once one of them is known. To illustrate this fact, let us start the Xerox problem over again. We begin as last time using the first formula in Figure 19.3 to calculate L:

$$L = \frac{\lambda}{\mu - \lambda} = \frac{0.05}{0.10 - 0.05} = 1$$

Now rather than using the other formulas in Figure 19.3 that are specifically for the basic model, we will use the two general results that we have just presented. First from Little's flow equation (19.2) we know that $L = \lambda W$. Thus, knowing $L = 1$ and $\lambda = 0.05$, we obtain $W = L/\lambda = 20$. Then, turning to (19.5), we see that

$$W = W_q + 1/\mu$$
$$W_q = W - 1/\mu = 20 - 1/0.10 = 10$$

Finally, (19.4) shows that

$$L_q = \lambda W_q = 0.05 \times 10 = 0.5$$

This alternative method of obtaining numerical results will turn out to be most useful when analyzing more complicated systems.

19.4

PROBLEM 1: A MULTIPLE-CHANNEL QUEUE (HEMATOLOGY LAB)

Recall that as we started this chapter, our stated goal was to attack three particular problems at St. Luke's with queuing models. In the preceding two sections we have laid the groundwork for this process. We have introduced, defined, and illustrated the characteristics of the systems that we will consider (e.g., expected number in queue, expected waiting time, etc.). We have also made some general results such as Little's flow equation available for use in future analysis. We are now in a position to turn our attention to Monte Jackson's problems.

The system described in Problem 1 of Section 19.1, the blood-testing problem, is illustrated in Figure 19.6. Note that each patient joins a common queue and when he arrives at the head of the line, he enters the first examining room that becomes available. This type of system must not be confused with a system in which a queue forms in front of each server as in the typical grocery store.

Figure 19.6
Multiple-Channel Queue

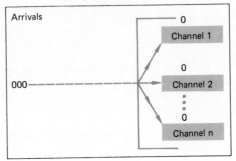

Parameters for the Problem

Assume that the interarrival time is given by an exponential distribution with parameter $\lambda = 0.20$. This implies that a new patient arrives every 5 minutes on the average, since

$$\text{mean interarrival time} = 1/\lambda = 1/0.20 = 5$$

Also, assume that each channel is identical and that each service time is given by an exponential distribution with parameter $\mu = 0.125$. This implies that the mean service time is 8 minutes, since

$$\begin{array}{l}\text{mean service time for}\\\text{an individual channel}\end{array} = 1/\mu = 1/0.125 = 8$$

Note that if there were only one channel, the queue would grow without limit, since $\lambda > \mu$ ($0.20 > 0.125$). For a multiple-channel queue, however, a steady state will exist as long as $\lambda < s\mu$, where s is the number of channels. For example, if we have two channels, $0.20 < 2(0.125)$ or $0.20 < 0.25$.

Probability the System Is Empty

As before, we want to find values L, L_q, W, and W_q. However, since this is a multiple-channel queue (not a single-channel queue as in the Xerox problem), we must use different formulas. To evaluate these formulas it is convenient to start with the expression for P_0, the probability that the system is empty. For this model

$$P_0 = \cfrac{1}{\displaystyle\sum_{n=0}^{s-1} \frac{(\lambda/\mu)^n}{n!} + \frac{(\lambda/\mu)^s}{s!}\left(\frac{1}{1 - (\lambda/s\mu)}\right)} \qquad (19.6)$$

and L_q, the expected number of people in the queue, is

$$L_q = P_0\left[\frac{\lambda^{s+1}}{\mu^{s-1}(s-1)!(\mu s - \lambda)^2}\right] \tag{19.7}$$

Equations (19.6) and (19.7) and the general results in (19.4) and (19.5) make it possible to calculate values for W_q, W, and L for any specified parameter values (μ and λ) and any number of channels (value of s).

Assume, for example, that Monte decided to hire two technicians. Then, since $s = 2$, $\lambda = 0.20$, and $\mu = 0.125$, we see that $\lambda/\mu = 0.20/0.125 = 1.6$, and $\lambda/s\mu = 0.20/2(0.125) = 0.8$. Equation (19.6) becomes[1]

$$P_0 = \frac{1}{1 + 1.6 + \frac{(1.6)^2}{2}\left(\frac{1}{1 - 0.8}\right)} = 0.11$$

Expected Number in Queue and the probability that the system is empty is 0.11. We can now use this result in (19.7) to find L_q.

$$L_q = 0.11\left[\frac{0.2^3}{0.125 \times 1 \times (0.250 - 0.20)^2}\right] = 2.82$$

that is, the expected number of people in the queue is somewhat less than 3. From (19.4), Monte knows that $L_q = \lambda W_q$. Thus,

$$W_q = \frac{L_q}{\lambda} = \frac{2.82}{0.20} = 14.10$$

or, on the average, a patient waits for 14.10 minutes before entering an examining room. Let us now look at the general observation that

expected waiting time = expected waiting time in queue + expected service time

We note that the expected service time in this expression is the expected time an individual will spend being served. This does not depend on the number of channels. It depends only on the amount of time an individual channel takes to do the job. In this case all channels are the same. Each has a mean service time of $1/\mu$. Thus we have

Expected Time in Hematology Area

$$W = W_q + 1/\mu = 14.10 + 1/0.125 = 22.10$$

On the average, then, a patient spends 22.10 minutes in the hematology area, waiting for a technician and having tests.

These calculations make the decision easy for Monte. With one technician, since $\lambda > \mu$, the system is unstable and the queue will steadily grow. This could be considered irresponsible. With two technicians, the average waiting time in the queue is less than 15

[1] To evaluate this expression, you must use the facts that $0! = 1$ and $(1.6)^0 = 1$.

minutes. By current hospital standards, this is a small and acceptable value. If, in some cases, the queue gets uncomfortably long (remember that W_q is an expected value and the actual time in queue will vary), the supervisors of the hematology laboratory can temporarily move one of the blood analysts to a technician's position. Monte thus feels comfortable with the idea of hiring two full-time technicians without performing a detailed cost analysis.

19.5
A TAXONOMY OF QUEUING MODELS

There is a large number of possible queuing models. For example, if the interarrival time in the basic model had been given a different distribution (not the exponential) we would have a different model, in the sense that the expressions for L, L_q, and so on, would no longer hold. To facilitate communication among those working on queuing models, D. G. Kendall proposed a taxonomy based on the following notation:

Kendall's
System

$$A/B/s$$

where A = arrival distribution
B = service distribution
s = number of channels

Different letters are used to designate certain distributions. By placing these in the A or the B position they indicate the arrival or the service distribution, respectively. The following conventions are in general use:

M = exponential distribution

D = deterministic number

G = any (a general) distribution of service times

GI = any (a general) distribution of arrival times

We can see, for example, that the Xerox problem is an $M/M/1$ model, that is, a single-channel queue with exponential interarrival and service times. Also, the model that Monte chose for Problem 1, the hematology lab problem, is an $M/M/2$ model, that is, a two-channel queue with exponential interarrival times and exponential service times for each channel.

19.6
ECONOMIC ANALYSIS OF QUEUING SYSTEMS

Monte selected the number of lab technicians to hire by looking at the probabilities and using his judgment. This is not an unusual approach in queuing models and is especially common in the not-for-profit sector. Monte realizes that he is balancing the cost of hiring more technicians against the costs he incurs by forcing the patients to wait. The cost of hiring additional technicians is fairly clear. The waiting cost is not.

Waiting
Cost

Monte first notes that the cost to the patient is irrelevant to his decision, except as it affects the patient's willingness to use the hospital. It really does not matter who is waiting—a tax lawyer who charges $200 per hour for his services or an unemployed person with no opportunity cost—unless the waiting time persuades the patient to use another health facility. This observation explains why certain monopolies like government bureaus and utilities can be so casual about your waiting time. There is no place else to go!

Besides the possible effect on demand, the hematology lab could cost the hospital money if it reduced the output of the hospital. Suppose, for example, that the outpatient clinics could process 50 new patients each day, but that the hematology lab could only handle 10. (This is clearly an extreme example to establish a point.) In this case, the hospital would be wasting a valuable resource, the doctors and other staff in the clinics, because of a bottleneck in the hematology lab. However, having stated this, it still is not easy to assess an explicit cost of a patient waiting.

If you are willing and able to estimate certain costs, you can build expected cost models of queuing systems. Consider, for example, the hematology lab problem (in general terms any multiple-channel queue with exponential interarrival and service times) and suppose that management is willing to specify two costs:

$$C_S = \text{cost per hour of having a channel available}$$

$$C_W = \text{cost per hour of having a person wait in the system}$$

Cost Components

With these it is possible to calculate the expected total costs associated with the decision to use any particular number of servers. Let us start by calculating the expected total cost of using two channels for an 8-hour day. There are two components.

$$\boxed{\text{channel cost} = (C_S)(2)(8)}$$

where C_S is the cost per hour for one channel, 2 is the number of channels, and 8 is the number of hours each channel works, and

$$\boxed{\text{waiting cost} = (C_W)(L(2))(8)}$$

This calculation may not be as obvious, but the rationale is the same as for the channel cost. If there are, on the average, $L(2)$ people waiting when the system has two channels then $L(2)$ times 8 is the average number of "waiting hours" per day. Hence, $(C_W)(L(2))(8)$ is the average waiting cost for the 8-hour day.

If we wanted to calculate the expected total cost of using four channels for a 6-hour day, we would take

$$\boxed{(C_S)(4)(6) + (C_W)(L(4))(6)}$$

We now define

Expected Total Cost per Hour with s Channels

$$TC(s) = \text{expected total cost per hour of using } s \text{ channels}$$

and we see that

$$TC(s) = (C_S)(s) + (C_W)(L(s))$$

Our goal is to choose s, the number of servers, to minimize this function.

Figure 19.7 shows the general shape of the function TC(s). This function is determined by plotting the two component parts, $(C_S)(s)$ and $(C_W)(L(s))$, and adding them together. We see that TC(s) assumes a minimum for some value s. Unfortunately it is not possible to derive a formula that gives the optimal value of s. (This is in contrast to

Figure 19.7
Costs in an *M/M/s* Queue

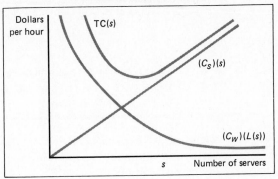

the EOQ model, where we can find the optimal order quantity, Q^*, with the equation $Q^* = \sqrt{2DC_0/C_h}$). It is, however, a relatively easy matter to attack a specific problem numerically, that is, by trying several values for s and selecting the value that yields the minimum total cost. Rather than pursuing this further, let us complete our examination of the hematology lab problem with these observations. We have seen how to find values for L, L_q, W, and W_q. These values were then used to select the appropriate number of technicians (channels). This decision might be made on intuitive grounds or on the basis of an explicit economic analysis. We now move on to Monte's second problem.

No Analytic Solution

19.7
PROBLEM 2: THE *M/G/s* MODEL WITH BLOCKED CUSTOMERS CLEARED (WATS LINES)

Do not be misled by the title of this section. It is devoted to Problem 2, Monte's attempt to select the appropriate number of WATS lines for St. Luke's. Fortunately, in this case he can expect help from the telephone company. They have a great deal of expertise in such matters, since queuing models have found extensive use in the field of telephone traffic engineering. The problem of how many lines are needed by a switchboard is typically attacked by using the *M/G/s* model, "with blocked customers cleared." You already know that this model is a multiple-channel queue with s channels (s lines), exponential interarrival times for the calls, and a general distribution for the service time, which in this case is the length of each call. The phrase "**blocked customers cleared**" is queuing jargon. It means that **when an arrival finds all the channels occupied (all of the lines busy), he does not get in a queue but simply leaves.** This phrase clearly describes the behavior of the traditional telephone switchboard. More sophisticated systems now provide for queuing of a finite number of customers, in some cases even providing the lucky customer the opportunity to enjoy a Muzak version of "You Light Up My Life," or "As Time Goes By."

Cleared Customers Do Not Join the Queue

The problem of selecting the appropriate number of lines (channels) is attacked by computing the steady-state probability that exactly j lines will be busy. This, in turn, will be used to calculate the steady-state probability that all s lines are busy. Clearly, if you have s lines and they are all busy, the next caller will not be able to place her call.

The steady-state probability that there are exactly j busy channels given that there are s lines (channels) available is given by the expression

$$P_j = \frac{(\lambda/\mu)^j/j!}{\sum\limits_{k=0}^{s} (\lambda/\mu)^k/k!} \qquad (19.8)$$

where λ = **arrival rate (the rate at which calls arrive)**
$1/\mu$ = **mean service time (the average length of a conversation)**
s = **number of channels (lines)**

The expression is called the *truncated Poisson distribution* or the *Erlang loss distribution*. It is noteworthy that although we are considering a general service-time distribution, the value P_j defined by (19.8) depends only on the mean of this distribution.

Consider a system in which $\lambda = 1$ (calls arrive at the rate of one per minute) and $1/\mu = 10$ (the average length of a conversation is 10 minutes). Here $\lambda/\mu = 10$. Suppose that we have five lines in the system ($s = 5$) and want to find the steady-state probability that exactly two are busy ($j = 2$). From (19.8) we see that

$$P_2 = \frac{(\lambda/\mu)^2/2!}{\sum\limits_{k=0}^{5} (\lambda/\mu)^k/k!}$$

$$= \frac{(10)^2/2 \cdot 1}{1 + 10^1/1 + 10^2/2 \cdot 1 + 10^3/3 \cdot 2 \cdot 1 + 10^4/4 \cdot 3 \cdot 2 \cdot 1 + 10^5/5 \cdot 4 \cdot 3 \cdot 2 \cdot 1}$$

$$= \frac{50}{1 + 10 + 50 + 166.67 + 416.67 + 833.33}$$

$$= \frac{50}{1477.67} = 0.034$$

In other words, on the average two lines would be busy 3.4% of the time.

The Probability
That All Lines
Are Busy

The more interesting question is: "What is the probability that all of the lines are busy?" since in this case a potential caller would not be able to place his call. To find the answer to this question, we simply set $j = s$ in (19.8). In our example $s = 5$ and we obtain

$$P_s = \frac{(\lambda/\mu)^5/5!}{\sum\limits_{k=0}^{5} (\lambda/\mu)^k/k!}$$

Using values that we calculated in our evaluation of P_2, we see that

$$P_s = \frac{833.33}{1477.67}$$

$$= 0.564$$

or on the average the system is totally occupied 56.4% of the time.

The probability that the system is totally occupied (all channels are busy) is important enough that its value has been calculated for a large range of values for λ/μ and s and the results recorded in graphs. The notation $B(s, \lambda/\mu)$ is used for thsi probability and its values for a variety of values of s and λ/μ are presented in Figure 19.8. Let us use this figure to find $B(5, 10)$, the steady-state probability that the system is busy if there are five lines and $\lambda/\mu = 10$. We proceed as follows:

Figure 19.8

$B(s, \lambda/\mu)$

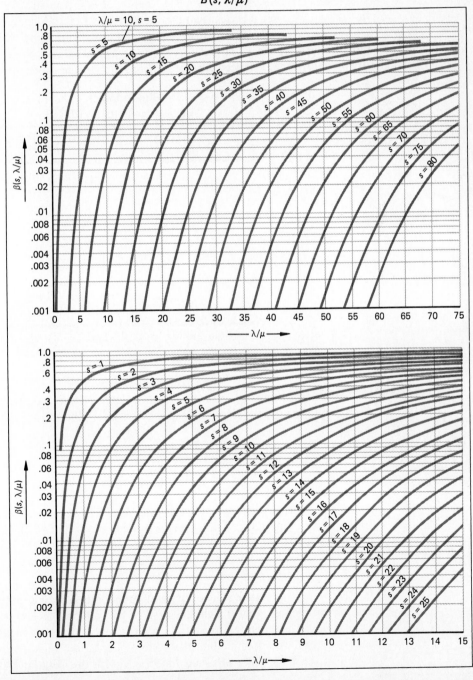

1. Find the value $\lambda/\mu = 10$ on the horizontal axis.
2. Follow this line up until it intersects with the curved contour $s = 5$.
3. Finally, read on the vertical axis the value of $B(s, \lambda/\mu)$ that corresponds to this intersection.

In this case ($s = 5$, $\lambda/\mu = 10$) the value of $B(5, 10)$ is approximately 0.56. We thus have obtained the same result with significantly less effort.

Purchasing additional lines obviously decreases the probability of finding the system busy, making $B(s, \lambda/\mu)$ smaller. Values of $B(s, 10)$ with 1 to 10 lines are recorded in Figure 19.9. Here it is clear that the marginal effect of adding more channels decreases. For example, adding a second line when there was one in service decreases the probability of the system being busy by 0.089, whereas adding the tenth line when there were already nine in service decreases this probability by 0.058.

Figure 19.9
$B(s, 10)$ for $s = 0, \ldots, 10$

s	$B(s, 10)$	DECREASE IN $B(s, 10)$[a]
0	1.000	
1	0.909	0.091
2	0.820	0.089
3	0.732	0.088
4	0.647	0.085
5	0.564	0.083
6	0.485	0.079
7	0.409	0.076
8	0.338	0.071
9	0.273	0.065
10	0.215	0.058

[a] The decrease in $B(s, 10)$ is defined as $B(s - 1, 10) - B(s, 10)$. It is the reduction in the probability of finding a busy system caused by adding the sth line.

Another interesting and useful quantity in the design of phone installations is the average number of busy lines. This quantity is called the *carried load* in queuing jargon.

The Average Number of Busy Lines

If $\bar{N}$ is the average number of busy lines, then

$$\bar{N} = (\lambda/\mu)[1 - B(s, \lambda/\mu)] \qquad (19.9)$$

Assume now that in Monte's problem with WATS lines for St. Luke's, $\lambda = 1$ and $\mu = 10$. Thus, if he purchases 10 lines, we see in Figure 19.9 that $B(10, 10) = 0.21$. It follows from (19.9) that

$$\bar{N} = 10(1 - 0.21) = 7.9$$

In other words, the system will be busy with probability 0.21 or about one-fifth of the time and, on the average, almost eight lines will be busy. Monte feels that this is a reasonable compromise. There does not seem to be a great deal of excess capacity, but, on the other hand, the probability of finding the system busy is in a region that he feels is appropriate for the hospital. If he is uncomfortable with this solution based on a subjective balancing of the number of lines and the probability of finding the system busy and is willing to specify a cost for each time a caller finds the system busy, he can select the number of lines to minimize the expected cost per hour. He would proceed in the same manner as in the $M/M/s$ system in Section 19.6.

19.8

PROBLEM 3: THE REPAIRMAN PROBLEM

In this problem Monte must decide how many repairmen to hire to maintain 20 pieces of electronic equipment. Repairmen deal with machines on a first-come (perhaps first-failed is more accurate), first-served basis.

A single repairman treats each broken machine. You can thus think of the failed machines as forming a queue in front of multiple channels (the repairmen).

This is another $M/M/s$ problem but it differs in a fundamental way from the $M/M/s$ system (the blood-testing problem) considered in Section 19.4. In this problem there is a limited number of items (20) which can join the queue, whereas in the hematology lab problem an unlimited number could potentially join the queue.

A Finite Calling Population A queuing problem, like the repairman problem, in which only a finite number of "people" are eligible to join the queue is said to have a *finite calling population*. Problems with an unlimited number of possible participants are said to have an *infinite calling population*.

Consider the problem with 20 machines and two repairmen. Assume that when a machine is running, the time between breakdowns has an exponential distribution with parameter $\lambda = 0.25$, that is, the average time between breakdowns is $1/\lambda = 4$ hours. Similarly, assume that the time it takes to repair a machine has an exponential distribution and that the mean repair time is 0.50 hour (i.e., $1/\mu = 0.50$). This problem is an $M/M/2$ problem with a maximum of 18 items in the queue (20 including the two in service) and a finite calling population. In this case the general equations for the steady state probability that there are n jobs in the system is a function of λ, μ, R (the number of repairmen) and M (the number of machines). In particular,

$$P_n = \frac{M!}{n!(M-n)!}(\lambda/\mu)^n P_0 \quad \text{for } 0 \le n \le R$$

$$P_n = \frac{M!}{(M-n)! \, R! \, R^{n-R}}(\lambda/\mu)^n P_0 \quad \text{for } R < n \le M$$

These equations plus the fact that

$$\sum_{n=0}^{M} P_n = 1$$

make it possible (if painful) to calculate values of P_n for any particular problem.

Expected Number in System There are, however, no simple (even by these standards) expressions for the expected number of jobs (broken machines) in the system or waiting. If the values for P_n are computed, then it is (truly) a simple task to find a numerical value for the expected number in the system. You must just calculate

$$\text{Expected number in system} = \sum_{n=0}^{M} n P_n$$

If God had intended man to perform this kind of calculation by hand, he would not have let computers be invented. Figure 19.10 shows the use of a computer routine that can be used to compute values of P_n, the expected number in the system, and the expected number waiting for a variety of different systems. As shown, the user enters the system parameters and the computer does the rest. In this case, "the rest" consists of numerically

Figure 19.10

Computer Analysis of the Repairman Problem

```
HOW MANY CHANNELS AND HOW MANY SPACES?
(SPACES MUST AT LEAST EQUAL CHANNELS)
2.20

INDICATE SERVICE TIME DISTRIBUTION TYPE
E (EXPONENTIAL) OR C (CONSTANT):
E

POPULATION SIZE (ENTER 0 IF INFINITE) =
20

ARRIVAL RATE AND MEAN SERVICE TIME?
0.25, 0.5
```

N.-IN-SYS.	PROBABILITY	CUMULATIVE-PROB
0	0.033	0.033
1	0.083	0.116
2	0.099	0.215
3	0.111	0.326
4	0.118	0.444
5	0.118	0.563
6	0.111	0.673
7	0.097	0.770
8	0.079	0.849
9	0.059	0.908
10	0.041	0.948
11	0.025	0.974
12	0.014	0.988
13	0.007	0.995
14	0.003	0.998
15	0.001	1.000
16	0.000	1.000
17	0.000	1.000
18	0.000	1.000

```
AVG.-NO.-IN-SYS. = 5.198
AVG.-NO.-WAITING = 3.348
PROBABILITY ALL SPACES FULL = 0.000
PROBABILITY FREE CHANNEL AVAILABLE = 0.116
AVG.-TIME-IN-SYS. FOR THOSE WHO GET SERVED = 1.405
AVG.-NO.-BUSY-CHANNELS = 1.850
STOP
```

evaluating the equations for P_n and using these results to find the expected number in the system. As you see in Figure 19.10, the computer stopped evaluating the number in the system at 18, since the probability was zero for any larger number. The summary data show that for this system, L_q, the average number of machines waiting for service, is 3.348 and W, the expected time in the system, is 1.405.

An on-line computer program such as the one used for the repairman problem is a convenient way to obtain quick numerical results for a number of queuing systems. Indeed, it could also have been used to solve Problems 1 and 2. Figure 19.11 shows the models that can be evaluated with this particular program.

Figure 19.11
Models in the Computer-Based System

QUEUING SYSTEM	QUEUE SIZE	CALLING POPULATION
$M/M/s$	Any specified number	Infinite
$M/M/s$	$N - s$	Finite, Say N
$M/G/\infty$	0	Infinite
$M/G/1$	Infinite	Infinite
$M/M/s$	0	Finite
$M/D/1$	0	Finite
$M/G/s$	0	Infinite

19.9
THE ROLE OF THE EXPONENTIAL DISTRIBUTION

There is an enormous body of literature concerning queuing systems and it is virtually impossible for a manager to be aware of all the results. There are, however, some general considerations that are useful in helping a manager think about the use of queuing models. One such consideration is the role of the exponential distribution in analytic queuing models.

There are essentially no analytic results for queuing situations that do not involve the exponential distribution either as the distribution of interarrival times or service times or both. This fact makes it important for a manager to recognize the set of circumstances in which it is reasonable to assume that an exponential distribution will occur.

Lack of
Memory

In an arrival process this property implies that the probability that an arrival will occur in the next few minutes is not influenced by when the last arrival occurred; that is, the system has no memory of what has just happened. This situation arises when (1) there are many individuals who could potentially arrive at the system, (2) each person decides to arrive independently of the other individuals, and (3) each individual selects his or her time of arrival completely at random. It is easy to see why the assumption of exponential arrivals fits the telephone system so well.

Small Service
Times

With an exponential distribution, small values of the service time are common. This can be seen in Figure 19.12. This figure shows the graph of the probability that the service time S is less than or equal to t (Prob $\{S \le t\}$) if the mean service time is ten, i.e., $\mu = 0.1$

and $1/\mu = 10$. Note that the graph rises rapidly and then slowly approaches the value 1.0. This indicates a high probability of having a short service time. For example, when $t = 10$, the probability that $S \le t$ is 0.632. In other words, more than 63 per cent of the service times are smaller than the average service time. This compares to a normal distribution where only 50 percent of the service times are smaller than the average. The practical implication of this fact is that an exponential distribution can best be used to model the distribution of service times in a system in which a large proportion of jobs take a very short time and only a few run for a long time.

Figure 19.12

A High Probability of Short Service Times

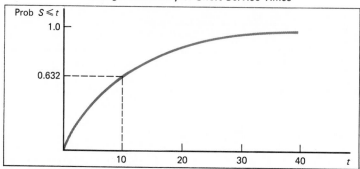

Relation to the Poisson Distribution

While introducing the basic model (Section 19.2) we noted the relationship between the exponential and Poisson distributions. In particular, if the time between arrivals has an exponential distribution with parameter λ, then in a specified period of time (say, T) the number of arrivals will have a Poisson distribution with parameter λT. Then if X is the number of arrivals during the time T, the probability that X equals a specific number (say n) is given by the equation

$$\text{Prob}\{X = n\} = \frac{c^{-\lambda T}(\lambda T)^n}{n!}$$

This equation holds for any integer value of n, i.e., $n = 0, 1, 2$, and so on.

The relationship between the exponential and the Poisson distributions plays an important role in the theoretical development of queuing theory. It also has an important practical implication. By comparing the number of jobs that arrive for service during a specific period of time with the number that the Poisson distribution suggests, the analyst is able to see if his or her choice of a model and parameter values for the arrival process is reasonable.

19.10

QUEUE DISCIPLINE

In the previous sections we have specified the arrival distribution, the service distribution, and the number of channels to define a queuing system. Queue discipline is still another characteristic that must be specified in order to define a queuing system. In all of the models that we have considered so far, we have assumed that arrivals were served on a first-come, first-served basis (often called FIFO, for "first-in, first-out"). This is certainly an appropriate assumption for telephone systems and for many systems where people are the arrivals. This is not necessarily the case for other systems, however. In an elevator the last person in is often the first out (LIFO). And in the repairmen model, there is really no reason for the repairmen to fix the machines in the same order as they break down. If a certain machine can be returned to production in 5 minutes, it seems like a good idea to do it first, rather than making it wait until a 1-hour job that broke down earlier is completed.

Adding the possibility of selecting a good queue discipline makes the queuing models more complicated. Problems of this sort are often referred to as scheduling problems and there is an extensive literature that deals with them.

19.11
NOTES ON IMPLEMENTATION

Queuing problems are everywhere. This fact is obvious even to the most casual observer. Airplanes "queue up" in holding patterns, waiting for a runway so they can land, and then they line up again to take off. People line up for tickets, to buy groceries, and, if they happen to live in England, for almost everything else. Jobs line up for machines, orders line up to be filled, and so on.

The models discussed in this chapter are useful representatives of only a small portion of the broad expanse of queuing problems. The results presented here in general require that either the time between arrivals, the service time, or both have an exponential distribution. They are important because they yield tight analytic results and because, in many circumstances, it is reasonable to assume that the arrival process is a Poisson process. In particular, we have noted that a large (essentially infinite) calling population in which individual members of the population decide at random to arrive at service facilities generates an exponential distribution for the time between arrivals. It is not surprising then that the analytic models are often used on systems with this type of arrival mechanism. Communication networks (especially the telephone system) and traffic control systems are two important examples of such systems.

Role of Simulation   Digital simulation is a popular approach for studying queuing problems that do not fit the analytic mold. Indeed, current programs such as GPSS (IBM's General Purpose Systems Simulator) have been created to facilitate the simulation process. A general discussion of simulation along with some specific comments on queuing simulators is included in Chapter 18.

19.12
MAJOR CONCEPTS QUIZ

True–False

1. T F The number of people in the system means the number waiting in line.
2. T F The waiting time includes the service time.
3. T F The exponential distribution is described by a mean and a standard deviation.

4. T F The mean interarrival time is the reciprocal of the mean arrival rate, and the mean service time is the reciprocal of the mean service rate.

5. T F The basic model is $M/M/1$.

6. T F As the number of channels increases, the cost of waiting generally increases.

7. T F The assumption that the mean service rate is less than the mean arrival rate is enough to eliminate the formation of infinitely long queues.

8. T F Little's flow equation states a directly proportional relationship between expected waiting time and expected number of people in the system.

9. T F The notation $G/M/2$ means the service distribution is general, the arrival distribution is exponential, and there are two channels.

Multiple Choice

10. Which of the following does not apply to the basic model?
  a. exponentially distributed arrivals
  b. exponentially distributed service times
  c. finite time horizon
  d. unlimited queue size
  e. the discipline is first-come, first-served

11. A major goal of queuing is to
  a. minimize the cost of providing service
  b. provide models which help the manager to trade off the costs of service and waiting
  c. maximize expected return
  d. optimize system characteristics

12. Characteristics of queues such as "expected number in the system"
  a. are relevant after the queue has reached a steady state
  b. may not actually be observed at a particular time
  c. depend on the specific model
  d. all of the above

13. In Little's flow equation, which of the following is *not* true?
  a. λ is the constant of proportionality between expected number in the queue and expected time in the queue.
  b. λ is the constant of proportionality between expected number in the system and expected time in the system.
  c. λ is the arrival rate, including those arrivals who choose not to join the system.

14. The most difficult aspect of performing a formal economic analysis of queuing systems is
  a. estimating the service cost
  b. estimating the waiting cost
  c. estimating use

15. In a multiple-channel system with blocked customers cleared, one of the following does not apply.
  a. When all channels are busy, new arrivals leave.
  b. Interesting characteristics are the probability that all channels are busy and the average number of busy channels.
  c. One would never do an expected cost per hour analysis.

16. For the exponential distribution, one of the following is *not* a characteristic.
  a. lack of memory
  b. a high probability of a long service time
  c. a single parameter

Answers

1. F	**7.** F	**12.** d
2. T	**8.** T	**13.** c
3. F	**9.** F	**14.** b
4. T	**10.** c	**15.** c
5. T	**11.** b	**16.** b
6. F		

19-1. Barges arrive at the La Crosse lock on the Mississippi River at an average rate of one every 2 hours. If the interarrival time has an exponential distribution:
(a) What is the value of λ?
(b) What is the mean interarrival time?
(c) What is the mean arrival rate?

19-2. Ninety-six cars arrived at Joe's Service Station during an 8-hour period. Assume that the interarrival time has an exponential distribution and use the given data to estimate
(a) The value of λ.
(b) The mean interarrival time.
(c) The mean arrival rate.

19-3. An immigration agent at Heathrow Airport in London could on the average process 120 entrants during her 8 hours on duty if she were busy all of the time. If the time to process each entrant is a random variable with an exponential distribution:
(a) What is the value of μ?
(b) What is the mean service time?
(c) What is the mean service rate?

19-4. On the average a complete tune-up (plugs, points, oil, etc.), at Fire Year takes 45 minutes. If the time to complete a tune-up is a random variable with an exponential distribution:
(a) What is the value of μ?
(b) What is the mean service time?
(c) What is the mean service rate?

19-5. Consider the immigration officer mentioned in Problem 19-3. Assume that the basic model is a reasonable approximation of her operation. Recall that if she were busy all the time she could process 120 entrants during her 8-hour shift. If on the average an entrant arrives at her station once every 6 minutes, find
(a) The expected number in the system.
(b) The expected number in the queue.
(c) The expected waiting time.
(d) The expected time in queue.
(e) The probability the system is empty.

19-6. Consider the La Crosse lock mentioned in Problem 19-1. Assume that the basic model is a reasonable approximation of its operation. The mean interarrival time is 2 hours for barges and on the average it takes 30 minutes to move a barge through the lock. Find
(a) The expected number in the system.
(b) The expected number in queue.
(c) The expected waiting time.
(d) The expected time in queue.
(e) The probability that the system is empty.

19-7. Consider a single-channel queue. Assume that the basic model is a reasonable approximation of its operation. Comment on the following scheme to estimate λ.
1. Let N equal the number of arrivals between 8:00 A.M. and 4:00 P.M.
2. Set $\lambda = 8/N$.

19-8. Consider a single-channel queue. Assume that the basic model is a reasonable approximation of its operation. Comment on the following scheme to estimate μ.
1. Let M equal the number of customers served between 8:00 A.M. and 4:00 P.M.
2. Set $\mu = M/8$.

19-9. Consider the basic model. Let $\mu = 10$ and plot the probability that the system is empty for $\lambda = 0, 1, \ldots, 10$.

19-10. Consider the basic model. Let $\mu = 10$ and plot the expected waiting time for $\lambda = 0, 1, \ldots, 10$.

19-11. Use Little's flow equation and the fact that $L = \lambda/(\mu - \lambda)$ in the basic model to derive the expression for W.

19-12. Use Little's flow equation, the expression for the mean service time, and the fact that $L = \lambda/(\mu - \lambda)$ in the basic model to derive the expression for W_q.

19-13. At the Homeburg Savings and Loan, customers who wish to buy certificates of deposit form a single line and are served on a first-come, first-served basis by a specific bank officer. Service time is normally distributed with a mean of 5 minutes and a standard deviation of 1 minute. Customers arrive at the rate of one every 8 minutes. A time study shows that customers spend an average of 10 minutes in the system (i.e., waiting and being served). What is the average number of people in the system?

19-14. A doctor schedules his patients to arrive at the rate of three per hour and treats them on a first-come, first-served basis. On the average he spends 15 minutes with each patient, but this time can vary anywhere from 5 to 40 minutes. If on the average there are five persons in his office (four waiting and one being served), how long on the average does a patient wait before he sees the doctor?

19-15. Assume that it was stated in Problem 19-14 that patients arrive at the rate of five per hour. Comment on this problem.

19-16. Assume that it was stated in Problem 19-13 that the mean service time was 10 minutes rather than 5. Comment on this problem.

19-17. The Homeburg Savings and Loan uses three tellers on Saturdays. The interarrival time and the service time for customers each has an exponential distribution. Customers arrive at the rate of 20 per hour and the mean service time is 6 minutes. Customers form a single queue and are served by the first available teller. Under steady-state conditions, find
(a) The probability that no customers are waiting or being served.
(b) The expected number of people in the queue.
(c) The expected waiting time in the queue.
(d) The expected waiting time.
(e) The expected number of people in the system.

19-18. The Business School reserves five ports on its on-line computer for faculty use. If a faculty member attempts to log in and all the ports are occupied she receives a busy signal. All calls are held in a queue and served by the first available open port on a first-come, first served basis. To estimate the system characteristics, the head of the computation center wants to know the steady-state values of the characteristics assuming an infinite calling population, an infinite queue, exponential interarrival times and service times, where jobs arrive at the rate of six per hour and the mean service time is 30 minutes. Find
(a) The probability that all ports are open.
(b) The expected number of people in the queue.
(c) The expected waiting time in the queue.
(d) The expected waiting time.
(e) The expected number in the system.

19-19. Describe a $M/D/3$ queuing system in words.

19-20. Describe a $GI/M/4$ queuing system in words.

19-21. STECO has 100 sales representatives in the United States. They call orders into a central office where an office worker using the central inventory control system confirms product availability, price, and delivery date. The representative calls directly from the customer's office before signing a contract. Calls are held in a queue and served by the first available office worker on a first-come, first-served basis. Calls arrive at the rate of 40 per hour and the mean service time is 6 minutes. Management estimates that it costs $20 per hour to have a sales representative wait and $12 per hour to employ an office worker. Model this situation as an $M/M/s$ queue with an infinite calling population and calculate the expected total cost per hour if STECO hires five office workers.

19-22. Find the expected total cost per hour for the system in Problem 19-21 if STECO hires six office workers.

19.23. A telephone exchange has seven lines. Calls arrive at the rate of two per minute and the interarrival time has an exponential distribution. Conversations have a normal distribution with a mean of 5 and a standard deviation of 1. When all seven lines are occupied, the caller simply receives a busy signal.

(a) What is the probability that exactly three lines are busy?

(b) What is the probability that the system is totally occupied?

(c) What is the average number of busy lines?

19-24. A market research group has four interviewers located in adjacent booths in a suburban shopping mall. A contact person meets people walking in the mall and asks them if they are willing to be interviewed. They estimate that customers willing to agree to the interview arrive at the rate of six per hour and the interarrival time has an exponential distribution. On the average the interview takes 30 minutes. If all booths are occupied, a person who has agreed to be interviewed will not wait and simply goes about his or her business.

(a) Comment on the following statement: Since $\lambda > \mu s$, this system will grow without bound.

(b) Calculate the probability that exactly one interviewer is occupied.

(c) Find the probability that all four interviewers are occupied.

(d) Find the average number of busy interviewers.

CHAPTER 20

Dynamic Programming

20.1
INTRODUCTION

Dynamic programming is a particular method of attacking certain decision problems. It is an approach that converts one large problem which has a large number of decision variables and is thus difficult to solve into a sequence of problems each of which has a smaller number of decision variables and is thus easier to solve. The technique is often applicable to dynamic problems in which a sequence of decisions must be made.

Comparison with LP

It may be useful, at the outset, to compare dynamic programming with linear programming. Linear programming has relatively tight restrictions on the form of the model: all the functions must be linear, all the decision variables must be continuous (as opposed to integer valued). These restrictions make it difficult or impossible to attack certain problems with LP. However, for those cases where a useful LP model can be constructed, the simplex algorithm can be used to solve the model quickly and cheaply. In contrast, a much greater variety of problems and cost functions can be modeled with dynamic programming, but in this case it will be seen that the solution process can be more complicated.

20.2
THE SHORTEST-ROUTE PROBLEM

We have discussed the shortest-route problem in Chapter 11. A quick review of that discussion reveals that the shortest-route problem can be modeled as a network problem and therefore an efficient algorithm exists to solve it. The problem is presented again here for pedagogical reasons. The shortest-route problem is an especially useful vehicle for motivating the concept and the notational formalities of dynamic programming.

The data for a typical shortest-route problem are presented in Figure 20.1. In this figure the squares (nodes) represent cities and the numbers attached to the arrows (arcs)

656

Figure 20.1
Shortest-Route Problem

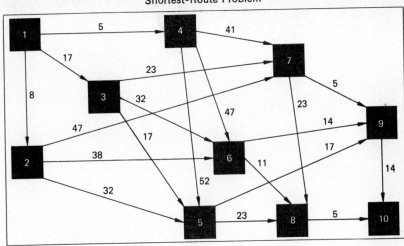

leading from one city to another are the tolls a traveler must pay to traverse that route. For example, it costs $23 to go from city 3 to city 7 and $17 to go from 5 to 9.

Our traveler starts in 1 and must make his way to 10. He would like to minimize the amount he has to pay in tolls. Which route should he take? As an example, we see that if he takes route 1–3–6–8–10 he will incur a cost of $17 + 32 + 11 + 5 = \$65$. The question is: Which route yields the minimum cost?

The minimum-cost route can be thought of as the shortest route from 1 to 10 simply by thinking of the tolls as distances. In general this type of problem is called the shortest-route problem but in a specific application the "distances" can be costs or times, or some other measure associated with each arc.

Complete Enumeration

One way to solve the shortest-route problem is by **complete enumeration**, that is, by listing all possible routes, calculating the cost for each route, and choosing the minimum-cost alternative. In general, this approach is not used because there are so many alternatives that it is too expensive in time and/or computing costs to evaluate all of them. In this example there are 18 possible routes. If you have enough patience you can list all of them and discover that the minimum cost route is 1–3–7–9–10, with a cost of $59. The worst you could do is to take the route 1–4–5–9–10 and incur a cost of $88.

Partial Enumeration

Dynamic programming is a method of **partial enumeration**: a method of finding the best alternative without listing all possible alternatives. To understand how dynamic programming works, suppose that our traveler seeks the aid of his cousin in solving this shortest-route problem. His cousin does not know the shortest route from city 1 to city 10, but he has traveled widely and he knows: (1) the shortest route from 2 to 10 and the cost of that route; (2) the shortest route from 3 to 10 and the cost of that route; and (3) the shortest route from 4 to 10 and the cost of that route. These data are presented in Figure 20.2.

Our traveler can easily use the data in Figure 20.2 to find the minimum cost route from 1 to 10. Suppose, for example, that he goes from 1 to 2. This costs $8. From Figure 20.2 we know that the minimum cost from 2 to 10 is $54. Therefore, the minimum-cost route from 1 to 10 *that passes through 2* is $8 + \$54 = \$62$.

Figure 20.2
Partial Solutions to the Shortest-Route Problem

CITY	MINIMUM-COST ROUTE TO 10	COST
2	2–6–8–10	$54
3	3–7–9–10	42
4	4–7–9–10	60

Minimum-Cost Route   When he leaves city 1 our traveler must go to 2, 3, or 4. He can evaluate the cost of each of these alternatives just as he evaluated the cost of going from 1 to 10 via 2. The cheapest of these three alternatives will be the minimum-cost route. In particular,

$$\text{min cost } 1\text{--}10 = \min \begin{Bmatrix} \text{cost 1 to 2} + \text{min cost 2--10} \\ \text{cost 1 to 3} + \text{min cost 3--10} \\ \text{cost 1 to 4} + \text{min cost 4--10} \end{Bmatrix} \qquad (20.1)$$

Substituting the minimum costs from Figure 20.2 and using the cost of the trips 1–2, 1–3, and 1–4 from Figure 20.1, the above expression yields

$$\text{min cost } 1\text{--}10 = \min \begin{Bmatrix} 8 + 54 \\ 17 + 42 \\ 5 + 60 \end{Bmatrix} = \min \begin{Bmatrix} 62 \\ 59 \\ 65 \end{Bmatrix} = \$59 \qquad (20.2)$$

We thus see that the minimum cost to get from 1 to 10 is 59. In (20.2) we see that to realize this cost our traveler must go from city 1 to 3. Combining this with the information in Figure 20.2, we see that the minimum cost route (the shortest route) is 1–3–7–9–10. We have thus reproduced the result originally achieved by complete enumeration.

20.3
RECURSIVE RELATIONSHIPS

In the preceding analysis we solved the 1–10 shortest-route problem by making use of the solutions to the 2–10, 3–10, and 4–10 shortest-route problems. We actually performed the *last step* in a dynamic programming solution to this problem. We will now repeat this analysis using the mathematical notation of dynamic programming.

    To formulate a problem as a dynamic programming problem, you must create a *recursive relationship*. The first step in this process is to define an appropriate function. For the purposes of introduction, it is better at the outset to illustrate this process than to attempt a general explanation, and thus we return to the shortest-route problem. Let

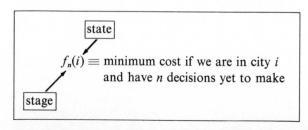

Stage and State

The *stage* and *state* are crucial parts of a function that will be used in a recursive relationship. Roughly, the stage is the number of sequential decisions that have yet to be made and the state describes the condition currently facing the decision maker. Thus, in this model, being in state i means being in city i. Finding an appropriate identity for the stage and state is the creative part of formulating a problem as a dynamic programming problem. Working your way through the examples in this chapter will introduce you to several of the most common types of dynamic programming models and you will start to develop skill in the art of formulation of these models.

In the shortest-route problem we know that our traveler starts in city 1. In addition, we see that each possible route from 1 to 10 includes four occasions when the traveler must decide which city to go to next. (Sometimes the decision is trivial, e.g., when the traveler is in city 9.) Nonetheless, four decisions must be made. In other words, the overall goal is to find $f_4(1)$, the minimum cost if the traveler is in city 1 with four decisions yet to make. You have already seen how we used the three solutions for shortest-route problems, with three decisions remaining, to find the solution to the shortest-route problem with four decisions remaining. In terms of the notation $f_n(i)$, we used $f_3(2), f_3(3)$, and $f_3(4)$ to find $f_4(1)$. We now repeat the process using the $f_n(i)$ notation. The data from Figure 20.2 are reproduced in Figure 20.3 with new labels.

Figure 20.3

Partial Solutions to the Shortest-Route Problem

CITY, i	MINIMUM-COST ROUTE TO 10	$f_3(i)$
2	2–6–8–10	54
3	3–7–9–10	42
4	4–7–9–10	60

If C_{ij} is the cost to go from city i to city j and we use $f_3(i)$ as defined above, then (20.1), which we used to find the minimum-cost route, takes a new appearance (same meaning) in the form of (20.3):

$$f_4(1) = \min \begin{cases} C_{12} + f_3(2) \\ C_{13} + f_3(3) \\ C_{14} + f_3(4) \end{cases} \tag{20.3}$$

Here we have a bona fide recursive relationship. *The minimum cost with four decisions to be made is found by using the minimum costs when there are three decisions to be made.*

So far our solution to the shortest-route problem with four decisions to be made depends on a mysterious cousin who knows the solution to three shortest-route problems with three decisions to be made. What actually happens in dynamic programming is that you use recursive relationships, starting with $f_1(i)$ to find $f_2(i)$, which in turn you use to find $f_3(i)$. The general recursive relationship is presented in (20.4).

General Recursive Relationship

$$f_n(i) = \min_{j \in D(i)} \{C_{ij} + f_{n-1}(j)\} \tag{20.4}$$

In this expression $D(i)$ is the set of all decisions that you can make if you are in state i. Thus, $D(1)$ is the set of cities you can move to if you are in city 1 [i.e., $D(1)$ consists of decisions to move to city 2, 3, or 4]. The symbol ϵ is read "is an element of." Thus, the phrase $\min_{j \in D(i)} \{\cdot\}$ says that we evaluate the expression in braces for every decision j that is an element of the set $D(i)$ and pick the smallest of them.

In this notation

$$f_4(1) = \min_{j \in D(1)} \{C_{1j} + f_3(j)\} \tag{20.5}$$

This is simply a shorthand way of writing (20.3). It says evaluate $C_{1j} + f_3(j)$ for $j = 2, 3, 4$ and pick the smallest of these three values. This is exactly what we did in (20.3).

We will now use the general recursive relationship, (20.4), to solve the shortest-route problem from the beginning.

Stage 1   Find $f_1(i)$ for $i = 8, 9$. We first note that when there is one decision (move) left to make, we must be in either city 8 or city 9. Thus, we do not have to worry about other states. Also, since we can only go to 10 from 8 and 9, there really is not a decision problem. In terms of the notation $D(8) = 10$ and $D(9) = 10$. We see that $f_1(8) = 5$ and $f_1(9) = 14$. In words, the cheapest (and in this case the only) route from 8 to 10 costs $5 and the cheapest route from 9 to 10 costs $14. This is hardly a revelation, but it is the first step in solving the problem with dynamic programming.

Stage 2   Here we will be able to use (20.4) and see how dynamic programming works. With two decisions to make, the traveler is in state 5, 6, or 7, where the state 5 is city 5, and so on. Now we wish to find $f_2(5), f_2(6)$, and $f_2(7)$. If the traveler is in state 5, 6, or 7, he can go to either city 8 or 9; thus, $D(5) = \{8, 9\}$, $D(6) = \{8, 9\}$, and $D(7) = \{8, 9\}$. Using these facts, we can employ a table to perform the calculations to find $f_2(i)$. Such a table is shown in Figure 20.4. In this table the rows are the possible

Figure 20.4
Finding $f_2(i)$

	$C_{ij} + f_1(j)$			
	j			
i	8	9	$f_2(i)$	$j^*(i)$
5	23 + 5 = 28	17 + 14 = 31	28	8
6	11 + 5 = 16	14 + 14 = 28	16	8
7	23 + 5 = 28	5 + 14 = 19	19	9

values for the states i. The columns up to the double bar are the possible decisions (j). That is, in this model decision j, taken in state i, means move from city i to city j. The entries are the cost of moving from i to j and from then on taking the minimum cost route, that is, the values of $C_{ij} + f_1(j)$ for the appropriate i and j; $f_2(i)$ is the minimum entry in each row and $j^*(i)$ is the optimal decision to make for each i. For example, if the traveler is in state 5 ($i = 5$), his minimum cost of getting to 10 is $28 and he must go through city 8 to obtain this cost.

Stage 3   We use the results of stage 2 to find $f_3(i)$ for $i = 2, 3, 4$ in exactly the same way in which we use the results of stage 1 to find $f_2(i)$ for $i = 5, 6, 7$. An appropriate table is shown in Figure 20.5.

Figure 20.5

Finding $f_3(i)$

	$c_{ij} + f_2(j)$				
	j				
i	5	6	7	$f_3(i)$	$j^*(i)$
2	32 + 28 = 60	38 + 16 = 54	47 + 19 = 66	54	6
3	17 + 28 = 45	32 + 16 = 48	23 + 19 = 42	42	7
4	52 + 28 = 80	47 + 16 = 63	41 + 19 = 60	60	7

Stage 4   The process for finding $f_4(1)$ is by now familiar but we repeat it here for completeness. An appropriate table is shown in Figure 20.6.

Figure 20.6

Finding $f_4(1)$

	$c_{ij} + f_3(j)$				
	j				
i	2	3	4	$f_4(i)$	$j^*(i)$
1	8 + 54 = 62	17 + 42 = 59	5 + 60 = 65	59	3

Stage 4 completes the dynamic programming solution to the shortest-route problem. We see (once again) that the minimum cost to go from 1 to 10 is $59. To find the optimal route we must work our way back through the tables. The table in Figure 20.6 tells us that we go from 1 to 3. The table in Figure 20.5 tells us that we go from 3 to 7. The table in Figure 20.4 tells us that we go from 7 to 9 and from stage 1 we know that we go from 9 to 10. Thus, again we see that the optimal route is 1–3–7–9–10.

20.4

THE KNAPSACK PROBLEM

The Hiker's Problem

An important class of dynamic programming problems derives its name from the *knapsack model* discussed in Chapter 11. Consider the following illustrative situation. A hiker can carry up to 11 pounds of food in his knapsack. He must select among four items, each of which comes in clearly marked but sealed packets. Data[1] on these items are presented in Figure 20.7.

Figure 20.7

Knapsack Stuffers

Item	Weight per Packet	Utility per Packet
A	1	2
B	2	5
C	3	6
D	4	12

The hiker would like to maximize his total utility subject to the constraint on total weight. He could, for example, select 11 packets of A and obtain a utility of 2 for each packet, or a total of 22. Alternatively, he could select 3 units of C and 1 unit of B for a total utility of $(3 \times 6) + 5 = 23$. The hiker is restricted to selecting full packets. For example, he cannot choose 11/4 packets of item D.

This problem can be formulated as a mathematical programming problem as follows. Let

Mathematical
Programming
Formulation

$$z_1 \equiv \text{number of packets of item A}$$
$$z_2 \equiv \text{number of packets of item B}$$
$$z_3 \equiv \text{number of packets of item C}$$
$$z_4 \equiv \text{number of packets of item D}$$
$$\max \quad 2z_1 + 5z_2 + 6z_3 + 12z_4$$
$$\text{s.t.} \quad 1z_1 + 2z_2 + 3z_3 + 4z_4 \leq 11$$
$$z_1, z_2, z_3, z_4 \geq 0 \text{ and integer}$$

This is *an integer programming model* since the decision variables $z_1, z_2, z_3,$ and z_4 are restricted to integer values. This enforces the conditions that only complete packets can be chosen.

This problem can be solved by dynamic programming. We know that the values of $z_1, \ldots, z_4$ must be selected so that the constraint is satisfied; thus, there is an interaction among the variables. However, in dynamic programming we think of selecting the values sequentially. Figure 20.8 illustrates the process. You can think of the process as evolving over time beginning at Start with stage 4 and ending at Finish with stage 1. In other words, first we select z_4, the number of packets of D to put in the knapsack. Then we select z_3, the number of packets of item C, and so on.

Defining the
State

The information produced at stage n is contained in the function $f_n(x)$. We thus need to define this function for the knapsack problem. We have, in Figure 20.8, identified the stages. However, we must still identify the state in order to define $f_n(x)$ and to create the recursive relationship. Think of it this way. Suppose that someone had already chosen $z_4, z_3,$ and z_2. What would you have to know about these decisions to choose z_1? If you answered "the total weight already assigned" or "the total weight left un-

---

[1] In this figure, interpret "utility per packet" to be some composite measure of preference in terms of taste, nourishment, energy, and any other relevant attributes.

Figure 20.8

Definition of Stages for Knapsack Problem

	Stage			
	4	3	2	1
Item being selected	D	C	B	A
Decision variable	z_4	z_3	z_2	z_1
Function being created	$f_4(x)$	$f_3(x)$	$f_2(x)$	$f_1(x)$

⇑
start

⇑
Finish

assigned," you are ready to start working on the recursive relationship. The state, at the beginning of stage n, will be denoted as x, which represents the amount of capacity still available (i.e., weight left unassigned).

As the first step in the formulation process, we define

$$f_n(x) = \text{maximum possible utility if we are in stage } n$$
$$\text{and } x \text{ pounds of capacity is still available}$$

Our goal is to find $f_4(11)$, the maximum possible utility when we must select the number of packets for all four items and all 11 pounds of capacity is available. To define the recursive relationship it is convenient to let

$$w_i = \text{weight in pounds per packet of the item dealt with at stage } i;$$
$$\text{thus, } w_1 \text{ is the weight per packet of item A (i.e., 1 pound)}$$

$$U_i = \text{utility per packet of the item dealt with at stage } i; \text{ thus,}$$
$$U_1 \text{ is the utility per packet of item A (i.e., 2)}$$

The Feasible Set

We must also develop some system to limit z_i to a feasible set of alternatives. Suppose, for example, that $x = 7$ at stage 3. This implies that 7 pounds of capacity is still available and we wish to select the optimal value for z_3, the number of packets of item C, to place in the knapsack. Since each packet of C weighs 3 pounds (i.e., $w_3 = 3$) and 7 pounds of capacity is available, we can decide to place 0, 1, or 2 packets in the knapsack (i.e., $z_3 = 0$ or 1 or 2). Any larger number of packets exceeds the capacity.

To introduce a general notation, let $[x/w_n]$ be the largest integer less than or equal to x/w_n. In our example $n = 3$; thus $w_n = 3$ and $x = 7$. Since $7/3 = 2.33$ we see that $[x/w_n] = 2$. We thus see that the feasible values for z_3 are the integers from 0 to $[x/w_n]$.

Recursive Relationship

With this notation we see that in general

$$f_n(x) = \max_{z_n = 0, 1, \ldots, [x_n/w_n]} \{U_n z_n + f_{n-1}(x - w_n z_n)\} \tag{20.6}$$

where the notation $\max_{z_n = 0, 1, \ldots, [x/w_n]}$ means we must select z_n to be one of the integers from 0 to $[x/w_n]$. In particular, when $n = 4$ and $x = 11$, (20.6) becomes

$$f_4(11) = \max_{z_4=0,1,2} \{12z_4 + f_3(11 - 4z_4)\} \tag{20.7}$$

To understand (20.7) recall that since $n = 4$ we are deciding how many units of D to put in the knapsack. Since $x = 11$ none of the capacity has been assigned. Now consider the term in braces. The $12z_4$ is the utility the hiker gets from putting z_4 units of D in his knapsack. The term $(11 - 4z_4)$ is the amount of the knapsack available to be assigned to the other three items and $f_3(11 - 4z_4)$ is the maximum utility that can be obtained with this unassigned capacity. The expression $\max_{z_4=0,1,2}$ tells us that we will set z_4 equal to 0, 1, or 2 depending on which value yields the maximum value of the sum in braces. The upper limit of 2 was selected because it is the largest integer less than or equal to $11/4$. If we attempted to put more than two packets of D in the knapsack we would exceed capacity.

To find $f_4(11)$ we start with $f_1(x)$ for $x = 0, 1, 2, \ldots, 11$ and work our way up through $f_2(x)$ and $f_3(x)$.

Stage 1 At this stage we are trying to decide how many packets of item A we should put in the knapsack as a function of the amount of the knapsack that is still available to be assigned. It is an easy problem. You simply fill up any available capacity with packets of A. Since each packet of A weighs 1 pound, $z_1^*(x) = x$; that is, we select one packet of A for each pound of available capacity. Also, since each packet has a utility of 2,

$$f_1(x) = 2x \qquad \{x = 0, 1, 2, \ldots, 11\}$$

Stage 2 The recursive relationship for stage 2 (or B units) is given by adapting the general equation (20.6) to this stage. Thus,

$$\boxed{f_2(x) = \max_{z_2=0,1,\ldots,[x/2]} \{5z_2 + f_1(x - 2z_2)\}} \tag{20.8}$$

The values of $f_2(x)$ could now be computed in a tabular format analogous to Figure 20.4. The rows would correspond to the states (the unassigned capacity) and thus assume the labels $0, 1, \ldots, 11$. As an illustration the row $x = 4$ is shown below.

	$z_2(x)$				
	0	**1**	**2**	$f_2(x)$	$z_2^*(x)$
$x = 4$	$0 + 8 = 8$	$5 + 4 = 9$	$10 + 0 = 10$	10	2

Each column up to the double bar corresponds to an allocation of the indicated number £ units of B to the knapsack. The entries in the table are calculated from the expression $5z_2 + f_1(x - 2z_2)$. To the right of the double bar we see that if at stage 2 there are 4 pounds of unassigned capacity, the 2 pounds of item B should be assigned $[z_2^*(4) = 2]$ and this assignment yields a utility of 10 $[f_2(4) = 10]$.

In this problem, however, we shall not make use of this tabular approach. We shall derive the function $f_2(x)$ analytically as contrasted to evaluating it at 11 specific points as we would be required to do in the tabular approach. Such an analytic approach is typically preferable since it involves much less computational effort. It is, however, not always possible to achieve. In this case it is easy to derive an analytic result because the utility associated with each item is directly proportional to the number of units assigned. In this problem recall that $f_1(x) = 2x$. It follows that $f_1(x - 2z_2) = 2(x - 2z_2)$.

$$f_2(x) = \max_{z_2=0,\ldots,[x/2]} \{5z_2 + 2(x - 2z_2)\}$$

$$= \max_{z_2=0,\ldots,[x/2]} \{2x + z_2\}$$

Clearly, the maximum is obtained by picking z_2 as large as possible; that is, set $z_2 =$ to $[x/2]$: in other words, $z_2^*(x) = [x/2]$ and $f_2(x) = 2x + [x/2]$. Values for $z_2^*(x)$ and $f_2(x)$ are presented in Figure 20.9.

Figure 20.9
Stage 2 Results

							x					
	0	1	2	3	4	5	6	7	8	9	10	11
$z_2^*(x)$	0	0	1	1	2	2	3	3	4	4	5	5
$f_2(x)$	0	2	5	7	10	12	15	17	20	22	25	27

Stage 3   Adapting (20.6) to stage 3 yields

$$f_3(x) = \max_{z_3=0,1,\ldots,[x/3]} \{6z_3 + f_2(x - 3z_3)\}.$$

Using the fact that $f_2(x) = 2x + [x/2]$, we have

$$f_2(x - 3z_3) = 2(x - 3z_3) + \left[\frac{x - 3z_3}{2}\right]$$

which gives

$$f_3(x) = \max_{z_3=0,1,\ldots,[x/3]} \left\{6z_3 + 2(x - 3z_3) + \left[\frac{x - 3z_3}{2}\right]\right\}$$

or

$$f_3(x) = \max_{z_3=0,1,\ldots,[x/3]} \left\{2x + \left[\frac{x - 3z_3}{2}\right]\right\}$$

From this result it is apparent that the quantity in brackets is maximized when z_3 is as small as possible. Hence, for each x, $z_3^*(x) = 0$ and

$$f_3(x) = 2x + [x/2]$$

These results are shown in Figure 20.10.

Figure 20.10

Stage 3 Results

							x					
	0	1	2	3	4	5	6	7	8	9	10	11
$z_3^*(x)$	0	0	0	0	0	0	0	0	0	0	0	0
$f_3(x)$	0	2	5	7	10	12	15	17	20	22	25	27

Stage 4 The recursive relationship for stage 4 was shown in (20.7). Since at this stage we know that all 11 pounds of capacity is available, we only have to find $f_4(11)$ and our table only has one row. The calculations are presented in Figure 20.11.

Figure 20.11

Finding $f_4(11)$

	$12z_4 + f_3(11 - 4z_4)$				
x	0	1	2	$f_4(11)$	$z_4^*(11)$
11	$0 + 27 = 27$	$12 + 17 = 29$	$24 + 7 = 31$	31	2

Finding the optimal solution (how many packets of each item to select) is achieved by working our way back down from stage 4 to stage 1. Figure 20.11 shows that the maximum total utility is 31 and that two packets of D should be selected. Since each packet of D weighs 4 pounds, this leaves 3 pounds of unused capacity.

Since $z_3^*(3)$ is 0 (see Figure 20.10), no packets of C are selected. This means that at the end of stage 3 there are still 3 pounds of unused capacity. Figure 20.9 reveals that $z_2^*(3)$ is 1; thus, 1 unit of B is selected. This leaves 1 unit of unused capacity. Since

The Optimal $z_1^*(x) = x$, $z_1^*(1) = 1$ and we select one packet of A.
Solution In summary:

optimal solution	
A	1 packet
B	1 packet
C	0 packet
D	2 packets
optimal value of objective function $= 31$	

The Budget Stuffing knapsacks is obviously not a manager's most important function. The knapsack
Allocation problem is important, however, because it is a paradigm of a process that is fundamen-
Problem tal to the management function—namely, allocating a budget (or effort) among various departments or projects. To obtain the best result from a budget, the manager must be able to specify what return he will obtain from each project for every possible allocation level.

To provide a specific structure, assume that there are three projects and let

$$g_i(x_i) = \text{return from project } i \text{ if } x_i \text{ dollars is invested in it}$$

Also assume that our manager has b dollars available to invest. The manager would like to invest his funds so as to maximize his total return. His problem then can be stated as the following mathematical programming problem:

$$
\begin{aligned}
\max \quad & g_1(x_1) + g_2(x_2) + g_3(x_3) \\
\text{s.t.} \quad & x_1 + x_2 + x_3 \le b \\
& 0 \le x_i \le b, \qquad i = 1, 2, 3
\end{aligned}
$$

In this context we should think of the manager making one decision about how much to allocate to each project.

Note that in the **knapsack problem** the return functions $g_i(x_i)$ were all linear functions, that is,

$$g_i(x_i) = U_i x_i$$

where U_i is a constant. In more general budget allocation problems these functions are not apt to be linear. Often return functions are characterized by *diminishing marginal returns*; that is, each dollar invested in a project yields a *marginal return* no larger than the previous dollar. Such a function is shown in Figure 20.12. Here we see that the increment in return from allocating an additional I dollars depends on how much has previously been allocated. In particular the incremental return starting at A is greater than the incremental return starting at B:

$$g_i(A + I) - g_i(A) \ge g_i(B + I) - g_i(B)$$

Since this relationship holds for every pair of points A and B for which $A \le B$, we see that returns increase at a decreasing rate. This characteristic is called diminishing marginal returns.

When the return functions are not linear or piecewise linear like Figure 20.12, the budget allocation problem cannot be attacked with linear programming. However, as

Figure 20.12
Diminishing Marginal Returns

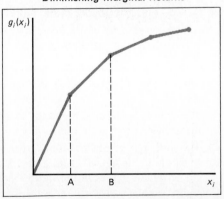

long as we know what the return will be for each project, for each possible investment, we can attack the problem with dynamic programming as follows. Define

$$f_n(x) = \text{maximum return if we have projects 1 through } n \text{ left to consider}$$
$$\text{and } x \text{ dollars available to invest}$$

Recursive Relationship

Then the recursive relationship is

$$f_n(x) = \max_{0 \le x_n \le x} \{g_n(x_n) + f_{n-1}(x - x_n)\}$$

Note that in the dynamic programming version of the budget allocation problem, the manager no longer decides on all the allocations simultaneously. He first decides on the best allocation for project 1 as a function of the funds that are available. He uses that information to find the best allocation for projects 2 and 1 as a function of the funds available, and so on. In other words, he proceeds in a sequential manner.

We thus see that the classic budget allocation problem can be attacked with dynamic programming. This statement is not intended to minimize the difficulty of developing the $g_i(x_i)$ functions, the return from a project as a function of the investment in the project. However, management must have an appreication of these functions; it must have an understanding of return as a function of investment if it is going to allocate its funds wisely. The point is that even with reasonable estimates of the profitability (return) of the various individual activities [i.e., even if you know the $g_i(x_i)$ functions], the question of how much to invest in each activity still remains.

In concluding this section one technical point deserves comment. In the problem above the decision variables x_n are continuous. Thus, we cannot use a tabular method to develop the functions $f_n(x)$. In this case, mathematical analysis must be employed. If the term $g_n(x_n) + f_{n-1}(x - x_n)$ is particularly simple (such as linear, as was the case with the knapsack example), then the optimization step is particularly easy. In more difficult cases, calculus must be employed. One advantage to having discrete (as opposed to continuous) decisions is that a tabular method will always produce results, no matter how complicated the functions are.

20.5

THE GENERAL MODEL

Having worked our way through the shortest-route and knapsack problems, it is now appropriate to consider dynamic programming in general. The diagram in Figure 20.13 illustrates the process by depicting stages n and $n - 1$. Consider stage n. Note that

1. All information about previous states and decisions is conveyed to stage n by the state x_n.

2. The state x_n determines the set of decisions $D(x_n)$ that are available to the decision maker. He selects a decision z_n from that set.

3. The state, x_n, and the decision, z_n, determine the impact of stage n on the objective function. In Figure 20.13 this is labeled $R(x_n, z_n)$ and called return. It could be a cost (to be minimized) as in the shortest-route problem, a utility (to be maximized) as in the knapsack problem, or some other measure of interest.

4. The state, x_n, and the decision, z_n, determine the state for the next stage, x_{n-1}. This new state is determined by the function $T(x_n, z_n)$, called the *transfer function*.

Figure 20.13
Dynamic Programming Process

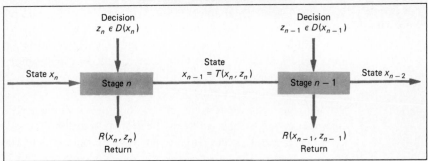

In some cases, as with the shortest-route problem, there is a "natural" sequential nature to the decision problem. Often the sequential relationship between decisions is provided by time; for example, you always make January's production decisions before February's. In other cases, as in the knapsack problem, all of the actual decisions will be made at one time. However, it may be useful to impose an arbitrary sequential structure on the problem so that it can be more readily attacked with dynamic programming. This is the procedure that was followed in the knapsack and budget allocation problem.

20.6

THE CURSE OF DIMENSIONALITY

*The State
as a Vector*

The curse of dimensionality is not the legacy of some obscure Count from Transylvania. It is management science jargon for the fact that a number of interesting and important problems can be formulated as dynamic programming problems but not solved in a reasonable amount of time. It is difficult to solve such problems because the number of states is so large that there is an enormous number of computations to be done. The problem typically occurs when the state is represented by a vector [say, $(x_1, x_2, \ldots, x_n)$]. This means that there are several state variables rather than a single one as has been the case in the problems we have seen to date. A vector (x_1, x_2) can be thought of as representing a point in two dimensions and a vector $(x_1, x_2, \ldots, x_n)$ represents a point in n dimensions. Since the computational problem typically occurs when the state is represented by a vector with several entries (that is, several dimensions), the difficulty has been dubbed the curse of dimensionality. To illustrate the curse, we will compare the number of states for a single-product and a multiple-product production planning model.

First consider a single-product model in which the state variable is the inventory on hand. In other words, all information about past production decisions and customer demands is included in the amount of inventory on hand. Also assume that, due to the physical constraints in the warehouse, no more than 199 of these units can be stored. Since the inventory on hand can be any of the integers $0, 1, \ldots, 199$, there are 200 states for this problem. This implies that if we were to construct a decision table like Figure 20.4 for this problem, it would have 200 rows. Although evaluating a decision table this large would be a painful experience for a person, it is a trivial task for a computer and dynamic programming problems of this size can be solved quickly and easily using a computer.

Now consider a multiproduct version of this production planning model. In particular, assume that there are five products that are produced on a single machine. Assume that the state variable is the amount of inventory on hand for each of these products. The state variable then is represented by the vector $(x_1, x_2, x_3, x_4, x_5)$, where x_1 is the amount of product 1 on hand, and so on. Once again assume that due to physical constraints, at most 199 of each of these products can be stored. As before this means that x_1 can assume any of the 200 integer values $0, 1, \ldots, 199$. The same statement can be made for x_2. The implication of these two facts is that there are $200 \times 200 = 40,000$ pairs of values for the first two elements in the vector. To see this, assume that x_1 is a specific number, say 4. The inventory for product 2 can be any of 200 values. This statement holds for every possible value of x_1; thus, there is a total of $200 \times 200 = 40,000$ pairs of values for the first two elements in the vector.

320 Billion Rows

By applying the same logic we see that the total number of states is

$$200 \times 200 \times 200 \times 200 \times 200 = 320,000,000,000$$

This implies that if we were to construct a decision table like Figure 20.4 for this problem, it would have 320 billion rows. Such a problem is simply too large to be solved on a computer in a reasonable amount of time. Thus the curse of dimensionality has struck.

This multiproduct example illustrates the main obstacle which can arise in using the dynamic programming technique. It is easy to find complex and important problems that can be modeled effectively with dynamic programming. Unfortunately, as soon as the state must be represented by a vector, the model can become computationally intractable. The skill in using this technique involves formulating your model with as few states as possible.

20.7

MAJOR CONCEPTS QUIZ

True–False

1. **T F** If the numbers attached to each arc in a shortest-route problem were reinterpreted as revenues and the goal was to maximize total revenue, you could not solve this problem with dynamic programming.

2. **T F** In the shortest-route problem, the cities are the states.

3. **T F** Once the optimal return is determined it is necessary to work back through the tables to determine the optimal decisions.

4. **T F** If a dynamic programming problem becomes too large to solve in a reasonable amount of time, it is typically because the number of stages is too large.

5. **T F** If an upper bound on the amount that could be invested in each project were added to the budget allocation problem, it could not be solved by dynamic programming.

6. **T F** In a dynamic programming model, the state variable must incorporate relevant information about the past performance of the system.

7. Dynamic programming
   a. is a method of partial enumeration
   b. relies on complete enumeration
   c. is used only on problems where the decisions occur sequentially over time
   d. none of the above

8. In the knapsack problem the state at stage n is
   a. the number of items yet to be considered
   b. the number of units of the item under consideration that are selected
   c. the unassigned capacity in the knapsack
   d. none of the above

9. In the knapsack problem the function $f_n(x)$ is measured in
   a. pounds
   b. units of utility
   c. unassigned capacity
   d. none of the above

10. The budget allocation problem
    a. requires a function for each project that yields return as a function of investment
    b. has a single constraint on the total budget
    c. has continuous variables
    d. all of the above

11. Suppose that a manager has to allocate both project directors and dollars to a set of potential projects. A dynamic programming model of this problem would have
    a. a vector with two variables to represent the state
    b. two constraints
    c. a return for each project that is a function of both dollars and the direction allocated to the project
    d. all of the above

12. The curse of dimensionality refers to
    a. the number of states
    b. the number of stages
    c. the number of solutions
    d. the estimation of parameters
    in a dynamic programming problem.

Answers

1. F	5. F	9. b
2. T	6. T	10. d
3. T	7. a	11. d
4. F	8. c	12. a

20.8
PROBLEMS

20-1. Consider the network shown in Figure 20.14. The numbers on the arcs are distances. We wish to find the shortest route from 1 to 12.
   (a) Specify the recursive relationship you would use to solve this problem with dynamic programming.
   (b) Find the optimal path and the cost of that route.
   (c) What is the optimal route from city 2 to 12 and the cost of that route?

Figure 20.14

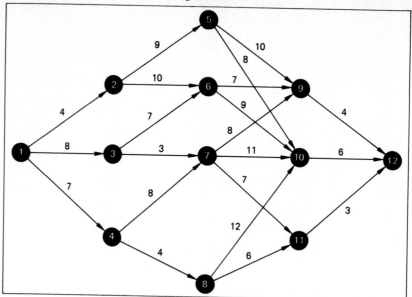

20-2. A trucker is presented with the chart in Figure 20.15. He can carry a truckload from the city he is in to any of the indicated cities for the profit indicated. He can go from city 1 to 2 for a profit of $7. Having arrived in city 2 he could go to city 7 for a profit of $12. The trucker starts in city 1 and wishes to find the most profitable route.
   (a) Specify the recursive relationship you would use to solve this problem with dynamic programming.
   (b) Find the optimal route and the profit from that route.
   (c) What route should the trucker follow if he started in city 3?

Figure 20.15

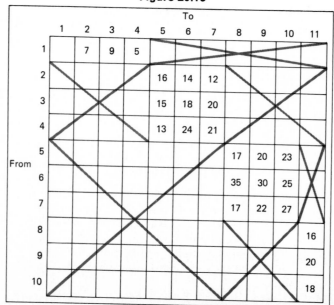

20-3. PROTRAC is making its annual allocation of salespersons to territories. A total of seven salespersons are available to assign to the four territories. The table in Figure 20.16 indicates sales revenues $R_n(j)$ (in \$100,000) in each territory as a function of the number of salespersons assigned.

Figure 20.16

Sales Revenues

TERRITORY	NUMBER OF SALESPERSONS							
	0	**1**	**2**	**3**	**4**	**5**	**6**	**7**
1	49	66	79	89	103	113	121	125
2	65	85	99	115	123	129	133	137
3	97	109	117	123	129	135	139	141
4	15	49	77	101	109	115	121	125

(a) Show the recursive relationship you would use to solve this problem by dynamic programming.

(b) Find the optimal allocation and the total sales revenue.

(c) What assignment would be optimal for territories 1, 2, and 3 if six salespersons were available for these three territories? What sales revenue would this allocation generate?

20-4. A firm can invest its funds in one of two development projects (project 2 and project 3) or in a joint venture (project 1). If \$y is invested in the joint venture, the present value of this investment is $1.15y$.

The possible investment levels for each project and the present value of each such investment is shown in Figure 20.17. The firm has \$9 million available.

Figure 20.17

PROJECT 2		PROJECT 3	
Investment	Present Value[a]	Investment	Present Value[a]
0	0	0	0
3	4.5	2	2.8
6	7.2	4	5.2
9	9.9	6	6.72

[a]All values are in millions of dollars.

(a) Show the recursive relationship you would use to solve this problem with dynamic programming.

(b) Find the optimal investment strategy and its present value.

(c) What is the optimal investment strategy and its present value if you have \$6 million to invest in projects 1 and 2?

20-5. PROTRAC is deciding how many turbo valves to produce in each of the next 4 weeks. The demand for these valves is shown in Figure 20.18. Note that in standard dynamic programming fashion: week 4 is next week, week 3 is two weeks from now etc. The cost of production is given by the equation

$$C(x) = 10 + 3x, \quad x > 0$$
$$= 0, \quad x = 0$$

Figure 20.18

	WEEK			
	Next Week 4	3	2	1
Demand	4	4	5	2

There is thus a setup cost of $10 to produce at all and a marginal cost per unit of $3. Assume that:

1. It costs $1 to carry a unit of inventory from one period to the next (i.e., there is a $1 charge assessed to ending inventory).
2. Production in week n as well as the inventory carried into week n can be used to satisfy demand in week n.
3. No inventory is available at the beginning of the problem.
4. All demand must be satisfied.

(a) Show the recursive relationship you would use to solve this problem with dynamic programming.
(b) What is the relationship between the state space for stage n and the total demand over the last n periods?
(c) Find the optimal production plan and its total cost.
(d) Can you tell without resolving the problem if the production plan found in part (c) would remain optimal if the marginal cost of production changed from $3 to $5, that is, if

$$C(x) = 10 + 5x, \qquad x > 0$$
$$= 0, \qquad\qquad x = 0$$

20-6. Consider the production planning problem presented in Problem 20-5. Assume that the cost of production varies from week to week. If $C_n(x)$ is the cost of producing x items in week n, then

$$C_n(x) = K_n + c_n \cdot x, \qquad x > 0$$
$$= 0, \qquad\qquad x = 0$$

The cost parameters and the demand for the next 4 weeks are given in Figure 20.19. Assume that it costs $2 to carry a unit of inventory from one week to the next and that there is no inventory on hand at the beginning of the problem.

Figure 20.19

	WEEK			
	Next Week 4	3	2	1
Setup cost, K_n	6	2	4	6
Production cost, C_n	6	5	3	5
Demand, d_n	4	2	1	2

(a) Show the recursive relationship you would use to solve this problem with dynamic programming.

(b) What is the size of the state space at stage 3?

(c) Find the optimal production plan and its cost.

20-7. A contractor needs a backhoe for the next two periods. At the beginning of each period he can purchase a hoe of age i, $i = 0$ (new), 1, 2, 3, for $P(i)$. At the same time he can sell the hoe he owns. This hoe will be of age j (where $j = 1, 2, 3, 4$) and will sell for $S(j)$. The cost of operating a hoe that starts a period at age i is $O(i)$ for that period. The data are shown in Figure 20.20. To illustrate, assume that at the beginning of a

Figure 20.20

	AGE, i				
	0	**1**	**2**	**3**	**4**
Purchase price $P(i)$	1000	700	490	340	
Sales price, $S(i)$		600	390	240	140
Operating cost, $O(i)$	100	200	400	600	

period the contractor sells his hoe that is two periods old and buys one that is one period old. His cost for the period will be

$$-390 + 700 + 200 = 510$$

Note that 390 is a negative cost since it is a revenue to the contractor. If at the start of a period the hoe is four periods old, the contractor must sell it and buy one of age 0, 1, 2, or 3. A hoe that starts a period at age i is age $i + 1$ at the beginning of the next period. When should the contractor buy and sell hoes over the two periods in order to minimize his cost during these periods? He cannot sell the hoe that he has on hand at the end of the last period. The diagram in Figure 20.21 illustrates the system. The contractor starts with a hoe of age 3. He sells it for $240 and buys one of age 1 for $700. During the period he incurs an operating cost of $200. In the last period he keeps the machine (now of age 2). There is thus only an operating cost of $400. He cannot make a decision at time 0.

(a) Show the recursive relationship you would use to solve this problem with dynamic programming.

(b) Finding the optimal policy and its cost if he starts with a hoe of age 3.

Figure 20.21

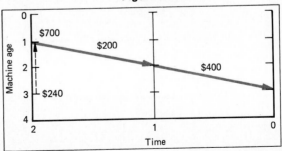

20-8. (a) and **(b).** Answer Problem 20-7 if the contractor can sell the hoe he has on hand at the end of the last period. To illustrate, the diagram in Figure 20.22 repeats the illustration started in Problem 20-7 with the new condition that the hoe can be sold at the end of the last period. Note that at time 0 the contractor can sell the hoe now age 3 for $240.

(c) Compare the answers to Problem 20-7 and parts (a) and (b).

Figure 20.22

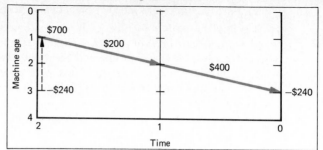

20-9. Consider the network in Figure 20.23. A router must send a message from A to H. The number on each arc indicates the probability that the circuit will *not* be busy when he tries to send (i.e., 0.95 is the probability that the router can successfully send a message from A to C). The probability that he can successfully send a message from A to H via the route A–C–F–H is $0.95 \times 0.97 \times 0.93 = 0.857$. The router wishes to find the route that maximizes the probability of successfully sending the message.

Figure 20.23

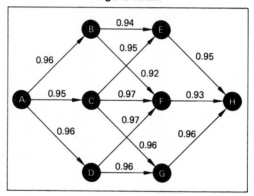

(a) Show the recursive relationship you would use to solve this problem.
(b) Find the optimal route and the probability of successfully sending the message.

20-10. The table in Figure 20.24 gives the probabilities of successfully sending a message from one station to another. For example, the probability of successfully sending a message

Figure 20.24

FROM	TO								
	B	C	D	E	F	G	H	I	J
A	0.8	0.7							
B			0.6	0.5	0.8	0.7			
C			0.7	0.4	0.9	0.6			
D							0.9	0.8	
E							0.8	0.9	
F							0.7	0.6	
G							0.6	0.7	
H									0.9
I									0.8

from G to H is 0.6 and the probability of successfully sending a message from A to J via the route A–B–D–H–J is $0.8 \times 0.6 \times 0.9 \times 0.9 = 0.3888$. What route should you take to maximize the probability of successfully sending a message from A to J?

(a) Show the recursive relationship you would use to solve this problem.

(b) Find the optimal route and its probability.

APPENDIX A

The Simplex Algorithm

The purpose of this appendix is to illustrate the basics of the most important *algorithm* in management science. This algorithm, used to solve linear programs, is called the simplex method and was created by George B. Dantzig in the late 1940s. Since then, George Dantzig and others have advanced its development and demonstrated its applicability to a myriad of real-world scenarios. It is a systematic way of examining the corners (also called *vertices*, or *extreme points*) of an LP constraint set in search of an optimal solution. In particular, the algorithm first seeks an initial corner. This is called *phase I*. If the problem is *inconsistent*, phase I will discover this fact. Otherwise, an initial corner is found and phase I is complete. Then the algorithm proceeds to generate a sequence of *adjacent* corners with the property that the objective function will either remain the same or improve in value (e.g., increase for a max model, decrease for a min model) at each successive corner. If the problem is unbounded, the algorithm will discover this during its execution. The mathematics of the uphill move from one corner to an adjacent corner requires a so-called *pivoting operation* on a tableau (i.e., a formal display) of data. When an optimal corner has been reached the algorithm terminates. Optimal solutions to both the primal and dual problems are provided.

We shall illustrate the algorithm on the following problem:

$$
\begin{aligned}
\max \quad & x_1 + 2x_2 \\
\text{s.t.} \quad & x_1 - 2x_2 \leq 2 \\
& 2x_1 - x_2 \leq 7 \\
& 4x_1 + x_2 \leq 29 \\
& -2x_1 + 3x_2 \leq 17 \\
& -3x_1 + 2x_2 \leq 8 \\
& x_1, x_2 \geq 0
\end{aligned}
$$

The constraint set corresponding to this problem is shown in Figure A.1. The objective contour is also shown. Note that the solution is at corner *D*.

In order to apply the simplex algorithm, this problem must first be converted to standard equality-constraint form. Normally, a computer would make this conversion

678

Figure A.1
Constraint Set and Objective Contour

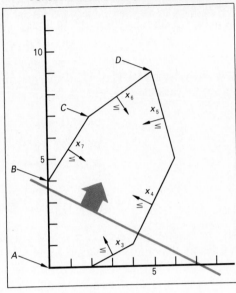

for you. However, since in this example we will not use the computer, it is necessary for us to perform the transformation explicitly. This will be accomplished by adding a non-negative slack variable to each constraint and converting the $\leq$ to $=$. In this way we obtain the problem

$$
\begin{aligned}
\max \quad & x_1 + 2x_2 \\
\text{s.t.} \quad & x_1 - 2x_2 + x_3 && = 2 \\
& 2x_1 - x_2 + x_4 && = 7 \\
& 4x_1 + x_2 + x_5 && = 29 \\
& -2x_1 + 3x_2 + x_6 && = 17 \\
& -3x_1 + 2x_2 + x_7 && = 8 \\
& x_j \geq 0 \quad j = 1, \ldots, 7
\end{aligned}
\tag{1}
$$

In mathematical terms, the set of points described by linear equations in nonnegative variables, such as system (1), is called a *convex polytope*. Before describing the simplex algorithm, we state several important facts about m linear equations in n nonnegative variables:

1. At each corner of the convex polytope described by these equations there are at most m positive variables. Under a nondegeneracy assumption there will, at each corner, be a *unique* set of exactly m positive variables. These variables are called **basic**. The remaining variables (which are zero in value) are **nonbasic**.

2. Given any set of linear equations and any set of basic variables, the equations can be solved explicitly for the basic variables in terms of the nonbasic variables.

We will employ these facts in illustrating the simplex algorithm in the above problem. Let us note that there is a one-to-one correspondence between the corners of the convex polytope described by system (1) (a polytope that resides in seven-dimensional space) and the corners in Figure A.1. This correspondence will be useful in showing the geometric analogue of the simplex calculations. For convenience, we shall circumvent phase I by arbitrarily selecting the corner denoted A as the initial corner, and noting that in Figure A.1 the basic variables at the origin are x_3, x_4, x_5, x_6, x_7. It is particularly easy to solve the equations of system (1) for these basic variables in terms of the nonbasic variables. In fact, the purpose of phase I is to obtain an explicit representation of *some* set of basic variables (corresponding to some corner) in terms of nonbasic variables. We must have such a representation in order to construct our first tableau. The representation for the basic variables at corner A is

$$\text{(row 1)} \quad x_3 = 2 - x_1 + 2x_2$$
$$\text{(row 2)} \quad x_4 = 7 - 2x_1 + x_2$$
$$\text{(row 3)} \quad x_5 = 29 - 4x_1 - x_2$$
$$\text{(row 4)} \quad x_6 = 17 + 2x_1 - 3x_2$$
$$\text{(row 5)} \quad x_7 = 8 + 3x_1 - 2x_2$$

Clearly, any nonnegative set of x values satisfies the equality constraints (1) if and only if they satisfy the above equivalent equality system.

Let us now use the symbol Z to denote the objective function. Given any representation of basic variables in terms of nonbasic, we can substitute into the objective function so that it is expressed exclusively in terms of nonbasic variables. That is, suppose

$$Z = \sum_{j \in 1}^{n} c_j x_j$$

is our objective function. Suppose that we have identified a particular corner at which the set of basic variables is $x_j, j \in B$, and the set of nonbasic variables is $x_j, j \in N$. Suppose that, as above, each basic x_j, is explicitly solved for in terms of the nonbasic variables. Then there are numbers z_0 and $\hat{c}_j, j \in N$, for which

$$Z = z_0 + \sum_{j \in N} \hat{c}_j x_j$$

In other words, at *any* feasible point the same objective value is produced by either of the expressions

$$\sum_{j=1}^{n} c_j x_j \quad \text{or} \quad z_0 + \sum_{j=N} \hat{c}_j x_j$$

For our particular example, the nonbasic variables corresponding to corner A are x_1 and x_2. Thus the objective function as initially given is in terms of only nonbasic variables, and noting that in this case $z_0 = 0$ we have

$$Z = x_1 + 2x_2$$

At the corner corresponding to $x_1 = x_2 = 0$, the value of Z, the objective function, is zero. Increasing either x_1 or x_2 will increase the objective function. Since a per-unit increase in x_2 yields two units of return, as opposed to one unit return per unit increase in x_1, let us increase x_2 and continue to keep x_1 at the value zero. In Figure A.1 this corresponds to moving vertically from the origin. We shall call x_2 the enter variable since its previous value (at corner A) was zero and now it is becoming positive.

It is seen from the geometry that x_2 can be increased until reaching corner B, at which x_1 and x_7 are nonbasic. That is, we have moved to a new corner at which x_2 and x_7 have exchanged roles. The previously nonbasic variable x_2 has become basic and x_7, which was previously basic, has become nonbasic. The other basic and nonbasic variables at corner B are the same as at corner A.[1] In looking at the above five equations for the basic variables, it is seen that as x_2 gradually becomes positive, x_3 and x_4 will increase but x_5, x_6, and x_7 will decrease from their values at the first corner (where $x_5 = 29$, $x_6 = 17$, $x_7 = 8$). It turns out that x_7 is the first of these variables to hit zero. That is,

$$x_5 = 29 - x_2 = 0 \implies x_2 = 29$$
$$x_6 = 17 - 3x_2 = 0 \implies x_2 = \frac{17}{3}$$
$$x_7 = 8 - 2x_2 = 0 \implies x_2 = \frac{8}{2}$$

Consequently, when x_2 increases to the value 4, the variable x_7 becomes zero, and this is the variable that becomes nonbasic at the new corner. Let us call this the *exit* variable. The formal rules for obtaining the enter and exit variables can be easily stated if we first rewrite the above data in the **tableau format** shown in Figure A.2.

Figure A.2
Tableau at Corner A

		x_1	x_2	x_3	x_4	x_5	x_6	x_7	
x_3	2	1	-2	1	0	0	0	0	
x_4	7	2	-1	0	1	0	0	0	
x_5	29	④	①	0	0	1	0	0	
x_6	17	-2	3	0	0	0	1	0	
x_7	8	[-3]	[2]	0	0	0	0	1	→
Z	0	-1	-2	0	0	0	0	0	
			↑						

The first row of the tableau, for example, is read "$2 = x_1 - 2x_2 + x_3$," which is equivalent to row 1 above. The last row is read "$0 = Z - x_1 - 2x_2$." It is to be noted that the last row is read differently than the other rows. This situation could be redressed by adding a Z column with all zeros except for a one in the Z row. However, our approach is traditional. You may wish to "imagine" the existence of such a column when reading the last row. We now state the following rules:

Enter rule: The variable to enter is the one that has the most negative entry in the last row.

Exit rule: Consider the ratio of each number in the first column to the corresponding number in the enter column, for which the enter column number is positive. The variable corresponding to the row with a minimum ratio is the exit variable.

In accordance with the exit rule above, we consider the ratios $\frac{29}{1}$, $\frac{17}{3}$, $\frac{8}{2}$. The minimum ratio is $\frac{8}{2}$, which identifies the exit variable as x_7.

The next step in the simplex algorithm is to obtain an updated tableau corresponding to corner B. Since x_2, x_3, x_4, x_5, and x_6 are basic at corner B, we want to solve the initial system of equations for these basic variables in terms of the nonbasic variables x_1 and x_7. The arithmetic for doing this is called **Gaussian elimination**. It turns out that

[1] This does not mean that these variables remain the same in *value*. For example, Figure A.1 indicates that x_6 is basic at each of the corners A and B, but it has a larger value at A than at B.

the new set of equations can be obtained by a sequence of mechanical operations on the tableau in Figure A.2 as follows:

1. The entry in the enter column and the exit row is called the **pivot element**. Divide each entry in the exit row by this element and replace the exit variable in the row labels with the entering variable. We now have the row of the new tableau corresponding to the entering variable. That is, the row label x_7 is replaced with x_2 and the entries in that row become $4, -\frac{3}{2}, 1, 0, 0, 0, 0, \frac{1}{2}$. (See the x_2 row of Figure A.3.)

2. The *columns* under each former basic variable other than the exit variable remain the same. Hence the columns labeled x_3, x_4, x_5, x_6 remain the same. (See the x_3, x_4, x_5, x_6 columns of Figure A.3.)

3. By virtue of the first step above, the new enter column already contains a 1. Make the remaining entries zero. (See the x_2 column of Figure A.3.)

Using steps 1, 2, and 3, we now have obtained the partial tableau in Figure A.3.

Figure A.3
Partial Update of Figure A.2. Former Basic Variables
Were x_3, x_4, x_5, x_6, x_7; x_2 and x_7 Have Exchanged Roles.

	x_1	x_2	x_3	x_4	x_5	x_6	x_7
x_3			1	0	0	0	
x_4			0	1	0	0	
x_5			0	0	1	0	
x_6			0	0	0	1	
x_2	4	$-\frac{3}{2}$	1	0	0	0	$\frac{1}{2}$
Z			0	0	0	0	

The remaining entries are obtained by the so-called **pivot rule**, which works as follows. Suppose that we want the new entry in the x_5 row and the x_1 column. In Figure A.2, it is seen that the former entry is a 4. This number, along with the pivot element (in the x_7 row, the x_2 column), can be used to define a rectangle whose corners ared istinguished in Figure A.2. The *pivoting operation* consists of the following opposite corner rule:

$$\textbf{new entry} = \textbf{old entry} - \frac{\textbf{product of opposite corners}}{\textbf{pivot element}}$$

Thus, we have

$$\text{new entry} = 4 - \frac{(1)(-3)}{2} = 5\frac{1}{2}$$

We use the same rule to obtain the new entry in, for example, the x_3 row, x_7 column. This gives

$$\text{new entry} = 0 - \frac{(1)(-2)}{2} = 1$$

The new entry in the Z row, the first column, is given by

$$\text{new entry} = 0 - \frac{(-2)(8)}{2} = 8$$

The entire tableau is completed in this fashion as shown in Figure A.4.

Figure A.4
Tableau at Corner B

		x_1	x_2	x_3	x_4	x_5	x_6	x_7	
x_3	10	-2	0	1	0	0	0	1	
x_4	11	$\frac{1}{2}$	0	0	1	0	0	$\frac{1}{2}$	
x_5	25	$5\frac{1}{2}$	0	0	0	1	0	$-\frac{1}{2}$	
x_6	5	$\boxed{2\frac{1}{2}}$	0	0	0	0	1	$-\frac{3}{2}$	$\rightarrow$
x_2	4	$-\frac{3}{2}$	1	0	0	0	0	$\frac{1}{2}$	
Z	8	-4	0	0	0	0	0	1	

$\uparrow$

The first five equations represented by Figure A.4 are read as follows:

$$10 = -2x_1 + x_3 + x_7 \quad \text{or} \quad x_3 = 10 + 2x_1 - x_7$$
$$11 = \tfrac{1}{2}x_1 + x_4 + \tfrac{1}{2}x_7 \quad \text{or} \quad x_4 = 11 - \tfrac{1}{2}x_1 - \tfrac{1}{2}x_7$$
$$\vdots \qquad\qquad\qquad \vdots$$
$$4 = -\tfrac{3}{2}x_1 + x_2 + \tfrac{1}{2}x_7 \quad \text{or} \quad x_2 = 4 + \tfrac{3}{2}x_1 - \tfrac{1}{2}x_7$$

These equations are equivalent to those in system (1) and to the first five equations in Figure A.2. We have simply obtained a new representation of the same conditions. This new representation corresponds to corner B because x_1 and x_7 are the nonbasic variables, both in the equations and at corner B. The equations express the basic variables at corner B explicitly in terms of x_1 and x_7. For example, the first equation says that at corner B, where $x_1 = x_7 = 0$, the slack variable x_3 has the value 10. But the equation also says much more. In particular, at *any* feasible point in Figure A.1, if we determine the x_1 value and the value of the slack variable x_7, then the first equation says that the value of x_3 at that point will be given by $10 + 2x_1 - x_7$. The remaining equations have analogous interpretations.

The last row of Figure A.4 is read "$8 = Z - 4x_1 + x_7$," which says that the objective function is given by

$$Z = z_0 + \sum_{j \in N} \hat{c}_j x_j = 8 + 4x_1 - x_7$$

This means that the value of the original objective function at any point on the feasible set can be expressed by $x_1 + 2x_2$ or by $8 + 4x_1 - x_7$. This is because, at any feasible point, Figure A.4 says that

$$x_2 = 4 + \tfrac{3}{2}x_1 - \tfrac{1}{2}x_7$$

Hence, $2x_2 = 8 + 3x_1 - x_7$, and $x_1 + 2x_2 = 8 + 4x_1 - x_7$.

The above expression for Z indicates that the objective function can be increased by increasing x_1 as much as possible while keeping x_7 at the value zero. This corresponds to a motion along the edge from corner B to corner C in Figure A.1. Note that at corner C the variable x_6 becomes nonbasic. Any additional increase in x_1, while keeping x_7 fixed at zero, would force x_6 to become negative, which means we would be leaving the feasible region. Hence we see that x_1 should enter and x_6 should exit. Let us now apply the enter and exit rules to Figure A.4 to obtain this same result. The most negative entry in the Z row is -4, and hence the rule says that x_1 enters. To find the exit variable we must check the ratios

$$11/0.5, \quad 25/5.5, \quad 5/2.5$$

The minimum ratio is $5/2.5 = 2$. Accordingly, the rule says that x_6 exits, and $2\frac{1}{2}$ is the pivot element.

Using the above steps 1, 2, 3, and the opposite corner rule, we obtain Figure A.5.

Figure A.5

Tableau at Corner C. Former Basic Variables Were x_2, x_3, x_4, x_5, x_6; x_1 and x_6 Have Exchanged Roles.

		x_1	x_2	x_3	x_4	x_5	x_6	x_7
x_3	14	0	0	1	0	0	$\frac{4}{5}$	$-\frac{1}{5}$
x_4	10	0	0	0	1	0	$-\frac{1}{5}$	$\frac{4}{5}$
x_5	14	0	0	0	0	1	$-\frac{11}{5}$	$\boxed{\frac{14}{5}}$
x_1	2	1	0	0	0	0	$\frac{2}{5}$	$-\frac{3}{5}$
x_2	7	0	1	0	0	0	$\frac{3}{5}$	$-\frac{2}{5}$
Z	16	0	0	0	0	0	$\frac{8}{5}$	$-\frac{7}{5}$

This tableau indicates that x_7 should enter the basis because $-\frac{7}{5}$ is the most negative entry in the Z row. The ratios

$$14/(14/5), \quad 10/(4/5)$$

indicate that x_5 should exit, and $\frac{14}{5}$ is the pivot element. The tableau is now updated to to obtain the tableau corresponding to corner D, shown in Figure A.6. This last tableau is

Figure A.6

Optimal Solution at Corner D. Former Basic Variables Were x_1, x_2, x_3, x_4, x_5; x_7 and x_5 Have Exchanged Roles.

		x_1	x_2	x_3	x_4	x_5	x_6	x_7
x_3	15	0	0	1	0	$\frac{1}{14}$	$\frac{9}{14}$	0
x_4	6	0	0	0	1	$-\frac{2}{7}$	$\frac{3}{7}$	0
x_7	5	0	0	0	0	$\frac{5}{14}$	$-\frac{11}{14}$	1
x_1	5	1	0	0	0	$\frac{3}{14}$	$-\frac{1}{14}$	0
x_2	9	0	1	0	0	$\frac{1}{7}$	$\frac{2}{7}$	0
Z	23	0	0	0	0	$\frac{1}{2}$	$\frac{1}{2}$	0

said to be **optimal** because all the entries in the last row are nonnegative. In this case, the last row tells us that $Z = 23 - \frac{1}{2}x_5 - \frac{1}{2}x_6$. Remember that this equation indicates the value of the objective function at *any* feasible point. Hence, the value is a maximum when $x_5 = x_6 = 0$, and this maximum value is 23. The tableau also gives the optimal values of the basic variables, namely

$$x_1^* = 5, \ x_2^* = 9, \ x_3^* = 15, \ x_4^* = 6, \ x_7^* = 5$$

We now state a number of additional facts about the simplex algorithm:

1. An optimal set of dual variables (an optimal solution to the dual problem) appears in the last row under the slack variable columns. In this case the slack variables are x_3, x_4, x_5, x_6, x_7, corresponding to constraints 1 through 5 of the problem we have solved. Letting $y_1, y_2, \ldots, y_5$ be the dual variables, we read from Figure A.6 that

$$y_1^* = 0, \ y_2^* = 0, \ y_3^* = \tfrac{1}{2}, \ y_4^* = \tfrac{1}{2}, \ y_5^* = 0$$

You can verify that these values are dual feasible and provide a value of 23 for the dual objective function, which is the same as the optimal primal objective value. It follows then from the dual theorem that the y_i^* values are optimal.

2. If a degenerate corner is reached there will not be a unique minimum ratio in seeking the exit vector. A number of formal tie-breaking rules exist, the simplest of which is to remove the variable with the smallest subscript.

3. The enter rule assures that the objective function will not decrease (and in the absence of degeneracy will increase) as the algorithm moves from corner to corner. In fact, this will be true if we bring in *any* variable whose entry in the last row is negative, as opposed to the *most* negative. It may happen that a column occurs with the following property: the bottom entry is negative and all other entries are nonpositive. This indicates that the problem is unbounded. Moreover, any unbounded problem will produce such a signal.

4. In order to solve a min problem, multiply the objective function by −1 and solve as a max problem. The solution so obtained will also solve the min model. The optimal objective value for the min problem will be the negative of the OV obtained for the max problem.

5. Alternative optima are revealed by discovering, in the optimal tableau, a nonbasic variable with a zero entry in the bottom row. Such a variable can be entered without changing the objective value.

6. When the constraints are all of the form

$$\sum_{j=1}^{n} a_{ij}x_j \leq b_i \qquad b_i \geq 0$$

then the slack variables will provide an initial set of basic variables, as illustrated for the above problem. The following phase I technique will find an initial set of basic variables (i.e., an initial corner) under more general conditions, such as the presence of equality constraints, or $\leq$ constraints with a negative RHS. For the ith such constraint, convert it to standard equality form, in the usual way, and then express it in such a way that the RHS is ≥ 0. Then add an *artificial variable*, z_i. Include each artificial variable in the objective function with a large negative coefficient.

For example, consider the problem

$$\max \quad x_1 + 6x_2 - 3x_3 + 4x_4$$

$$
\begin{aligned}
\text{s.t.} \quad 2x_1 - 3x_2 + x_3 &\leq -3 \\
3x_1 + x_2 + 4x_3 + x_4 &= 6 \\
-8x_1 + 6x_3 &= 7 \\
3x_1 + 4x_2 &\geq 3 \\
8x_2 - 12x_3 &\leq 6
\end{aligned}
$$

$$x_1, x_2, x_3, x_4 \text{ all nonnegative}$$

In order to apply the simplex method, we first convert to standard equality-constraint form. This gives

$$\begin{aligned}
\max \quad & x_1 + 6x_2 - 3x_3 + 4x_4 \\
\text{s.t.} \quad & 2x_1 - 3x_2 + x_3 \qquad\qquad + x_5 \qquad\qquad\qquad = -3 \\
& 3x_1 + x_2 + 4x_3 + x_4 \qquad\qquad\qquad\qquad = 6 \\
& -8x_1 \qquad\quad + 6x_3 \qquad\qquad\qquad\qquad\qquad = 7 \\
& 3x_1 + 4x_2 \qquad\qquad\qquad\quad - x_6 \qquad\qquad = 3 \\
& \qquad 8x_2 - 12x_3 \qquad\qquad\qquad\qquad + x_7 = 6 \\
& x_j \geq 0 \qquad \text{all } j
\end{aligned}$$

We next restate this in such a way that all right-hand sides are nonnegative. We obtain

$$\begin{aligned}
\max \quad & x_1 + 6x_2 - 3x_3 + 4x_4 \\
\text{s.t.} \quad & -2x_1 + 3x_2 - x_3 \qquad\quad - x_5 \qquad\qquad\quad = 3 \\
& 3x_1 + x_2 + 4x_3 + x_4 \qquad\qquad\qquad\quad = 6 \\
& -8x_1 \qquad\quad + 6x_3 \qquad\qquad\qquad\qquad\quad = 7 \\
& 3x_1 + 4x_2 \qquad\qquad\qquad\quad - x_6 \qquad\quad = 3 \\
& \qquad 8x_2 - 12x_3 \qquad\qquad\qquad\qquad + x_7 = 6 \\
& x_j \geq 0 \qquad \text{all } j
\end{aligned}$$

Certainly it is true that any LP problem can be expressed in such a form. Any variable that appears only in a single constraint and that has a coefficient of $+1$ in that constraint can be used as part of an initial set of basic variables. Thus, x_4 and x_7 qualify (and note that x_4 is not a slack variable since it appears in the objective function). To obtain a complete initial set of basic variables we add artificial variables to the first, third, and fourth equations. These variables are included in the objective function with a large negative coefficient, say -10^6. Hence, we obtain

$$\begin{aligned}
\max \quad & x_1 + 6x_2 - 3x_3 + 4x_4 - 10^6 z_1 - 10^6 z_2 - 10^6 z_3 \\
\text{s.t.} \quad & -2x_1 + 3x_2 - x_3 \qquad\quad - x_5 \qquad\qquad + z_1 \qquad\qquad = 3 \\
& 3x_1 + x_2 + 4x_3 + x_4 \qquad\qquad\qquad\qquad\qquad\qquad = 6 \\
& -8x_1 \qquad\quad + 6x_3 \qquad\qquad\qquad\qquad + z_2 \qquad\quad = 7 \\
& 3x_1 + 4x_2 \qquad\qquad\qquad\quad - x_6 \qquad\qquad + z_3 = 3 \\
& \qquad 8x_2 - 12x_3 \qquad\qquad\qquad + x_7 \qquad\qquad\qquad = 6 \\
& x_i \geq 0, i = 1, \ldots, 7; z_i \geq 0, i = 1, 2, 3
\end{aligned}$$

The variables x_4, x_7, z_1, z_2, z_3 provide an initial set of basic variables. However, before writing the first tableau we must replace each basic variable in the objective function with nonbasic variables, as follows. Since, from the equations above,

$$\begin{aligned}
z_1 &= 3 + 2x_1 - 3x_2 + x_3 + x_5 \\
z_2 &= 7 + 8x_1 - 6x_3
\end{aligned}$$

$$z_3 = 3 - 3x_1 - 4x_2 + x_6$$
$$x_4 = 6 - 3x_1 - x_2 - 4x_3$$

the objective function becomes

$$Z = x_1 + 6x_2 - 3x_3 + 4(6 - 3x_1 - x_2 - 4x_3) - 10^6(3 + 2x_1 - 3x_2 + x_3 + x_5)$$
$$\quad - 10^6(7 + 8x_1 - 6x_3) - 10^6(3 - 3x_1 - 4x_2 + x_6)$$
$$= [-11 - 7(10^6)]x_1 + [2 + 7(10^6)]x_2 + [-19 + 5(10^6)]x_3 - 10^6 x_5 - 10^6 x_6$$
$$\quad - 13(10^6) + 24$$
$$= -13(10^6) + 24 - [11 + 7(10^6)]x_1 - [-2 - 7(10^6)]x_2 - [19 - 5(10^6)]x_3$$
$$\quad - 10^6 x_5 - 10^6 x_6$$

Now we obtain the first tableau as shown in Figure A.7. This tableau is then transformed by a series of updates in exactly the way we described above. For example, x_2 is the first variable to enter, and either z_3 or x_7 can be chosen to exit. Each time an artificial variable

Figure A.7
First Tableau with Artificial Variables

		x_1	x_2	x_3	x_4	x_5	x_6	x_7	z_1	z_2	z_3
z_1	3	-2	3	-1	0	-1	0	0	1	0	0
x_4	6	3	1	4	1	0	0	0	0	0	0
z_2	7	-8	0	6	0	0	0	0	0	1	0
z_3	3	3	4	0	0	0	-1	0	0	0	1
x_7	6	0	8	-12	0	0	0	1	0	0	0
Z	24	11	-2	19	0	0	0	0	0	0	0
$\times 10^6$	-13	7	-7	-5	0	1	1	0	0	0	0

exits, the corresponding column can thereafter be ignored. When all artificial variables have exited, phase I is complete and the pivoting algorithm is continued until either an optimality signal or an unbounded signal occurs.

If an optimality signal occurs before all artificial variables have been removed, then the initial problem is infeasible.

The use of artificial variables is illustrated in Example 1 below.

In concluding this brief illustration of the simplex algorithm, we wish to stress that the LP software carried by the large computers employs much more sophisticated computations than those outlined above. The phase I procedure often allows the user to preselect a set of variables to be included in the initial set of basic variables. Product inverse computation methods are usually employed in the pivoting procedure, and the codes are often of an in-core-out-of-core variety. Nevertheless, at the heart of the simplex method is the above-described concept of pivoting, in order to update each tableau, thereby moving uphill from extreme point to adjacent extreme point on the underlying convex polytope. However, the efficient computational implementation of the algorithm becomes quite complicated and is a topic worthy of study in its own right.

Example 1

Use the simplex method to solve the following linear program:

$$\begin{aligned} \max \quad & -3x_1 + 4x_2 + 6x_3 \\ \text{s.t.} \quad & -3x_1 - x_2 + 3x_3 = -20 \\ & 6x_1 - x_2 \geq 12 \\ & x_1, x_2, x_3 \geq 0 \end{aligned}$$

Solution to Example 1

First, convert to the form

$$\begin{aligned} \max \quad & -3x_1 + 4x_2 + 6x_3 \\ \text{s.t.} \quad & 3x_1 + x_2 - 3x_3 = 20 \\ & 6x_1 - x_2 - x_4 = 12 \\ & x_j \geq 0 \quad \text{all } j \end{aligned}$$

To obtain an initial set of basic variables, we employ artificial variables z_1, z_2 with very negative coefficients in the objective function, say -10^6. This gives

$$\begin{aligned} \max \quad & -3x_1 + 4x_2 + 6x_3 - 10^6 z_1 - 10^6 z_2 \\ \text{s.t.} \quad & 3x_1 + x_2 - 3x_3 + z_1 = 20 \\ & 6x_1 - x_2 - x_4 + z_2 = 12 \\ & x_1, x_2, x_3, x_4, z_1, z_2 \geq 0 \end{aligned}$$

In the first tableau, the basic variables will be z_1, z_2 and the nonbasic variables are x_1, x_2, x_3, and x_4. The equations are used to substitute for z_1 and z_2 in the objective function to obtain

$$\begin{aligned} Z &= -3x_1 + 4x_2 + 6x_3 - 10^6(20 - 3x_1 - x_2 + 3x_3) - 10^6(12 - 6x_1 + x_2 + x_4) \\ &= -32(10^6) - [3 - 9(10^6)]x_1 - (-4)x_2 - [-6 + 3(10^6)]x_3 - 10^6 x_4 \end{aligned}$$

The first tableau is given in Figure A.8. The variable x_1 enters, z_2 exits, and 6 is the pivot element.

Figure A.8
First Tableau for Example 1

		x_1	x_2	x_3	x_4	z_1	z_2	
z_1	20	3	1	−3	0	1	0	
z_2	12	[6]	−1	0	−1	0	1	→
Z	0	3	−4	−6	0	0	0	
$\times 10^6$	−32	−9	0	3	1	0	0	
		↑						

The second tableau is shown in Figure A.9, where we have omitted the z_2 column since z_2, an artificial variable, is no longer basic. Now x_2 enters, z_1 exits, and $\frac{3}{2}$ is the pivot element. The new tableau is shown in Figure A.10.

Now phase I is complete for the artificial variables are completely eliminated. The new entry variable is x_3 (because of the -13 in the Z row), but the x_3 column consists of

Figure A.9
Second Tableau for Example 1

		x_1	x_2	x_3	x_4	z_1	
z_1	14	0	$\boxed{\frac{3}{2}}$	-3	$\frac{1}{2}$	1	$\rightarrow$
x_1	2	1	$-\frac{1}{6}$	0	$-\frac{1}{6}$	0	
Z	-6	0	$-3\frac{1}{2}$	-6	$\frac{1}{2}$	0	
$\times 10^6$	-14	0	$-\frac{3}{2}$	3	$-\frac{1}{2}$	0	

Figure A.10
Third Tableau for Example 1

		x_1	x_2	x_3	x_4
x_2	$\frac{28}{3}$	0	1	-2	$\frac{1}{3}$
x_1	$3\frac{5}{9}$	1	0	$-\frac{1}{3}$	$-\frac{1}{9}$
Z	$\frac{80}{3}$	0	0	-13	$\frac{5}{3}$
$\times 10^6$	0	0	0	0	0

all negative entries, and hence the original problem is unbounded. It can be seen from the final tableau that if the variable x_4 is fixed at zero, with x_3 increased arbitrarily, the variables x_2 and x_1 will remain nonnegative, that is,

$$x_2 = \tfrac{28}{3} + 2x_3, \, x_1 = 3\tfrac{5}{9} + \tfrac{1}{3}x_3$$

and the objective function

$$Z = \tfrac{80}{3} + 13x_3$$

will grow arbitrarily large.

INDEX

QUANTITATIVE CONCEPTS FOR MANAGEMENT, 2/E

by

G. D. Eppen and F. J. Gould

Errata

Page 690 does not appear in the book; see the reverse side
of this page for the missing information.

APPENDIX B

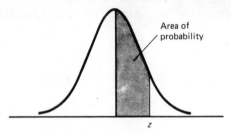

Area of probability

TABLE T.1 AREAS FOR THE STANDARD NORMAL DISTRIBUTION

Entries in the table give the area under the curve between the mean and z standard deviations above the mean. For example, for $z = 1.25$ the area under the curve between the mean and z is 0.3944.

z	0.00	0.01	0.02	0.03	0.04	0.05	0.06	0.07	0.08	0.09
0.0	0.0000	0.0040	0.0080	0.0120	0.0160	0.0199	0.0239	0.0279	0.0319	0.0359
0.1	0.0398	0.0438	0.0478	0.0517	0.0557	0.0596	0.0636	0.0675	0.0714	0.0753
0.2	0.0793	0.0832	0.0871	0.0910	0.0948	0.0987	0.1026	0.1064	0.1103	0.1141
0.3	0.1179	0.1217	0.1255	0.1293	0.1331	0.1368	0.1406	0.1443	0.1480	0.1517
0.4	0.1554	0.1591	0.1628	0.1664	0.1700	0.1736	0.1772	0.1808	0.1844	0.1879
0.5	0.1915	0.1950	0.1985	0.2019	0.2054	0.2088	0.2123	0.2157	0.2190	0.2224
0.6	0.2257	0.2291	0.2324	0.2357	0.2389	0.2422	0.2454	0.2486	0.2518	0.2549
0.7	0.2580	0.2612	0.2642	0.2673	0.2704	0.2734	0.2764	0.2794	0.2823	0.2852
0.8	0.2881	0.2910	0.2939	0.2967	0.2995	0.3023	0.3051	0.3078	0.3106	0.3133
0.9	0.3159	0.3186	0.3212	0.3238	0.3264	0.3289	0.3315	0.3340	0.3365	0.3389
1.0	0.3413	0.3438	0.3461	0.3485	0.3508	0.3531	0.3554	0.3577	0.3599	0.3621
1.1	0.3643	0.3665	0.3686	0.3708	0.3729	0.3749	0.3770	0.3790	0.3810	0.3830
1.2	0.3849	0.3869	0.3888	0.3907	0.3925	0.3944	0.3962	0.3980	0.3997	0.4015
1.3	0.4032	0.4049	0.4066	0.4082	0.4099	0.4115	0.4131	0.4147	0.4162	0.4177
1.4	0.4192	0.4207	0.4222	0.4236	0.4251	0.4265	0.4279	0.4292	0.4306	0.4319
1.5	0.4332	0.4345	0.4357	0.4370	0.4382	0.4394	0.4406	0.4418	0.4429	0.4441
1.6	0.4452	0.4463	0.4474	0.4484	0.4495	0.4505	0.4515	0.4525	0.4535	0.4545
1.7	0.4554	0.4564	0.4573	0.4582	0.4591	0.4599	0.4608	0.4616	0.4625	0.4633
1.8	0.4641	0.4649	0.4656	0.4664	0.4671	0.4678	0.4686	0.4693	0.4699	0.4706
1.9	0.4713	0.4719	0.4726	0.4732	0.4738	0.4744	0.4750	0.4756	0.4761	0.4767
2.0	0.4772	0.4778	0.4783	0.4788	0.4793	0.4798	0.4803	0.4808	0.4812	0.4817
2.1	0.4821	0.4826	0.4830	0.4834	0.4838	0.4842	0.4846	0.4850	0.4854	0.4857
2.2	0.4861	0.4864	0.4868	0.4871	0.4875	0.4878	0.4881	0.4884	0.4887	0.4890
2.3	0.4893	0.4896	0.4898	0.4901	0.4904	0.4906	0.4909	0.4911	0.4913	0.4916
2.4	0.4918	0.4920	0.4922	0.4925	0.4927	0.4929	0.4931	0.4932	0.4934	0.4936
2.5	0.4938	0.4940	0.4941	0.4943	0.4945	0.4946	0.4948	0.4949	0.4951	0.4952
2.6	0.4953	0.4955	0.4956	0.4957	0.4959	0.4960	0.4961	0.4962	0.4963	0.4964
2.7	0.4965	0.4966	0.4967	0.4968	0.4969	0.4970	0.4971	0.4972	0.4973	0.4974
2.8	0.4974	0.4975	0.4976	0.4977	0.4977	0.4978	0.4979	0.4979	0.4980	0.4981
2.9	0.4981	0.4982	0.4982	0.4983	0.4984	0.4984	0.4985	0.4985	0.4986	0.4986
3.0	0.4986	0.4987	0.4987	0.4988	0.4988	0.4989	0.4989	0.4989	0.4990	0.4990